An American Family

History and Descendants of Michael Arbogast

Born September 27 1732 in
Freiburg, Baden-Württemberg, Germany

VOLUME THREE

Descendants of children

Henry (b 1770 – d 1844),
Peter (b. 1770 – d.1842)
John (b. 1771 – d.1821
George (b 1772 – d 1844),

Curtis Sharp, Eight Generation

Both justice and decency require that we should bestow on our forefathers an honorable remembrance.
Thucydides

Hath this been in your days, or even in the days of your fathers? Tell your children of it, and let your children tell their children, and their children another generation - Joel 1:1-3

Published 2017
CeateSpace

Contents

Introduction

Accumulating data on the ancestors of of my grandmother Nancy Elizabeth Arbogast, who Married William Alexander Gilmer Sharp September 24, 1868 started in 1995 and initiated an effort to honor all my grand parents by researching their history and identifying their descendants. The Sir names of my grandparents are Sharp, Morrison, Hill and Arbogast. How fascinating that I should be the off spring of four pioneering families who settled in the heart of the Alleghany Mountains.

The collection phase continued through the first dozen years of the 21 century. The not-to-be-ignored shadows of the tombs of my ancestors compelled me to lay aside the searching and pursue making the results available through the print media. This has been accomplished for my parents families, the Sharp and Morrison. Now the Arbogast, where the greatest amount of work by others resided. Fortunately the fruits of earlier and more diligent researchers were available. All are recognized in Acknowledgements. starting on page 7.

Michael Arbogast came, and settled in the central Allegany's, and as the pages of countless documents, testify, the struggle for that elusive 'better life 'continued. But is it really important that we know our ancestors, why is it necessary or even desirable to count or identify them? On the other hand, why would one not do this? Didn't some not-to-be-forgotten Arbogast sail the stormy Atlantic and survive in the wilderness so that I might exist. If any thread of my emigrate ancestors had wiggled ever so much from the path they followed, I, Curtis Sharp, would have experienced an eternity of nonexistence.

It is not surprising, there are others with strong opinions of why we should count or identify our ancestors.

Leonard Morrison[1] offers a full and logical explanation in his1880 publication The History of the Morison or Morrison Family.

> *"Our ancestors labored and suffered much for the attainment of the rich blessings which we enjoy. They rest from their labors; they have found "Sleep after toyle, port after stormie seas." It is not right in their descendants to allow their names and deeds to perish from the earth. To permit it would be unjust to the living and the dead; to those who have gone before us, and those who shall come after us. To prevent such a result is this volume published. It is a family record; to preserve its traditions, gathering up the fading memorials of its past, and transmit them to those who shall succeed us."*

Thucydides [2] put it another way.

> *"Both justice and decency require that we should bestow on our forefathers an honorable remembrance".*

This closely parallels that offered by Dr. William T. Price[3] author of Historical Sketches of Pocahontas County, West Virginia.

> *"Persons knowing but little of those gone before is very likely to care but little of those coming after them."*

Arthur C. Morrison[4], whose work made significant contributions to this book, observed in his introductory comments

> *"This book seeks to reunite descendants under a single roof."*

Another Morrison suggests[5]

> *"May we ever keep green the graves, and fresh in our memories the lives of our dear ones who have proceeded us to the beyond"*

And so Michael Arbogast came, leaving the hinder land of Baden-Württemberg, Germany. He put down roots in the heart of the Allegany Mountains near the head waters of eastern flowing rivers and western flowing rivers, straddling the Eastern North America continental divide in what is now Highland County. Here his family came into existence and expanded well over 15,000 ancestors.

Volumes II and III on the *History and Descendants of Michael Arbogast* eliminates some detail on the history of the Arbogast name, and the life of the pioneer Michael and needs to be reviewed to get a fuller history and appreciation of the family. This Volume (III) concentrates on the descendants of four of his children; Henry, Peter, John and George and does not contain a full review of the pioneer Michael. Volume Two contains the descendants of his children David, Mary Elizabeth, Michael and Dorothy.

All descendants of Michael Arbogast are a part of this history. This seems to diminish the rational of excluding any known descendants. Consequently, this volume includes some living persons. Other supporting points for doing this are:

(1) The *History of Pocahontas County West Virginia 1980,* references many living persons in this volume and is about ancestors and living family members;

(2) Some genealogy internet sites are now including birth dates of living persons[6]

(3) Current proliferation and instant availability of information through the social media, and the on-line search capabilities, expand, rather than diminish, the availability of personal data.

It is inevitable that omissions, errors and deficiency are present in any book of this type and certainly in this one. We know many descendants are missing, and the data are not complete and may contain errors. As a matter of fact, considering all the potential data points that might be recorded for the nearly 30,000 descendants and spouses in all three volumes. , it is likely that more are missing than are present. It is appropriate to repeat the final words from the often-cited *Historical Sketches of Pocahontas County*."[i] "In submitting this book to the public, we are aware that there are imperfections and omissions that will be apparent to many readers."

---

[1] The History of the Morison or Morrison Family by Leonard A. Morrison, Frederick William Leopold Thomas A. Williams & Company, 1880 - 468 p.

[2] Thucydides, The history of the Peloponnesian war, Vol. I, John Watts, 1753

[3] William T. Price, Historical Sketches of Pocahontas County, West Virginia, 1901, Heritage Books, 2003 .

[4] Arthur C. Morrison, Descendants of Nathanial Morrison of Virginia, 6th Edition, Glendora, CA, 198

[5] Morrison Genealogy, A History of a Branch of the Morrison Family by Granville Price Morrison, 1928.

[6] Family Tree Maker, http://familytreemaker.genealogy.com/users/d/r/a/Angela-Draper/GENE8-0009.html#CHILD37, accessed Nov 16, 2014.

The identified descendants of first son Odessus Adam (Volume One) nearly equal all the descendants from the other eight children. The table below lists the descendants and spouses associated with each of the nine children of Michael Arbogast that is included in these three volumes. The are listed in birth order.

Child	descendent of each child	spouses of descendants
Adam	8706	4619
David	261	101
Mary	1653	858
Michael	529	253
Dorothy	1011	436
Henry	1242	660
Peter	1420	741
John	2701	1338
George	1951	1054

Front and back cover pictures:
Front upper left: Mitchell Sharp and wife Edyth Morrison Sharp and son Warren.
Front upper center; Sketch of the pioneer Michael Arbogast
Front upper right: Christopher Wickline Dilley and wife Nancy Elizabeth Sharp Dilley. Nancy's mother was an Arbogast.
Front lower left: Norval Wilson Arbogast
Front lower center: Arbogast Crest
Front lower right: Estol Harry Arbogast, child of Thomas Arbogast and Hallie Jane Young.
Back upper left: John Clark Hartman, children John and Sidney Hartman, and Minerva Octavia E. Sponaugle Hartman.
Back upper right: Henry Clay Arbogast and wife Gertrude Ellen Teter with part of family
Back lower left: William Arbogast (of Henry Miles Arbogast) and sons. Their mother was Elizabeth Newcomb.
Back lower middle: Asgil Stevenson Will and the female members of his family
Back lower right: Rachel Frances Arbogast who married Samuel Jacob Sutton.

Acknowledgements, Data Sources, Contributors

Typically this subject area would appear near the end of the book. However, since much of the data collection for these Arbogast volumes was done by others, and early recognition of those responsible is totally justified.. First, volumes by Charles Joseph Eades are a most extensive accumulation of Arbogast data. And his able research assistant Amanda Arbogast Forbes warrants equal recognition. These contributions exceed all other

Their Work also contains excellent source documentation. Frequently there was multiple source documentation for each descendant, resulting in the source data greatly exceeding the data. Unfortunately, publisher imposed space limitation mandated the removal of the source data for each piece of data. However, to be sure each individual contribution is recognized all the source citations have been accumulated and are presented here in Acknowledgements, Data Sources, and Contributor. Also included in Acknowledgements, Data Sources, and Contributors, are numerous other citations not included in the work by Eades, such as the footnotes.

Dates from sources such as b. Wft Est. 1813-1850 or d. Wft Est. 1819-1887 have been deleted. Such dates provide no useful information. Many of these with Wft Est. born an death dates span in excess of 100 years. The reader can estimate better than this by observing birth, and marriage dates of the parents or grandparents. For example (b. Wft Est. 1848-1885, d. Wft Est. 1874-1965) this information says this person could have died nine years before they were born or lived to be 117 years old. What it really says is "We don't know when they were born or died"

- Arbogast Chorba of New Vernon, New Jersey Ref: Stalnaker 249 S/o Boston and Margaret (Hamilton) Stalnaker.
- A dozen Arbogast reunions who individually contributed data.
- **Amanda Arbogast Forbes** (AAF) research includes papers of Wilma Harper, 1850 and 1880 Census of Pendleton County, Court Records and County histories.
- (Amanda Arbogast Forbes AAF) research and papers, copy, Pendleton Co. Marriage Record. A.k.a. Eliza Ann & Ann Elizabeth. Ref: WBH; children and spouses from grandson Dr. William Kerr of Burnsville, WV. Lived in Burnsville, Upshur Co.
- Amanda Arbogast Forbs, (AAF) Principal Researcher for: Eades, Charles Joseph author of "Descendants of Michael Arbogast". +
- Ames Edward and Rita Wooddell for compiling the Pocahontas County Marriage Bonds 1822-52, and Minister Returns.
- Ancestry Family Trees Note: http://www.Ancestry.com/AMTCitationRedir.aspx? tid=16931876&pid=107>.
- Ancestry Family Trees Publication: Online publication - Provo, UT, USA: Ancestry.com. Original data: Family Tree files submitted by Ancestry members. Note: This information comes from 1 or more individual Ancestry Family Tree files. This source citation points you to a current version of those files. Note: The owners of these tree files may have removed or changed information since this source citation was created. Page: Ancestry Family Trees Note: Data: Repository: R2170648939 Name: Ancestry.com Address: <http://www.Ancestry.com> Note: Text: <http://trees.ancestry.com/pt/AMTCitationRedir.aspx?tid=16931876&pid=107>.
- Arthur C. Morrison, Descendants of Nathanial Morrison of Virginia, 6th Edition, Glendora, CA, 1988.
- Augusta Co. Marriage records
- Augusta county entry book 31 PG 64, 1765.
- Augusta County Courthouse Records, Staunton, VA.
- Barbara Black Lawyer, Industry, IL.
- Bockstruck, Lloyd D., "Naturalizations and Denizations in Colonial Virginia." In National Genealogical Society Quarterly, vol. 73:2 (June 1985), pp. 109-116.
- Capt. Peter Hull's Company of Cavalry. AAF's DAR Nat'l. #-484839. 1781
- Chalkleys Abstracts, Vol. I, p. 161.
  In National Genealogical Society Quarterly, vol. 73:2 (June 1985), pp. 109-116.
- Colonel Dean C. Davisson, Dayton, OH for his major contributions to sons David Michael and Peter
- Court Records Augusta County Virginia; August 22, 1770, page 117, Michael Arbocoast naturalized.
- DAR ancestor # A002973, Michael Arbogast Service, Birth and Death Records.
- Daughter of Richard David and Matilda Amanda (Meade) Robinson
- Daughter of Wilburn A. and Ellen Ivory (Hammond) Russell.
- Daughter. of Samuel Elliott and Josie Lee (Taylor) Elliott, Green Bank
- Deed Book 19, page 267, 130 acres on head of South Branch of Potowmack, Highland County, VA, patented to Michael Arbogast, undated, but adjacent entries indicate the year was 1773; Augusta Co., VA.
- Deed Book 23, page 90, 17 Aug 1779, is conveying property to Michael Armingcost.
- Descendants, by Mary Elizabeth (Nottingham) Skelton of Jamestown, = Durbin, WV.
- Doris (Snyder) Beverage.
- Dozens, hundreds even, of individuals that contributed single or multiple pieces of data and did not receive credit. You know who you are.
- Dr. Francis Yeager Dunham for preserving the records of Wilma Beard Harper.
- **Eades, Charles Joseph**, and Dunham, PhD, Frances (Yeager) et.al. "Descendants of Michael Arbogast (ca. 1734-1812), Vol. I-V, 1995-1996; Westbrook Publishing Co., 121 Yorktown Rd., Franklin, TN, 37064-3277AAT =
- Family and descendants from Tommie Arbogast Huggins and The Galford Ancestry, by Lloyd Pritt Galford, 1981, Gateway Press, Baltimore, MD.

- Find A Grave, all sites available of Michael Arbogast descendants
- From family records of Merle Arbogast Chorba of New Vernon, New Jersey, daughter of Dr. Hoyt Bailey Arbogast. Ref: Morton's Highland 344 S/o John and Matilda (Slaven) Wade.
- From Geo. O. Wilson, Jr., brother, Bridgewater, VA, 1995. Mary = children of Geo. Osborne Wilson and Bonnie Grace Gum.
- From obituary. She Married MAR 1916 in Elkins, Randolph Co., WV, Donald Harper, b. Jun 1 1892 in Tucker Co., WV, d. Feb 4 1974, buried in Maplewood Cem., Elkins, Randolph Co., WV
- From research and papers of Helen Rex Arbogast Huggins,
- From Wm. C. Varner
- From, The Lunsford Family, by Mrs. Ralph Lunsford, Cortland, OH, = undated, but believed to be written in 1982. Copy from =,
- From, William Nottingham, Jr. & Mary Arbogast of Pocahontas Co., = Descendants, by Mary Elizabeth (Nottingham) Skelton of Jamestown
- Glenn Huffman, Bridgewater, VA for his major contributions Highland and Pendleton Counties
- Highland County Courthouse Records, Monterey, VA.
- Highland History, Page 290.
- *Historical Sketches of Pocahontas County, West Virginia* William T. Price, Price Brothers Publishers, Marlinton, West Virginia, 1901
- *History of Pendleton (Highland) Co.*, by Morton, pages 257 332.
- Information from Avis Irene (Wimer) Arbogast family of Newport, PA
- Information from family records of Dolores J. Tacy Russell.
- Information from family records of James Collins, Essex, MD, a descendant.
- Information from family records of Lillian McCauley Griffith of = file. Daughter of John Horace and Gussie Belle (Evans) Gray.
- Information from Mrs. Sylvia (Taylor) Gum of Green Bank, WV
- Information from Pocahontas Co., WV, History, 1981, by Brambel Tracy.
- Information from records of Dolores Tacy Russell of Lebanon, PA
- Information from Tommie Arbogast Huggins and The Galford Ancestry, by Lloyd Pritt Galford, 1981, The Gateway Press, Baltimore, MD.
- Jane Weber Mason, Morgantown, WV
- Marriage and death date from A. Arbogast Forbes Papers.
- Mary E. (Nottingham) Skelton of Jamestown, PA
- Naturalized in Augusta Co., VA, 22 Aug 1770, #117, Chalkley's Abstracts, Vol. I, p. 161.zz
- Odessus Adam Arbogast Date and place of marriage from Pension Record, War of 1812. See deed of heirs, Deed Book 6, pp. 303 & 304 Pocahontas County Court Records. Storekeeper in Green Bank. AAF # A-7. (Amanda Arbogast Forbs file id.)
- Odessus Adam Arbogast, Birth 1759/60 from Rev. War Pension Applications.
- Peter Hull's Capt. 1781. Company of Cavalry. AAF's DAR Nat'l. #-484839.
- Pendleton County Courthouse Records, Franklin, VA
- *Pennsylvania German Pioneers*, 1993 edition, Strassberger, Ralph Beaver and Hincke, William John, editor of 1934 edition, pp. 410,411, Port of Philadelphia.
- Philip D. Arbogast letter. Daughter of Koichi and Yo (Kimura) Ido, Japan.
- Philip D. Arbogast. Lives in Tucson, AZ.
- Phyllis and John, Clendenin, WV, 1996.
- Real Estate Sources: See Deed Book 19, page 267, 130 acres on head of South Branch of Potowmack, Highland County, VA, patented to Michael Arbogast, undated, but adjacent entries indicate the year was 1773; Augusta Co., VA. Also Deed Book 23, page 90, 17 Aug 1779, conveying property to Michael Armingcost. This area is now Blue Grass, Highland Co., VA.
- Record from Evangelical Lutheran Church Records, Kehl, Baden, Germany
- Records of Augusta Co., VA, Page 195, citing Will Book VI, records appraisement of the estate of Barnet Lance by Peter Hull, Jno. Gum, Sr. and Michael Armengash, 20 Sep 1791.
- Records of Augusta Co., VA, Vol. III, by Chalkley, p.531, 560.
- Records of Jim and Rita Wooddell, January 1994. (These were extensive)
- Records of Sylvia (Taylor) Gum of Green Bank, WV
- Ref: Stalnaker 254.
- Robert B. Jordan, Brooklyn, NY, descendant. Married Wanda Watt. Children are Frank Cleland, Ruth Ann, and Mark Donavan Jordan.
- See Virginia Militia in the Revolutionary War, by McAllister, page 235. Adam received pension for service as Virginia Militiaman, living 1835. Also page 19, Indian Spy, 1776 or 1777; page 22, Pvt., Capt. Peter Hull's Co. during Yorktown Campaign, 1781; and, page 148, Muster Roll of that Company in 1779.See Pocahontas Co. History, by Price.
- Sharp, William Curtis, 2013 Author of these Arbogast volumes also wrote *John Sharp and Margaret Blain Sharp Family History*, .WC Sharp and MC Sharp and is the grandson of Nancy Elizabeth Arbogast.
- Sharron Wilkinson McNeeley, Dearborn Heights, MI
- Shirley Colaw Howell, Sumter, SC
- Source is AAF record A-371146, i.e. Amanda Arbogast Forbs.
- Stalnaker Son of George Washington Salisbury and Mary Blaine (Mace) Salisbury.
- Sylvia (Arbogast) Arndorff, daughter of Fountain, Marlinton, WV, to Amanda (Arbogast) Forbes, 1991.
- The Church of Jesus Christ of Latter-day Saints, Ancestral File (R) (Copyright (c) 1987, June 1998, data as of 5 January 1998).
- The Family of John P. and Dinah (Nottingham) Varner, = Varner, R#1, Dayton, VA, in about 1962.
- The Galford Ancestry, by Lloyd Pritt Galford, 1981.

- *The History of the Morison or Morrison Family* by Leonard A. Morrison, Frederick William Leopold Thomas A. Williams & Company, 1880 - 468 p. Thucydides, *The history of the Peloponnesian war*, Vol. I, John Watts, 1753.
- The *Samuels Family Story*, Virginia, Kentucky, Indiana and Illinois, 1971 by Murial (Martens) Hoffman.
- The WBH is so often cited in this volume is Wilma Beard Harper.
- This information from, Records of Augusta Co., VA, Vol. III, by Chalkley, p.531, 560. Page 195, citing Will Book VI, records appraisement of the estate of Barnet Lance by Peter Hull, Jno. Gum, Sr. and Michael Armengash, 20 Sep 1791.
- Title: Ancestry Family Trees Publication: Online publication - Provo, UT, USA: Ancestry.com. Source: S2170648941 Repository: #R2170648939. Original data: Family Tree files submitted by Ancestry members. Note: This information comes from 1 or more individual Ancestry Family Tree files.
- Wesley Mullenneix of Naches, WA and Salton City, CA representing the Molynrux Family Association.
- Will recorded in Pocahontas Co. Will Book 3, page 4, copy Jacob Hull Arbogast is named as son in all histories but was not in will. Will probated in June 1852 term of Court, actual date of death unknown. Tombstone indicates 1760 birth.
- William Nottingham, Jr. & Mary Arbogast of Pocahontas

Immediate Family of Michael Arbogast and Mary Elizabeth Samuels.

The details and descendants of each child is presented in this Volume or in Volumes I and II

			Children
+	2	i.	Odessus Adam2 Arbogast b. Oct 25 1759.
+	3	ii.	David Arbogast b. C 1761.
+	4	iii.	Mary Elizabeth Arbogast b. C 1765.
+	5	iv.	Michael Arbogast b. C 1768.
+	6	v.	Dorothy "Dolly" Arbogast b. 1765/1769.
+	7	vi.	Henry Arbogast b. Aug 22 1770.
+	8	vii.	Peter Arbogast b. Aug 22 1770.
+	9	viii.	John C. Arbogast b. C 1771.
+	10	ix.	George Arbogast b. Jun 09 1772.

How best to use these listing

Each descendant of of Adam Odessus Arbogast in all generations has been assigned a unique, person number. Following the unique number the descendant's name will appear in the listings, followed by, in parenthesis, the genealogical track of the person back to Adam **Odessus** Arbogast, who is person number 1. Following that in the paragraph is the personal information (birth, death, burial, notes, etc.) about the individual, their spouse(s), with the same information about them, and their children. Here is an example using the family of one of Adam's children Mary.

3. **Mary^{2} Arbogast** (1.Odessus Adam^{1}), b. Jun 15 1782 in Augusta Co., VA, d. Oct 23 1858 in Siltington Creek, Pocahontas Co., WV, buried in Family Cem., Glade Hill, Pocahontas Co., WV.
She Married **William Nottingham, Jr.**, b. Nov 5 1778 in Augusta Co., VA (son of William Nottingham, Sr. and Susannah O'Brien), d. Apr 14 1857 in Pocahontas Co., WV, buried in Family Cem., Glade Hill, Pocahontas Co., WV

+	16	i.	Henry^{3} Nottingham b. Jul 13 1804.
+	17	ii.	Margaret Nottingham b. Sep 25 1806.
+	18	iii.	Nancy Jane Nottingham b. Feb 14 1808.
+	19	iv.	Adam Nottingham b. Sep 12 1809.
+	20	v.	Mahalia Patsy Nottingham b. Jul 12 1811.
+	21	vi.	William Nottingham III b. Dec 25 1812.
	22	vii.	Mary Nottingham b. May 20 1814 in Bath Co., VA, buried in Family Cem., Glade Hill, Pocahontas Co., WV, d. 1840 in Pocahontas Co., WV.
+	23	viii.	Addison Nottingham b. Apr 2 1817.

Here, Mary Arbogast, who's unique number is "3", in front of her name is followed by her personal information and spouse, which will always be in bold, followed by her children. Note the superscript 2following her name, meaning she is the second generation from Adam, being number one. Note that seven of her listed children have a plus (+) symbol in front of their unique number and one does not. Those with a (+) symbol in front of their unique number means they were Married with children and will appear later in the document identified by their unique number with their, spouse and children. The name of those descendants which did not have children (i.e. no + symbol in front of their name) appears once as a child below their parents names. If those descendants had a spouse it will appear with them in bold as well as the paragraph of personal information (birth, death, burial, notes, etc.). Their unique number or name will not appear again except in the index.

Those descendants who are parents of children (have a + symbol, to the left of their name) will initially only have their unique number, name and birth date (if available). However, the child's number and name will appear as a paragraph heading in the next generation, along with, in parenthesis, the genealogical track back to Adam Arbogast, personal information (birth, death, burial, notes, etc.), their spouse(s) and parents of the spouse(s) if available, notes about them, and their children, if any. Within the child's name will have a superscript number indicating which generation they are in.

Within those families with children, the children will be numbered i, ii, etc. The first child of a family will have a superscript showing their generation, and that of their siblings. This process repeats itself through all generations.

See in the example above. Mary is a second generation family and their third generation children. First is a person number. Then the person's name with a superscript number showing their generation from Adam. Following her name and within a set of parenthesis are the ancestors of the person back to Adam[1], then the descendants birth, death, etc. details, followed by any notes about the person. If the person has a spouse(s) it will be next in bold, followed by the parents of the spouse(s), and then their children, (numbered i, ii, etc.). In our example the family has eight children, each with its own unique number. Seven of the eight have a + symbol in front of their name, meaning it will appear in the next generation with their spouse and offspring. The children without a + symbol as well as their spouse, which will be in bold, if there is one, will not appear again in a listing. This process will repeat itself until all persons and all generations are listed.

Notice the first child in the listing has a superscript number. This indicates the number of generations this child is away from Adam Arbogast. For example Henry[3] Nottingham is three generation away, as is shown by the superscript [3].

Descendants of Henry Arbogast, Sixth Child of Michael Arbogast and Mary Elizabeth Samuels

Generation One

1. **Henry[1] Arbogast**, b. Aug 22 1770 in Crabbottom, Highland Co., VA (son of Michael Arbogast and Mary Elizabeth Samuels Amanapas), d. Apr 00 1844 in Crabbottom, Highland Co., VA.
May have been Married more than two times, had 17 children. Henry remained in community of father, Dry Run, near Crabbottom, now Blue Grass, and VA. He may have inherited or otherwise acquired his father's homestead because his descendants owned the property as late as 1971 per Amanda Crawford Arbogast Forbes research.
WILL: Pendleton Co. Court Records Will Book 4, pp.236-237, children's names. Copy of will in file also names wife, Elizabeth. Probated 4 Apr 1844, written Feb. 1844. Son, Ephraim not in will, previously deeded 375ac to him in 1840.

TRANSCRIPT OF WILL OF HENRY Arbogast

From Will Book 4, pp. 236-237 Pendleton County, Virginia In the name of God, Amen, I Henry Arbogast of the county of Pendleton, and State of Virginia, weak in body but of perfectly sound mind and memory, calling to mind the mortality of all flesh, do make and and ordain this my last will and testament and, first of all, I will and recommend my soul into the hands of God who gave it and my body I recommend to the earth from whom it was taken, to be buried in a Christian like manner, nothing doubting but in the general resurrection of the last day I shall receive it again. And, as touching these worldly goods wherewith it has pleased God to bless me in this life, I will and bequeath of in the following manner. That is to say, I will and devise as follows: To Wit: I will my part of the Keep place to my two sons, Levi and George, to be equally divided between them. Two, I also will my home place which contains four trusts to my sons Benjamin and Henry, to be equally divided between them, and they for their part must keep my wife as long as she may live, to furnish her plenty of all such things as she may need or want plentifully, firewood cut and hauled and fires made and in all states of life to keep her decent and comfortable and plentifully and to let her have the room and fireplace to the East end of the house we live in. And I will to my wife, Elizabeth, all the household and kitchen furniture to hold it as long as she lives and after that to be sold at public sale and the money to be equally divided amongst all my daughters; and I also will to my four sons Levi, George, Benjamin and Henry, all my living property and farming tools of every kind; and for my two sous, that is Levi and George, to have equal February 1844.
Witnesses: Sampson Zukefoose his

William W. Will Henry X Arbogast

mark
At a court held for the County of Pendleton 4th day April 1844, the last will and testament of Henry Arbogast, deceased, was presented to Court and proved by the oaths of Samuel Zukefoose and William E. Will, the subscribing witnesses thereto, and ordered to be recorded. Teste: Z. Dyer C.C.

Birth estimated from Pendleton Co., VA census of 1810,20, 30 and 40.
See Pendleton (Highland) Co. History, by Morton
Name appears frequently in Pendleton Co. Court Records.
All information herein from Amanda Arbogast Forbes research,
Sons of Michael Arbogast Henry and Peter were twin.
Marriage bond for first wife, Sophia Wade, dated 17 Jan. 1792.

(1) Married Jan 17 1792 in Pendleton Co., WV, **Sophia Wade**, b. About 1772 in Maryland (daughter of William Wade and Mary (Unknown)), d. About 1803 in Crabbottom, Highland Co., VA. **Sophia**: Source is Amanda Arbogast Forbes research and family group records in file. According to History of Highland Co., Virginia, by Morton, the Wade family came from Maryland to Virginia about 1780. The parents of Sophia are not known however she is the granddaughter of John Wade (1723-1815) and Sophia (Howard) Wade (1727-1816) who came from England to Maryland to Augusta Co., Virginia about 1780. Sophia (Wade) Arbogast's birth and death dates are approximated from available information.

Children:

\+ 2 i. Eleanor[2] Arbogast b. 1792.

3 ii. Margaret (Pukey) Arbogast, b. About 1794 in Pendleton Co., WV, d. About 1860 in Barbour Co., WV.
VA/WV census of 1860, age 67, not located thereafter.
Married Jan 03 1817 in Pendleton Co., WV, **John Gall**, d. c 1860 in Barbour Co., WV.

+ 4 iii. Mary Arbogast b. 1796.

+ 5 iv. Phebe Arbogast b. Feb 01 1798.

+ 6 v. Sophia Arbogast b. About 1800.

+ 7 vi. Andrew Arbogast b. ABT 1800.

(2) Married About 1805 in Pendleton Co., WV, **Elizabeth Seybert**, b. About 1785 in Augusta Co., VA (daughter of George Seybert and Mary Pickle), d. About 1844 in Pendleton Co., WV. **Elizabeth**: Source is Amanda Arbogast Forbes research and family group record with references to Pendleton Co. census of 1810, 20, 30 and 40, Seybert Fam. Ms. and Seybert Family by Charles Beverage in the Highland Recorder April 1991. Elizabeth is in Henry's will and not on 1850 census. The area of Augusta Co., VA where Elizabeth was born later became Pendleton Co., VA and finally Highland Co., VA.

Children:

+ 8 vii. Ephraim Arbogast b. Dec 08 1806.

9 viii. Lavinia Arbogast, b. About 1809 in Crabbottom, Highland Co., VA, d. About 1881 in Crabbottom, Highland Co., VA.
Source AFA research and family group record with references to 1850-1880 Highland Co., VA census, estate settled 1881 Highland Co., VA and divorce by legislative petition from Charles Gum 26 Nov 1834. Pendleton Co., VA marriage bonds for second marriage. "Winney" in father's will.
(1) Married Nov 07 1845 in Pendleton Co., WV, **John Chew**.
(2) Married May 28 1825 in Pendleton Co., WV, **Charles Gum**.

+ 10 ix. Levi Arbogast b. About 1810.

+ 11 x. Sarah Arbogast b. About 1812.

+ 12 xi. George W. Arbogast b. Feb 01 1812.

+ 13 xii. Catherine Arbogast b. About 1818.

14 xiii. Benjamin Arbogast, b. About 1821 in Crabbottom, Highland Co., VA, d. Feb 21 1887 in Crabbottom, Highland Co., VA, buried in Blue Grass Cem., Highland Co., VA.
Source is AAF research with references to tombstone record at cemetery and will filed in 1887 in Highland Co., VA. No children known to be born to this marriage. 1880 Census, Blue Grass Dist., Highland Co., VA, Benjamin age 58 born VA, Amelia, wife, age 49, and 4 servants.
Married Nov-25-1847 in Highland Co., VA, **Amelia Mildred Gray**, b. 1831.

+ 15 xiv. Henry A. Arbogast b. Jul 00 1821.

+ 16 xv. Hester Arbogast b. About 1823.

+ 17 xvi. Elizabeth Arbogast b. May 13 1826.

+ 18 xvii. Alcinda Arbogast b. About 1828.

Generation Two

2. **Eleanor[2] Arbogast** (1.Henry[1]), b. 1792 in Crabbottom, Highland Co., VA, d. Jul 17 1853 in Pendleton Co., WV.
Married Sep 5 1810 in Pendleton Co., WV, **Jonas Lantz**, b. 1787 in Pendleton Co., WV, d. Jul 17 1853 in Pendleton Co., WV.

Children:

19 i. Margaret[3] Lantz b. 1811 in Pendleton Co., WV.
Married Jul 12 1832 in Pendleton Co., WV, **Andrew Brown**, b. 1807.

20 ii. Magdalena Lantz b. 1817 in Pendleton Co., WV.
Married Dec 31 1840 in Pendleton Co., WV, **Jacob Jordan**, b. 1813.

21 iii. Elizabeth Lantz b. 1820 in Pendleton Co., WV, d. in Missouri.

+ 22 iv. Phoebe Lantz b. 15 March 1820.

+ 23 v. Mary Lantz b. Oct 2 1822.

+ 24 vi. Susannah Lantz b. Jul 1824.

25 vii. Ephraim Lantz b. 1828 in Pendleton Co., WV.
He Married Mary **Ellen Snyder**.

26 viii. Eleanor Lantz b. 1830 in Pendleton Co., WV, d. in Missouri.
Married Jan 2 1841, **Amos Wimer**.

27 ix. Andrew J. Lantz b. 1832 in Pendleton Co., WV.

4. **Mary[2] Arbogast** (1.Henry[1]), b. 1796 in Pendleton Co., WV, d. Mar 25 1870 in Champaign Co., OH, buried in Halterman Cem., Adams Twp., Champaign Co., OH.
Married May 22 1870 in Highland Co., VA, **Peter S. Halterman**, b. 1797 in Highland Co., VA, d. Dec 6 1855 in Champaign Co., OH, buried in Halterman Cem., Adams Twp., Champaign Co., OH.

Children:

+	28	i.	Elizabeth[3] Halterman b. ABT 1821.
+	29	ii.	Samuel Halterman b. 1822.
+	30	iii.	Eli Halterman b. 1823.
	31	iv.	Lavinia Halterman b. 1825. She Married **Samuel McCrosky**.
	32	v.	William Halterman b. 1825 in Ohio. Married Nov 14 1867, **Margaretta Dodson**.
+	33	vi.	Amos Halterman b. ABT 1825.
+	34	vii.	Allen Halterman b. ABT 1831.
+	35	viii.	Ephraim Halterman b. ABT 1834.

5. **Phebe[2] Arbogast** (1.Henry[1]), b. Feb 01 1798 in Pendleton Co., WV, d. Nov 14 1889 in Pendleton Co., WV.
Source is AAF research and family group record with references to 1850 census (not found) with daughter Margaret (Mrs. Nicholas Harperon 1860 and 70 Pendleton Co., WV census. Death record in Pendleton Co., WV. 1850 census Lewis Co. age 56 under spouse notes indicates possible earlier birth in 1794.
Pend. Co. grave register, p. 67, 2nd vol. indicates Phebe died 14 Nov 1889 at the age of 94 yrs., 9 mos., 14 days which would indicate birth at 31 Jan 1795 by the Gregorian calendar.
Married 1821, **John Rexrode**.

Children:

	36	i.	Margaret[3] Rexroad b. About 1819 in Pendleton Co., WV, d. 1903. Married Jan 27 1842, **Nicholas Harper, Jr.,** d. 1891 in Pendleton Co., WV.
+	37	ii.	John J Rexroad b. May 18 1826.
+	38	iii.	Nathan N Rexroad b. Oct 10 1826.
+	39	iv.	William Harrison Rexroad b. Dec 16 1831.
+	40	v.	Phebe Rexroad b. Oct 16 1833.
	41	vi.	Sophia Rexroad b. About 1835. Married Jun 21 1868 in Wood Co., WV, **Noah Hoover**.
	42	vii.	McGraw Rexroad b. Nov 19 1838.

6. **Sophia[2] Arbogast** (1.Henry[1]), b. About 1800 in Crabbottom, Highland Co., VA, d. About 1861 in Tiffin, Seneca Co., OH.
Source is AAF research and family group record with references to Centennial Biographical History of Seneca Co., OH, p. 344 and Sophia named in father's will. Sophia's husband Peter Arbogast is not a son of of Henry Arbogast. We are unable at this time to identify his parents. For Peter Arbogast, son of Henry, of David, see RIN # 8883. Extracts from Seneca County Land Records and deeds, sent to me by Barbara Lawyer, in file, indicate several real property transactions. One, a deed, from Christian Stoner and Anna Maria Stoner his wife, recorded on page 78, is of particular interest since Stoner and Arbogast families Married at least twice, **Jesse Arbogast** #3716, to Susan Stoner and Michael Arbogast #3712, to Jane R. Stoner, a.k.a. Jane Rebecca and Rebecca Jane. Sophia Arbogast Married 2nd, **David Speilman** or Speelman, 27 Oct 1834.

In a civil action in Seneca Co., OH, Common Pleas Court, filed 31 Oct 1833, having to do with Peter's estate, Sophia represents that Jesse, Phebe, Christina, and Michael are her children and Peter's. Page 220 of court records.

1830 census, Hopewell Twp., Seneca Co., OH, Sophia, age bracket 30-40, so her birth could be before 1800.

Married Apr 16 1823 in Blue Grass, Highland Co., WV, **Peter Arbogast Jr.** (son of Peter Arbogast and Sarah Henderson), d. Jun 09 1833 in Tiffin, Seneca Co., OH, b. About 1781 in Augusta Co., VA.
Source is AAF file with reference to correspondence with Grace Emahiser of Fostoria, OH. Tombstone indicates death at 39 yrs. *Centennial Biographical History of Seneca Co., OH* indicates death in 1835. Same history lists children Phoebe, Christina, Jesse and Michael. Grace's husband is Geo. Clifton Emahiser, a descendant of Andrew, #2803, and Barbara (Wimer) Arbogast. Tiffin-Seneca County Public Library, 76569-85. Page 552, Pioneers and Incidents of Pioneer Times..."Peter Arbogast, who died in 1833, owned the west half of southwest quarter of Section 16, Township 2 north, Range 14 east. He settled here in 1826. Mrs. Sophia Arbogast died in 1861. Michael Arbogast, born in Virginia in 1824, came here when two years old, and is now a resident of Seneca Township. Page 987, Michael Arbogast, farmer, P.O. Tiffin, was born in Virginia, 1 Aug 1824, a son

of Peter and Sophia Arbogast, natives of Virginia, where they first settled; thence came to this county in 1826, locating in Hopewell Township, where they lived and died, the former in 1833, and the latter in 1861. Our subject (Michael, ed.) was united in marriage, 19 Dec 1847, with Jane Gedulting, born in Frederick Co., MD, a daughter of Jacob and Elizabeth Gedulting. Mrs. Arbogast departed this life 6 Jan 1849, and our subject then Married, 11 Mar 1852, for his second wife, Jane R. Stoner, born in Frederick Co., MD, 18 Jan 1825, a daughter of Henry and Sarah Stoner. Father of nine children, all named except an infant, as recorded, six living in 1886. Jane R. (Stoner) Arbogast died 23 Jun 1882. Our subject has met with fair success and now owns 300 acres of land". A photo of Michael appears therein. Peter is obviously a descendant of Michael Arbogast, unplaced at this time. On 1830 census, Seneca Co., OH, age 30-40 bracket. Also two males age 20-30 bracket unidentified.

Children:

+ 43 i. Jesse[3] Arbogast b. Apr 01 1815.
44 ii. Phebe Arbogast b. About 1818 in Blue Grass, Highland Co., WV, d. in Ohio.
She Married **Thomas J. Windsor**.
45 iii. Christina Arbogast b. About 1821 in Blue Grass, Highland Co., WV, d. About 1849 in Seneca Co., OH
She Married **Aaron Carr**.
+ 46 iv. Michael Arbogast b. Aug 01 1824.

7. **Andrew[2] Arbogast** (1.Henry[1]), b. ABT 1800 in Pendleton Co., WV, d. BEF 1880.
On May 7th, 1865 Andrew purchased lots 22 and 23 in Milton Center, Wood County, Ohio from James F. and Elizabeth Dubbs for the sum of forty dollars. However, the sale of this land was not recorded until April 16, 1880 at which time two additional transactions were also filed and recorded at the County Recorder's Office in Wood Co, Ohio. Those being: (1) March 24, 1880 the sale by Henry and Catherine Arbogast to Ellen Morrison, their interest in lots 22 and 23 in Milton Center for the sum of 1 dollar. (2) The sale of Lots 22 and 23 for the sum of 50 dollars to A. J. Rickard by Ellen Morrison on March 22, 1880. Note that Ellen sold the land two days before her brother signed over his share in the property.
Married Jun 5 1821 in Pendleton Co., WV, **Barbara Ellener Wimer**, b. Mar 9 1793 in Pennsylvania, d. Jan 15 1862 in Wood Co., OH, buried in Milton Township Cem.; Wood County OH.

Children:

+ 47 i. Barbara Ellen[3] Arbogast b. Apr 2 1822.
+ 48 ii. Henry Arbogast b. Feb 13 1825.

8. **Ephriam[2] Arbogast** (1.Henry[1]), b. Dec 08 1806 in Crabbottom, Highland Co., VA, d. Mar 08 1866 in Crabbottom, Highland Co., VA.
Source is AAF research and family group record with references to death record naming parents, 1850 and 60 Highland Co., VA census, vital records of Highland Co., VA by Matheny and deed from Henry and Elizabeth of375 ac. to Ephraim on 14 Mar 1840, thus Ephraim not in will of father. Will is recorded in deed book 13, p. 94. This property is situated on South Branch, Seybert Gap conveyed in 1809 by Nicholas Seybert to George Seybert and later conveyed to Henry Arbogast. Ephraim was a farmer.
Married 1837 in Rockingham Co., VA, **Grace Allen**.

Children:

+ 49 i. Elizabeth Jane[3] Arbogast b. Oct-12-1842.
+ 50 ii. William M. Arbogast b. 1854.
51 iii. Jane Arbogast.
She Married **Danial Grogg.**

10. **Levi[2] Arbogast** (1.Henry[1]), b. About 1810 in Crabbottom, Highland Co., VA, d. Nov 18 1887 in Crabbottom, Highland Co., VA.
Source is AAF research and references to 1850 - 1870 census of Highland Co., VA and tombstone in family cemetery on a hill near Blue Grass, VA. Date of birth on tombstone of 1817 does seem correct.
(1) Married 1850, **Catharine Penninger**, b. May 15 1830 in Crabbottom, Highland Co., VA, d. Jun 30 1864 in Crabbottom, Highland Co., VA.

Children:

52 i. Mary A.[3] Arbogast b. Nov 08 1852.
Married About 1870, **Richard Morgan Hildebrand**, b. Nov 02 1850, d. Dec 27 1930.
+ 53 ii. Martha J. Arbogast b. About 1856.
54 iii. Charles Arbogast b. About 1860.
Married May 18 1876 in Crabbottom, Highland Co., VA, **Francis A. Gum**, b. About 1860 in Highland Co., VA.

(2) Married Nov 25 1867 in Pendleton Co., WV, **Catherine Eackle** (daughter of Christian Eackle and Jane Cook).

11. **Sarah[2] Arbogast** (1.Henry[1]), b. About 1812 in Crabbottom, Highland Co., VA, d. About 1870 in Lewis Co., WV.
Sources AAF research with reference to 1870 Lewis Co., WV census, age 58.
Married 1834, **Andrew Jordan**, b. 1810.

55 i. Elizabeth A.[3] Jordan b. 1837.
She Married **McBride Gum.**
56 ii. Lavinia Jordan b. 1839.
She Married **William Taylor**.
57 iii. George W. Jordan b. 1841.
58 iv. Mary E. Jordan b. 1850.
59 v. Samuel B. Jordan.
He Married **Leah Virginia Arbogast**, b. About 1848 in Highland Co., VA (daughter of Henry A. Arbogast and Mary Margaret Sullenberger).
60 vi. Benjamin A. Jordan b. 1851.
(1) He Married **Rebecca Burnside.**
(2) He Married **Mary Bennett**.

12. **George W.[2] Arbogast** (1.Henry[1]), b. Feb 01 1812 in Crabbottom, Highland Co., VA, d. Feb 26 1892 in Crabbottom, Highland Co., VA.
Source is AAF research and references to tombstone in family cemetery near village of Blue Grass, VA and will proven in May 1892. Cemetery records from Vital Records of Highland Co., VA. Will names wife Eunice and children Wm. H., Mary Catherine and Virginia.
(1) Married 1840, **Lavinia L. Ervine**.
(2) Married 1846, **Eunice Peninger**.

\+ 61 i. William Henry[3] Arbogast b. Dec 11 1848.
\+ 62 ii. Mary Catherine Arbogast b. 1879.
\+ 63 iii. Sarah Virginia Arbogast.

13. **Catherine[2] Arbogast** (1.Henry[1]), b. About 1818 in Crabbottom, Highland Co., VA, d. 1812 in Lincoln Co., MO.
Sources Amanda Arbogast Forbes research with references to 1850 Highland Co. census and Highland Co., VA History, by Morton. Left Virginia about 1855 with a group of other families who went to McLean Co., IL (near Lexington). Records indicate they lived there for some time and then went to Missouri.
She Married **Jessie Colaw**.

64 i. Sarah Taylor[3] Colaw.
She Married **Samuel Taylor.**
65 ii. Elmira Colaw.
66 iii. Jane Colaw.
67 iv. Hester Hestera Colaw, b. Aug-15-1841, d. Aug-25-1925.
68 v. James Colaw.
69 vi. Catharine Colaw.
70 vii. Margaret Colaw.
71 viii. Hannah Colaw.
72 ix. Benton Colaw.

15. **Henry A.[2] Arbogast** (1.Henry[1]), b. Jul 00 1821 in Crabbottom, Highland Co., VA, d. Dec 06 1901 in Crabbottom, Highland Co., VA, buried in Blue Grass Cem., Highland Co., VA.
Sources AAF research with references to cemetery records, 1900 Highland Co., VA census and Vital Records of Highland Co., VA, by Matheny. Also 1850-1880 census of Highland Co., VA.
Married Dec 23 1843 in Pendleton Co., WV, **Mary Margaret Sullenberger**, b. May 20 1827 in Pendleton Co., WV (daughter of Samuel Sollenberger and Martha (Patsy) Scott), d. Mar 22 1908 in Highland Co., VA.

Children:

\+ 73 i. Samuel Walton[3] Arbogast b. Nov 07 1845.
74 ii. Leah Virginia Arbogast b. About 1848 in Highland Co., VA.
She Married **Samuel B. Jordan** (son of Andrew Jordan and Sarah Arbogast).
75 iii. William Arbogast b. Aug 03 1854 in Highland Co., VA.
He Married **(unknown) Houchin**.

76 iv. Elizabeth Arbogast b. About 1857 in Highland Co., VA.
She Married **James Kemper**.

77 v. Benjamin S. Arbogast b. Jan 04 1859 in Pendleton Co., WV.

78 vi. Sarah S. Arbogast b. 1860 in Highland Co., VA.
She Married **John K. Kramer.**

+ 79 vii. Abraham (Able) Pryor Arbogast b. Oct 07 1861.

+ 80 viii. John David Arbogast b. About 1863.

81 ix. Mary (Molly) Arbogast b. 1866 in Highland Co., VA, d. 1924, buried in Arbogast Cem., Blue Grass, Highland Co., VA.
(1) She Married **Jessie Patterson.**
(2) Married Dec 23 1901, **Solomon Harper.**

82 x. Charles G. Arbogast b. May 12 1870 in Highland Co., VA, d. Aug 09 1889 in Crabbottom, Highland Co., VA, buried in Arbogast Cem., Blue Grass, Highland Co., VA.

16. **Hester[2] Arbogast** (1.Henry[1]), b. About 1823 in Crabbottom, Highland Co., VA, d. BEF NOV-1844 in Crabbottom, Highland Co., VA.
Source is AAF research with references to; not found on census records so dates are estimated, probably died before 1849 when husband remarried and may have had one child born about 1845. From, *Teter Descendants*, by Eva A. Winfield, Ridgeley, WV, Hester was his first wife, Jane Bland his second. He had a son with Hester, Henry T. Waybright. Jesse was ambushed outside his home during the Civil War.
See #3973 for marriage and son, Henry T. Waybright.
She Married **Jesse Waybright**, b. 1817 in Pendleton Co., WV (son of Daniel Waybright and Rachel Arbogast), d. 1864 in Pendleton Co., WV, buried in Warner Cem., Hunting Ground, Pendleton Co., VA/WV.

Children:

83 i. Henry Teter[3] Waybright b. 1844 or prior to. in Pendleton Co., WV.

17. **Elizabeth[2] Arbogast** (1.Henry[1]), b. May 13 1826 in Crabbottom, Highland Co., VA, d. AUG-1902 in Plattsburg, Clinton Co., MO.
Source is AAF research with reference to information from Eula Will Gallatin, Thomas J. Will in Van Nuys, CA and Ellen Sparks. Elizabeth died on a visit to see son Asgil. Another son, Asbury S. Will b. 1850 #21813 married Barbara E. Harold in 1870.
She Married **William W. Will**.

Children:

+ 84 i. William Perkey[3] Will.

18. **Alcinda[2] Arbogast** (1.Henry[1]), b. About 1828 in Crabbottom, Highland Co., VA, d. AFT 1895 in Barbour Co., WV.
From Amanda Arbogast Forbes research and parents family record. Reference is to 1850 Highland Co., VA census and Pendleton Co. marriage records. Letter from Mrs. Doris V. Bias, Barboursville, WV provides data on parents of Harvey Vance. Doris is descended from Harvey's sister Mary Lucinda Vance who Married **Henry Stinespring**.
Married Nov 22 1844 in Pendleton Co., WV, **Harvey Vance**, b. 1813 in Pendleton Co., WV.

Children:

85 i. Mary C.[3] Vance b. 1845 in Highland Co., VA.

86 ii. James K. Vance b. in Highland Co., VA.

87 iii. Newborn Vance b. 1850 in Highland Co., VA.

Generation Three

22. **Phoebe[3] Lantz** (2.Eleanor[2] Arbogast, 1.Henry[1]), b. 15 March 1820 in Crabbottom, Highland Co., VA, d. May 7 1905 in La Monte, Pettis Co., MO.
Albert Washington b 1-20-1842 d 1-22-1913 m Susan Fisher, Sarah Carolina b 11-19-1843 d 5-9-1924 m Pleas Oglesby 1-19-1862, James Polk, David Jasper b10-18-1847 m Callie Sebring 3-19-1871,Susan Jane b 8-14-1849 d 4-29-1852, Amber b 10-5-1851, m Ella Johnson, Asher Franklin b 8-5-1853 m Mary Craighead 12-23-1875, Lucy Isabel b 5-1-1856 m Troup Fisher.
Married Jan 7 1841 in Crabbottom, Highland Co., VA, **Amos Wimer**, b. 6July 1819 in Crabbottom, Highland Co., VA, (son of Susan Judy), d. 7 July 1876 in SE Wellington, KS, buried in Jordan Cem., SE of Wellington, KS. **Amos**: moved to Pettis Co, Mo

1850's. He and wife visiting son SE of Wellington and while helping neighbor with heavy work was injured, and died. Amos was member of the first Grand Jury in Highland County.

Children:

+ 88 i. James Polk^{4} Wimer b. Nov 10 1845.

23. **Mary^{3} Lantz** (2.Eleanor^{2} Arbogast, 1.Henry^{1}), b. Oct 2 1822 in Crabbottom, Highland Co., VA, d. Feb 23 1901 in Crabbottom, Highland Co., VA, buried in Swecker Family Cem., Swecker Farm, Pendleton Co., VA.
Married Sep 7 1858, **Ambrose Swecker**, b. 1822 in Crabbottom, Highland Co., VA, d. Nov 2 1882 in Crabbottom, Highland Co., VA.

Children:

+ 89 i. John C.^{4} Swecker.

24. **Susannah^{3} Lantz** (2.Eleanor^{2} Arbogast, 1.Henry^{1}), b. Jul 1824 in Pendleton Co., WV, d. Apr 1879 in Blue Grass Cem., Highland Co., VA, buried in Blue Grass Cem., Highland Co., VA.
Married Nov 22 1849 in Pendleton Co., WV, **Peter Waybright**, b. Dec 1824 in Pendleton Co., WV, d. Apr 1883 in Highland Co., VA, buried in Blue Grass Cem., Highland Co., VA.

Children:

90 i. Joseph^{4} Waybright b. 4 Oct 185 in Pendleton Co., WV.
+ 91 ii. Mary Elizabeth Waybright b. Sep 5 1850.
+ 92 iii. Irene Elizabeth Waybright b. Mar 3 1852.
+ 93 iv. David Jasper Waybright b. Oct 8 1853.

28. **Elizabeth^{3} Halterman** (4.Mary^{2} Arbogast, 1.Henry^{1}), b. ABT 1821 in Ohio, d. AFT 6 Mar 1890 in Christian Co., IL.
Elizabeth was said to be 39 in the 1860 Census.
Married Dec 12 1844 in Champaign Co., OH, **Ezekiel Sargeant Jr.**, b. 1825 in Green Twp., Shelby Co., OH, d. in Unknown.
Ezekiel: Ezekiel was said to be 35 and born in Ohio in the 1860 Census.

Children:

+ 94 i. Eli^{4} Sargeant b. Jan 6 1846.
95 ii. Mary J. Sargeant b. ABT 1849 in Christian Co., IL, d. 1854 in Mount Auburn Cem., Mount Auburn, IL, buried 1854 in Mt. Auburn Cem., Greenville, Christian Co., IL
96 iii. John Frank Sargeant b. ABT 1852 in Mt. Auburn Cem., Greenville, Christian Co., IL.
John F. Sargeant was about 6 1/2 months old in the 1850 Christian County, Illinois Census.
John F. was said to be 8 and born in Illinois in the 1860 Census.
Married Sep 27 1874 in Christian Co., IL, **Louise Ann Morgan**, b. 1857, d. AFT 1915.

29. **Samuel^{3} Halterman** (4.Mary^{2} Arbogast, 1.Henry^{1}), b. 1822 in Ohio, d. in Unknown.
Samuel Halterman is listed in the 1850 census as being 28 years old, a carpenter, value of property $100.00 and living with his wife Elizabeth Halterman.
Married May 22 1870 in Pendleton Co., WV, **Elizabeth McAlexander**, b. 1825, d. in Unknown.

Children:

97 i. Ann E.^{4} Halterman b. 1849, d. in Unknown.

30. **Eli^{3} Halterman** (4.Mary^{2} Arbogast, 1.Henry^{1}), b. 1823 in Ohio, d. BEF 24 Nov 1857.
Eli HALTERMAN is listed in the 1850 Census under the name Eli Hotderman, age 27 years, a shoemaker, born in Ohio and living with his wife Margaret Halterman, son Jesse F. Halterman and daughter Mary E. Halterman.
Married 1844, **Margaret Miller**.

Children:

+ 98 i. Jesse Franklin^{4} Halterman b. Apr 13 1845.
+ 99 ii. Mary Ellen Halterman b. ABT 1847.
+ 100 iii. William Hershel Halterman b. 1854.

33. **Amos^{3} Halterman** (4.Mary^{2} Arbogast, 1.Henry^{1}), b. ABT 1825 in Ohio, d. AFT 6 Mar 1890.
He Married **Margaret Swisher**, b. 1830 in Ohio, d. in Unknown.

Children:

101 i. Mary S.^{4} Halterman b. ABT 1850, d. in Unknown.

34. **Allen[3] Halterman** (4.Mary[2] Arbogast, 1.Henry[1]), b. ABT 1831 in Champaign Co., OH, d. 1884 in Porterville, Tulare Co., CA.
Married 1869 in Highland Co., VA, **Mercy Ann Snedeker**.

Children:

102 i. Leah Nora[4] Halterman b. Sep 17 1859 in Quincy, Champaign Co., OH, d. Dec 7 1917.
103 ii. Rebecca Halterman b. Jul 17 1872 in Grundy Co., MO, d. Dec 24 1941.

35. **Ephraim[3] Halterman** (4.Mary[2] Arbogast, 1.Henry[1]), b. ABT 1834 in Ohio, d. in Unknown.
He Married **Samantha Jane Martz**, d. in Unknown.

Children:

104 i. Versalius Pierce[4] C b. 1855.
He Married **Sarah Francis Grammer**.
105 ii. Temperance Halterman b. 1857.
106 iii. Mary S. Halterman b. 1857.
\+ 107 iv. Ephraim Vandlandingham Halterman b. Nov 8 1859.

37. **John J[3] Rexroad** (5.Phebe[2] Arbogast, 1.Henry[1]), b. May 18 1826 in Pendleton Co., WV, d. Jan 09 1895 near Hutchinson, Reno Co., KS.
Married Dec 22 1853 in Lewis Co., WV, **Sarah W Campbell**, b. Dec 05 1827 in Amherst Co., VA, d. Apr 14 1904 in Reno Co., KS.

Children:

108 i. Martha A[4] Rexroad b. Sep 16 1853, d. Sep 25 1927.
\+ 109 ii. William Wyatt Rexroad b. Nov 04 1854.
110 iii. John Amby Rexroad b. Dec 31 1855.
\+ 111 iv. George Nathen Rexroad b. Sep 21 1857.
112 v. Benjamin S Rexroad b. Aug 23 1859, d. Mar 27 1927.
He Married **Ida Crippen**.
113 vi. James M Rexroad b. Feb 11 1861, d. Feb 28 1946.
114 vii. Joseph Samuel Rexroad b. May 02 1863, d. Oct 25 1926.
Married Dec 18 1888, **Dora Bell Thorp.**
115 viii. Henry Jackson Rexroad b. Oct 10 1866, d. Oct 30 1938.
Married Sep 18 1889, **Mary Ann Ferguson**.
116 ix. Francis Marion Rexroad b. Mar 25 1868, d. Aug 18 1939.
She Married **Elizabeth Goatley.**

38. **Nathan N[3] Rexroad** (5.Phebe[2] Arbogast, 1.Henry[1]), b. Oct 10 1826 in Virginia, d. Jul 13 1900 in Upshur Co., WV.
Married Dec 26 1848 in Lewis Co., WV, **Nancy A Campbell**, b. 1828 in Virginia.

Children:

117 i. Phebe E[4] Rexroad b. April 1850 in Virginia.

39. **William Harrison[3] Rexroad** (5.Phebe[2] Arbogast, 1.Henry[1]), b. Dec 16 1831, d. Jun 27 1908.
Married Apr 20 1854 in Lewis Co., WV, **Mathilda Badgett**.

Children:

118 i. Charles[4] Rexroad.
He Married Martha Lamb.
\+ 119 ii. Perry Nelson Rexroad.
120 iii. John Rexroad.
121 iv. William Rexroad.
He Married **Nellie Cobley**.
122 v. James Rexroad.
He Married **Nannie Hewlin**.
123 vi. Robert Rexroad.

40. **Phebe[3] Rexroad** (5.Phebe[2] Arbogast, 1.Henry[1]), b. Oct 16 1833, d. Nov 24 1904.
Married Aug 11 1859 in Ritchie Co., WV, **Aaron Simmons**, b. 1838, d. Oct 19 1924 in Mahoney. Ohio Co., WV.

Children:

\+ 124 i. Andrew Lincoln[4] Simmons b. Jun 11 1865.

43. **Jesse[3] Arbogast** (6.Sophia[2], 1.Henry[1]), b. Apr 01 1815 in Harrison Co., WV, d. Sep 23 1874 in Bushnell, Walnut Grove Twp., McDonough Co., IL.
He Married **Susan Stoner**, b. Mar 05 1820 in Baltimore, Baltimore Co., MD, d. Nov 06 1891 in Bushnell, Walnut Grove Twp., McDonough Co., IL, buried in Prairie City Cem., Pierce Co., WA.

Children:

+ 125 i. Sophia[4] Arbogast b. Jul 18 1838.
  126 ii. Ann Eliza Arbogast b. About1842 in Wabash Co., IN, d. Jul 06 1920 in Prairie City, McDonough Co., IL. Married Apr 19 1856, **James Wilson.**
+ 127 iii. Louis Peter Arbogast b. Jan 01 1844.
+ 128 iv. Mary Jane Arbogast b. Jan 15 1845.
+ 129 v. Henry S. Arbogast b. Mar 18 1847.
  130 vi. Angeline Arbogast b. Abourt1849, d. About 1850.
+ 131 vii. Sarah Arbogast b. Apr 23 1851.
+ 132 viii. Cynthia Arbogast b. About 1853.
+ 133 ix. Frances Arbogast b. Jul 20 1856.
+ 134 x. Stephen Aaron Douglas Arbogast b. Jun 18 1859.
  135 xi. Marion Arbogast b. ABOUT 1864 in Walnut Grove Twp., Knox Co., IL, d. in Grand Island, Hall Co., NE.

46. **Michael[3] Arbogast** (6.Sophia[2], 1.Henry[1]), b. Aug 01 1824 in Seneca Co., OH, d. Oct 11 1902 in Seneca Co., OH.
(1) Married Mar 11 1852 in Seneca Co., OH, **Jane Stoner**, b. Jan 18 1825 in Frederick Co., MD, d. Aug 23 1882 in Seneca Co., OH. Michael Arbogast, the youngest child of Peter and Sophia Arbogast, 0was only two years of age when brought by his parents to Seneca County, where he spent all the years of his childhood and manhood. He aided in the difficult task of clearing the farm and preparing the fields for cultivation, and when the land became arable he bore his part in the work of plowing, planting and harvesting. As his father died when he was only nine years of age, he and his mother carried on the work of the farm, with the aid of an ox team. It was in 1855 that he took up his abode upon the place where he would live out his life. On the 11th of March in 1852, Michael was united in marriage to Miss Jane R. Stoner, a daughter of Henry and Sara (Reagan) Stoner. They were blessed with nine children before her death on June 23, 1882. They are: Alice, who Married **Jacob Staib**, is now deceased; John F. was a resident of Seneca township; Nettie became the wife of Robert E. Lutz, of Oklahoma; Lewis was a mechanic and resided in Tiffin; Charles resided near Bushnell, Illinois; Rush operated the homestead farm; and three sons passed away in childhood. Mr. Arbogast put forth every effort to make a comfortable home for his family and to give his children the opportunity to prepare themselves for the practical and responsible duties of life. In 1854 he purchased one hundred and twenty-three acres of land, the improvements on which consisted of a log house and a log barn. He went in debt for the entire amount, $3690, and this was all paid in three years time. Fifty acres had been cleared and in the course of time his fields were green with the crops that promised golden harvests. As his financial resources increased he added to his landed possessions until the home farm comprised of two hundred acres. He also owned another farm, of one hundred acres, in Seneca Township and had made excellent improvements on both. In 1875 he erected one of the most pretentious brick residences in the vicinity. He used the latest machinery for facilitating farm work and erected good barns and outbuildings for the shelter of grain and stock. His residence in the county covered more than three-quarters of a century and the present generation cannot realize the changes which had occurred during this period. Michael Arbogast remembered seeing many Indians in the locality and had driven through tiffin with an ox team many a time when the mud came up to the hubs of the wagon wheels. The flourishing city then contained only a few pioneer cabins and the county gave little promise of its present developments. However, the pioneers had laid broad and deep the foundations for its present progress, with Mr. Arbogast performing his full share in the work of citizenship. He favored reform and improvement, and his labors were effective in promoting the general welfare. Owing to his father's death he early had to take up the responsibilities of a business career, and industry, economy, and honesty were salient features in his history, enabling him to advance steadily until he occupied a prominent place on the plane of affluence. aken from the Centennial Biographical History pgs. 344,345,346.

Children:

  136 i. Warren D.[4] Arbogast b. May 11 1852, d. 1886.
+ 137 ii. Alice M. Arbogast b. Nov 30 1853.
+ 138 iii. John Franklin Arbogast b. Oct 18 1855.
+ 139 iv. Lewis Heenan Arbogast b. 1862.
+ 140 v. Annette A. Arbogast.
+ 141 vi. Charles Sayers Arbogast b. Oct 13 1864.
+ 142 vii. Rush Arlington Arbogast b. Aug 15 1867.
  143 viii. (infant) Arbogast.

(2) Married Dec 19 1847 in Frederick Co., MD, **Jane Gedulding**, b. Mar 21 1827 in Frederick Co., MD, d. Oct 11 1902 in Seneca Co., OH.

Children:

144 ix. Henry W. Arbogast b. Jan 06 1849 in Seneca Co., OH, d. May 24 1949 in Seneca Co., OH.

47. **Barbara Ellen[3] Arbogast** (7.Andrew[2], 1.Henry[1]), b. Apr 2 1822 in Pendleton Co., WV, d. Sep 24 1893 in Jackson Twp., Wood County OH.
Married May 24 1845 in Lucas Co., OH, **Thomas Morrison**, b. About 1815 in Wales, d. May 22 1877 in Farnham Station, Milton Twp., Wood County OH, buried May 24 1877 in Milton Township Cem.; Wood County OH.

Children:

145 i. Edward[4] Morrison b. About 1846.
\+ 146 ii. Mary Anna Morrison b. Aug 7 1849.
147 iii. Rebecca Morrison b. About 1852 in Ohio, d. About 1932.
Married Mar 24 1872 in Wood Co., OH, **Joseph Blyth.**
148 iv. Emma J. Morrison b. About 1855, d. About 1919.
Married Mar 24 1872 in Wood Co., OH, **Philander J. Husted**.
149 v. Thomas H. Morrison b. Aug 05 1858 in Wood Co., OH, d. Nov 09 1930 in Findlay, Hancock Co., OH.
Married Dec 07 1884 in Wood Co., OH, **Martha Ann Mellott**.
150 vi. George Morrison b. 1860 in Ohio, d. About 1934.
Married in Seneca Co., OH, **Elmina Fuller,** b. Sep 1835 in Ohio.
151 vii. Della Morrison b. About 1863.

48. **Henry[3] Arbogast** (7.Andrew[2], 1.Henry[1]), b. Feb 13 1825 in Pennsylvania, d. Mar 9 1901 in Tiffin, Seneca Co., OH, buried in Greenlawn Cem.; Seneca County OH.
Married Mar 13 1855, **Catharine Crooks**, b. ABT 1835.

Children:

152 i. Flavius Josephus[4] Arbogast b. ABT 1856, d. Oct 22 1921 in Tiffin, Seneca Co., OH.
(1) Married Aug 26 1879 in Tiffin, Seneca Co., OH, **Martha E Gasser**, b. Sep 20 1853 in Tiffin, Seneca Co., OH, d. Jan 05 1901.
(2) Married May-27-1903, **Anna Katherine Zink**,.
153 ii. Adolphus Arbogast b. Abt 1859.
\+ 154 iii. Jennie Arbogast b. Abt 1865.

49. **Elizabeth Jane[3] Arbogast** (8.Ephriam[2], 1.Henry[1]), b. Oct-12-1842 in Crabbottom, Highland Co., VA, d. Oct-06-1906 in Pendleton Co., VA.
Married Nov 25 1857 in Highland Co., VA, **George Harper**, b. About 1839 in Pendleton Co., WV, d. After 1880.

Children:

155 i. Grace[4] Harper b. 1861 in Pendleton Co., WV, d. 1937.
Married Oct-25-1880, **J.D. Swank**.
156 ii. William M. Harper b. 1863 in Pendleton Co., WV.
Married Dec-20-1885, **Sallie C. Tingler.**
\+ 157 iii. Howard Harper b. Jan 04 1865.
158 iv. Louella M. Harper b. Jun 20 1871, d. Mar 18 1942.
She Married **Charles B Wimer**.
159 v. Mattie Harper b. 1877, d. 1948.
She Married **Frank Allen**.
160 vi. (infant) Harper b. 1879, d. 1879.

50. **William M.[3] Arbogast** (8.Ephriam[2], 1.Henry[1]), b. 1854 in Pendleton Co., WV, d. Feb-25-1928 in Highland Co., VA.
Married Dec-26-1886 in Highland Co., VA, **Lucy D. Harting**, b. 1886.

Children:

161 i. Flemmie[4] Arbogast.
She Married **Marvin E. Fitzwater**.
162 ii. Hubert Arbogast.
163 iii. Nannie Arbogast.
164 iv. Sarah Arbogast.
165 v. Raymond Arbogast.
He Married **Adrey Wooddell**.

166 vi. Benjamin Arbogast.
167 vii. Evelyn Arbogast.
168 viii. William Arbogast.

53. **Martha J.[3] Arbogast** (10.Levi[2], 1.Henry[1]), b. About 1856, d. About 1939.
She Married **Henry Ephraim Colaw**, b. Feb 20 1854, d. About 1921.

Children:

169 i. Virginia[4] Colaw.

61. **William Henry[3] Arbogast** (12.George W.[2], 1.Henry[1]), b. Dec 11 1848 in Crabbottom, Highland Co., VA, d. Jul-28-1912 in Highland Co., VA, buried in Arbogast Cem., Blue Grass, Highland Co., VA.
Source is Amanda Arbogast Forbes research and family group records.
Married Apr 21 1874 in Crabbottom, Highland Co., VA, **Barbara Ellen Fleiisher**, b. Aug 29 1857 in Crabbottom, Highland Co., VA, d. Jul-29-1940 in Crab Orchard, Raleigh Co., WV, buried in Arbogast Cem., Blue Grass, Highland Co., VA.

Children:

170 i. Fay Fleishner[4] Arbogast b. Feb 10 1875 in Crabbottom, Highland Co., VA, d. Mar 20 1904 Crabbottom, Highland Co., VA.
Source is Amanda Arbogast Forbes research and family group records.
\+ 171 ii. Gay G. Arbogast b. Apr 08 1877.
\+ 172 iii. Ollie A. Arbogast b. Nov 23 1879.
\+ 173 iv. Cameron Eldridge Arbogast b. Sep 05 1881.
\+ 174 v. Manie Catherine Arbogast b. Aug 08 1883.
\+ 175 vi. Martha Mae Arbogast b. Jun 19 1887.
\+ 176 vii. William Lurty Arbogast b. Sep 21 1889.

62. **Mary Catherine[3] Arbogast** (12.George W.[2], 1.Henry[1]), b. 1879 in Crabbottom, Highland Co., VA, d. in Pendleton Co., VA.
Married Feb-19-1979, **James M. Kee**. **James**: Source is Amanda Arbogast Forbes research and family group records.

Children:

\+ 177 i. William Arbogast[4] Kee b. Apr-04-1946.
178 ii. Maude Kee.

63. **Sarah Virginia[3] Arbogast** (12.George W.[2], 1.Henry[1]).
She Married **Harmon Hiner Seybert**, b. Apr 12 1850 in Seybert Hills, Highland Co., VA.

Children:

179 i. Clara Hester[4] Seybert b. May 12 1881 in Seybert Hills, Highland Co., VA.

73. **Samuel Walton[3] Arbogast** (15.Henry A.[2], 1.Henry[1]), b. Nov 07 1845 in Pendleton Co., WV, d. Oct 18 1914 in Freemansburg, Lewis Co., WV.
Married Sep-21-1879 in Lewis Co., VA, **Canzada Eglinton Riley**, b. Feb 28 1858 in Freemansburg, Lewis Co., WV (daughter of William R. Riley and Melinda Bartlett), d. Mar 30 1933 in Jackson Mill, Lewis Co., WV.

Children:

180 i. Pryor W.[4] Arbogast b. Jul 24 1880 in Freemansburg, Lewis Co., WV, d. Nov 06 1963 in Clarksburg, Harrison Co., WV.
Married Jun-19-1910, **Melisa Furby.**
181 ii. Charles D. Arbogast b. Mar 23 1882 in Freemansburg, Lewis Co., WV, d. Apr 12 1963 in Weston, Lewis Co., WV.
Married Dec-03-1932, **Georgia Kearns.**
\+ 182 iii. Eugenious Riley Arbogast b. Feb 22 1884.
183 iv. Essie M. Arbogast b. Mar 31 1887 in Freemansburg, Lewis Co., WV, d. Dec. 1976.
184 v. Willis Thurman Arbogast b. Sep 17 1889 in Freemansburg, Lewis Co., WV, d. Mar 09 1972.
185 vi. Francis Arbogast b. Oct 23 1892 in Freemansburg, Lewis Co., WV, d. Apr 05 1955.
186 vii. Heber M. Arbogast b. Apr 27 1895 in Freemansburg, Lewis Co., WV, d. March 1972.
He Married Elvira Stutler.
187 viii. Jackson E, Arbogast b. Feb 21 1899 in Freemansburg, Lewis Co., WV, d. Mar 1972.
188 ix. Martha Ruth Arbogast b. Sep 08 1902 in Freemansburg, Lewis Co., WV, d. Nov 15 1955.
Married Jul 15 1922, Robert Brum lay.

79. **Abraham (Able) Pryor[3] Arbogast** (15.Henry A.[2], 1.Henry[1]), b. Oct 07 1861 in Highland Co., VA.

Married 1888, **Amanda E. Skecker**.

Children:

189 i. Margaret L.[4] Arbogast b. Sep 04 1889 in Crabbottom, Highland Co., VA.
190 ii. Ollie Arbogast b. Jul 26 1891 in Crabbottom, Highland Co., VA, d. Nov 24 1895 in Crabbottom, Highland Co., VA.
191 iii. Sula Arbogast b. Nov 18 1892 in Crabbottom, Highland Co., VA, buried in Arbogast Cem., Blue Grass, Highland Co., VA.
192 iv. Arlie R. Arbogast b. Aug 13 1894 in Crabbottom, Highland Co., VA, d. Sep 26 1894, buried in Arbogast Cem., Blue Grass, Highland Co., VA.
193 v. Octavia E. Arbogast b. Sep 24 1895 in Crabbottom, Highland Co., VA, d. 1949, buried in Arbogast Cem., Blue Grass, Highland Co., VA.
+ 194 vi. Ruth Arbogast b. Aug 07 1897.
+ 195 vii. Robert Lester Arbogast b. Aug 07 1899.
196 viii. Polly Swacker Arbogast b. Apr 05 1902 in Crabbottom, Highland Co., VA, d. Jun 28 1986 in Churchville, Pendleton Co., WV, buried in Arbogast Cem., Blue Grass, Highland Co., VA.
She Married **Wilber E. Halterman**.
197 ix. (infant) Arbogast b. Feb 14 1903 in Crabbottom, Highland Co., VA, d. Feb 21 1903 in Crabbottom, Highland Co., VA, buried in Arbogast Cem., Blue Grass, Highland Co., VA.
+ 198 x. Frederick Lee Arbogast b. Jul 06 1904.
+ 199 xi. Carl Arbogast b. Oct 28 1906.
200 xii. Russell Arbogast b. Aug 27 1908 in Crabbottom, Highland Co., VA, d. July 1994.
+ 201 xiii. Mary Mildred Arbogast b. Mar 14 1911.

80. **John David[3] Arbogast** (15.Henry A.[2], 1.Henry[1]), b. About 1863 in Highland Co., VA, d. May 24 1888 in Crabbottom, Highland Co., VA, buried in Arbogast Cem., Blue Grass, Highland Co., VA.
Married Oct 25 1884 in Crabbottom, Highland Co., VA, **Susan S. Wimer**.

Children:

202 i. John[4] Arbogast.
203 ii. Virginia Arbogast.

84. **William Perkey[3] Will** (17.Elizabeth[2] Arbogast, 1.Henry[1]).
He Married **Lola Newman**.

Children:

204 i. Lula Lee[4] Will b. Apr 14 1906 in Crabbottom, Highland Co., VA, d. Apr 12 1983, buried in Arbogast Cem., Blue Grass, Highland Co., VA.
Married Sep 16 1925, **Robert L. Gallatin**, d. Nov 20 1974.
205 ii. Geneva Will.
206 iii. Genoa Will.
207 iv. Lola Iasbel Will.
208 v. William C. Will.

Generation Four

88. **James Polk[4] Wimer** (22.Phoebe[3] Lantz, 2.Eleanor[2] Arbogast, 1.Henry[1]), b. Nov 10 1845 in Crabbottom, Highland Co., VA, d. 9 June 1923 in Wellington, KS.
Moved from Crabbottom VA age 12 to Pettis Co, Mo, worked on farm until 21-farmed 1 yr. in Mo. after marrying Betty on 23rd then kept hotel at Sweet Springs, Mo. 1873 came to Ks, homesteaded 160 acres 7 1/2 miles SE Wellington-2 sons born in Mo. in winter74-75 LOA from claim, back to Mo. where Lutie born, back to claim at end of LOA rest of children born there. Moved into Wellington in 1900.
Married 11-10-1868 in Dunksburg, Johnson Co., MO, **Elizabeth Ellen Chipman**, b. Nov 7 1851 in Pettis Co., MO, d. 14 April 1940 in Wellington, KS. **Elizabeth**: after moving into Wellington, sister Lute and her daughter Eula Grubbs moved from Mo to Wellington. Had adjoining houses and with another
pioneer neighbor were call "The Three Graces" by the young people. Elizabeth and Lute were only children left.

Children:

209 i. William Eugene[5] Wimer b. 10-7-1871 in Missouri, d. 3-9-1872 in Missouri.

+ 210 ii. Lutie May Wimer b. Jan 14 1875.
211 iii. Emmet Bartlett Wimer b. Jan 22 1876 in Missouri, d. 11-14-1904.
Married Mar 1 1904 in Highland Co., VA, **Lemuel Benjamin Waybright**, b. May 27 1859 in Pendleton Co., WV (son of Morgan Waybright and Lucinda Arbogast), d. Nov 18 1913.
212 iv. Odie Ellen Wimer b. 5-7-1877 in Summers Co., WV, d. 1981 in Enid, Garfield Co., OK.
213 v. Celia Forest Wimer b. 9-29-1879 in Summers Co., WV, d. July 1984 in Oxford, Sumner Co., KS.
214 vi. James Elmer Wimer b. 7-20-1881 in Summers Co., WV, d. 5-5-1883 in Summers Co., WV.
215 vii. Lena Pearl Wimer b. 9-3-1883 in Summers Co., WV, d. 6-24-1992 in Missouri.

89. **John C.[4] Swecker** (23.Mary[3] Lantz, 2.Eleanor[2] Arbogast, 1.Henry[1]).
s/o Ambrose and Mary (Lantz) Swecker. Same person as #22686, a = Henry Arbogast, of Michael. See Vol. III for his lineage.
Married in Unsure, **Susan Arabella Keller**, b. DEC 1853 in Pocahontas Co., WV (daughter of Abraham Keller and Martha V. Arbogast), d. Jun 7 1937.

Children:

+ 216 i. Virgie Belle[5] Swecker b. Apr 08 1894.

91. **Mary Elizabeth[4] Waybright** (24.Susannah[3] Lantz, 2.Eleanor[2] Arbogast, 1.Henry[1]), b. Sep 5 1850 in Pendleton Co., WV, d. Jul 9 1932 in Highland Co., VA.
(1) Married May 22 1870 in Pendleton Co., WV, **William Clark Rexrode**, b. Apr 18 1846 in Pendleton Co., WV, d. May 14 1927 in Highland Co., VA.

Children:

217 i. Harriet[5] Rexrode.
Married Sep 22 1896, **Edward R. Hull.**
218 ii. William K. Rexrode.
219 iii. Nettie Rexrode b. 1871.
She Married **Joseph W. Varner**.
220 iv. Lottie Rexrode b. Jan 23 1875, d. Jan 16 1969.
Married May 10 1896, **James Wiley Hull**, b. Aug 18 1876, d. Jan 25 1959.
221 v. Artie Rexrode b. Mar 13 1877.
Married Apr 10 1895, **Luther Clarence Hull.**
222 vi. Sarah Rexrode b. 1881, d. 1934.
Married Nov 23 1897, Jacob Walter Newman.
223 vii. Clyde Charles Rexrode b. Apr 1883, d. 1950.
Married Apr 19 1922, **Ollie Kathryn Simmons,** b. 1893, d. 1938.
+ 224 viii. Eva C. Rexrode b. Apr 1884.
225 ix. Lula M. Rexrode b. May 30 1885, d. Apr 5 1919.
Married Nov 7 1906, **Hiram Linus Simmons**, b. Oct 31 1886, d. Aug 28 1970.
226 x. Richard R. Rexrode b. Oct 30 1887.
227 xi. Arlie B Rexrode b. 1888, d. 1913.
228 xii. Anna L. Rexrode b. 1890.
Married Feb 23 1911, **Alden Keiffer Evick**, b. 1883, d. 1964, buried in Monterey Cem., Monterey, Highland Co., VA.
229 xiii. Ruth Rexrode b. Aug 1895, d. Mar 17 1896.

92. **Irene Elizabeth[4] Waybright** (24.Susannah[3] Lantz, 2.Eleanor[2] Arbogast, 1.Henry[1]), b. Mar 3 1852 in Pendleton Co., WV, d. Jan 19 1920.
(1) Married Nov 14 1867, **David W Palmer**, b. 1847 in Pendleton Co., WV.

Children:

230 i. William S.[5] Palmer b. 1873 in Highland Co., VA, d. 1952.
He Married Ida Rexrode, b. 1866 in Highland Co., VA, d. 1962.

(2) Married 1869 in Highland Co., VA, **Jacob G. Hevener**, b. Jun 17 1846 in Hightown, Highland Co., VA, d. Jan 13 1908.

93. **David Jasper[4] Waybright** (24.Susannah[3] Lantz, 2.Eleanor[2] Arbogast, 1.Henry[1]), b. Oct 8 1853 in Pendleton Co., WV, d. Jun 7 1927 in Calverton Fauquier Co., VA, buried in Warrenton Cem., Fauquier Co., VA.
David was a Engineer for the Railroad.
Married 1876 in Highland Co., VA, **Mary Ellen Snyder**, b. Mar 24 1858 in Pendleton Co., WV, d. Aug 9 1935, buried in Warrenton Cem., Fauquier Co., VA.

Children:

+ 231 i. Myrtle[5] Waybright b. Oct 23 1877.

232 ii. Johnny O. Waybright b. Oct 3 1879 in Crabbottom, Highland Co., VA, d. Dec 7 1880, buried in Waybright Cem., Blue Grass, Highland Co., VA.

233 iii. James Carl Waybright b. Dec 6 1881 in Crabbottom, Highland Co., VA, d. Feb 13 1947 in Staunton, Augusta Co., VA, buried in Thornrose Cem., Staunton, Augusta Co., VA.
Married Bef 1940, **Lee Collins.**

+ 234 iv. Matie Pearl Waybright b. Jun 12 1884.

+ 235 v. William Wellington Waybright b. Oct 25 1885.

236 vi. Mary J. Waybright b. 1889, d. 1901.

237 vii. Annie M. Waybright b. 1892, d. Sep 6 1916, buried in Warrenton Cem., Fauquier Co., VA.

94. **Eli[4] Sargeant** (28.Elizabeth[3] Halterman, 4.Mary[2] Arbogast, 1.Henry[1]), b. Jan 6 1846 in Champaign Co., OH, d. Jul 4 1928 in Perry Co., AL, buried AFT 4 Jul 1928 in Fellowship Baptist Church Cem., Morgan Springs, Perry Co., AL.
Eli Sargeant Jan. 6, 1846 July 4, 1928 born Champaign Co., Ohio

This is a letter from Emory Holston Booth written in March? of 1997. Emory is the daughter of Henrietta Holston-daughter of Eli and Virginia Payne Sargeant.

Eli was born and raised in Illinois. (Mother was never in Ill.) Towns I remember Mother saying was Springfield, Taylorville, and
Champaign.

Virginia was born in Dallas County, Alabama. Her parents died when she was young, and she went to live with an aunt in Illinois. There she met Eli, a widower with 3 children. they Married (probably in the late 1880's.) Eli had arthritis bad. He decided to move to a warmer climate, as Virginia was from Ala. they decided to sell his f arm in Ill. and move to Ala. He bought a farm near Marion in Perry County, Alabama. Mother was born here.

(I think) Eliza (Rolley" s mother) was married at this time. And stayed in Ill. Gussie (I think Augusta) and Chester (J. C.) moved to Alabama. Gussie Married but I can not think of his name. She died before Mother was born.

Chester & family moved to Florida when Mother was a young girl. She did not see him again until about 1945. Joseph had went down in Perry Co. and found where Mother was living and came to see her in the late 1930-as long as he lived he came to see her and kept in touch with her-when Joseph died Stanley started to sending Mother fruit every Christmas. She sure appreciated them thinking of her-and I do too. She never heard from Chester and could not let him know when Granddaddy died. After Granddaddy died Mother had to move as Granddad had sold his property to Ray Crawford, and got money to live on as long as he lived.

Mother lived and helped a Cousin in Hale County until she moved t o Helena in Shelby Co. to live with her mother's half sister. After my Great aunt died, She (Mother) kept house for her sons-one died and the other Married

I can remember Grandda sitting in a chair and couldn't walk for three years. I remember Mother getting him up in a straight chair and pulling him to a big rocker to sit in. I remember getting him water and other d. She came and lived with my husband and I- I'm so glad she knew, she had a home at last. things. He would read to me, and taught me to read and spell.

The last memory I have of him, is walking behind his casket tot he church and cemetery. Their house was near the church & cemetery. (Old Fellowship Church). Granddad had been a deacon in this Baptist Church.

Ely was said to be 14 and born in Ohio in the 1860 Census.
(1) Married Nov 28 1872 in Christian Co., IL, **Isola W. Arnold**, b. 1853, d. 1889 in Mount Auburn Cem., Mount Auburn, IL, buried 1889 in Mt. Auburn Cem., Greenville, Christian Co., IL.

Children:

+ 238 i. Ida Bell "Eliza"[5] Sargeant b. Oct 25 1873.

239 ii. Augusta L. "Gussie" Sargeant b. Mar 30 1879 in Mt. Auburn Cem., Greenville, Christian Co., IL, d. Nov 4 1895 in Perry Co., AL, buried AFT 4 Nov 1895 in Providence Church Cem., Perry Co., AL.
She Married **Victor Kelly Spencer**, b. Oct 21 1876, d. Dec 14 1950, buried in Mt. Hermon Church Cem., Hale Co., AL.

+ 240 iii. Joseph Chester Sargeant b. Sep 24 1884.

(2) Married Dec 4 1889 in Christian Co., IL, **Mary Virginia Payne**, b. Jul 18 1859 in Perry Co., AL, d. Sep 2 1925. **Mary**: Virginia P. Sargeant July 18, 1859 Sept. 2, 1925 born in Uniontown,
Ala.

Children:

241 iv. Charles Sargeant d. 1893 in Mount Auburn Cem., Mount Auburn, IL, buried 1893 in Mt. Auburn Cem., Greenville, Christian Co., IL.

242 v. Henrietta "Etta" Sargeant b. Jun 23 1900 in Perry Co., AL, d. Nov 22 1986, buried in Cedar Grove Cem., Alabaster, Shelby Co., AL.

She Married **Henry Douglas Holston**, b. Mar 28 1890, d. Jun 1971 in Greensboro, Hale Co., AL.

98. **Jesse Franklin[4] Halterman** (30.Eli[3], 4.Mary[2] Arbogast, 1.Henry[1]), b. Apr 13 1845 in Ohio, d. Oct 8 1915 in Mt. Vernon, Putnam Co., MO., buried in Mt. Vernon Cem., Glade Creek, Nicholas Co., WV.
See Biography for Jesse.
(1) Married 1872 in Indiana, **Mary Mollie Guy**, b. ABT 1851, d. Feb 22 1884, buried in Mt. Vernon, Putnam Co., MO.

Children:

243 i. Arthur[5] Halterman b. Feb 13 1873 in Ohio, d. Jan 6 1897.
244 ii. Adrain Guy Halterman b. ABT 1875.
He Married **Elsie McMillen**.
245 iii. Harry O. Halterman b. ABT 1878.
He Married **Catherine Skinner**.
246 iv. Amos Halterman b. AFT. 1880. died as an infant.
247 v. Lillie Halterman b. AFT. 1880.
She Married **Emery Alexander. Emery**:

(2) Married Sep 29 1886, **Adaline A. Wicks**, b. 1865, d. 1948, buried in Mt. Vernon, Putnam Co., MO.

Children:

248 vi. Ike Halterman.
249 vii. Franklin Halterman.
250 viii. Mary E. Halterman.
She Married **Edgar Hill**.
251 ix. Isaac Halterman.

99. **Mary Ellen[4] Halterman** (30.Eli[3], 4.Mary[2] Arbogast, 1.Henry[1]), b. ABT 1847 in Ohio, d. in Missouri, buried in Spring River Cem., Lawrence Co., MO.
Married Jan 26 1865, **Hiram Martz**, b. ABT 1846 in Ohio, d. in Missouri, buried in Spring River Cem., Lawrence Co., MO.

Children:

252 i. Shirley[5] Martz b. 1875.

100. **William Hershel[4] Halterman** (30.Eli[3], 4.Mary[2] Arbogast, 1.Henry[1]), b. 1854.
Married Dec 2 1880 in Lawrence Co., MO, **Elizabeth (Betty) Howard**.

Children:

253 i. Amy[5] Halterman.
254 ii. John Halterman.
255 iii. Herbert Halterman.

107. **Ephraim Vandlandingham[4] Halterman** (35.Ephraim[3], 4.Mary[2] Arbogast, 1.Henry[1]), b. Nov 8 1859 in Careysville Co., OH, d. Aug 30 1931 in Aurora, Lawrence Co., MO.
Known as "Bose".
(1) Married Jul 27 1881 in Champaign Co., OH, **Ella Poorman**, b. Mar 4 1860 in Careysville Co., OH, d. Apr 23 1886 in Careysville Co., OH.

Children:

256 i. John W.[5] Halterman b. Dec 26 1883 in Ohio.
He Married Winnie Beauenta Browning, b. Sep 18 1881, d. Aug 26 1937.

(2) Married May 7 1890 in Verona, Lawrence Co., MO, **Martha Ann Grammer**, b. DEC 1862 in Lawrence Co., MO, d. Jun 7 1908 in Verona, Lawrence Co., MO.

Children:

257 ii. Flossie Madora Halterman b. Feb 3 1891 in Verona, Lawrence Co., MO, d. JUN 1972 in Nashville, Davidson Co., TN.
258 iii. Elston "Jack" Grammer Halterman b. Feb 2 1895 in Champaign Co., OH, d. MAR 1985 in Los Angeles, Los Angeles Co., CA.
\+ 259 iv. Rex Hiram Halterman b. Jul 27 1897.
260 v. Orlena Halterman b. APR 1900 in Verona, Lawrence Co., MO, d. UNKNOWN in Verona, Lawrence Co., MO.
261 vi. Sara Halterman b. Dec 27 1902 in Verona, Lawrence Co., MO, d. DEC 1982 in Los Angeles, Los Angeles Co., CA.

She Married John Detwiler.

109. **William Wyatt[4] Rexroad** (37.John J[3], 5.Phebe[2] Arbogast, 1.Henry[1]), b. Nov 04 1854 in Lewis Co., WV, d. Feb 26 1937 in Wichita, Sedgwick Co., KS.
Married Feb 25 1886 in Kingman Co., KS, **Minnie Jane Bailey**, b. Aug 14 1866 in Clearfield Co., PA, d. in Wichita, Sedgwick Co., KS.

Children:

262 i. Lottie[5] Rexroad b. Apr 13 1887 in Reno Co., KS, d. Feb 08 1975.
Married May 26 1909, **Charles Elmer Terry**.
263 ii. Raymond Rexroad b. Jan 17 1889 in Darlow, Reno Co., KS, d. Oct 29 1968 in Springdale, Benton county, AR.
Married Oct 14 1914, **Ida Montgomery**.
\+ 264 iii. Carl Newton Rexroad b. Sep 03 1896.
265 iv. John Edward Rexroad b. May 13 1898, d. Jun 14 1963.
Married Sep 20 1920, **Bertha Hiebert**.
266 v. Anna Ruth Rexroad b. Jun 12 1902.
Married Oct 16 1948 in Wichita, Sedgwick, County KS, **Elsworth Garnett**.
267 vi. Dorothy Hazel Rexroad b. Jul 16 1906, d. Dec 21 1935.
Married Dec 21 1926, **Murl Broyles**.

111. **George Nathen[4] Rexroad** (37.John J[3], 5.Phebe[2] Arbogast, 1.Henry[1]), b. Sep 21 1857, d. Apr 01 1926.
He Married **Hattie Duckworth**

Children:

268 i. Earl[5] Rexroad.
269 ii. Mae Rexroad.

119. **Perry Nelson[4] Rexroad** (39.William Harrison[3], 5.Phebe[2] Arbogast, 1.Henry[1]).
He Married **Lydia C Lamb**.

Children:

270 i. George Elbert[5] Rexroad.
271 ii. Jesse Lee Rexroad.
272 iii. Perry Smith Rexroad.
273 iv. Grace Rexroad.
274 v. Lydia Rexroad.
275 vi. Effie Rexroad.
276 vii. Leta Rexroad.

124. **Andrew Lincoln[4] Simmons** (40.Phebe[3] Rexroad, 5.Phebe[2] Arbogast, 1.Henry[1]), b. Jun 11 1865 in Ritchie Co., WV, d. Jan 13 1944 in Algonac, St. Clair Co., MI.
Andrew was a Methodist Minister.
(1) Married Jul 11 1889 in Ritchie Co., WV, **Susan L Cokeley**, b. Oct 15 1867 in Ritchie Co., WV, d. Dec 19 1892 in Ritchie Co., WV.

Children:

277 i. Susie[5] Simmons b. Sep 04 1890, d. May 20 1971.

(2) Married Mar 29 1899 in Ritchie Co., WV, **Elspeth Leeton**, b. Sep 10 1876 in Wood Co., WV, d. Jan 16 1944 in Algonac, St. Clair Co., MI.

Children:

\+ 278 ii. Walter Raymond Simmons b. Jun 04 1902.
\+ 279 iii. Melvin Andrew Simmons b. Aug 22 1904.

125. **Sophia[4] Arbogast** (43.Jesse[3], 6.Sophia[2], 1.Henry[1]), b. Jul 18 1838 in Seneca Co., OH, d. Apr 30 1912 in Good Hope, Walnut Grove, Putnam Co., IL.
Married Aug 18 1858 in Rock Island, Rock Island Co., IL, **Josiah W Morrison**, b. 1836 in Pennsylvania, d. in McDonough Co., IL.

Children:

280 i. Catherine[5] Morrison b. 1853 in Good Hope, Walnut Grove, Putnam Co., IL.
\+ 281 ii. Mary Morrison b. Aug 01 1859.

282 iii. Warren Morrison b. 1862 in Good Hope, Walnut Grove, Putnam Co., IL.
283 iv. Margaret Morrison b. 1865 in Good Hope, Walnut Grove, Putnam Co., IL.
284 v. Charlotte Morrison b. 1867 in Good Hope, Walnut Grove, Putnam Co., IL.
\+ 285 vi. Rose Morrison b. Oct 18 1869.
286 vii. Rhoda Morrison b. Oct 10 1872 in Good Hope, Walnut Grove, Putnam Co., IL, d. May 19 1942.
She Married **Elmer Ellaberry**.
\+ 287 viii. Ida Morrison b. 1875.

127. **Louis Peter[4] Arbogast** (43.Jesse[3], 6.Sophia[2], 1.Henry[1]), b. Jan 01 1844 in Wabash Co., IN, d. Jul 13 1911 in Salem Twp., Knox Co., IL.
Married Feb 18 1875 in Galesburg, Knox Co., IL, **Easter E Potter**, b. in Salem Twp., Knox Co., IL.

Children:

288 i. Norman P[5] Arbogast b. Jun 18 1882 in Salem Twp., Knox Co., IL.

128. **Mary Jane[4] Arbogast** (43.Jesse[3], 6.Sophia[2], 1.Henry[1]), b. Jan 15 1845 in Wabash Co., IL, d. Nov 28 1927 in McComb, McDonough Co., IL.
Married Mar 03 1872 at St. Clair Co., IL, **Andrew Taylor Brown**, b. Aug 23 1843 in Caress, Braxton Co., VA, d. Sep 09 1891 in McComb, McDonough Co., IL.

Children:

\+ 289 i. Amy[5] Brown b. Feb 06 1873.
290 ii. Carl Ivan Brown b. Jul 20 1874 in McComb, McDonough Co., IL, d. Jul 20 1916.
\+ 291 iii. Ethel Clare Brown b. Sep 03 1875.
292 iv. Edith Nora Brown b. Nov 10 1876 in McComb, McDonough Co., IL, d. Jan 04 1962.
\+ 293 v. Lois Irene Brown b. Feb 11 1880.
294 vi. Beatrice Brown b. Mar 17 1882 in McComb, McDonough Co., IL, d. Jan 05 1965.
Married in Divorced, **Cliff Anderson**.
\+ 295 vii. Mertice Loine Brown b. Oct 29 1886.
296 viii. Berdie Brown b. Aug 22 1889 in McComb, McDonough Co., IL, d. Feb 02 1980.
Married in Divorced, **Alfred Homer**.

129. **Henry S.[4] Arbogast** (43.Jesse[3], 6.Sophia[2], 1.Henry[1]), b. Mar 18 1847 in Wabash Co., IL, d. in Idaho.
C Co., 151st IL during Civil War.
Married Jan 01 1871 in Warren Co., IL, **Marietta Warden**, b. 1853 in Swan Lake, Warren Co., IL.

Children:

297 i. Marion S.[5] Arbogast b. About 1877.
298 ii. Ira E. Arbogast b. About 1879.
299 iii. Donald E. Arbogast.

131. **Sarah[4] Arbogast** (43.Jesse[3], 6.Sophia[2], 1.Henry[1]), b. Apr 23 1851 in Wabash Co., IL, d. May 27 1927 in Scioto Twp., McDonough Co., IL.
Married Jul 30 1873, **Green Berry Howard**, b. Sep 15 1848 in Tompkinsville, Monroe Co., KY, d. May 30 1925 in Scioto Twp., McDonough Co., IL, buried in Macomb, McDonough Co., IL.

Children:

300 i. Hubert[5] Howard b. 1870.
Married Oct 07 1891 in McComb, McDonough Co., IL, Mary Cambell, b. 1870.
\+ 301 ii. Mae Howard b. May 01 1874.

132. **Cynthia[4] Arbogast** (43.Jesse[3], 6.Sophia[2], 1.Henry[1]), b. About 1853 in Terra Haute, Vigo Co., IN.

Married Oct 26 1887 in McDonough Co., IL, **Hugh Gilworth**, b. Apr 03 1857 in McComb, McDonough Co., IL, d. Aug 1946 in Duncan, Stephens Co., OK.

Children:

302 i. Edna M.[5] Gilworth b. Apr 19 1891 in McComb, McDonough Co., IL, d. Apr 12 1955 in Duncan, Stephens Co., OK.
She Married **Van Gaston Denman**, b. 1887, d. Jul 15 1946.
303 ii. Joseph Victory Gilworth b. Oct 14 1893 in Linn Co., MO, d. Nov 23 1918 in Camp Cody, Deming, Luna Co., NM.

133. **Frances[4] Arbogast** (43.Jesse[3], 6.Sophia[2], 1.Henry[1]), b. Jul 20 1856 in Walnut Grove Twp., Knox Co., IL, d. Jun 12 1909 in Walnut Grove Twp., Knox Co., IL.
She Married **Franklin King Smith**, b. 1853.

Children:

+ 304 i. Neil[5] Smith b. Dec 08 1877.
+ 305 ii. Emerson Eugene Smith.
306 iii. Charles Smith b. 1881 in Good Hope, Walnut Grove, Putnam Co., IL, d. 1936.
+ 307 iv. Jessie Smith.
308 v. Jesse N. Smith b. 1885 in Good Hope, Walnut Grove, Putnam Co., IL, d. 1956.
He Married **Tessie N. Smith**.
+ 309 vi. June Smith b. Jun 1887.
+ 310 vii. Myrtle Smith b. Dec 17 1896.

134. **Stephen Aaron Douglas[4] Arbogast** (43.Jesse[3], 6.Sophia[2], 1.Henry[1]), b. Jun 18 1859 in Walnut Grove Twp., Knox Co., IL, d. Mar 21 1930 in Silver Creek, Merrick Co., NE.
Married Apr 04 1888, **Cora Maud Dille**, b. Jun 27 1872 in Lagrange Co., IN, d. Mar 21 1930 in Silver Creek, Merrick Co., NE.

Children:

+ 311 i. Clyde Stewart[5] Arbogast b. Feb 03 1891.
312 ii. George Dille Arbogast b. Apr 18 1894 in Rising City, Butler Co., NE, d. Apr 28 1950.
+ 313 iii. Nellie Millicent Arbogast b. Sep 22 1898.
+ 314 iv. Gladys Mary Arbogast b. May 18 1901.
+ 315 v. Harold Edson Arbogast b. Nov 30 1912.

137. **Alice M.[4] Arbogast** (46.Michael[3], 6.Sophia[2], 1.Henry[1]), b. Nov 30 1853, d. Dec 11 1918.
She Married **Jacob Staib**. .

Children:

316 i. Alverta[5] STAIB.
She Married **Thomas Barclay**.
317 ii. Victor J. Staib.
He Married **Mabel Gibbs**. .
+ 318 iii. Lorenzo Staib b. Feb 08 1892.
+ 319 iv. Nettie Staib.

138. **John Franklin[4] Arbogast** (46.Michael[3], 6.Sophia[2], 1.Henry[1]), b. Oct 18 1855 in Seneca Co., OH, d. 1949 in Seneca Co., OH.
He Married **Henrietta Calra Hiser**, b. 1861 in Seneca Co., OH, d. 1955 in Seneca Co., OH, buried in Tiffin, Seneca Co.,

Children:

+ 320 i. Jessie L.[5] Arbogast b. Aug 20 1880.
321 ii. Franklin Seymore Arbogast b. 1883.
He Married **Mary Weller**, b. 1889.
322 iii. Ward Arbogast.

139. **Lewis Heenan[4] Arbogast** (46.Michael[3], 6.Sophia[2], 1.Henry[1]), b. 1862, d. 1944 in Seneca Co., OH.
He Married **Flora Caroline Sohn**, b. Jul 25 1864. .

Children:

323 i. Hazel[5] Arbogast b. Apr 01 1888, d. c 1981.
She Married **Robert Haskins**. .
324 ii. Russel Arbogast b. May 14 1892, d. Apr 29 1957.
He Married **Jane Vanderstoop**. .
+ 325 iii. James Warren Arbogast b. Dec 29 1896.
326 iv. Herbert Arbogast.
He Married **Garnet Warren**. .

140. **Annetta A.[4] Arbogast** (46.Michael[3], 6.Sophia[2], 1.Henry[1]).
She Married **Robert Lutz**. .

Children:

327 i. Floyd[5] LUTZ.
328 ii. Hazel Lutz.

329 iii. Fern Lutz.
She Married **Robert Brown**.
330 iv. Ernest Lutz.
331 v. Ivy Lutz.
332 vi. Stanley Lutz.

141. **Charles Sayers[4] Arbogast** (46.Michael[3], 6.Sophia[2], 1.Henry[1]), b. Oct 13 1864 in Seneca Co., OH, d. Oct 18 1931 in Calgary, Alberta.
He Married **Eva Maud Hudson**, b. Nov 01 1866 in Yates City, Knox Co., IL, d. Apr 20 1939 in Calgary, Alberta.

Children:

\+ 333 i. James Michael[5] Arbogast b. Dec 16 1887.
\+ 334 ii. Alice Arbogast.
335 iii. Louise Arbogast.
She Married **Percy McCarthy**.
336 iv. Olind Ray Arbogast b. 1891, d. 1905.

142. **Rush Arlington[4] Arbogast** (46.Michael[3], 6.Sophia[2], 1.Henry[1]), b. Aug 15 1867 in Seneca Co., OH, d. Apr 08 1965.

He Married **Clara Kingseed**. Rush Arbogast was born in a log cabin to Michael and Jane (Stoner) Arbogast. The log cabin was located where now, in 1986, is the grain handling facilities for Kingland Farms. He was their sixth child, having three older brothers and two sisters, plus three younger brothers who died in childhood. In 1875, when he was eight years old the family moved into their new large brick home which had been built several hundred feet northeast of the cabin. His mother passed away in June 1882. He resided with his father and in January 1892 he Married Clara Kingseed and they started housekeeping with his father Rush and Clara were the parents of three children: Frances, who later Married Louis Smith and had 11 children; Charles, who Married Loretta Reinhart and had 11 children, one who died at birth; and Clarence, who Married Aleta Talley and had one son and one daughter. His father passed away in 1902. He continued to reside there and his wife passed away in 1938. About 1942 his son Clarence, with his wife Aleta and their two children, James and Naomi, moved in to take over farming the 127-acre farm. His son Clarence passed away in January 1944. A short while later his daughter-in-law and her two children moved out leaving him to reside alone until his death in April 1965.

Children:

\+ 337 i. Clarence James[5] Arbogast b. Jun-08-1904.
\+ 338 ii. Charles Anthony Arbogast b. Sep-11-1900.
\+ 339 iii. Frances Marie Arbogast b. Dec 28 1892.

146. **Mary Anna[4] Morrison** (47.Barbara Ellen[3] Arbogast, 7.Andrew[2], 1.Henry[1]), b. Aug 7 1849 in Milton Twp., Wood County OH, d. Mar 13 1931 in Deshler, Henry Co., OH, buried in Milton Township Cem.; Wood County OH.
Married Dec 6 1866 in Weston, Wood County OH, **Dexter Ashley McMaster**, b. Dec 20 1842 in Greenfield Twp., Huron Co., OH, d. Mar 24 1925 in Deshler, Henry Co., OH, buried in Milton Township Cem.; Wood County OH.

Children:

340 i. Sylvester[5] Mahoney.
\+ 341 ii. Charity Ellen McMaster b. Sep 14 1869.
\+ 342 iii. William Dexter McMaster b. Mar 26 1871.
\+ 343 iv. Charles Henry McMaster b. Jan 26 1873.
344 v. Frederick Ashley McMaster b. Mar 20 1875, d. DEC 1947 in Custer, Wood Co., OH.
Married Apr 7 1896, **Catherine Rigby**.
345 vi. Frank Nuton McMaster b. Dec 18 1878 in Jackson Twp., Wood County OH, d. OCT 1951 in Findlay, Hancock Co., OH.
346 vii. Oura Alice McMaster b. Mar 30 1882, d. 1916.
\+ 347 viii. George Herman McMaster b. Aug 16 1884.
\+ 348 ix. Myron Edward McMaster b. Jun 11 1887.
349 x. Beulah Ethel McMaster b. Nov 28 1890.
She Married **Fred Taylor**.
350 xi. Mabel Luella McMaster b. Feb 6 1893, d. NOV 1977 in Gallipolis, Gallia Co., OH.
Married Aug 3 1916, **John S. Rumbaugh**.

154. **Jennie[4] Arbogast** (48.Henry[3], 7.Andrew[2], 1.Henry[1]), b. ABT 1865, buried in Greenlawn Cem., Tiffin, Seneca Co., OH.
Married Aug 02 1879 in Tiffin, Seneca Co., OH, **Owen E Ohie**.

Children:

351 i. William[5] Ohie.
352 ii. Charles Ohie.
353 iii. Laura Ohie b. 1871, d. 1891.
354 iv. Henry Ohie.

157. **Howard[4] Harper** (49.Elizabeth Jane[3] Arbogast, 8.Ephriam[2], 1.Henry[1]), b. Jan 04 1865 in Pendleton Co., WV, d. Sep 30 1937 in Pendleton Co., WV.
Married Feb 18 1894 in Pendleton Co., WV, **Gertie Elizabeth Moyers**, b. in Pendleton Co., WV.

Children:

\+ 355 i. Luther Glen[5] Harper b. Oct 01 1897.

171. **Gay G.[4] Arbogast** (61.William Henry[3], 12.George W.[2], 1.Henry[1]), b. Apr 08 1877 in Crabbottom, Highland Co., VA, d. Apr 14 1942 Highland Co., VA.
Married Sep-20-1899 in Highland Co., VA, **Frank C. Beverage**, b. Jun-20-1870, d. Jan-25-1923 in Highland Co., VA. **Frank**: ranks daughter Thelma Married Harry Hale Hollingsworth, no kin.

Children:

356 i. Thelma Flesher[5] Beverage b. Mar-02-1909, d. Feb-02-1980.
She Married **Harry Hale Hollingsworth**, b. Aug 1900, d. Sept 1978.

172. **Ollie A.[4] Arbogast** (61.William Henry[3], 12.George W.[2], 1.Henry[1]), b. Nov 23 1879 in Crabbottom, Highland Co., VA, d. Feb 01 1963 in Highland Co., VA.
Married May-04-1898 in Highland Co., VA, **Kenton L. Mullenax**, b. Dec 10 1865 (son of Henry Clay Mullenax and Lucinda Simmons), d. 1946 in Camille, Prince George's Co., MD.

Children:

\+ 357 i. Mavis A.[5] Mullenax b. Apr-28-2005.
358 ii. Ronald Jones Arbogast b. Apr-19-1908, d. Sep-24-1970.
He Married **Rebecca M. Cox**, d. 17 Dec 1957.
\+ 359 iii. Claris Ella Mullenax b. Oct-15-1910.
360 iv. Ruby Mae Mullenax b. Feb-15-1915.
Married May-07-1960, **Leonard Christebson**.
\+ 361 v. Kenton Dexter Mullenax b. Jul-11-1917.

173. **Cameron Eldridge[4] Arbogast** (61.William Henry[3], 12.George W.[2], 1.Henry[1]), b. Sep 05 1881 in Crabbottom, Highland Co., VA.. Source is AAF research and family group records.
(1) Married 1916, **Annie R. Colaw**, b. Feb-10-1896 in Crabbottom, Highland Co., VA, d. Apr-13-1929.

Children:

\+ 362 i. Martin Dwight[5] Arbogast b. Jun-16-0117.
363 ii. William Blair Arbogast b. Aug-11-1919, d. Aug-17-1939.
(2) He Married **Annia Puffenburger Woofter**, b. Sep-29-1988, d. Feb-26-1976.

174. **Manie Catherine[4] Arbogast** (61.William Henry[3], 12.George W.[2], 1.Henry[1]), b. Aug 08 1883 in Crabbottom, Highland Co., VA, d. Nov 08 1969.
She Married **John David Waybright**, b. Aug-06-1882 in Crabbottom, Highland Co., VA, buried in Blue Grass Cem., Highland Co., VA, d. Nov-08-1969 in Staunton, Augusta Co., VA.

Children:

\+ 364 i. Virginia Ella[5] Waybright b. Aug-21-1915.
\+ 365 ii. William Samuel Waybright b. May-12-1917.
\+ 366 iii. Jeanette Blair Waybright b. Jun-20-1919.

175. **Martha Mae[4] Arbogast** (61.William Henry[3], 12.George W.[2], 1.Henry[1]), b. Jun 19 1887 in Crabbottom, Highland Co., VA, d. Nov 16 1921.
Married Sep-22-1915 in Highland Co., VA, **Abrm Dave Mullenax**.

Children:

367 i. Henry Leon[5] Mullenax b. Nov-13-1916, d. Mar-15-1976.
He Married **Elizabeth Hurley**.
\+ 368 ii. Max Marlin Mullenax b. Jul-10-1919.

176. **William Lurty⁴ Arbogast** (61.William Henry³, 12.George W.², 1.Henry¹), b. Sep 21 1889 in Crabbottom, Highland Co., VA, d. Nov 28 1973.
Married Sep-15-1915 in Highland Co., VA, **Esther Rebecca Chew**, b. Jun-19-1894 in Blue Grass, Highland Co., WV (daughter of Letcher Chew), d. Aug-11-1981 in Staunton, Augusta Co., VA.

Children:

+ 369 i. William Royce⁵ Arbogast b. Jun-05-1916.
+ 370 ii. Wilton Dale Arbogast b. Oct-07-1918.
+ 371 iii. June Lenore Arbogast b. Mar-30-1922.
372 iv. Lurty Chew Arbogast b. Aug-03-1927.
(1) Married Mar-30-1949, **Mary Francis Pannell**.
(2) Married 0741975, **Betty Taylor James**.

177. **William Arbogast⁴ Kee** (62.Mary Catherine³ Arbogast, 12.George W.², 1.Henry¹), b. Apr-04-1946, d. Apr-04-1996.
Married Jul-19-1967, **Lucy Wilson Crigler**, b. Dec-17-1893 in Franklin, Pendleton Co., WV (daughter of henry Crigler), d. 03.

Children:

373 i. Mildred Lee⁵ Kee.
She Married **Hinkle Dice**.
374 ii. Carl Kee.
375 iii. James William Kee.

182. **Eugenious Riley⁴ Arbogast** (73.Samual Walton³, 15.Henry A.², 1.Henry¹), b. Feb 22 1884 in Freemansburg, Lewis Co., WV, d. Apr 14 1947 in Weston, Lewis Co., WV.
Married Jan 29 1911, **Ethel Garrison**.

Children:

376 i. Dorothy⁵ Arbogast b. Jul 24 1913 in Freemansburg, Lewis Co., WV.

194. **Ruth⁴ Arbogast** (79.Abraham (Able) Pryor³, 15.Henry A.², 1.Henry¹), b. Aug 07 1897 in Crabbottom, Highland Co., VA, buried in Arbogast Cem., Blue Grass, Highland Co., VA.
Married Jul 4 1913 in Highland Co., VA, **Wendell Wilfong**, b. 1896 in Highland Co., VA (son of John Ellis Wilfong and Josephine Varner).

Children:

+ 377 i. Roscoe Thomas⁵ Wilfong b. Jun 6 1915.
378 ii. Sharlene Wilfong.
379 iii. Geraldine Wilfong.
380 iv. Dolly Wilfong.
She Married **Ralph Tacy** (son of Robert Jacob Tacy and Virginia Ruth Gear).
381 v. Mary Wilfong.
382 vi. Evone Wilfong.

195. **Robert Lester⁴ Arbogast** (79.Abraham (Able) Pryor³, 15.Henry A.², 1.Henry¹), b. Aug 07 1899 in Crabbottom, Highland Co., VA, d. Aug 20 1959 in Blue Grass, Highland Co., WV.
He Married **Lottie May Propst**.

Children:

383 i. Robert M.⁵ Arbogast d. in Blue Grass, Highland Co., WV.

198. **Frederick Lee⁴ Arbogast** (79.Abraham (Able) Pryor³, 15.Henry A.², 1.Henry¹), b. Jul 06 1904 in Crabbottom, Highland Co., VA, d. Sep 26 1986 in Millboro, Bath Co., VA, buried in Millboro, Bath Co., VA.
Married Jan 19 1929 in Durbin, Pocahontas Co., WV, **Florence Loid Carlson**, b. Oct 27 1910 in Boyer, Pocahontas Co., WV, d. Sep 03 1988 in Staunton, Augusta Co., VA, buried in Millboro, Bath Co., VA.

Children:

384 i. Ruth Elaine⁵ Arbogast b. 1928.
385 ii. Mildred Lee Arbogast b. Sep 05 1929 in Millboro, Bath Co., VA.
386 iii. Nancy Lee Arbogast b. Sep 16 1929 in Millboro, Bath Co., VA.
387 iv. Betty Dare Arbogast b. Oct 21 1935 in Millboro, Bath Co., VA.
Married Jun 06 1959, Earl Blaine Haddix.
388 v. Freddie Carlson Arbogast b. Jun 04 1944 in Millboro, Bath Co., VA.

Married Dec 24 1966 in McDowell, Highland Co., VA, **Mary Catherine Simmons**.

389 vi. Johnny Reid Arbogast b. Nov 03 1953 in Clifton Forge, Allegheny Co., VA.
Married Feb 29 1976 in Grundy, Buchanan Co., VA, **Geneva Howard**.

199. **Carl[4] Arbogast** (79.Abraham (Able) Pryor[3], 15.Henry A.[2], 1.Henry[1]), b. Oct 28 1906 in Crabbottom, Highland Co., VA, d. Nov 28 1984 in Staunton, Augusta Co., VA.
Married Jun 11 1937 in Blue Grass, Highland Co., WV, **Mattie Marie Waggner**.

Children:

390 i. Gail[5] Arbogast.
391 ii. Doris Arbogast.
392 iii. Carylon Arbogast.
393 iv. Ralph Arbogast.

201. **Mary Mildred[4] Arbogast** (79.Abraham (Able) Pryor[3], 15.Henry A.[2], 1.Henry[1]), b. Mar 14 1911 in Crabbottom, Highland Co., VA, d. Jul -3 1994.
She Married **Albert Martin Lotts**.

Children:

394 i. Albert Martin[5] Lotts, Jr..
395 ii. David Lotts.
396 iii. Leon Lotts.
397 iv. Eugene Lotts.
398 v. Kenneth Lotts.
399 vi. William Lotts.

Generation Five

210. **Lutie May[5] Wimer** (88.James Polk[4], 22.Phoebe[3] Lantz, 2.Eleanor[2] Arbogast, 1.Henry[1]), b. Jan 14 1875 in Sweet Springs, Saline Co., MO, d. 28June 1962 in Minnesota.
Member American Legion Auxiliary, Charter member Chapter ET, P.E.O., Trustee of Methodist Episcopal Church, Mayflower Descendants, Colonial Dames of America, Daughter of American Colonists, Daughter of Colonial Wars, Daughter of American Revolution and War of 1812.
Married 11-3-1897 in Wellington, KS, **Edwin Albert Rothrock**.

Children:

\+ 400 i. Ray Russel[6] Rothrock b. 25July 1898.
401 ii. Helen Rothrock b. 9-23-1903 in Wellington, KS, d. 12-5-1918 in Wellington, KS.
Died during influenza epidemic.

216. **Virgie Belle[5] Swecker** (89.John C.[4], 23.Mary[3] Lantz, 2.Eleanor[2] Arbogast, 1.Henry[1]), b. Apr 08 1894, d. May 09 1985 in Blue Grass, Highland Co., WV.
She Married **George E Colaw**, d. Jun 12 1967.

Children:

402 i. Virginia[6] Colaw.
403 ii. Mary Margaret Colaw.
404 iii. Dorothy Colaw.
405 iv. Rebecca Colaw.
406 v. George J Colaw.
407 vi. Paul Colaw.
408 vii. John D Colaw.
409 viii. Wayne Colaw.

224. **Eva C.[5] Rexrode** (91.Mary Elizabeth[4] Waybright, 24.Susannah[3] Lantz, 2.Eleanor[2] Arbogast, 1.Henry[1]), b. Apr 1884.
She Married **John Roston Hively**.

Children:

\+ 410 i. Don Ralston[6] Hively b. Nov 30 1929.

231. **Myrtle[5] Waybright** (93.David Jasper[4], 24.Susannah[3] Lantz, 2.Eleanor[2] Arbogast, 1.Henry[1]), b. Oct 23 1877 in Crabbottom, Highland Co., VA, d. May 18 1950 in Pocahontas County Memorial Hospital, Marlinton, WV, buried in Mountain View Cem., Marlinton, Pocahontas Co., WV.
Married Jan 15 1896 in Highland Co., VA, **Claude Davis Newman**, b. Oct 7 1875 in Crabbottom, Highland Co., VA, d. May 19 1952 in Knapps Creek, Pocahontas Co., WV, buried in Mountain View Cem., Marlinton, Pocahontas Co., WV.

Children:

411 i. Emerson S.[6] Newman b. Oct 29 1897 in McDowell, Highland Co., VA, d. Oct 1975 in Buckeye, Pocahontas Co., WV.
Married Jun 20 1931, Blanche Pritchard, b. Nov 22 1895, d. Jun 1977.
412 ii. Annie Ellen Newman b. Oct 2 1899 in Crabbottom, Highland Co., VA, d. Feb 1 1919.
413 iii. Hazel Newman b. May 29 1901 in Crabbottom, Highland Co., VA, d. Jan 27 1993.
414 iv. Clarence Newman b. Oct 10 1903 in Crabbottom, Highland Co., VA, d. Dec 20 1973, buried in Mountain View Cem., Marlinton, Pocahontas Co., WV.
Married Dec 24 1931, **Helen Hansford**, b. Jan 16 1910 in Parsons, Tucker Co., WV, d. Jul 1 1934 in Marlinton, Pocahontas Co., WV, buried in Mountain View Cem., Marlinton, Pocahontas Co., WV.
415 v. Thelma Newman b. Aug 29 1905 in Crabbottom, Highland Co., VA, d. Feb 22 1995 in Marlinton, Pocahontas Co., WV.
Married Sep 21 1935, **Dock R. Hannah**.
416 vi. Dorothy Newman b. Oct 29 1907 in Crabbottom, Highland Co., VA, d. Feb 22 1996.
Married Dec 25 1929, **Edward Young**.
+ 417 vii. Mary Edith Newman b. Jul 30 1909.
418 viii. Alda Newman b. Aug 23 1911 in Knapps Creek, Pocahontas Co., WV, d. Jun 6 1958.
Married Apr 20 1940, **George E. Diament**.
419 ix. Donald P Newman b. Jul 29 1914 in Knapps Creek, Pocahontas Co., WV.
He Married **Alice Evans**.
420 x. Claude Carnell Newman b. May 12 1916 in Knapps Creek, Pocahontas Co., WV, d. Jun 6 1994 in Richmond, Henrico Co., VA.
Married Jul 23 1938, **Ernestine Sale**.
421 xi. Virginia Newman b. Sep 29 1918 in Knapps Creek, Pocahontas Co., WV.
Married Jan 1 1946, **George William Branett**.
422 xii. Sally Newman b. May 26 1920 in Knapps Creek, Pocahontas Co., WV.
Married May 26 1941, **Byron N. Baer**.

234. **Matie Pearl[5] Waybright** (93.David Jasper[4], 24.Susannah[3] Lantz, 2.Eleanor[2] Arbogast, 1.Henry[1]), b. Jun 12 1884 in Augusta Co., VA, d. May 28 1948, buried in Warrenton Cem., Fauquier Co., VA.
She Married **William Howard Spicer**, b. Jul 31 1869, d. Nov 9 1943, buried in Warrenton Cem., Fauquier Co., VA.

Children:

423 i. Frances[6] Spicer b. in Calverton Fauquier Co., VA.
She Married **George Miller**.
424 ii. William Howard Spicer b. Sep 16 1918 in Calverton Fauquier Co., VA.
Married Jun 1941, **Thelma Mae Crandall**, b. Oct 26 1917.

235. **William Wellington[5] Waybright** (93.David Jasper[4], 24.Susannah[3] Lantz, 2.Eleanor[2] Arbogast, 1.Henry[1]), b. Oct 25 1885 in Highland Co., VA, d. Oct 17 1933 in Alexandria, Fairfax Co., VA, buried in Alexandria, Fairfax Co., VA.
Married Sep 26 1906 in Highland Co., VA, **Maude Mabel Kramer**, b. Aug 15 1885 in Texas, d. May 2 1951 in Alexandria, Fairfax Co., VA.

Children:

425 i. John David[6] Waybright b. Jan 22 1908 in Alexandria, Fairfax Co., VA, d. Aug 23 1970 in New Market, Shenandoah Co., VA, buried Aug 26 1970 in St Matthews Cem., New Market, Shenandoah Co., VA.
Married Jun 9 1936 in Hagerstown, Washington Co., MD, Alma Lynn Galladay, b. Feb 10 1904 in Shenandoah Co., VA, d. May 21 1956 in New Market, Shenandoah Co., VA, buried May 23 1956 in St Matthews Cem., New Market, Shenandoah Co., VA.
+ 426 ii. Everett Payne Waybright b. Nov 18 1909.
427 iii. Richard Kramer Waybright b. Feb 17 1911 in Alexandria, Fairfax Co., VA, d. Jul 13 1956 in Alexandria, Fairfax Co., VA.
428 iv. Mary Virginia Waybright b. Jul 11 1913 in Alexandria, Fairfax Co., VA, d. Sep 28 1919 in Alexandria, Fairfax Co., VA, buried in Bethel Cem., Alexandria, Fairfax, VA.

429 v. Louise Mabel Waybright b. Mar 29 1916 in Alexandria, Fairfax Co., VA, d. Mar 8 1994 in Warrenton Fauquier Co., VA, buried in Bethel Cem., Alexandria, Fairfax, VA.

430 vi. Helen Grace Waybright b. Feb 4 1921 in Alexandria, Fairfax Co., VA.
Married Aug 19 1940 in Fairfax, Fairfax Co., VA, **Thomas Paul Cooper**, b. Feb 23 1917 in Walkersville, Braxton Co., WV.

238. **Ida Bell "Eliza"^{5} Sargeant** (94.Eli^{4}, 28.Elizabeth^{3} Halterman, 4.Mary^{2} Arbogast, 1.Henry^{1}), b. Oct 25 1873 in Mount Auburn Cem., Mount Auburn, IL, d. Sep 8 1894 in Taylorsville, Christian Co., IL, buried in Mount Auburn Cem., Mount Auburn, IL.
Married Feb 7 1889 in Christian Co., IL, **Ezra Garland**, b. Sep 21 1856, d. Aug 13 1931, buried in Mount Auburn Cem., Mount Auburn, IL.

Children:

\+ 431 i. Rolley^{6} Garland b. Jan 23 1890.

240. **Joseph Chester^{5} Sargeant** (94.Eli^{4}, 28.Elizabeth^{3} Halterman, 4.Mary^{2} Arbogast, 1.Henry^{1}), b. Sep 24 1884 in Mount Auburn Cem., Mount Auburn, IL, d. Aug 6 1949 in Lakeland, Polk Co., FL, buried Aug 8 1949 in Elmwood Cem., Birmingham, Jefferson Co., AL.J. C. died of Uremia, Chronic glomerulonephritis and Arteriosclerotic heart disease.

This is the obituary from the Birmingham, Alabama newspaper: J. C.
Sargeant, Sr.

A Birmingham resident who left the city in the early 1920's for Florida, will be returned here for burial.

J. C. Sargeant, Sr. died Saturday in Lakeland, Fla. Funeral services were held today at the Duke-Steen Funeral Chapel in Lakeland.

A native of Illinois, he was in the mercantile business here for 12 years. He moved to Lakeland in 1921 where he became a citrus fruit grower. He was president of the Sargeant Farms, and president of Polk Dairies in Florida.

Surviving are his widow, Mrs. Mattie Pearl Mackey Sargeant; four sons, J.C. Sargeant, Jr., Birmingham; Ralph G. Sargeant, John Sargeant and Stanley Sargeant, all of Lakeland.

Johns Funeral Home will be in charge of burial at Elmwood Cemetery.

Children:

432 i. Joseph Chester "Jody"^{6} Sargeant Jr. b. Nov 4 1909 in Birmingham, Jefferson Co., AL, d. Nov 12 1976 in Lakeland, Polk Co., FL, buried in Elmwood Cem., Birmingham, Jefferson Co., AL.

433 ii. Ralph George Sargeant b. Jan 24 1913 in Birmingham, Jefferson Co., AL, d. Mar 11 1977 in Lakeland, Polk Co., FL, buried Mar 14 1977 in Lakeland Memorial Gardens, Lakeland, Polk Co., FL.
Married 1939, **Margaret Lowry**, b. Jan 18 1920 in Eugene, Lane Co., OR, d. Jan 26 1995 in Lakeland, Polk Co., FL, buried Jan 30 1995 in Lakeland Memorial Gardens, Lakeland, Polk Co., FL.
Born in Eugene, Ore., on Jan. 18, 1920, she moved from Winter Haven to Lakeland in 1951. She was a member of the Daughters of the American Revolution. She was a member of the First Methodist Church of Lakeland.

434 iii. John Boyd Sargeant Sr. b. May 29 1915 in Birmingham, Jefferson Co., AL, d. Mar 6 1989 in Lakeland, Polk Co., FL, buried Mar 9 1989 in Lakeland Memorial Gardens, Lakeland, Polk Co., FL.

259. **Rex Hiram^{5} Halterman** (107.Ephrain Vandlandingham^{4}, 35.Ephraim^{3}, 4.Mary^{2} Arbogast, 1.Henry^{1}), b. Jul 27 1897 in Verona, Lawrence Co., MO, d. Aug 4 1978 in Aurora, Lawrence Co., MO.
Married Mar 5 1927 in Aurora, Lawrence Co., MO, **Crete Reitha Bouyer**, b. Mar 26 1904 in Aurora, Lawrence Co., MO, d. Aug 29 2000 in Aurora, Lawrence Co., MO.

Children:

435 i. Danny Rex Sr.^{6} Halterman b. Sep 22 1927 in Aurora, Lawrence Co., MO, d. Mar 14 1998 in Springfield, Greene Co., MO.

436 ii. Russel Lee Halterman b. Dec 31 1931 in Aurora, Lawrence Co., MO, d. Jul 30 1996 in Springfield, Greene Co., MO.

264. **Carl Newton^{5} Rexroad** (109.William Wyatt^{4}, 37.John J^{3}, 5.Phebe^{2} Arbogast, 1.Henry^{1}), b. Sep 03 1896 in Darlow, Reno Co., KS, d. Feb 20 1965 in Columbia, Boone Co., MO.
Married Jun 12 1924 in New Haven Co., CT, **May Christine Buckner**, b. Mar 03 1897 in East Hampton, MS (daughter of George Stephen Buckner and Amelia Vogel), d. Jun 26 1987 in Columbia, Boone Co., MO.

Children:

437 i. Carl Buckner^{6} Rexroad b. Apr 02 1925.
Married Apr 07 1951 in Ruston, Lincoln Parish, LA, **Edythe Rose Evens**.

438 ii. Bonnie Sue Rexroad b. Jul 01 1930 in Columbia, Boone Co., MO.
Married Nov 16 1951 in Bentonville, Benton Co., AR, **Donald Kemper Reid**.

278. **Walter Raymond^5 Simmons** (124.Andrew Lincoln^4, 40.Phebe^3 Rexroad, 5.Phebe^2 Arbogast, 1.Henry^1), b. Jun 04 1902 in Gainesville, Ozark Co., MO, d. Feb 24 1931.
Married Dec 01 1920 in Detroit, Wayne Co., MI, **June Elizabeth Putman**, b. Jun 20 1902 in Henning, Vermilion Co., IL.

Children:

+ 439 i. Wallace Raymond^6 Simmons b. Jun 26 1921.
+ 440 ii. Paul Herbert Simmons b. Jan 25 1925.

279. **Melvin Andrew^5 Simmons** (124.Andrew Lincoln^4, 40.Phebe^3 Rexroad, 5.Phebe^2 Arbogast, 1.Henry^1), b. Aug 22 1904 in Gainesville, Ozark Co., MO, d. Apr 07 1947 in Dearborn, Wayne County OH.
He Married **Alma Alice Ingram**, b. Dec 22 1919 in Bay City, Bay Co., MI.

Children:

441 i. Dorothy Jean^6 Simmons b. Mar 10 1937 in Argyle, Sanilac Co., MI.
Married Feb 15 1955 in Wayne Co., MI, **James Howard Copper**.
+ 442 ii. Robert Walter Simmons b. Mar 30 1939.

281. **Mary^5 Morrison** (125.Sophia^4 Arbogast, 43.Jesse^3, 6.Sophia^2, 1.Henry^1), b. Aug 01 1859 in Good Hope, Walnut Grove, Putnam Co., IL.
(1) Married Dec 01 1876 in Monmouth, Warren Co., IL, **Edward Earl Payne**, b. Jul 15 1849 in Pleasant Valley, Scott Co., IA (son of Jeremiah E. Payne and Letitia Orr), d. Jan 01 1886 in Hannah, Henry Co., IL.

Children:

+ 443 i. William Charles^6 Payne b. Feb 02 1878.
444 ii. Ida Mae Payne b. Feb 24 1879 in Good Hope, Walnut Grove, Putnam Co., IL, d. Feb 20 1902.
Died of tuberculosis.
445 iii. Ada Letitia Payne b. Aug 04 1882 in Good Hope, Walnut Grove, Putnam Co., IL, d. Oct 24 1902.
Died of tuberculosis.
446 iv. Leroy L Payne b. Oct 30 1882 in Good Hope, Walnut Grove, Putnam Co., IL, d. 1945.
He Married **Bessie E Stump**.
447 v. Walter Scott Payne b. Jun 04 1884 in Good Hope, Walnut Grove, Putnam Co., IL, d. Jul 22 1906.
Died of tuberculosis.

(2) Married Aug 19 1890 in McComb, McDonough Co., IL, **Lafayette Powers**. **Lafayette**: Moved to Sedalia, MO 1n 1898.

285. **Rose^5 Morrison** (125.Sophia^4 Arbogast, 43.Jesse^3, 6.Sophia^2, 1.Henry^1), b. Oct 18 1869 in Good Hope, Walnut Grove, Putnam Co., IL, d. Oct 03 1954 in McComb, McDonough Co., IL.
Married 1892, **Isaac Woolverton**.

Children:

+ 448 i. Harry^6 Woolverton.

287. **Ida^5 Morrison** (125.Sophia^4 Arbogast, 43.Jesse^3, 6.Sophia^2, 1.Henry^1), b. 1875 in Good Hope, Walnut Grove, Putnam Co., IL.
She Married **Ed Reipen**.

Children:

449 i. Helen^6 Reipen.
450 ii. Lottie Reipen.

289. **Amy^5 Brown** (128.Mary Jane^4 Arbogast, 43.Jesse^3, 6.Sophia^2, 1.Henry^1), b. Feb 06 1873 in McComb, McDonough Co., IL, d. Jun 20 1947.
Married Dec 19 1900, **George Carl Clarke**, b. 1878.

Children:

+ 451 i. Bernice^6 Clarke b. Jul 30 1912.
+ 452 ii. Carl C Clarke b. Oct 04 1915.

291. **Ethel Clare^5 Brown** (128.Mary Jane^4 Arbogast, 43.Jesse^3, 6.Sophia^2, 1.Henry^1), b. Sep 03 1875 in McComb, McDonough Co., IL, d. Apr 30 1957.
Married Sep 19 1904, **Harold Mitchell**, b. 1877, d. 1961.

Children:

+ 453 i. R Taylor^6 Mitchell b. Nov 09 1908.

293. **Lois Irene^5 Brown** (128.Mary Jane^4 Arbogast, 43.Jesse^3, 6.Sophia^2, 1.Henry^1), b. Feb 11 1880 in McComb, McDonough Co., IL, d. Dec 08 1966.

Married Oct 13 1910, **Charles Frary**, b. Mar 15 1883, d. Apr 04 1966.

Children:

	454	i.	Robert Orlando[6] Frary b. Dec 11 1911. Married Jan 23 1944, **Delores Samuelson**.
+	455	ii.	Thelma Hannah Frary.
+	456	iii.	Alice Lucille Frary b. Jul 20 1914.
	457	iv.	Virginia Elizabeth Frary b. Oct 03 1916, d. Aug 20 1919.

295. **Mertice Loine[5] Brown** (128.Mary Jane[4] Arbogast, 43.Jesse[3], 6.Sophia[2], 1.Henry[1]), b. Oct 29 1886 in McComb, McDonough Co., IL, d. Mar 19 1932.
She Married **Harry Mikesell**, b. Oct 12 1884, d. Oct 24 1954.

Children:

+	458	i.	Lewis[6] Mikesell b. Nov 14 1912.
+	459	ii.	Osmond Mikesell b. Feb 13 1914.
+	460	iii.	Weist Lamoine Mikesell b. May 15 1916.
+	461	iv.	Orth Arbogast Mikesell b. Nov 14 1919.
+	462	v.	Betty Lou Mikesell b. Jun 17 1921.
+	463	vi.	Erwin Claire Mikesell b. Apr 08 1924.

301. **Mae[5] Howard** (131.Sarah[4] Arbogast, 43.Jesse[3], 6.Sophia[2], 1.Henry[1]), b. May 01 1874 in Scioto Twp., McDonough Co., IL, d. Dec 28 1932.
Married Feb 08 1898 in Good Hope, Walnut Grove, Putnam Co., IL, **William Oscar Cozad**, b. Jun 01 1868 in Ellisville, Fulton Co., IL, d. Jun 31 1949 in McComb, McDonough Co., IL.

Children:

+	464	i.	Sarah Fern[6] Cozad b. Jul 24 1899.
+	465	ii.	Faun Elizabeth Cozad b. Jun 12 1902.

304. **Neil[5] Smith** (133.Frances[4] Arbogast, 43.Jesse[3], 6.Sophia[2], 1.Henry[1]), b. Dec 08 1877, d. Jan 03 1942 in Bayless, Pike Co., IL.
She Married **Thomas R. Askew**, b. Jan 19 1874, d. Oct 1952.

Children:

	466	i.	Wayne F[6] Askew b. Sep 12 1915 in Dahlgren, Hamilton Co., IL. Married Jun 01 1937, **Mary K. Johnson**.

305. **Emerson Eugene[5] Smith** (133.Frances[4] Arbogast, 43.Jesse[3], 6.Sophia[2], 1.Henry[1]).
He Married **Aletha Bryan Morris**.

Children:

+	467	i.	Margaret[6] Smith b. Apr 06 1911.
	468	ii.	Caroline Smith b. May 31 1916. She Married **James Wicks**.
+	469	iii.	Russell Smith b. May 31 1916.

307. **Jessie[5] Smith** (133.Frances[4] Arbogast, 43.Jesse[3], 6.Sophia[2], 1.Henry[1]).
She Married **Ezra Huffman**.

Children:

	470	i.	Irena[6] Huffman.
	471	ii.	Ruth Huffman.
	472	iii.	Glen Huffman.

309. **June[5] Smith** (133.Frances[4] Arbogast, 43.Jesse[3], 6.Sophia[2], 1.Henry[1]), b. Jun 1887, d. Oct 31 1984.
Married Nov 21 1920, **Oscar Olson**, d. 1972.

Children:

	473	i.	Maxwell Terry[6] Olson.
	474	ii.	Francis Nels Olson.
	475	iii.	Marlin Jean Olson.
	476	iv.	Oscar George Olson.

310. **Myrtle[5] Smith** (133.Frances[4] Arbogast, 43.Jesse[3], 6.Sophia[2], 1.Henry[1]), b. Dec 17 1896, d. Dec 15 1982.

Married Oct 03 1909, **George Harold Fox**, b. Nov 10 1885, d. Jan 22 1961.

Children:

+ 477 i. Keith Leroy[6] Fox b. Oct 15 1911.
+ 478 ii. Ralth Wilton Fox b. May 01 1913.

311. **Clyde Stewart[5] Arbogast** (134.Stephen Aaron Douglas[4], 43.Jesse[3], 6.Sophia[2], 1.Henry[1]), b. Feb 03 1891 in Rising City, Butler Co., NE, d. Aug 11 1965 in Burley, Cassia Co., ID.
Married Mar 24 1905, **Anta Marie Conkling**, b. Dec 18 1889 in Shelley, Bingham Co., ID, d. Jan 22 1927 in Maple Grove Cem., Rochester, Olmsted Co., MN.

Children:

+ 479 i. Theodore Fenton[6] Arbogast b. Sep 11 1905.
480 ii. Clare Eleanor Arbogast b. Nov 05 1910 in Silver Creek, Blaine Co., ID, d. Apr 01 1927.
+ 481 iii. Helen Elene Arbogast b. Aug 15 1912.
+ 482 iv. Allen Sterart Arbogast b. Jul 02 1914.
+ 483 v. Gladys Catherine Arbogast b. Aug 27 1917.
484 vi. Dorothy Dare Arbogast b. May 20 1920 in Burley, Cassia Co., ID, d. 1937.
+ 485 vii. Marilyn Inez Arbogast b. Jun 03 1924.

313. **Nellie Millicent[5] Arbogast** (134.Stephen Aaron Douglas[4], 43.Jesse[3], 6.Sophia[2], 1.Henry[1]), b. Sep 22 1898 in Rising City, Butler Co., NE, d. Aug 16 1991 in Grand Island, Hall Co., NE.
Married Nov 02 1920, **Gilfford E. Hutchison**, b. Dec 15 1896 in Ashland, Saunders Co., NE, d. Mar 11 1973 in Grand Island, Hall Co., NE.

Children:

+ 486 i. Carolyn Jean[6] Hutchison b. Aug 14 1921.
+ 487 ii. Betty Jane Hutchison b. Feb 04 1924.

314. **Gladys Mary[5] Arbogast** (134.Stephen Aaron Douglas[4], 43.Jesse[3], 6.Sophia[2], 1.Henry[1]), b. May 18 1901 in Silver Creek, Merrick Co., NE.
She Married **John Gerber**.

Children:

+ 488 i. Marjorie Elaine[6] Gerber b. May 17 1921.
489 ii. Mary Lois Gerber b. Feb 24 1925 in Silver Creek, Merrick Co., NE, d. Aug 16 1977 in Chicago, Cook Co., IL.
Married Oct 06 1944 in Florida, **Emil Kupcik**.

315. **Harold Edson[5] Arbogast** (134.Stephen Aaron Douglas[4], 43.Jesse[3], 6.Sophia[2], 1.Henry[1]), b. Nov 30 1912 in Silver Creek, Merrick Co., NE, d. Oct 09 1963 in Nyssa, OR.
He Married **Nellie Hokanson**, b. Sep 26 1917 in Thayne, Lincoln Co., WY.

Children:

490 i. Patricia Ann[6] Arbogast b. Nov 29 1939 in Afton, Lincoln Co., WY.
Married Jun 23 1955, **Brent J. Harrison.**
491 ii. Liola Arbogast b. Mar 20 1941 in Afton, Lincoln Co., WY.
Married Oct 04 1957, **Rex N. Leavitt**.
492 iii. Gloria Arbogast b. Oct 26 1942 in Afton, Lincoln Co., WY.
Married Jun 24 1958, **Edward Stumpp**.

318. **Lorenzo[5] STAIB** (137.Alice M.[4] Arbogast, 46.Michael[3], 6.Sophia[2], 1.Henry[1]), b. Feb 08 1892, d. Sep 25 1970.
He Married **Mary Dartz**.

Children:

493 i. Lewis Victor[6] Staib.
494 ii. Alice Kay Staib.

She Married **Wilber Kenny**.
495 iii. Jean Staib.
She Married **Charles Hughes.**
496 iv. Paul Staib.
497 v. Helen Rose Staib.

319. **Nettie^5 STAIB** (137.Alice M.^{4} Arbogast, 46.Michael^3, 6.Sophia^2, 1.Henry^1).
She Married **Charles Kingseed**.

Children:

498 i. Carl^6 Kingseed.

320. **Jessie L.^{5} Arbogast** (138.John Franklin^4, 46.Michael^3, 6.Sophia^2, 1.Henry^1), b. Aug 20 1880 in Seneca Co., OH, d. Mar 13 1958 in Seneca Co., OH.
He Married **Etta Margaret Estep**, b. About 1881, d. About 1946, buried in Tacoma, Pierce Co., WA.

Children:

499 i. Howard^6 Arbogast.
500 ii. Edgar Allen Arbogast b. Oct 24 1904, d. Nov 18 1980 in Tiffin, Seneca Co., OH.
501 iii. Merlin M. Arbogast b. About 1905, d. About 1937 in Tiffin, Seneca Co., OH.
502 iv. Neva Arbogast.
She Married **Myron Tuttle.**
503 v. Annabelle Arbogast.
\+ 504 vi. Dwight Arbogast b. Jul 13 1911.
505 vii. Loris Arbogast b. About 1914 in Seneca Co., OH, d. About 1946 in Seneca Co., OH.
He Married Mary **Lou Fosnaugh**.

325. **James Warren^5 Arbogast** (139.Lewis Heenan^4, 46.Michael^3, 6.Sophia^2, 1.Henry^1), b. Dec 29 1896, d. Jan 20 1981.
Married Oct 16 1920, **Mildred Hovis**.

Children:

506 i. Ann^6 Arbogast.
507 ii. Sharlin Arbogast.
She Married **Paul Troxell**.
508 iii. Joan Arbogast.
She Married **Marion Miller.**

333. **James Michael^5 Arbogast** (141.Charles Sayers^4, 46.Michael^3, 6.Sophia^2, 1.Henry^1), b. Dec 16 1887 in Walnut Grove, Knox Co., IL, d. July 1965.
He Married **Tola Merle McGee**, b. Sep 11 1890.

Children:

\+ 509 i. Lois Alberta^6 Arbogast.
\+ 510 ii. Gayl Jane Arbogast b. Oct 14 1921.
\+ 511 iii. Charles Sayers Arbogast b. Jul 29 1925.

334. **Alice^5 Arbogast** (141.Charles Sayers^4, 46.Michael^3, 6.Sophia^2, 1.Henry^1).
She Married **Chauncey Brewster Heath**. .

Children:

\+ 512 i. James Kenneth^6 Heath b. Jan 08 1913.
\+ 513 ii. Marion E. Heath b. Nov 18 1917.

337. **Clarence James^5 Arbogast** (142.Rush Arlington^4, 46.Michael^3, 6.Sophia^2, 1.Henry^1), b. Jun-08-1904, d. Jan-21-1904.
He Married **Aleta Talley**, b. 1902, d. 1976..

Children:

\+ 514 i. James Clarence^6 Arbogast b. Mar 13 1927.
\+ 515 ii. Naomi Agnus Arbogast b. Jun 06 1938.

338. **Charles Anthony^5 Arbogast** (142.Rush Arlington^4, 46.Michael^3, 6.Sophia^2, 1.Henry^1), b. Sep-11-1900, d. 1171982 in Seneca Co., OH.
Married Nov-22-1921, Married Feb-22-1975, **Loretta Rose Rhinehart**, b. Sep-11-1900.

Children:

\+ 516 i. Paul Joseph^6 Arbogast b. Sep-06-1922.
\+ 517 ii. Lawrence Anselm Arbogast b. Dec-20-1924.
\+ 518 iii. Urban Anthony Arbogast b. Mar-20-1926.

+ 519 iv. Eugene Jerome Arbogast b. Oct 24 1928.
+ 520 v. Marion Victor Arbogast b. Apr 16 1930.
+ 521 vi. Marguerite Elenora Arbogast b. Apr 30 1934.
+ 522 vii. Harlan Clarence Arbogast b. Nov 24 1936.
+ 523 viii. Lester Michael Arbogast b. Jul 21 1938.
+ 524 ix. Rita Mae Arbogast b. Nov-26-1941.
+ 525 x. Louis Cyril Arbogast b. Aug-01-1944.
526 xi. Joseph Arbogast b. Aug-01-1944, d. Aug-01-1944.

339. **Frances Marie[5] Arbogast** (142.Rush Arlington[4], 46.Michael[3], 6.Sophia[2], 1.Henry[1]), b. Dec 28 1892, d. Jan 29 1967.

Married Jan 26 1915, **Louis Joseph Smith**.

Children:

+ 527 i. Clarence Louis[6] SMITH b. Nov 17 1915.
+ 528 ii. Rita Theresa Smith b. Nov 07 1916.
+ 529 iii. Richard Joseph Smith b. Mar 12 1920.
530 iv. Dorothy Clara Smith b. Jul 29 1921, d. Jul 05 1950.
Married Jan 16 1946, **Bernard Joseph Frankart**, b. Mar 22 1919, d. Feb 19 1980.
+ 531 v. Marjorie Mary Smith b. Oct 17 1922.
+ 532 vi. Robert Eugene Smith b. Sep 19 1925.
+ 533 vii. Helen Francis Smith b. Sep 28 1927.
+ 534 viii. Bernard Charles Smith b. May 30 1929.
+ 535 ix. Leo Frederick Smith b. Feb 19 1931.
+ 536 x. Catherine Louise Smith b. Dec 20 1935.
+ 537 xi. Rosemary Smith b. Jan 22 1938.

341. **Charity Ellen[5] McMaster** (146.Mary Anna[4] Morrison, 47.Barbara Ellen[3] Arbogast, 7.Andrew[2], 1.Henry[1]), b. Sep 14 1869 in Milton Twp., Wood County OH, d. Nov 1 1953 in Fostoria, Seneca County OH, buried in Milton Twp., Wood County OH. Married Jul 19 1890 in Bowling Green, Henry County OH, **Clifton Burr Emahiser**, b. Mar 19 1866 in Morrow Co., OH, d. in Deshler, Henry Co., OH, buried in Milton Twp., Wood County OH.

Children:

538 i. (unknown)[6] Emahiser.
She Married **Emmet Leffel**, b. 1893, d. Nov 2 1970.
+ 539 ii. Lawrence Owen Emahiser b. Apr 6 1891.
540 iii. Elizabeth Grace Emahiser b. Nov 5 1892, d. Feb 25 1978.
She Married **Frank Lahr**, b. Mar 22 1891, d. May 28 1974.
+ 541 iv. Roscoe Emahiser b. Mar 19 1894.
542 v. Blanche Marie Emahiser b. Mar 18 1896 in Deshler, Henry Co., OH, d. OCT 1975 in Fostoria, Seneca County OH.
Married Apr 15 1914 in Fostoria, Seneca County OH, **Russell Hamilton Stiles**, b. Jan 17 1895 in Columbus Grove, Putnam Co., OH, d. Jan 3 1965 in Fostoria, Seneca County OH, buried in Fostoria, Seneca County OH.
543 vi. Laura Bernice Emahiser b. Jul 1 1897, d. Jun 18 1982.
She Married **John Crouch**, b. Jan 30 1897, d. Feb 20 1973.
544 vii. Florence Ethel Emahiser b. May 4 1899, d. Jan 3 1979.
Married Jun 22 1919, **Hobson Kline**, b. Apr 24 1898, d. Mar 7 1974.
545 viii. Dexter Ashley Emahiser b. Apr 19 1901, d. Oct 29 1983 in Dearborn, Wayne County OH.
Married AUG 1925, **Alice Marie Vandembussche**, b. Aug 18 1904, d. Oct 2 1974 in Dearborn, Wayne County OH.
+ 546 ix. George Clifton Emahiser b. Feb 1 1903.
547 x. Alice Irene Emahiser b. Oct 9 1904, d. Mar 9 1986.
Married Mar 15 1923, **Leo Maloch**, b. MAY 1901, d. 1989.
548 xi. Charles Raymond Emahiser b. Jul 30 1906 in Custer, Wood Co., OH, d. Oct 5 1985 in Fostoria, Seneca County OH, buried in Fountain Cem.; Fostoria, Seneca County OH.
(1) He Married **Ethel Mae Perry**, b. Jun 23 1919, buried in Eagle Creek Cem.
(2) He Married (unknown) Perry.
(3) Married Dec 3 1928 in Arcadia, Hancock County OH, **Marie Mae Moon**, b. Mar 24 1909 in Fostoria, Seneca County OH, d. Feb 5 1967 in Fostoria, Seneca County OH.

549 xii. Arthur Leland Emahiser b. Sep 7 1911 in Deshler, Henry Co., OH, d. Dec 13 1977 in Hancock County OH, buried in Maplewood Cem.; North Baltimore, OH.
He Married **(unknown) King**.

550 xiii. Marvel Oda Emahiser b. Jun 17 1915, d. Apr 12 1990 in Hancock County OH.
Married Jun 14 1935, **Hershel Haley**, b. FEB 1913, d. Jan 6 1976.

342. **William Dexter[5] McMaster** (146.Mary Anna[4] Morrison, 47.Barbara Ellen[3] Arbogast, 7.Andrew[2], 1.Henry[1]), b. Mar 26 1871, d. 1960, buried in Young's Cem., Liberty Twp., Henry Co., OH.
He Married **Sarah Matilda Emahiser**, b. Apr 12 1877, d. 1961, buried in Young's Cem., Liberty Twp., Henry Co., OH.

Children:

551 i. Elizabeth[6] McMaster.
She Married **(unknown) Thorn.**

343. **Charles Henry[5] McMaster** (146.Mary Anna[4] Morrison, 47.Barbara Ellen[3] Arbogast, 7.Andrew[2], 1.Henry[1]), b. Jan 26 1873 in Jackson Twp., Wood County OH, d. Jul 14 1944 in McComb, Hancock County OH.
Married Apr 22 1895, **Myrta Mae Funk**.

Children:

552 i. Raymond L.[6] McMaster b. About 1908.

553 ii. Howard G. McMaster b. About 1913.

554 iii. Homer E. McMaster b. About 1917.

347. **George Herman[5] McMaster** (146.Mary Anna[4] Morrison, 47.Barbara Ellen[3] Arbogast, 7.Andrew[2], 1.Henry[1]), b. Aug 16 1884 in Wood Co., OH, d. Jul 15 1967 in Wood County Hospital, Bowling Green, Wood Co., OH, buried in Woodlawn Cem.; Barlow Twp., Henry County OH.
Married in Monroe, Monroe Co., MI, **Nancy Lauretta Butler**, b. Dec 12 1893, d. Sep 25 1970 in Wood County Hospital, Bowling Green, Wood Co., OH.

Children:

555 i. Earl Darrold[6] McMaster b. ABT 1913 in Deshler, Henry Co., OH, d. in Deshler, Henry Co., OH.

556 ii. Bertha Mary McMaster b. Jan 5 1914 in Deshler, Henry Co., OH.
Married Apr 18 1937, **Ed Rutter**, b. Jan 9 1917, d. ABT 1965.

557 iii. Harold Ashley McMaster b. Jul 21 1916 in Deshler, Henry Co., OH.
Married Apr 30 1937 in Ohio, **Helen Elizabeth Clark**, b. Dec 13 1916 in Ohio.

558 iv. Hazel Iona McMaster b. May 6 1918 in Deshler, Henry Co., OH.
Residence: built; sold to Dexter & Marilyn.
Married Mar 30 1940 in Sandusky, Sanilac Co., OH, Frank Austin Larimer, b. Dec 25 1915 in Sandusky, Sanilac Co., OH, d. Oct 7 2002 in Ohio, buried Oct 10 2002 in Fort Meigs Cem.; Perrysburg, Wood Co., OH. Frank: The Toledo Blade
October 8, 2002
Frank A. Larimer, age 86 of Perrysburg, died Monday, October 7, 2002, in his daughter's home. He was born December 25, 1915, in Sandusky, Ohio, to Fred and Anna (Berry) Larimer and was Married March 30, 1940, to Hazel I. McMaster. Frank attended Baldwin-Wallace College in Cleveland, Ohio, where he was a member of Phi Kappa Phi and was later inducted into Athletic Hall of Fame.
Frank's career in the glass industry began at Perma glass, in Genoa, OH, as sales manager with Harold McMaster and Norm Nitschke. He later served with them as Vice-President-Treasurer at Glasstech, Inc. In the interim Frank worked for Tempglass, Inc. Frank's passion was golf. As a smooth swinger he was well known for consistently shooting a score lower than his age. He was a member of Belmont Country Club in Perrysburg, OH, and Briarwood Country Club in Sun City West, AZ. He was also a generous contributor and supporter of all their employees.
Frank established several scholarships and gave abundantly to Baldwin-Wallace College and the University of Toledo, where a state of the art educational complex was named after him, the Larimer Athletic Complex. His donations to the Way Public Library set up the Larimer Family Book Collection which were made available to many teachers as mobile educational units. He was also actively involved and supported the Sun City West Sundome in AZ.
He leaves to cherish his memory his wife, Hazel I. Larimer; children, Drack A. (Janet) Larimer of Jackson Hole, WY, and Susan J. Goliver of Perrysburg, OH; grandchildren, Doug and Amy Larimer, Patrick Johnson, Jake and Kaie Goliver and his brother's son, Jake Larimer. He was preceded in death by his parents, and brother, Arthur Larimer.

Friends will be received from 4-9 p.m. Wednesday in the Witzler-Shank Funeral Home, 222 E. South Boundary, Perrysburg (419-874-3133) when funeral service will be held 1 p.m. Thursday, October 10, 2002, with Rev. Hal Mills, officiating. Burial will follow in Fort Meigs Cemetery. Those planning an expression of sympathy are asked to consider a charity of the donor's choice.

559 v. Leona Eloise McMaster b. Jun 6 1920 in Deshler, Henry Co., OH.
Married May 16 1964, **Arthur Schwartz**, b. May 24 1917, d. Feb 25 1987.

560 vi. Erma Mae McMaster b. Oct 1 1922 in Deshler, Henry Co., OH.
(1) Married Dec 24 1941, **James Frederick Buhler**:
(2) Married Aug 24 1952, **Delbert Cluckey**, b. Jan 9 1923, d. Feb 15 1990.

561 vii. Dexter Herman McMaster b. Nov 5 1924 in Deshler, Henry Co., OH.

562 viii. Clarence Owen McMaster b. Aug 1 1926 in Deshler, Henry Co., OH.

563 ix. Reva Jean McMaster b. Dec 12 1927 in Deshler, Henry Co., OH.
Married Aug 17 1947, **Dalton Christman**, b. Jul 9 1927.

564 x. June Eileen McMaster b. Jun 17 1929 in Deshler, Henry Co., OH, d. Jan 24 1938 in Deshler, Henry Co., OH.

348. **Myron Edward[5] McMaster** (146.Mary Anna[4] Morrison, 47.Barbara Ellen[3] Arbogast, 7.Andrew[2], 1.Henry[1]), b. Jun 11 1887 in Wood Co., OH, d. Mar 4 1933 in Bartow Twp., Deshler Village, Henry County OH.
Married Jun 14 1908, **Sarah Almeda Russell**, b. Dec 25 1886 in Jackson Twp., Wood County OH, d. Apr 27 1925 in Barlow Twp., Deshler Village, Henry County OH.

Children:

\+ 565 i. Mary Luella[6] McMaster b. May 06 1909.

\+ 566 ii. Alvie Clifford McMaster.

567 iii. (unknown) McMaster.
She Married **(unknown) Marksch**.

568 iv. John Dexter McMaster b. Mar 23 1914 in Dashler, Barlow Twp., Henry Co., OH, d. May 29 1967 in Norfolk, VA.
Married About 1944 in Bremerton, Kitsap Co., WA, **Avonell Swope**, d. About 1993 in Norfolk, VA.

\+ 569 v. Alice May McMaster b. Feb 19 1917.

570 vi. (unknown) McMaster.
She Married **(unknown) Miller**.

571 vii. (unknown) McMaster.

\+ 572 viii. Imo-Geraldine McMaster b. Sep 22 1921.

355. **Luther Glen[5] Harper** (157.Howard[4], 49.Elizabeth Jane[3] Arbogast, 8.Ephriam[2], 1.Henry[1]), b. Oct 01 1897 in Pendleton Co., WV, d. Sep 14 1979 in Morgantown, Monongalia Co., WV.
Married Apr 02 1920 in Franklin Co., WV, **Montie Fleisher**.

Children:

573 i. Irene[6] Harper.

574 ii. Louise Harper.

357. **Mavis A.[5] Mullenax** (172.Ollie A.[4] Arbogast, 61.William Henry[3], 12.George W.[2], 1.Henry[1]), b. Apr-28-2005 in Crabbottom, Highland Co., VA, d. Mar-14-1952 in Highland Co., VA.
Married Sep-13-1920, **John H. Hevener**.

Children:

575 i. Kathleen Hope[6] Hevener b. Jul-20-1921 in NY.
Married May-11-1944, **Ernest A. Thompson**.

\+ 576 ii. Madelyn Gayle Hevener b. Feb-03-1923.

359. **Claris Ella[5] Mullenax** (172.Ollie A.[4] Arbogast, 61.William Henry[3], 12.George W.[2], 1.Henry[1]), b. Oct-15-1910.
Married Feb-11-1931, **James Arthur Jerman**.

Children:

577 i. James Arthur[6] Jerman, Jr. b. Oct-24-1931, d. Feb-14-1968.

361. **Kenton Dexter[5] Mullenax** (172.Ollie A.[4] Arbogast, 61.William Henry[3], 12.George W.[2], 1.Henry[1]), b. Jul-11-1917.
Married Jun-17-1941, **Gertrude Maequess**, d. Oct-15-1956.

Children:

\+ 578 i. Wanda Dran[6] Mullenax b. Feb-27-1944.

579 ii. Kenton Dexter Mullenax, Jr. b. Apr-16-1952.

(1) Married Nov-16-1981, **Donna Cotherman.**
(2) He Married **Helen Gregory.**

362. **Martin Dwight[5] Arbogast** (173.Cameron Eldridge[4], 61.William Henry[3], 12.George W.[2], 1.Henry[1]), b. Jun-16-0117, buried in Eastlawn Memorial Gardens, Harrisonburg, Rockingham Co., VA, d. Nov-28-1986 in Timberville, VA.
Operated the Arbogast Grain Elevator in Timberville, VA.
Married Aug-07-1954, **Merten Self**, b. Aug-20-1928.

Children:

580 i. W. Wayne[6] Arbogast b. Sep-30-1957.
Married Aug-01-1981, **Donna Gladden**.
581 ii. W. Bradley Arbogast b. Apr-17-1959.
Married Feb-02-1980, **Sheila Liskey**.
582 iii. Teresea Lynn Arbogast b. Feb-19-1963.
She Married **Anthony Whetzel**.
583 iv. Jerry Arbogast b. Jan-06-1967.

364. **Virginia Ella[5] Waybright** (174.Manie Catherine[4] Arbogast, 61.William Henry[3], 12.George W.[2], 1.Henry[1]), b. Aug-21-1915, d. Oct 1930.
She Married **Erskine Pierce Newman**, b. Jan-25-1910 in Blue Grass, Highland Co., WV, buried in Blue Grass Cem., Highland Co., VA, d. Dec-14-1992 in Staunton, Augusta Co., VA.

Children:

\+ 584 i. Shirley Rae[6] Newman b. Apr-13-1937.

365. **William Samuel[5] Waybright** (174.Manie Catherine[4] Arbogast, 61.William Henry[3], 12.George W.[2], 1.Henry[1]), b. May-12-1917.
Married Jun-05-1947, **Virginia Gay Sites**.

Children:

\+ 585 i. Gae Lou[6] Waybright b. Aug-10-1948.
586 ii. Virginia Ann Waybright b. Oct-23-1950.
Married Sep-05-1974, **Lewis Gilmore Sines**.

366. **Jeanette Blair[5] Waybright** (174.Manie Catherine[4] Arbogast, 61.William Henry[3], 12.George W.[2], 1.Henry[1]), b. Jun-20-1919, d. Jun-12-1942.
She Married **RoyStuart Clemmer**, b. Jun-29-1914.

Children:

\+ 587 i. James Stuart[6] Clemmer b. Apr-15-1944.
\+ 588 ii. Joan Marie Clemmer b. Oct-13-1949.

368. **Max Marlin[5] Mullenax** (175.Martha Mae[4] Arbogast, 61.William Henry[3], 12.George W.[2], 1.Henry[1]), b. Jul-10-1919, d. Jun-01-1973.
Married Mar-27-1948, **Theresa January Neary**.

Children:

\+ 589 i. Marilyn Louise[6] Mullenax b. Jul-31-1945.

369. **William Royce[5] Arbogast** (176.William Lurty[4], 61.William Henry[3], 12.George W.[2], 1.Henry[1]), b. Jun-05-1916.
(1) Married Jul-16-1949, **Nancy Wilson**.

Children:

590 i. Dixie Gayle[6] Arbogast b. 0523152.
591 ii. Kelly Claek Arbogast b. 03, buried ___-19-1955.
592 iii. Terry Mark Arbogast b. Mar-23-1955.

(2) Married Jul-17-1982, **Deborah Hoover**.

370. **Wilton Dale[5] Arbogast** (176.William Lurty[4], 61.William Henry[3], 12.George W.[2], 1.Henry[1]), b. Oct-07-1918 in Blue Grass, Highland Co., VA, buried in Thornrose Cem., d. Jun-15-1984 in Stuart Draft, Augusta Co., VA.
Married Aug-03-1946 in Highland Co., VA, **Genevieve Mullenax**, b. May-11-1926.

Children:

593 i. Steven Dale[6] Arbogast b. May-29-1962.
Married 020701981, Teresa Antinori.
594 ii. Faye Alta Arbogast b. Dec-07-1954.
Married Sep-18-1982, **Loraine Ann MacDowell**.
595 iii. Blair Lurty Arbogast b. Mar-19-1958.

371. **June Lenore[5] Arbogast** (176.William Lurty[4], 61.William Henry[3], 12.George W.[2], 1.Henry[1]), b. Mar-30-1922.
Married Jun-29-1945 in Staunton, Augusta Co., VA, **Harry Clement Lunsford, Jr.**, b. Sep-18-1917, d. Feb-23-1974.

Children:

\+ 596 i. HarryClement[6] Lunsford, III b. Jun-12-1950.
597 ii. William Bryce Lunsford b. Jul-15-1974.

377. **Roscoe Thomas[5] Wilfong** (194.Ruth[4] Arbogast, 79.Abraham (Able) Pryor[3], 15.Henry A.[2], 1.Henry[1]), b. Jun 6 1915 in Covington, Allegheny Co., VA.
Married Oct 4 1935, **Viola Harris**, b. Apr 3 1918, d. Feb. 1985.

Children:

598 i. Elaine[6] Wilfong.
599 ii. Kathleen Wilfong.
600 iii. Vonda Wilfong.
601 iv. Juanita Wilfong.
602 v. Boyd Lloyd Wilfong.
603 vi. Fred Allen Wilfong.
604 vii. Gary Lynn Wilfong.
605 viii. Thomas Dwight Wilfong.

Generation Six

400. **Ray Russel[6] Rothrock** (210.Lutie May[5] Wimer, 88.James Polk[4], 22.Phoebe[3] Lantz, 2.Eleanor[2] Arbogast, 1.Henry[1]), b. 25July 1898 in Wellington, KS, d. 28January 1944 in Wichita, Sedgwick Co., KS.
Married 16 Aug,1921, **Rachael Janet Renn**, b. Dec 19 1900 in Peoria, Peoria Co., IL, d. June 18, 1964 in Miltona, Douglas Co., MN. **Rachael**: Helen Renn and Van Edwin were children. Van died 1987 during heart bypass surgery.

Children:

606 i. Helen Renn[7] Rothrock b. 11July 1924 in Wellington, KS.
Married 29 Dec1943 in Jefferson Barracks, St. Louis, MO, **William Ted Clark**, b. 31March 1923 in Scott City , Scott Co., KS, d. 29Dec 1993 in Wellington, KS. William: proud of making parts for the lunar rover that was left on moon after Apollo project finished makes parts used on booster rocket for the space shuttle
607 ii. Van Edwin Rothrock b. 29Nov 1929 in Wellington, KS, d. 22Jan1987 in Kansas City, Jackson Co., MO.

410. **Don Ralston[6] Hively** (224.Eva C.[5] Rexrode, 91.Mary Elizabeth[4] Waybright, 24.Susannah[3] Lantz, 2.Eleanor[2] Arbogast, 1.Henry[1]), b. Nov 30 1929.
Married Dec 25 1954, **Manota Yvonne Carpenter**, b. Oct 11 1937 (daughter of James Lawrence Carpenter and Ida Faye Kerr).

Children:

608 i. Keith Curtis[7] Hively b. Feb 22 1958.
(1) He Married **Rejetta Lynn Cassell**, b. Mar 23 1963 (daughter of Caroline Tacy and Dana Cassell).
(2) Married Aug 8 1998, **Tammy L. Armstrong**.
609 ii. Nida Dawn Hively b. Jul 31 1970.
Married Sep 21 2002 in Snowshoe, Pocahontas Co., WV, **Steve Fred Mullins**.

417. **Mary Edith[6] Newman** (231.Myrtle[5] Waybright, 93.David Jasper[4], 24.Susannah[3] Lantz, 2.Eleanor[2] Arbogast, 1.Henry[1]), b. Jul 30 1909 in Crabbottom, Highland Co., VA.
Married Aug 27 1932 in Pocahontas Co., WV, **Ward Elton Harper**, b. About 1897 (son of James Cosby Harper and Myrtle Florence Hannah).

Children:

\+ 610 i. Samuel Elton[7] Harper b. Feb 28 1924.

\+ 611 ii. Vincent Bryson Harper b. Jan 30 1936.
612 iii. Marilyn Harper.

426. **Everett Payne^{6} Waybright** (235.William Wellington^{5}, 93.David Jasper^{4}, 24.Susannah^{3} Lantz, 2.Eleanor^{2} Arbogast, 1.Henry^{1}), b. Nov 18 1909 in Alexandria, Fairfax Co., VA, d. Apr 10 1985 in Anniston, Calhoun Co., AL, buried in Bethel Cem., Alexandria, Fairfax, VA.
He Married **Helen Marie Armel**, b. Apr 27 1914 in Pennsylvania, d. Mar 27 1977 in Alexandria, Fairfax Co., VA.

Children:

613 i. John Richard^{7} Waybright b. Jul 21 1935 in Alexandria, Fairfax Co., VA, d. Sep 18 1997 in Bedford, Bedford Co., PA.
614 ii. Carole Ann Waybright b. Apr 15 1940 in Alexandria, Fairfax Co., VA, d. Dec 13 1988 in Roanoke, Randolph Co., AL.

431. **Rolley^{6} Garland** (238.Ida Bell "Eliza"^{5} Sargeant, 94.Eli^{4}, 28.Elizabeth^{3} Halterman, 4.Mary^{2} Arbogast, 1.Henry^{1}), b. Jan 23 1890 in Christian Co., IL, d. Feb 25 1990 in Taylorsville, Christian Co., IL, buried in Mount Auburn Cem., Mount Auburn, IL.
ROLLEY GARLAND IS MARKING 90th BIRTHDAY ANNIVERSARY
Rolley Garland of this city, today is marking his 90th birthday anniversary. He was honored at a family dinner Monday, in celebration of the occasion.
Mr. Garland is in good health and walks to town every day and quite often travels to Springfield by bus where he visits a doctor and sometimes goes shopping. He is an avid reader and especially the sport section of the newspaper and listens to all ballgames on the radio being a Cardinal fan.
Mr. Garland was born January 23, 1890 in Christian County, a son of Ezra and Elisa Sargeant Garland, and many years ago he was Married to Erna Greer, who died in 1971. He has resided his entire lifetime in Christian County where he was employed as a coal miner prior to his retirement. He is the father of twin children, Mrs. Catherine Cummings of Taylorville, and Francis Marion (Bud) Garland of Vandalia. He also has three grandchildren, one great-grandchild and two great-great-grandchildren.
This is an article from an Illinois newspaper published January 23, 1980.
Married Sep 18 1912, **Erna Greer**, d. 1971.

Children:

615 i. Francis Marion^{7} Garland b. Mar 11 1915 in Christian Co., IL, d. Feb 13 1994 in Vandalia, Fayette Co., IL.
He was a twin to Catherine Marie Garland.
616 ii. (unknown) Garland b. 1923, d. 1923.

439. **Wallace Raymond^{6} Simmons** (278.Walter Raymond^{5}, 124.Andrew Lincoln^{4}, 40.Phebe^{3} Rexroad, 5.Phebe^{2} Arbogast, 1.Henry^{1}), b. Jun 26 1921 in Detroit, Wayne Co., MI.
Married Aug 20 1949, **Ruth Wheeler**, b. Aug 28 1923 in Enfield, Broome Co., IL.

Children:

617 i. Beverly Ann^{7} Simmons b. Apr 24 1953 in Joliet, Will Co., IL.
She Married **Jeffery French**.
618 ii. Wallace Randell Simmons b. Apr 09 1956 in Joliet, Will Co., IL.

440. **Paul Herbert^{6} Simmons** (278.Walter Raymond^{5}, 124.Andrew Lincoln^{4}, 40.Phebe^{3} Rexroad, 5.Phebe^{2} Arbogast, 1.Henry^{1}), b. Jan 25 1925 in Henning, Vermilion Co., IL.
Married Dec 27 1946 in Detroit, Wayne Co., MI, **Josephine Blanche Martin**.

Children:

619 i. Nancy^{7} Simmons.
She Married **(unknown) Robertson**.

442. **Robert Walter^{6} Simmons** (279.Melvin Andrew^{5}, 124.Andrew Lincoln^{4}, 40.Phebe^{3} Rexroad, 5.Phebe^{2} Arbogast, 1.Henry^{1}), b. Mar 30 1939 in Detroit, Wayne Co., MI.
Married Apr 02 1960 in Croswell, Sanilac Co., MI, **Rosemary English**, b. Apr 02 1940 in Detroit, Wayne Co., MI.

Children:

\+ 620 i. Ramona Sue^{7} Simmons b. Nov 12 1960.
\+ 621 ii. Regan Andrew Simmons b. Aug 08 1962.
\+ 622 iii. Ryan William Simmons b. Nov 16 1963.
623 iv. Randell Lee Simmons b. Oct 09 1969 in Schenectady Co., NY.
\+ 624 v. Ronda Jean Simmons b. Oct 09 1969.

443. **William Charles^{6} Payne** (281.Mary^{5} Morrison, 125.Sophia^{4} Arbogast, 43.Jesse^{3}, 6.Sophia^{2}, 1.Henry^{1}), b. Feb 02 1878 in Prairie City, McDonough Co., IL, d. May 13 1957 in Delta Co., CO.
Married May 16 1901 in Oswego, Labette Co., KS, **Ida Mae Hail**, b. Jan 27 1882 in Keokuk, Lee Co., IA, d. Nov 17 1971 in Montrose Co., CO.

Children:

625 i. Grace^{7} Payne b. Jul 24 1902 in Parsons, Labette Co., KS.
Married Dec 15 1919, **Robert Willard Grant**.
626 ii. Djahlma Payne b. Feb 27 1904 in Parsons, Labette Co., KS, d. May 01 1979.
He Married **Mary Owens**.
627 iii. Philman Earl Payne b. Jun 19 1908 in Gracemont, Caddo Co., OK, d. Jul 17 1984.
Married Nov 08 1933, **Merle Ann Howard**.
\+ 628 iv. Alma Joyce Payne b. Apr 10 1912.
629 v. Romala Payne b. in Gracemont, Caddo Co., OK.
She Married **Arthur Davis**.
630 vi. Erma Ruth Payne b. Nov 14 1916 in Gracemont, Caddo Co., OK.
Married Apr 21 1935, **Wilber Seath Adams**.
631 vii. Aletha Payne b. Aug 13 1919.
Married Oct 20 1936, **George Ball**.
\+ 632 viii. Marcia Roberta Payne b. May 16 1921.
\+ 633 ix. Morris R Payne b. Aug 15 1923.
634 x. Loretta Blanch Payne b. Jan 19 1926 in Delta Co., CO.
Married Jul 13 1946, John **Thomas Williams**.

448. **Harry^{6} Woolverton** (285.Rose^{5} Morrison, 125.Sophia^{4} Arbogast, 43.Jesse^{3}, 6.Sophia^{2}, 1.Henry^{1}), d. Oct 19 1982 in McComb, McDonough Co., IL.
He Married **Alice Wright**, d. 1981.

Children:

635 i. Eloise^{7} Woolverton.
\+ 636 ii. Duane Woolverton b. May 11 1929.

451. **Bernice^{6} Clarke** (289.Amy^{5} Brown, 128.Mary Jane^{4} Arbogast, 43.Jesse^{3}, 6.Sophia^{2}, 1.Henry^{1}), b. Jul 30 1912.
She Married **Glenn McMillian**, b. Jul 30 1912.

Children:

\+ 637 i. Marlin Glenn^{7} McMillian b. Feb 22 1934.
\+ 638 ii. Merrill Gene McMillian b. Jun 15 1935.

452. **Carl C^{6} Clarke** (289.Amy^{5} Brown, 128.Mary Jane^{4} Arbogast, 43.Jesse^{3}, 6.Sophia^{2}, 1.Henry^{1}), b. Oct 04 1915.
He Married **Marjorie Taylor**, b. 1917 in McComb, McDonough Co., IL.

Children:

\+ 639 i. Terry^{7} Clarke b. 1944.
\+ 640 ii. Gary Taylor Clarke b. Jan 16 1949.
\+ 641 iii. Richard Allison Clarke b. Feb 23 1950.

453. **R Taylor^{6} Mitchell** (291.Ethel Clare^{5} Brown, 128.Mary Jane^{4} Arbogast, 43.Jesse^{3}, 6.Sophia^{2}, 1.Henry^{1}), b. Nov 09 1908.
Married May 31 1938, **Carle Ivan**.

Children:

642 i. Liliam^{7} Mitchell b. 1940.
643 ii. Dan Gillin Mitchell b. Oct 13 1944.
Married Nov 23 1966, **Margaret Sistler**, b. May 05 1944.

455. **Thelma Hannah^{6} Frary** (293.Lois Irene^{5} Brown, 128.Mary Jane^{4} Arbogast, 43.Jesse^{3}, 6.Sophia^{2}, 1.Henry^{1}).
Married c 1931, **Homer Kincaid**, b. Nov 03 1909.

Children:

\+ 644 i. Jack Edward^{7} Kincaid b. Nov 27 1932.
\+ 645 ii. William Gerald Kincaid b. Sep 19 1934.
646 iii. Judith Alice Kincaid b. Mar 25 1936.
She Married **Bill Carmichael**, b. Jan 21 1935.

+ 647 iv. James Richard Kincaid b. Aug 09 1943.

456. **Alice Lucille[6] Frary** (293.Lois Irene[5] Brown, 128.Mary Jane[4] Arbogast, 43.Jesse[3], 6.Sophia[2], 1.Henry[1]), b. Jul 20 1914.
She Married **Claude Miller**, b. Aug 11 1902.

Children:

+ 648 i. Elizabeth Ann[7] Miller b. Feb 19 1938.

458. **Lewis[6] Mikesell** (295.Mertice Loine[5] Brown, 128.Mary Jane[4] Arbogast, 43.Jesse[3], 6.Sophia[2], 1.Henry[1]), b. Nov 14 1912, d. Jan 15 1980.
He Married **Susan Bland**.

Children:

+ 649 i. Jan Erwin[7] Mikesell b. Feb 14 1943.

459. **Osmond[6] Mikesell** (295.Mertice Loine[5] Brown, 128.Mary Jane[4] Arbogast, 43.Jesse[3], 6.Sophia[2], 1.Henry[1]), b. Feb 13 1914, d. Dec 19 1969.
He Married **Mary Barnes**.

Children:

+ 650 i. Norma Jean[7] Mikesell b. Mar 01 1936.
651 ii. Betty Lou Mikesell b. Nov 22 1937.
She Married **Thomas Dillon.**

460. **Weist Lamoine[6] Mikesell** (295.Mertice Loine[5] Brown, 128.Mary Jane[4] Arbogast, 43.Jesse[3], 6.Sophia[2], 1.Henry[1]), b. May 15 1916.
He Married **Louise Bubb**, b. Jun 17 1917.

Children:

+ 652 i. Ralph[7] Mikesell b. Dec 04 1936.
+ 653 ii. Herbert Mikesell b. Jul 20 1938.

461. **Orth Arbogast[6] Mikesell** (295.Mertice Loine[5] Brown, 128.Mary Jane[4] Arbogast, 43.Jesse[3], 6.Sophia[2], 1.Henry[1]), b. Nov 14 1919.
Married Nov 21 1940, **Delores Stenger**, b. May 07 1922.

Children:

654 i. Gary Lewis[7] Mikesell b. Jan 03 1943, d. Jun 10 1944.
+ 655 ii. Gayle Lynn Mikesell b. May 17 1945.
656 iii. Gloria Kay Mikesell b. Jul 15 1948.
Married Dec 31 1972, **Connie Watt, Jr..**

462. **Betty Lou[6] Mikesell** (295.Mertice Loine[5] Brown, 128.Mary Jane[4] Arbogast, 43.Jesse[3], 6.Sophia[2], 1.Henry[1]), b. Jun 17 1921.
She Married **Robert E Moore**, b. Jul 06 1920, d. Jan 14 1979.

Children:

657 i. Thomas[7] Moore b. Jun 21 1955.

463. **Erwin Claire[6] Mikesell** (295.Mertice Loine[5] Brown, 128.Mary Jane[4] Arbogast, 43.Jesse[3], 6.Sophia[2], 1.Henry[1]), b. Apr 08 1924.
Married Apr 23 1955, **Grace Pawlicki**, b. Mar 03 1928.

Children:

658 i. Erwin Claire[7] Mikesell, Jr. b. May 30 1959.
659 ii. Chris John Mikesell.

464. **Sarah Fern[6] Cozad** (301.Mae[5] Howard, 131.Sarah[4] Arbogast, 43.Jesse[3], 6.Sophia[2], 1.Henry[1]), b. Jul 24 1899 in Roseville, Warren Co., IL, d. Mar 28 1991 in McComb, McDonough Co., IL.
She Married **Alva Brewer**, b. in Bushnell, Walnut Grove Twp., McDonough Co., IL, d. Feb 06 1986 in McComb, McDonough Co., IL.

Children:

+ 660 i. Richard Gene[7] Brewer b. Jul 07 1930.

465. **Faun Elizabeth[6] Cozad** (301.Mae[5] Howard, 131.Sarah[4] Arbogast, 43.Jesse[3], 6.Sophia[2], 1.Henry[1]), b. Jun 12 1902 in Roseville, Warren Co., IL, d. Mar 07 1983.

Married Sep 17 1919 in Quincy, Adams Co., IL, **Harold Black**, b. Nov 27 1899, d. 1987.

Children:

+ 661 i. Barbara Mae[7] Black b. Oct 07 1922.
+ 662 ii. William Howard Black b. May 19 1925.

467. **Margaret[6] Smith** (305.Emerson Eugene[5], 133.Frances[4] Arbogast, 43.Jesse[3], 6.Sophia[2], 1.Henry[1]), b. Apr 06 1911.
She Married **Robert Maxey**.

Children:

663 i. Joan[7] Maxey.
664 ii. Susan Maxey.
665 iii. Charles Eugene Maxey.

469. **Russell[6] Smith** (305.Emerson Eugene[5], 133.Frances[4] Arbogast, 43.Jesse[3], 6.Sophia[2], 1.Henry[1]), b. May 31 1916 in Good Hope, Walnut Grove, Putnam Co., IL.
Married Dec 31 1939, **Lois Penvarvis**, b. Mar 1918.

Children:

+ 666 i. Judy[7] Smith.

477. **Keith Leroy[6] Fox** (310.Myrtle[5] Smith, 133.Frances[4] Arbogast, 43.Jesse[3], 6.Sophia[2], 1.Henry[1]), b. Oct 15 1911, d. Oct 16 1991.
Married Jul 20 1933 in Divorced, **Elsie Pauline Herchenroder**, b. Feb 02 1915.

Children:

+ 667 i. Kathryn Louise[7] Fox b. Oct 10 1934.
+ 668 ii. Dean Edward Fox b. Oct 08 1935.
+ 669 iii. Carol Jean Fox b. Mar 23 1938.
670 iv. Marylyn Kay Fox b. Aug 24 1939.
Married Jun 22 1957, Gerald Cole, b. May 22 1935.
+ 671 v. George Leroy Fox b. Jun 27 1941.
+ 672 vi. Beverly Jane Fox b. Dec 23 1942.
+ 673 vii. James Keith Fox b. Mar 16 1944.
+ 674 viii. Kenneth Lee Fox b. Jul 15 1949.

478. **Ralth Wilton[6] Fox** (310.Myrtle[5] Smith, 133.Frances[4] Arbogast, 43.Jesse[3], 6.Sophia[2], 1.Henry[1]), b. May 01 1913.
Married Mar 25 1955, **Mildred Welty**, b. Sep 03 1924.

Children:

+ 675 i. David Bruce[7] Fox b. Sep 19 1956.
+ 676 ii. Joni Sue Fox b. Feb 04 1959.
677 iii. Cheryl Ann Fox b. Feb 20 1962.
Married Aug 12 1989, **William Michael Barrett.**

479. **Theodore Fenton[6] Arbogast** (311.Clyde Stewart[5], 134.Stephen Aaron Douglas[4], 43.Jesse[3], 6.Sophia[2], 1.Henry[1]), b. Sep 11 1905 in Silver Creek, Merrick Co., NE, d. Jun 28 1980 in Twin Falls Co., ID.
Married Aug 13 1932 in Blaire, Washington Co., NE, **Esther Wilhelmina Lallman**, b. Apr 16 1912 in Arlington, Washington Co., NE, d. Nov 23 1993 in Idaho Falls, Bonneville Co., ID.

Children:

+ 678 i. Richard Francis[7] Arbogast b. Feb 10 1934.
+ 679 ii. Patricia Ann Arbogast b. May 28 1935.
680 iii. Nancy Lou Arbogast b. Dec 03 1936.
+ 681 iv. Gerald Lee Arbogast b. Apr 13 1936.
+ 682 v. Theodore Clyde Arbogast b. Dec 31 1937.

481. **Helen Elene[6] Arbogast** (311.Clyde Stewart[5], 134.Stephen Aaron Douglas[4], 43.Jesse[3], 6.Sophia[2], 1.Henry[1]), b. Aug 15 1912 in Silver Creek, Blaine Co., ID.
She Married **Arndt Andrew Oscar Chelberg**, b. Feb 16 1910 in Malmo, Saunders Co., NE.

Children:

+ 683 i. Larry Arndt[7] Chelberg b. Mar 13 1938.
+ 684 ii. Gary Allen Chelberg b. Nov 13 1939.

482. **Allen Sterart[6] Arbogast** (311.Clyde Stewart[5], 134.Stephen Aaron Douglas[4], 43.Jesse[3], 6.Sophia[2], 1.Henry[1]), b. Jul 02 1914 in Silver Creek, Merrick Co., NE, d. Apr 08 1994 in Eugene, Lane Co., OR.
Married Apr 21 1940 in Rupert, Minidoka Co., ID, **Ilene Johnson**, b. Apr 13 1923 in Burley, Cassia Co., ID.

Children:

+ 685 i. Roland Allen[7] Arbogast b. Nov 19 1940.
+ 686 ii. Calvin Stewart Arbogast b. Jun 04 1942.
+ 687 iii. Sherry Lorraine Arbogast b. Apr 21 1944.
+ 688 iv. Leland G. Arbogast b. Mar 06 1946.
+ 689 v. Darrell Ray Arbogast b. Jan 28 1948.

483. **Gladys Catherine[6] Arbogast** (311.Clyde Stewart[5], 134.Stephen Aaron Douglas[4], 43.Jesse[3], 6.Sophia[2], 1.Henry[1]), b. Aug 27 1917 in Cedar Bluffs, Saunders Co., NE.
(1) Married Mar 19 1934, **John H. Holmes**, b. Feb 03 1908 in Elgin, Kane Co., IL, d. Jul 01 1936 in Burley, Cassia Co., ID.

Children:

+ 690 i. John Stewart[7] Holmes b. Oct 13 1934.

(2) She Married **Milford Milton Coons**, b. in Canton, McPherson Co., KS, d. May 14 1989 in Chico, Butte Co., CA.

Children:

+ 691 ii. David Coons b. Sep 22 1951.

485. **Marilyn Inez[6] Arbogast** (311.Clyde Stewart[5], 134.Stephen Aaron Douglas[4], 43.Jesse[3], 6.Sophia[2], 1.Henry[1]), b. Jun 03 1924 in Cedar Bluffs, Saunders Co., NE.
(1) She Married **Robert Allen Sagarra**.

Children:

692 i. Robert Craig[7] Sagarra b. Feb 15 1948 in Los Angeles, Los Angeles Co., CA.
+ 693 ii. Karen Sue Sagarra b. Feb 17 1951.
694 iii. Diane Lyn Sagarra b. Jun 04 1962 in Los Altos, Santa Clara Co., CA.

She Married Jeff Sanders.

(2) Married Aug 17 1968, **Anthony Janulis**.

486. **Carolyn Jean[6] Hutchison** (313.Nellie Millicent[5] Arbogast, 134.Stephen Aaron Douglas[4], 43.Jesse[3], 6.Sophia[2], 1.Henry[1]), b. Aug 14 1921 in Silver Creek, Merrick Co., NE, d. May 19 1989 in Kearney, Buffalo Co., NE.
Married Jun 14 1942 in Yuma Co., AZ, **Richard A. House**, b. May 21 1921 in Silver Creek, Merrick Co., NE.

Children:

695 i. Andra Kay[7] House b. Apr 13 1945 in Stormberg, Polk Co., NE.
She Married **Cohn Cobb**.
696 ii. Cinda Rea House b. Mar 05 1949 in Grand Island, Hall Co., NE.
Married Apr 23 1971, **Gale Bertrand**.
697 iii. Belinda Jane House b. Jul 24 1951 in Grand Island, Hall Co., NE.
Married Apr 03 1971, **Gilbert Rude**.
698 iv. Marcia Lynn House b. Sep 10 1952 in Grand Island, Hall Co., NE.
Married Nov 23 1971, **Larry Trompke.**
699 v. Patti Jean House b. Jul 31 1956 in Grand Island, Hall Co., NE.
She Married **David Swift**, b. Feb 07 1976.
700 vi. Richard Gary House b. May 27 1960 in Sioux Falls, Minnehaha Co., SD.

487. **Betty Jane[6] Hutchison** (313.Nellie Millicent[5] Arbogast, 134.Stephen Aaron Douglas[4], 43.Jesse[3], 6.Sophia[2], 1.Henry[1]), b. Feb 04 1924 in Silver Creek, Merrick Co., NE.
She Married **George I. Slone**, b. Aug 04 1922.

Children:

701 i. Donald Lynn[7] Slone b. Dec 14 1949 in Lincoln, Lancaster Co., NE.
Married Jul 18 1971 in Colorado Springs, El Paso Co., CO, **Charlene Taylor**.
702 ii. Robert Dean Slone b. Feb 06 1952 in Syracuse, Otoe Co., NE.
Married Aug 26 1981 in Seattle, King Co., WA, **Julianna Uerling.**
703 iii. Gregg Ivan Slone b. Jun 19 1953 in Neligh, Antelope Co., NE.

Married in Glenwood Springs, Garfield Co., CO, **Susan Richards.**

704 iv. Bryan Eugene Slone b. Jul 28 1957 in Wayne Co., NE.
Married Oct 29 1984 in Lincoln, Lancaster Co., NE, **Leslie Shaner.**

488. **Marjorie Elaine[6] Gerber** (314.Gladys Mary[5] Arbogast, 134.Stephen Aaron Douglas[4], 43.Jesse[3], 6.Sophia[2], 1.Henry[1]), b. May 17 1921 in Silver Creek, Merrick Co., NE, d. Aug 1959 in Denver, Arapaho Co., CO.
She Married **Lambert Bukacek**.

Children:

705 i. Darrell Gene[7] Bukacek.
706 ii. Jerry Dean Bukacek.
707 iii. Jody Ann Bukacek.

504. **Dwight[6] Arbogast** (320.Jessie L.[5], 138.John Franklin[4], 46.Michael[3], 6.Sophia[2], 1.Henry[1]), b. Jul 13 1911.
He Married **Helen Louise Shely**.

Children:

\+ 708 i. John Allen[7] Arbogast.
\+ 709 ii. Carol Jean Arbogast.
\+ 710 iii. Rual Arbogast.

509. **Lois Alberta[6] Arbogast** (333.James Michael[5], 141.Charles Sayers[4], 46.Michael[3], 6.Sophia[2], 1.Henry[1]), b. in Richdale, Alberta, CA.
Married Jan 12 1941, **Douglas Earl Slater**.

Children:

\+ 711 i. Brian Earl[7] Slater b. Nov 02 1946.
\+ 712 ii. Lynn Marie Slater b. Oct 10 1948.

510. **Gayl Jane[6] Arbogast** (333.James Michael[5], 141.Charles Sayers[4], 46.Michael[3], 6.Sophia[2], 1.Henry[1]), b. Oct 14 1921, d. Nov 27 1967.
She Married **Charles Arthur Armour**.

Children:

\+ 713 i. Patricia Leigh[7] Armour b. Jan 24 1943.
714 ii. Arthur Glenn Armour b. Dec 15 1944, d. Jun 04 1969.
715 iii. Myrna Rea Armour b. Aug 03 1946.

511. **Charles Sayers[6] Arbogast** (333.James Michael[5], 141.Charles Sayers[4], 46.Michael[3], 6.Sophia[2], 1.Henry[1]), b. Jul 29 1925, d. Feb 04 1992.
He Married **Ruth Pedersen**.

Children:

716 i. Carol Annetta[7] Arbogast b. May 07 1954.
She Married **Ivor Oberholtzer**.
717 ii. Craig Sayers Arbogast b. Sep 28 1955, d. Dec 21 1973.
718 iii. Dale Scott Arbogast b. Nov 29 1958.
He Married **Wanda Gorman**.

512. **James Kenneth[6] Heath** (334.Alice[5] Arbogast, 141.Charles Sayers[4], 46.Michael[3], 6.Sophia[2], 1.Henry[1]), b. Jan 08 1913 in Canada, d. Jan 02 1988 in Good Hope, Walnut Grove, Putnam Co., IL.
He Married **Josephine Bobrick**, b. Nov 18 1913 in Van Meter, Westmoreland Co., PA.

Children:

\+ 719 i. John[7] Heath b. Jul 05 1946.
720 ii. Joseph Heath b. Jun 15 1949 in McComb, McDonough Co., IL.
He Married **Shirley Lensch**.
\+ 721 iii. Susan Heath b. Dec 08 1952.

513. **Marion E.[6] Heath** (334.Alice[5] Arbogast, 141.Charles Sayers[4], 46.Michael[3], 6.Sophia[2], 1.Henry[1]), b. Nov 18 1917.
(1) She Married **Charles Thomas Buell**, b. Jul 1917.

(2) She Married **Newburn Bates**, b. Apr 04 1919 at Eva, Morgan Co., AL, d. Jul 07 1960 in Peoria, Peoria Co., IL.

Children:

+ 722 i. Danial Claude[7] Bates b. Jan 20 1946.
+ 723 ii. Donna Ruth Bates b. Nov 21 1949.

514. **James Clarence[6] Arbogast** (337.Clarence James[5], 142.Rush Arlington[4], 46.Michael[3], 6.Sophia[2], 1.Henry[1]), b. Mar 13 1927 in Seneca Co., OH, d. Jul 1 1982 in Tiffin, Seneca Co., OH, buried in St. Mary's Cem., Tiffin, Seneca Co., OH.
Married Oct 25 1947 in Tiffin, Seneca Co., OH, **Margery Louise Shaull**, b. Jan 25 1929. **Margery**: Nickname:<NICK> Marge

Children:

+ 724 i. Suzanne Marie[7] Arbogast b. Nov 2 0052.
+ 725 ii. Teresa Kay Arbogast b. May 6 0055.
726 iii. Michael James Arbogast b. Jun 1 0058 in Tiffin, Seneca Co., OH.
Married May 29 1981, **Rosann Kessler**, b. May 15 1960.
+ 727 iv. Gregory Charles Arbogast b. Mar 1 0062.
728 v. Brett Arbogast b. May 22 0065 in Tiffin, Seneca Co., OH.
729 vi. Karen Ann Arbogast b. Oct 21 1948.
Married Sep 03 1971, **James Lynn Mars**, b. Mar 12 1949.
+ 730 vii. Anita Louise Arbogast b. Aug 14 1960.
731 viii. Laura Jenne Arbogast b. May 01 1962.
This Family has 4 living children as of 2005.
Married Aug 25 1984, **Randal W. Brickner**, b. Sep 19 1960.

515. **Naomi Agnus[6] Arbogast** (337.Clarence James[5], 142.Rush Arlington[4], 46.Michael[3], 6.Sophia[2], 1.Henry[1]), b. Jun 06 1938.
Married Sep 05 1959, **Peter Eugene Hankish**, b. Feb 10 1932.

Children:

732 i. Deborah Sue[7] Hankish b. Nov 16 1960.
733 ii. Steven Michael Hankish b. Apr 01 1963.
734 iii. Timothy Joseph Hankish b. Jul 17 1966.

516. **Paul Joseph[6] Arbogast** (338.Charles Anthony[5], 142.Rush Arlington[4], 46.Michael[3], 6.Sophia[2], 1.Henry[1]), b. Sep-06-1922.
He Married **Florence Clouse**.

Children:

+ 735 i. Jane[7] Arbogast.
+ 736 ii. Dean Lawrence Arbogast.
+ 737 iii. Ruth Ann Arbogast.
+ 738 iv. Judith Carol Arbogast.
739 v. Carl Arbogast.
+ 740 vi. Mark Anthony Arbogast b. Sep 30 1963.

517. **Lawrence Anselm[6] Arbogast** (338.Charles Anthony[5], 142.Rush Arlington[4], 46.Michael[3], 6.Sophia[2], 1.Henry[1]), b. Dec-20-1924.
He Married **Marion Schullenburger**. .

Children:

+ 741 i. Daria[7] Arbogast b. Apr 29 1953.
742 ii. Lydia Ann Arbogast b. Oct 15 1954.
743 iii. Clara Ellen Arbogast b. Jan 07 1956.
+ 744 iv. Paula Louise Arbogast b. Sep 15 1958.
745 v. Peter Eugene Arbogast b. Mar 26 1966.
Married Jun 06 1978, **Carol Sue Kimbell.**
746 vi. Mariea Rose Arbogast b. Mar 28 1968.
747 vii. Elmer Lester Arbogast b. Mar 31 1971.
748 viii. Anita Arbogast b. Sep 05 1974.

518. **Urban Anthony[6] Arbogast** (338.Charles Anthony[5], 142.Rush Arlington[4], 46.Michael[3], 6.Sophia[2], 1.Henry[1]), b. Mar-20-1926.
Married Oct 16 1948 in Seneca Co., OH, **Dorothy Ann Daniels**, b. Jun 05 1928 in Seneca Co., OH. .

Children:

+ 749 i. Virginia Ann[7] Arbogast b. Oct 11 1949.
+ 750 ii. Alice Rose Arbogast b. Sep 10 1950.

+ 751 iii. Pauline Mary Arbogast b. Sep 06 1951.
+ 752 iv. Helen Lucille Arbogast b. Mar 16 1953.
+ 753 v. Susan Theresa Arbogast b. Mar 29 1953.
+ 754 vi. Doris Mae Arbogast b. May 04 1955.
+ 755 vii. Angela Marie Arbogast b. May 21 1956.
+ 756 viii. Janice Eileen Arbogast b. May 17 1958.
+ 757 ix. Patricia Louise Arbogast b. May 05 1960.
+ 758 x. June Ellen Arbogast b. Jun 04 1961.
+ 759 xi. Linda Kay Arbogast b. Oct 27 1966.
760 xii. Betty Jean Arbogast b. Aug 13 1968.
Married Jun 05 1992, **James Basset**, b. Jan 03 1961.
761 xiii. David Anthony Arbogast b. Jun 25 1971, d. Aug 15 1971.

519. **Eugene Jerome[6] Arbogast** (338.Charles Anthony[5], 142.Rush Arlington[4], 46.Michael[3], 6.Sophia[2], 1.Henry[1]), b. Oct 24 1928.
Married Mar 17 1952, **Eileen Wagner**, b. Dec 25 1932, d. Oct 16 1966. .

Children:

+ 762 i. Marilyn Ann[7] Arbogast b. Dec 05 1952.
763 ii. Ronald Marion Arbogast b. Jan 23 1954.
Married Aug 24 1985, **Brenda Niue,** b. Apr 04 1961.
+ 764 iii. Barbara Jean Arbogast b. Nov 27 1957.
+ 765 iv. Kenneth Arbogast b. Mar 30 1959.
766 v. Gary Arbogast b. Sep 15 1960.
+ 767 vi. Lois Marie Arbogast b. Jul 05 1962.

520. **Marion Victor[6] Arbogast** (338.Charles Anthony[5], 142.Rush Arlington[4], 46.Michael[3], 6.Sophia[2], 1.Henry[1]), b. Apr 16 1930.
Married Jun 18 1955, **Kathleen Marie Wilhelm**, b. Nov 27 1931.

Children:

+ 768 i. Diane Ruth[7] Arbogast b. Jan 10 1956.
769 ii. Roxanne Marguerite Arbogast b. Feb 25 1957.
She Married **Timothy Ferrell**.
770 iii. Nancy Eileen Arbogast b. Aug 02 1958.
771 iv. Norma Mae Arbogast b. Dec 27 1959, d. Apr 22 1962.
772 v. Sharon Marie Arbogast b. May 02 1961.
Married May 05 1984, **Daniel Eugene George**, b. Jan 21 1957.

521. **Marguerite Elenora[6] Arbogast** (338.Charles Anthony[5], 142.Rush Arlington[4], 46.Michael[3], 6.Sophia[2], 1.Henry[1]), b. Apr 30 1934.
She Married **Eugene Boes**

Children:

+ 773 i. Theresa Marie[7] Boes b. Jun 15 1954.
774 ii. Michael Eugene Boes b. Sep 06 1957.
Married Apr 14 1984, **Sandra Watson**.
775 iii. John Charles Boes b. Aug 26 1959.
776 iv. Donald Marion Boes b. Oct 05 1961.
777 v. Mary Irene Boes b. Aug 26 1965.
Married Sep 13 1986, G**regory Scott Bussing.**

522. **Harlan Clarence[6] Arbogast** (338.Charles Anthony[5], 142.Rush Arlington[4], 46.Michael[3], 6.Sophia[2], 1.Henry[1]), b. Nov 24 1936.
Married Jan 31 1959, **Rosemary Schriner**, b. Feb 07 1940. .

Children:

+ 778 i. Mary Catherine[7] Arbogast b. Aug 17 1959.
+ 779 ii. Carol Sue Arbogast b. Sep 10 1960.
+ 780 iii. Sandra Marie Arbogast b. May 23 1962.
781 iv. Steven Joseph Arbogast b. Jun 08 1963.
Married Jun 08 1985, **Yvonne Haubert**.
782 v. Phillis Jean Arbogast.
Married Jul 30 1988, **Brian Ream**.
783 vi. James Lester Arbogast b. Jun 23 1965.

784 vii. Tina Rose Arbogast b. Nov 11 1967.
785 viii. Roger Urban Arbogast b. Feb 04 1969.
Married May 07 1988, **Lori Bigley**.
+ 786 ix. Wanda Ann Arbogast b. Jun 23 1970.
787 x. Joanna Mary Arbogast b. Feb 25 1972.
788 xi. Justin Lee Arbogast b. Mar 10 1973.
789 xii. Dennis Larry Arbogast b. Mar 20 1975.
790 xiii. Melissa Ann Arbogast b. Jul 27 1976.
791 xiv. Bruce Dean Arbogast b. Jul 27 1976.
792 xv. Douglas Ronald Arbogast b. Aug 07 1978.
793 xvi. Jessica Lynn Arbogast b. Oct 01 1980.

523. **Lester Michael[6] Arbogast** (338.Charles Anthony[5], 142.Rush Arlington[4], 46.Michael[3], 6.Sophia[2], 1.Henry[1]), b. Jul 21 1938.
Married Sep-26-1942, **Eloise Marie Piper**, b. Sep 26 1942.

Children:

794 i. Kevin Michael[7] Arbogast b. Sep 23 1963.
795 ii. Brian James Arbogast b. Mar 08 1965.
He Married **Dawn Marie Kuhn**.
796 iii. Randel Louis Arbogast b. Mar 19 1969.
797 iv. Laura Marie Arbogast b. Jun 14 1973.

524. **Rita Mae[6] Arbogast** (338.Charles Anthony[5], 142.Rush Arlington[4], 46.Michael[3], 6.Sophia[2], 1.Henry[1]), b. Nov-26-1941.
She Married **Robert Joseph Kelbley**.

Children:

798 i. Deborah Louise[7] Kelbley b. Mar 13 1961.
799 ii. Lynn Edward Kelbley b. Jun 02 1962.
Married Jul 12 1986, **Rebecca J. Smith**.
800 iii. Pamela Jane Kelbley b. May 07 1964.
+ 801 iv. Neil Eugene Kelbley b. Jun 07 1965.

525. **Louis Cyril[6] Arbogast** (338.Charles Anthony[5], 142.Rush Arlington[4], 46.Michael[3], 6.Sophia[2], 1.Henry[1]), b. Aug-01-1944.
Married Jul 22 1967, **Jeannette An Hammer**, b. Apr 11 1947.

Children:

802 i. Leonard Michael[7] Arbogast b. May 12 1968.
803 ii. Amy Jo Arbogast b. May 02 1969.
804 iii. Karen Ann Arbogast b. Jun 24 1970.
Married Nov 19 1988, **James McNulty**, b. Apr 18 1960.
805 iv. Gene Blaser Arbogast b. Oct 13 1972.
806 v. Eli Victor Arbogast b. Feb 26 1973.

527. **Clarence Louis[6] SMITH** (339.Frances Marie[5] Arbogast, 142.Rush Arlington[4], 46.Michael[3], 6.Sophia[2], 1.Henry[1]), b. Nov 17 1915.
Married May 13 1938, **Rita Margaret Sendelbach**.

Children:

+ 807 i. Elmo Harold[7] Smith b. Jan 25 1941.
+ 808 ii. Norman Paul Smith b. Sep 27 1943.
+ 809 iii. Nancy Smith b. Feb 13 1945.
+ 810 iv. Ramona Teresita Smith b. Jan 07 1950.

528. **Rita Theresa[6] SMITH** (339.Frances Marie[5] Arbogast, 142.Rush Arlington[4], 46.Michael[3], 6.Sophia[2], 1.Henry[1]), b. Nov 07 1916.
Married Nov 25 1937, **James Allen King**, b. Aug 21 1910, d. Mar 15 1979. .

Children:

+ 811 i. Louis James[7] KING b. Dec 04 1938.
+ 812 ii. Marjorie Ann King b. Nov 23 1941.

529. **Richard Joseph[6] SMITH** (339.Frances Marie[5] Arbogast, 142.Rush Arlington[4], 46.Michael[3], 6.Sophia[2], 1.Henry[1]), b. Mar 12 1920.

Married Feb 02 1943, **Margaret Dorothy Sloma**, b. Aug 04 1921. .

Children:

+ 813 i. Deanna Rose^{7} SMITH b. Nov 24 1943.
+ 814 ii. Allan Peter Smith b. Jan 07 1945.
+ 815 iii. Alice Mary Smith b. Feb 23 1949.
+ 816 iv. Jane Margaret Smith b. Dec 30 1949.

531. **Marjorie Mary^{6} SMITH** (339.Frances Marie^{5} Arbogast, 142.Rush Arlington^{4}, 46.Michael^{3}, 6.Sophia^{2}, 1.Henry^{1}), b. Oct 17 1922.
She Married **Calvin James Adams**, b. Apr 17 1921. .

Children:

+ 817 i. Gloria Jean^{7} Adams b. Dec 11 1946.
818 ii. Carol Ann Adams b. Aug 19 1948.
She Married **Gary Wilson.**
+ 819 iii. Gerald Edwards Adams b. Feb 12 1954.

532. **Robert Eugene^{6} SMITH** (339.Frances Marie^{5} Arbogast, 142.Rush Arlington^{4}, 46.Michael^{3}, 6.Sophia^{2}, 1.Henry^{1}), b. Sep 19 1925.
Married Aug 28 1947, **Clarice M. Keller**, b. Dec 17 1925.

Children:

+ 820 i. Cheryl Lajean^{7} SMITH b. Aug 27 1949.
+ 821 ii. Patricia Ann Smith b. Nov 29 1954.

533. **Helen Francis^{6} SMITH** (339.Frances Marie^{5} Arbogast, 142.Rush Arlington^{4}, 46.Michael^{3}, 6.Sophia^{2}, 1.Henry^{1}), b. Sep 28 1927, d. Sep 29 1959.
She Married **Herbert Hammer**..

Children:

+ 822 i. David Eugene^{7} HAMMER b. Aug 21 1947.
+ 823 ii. Thomas Herbert Hammer b. Sep 13 1948.
+ 824 iii. William Joseph Hammer b. Feb 11 1951.
+ 825 iv. Donald Lee Hammer b. May 29 1953.
+ 826 v. Kenneth Lewis Hammer b. May 29 1953.
+ 827 vi. Mary Alice Hammer b. Sep 02 1955.
+ 828 vii. Eileen Marie Hammer b. Mar 16 1957.
+ 829 viii. Roger Francis Hammer b. Sep 28 1958.
830 ix. Michael Paul Hammer b. Sep 29 1959.
He Married **Judith Ann Bonham**.

534. **Bernard Charles^{6} SMITH** (339.Frances Marie^{5} Arbogast, 142.Rush Arlington^{4}, 46.Michael^{3}, 6.Sophia^{2}, 1.Henry^{1}), b. May 30 1929.
He Married **Carolyn Smith**.

Children:

831 i. Michael Lynn^{7} SMITH b. Oct 13 1953.
He Married **Victoria Kersch**.
832 ii. Joseph Lynn Smith b. Oct 28 1954.
He Married .
833 iii. Lorraine Ann Smith b. Feb 26 1956.
834 iv. Steven Patrick Smith b. Sep 18 1957.
He Married **Linda Elchert**.
+ 835 v. Jill Christine Smith.
836 vi. John Damian Smith b. Feb 23 1964.
837 vii. Michelle Marie Smith b. Sep 05 1967.

535. **Leo Frederick^{6} SMITH** (339.Frances Marie^{5} Arbogast, 142.Rush Arlington^{4}, 46.Michael^{3}, 6.Sophia^{2}, 1.Henry^{1}), b. Feb 19 1931.
He Married **Elizabeth Zole**.

Children:

838 i. Thomas Joseph[7] SMITH b. Apr 09 1957.
+ 839 ii. Edward Louis Smith.
840 iii. Virginia Marie Smith b. Jan 07 1963.
841 iv. Christopher Lee Smith b. Apr 24 1964.
842 v. Deborah Sue Smith b. Feb 02 1966.
843 vi. Donna Jean Smith b. Apr 24 1968.
844 vii. Jude Ann Smith b. Oct 14 1980.

536. **Catherine Louise[6] SMITH** (339.Frances Marie[5] Arbogast, 142.Rush Arlington[4], 46.Michael[3], 6.Sophia[2], 1.Henry[1]), b. Dec 20 1935.
She Married **Frederick Tiell**.

Children:

845 i. Steven Joseph[7] Tiell b. Jul 14 1961.
846 ii. Susan Lynn Tiell b. Sep 13 1969.

537. **Rosemary[6] SMITH** (339.Frances Marie[5] Arbogast, 142.Rush Arlington[4], 46.Michael[3], 6.Sophia[2], 1.Henry[1]), b. Jan 22 1938.
She Married **Thomas Widmam**, b. Apr 17 1933

Children:

847 i. Mark Thomas[7] Widmam b. Feb 12 1961.
848 ii. Jean Marie Widman b. Jun 20 1963.
849 iii. Sharon Rose Widman b. Sep 08 1965.
850 iv. Anna Kristin Widman b. Mar 10 1970.

539. **Lawrence Owen[6] Emahiser** (341.Charity Ellen[5] McMaster, 146.Mary Anna[4] Morrison, 47.Barbara Ellen[3] Arbogast, 7.Andrew[2], 1.Henry[1]), b. Apr 6 1891 in Barlow Twp., Deshler Village, Henry County OH, d. Dec 2 1976 in Findlay, Hancock Co., OH, buried in Memory Gardens; Arcadia, Hancock Co., OH.
Married Dec 22 1915, **Florence O. Fenstermaker**, b. Mar 28 1895 in Putnam Co., OH, d. AUG 1984 in Findlay, Hancock Co., OH, buried in Memory Gardens; Arcadia, Hancock Co., OH.

Children:

851 i. Donald Owen[7] Emahiser d. Aug 15 1989.
852 ii. Paul Wayne Emahiser b. Apr 22 1919, d. OCT 1965 in Oregon.
He Married **Mildred M. Drummelsmith**, b. Sep 21 1919 in Miller City, Putnam Co., OH, d. MAY 1985 in Ohio, buried in Restlawn Cem.; Stony Ridge, Wood Co., OH.

541. **Roscoe[6] Emahiser** (341.Charity Ellen[5] McMaster, 146.Mary Anna[4] Morrison, 47.Barbara Ellen[3] Arbogast, 7.Andrew[2], 1.Henry[1]), b. Mar 19 1894 in Wood Co., OH, d. Jan 16 1949 in Risingsun, Wood County OH, buried in Graham Cem., Wayne Co., OH.
(1) He Married **Esther Woodruff**, b. Aug 14 1899, d. OCT 1979 in Fostoria, Seneca County OH, buried in Graham Cem., Wayne Co., OH.

Children:

853 i. (unknown)[7] Emahiser.
She Married **(unknown) Kern**.
854 ii. (unknown) Emahiser.

(2) He Married **Nan Powell**.
(3) He Married **Mildred Smith**.

546. **George Clifton[6] Emahiser** (341.Charity Ellen[5] McMaster, 146.Mary Anna[4] Morrison, 47.Barbara Ellen[3] Arbogast, 7.Andrew[2], 1.Henry[1]), b. Feb 1 1903, d. Feb 10 1997 in Fostoria, Seneca County OH.
He Married **Grace U. Keiser**, b. Oct 23 1910, d. Dec 29 1994 in Fostoria, Seneca County OH.

Children:

855 i. (unknown)[7] Emahiser.
He Married Trillis **Amina Moelman**, b. May 10 1929, d. SEP 1993 in Fostoria, Seneca County OH.

565. **Mary Luella[6] McMaster** (348.Myron Edward[5], 146.Mary Anna[4] Morrison, 47.Barbara Ellen[3] Arbogast, 7.Andrew[2], 1.Henry[1]), b. May 06 1909 in Dashler, Barlow Twp., Henry Co., OH, d. Oct 03 1971 in Dashler, Barlow Twp., Henry Co., OH.
(1) She Married **Boyd Kidwell. Boyd**: .

Children:

856 i. Boyd[7] Kidwell b. May 1928, d. Before 1933.
857 ii. Benjamin Kiudwell b. Dec 1929.

(2) She Married **Walter Newton**.

566. **Alvie Clifford[6] McMaster** (348.Myron Edward[5], 146.Mary Anna[4] Morrison, 47.Barbara Ellen[3] Arbogast, 7.Andrew[2], 1.Henry[1]).
(1) Married About 1941 in Cardington Twp., Morrow Co., OH, **Edyth Smith**, d. After 2001 in Indiana
(2) Married About 1934 in Montana, **Mrs. Morgan Jones**, d. Before 1937.

Children:

858 i. (unknown)[7] Jones b. About 1935 in Mt. Auburn Cem., Greenville, Christian Co., IL, d. 1935 in Mt. Auburn Cem., Greenville, Christian Co., IL.

569. **Alice May[6] McMaster** (348.Myron Edward[5], 146.Mary Anna[4] Morrison, 47.Barbara Ellen[3] Arbogast, 7.Andrew[2], 1.Henry[1]), b. Feb 19 1917, d. About 1985.
(1) Married About 1930, **Henry Bruce Kinder**. **Henry**:

. ***Children:***

859 i. (unknown)[7] Kinder b. About 1936, d. About 1936 in Stillborn.

(2) Married About 1944 in Henry Co., OH, **Clarence Bennett**, d. About 2001 in Hancock Co., OH.

572. **Imo-Geraldine[6] McMaster** (348.Myron Edward[5], 146.Mary Anna[4] Morrison, 47.Barbara Ellen[3] Arbogast, 7.Andrew[2], 1.Henry[1]), b. Sep 22 1921 in Dashler, Barlow Twp., Henry Co., OH.
Married Dec 26 1939 in Aldridge farm, Portage Twp., Hancock Co., OH,, **James Allen Siverling**, b. Apr 26 1916 in Youngstown, Mahoning Co., OH (son of Abraham Buel Siverling and Catherine Josephine Schilling), d. Aug 2 1993 in Ann Arbor, Washtenaw Co., MI, buried in Pleasant Hill Cem., Hancock Co., OH.

Children:

860 i. Linda Ann[7] Siverling b. Mar 18 1941 in Miller McComb Hospital, Hancock Co., OH, d. Mar 18 1941 in Miller McComb Hospital, Hancock Co., OH.
861 ii. Roberta Jean Siverling b. Mar 18 1941 in Miller McComb Hospital, Hancock Co., OH, d. Mar 18 1941 in Miller McComb Hospital, Hancock Co., OH.

576. **Madelyn Gayle[6] Hevener** (357.Mavis A.[5] Mullenax, 172.Ollie A.[4] Arbogast, 61.William Henry[3], 12.George W.[2], 1.Henry[1]), b. Feb-03-1923 in MD.
Married Jun-18-1942, **Russell C Turner, Jr.**.

Children:

862 i. Sharron Lee[7] Turner b. Oct-04-1945.
863 ii. Sondra Jat Turner b. May-02-1948.

578. **Wanda Dran[6] Mullenax** (361.Kenton Dexter[5], 172.Ollie A.[4] Arbogast, 61.William Henry[3], 12.George W.[2], 1.Henry[1]), b. Feb-27-1944.
Married May-06-1961, **Richard Theodore Hebb**.

Children:

864 i. Richard[7] Kenton b. 0211962.
Married Aug-28-1981, Belinda Hix.
865 ii. Sherry Lynn Hebb b. Sep-16-1964.

584. **Shirley Rae[6] Newman** (364.Virginia Ella[5] Waybright, 174.Manie Catherine[4] Arbogast, 61.William Henry[3], 12.George W.[2], 1.Henry[1]), b. Apr-13-1937.
Married Dec-10-1961, **Hal Dalton Ragland**.

Children:

866 i. Leslie Carol[7] Ragland b. Mar-02-1968.

585. **Gae Lou[6] Waybright** (365.William Samuel[5], 174.Manie Catherine[4] Arbogast, 61.William Henry[3], 12.George W.[2], 1.Henry[1]), b. Aug-10-1948.
Married Aug-17-1968, **Tonald Gene Bowersock**.

Children:

867 i. Ronald Michael^{7} Bowersock b. Dec-27-1969.
868 ii. Scott David Bowersock b. May-30-1974.

587. **James Stuart^{6} Clemmer** (366.Jeanette Blair^{5} Waybright, 174.Manie Catherine^{4} Arbogast, 61.William Henry^{3}, 12.George W.^{2}, 1.Henry^{1}), b. Apr-15-1944.
Married Mar-03-1973, **Sandra Kay Cook**.

Children:

869 i. Elizabeth stuart^{7} Clemmer b. Jan-18-1977.

588. **Joan Marie^{6} Clemmer** (366.Jeanette Blair^{5} Waybright, 174.Manie Catherine^{4} Arbogast, 61.William Henry^{3}, 12.George W.^{2}, 1.Henry^{1}), b. Oct-13-1949.
Married Jun-09-1971, **Guy Michel Wright**.

Children:

870 i. David Christipher^{7} Clemmer b. Nov-28-1975.
871 ii. Catherine Scott Clemmer b. Jul-02-1977.

589. **Marilyn Louise^{6} Mullenax** (368.Max Marlin^{5}, 175.Martha Mae^{4} Arbogast, 61.William Henry^{3}, 12.George W.^{2}, 1.Henry^{1}), b. Jul-31-1945.
Married Dec-02-1972, **John Wierrnga**.

Children:

872 i. Gregory^{7} Mullenax b. Apr-09-1976.

596. **HarryClement^{6} Lunsford, III** (371.June Lenore^{5} Arbogast, 176.William Lurty^{4}, 61.William Henry^{3}, 12.George W.^{2}, 1.Henry^{1}), b. Jun-12-1950.
Married Dec-19-1971, **Melanie Sullenburger**.

Children:

873 i. Matthew Clement^{7} Lunsford b. Jun-24-1979.
874 ii. Brail Joseph Lunsford b. Oct-17-1981.

Generation Seven

610. **Samuel Elton^{7} Harper** (417.Mary Edith^{6} Newman, 231.Myrtle^{5} Waybright, 93.David Jasper^{4}, 24.Susannah^{3} Lantz, 2.Eleanor^{2} Arbogast, 1.Henry^{1}), b. Feb 28 1924 in Pocahontas Co., WV, d. Sep 11 2000 in Pocahontas Co., WV.
He Married **Maxine Thomas**.

Children:

875 i. Beth^{8} Harper.

611. **Vincent Bryson^{7} Harper** (417.Mary Edith^{6} Newman, 231.Myrtle^{5} Waybright, 93.David Jasper^{4}, 24.Susannah^{3} Lantz, 2.Eleanor^{2} Arbogast, 1.Henry^{1}), b. Jan 30 1936 in Knapps Creek, Pocahontas Co., WV, d. May 27 1985 in Knapps Creek, Pocahontas Co., WV.
He Married **Priscilla Jean Shinaberry**, b. Dec 5 1935 (daughter of Sterl Washington Shinaberry and Maude Geraldine McLaughlin).

Children:

\+ 876 i. Bradley Michael^{8} Harper b. Feb 2 1966.
877 ii. Richard Bryson Harper.
878 iii. Candace Sue Harper.
Married Jun 21 1980 in Marlinton, Pocahontas Co., WV, **Oran Arbie McLaughlin**.

620. **Ramona Sue^{7} Simmons** (442.Robert Walter^{6}, 279.Melvin Andrew^{5}, 124.Andrew Lincoln^{4}, 40.Phebe^{3} Rexroad, 5.Phebe^{2} Arbogast, 1.Henry^{1}), b. Nov 12 1960 in San Diego, San Diego Co., CA.
Married Apr 27 1985 in Richmond, Henrico Co., VA, **James Paul Neifeld**, b. Jun 05 1948 in Patterson, Passaic Co., NJ.

Children:

879 i. Emily Clair^{8} Neifeld b. Aug 31 1986 in Richmond, Henrico Co., VA.
880 ii. Julian Rose Neifeld b. Nov 29 1989 in Richmond, Henrico Co., VA.

621. **Regan Andrew[7] Simmons** (442.Robert Walter[6], 279.Melvin Andrew[5], 124.Andrew Lincoln[4], 40.Phebe[3] Rexroad, 5.Phebe[2] Arbogast, 1.Henry[1]), b. Aug 08 1962 in Saratoga Springs, Saratoga Co., NY.
(1) Married May 30 1981 in Nichols, Tioga Co., NY, **Leeann Marie Thomas**.
(2) He Married **Christina Torres**, b. Feb 07 1972 in Philippine Islands. **Christina**: Christina had a child by a previous marriage, Karen Romines, (b 02/25/1987), being adopted by Regan.

Children:

881 i. Rhea Marie[8] Simmons b. Mar 26 1991 in Subic Bay, Philippine Islands.

622. **Ryan William[7] Simmons** (442.Robert Walter[6], 279.Melvin Andrew[5], 124.Andrew Lincoln[4], 40.Phebe[3] Rexroad, 5.Phebe[2] Arbogast, 1.Henry[1]), b. Nov 16 1963 in Norwich, New London Co., CT.
Married Jan 01 1984 in Nichols, Tioga Co., NY, **Julie Rena Thomas**, b. Mar 26 1965 in Waverly, Tioga Co., NY.

Children:

882 i. Kasandra Julieann[8] Simmons b. Oct 08 1987 in Sayer, NY.
883 ii. Kellen Ryan Simmons b. Mar 16 1989 in Sayer, NY.
884 iii. Kaleen Olivia Simmons b. Apr 30 1990 in Sayer, NY.

624. **Ronda Jean[7] Simmons** (442.Robert Walter[6], 279.Melvin Andrew[5], 124.Andrew Lincoln[4], 40.Phebe[3] Rexroad, 5.Phebe[2] Arbogast, 1.Henry[1]), b. Oct 09 1969 in Ithaca, Tompkins Co., NY.
She Married **Michael Karl Haight**, b. Oct 15 1969 in Tonawanda, Erie Co., NY.

Children:

885 i. Samantha Tayren[8] Haight b. Jul 22 1988 in Richmond, Henrico Co., VA.
886 ii. Kristin Jordan Haight b. Jul 22 1988 in Richmond, Henrico Co., VA.
887 iii. Mackay Simmons Haight b. Oct 15 1994 in Richmond, Henrico Co., VA.

628. **Alma Joyce[7] Payne** (443.William Charles[6], 281.Mary[5] Morrison, 125.Sophia[4] Arbogast, 43.Jesse[3], 6.Sophia[2], 1.Henry[1]), b. Apr 10 1912 in Gracemont, Caddo Co., OK.

Married Nov 09 1930 in Montrose Co., CO, **Isham Reese Hamilton**, b. Mar 24 1909 in Kearney, Buffalo Co., NE, d. Jan 13 1977 in Montrose Co., CO.

Children:

888 i. Glen Dean[8] Hamilton b. Aug 06 1931 in Delta Co., CO.
He Married Norma Campbell, b. Jun 06 1960 in Grand Junction, Mesa Co., CO.
889 ii. Eddie Lee Hamilton b. Jun 23 1934 in Delta Co., CO.
Married Jun 09 1968 in Montrose Co., CO, **Lila David**.
\+ 890 iii. Lois Nadine Hamilton b. Dec 14 1936.
891 iv. Kit J Hamilton b. Jan 21 1938 in Delta Co., CO.
She Married **Sue Dickerson**, b. Sep 29 1973 in New York City, NY.
892 v. Corliss Ann Hamilton b. Feb 07 1940 in Delta Co., CO.
(1) Married Dec 24 1958 in Divorced, **William Fredricks**.
(2) Married May 62 1967, **George Butler**, d. Jun 24 1973.
(3) Married Apr 11 1977, **Seebert Smith.**

632. **Marcia Roberta[7] Payne** (443.William Charles[6], 281.Mary[5] Morrison, 125.Sophia[4] Arbogast, 43.Jesse[3], 6.Sophia[2], 1.Henry[1]), b. May 16 1921 in Gracemont, Caddo Co., OK.
Married Jun 09 1939 in Delta Co., CO, **Charles Russell Robertson**, b. Jan 37 1914 in Denison, Grayson Co., TX.

Children:

\+ 893 i. Charles Ronald[8] Robertson b. Jul 01 1941.
894 ii. Jay Douglas Robertson b. Oct 24 1943 in Eugene, Lane Co., OR, d. May 26 1974 in Scotts Valley, Santa Cruz Co., CA.
He Married **Brenda Sue Mayberry**.
\+ 895 iii. John Ralph Robertson b. Mar 07 1952.

633. **Morris R[7] Payne** (443.William Charles[6], 281.Mary[5] Morrison, 125.Sophia[4] Arbogast, 43.Jesse[3], 6.Sophia[2], 1.Henry[1]), b. Aug 15 1923.
Married Jun 09 1946 in Ouray, Ouray Co., CO, **Dema Mae Bullock**, b. Mar 10 1926 in Maple City, Cowley Co., KS.

Children:

896 i. Mary Ann[8] Payne b. Jul 26 1949 in Alameda, Alameda Co., CA.

897 ii. Richard Charles Payne b. Feb 01 1956 in Alameda, Alameda Co., CA.
898 iii. Kenneth Bernard Payne b. Mar 29 1960 in Alameda, Alameda Co., CA.

636. **Duane^{7} Woolverton** (448.Harry^{6}, 285.Rose^{5} Morrison, 125.Sophia^{4} Arbogast, 43.Jesse^{3}, 6.Sophia^{2}, 1.Henry^{1}), b. May 11 1929.
He Married **Ann Lou Harl**, b. Jul 13 1928.

Children:

899 i. Wayne Harl^{8} Woolverton b. Dec 31 1950 in Illinois.
900 ii. Gary Allen Woolverton b. May 13 1953 in Illinois.
+ 901 iii. Donald Ralph Woolverton b. Jul 20 1954.
902 iv. Ned Wayne Woolverton b. Jun 25 1958.

637. **Marlin Glenn^{7} McMillian** (451.Bernice^{6} Clarke, 289.Amy^{5} Brown, 128.Mary Jane^{4} Arbogast, 43.Jesse^{3}, 6.Sophia^{2}, 1.Henry^{1}), b. Feb 22 1934.
He Married **Carol Peterson**.

Children:

903 i. Norman Wayne^{8} McMillian.
904 ii. Michael Kevin McMillian b. Aug 10 1957.
905 iii. Kim Reese McMillian b. 1959.

638. **Merrill Gene^{7} McMillian** (451.Bernice^{6} Clarke, 289.Amy^{5} Brown, 128.Mary Jane^{4} Arbogast, 43.Jesse^{3}, 6.Sophia^{2}, 1.Henry^{1}), b. Jun 15 1935.
He Married **Wanda Bush**.

Children:

906 i. Shelby^{8} McMillian b. Jul 24 1958.
907 ii. Mitchell Glenn McMillian b. Dec 07 1960.
908 iii. Stacey Diane McMillian b. Feb 20 1969.

639. **Terry^{7} Clarke** (452.Carl C^{6}, 289.Amy^{5} Brown, 128.Mary Jane^{4} Arbogast, 43.Jesse^{3}, 6.Sophia^{2}, 1.Henry^{1}), b. 1944.
Married Jan 16 1964, **Jayne Coddington**, b. 1945.

Children:

909 i. Del^{8} Clarke b. 1965.
910 ii. Penny Jane Clarke b. Feb 08 1970.

640. **Gary Taylor^{7} Clarke** (452.Carl C^{6}, 289.Amy^{5} Brown, 128.Mary Jane^{4} Arbogast, 43.Jesse^{3}, 6.Sophia^{2}, 1.Henry^{1}), b. Jan 16 1949.
Married Apr 14 1970, **Sally Wright**.

Children:

911 i. Jason Carl^{8} Clarke.

641. **Richard Allison^{7} Clarke** (452.Carl C^{6}, 289.Amy^{5} Brown, 128.Mary Jane^{4} Arbogast, 43.Jesse^{3}, 6.Sophia^{2}, 1.Henry^{1}), b. Feb 23 1950.
He Married **Becky Creek**, b. Nov 28 1946.

Children:

912 i. Jason Parrish^{8} Clarke b. May 06 1973.

644. **Jack Edward^{7} Kincaid** (455.Thelma Hannah^{6} Frary, 293.Lois Irene^{5} Brown, 128.Mary Jane^{4} Arbogast, 43.Jesse^{3}, 6.Sophia^{2}, 1.Henry^{1}), b. Nov 27 1932.
Married May 11 1959, **Sandra Wagader**.

Children:

913 i. John Edward^{8} Kincaid b. Aug 01 1961.
914 ii. Susan Jean Kincaid b. May 07 1964.

645. **William Gerald^{7} Kincaid** (455.Thelma Hannah^{6} Frary, 293.Lois Irene^{5} Brown, 128.Mary Jane^{4} Arbogast, 43.Jesse^{3}, 6.Sophia^{2}, 1.Henry^{1}), b. Sep 19 1934.
He Married **Patricia Fabricia**, b. Aug 12 1933.

Children:

915 i. Craig William^{8} Kincaid b. Feb 27 1961.

647. **James Richard^{7} Kincaid** (455.Thelma Hannah^{6} Frary, 293.Lois Irene^{5} Brown, 128.Mary Jane^{4} Arbogast, 43.Jesse^{3}, 6.Sophia^{2}, 1.Henry^{1}), b. Aug 09 1943.
He Married **Deana Rusk**.

Children:

916 i. Brian Richard^{8} Kincaid b. Mar 20 1961.

648. **Elizabeth Ann^{7} Miller** (456.Alice Lucille^{6} Frary, 293.Lois Irene^{5} Brown, 128.Mary Jane^{4} Arbogast, 43.Jesse^{3}, 6.Sophia^{2}, 1.Henry^{1}), b. Feb 19 1938.
She Married **Wendell Meyer**, b. Feb 13 1936.

Children:

917 i. Mark Allen^{8} Meyer b. Apr 25 1958.
918 ii. Sandra Meyer b. Dec 29 1961.
919 iii. Lisa Meyer b. Feb 17 1963.

649. **Jan Erwin^{7} Mikesell** (458.Lewis^{6}, 295.Mertice Loine^{5} Brown, 128.Mary Jane^{4} Arbogast, 43.Jesse^{3}, 6.Sophia^{2}, 1.Henry^{1}), b. Feb 14 1943.
He Married **Pamela Priestwood**.

Children:

920 i. Shalee^{8} Mikesell.
921 ii. Doni Mikesell.

650. **Norma Jean^{7} Mikesell** (459.Osmond^{6}, 295.Mertice Loine^{5} Brown, 128.Mary Jane^{4} Arbogast, 43.Jesse^{3}, 6.Sophia^{2}, 1.Henry^{1}), b. Mar 01 1936.
Married in Divorced, **Stanley Creech**.

Children:

922 i. Sharon Deane^{8} Creech b. Mar 30 1962.
923 ii. Steven David Creech b. Mar 30 1962.

652. **Ralph^{7} Mikesell** (460.Weist Lamoine^{6}, 295.Mertice Loine^{5} Brown, 128.Mary Jane^{4} Arbogast, 43.Jesse^{3}, 6.Sophia^{2}, 1.Henry^{1}), b. Dec 04 1936.
He Married **Nancy Mathers**, b. Apr 17 1937.

Children:

924 i. Victoria^{8} Mikesell b. Jul 30 1956.
925 ii. Steven Mikesell b. Apr 06 1958.
926 iii. Christopher Mikesell b. Oct 21 1959.
927 iv. Timothy Mikesell b. Aug 08 1961.
928 v. David Mikesell b. Mar 12 1962, d. Nov 10 1976.

653. **Herbert^{7} Mikesell** (460.Weist Lamoine^{6}, 295.Mertice Loine^{5} Brown, 128.Mary Jane^{4} Arbogast, 43.Jesse^{3}, 6.Sophia^{2}, 1.Henry^{1}), b. Jul 20 1938.
He Married **Elizabeth Cosello**, b. Nov 28 1938.

Children:

929 i. Joel Eugene^{8} Mikesell b. Jan 16 1966.
930 ii. Mary Elizabeth Mikesell b. Apr 08 1971.

655. **Gayle Lynn^{7} Mikesell** (461.Orth Arbogast^{6}, 295.Mertice Loine^{5} Brown, 128.Mary Jane^{4} Arbogast, 43.Jesse^{3}, 6.Sophia^{2}, 1.Henry^{1}), b. May 17 1945.
Married Aug 30 1964, **Jim Garrison**, b. Mar 21 1945.

Children:

931 i. Angela Lynn^{8} Garrison b. Jul 14 1970.
932 ii. Todd James Garrison b. Jun 26 1972.
933 iii. Melanie Ann Garrison b. Apr 12 1978.

660. **Richard Gene^{7} Brewer** (464.Sarah Fern^{6} Cozad, 301.Mae^{5} Howard, 131.Sarah^{4} Arbogast, 43.Jesse^{3}, 6.Sophia^{2}, 1.Henry^{1}), b. Jul 07 1930.
Married Sep 09 1950, **Carolyn May Mochel**, b. Apr 30 1930 in Downers Grove, DuPage Co., IL.

Children:

934 i. Dennis Gene^{8} Brewer b. May 09 1953 in Avon, Fulton Co., IL.
\+ 935 ii. David Lee Brewer b. Aug 13 1955.

661. **Barbara Mae^{7} Black** (465.Faun Elizabeth^{6} Cozad, 301.Mae^{5} Howard, 131.Sarah^{4} Arbogast, 43.Jesse^{3}, 6.Sophia^{2}, 1.Henry^{1}), b. Oct 07 1922 in Colchester, McDonough Co., IL.
Married Dec 24 1941, **Donovan Kinkade Lawyer**, b. Jan 23 1921 in Industry, McDonough Co., IL, d. May 24 1991 in McComb, McDonough Co., IL.

Children:

\+ 936 i. Donna Kay^{8} Lawyer b. Apr 10 1945.
\+ 937 ii. Linda Lou Lawyer b. Mar 08 1950.

662. **William Howard^{7} Black** (465.Faun Elizabeth^{6} Cozad, 301.Mae^{5} Howard, 131.Sarah^{4} Arbogast, 43.Jesse^{3}, 6.Sophia^{2}, 1.Henry^{1}), b. May 19 1925 in Good Hope, Walnut Grove, Putnam Co., IL.
He Married **Nita Orlayne Toland**, b. Apr 19 1926 in Industry, McDonough Co., IL.

Children:

\+ 938 i. William Authur^{8} Black b. Dec 09 1947.
\+ 939 ii. Susan Elizabeth Black b. Sep 11 1948.
\+ 940 iii. Rex Eugene Black b. Jul 04 1950.
941 iv. Scott Black b. Oct 01 1952.

666. **Judy^{7} Smith** (469.Russell^{6}, 305.Emerson Eugene^{5}, 133.Frances^{4} Arbogast, 43.Jesse^{3}, 6.Sophia^{2}, 1.Henry^{1}), b. in McComb, McDonough Co., IL.
She Married **Robert Worman**.

Children:

942 i. Emma^{8} Worman.
She Married **Kent Poulter.**
943 ii. Kate Worman.

667. **Kathryn Louise^{7} Fox** (477.Keith Leroy^{6}, 310.Myrtle^{5} Smith, 133.Frances^{4} Arbogast, 43.Jesse^{3}, 6.Sophia^{2}, 1.Henry^{1}), b. Oct 10 1934 in Ellisville, Fulton Co., IL.
She Married **Marion Frank Huston**, b. Jul 08 1928 in McDonough Co., IL.

Children:

\+ 944 i. Harold William^{8} Huston b. Jun 24 1959.

668. **Dean Edward^{7} Fox** (477.Keith Leroy^{6}, 310.Myrtle^{5} Smith, 133.Frances^{4} Arbogast, 43.Jesse^{3}, 6.Sophia^{2}, 1.Henry^{1}), b. Oct 08 1935 in Hartsburg, Logan Co., IL.
He Married **Maxine Starkley**, b. Mar 01 1935.

Children:

\+ 945 i. Tracie Gaye^{8} Fox b. Dec 03 1958.
\+ 946 ii. Dale Edward Fox b. Sep 30 1967.
\+ 947 iii. Amy Suzanne Fox.

669. **Carol Jean^{7} Fox** (477.Keith Leroy^{6}, 310.Myrtle^{5} Smith, 133.Frances^{4} Arbogast, 43.Jesse^{3}, 6.Sophia^{2}, 1.Henry^{1}), b. Mar 23 1938.
Married Mar 23 1957 in Divorced, **James Joseph Schulte**, b. Dec 01 1935.

Children:

\+ 948 i. Randy Joe^{8} Schulte b. Jul 07 1957.
949 ii. James Kent Schulte b. May 23 1959, d. Dec 01 1984.
Married Aug 09 1980, **Wendy Woodward**, b. Sep 28 1959.
950 iii. Matthew Schulte b. Apr 06 1960, d. Apr 06 1960.
951 iv. Mark Schulte b. Apr 06 1960, d. Apr 06 1960.
952 v. Kelly Jean Schulte b. Sep 04 1962.
Married Sep 10 1983 in Divorced, **Gary Tueschmann**.

671. **George Leroy^{7} Fox** (477.Keith Leroy^{6}, 310.Myrtle^{5} Smith, 133.Frances^{4} Arbogast, 43.Jesse^{3}, 6.Sophia^{2}, 1.Henry^{1}), b. Jun 27 1941.

Married in Divorced, **Victoria Ann Woerly**, b. Aug 02 1944.

Children:

953 i. Tori Lynn[8] Fox b. May 06 1967.
She Married **Robert Sumter**, b. Apr 14 1990.

954 ii. Michael George Fox b. Sep 10 1970.

672. **Beverly Jane[7] Fox** (477.Keith Leroy[6], 310.Myrtle[5] Smith, 133.Frances[4] Arbogast, 43.Jesse[3], 6.Sophia[2], 1.Henry[1]), b. Dec 23 1942.
Married Nov 17 1960 in Divorced, **William Clark**, b. Feb 06 1943.

Children:

\+ 955 i. Barbara Jo[8] Clark b. Jun 26 1961.
\+ 956 ii. Linda Kay Clark b. May 15 1962.
\+ 957 iii. Carol Ann Clark b. May 25 1963.
\+ 958 iv. Dorothy Elaine Clark b. Apr 28 1965.

673. **James Keith[7] Fox** (477.Keith Leroy[6], 310.Myrtle[5] Smith, 133.Frances[4] Arbogast, 43.Jesse[3], 6.Sophia[2], 1.Henry[1]), b. Mar 16 1944.
James Married twice more, divorced each time.
(1) Married Apr 18 1964, **Kathy (Unknown). Kathy**: One child to this marriage.

Children:

959 i. James Todd[8] Fox b. Feb 13 1966.

(2) Married in Divorced, **Tannie Wilson**.

Children:

960 ii. Brian Keith Fox b. Jul 17 1972.

674. **Kenneth Lee[7] Fox** (477.Keith Leroy[6], 310.Myrtle[5] Smith, 133.Frances[4] Arbogast, 43.Jesse[3], 6.Sophia[2], 1.Henry[1]), b. Jul 15 1949.
He Married **Shirley Ann Sauvageau**.

Children:

961 i. Sandra Jane[8] Fox b. Feb 07 1972.
962 ii. Carrie Lynn Fox b. May 08 1975.
963 iii. Lori Ann Fox b. Oct 24 1976.
964 iv. Kristy Loreen Fox b. Jun 30 1978.
965 v. Norleen Lynette Fox b. Apr 01 1980.

675. **David Bruce[7] Fox** (478.Ralth Wilton[6], 310.Myrtle[5] Smith, 133.Frances[4] Arbogast, 43.Jesse[3], 6.Sophia[2], 1.Henry[1]), b. Sep 19 1956.
Married in Divorced 1988, **Lori Sears**, b. Jun 11 1961.

Children:

966 i. Cassandra June[8] Fox b. Nov 07 1982.
967 ii. Mallary Erin Fox b. Jul 23 1985.

676. **Joni Sue[7] Fox** (478.Ralth Wilton[6], 310.Myrtle[5] Smith, 133.Frances[4] Arbogast, 43.Jesse[3], 6.Sophia[2], 1.Henry[1]), b. Feb 04 1959.
She Married **James Calvin Poisel, Jr.**.

Children:

968 i. Heather[8] Poisel b. Sep 21 1982.
969 ii. Jessica Dawn Poisel b. Oct 30 1984.
970 iii. Jenna Rose Poisel b. Jun 21 1989.
971 iv. Janelle Christine Poisel b. Mar 20 1991.

678. **Richard Francis[7] Arbogast** (479.Theodore Fenton[6], 311.Clyde Stewart[5], 134.Stephen Aaron Douglas[4], 43.Jesse[3], 6.Sophia[2], 1.Henry[1]), b. Feb 10 1934 in Silver Creek, Merrick Co., NE.
Married Nov 10 1960 in Burley, Cassia Co., ID, **Donna Hutchinson Williams**, b. Mar 01 1920 in Evanston, Uinta Co., WY.

Children:

\+ 972 i. Donna Esther[8] Arbogast b. Jan 08 1962.

679. **Patricia Ann^{7} Arbogast** (479.Theodore Fenton^{6}, 311.Clyde Stewart^{5}, 134.Stephen Aaron Douglas^{4}, 43.Jesse^{3}, 6.Sophia^{2}, 1.Henry^{1}), b. May 28 1935 in Burley, Cassia Co., ID.
Married Aug 23 1955 in Elko, Elko Co., NV, **Price Ray Howard**, b. Apr 14 1935 in Lewisburg, Greenbrier Co., WV.

Children:

+ 973 i. Richard Ray^{8} Howard.

681. **Gerald Lee^{7} Arbogast** (479.Theodore Fenton^{6}, 311.Clyde Stewart^{5}, 134.Stephen Aaron Douglas^{4}, 43.Jesse^{3}, 6.Sophia^{2}, 1.Henry^{1}), b. Apr 13 1936 in Burley, Cassia Co., ID.
Married Apr 16 1966 in Rupert, Minidoka Co., ID, **Sandra Kay Dozer**, b. Oct 17 1947.

Children:

974 i. Nicole Ann^{8} Arbogast b. Nov 28 1969 in Oxnard, Ventura Co., CA.
Married Sep 11 1992, Clyde Lay.
975 ii. Rebecca Ann Arbogast b. Aug 26 1971 in Burley, Cassia Co., ID.

682. **Theodore Clyde^{7} Arbogast** (479.Theodore Fenton^{6}, 311.Clyde Stewart^{5}, 134.Stephen Aaron Douglas^{4}, 43.Jesse^{3}, 6.Sophia^{2}, 1.Henry^{1}), b. Dec 31 1937 in Burley, Cassia Co., ID.
Married Jun 19 1958 in Rupert, Minidoka Co., ID, **Lorna Karen Rasmussen**, b. Dec 31 1937.

Children:

+ 976 i. Kathleen K.^{8} Arbogast b. Jun 19 1959.
977 ii. Jeffery C. Arbogast b. Nov 20 1961.
Married Oct 25 1986, **Kathy Shipuro**.
978 iii. Gregory T. Arbogast b. Feb 19 1964.
Married Jun 04 1994, **Sherry Risa Lee Hooper**.

683. **Larry Arndt^{7} Chelberg** (481.Helen Elene^{6} Arbogast, 311.Clyde Stewart^{5}, 134.Stephen Aaron Douglas^{4}, 43.Jesse^{3}, 6.Sophia^{2}, 1.Henry^{1}), b. Mar 13 1938 in Wahoo, Saunders Co., NE.
Married Jan 31 1959 in Wahoo, Saunders Co., NE, **Mary Kay Kacirck**.

Children:

979 i. Craig Allen^{8} Chelberg b. Jul 13 1959 in Omaha, Douglas Co., NE.
980 ii. Leann Chelberg b. Aug 19 1960 in Omaha, Douglas Co., NE.
981 iii. Steven Michael Chelberg b. Dec 31 1961 in Omaha, Douglas Co., NE.
982 iv. Mark Lee Chelberg b. Apr 27 1965 in Omaha, Douglas Co., NE.
Married Jun 14 1989, **Penny Heidt**.

684. **Gary Allen^{7} Chelberg** (481.Helen Elene^{6} Arbogast, 311.Clyde Stewart^{5}, 134.Stephen Aaron Douglas^{4}, 43.Jesse^{3}, 6.Sophia^{2}, 1.Henry^{1}), b. Nov 13 1939 in Neligh, Antelope Co., NE.
Married Dec 28 1960 in Wahoo, Saunders Co., NE, **Jean Berry**.

Children:

983 i. Pamela Renae^{8} Chelberg b. May 30 1961.
Married Apr 30 1983, **Les Kotera.**
984 ii. Scott Allen Chelberg b. Sep 18 1962 in David City, Butler Co., NE.
Married Oct 14 1989, **Barbara Jean Lewsin.**

685. **Roland Allen^{7} Arbogast** (482.Allen Sterart^{6}, 311.Clyde Stewart^{5}, 134.Stephen Aaron Douglas^{4}, 43.Jesse^{3}, 6.Sophia^{2}, 1.Henry^{1}), b. Nov 19 1940 in Burley, Cassia Co., ID.

Married Apr 28 1961 in Caldwell, Canyon Co., ID, **Judith Marie Reynolds**, b. Jul 20 1941 in Denver, Arapaho Co., CO.

Children:

+ 985 i. Karen Diane^{8} Arbogast b. Jan 18 1962.
+ 986 ii. Susan Lynn Arbogast b. Jun 04 1963.
987 iii. Nancy Anne Arbogast b. May 11 1965.
Married Feb 25 1989 in Eugene, Lane Co., OR, **Bradley Zakes.**
988 iv. Janet Kay Arbogast b. Jul 09 1968 in Portland, Multnomah Co., OR.
989 v. Steven Craig Arbogast b. Oct 03 1975 in Portland, Multnomah Co., OR.

686. **Calvin Stewart^{7} Arbogast** (482.Allen Sterart^{6}, 311.Clyde Stewart^{5}, 134.Stephen Aaron Douglas^{4}, 43.Jesse^{3}, 6.Sophia^{2}, 1.Henry^{1}), b. Jun 04 1942.
(1) Married Sep 16 1962 in Lebanon, Linn Co., OR, **Leona May Stenberg**, b. Jan 21 1943.

Children:

990 i. Dawn Deann[8] Arbogast b. Feb 28 1969 in Cottage Grove. Lane Co., OR.

(2) Married Aug 04 1978 in Salem, Marion Co., OR, **Leila May Corrasco**, b. Aug 25 1949 in Cotabato, Philippines.

Children:

991 ii. Brent Tyler Arbogast b. Nov 25 1988 in Kent, King Co., WA.
992 iii. Bryce Taylor Arbogast b. Nov 25 1988 in Kent, King Co., WA.

687. **Sherry Lorraine[7] Arbogast** (482.Allen Sterart[6], 311.Clyde Stewart[5], 134.Stephen Aaron Douglas[4], 43.Jesse[3], 6.Sophia[2], 1.Henry[1]), b. Apr 21 1944 in Burley, Cassia Co., ID.
Married Jan 25 1963 in Albany, Linn Co., OR, **James Jordon May**, b. Mar 22 1943.

Children:

993 i. Nathan James[8] May b. Aug 11 1963 in Lebanon, Linn Co., OR.
994 ii. Jordon Michael May b. May 21 1966 in Lebanon, Linn Co., OR.
995 iii. Lewis Vandiver May b. Nov 02 1968 in Kenie, AR.
996 iv. Leland George May b. Jul 21 1971 in Soldotna, Kenai Peninsula Borough, AK.

688. **Leland G.[7] Arbogast** (482.Allen Sterart[6], 311.Clyde Stewart[5], 134.Stephen Aaron Douglas[4], 43.Jesse[3], 6.Sophia[2], 1.Henry[1]), b. Mar 06 1946.
He Married **Diane Alice Beck**, b. Jan 09 1945 in Lebanon, Linn Co., OR.

Children:

997 i. Jason Allen[8] Arbogast b. May 06 1970 in Cottage Grove. Lane Co., OR.
998 ii. Justin Lee Arbogast b. Jul 01 1973 in Cottage Grove. Lane Co., OR.

689. **Darrell Ray[7] Arbogast** (482.Allen Sterart[6], 311.Clyde Stewart[5], 134.Stephen Aaron Douglas[4], 43.Jesse[3], 6.Sophia[2], 1.Henry[1]), b. Jan 28 1948 in Burley, Cassia Co., ID.
Married Apr 08 1972 in Corvallis, Benton Co., OR, **Janet Louise Stiles**, b. Aug 13 1950 in Tacoma, Pierce Co., WA.

Children:

999 i. Alicia Dawn[8] Arbogast b. Nov 03 1974 in Albany, Linn Co., OR.
1000 ii. Brian Loren Arbogast b. Dec 30 1976 in Springfield, Lane Co., OR.
1001 iii. Kristin Ilene Arbogast b. Dec 28 1978 in Eugene, Lane Co., OR.

690. **John Stewart[7] Holmes** (483.Gladys Catherine[6] Arbogast, 311.Clyde Stewart[5], 134.Stephen Aaron Douglas[4], 43.Jesse[3], 6.Sophia[2], 1.Henry[1]), b. Oct 13 1934 in Lincoln, Lancaster Co., NE.
Married Oct 30 1955 in Lincoln, Lancaster Co., NE, **Janice Rae Street**.

Children:

1002 i. Jeffery[8] Holmes b. Nov 02 1957 in Santa Monica, Los Angeles Co., CA.
1003 ii. Kristin Holmes b. Jan 01 1961 in Santa Monica, Los Angeles Co., CA.
Married May 30 1987, **Jeffery Fafara**.
1004 iii. John Steven Holmes b. Aug 26 1964 in Santa Monica, Los Angeles Co., CA.

691. **David[7] Coons** (483.Gladys Catherine[6] Arbogast, 311.Clyde Stewart[5], 134.Stephen Aaron Douglas[4], 43.Jesse[3], 6.Sophia[2], 1.Henry[1]), b. Sep 22 1951 in Lincoln, Lancaster Co., NE.
He Married **Pamela Elaine Johnston**, b. Nov 04 1954 in Ft. Worth, Tarrant Co., TX.

Children:

1005 i. Rachel Leigh[8] Coons b. Jul 09 1986 in Lubbock, Lubbock Co., TX.

693. **Karen Sue[7] Sagarra** (485.Marilyn Inez[6] Arbogast, 311.Clyde Stewart[5], 134.Stephen Aaron Douglas[4], 43.Jesse[3], 6.Sophia[2], 1.Henry[1]), b. Feb 17 1951 in Los Angeles, Los Angeles Co., CA.
She Married **Steven Knorpp**.

Children:

1006 i. Benjamin S[8] Knorpp b. Mar 25 1971.

708. **John Allen[7] Arbogast** (504.Dwight[6], 320.Jessie L.[5], 138.John Franklin[4], 46.Michael[3], 6.Sophia[2], 1.Henry[1]).
He Married **Sue Mitten**.

Children:

1007 i. Jo[8] Arbogast.

She Married **Albert Schank.**
1008 ii. Steve Arbogast.
He Married **Carol Fleetwood.**
1009 iii. John Arbogast.
He Married **Kerry Fredericks.**
1010 iv. James Arbogast.
1011 v. Susan Arbogast.
She Married **Peter Galipeau**.

709. **Carol Jean^{7} Arbogast** (504.Dwight^{6}, 320.Jessie L.^{5}, 138.John Franklin^{4}, 46.Michael^{3}, 6.Sophia^{2}, 1.Henry^{1}).
She Married **Joseph Engle**.

Children:

1012 i. Melissa^{8} Engle.
1013 ii. Louise Engle.
1014 iii. James Engle.

710. **Rual^{7} Arbogast** (504.Dwight^{6}, 320.Jessie L.^{5}, 138.John Franklin^{4}, 46.Michael^{3}, 6.Sophia^{2}, 1.Henry^{1}), d. Nov 22 1978.
Married Jun 12 1837, **Walter Hill**, b. Jun 05 1808, d. Dec 25 1883.

Children:

1015 i. Patricia^{8} Hill.
She Married **Raymond Scherger**.
1016 ii. Bill Hill.

711. **Brian Earl^{7} Slater** (509.Lois Alberta^{6} Arbogast, 333.James Michael^{5}, 141.Charles Sayers^{4}, 46.Michael^{3}, 6.Sophia^{2}, 1.Henry^{1}), b. Nov 02 1946.
He Married **Sharon Rose Maddess**.

Children:

1017 i. Kari Rose^{8} Slater b. Aug 26 1978.
1018 ii. Curtis Earl Slater b. Mar 22 1980.

712. **Lynn Marie^{7} Slater** (509.Lois Alberta^{6} Arbogast, 333.James Michael^{5}, 141.Charles Sayers^{4}, 46.Michael^{3}, 6.Sophia^{2}, 1.Henry^{1}), b. Oct 10 1948.
She Married **Lorne Adamschek**.

Children:

1019 i. Jodi Lynn^{8} Adamschek b. Aug 07 1981.
1020 ii. Lisa Marie Adamschek b. Mar 14 1983.
1021 iii. Douglas Adamschek b. Jun 18 1985.

713. **Patricia Leigh^{7} Armour** (510.Gayl Jane^{6} Arbogast, 333.James Michael^{5}, 141.Charles Sayers^{4}, 46.Michael^{3}, 6.Sophia^{2}, 1.Henry^{1}), b. Jan 24 1943.
She Married **Gary Ritchie**.

Children:

\+ 1022 i. Terri^{8} Ritchie.
1023 ii. Todd Arthur Ritchie.
1024 iii. James Ritchie.

719. **John^{7} Heath** (512.James Kenneth^{6}, 334.Alice^{5} Arbogast, 141.Charles Sayers^{4}, 46.Michael^{3}, 6.Sophia^{2}, 1.Henry^{1}), b. Jul 05 1946.
He Married **Maxine Spicker**.

Children:

1025 i. Jason^{8} Heath.
1026 ii. Ryan Heath.
1027 iii. Jeremy Heath.

721. **Susan^{7} Heath** (512.James Kenneth^{6}, 334.Alice^{5} Arbogast, 141.Charles Sayers^{4}, 46.Michael^{3}, 6.Sophia^{2}, 1.Henry^{1}), b. Dec 08 1952 in McComb, McDonough Co., IL.
She Married **J Greg Hummel**.

Children:

1028 i. J. Chris^{8} Hummel.
1029 ii. Cara Hummel.
1030 iii. Cortney Hummel.

722. **Danial Claude^{7} Bates** (513.Marion E.^{6} Heath, 334.Alice^{5} Arbogast, 141.Charles Sayers^{4}, 46.Michael^{3}, 6.Sophia^{2}, 1.Henry^{1}), b. Jan 20 1946.
He Married **Susan Lee Miler**.

Children:

1031 i. Brian Michael^{8} Heath.

723. **Donna Ruth^{7} Bates** (513.Marion E.^{6} Heath, 334.Alice^{5} Arbogast, 141.Charles Sayers^{4}, 46.Michael^{3}, 6.Sophia^{2}, 1.Henry^{1}), b. Nov 21 1949.
She Married **Wayne Thomas Inman**, b. Nov 25 1943 in Wyandotte, Wayne Co., MI.

Children:

1032 i. Thomas D.^{8} Inman b. Nov 11 1982 in Peoria, Peoria Co., IL.

724. **Suzanne Marie^{7} Arbogast** (514.James Clarence^{6}, 337.Clarence James^{5}, 142.Rush Arlington^{4}, 46.Michael^{3}, 6.Sophia^{2}, 1.Henry^{1}), b. Nov 2 0052.
She Married **David Curlis**. .

Children:

1033 i. Trisha Lee^{8} CURLIS b. Jan 17 1980.
1034 ii. Adrienne Curlis b. Oct 09 1985.

725. **Teresa Kay^{7} Arbogast** (514.James Clarence^{6}, 337.Clarence James^{5}, 142.Rush Arlington^{4}, 46.Michael^{3}, 6.Sophia^{2}, 1.Henry^{1}), b. May 6 0055 in Tiffin, Seneca Co., OH.
Married Nov 25 1977, **Richard Burkett**, b. Nov 15 1953. .

Children:

1035 i. Benjamin^{8} BURKETT.
1036 ii. Katherine Burkett.
Nickname:<NICK> Katie.

727. **Gregory Charles^{7} Arbogast** (514.James Clarence^{6}, 337.Clarence James^{5}, 142.Rush Arlington^{4}, 46.Michael^{3}, 6.Sophia^{2}, 1.Henry^{1}), b. Mar 1 0062 in Tiffin, Seneca Co., OH.
He Married **Diane Louise Kessler**. .

Children:

1037 i. Brandy Rose^{8} Arbogast b. Oct 12 1984 in Tiffin, Seneca Co., OH.
1038 ii. Haili Nicole Arbogast b. in Tiffin, Seneca Co., OH.
1039 iii. Eric Gregory Arbogast b. in Tiffin, Seneca Co., OH.

730. **Anita Louise^{7} Arbogast** (514.James Clarence^{6}, 337.Clarence James^{5}, 142.Rush Arlington^{4}, 46.Michael^{3}, 6.Sophia^{2}, 1.Henry^{1}), b. Aug 14 1960.
Married Jun 08 1979, **Joseph Gosche**, b. Jun 30 1958.

Children:

1040 i. Heather Jo^{8} Gosche b. Dec 08 1982.
1041 ii. Nicholas James Gosche b. Jun 07 1985.

735. **Jane^{7} Arbogast** (516.Paul Joseph^{6}, 338.Charles Anthony^{5}, 142.Rush Arlington^{4}, 46.Michael^{3}, 6.Sophia^{2}, 1.Henry^{1}).
(1) She Married **Lawrence Sorg**, b. Dec 20 1946.

Children:

\+ 1042 i. Christina Rose^{8} Sorg b. May 03 1969.
1043 ii. Kelley Eugene Sorg b. Mar 30 1972.
1044 iii. Randy Alexander Sorg b. Feb 23 1975.

(2) She Married **Dan Gildermister**.

736. **Dean Larwence^{7} Arbogast** (516.Paul Joseph^{6}, 338.Charles Anthony^{5}, 142.Rush Arlington^{4}, 46.Michael^{3}, 6.Sophia^{2}, 1.Henry^{1}).
Married Feb 12 1972, **Mary Edith Lumberjack**.

Children:

1045 i. Wendy Ann^{8} Arbogast b. Mar 06 1973.
1046 ii. Chad Anthony Arbogast b. Apr 10 1975.
1047 iii. Denise Ellen Arbogast.
1048 iv. Kimberley Kay Arbogast b. Jun 05 1981.

737. **Ruth Ann^{7} Arbogast** (516.Paul Joseph^{6}, 338.Charles Anthony^{5}, 142.Rush Arlington^{4}, 46.Michael^{3}, 6.Sophia^{2}, 1.Henry^{1}).
Married Nov 07 1970, **Gary Lynn Hawk**.

Children:

1049 i. Victoria Lynn^{8} Hawk b. Jun 03 1971.
1050 ii. Matthew Glen Hawk b. Sep 25 1975.
1051 iii. Debra Ann Hawk b. May 17 1979.

738. **Judith Carol^{7} Arbogast** (516.Paul Joseph^{6}, 338.Charles Anthony^{5}, 142.Rush Arlington^{4}, 46.Michael^{3}, 6.Sophia^{2}, 1.Henry^{1}).
(1) Married Jan 12 1974, **Donald Staats**, d. Jan 07 1984.

Children:

1052 i. Stephanie Carol^{8} Staats b. May 11 1974.
1053 ii. Donald Christopher Staats b. Apr 20 1977.
1054 iii. Jenifer Renee Staats b. Jun 06 1980.

(2) She Married **Ralph Stearn**.

740. **Mark Anthony^{7} Arbogast** (516.Paul Joseph^{6}, 338.Charles Anthony^{5}, 142.Rush Arlington^{4}, 46.Michael^{3}, 6.Sophia^{2}, 1.Henry^{1}), b. Sep 30 1963.
Married Feb 28 1987, **Dorette Reguiti**.

Children:

1055 i. Ryan Anthony^{8} Arbogast b. Jan 20 1989.

741. **Daria^{7} Arbogast** (517.Lawrence Anselm^{6}, 338.Charles Anthony^{5}, 142.Rush Arlington^{4}, 46.Michael^{3}, 6.Sophia^{2}, 1.Henry^{1}), b. Apr 29 1953.
Married 1982, **Pat Walsh**.

Children:

1056 i. Edmund Anthony^{8} Walsh b. Aug 29 1983.

744. **Paula Louise^{7} Arbogast** (517.Lawrence Anselm^{6}, 338.Charles Anthony^{5}, 142.Rush Arlington^{4}, 46.Michael^{3}, 6.Sophia^{2}, 1.Henry^{1}), b. Sep 15 1958.
Married Dec 22 1979, **Martin Karlin**.

Children:

1057 i. James Francis^{8} Karlin b. Apr 14 1982.
1058 ii. Melissa Francine Karlin b. Dec 03 1983.
1059 iii. Virginia Winfred Karlin b. Mar 11 1985.

749. **Virginia Ann^{7} Arbogast** (518.Urban Anthony^{6}, 338.Charles Anthony^{5}, 142.Rush Arlington^{4}, 46.Michael^{3}, 6.Sophia^{2}, 1.Henry^{1}), b. Oct 11 1949.
Married Oct 26 1968, **Larry Charles Shock**, b. Mar 06 1947 in Seneca Co., OH.

Children:

1060 i. Denise Marie^{8} Shock b. Jul 19 1969.
1061 ii. Anthony Charles Shock b. Nov 10 1973.

750. **Alice Rose^{7} Arbogast** (518.Urban Anthony^{6}, 338.Charles Anthony^{5}, 142.Rush Arlington^{4}, 46.Michael^{3}, 6.Sophia^{2}, 1.Henry^{1}), b. Sep 10 1950.
Married Apr 04 1970, **Christopher Oscar Mugrage**.

Children:

1062 i. Phillip Anthony^{8} Mugrage b. Dec 26 1972.
1063 ii. Jason Michael Mugrage b. Jul 05 1974.

751. **Pauline Mary^{7} Arbogast** (518.Urban Anthony^{6}, 338.Charles Anthony^{5}, 142.Rush Arlington^{4}, 46.Michael^{3}, 6.Sophia^{2}, 1.Henry^{1}), b. Sep 06 1951.

(1) She Married **Samuel Fey**, b. Apr 01 1963.

Children:

1064 i. Samantha[8] Fey b. Jul 22 1986.
1065 ii. Dolly Fey b. Jan 20 1988.

(2) She Married **Michael Sparkman**, b. Feb 08 1952.

Children:

1066 iii. Honey Marie Sparkman b. May 25 1973.
1067 iv. Michael David Sparkman b. May 02 1976.

752. **Helen Lucille[7] Arbogast** (518.Urban Anthony[6], 338.Charles Anthony[5], 142.Rush Arlington[4], 46.Michael[3], 6.Sophia[2], 1.Henry[1]), b. Mar 16 1953.
Married Apr 28 1972, **James Lemmerman**, b. Feb 18 1950.

Children:

1068 i. Jami Jo[8] Lemmerman b. Oct 21 1972.
1069 ii. Joshua David Lemmerman b. Feb 19 1977.

753. **Susan Theresa[7] Arbogast** (518.Urban Anthony[6], 338.Charles Anthony[5], 142.Rush Arlington[4], 46.Michael[3], 6.Sophia[2], 1.Henry[1]), b. Mar 29 1953.
Married May 05 1973 in St. Aloysius Church, Mercer Co., OH, **David Lewis Robison**, b. Dec 29 1933.

Children:

1070 i. Toby David[8] Robison b. May 29 1975.
1071 ii. Christopher Shawn Robison b. Nov 29 1976.

754. **Doris Mae[7] Arbogast** (518.Urban Anthony[6], 338.Charles Anthony[5], 142.Rush Arlington[4], 46.Michael[3], 6.Sophia[2], 1.Henry[1]), b. May 04 1955.
Married Jul 12 1974, **Bruce Lambert**, b. Oct 20 1955.

Children:

1072 i. Melissa Ann[8] Lambert b. Sep 07 1978.
1073 ii. Laura Mae Lambert b. Nov 03 1979.
1074 iii. Matthew Paul Lambert b. Jul 27 1981.
1075 iv. Sheene Marie Lambert b. Jan 12 1983.

755. **Angela Marie[7] Arbogast** (518.Urban Anthony[6], 338.Charles Anthony[5], 142.Rush Arlington[4], 46.Michael[3], 6.Sophia[2], 1.Henry[1]), b. May 21 1956.
Married Jun 20 1975, **Dennis A. Roush**, b. Mar 11 1954.

Children:

1076 i. Eric David[8] Roush b. Dec 19 1979.
1077 ii. Aaron Patrick Roush b. Sep 21 1981.

756. **Janice Eileen[7] Arbogast** (518.Urban Anthony[6], 338.Charles Anthony[5], 142.Rush Arlington[4], 46.Michael[3], 6.Sophia[2], 1.Henry[1]), b. May 17 1958.
(1) Married Aug 20 1978, **Ronald Roush**, b. Sep 27 1957.

Children:

1078 i. Rhyn William[8] Roush b. Jun 01 1981.

(2) Married Aug 03 1983, **Kenneth Miller**, b. Aug 17 1954.

Children:

1079 ii. Christa Miller b. Aug 21 1975.
1080 iii. Bradley Alan Miller b. Jul 30 1986.
1081 iv. Timothy Joseph Miller b. Dec 15 1987.

757. **Patricia Louise[7] Arbogast** (518.Urban Anthony[6], 338.Charles Anthony[5], 142.Rush Arlington[4], 46.Michael[3], 6.Sophia[2], 1.Henry[1]), b. May 05 1960.
Married Oct 12 1984, **Stanley Tolbert**, b. Aug 10 1960.

Children:

1082 i. Cory Maurice[8] Tolbert b. Nov 02 1987.

1083 ii. Catrina Tolbert b. Apr 24 1989.

758. **June Ellen[7] Arbogast** (518.Urban Anthony[6] Arbogast, 338.Charles Anthony[5], 142.Rush Arlington[4], 46.Michael[3], 6.Sophia[2], 1.Henry[1]), b. Jun 04 1961.
(1) Married Aug 20 1978, **Joseph Conrad**.

Children:

1084 i. Kendall Owen[8] Conrad b. Oct 18 1981.

(2) Married Dec 22 1987, **Donald Eveland**, b. Sep 13 1959.

Children:

1085 ii. Nicole Eveland b. May 12 1993.

759. **Linda Kay[7] Arbogast** (518.Urban Anthony[6], 338.Charles Anthony[5], 142.Rush Arlington[4], 46.Michael[3], 6.Sophia[2], 1.Henry[1]), b. Oct 27 1966.
Married Nov 28 1987, **Christopher Barger**, b. Nov 07 1964.

Children:

1086 i. Amanda[8] Barger b. Sep 03 1993.

762. **Marilyn Ann[7] Arbogast** (519.Eugene Jerome[6], 338.Charles Anthony[5], 142.Rush Arlington[4], 46.Michael[3], 6.Sophia[2], 1.Henry[1]), b. Dec 05 1952.
Married Jun 18 1976, **John Gagen**.

Children:

1087 i. Jason Robert[8] Gagen b. Jan 04 1978.

764. **Barbara Jean[7] Arbogast** (519.Eugene Jerome[6], 338.Charles Anthony[5], 142.Rush Arlington[4], 46.Michael[3], 6.Sophia[2], 1.Henry[1]), b. Nov 27 1957.
Married Oct 14 1977, **Clifton Hicklin**.

Children:

1088 i. Christopher Lane[8] Hicklin b. Feb 27 1978.
1089 ii. Charles Andrew Hicklin b. Aug 01 1979.
1090 iii. Jeffery Wayne Hicklin b. May 02 1981.
1091 iv. Jermey Scott Hicklin b. Sep 02 1983.

765. **Kenneth[7] Arbogast** (519.Eugene Jerome[6], 338.Charles Anthony[5], 142.Rush Arlington[4], 46.Michael[3], 6.Sophia[2], 1.Henry[1]), b. Mar 30 1959.
Married Apr 27 1984, **Lori Schroeder**.

Children:

1092 i. Michelle Renee[8] Arbogast b. Jul 24 1984.
1093 ii. Brent Michael Arbogast b. Jun 18 1986.
1094 iii. Rachel Ann Arbogast b. Mar 18 1988.

767. **Lois Marie[7] Arbogast** (519.Eugene Jerome[6], 338.Charles Anthony[5], 142.Rush Arlington[4], 46.Michael[3], 6.Sophia[2], 1.Henry[1]), b. Jul 05 1962.
Married Aug 08 1981, **Dave McQuiston**.

Children:

1095 i. Kristin Eileen[8] McQuiston b. Dec 12 1981.

768. **Diane Ruth[7] Arbogast** (520.Marion Victor[6], 338.Charles Anthony[5], 142.Rush Arlington[4], 46.Michael[3], 6.Sophia[2], 1.Henry[1]), b. Jan 10 1956.
Married Aug 06 1976, **Michael Girdler**.

Children:

1096 i. Douglas Michael[8] Girdler b. Oct 22 1977.
1097 ii. Matthew Scot Girdler b. Apr 02 1981.
1098 iii. Steven Girdler b. Mar 13 1985.

773. **Theresa Marie[7] Boes** (521.Marguerite Elenora[6] Arbogast, 338.Charles Anthony[5], 142.Rush Arlington[4], 46.Michael[3], 6.Sophia[2], 1.Henry[1]), b. Jun 15 1954.
Married Feb 04 1984, **Jerry Barrett**.

Children:

1099 i. Alicia Marie[8] Boes b. Jul 09 1984.

778. **Mary Catherine[7] Arbogast** (522.Harlan Clarence[6], 338.Charles Anthony[5], 142.Rush Arlington[4], 46.Michael[3], 6.Sophia[2], 1.Henry[1]), b. Aug 17 1959.
Married Apr 29 1978, **Dennis Pierce**.

Children:

1100 i. Christopher Jason[8] Pierce b. Dec 01 1979.

779. **Carol Sue[7] Arbogast** (522.Harlan Clarence[6], 338.Charles Anthony[5], 142.Rush Arlington[4], 46.Michael[3], 6.Sophia[2], 1.Henry[1]), b. Sep 10 1960.
Married Sep 25 1982, **Dennis Lofat**.

Children:

1101 i. Nathan Carl[8] Lofat b. Aug 15 1983.
1102 ii. Andrea Rose Lofat b. Jan 24 1986.

780. **Sandra Marie[7] Arbogast** (522.Harlan Clarence[6], 338.Charles Anthony[5], 142.Rush Arlington[4], 46.Michael[3], 6.Sophia[2], 1.Henry[1]), b. May 23 1962.
Married Aug 14 1986, **Mark Sexton**.

Children:

1103 i. Allab Thomas[8] Sexton b. Nov 27 1984.
1104 ii. Renee Marie Sexton b. Aug 25 1986.

786. **Wanda Ann[7] Arbogast** (522.Harlan Clarence[6], 338.Charles Anthony[5], 142.Rush Arlington[4], 46.Michael[3], 6.Sophia[2], 1.Henry[1]), b. Jun 23 1970.

Children:

1105 i. Amanda Marie[8] Arbogast b. Dec 14 1988.

801. **Neil Eugene[7] Kelbley** (524.Rita Mae[6] Arbogast, 338.Charles Anthony[5], 142.Rush Arlington[4], 46.Michael[3], 6.Sophia[2], 1.Henry[1]), b. Jun 07 1965.
Married Sep 21 1985, **Brenda Haubert**, b. Dec 18 1966.

Children:

1106 i. Ashley Rose[8] Kelbley b. May 30 1984.
1107 ii. Andrew Jonathan Kelbley b. Dec 20 1986.

807. **Elmo Harold[7] SMITH** (527.Clarence Louis[6], 339.Frances Marie[5] Arbogast, 142.Rush Arlington[4], 46.Michael[3], 6.Sophia[2], 1.Henry[1]), b. Jan 25 1941.
(1) He Married **Bernice Stromme**.

Children:

1108 i. Brent Stromme[8] Smith b. Apr 02 1967.
1109 ii. Dena Stromme Smith b. May 07 1968.

(2) He Married **Jennett Mac Daniel**, b. Jun 09 1945, d. Sep 28 1974.

Children:

1110 iii. Geoffrey Quinton Smith b. Apr 27 1964.
1111 iv. Michele Renee Smith.
1112 v. Jennifer Ann Smith b. Jun 09 1972.

808. **Norman Paul[7] SMITH** (527.Clarence Louis[6], 339.Frances Marie[5] Arbogast, 142.Rush Arlington[4], 46.Michael[3], 6.Sophia[2], 1.Henry[1]), b. Sep 27 1943.
He Married **Jean Marie Nienberg**, b. Nov 25 1945.

Children:

1113 i. Teresa Lynn[8] Smith b. Jun 07 1966.
1114 ii. Todd Smith b. May 08 1967.
1115 iii. Matt Ross Smith b. Feb 26 1969.
1116 iv. Melinda Marie Smith b. May 29 1971.

809. **Nancy**^{7} **SMITH** (527.Clarence Louis^{6}, 339.Frances Marie^{5} Arbogast, 142.Rush Arlington^{4}, 46.Michael^{3}, 6.Sophia^{2}, 1.Henry^{1}), b. Feb 13 1945.
Married Aug 10 1968, **Richard Neile Heebsh**, b. Dec 17 1941.

Children:

1117 i. Brian William^{8} Heebsh b. Dec 29 1969.
1118 ii. Kevin Markwood Heebsh b. Jul 23 1971.

810. **Ramona Tereista**^{7} **SMITH** (527.Clarence Louis^{6}, 339.Frances Marie^{5} Arbogast, 142.Rush Arlington^{4}, 46.Michael^{3}, 6.Sophia^{2}, 1.Henry^{1}), b. Jan 07 1950.
Married May 02 1970, **Richard Peter Cleary**, b. Aug 19 1949.

Children:

1119 i. Christopher Sean^{8} Cleary b. Sep 10 1970.
1120 ii. April Joan Cleary b. Apr 12 1973.

811. **Louis James**^{7} **KING** (528.Rita Theresa^{6} SMITH, 339.Frances Marie^{5} Arbogast, 142.Rush Arlington^{4}, 46.Michael^{3}, 6.Sophia^{2}, 1.Henry^{1}), b. Dec 04 1938.
Married Jun 24 1962, **Joanne Kent**, b. Dec 23 1939. .

Children:

1121 i. Randall Joseph^{8} KING b. Apr 02 1962.
1122 ii. Lucenda Marie King b. Oct 25 1963.
1123 iii. Melissa Beth King b. Jul 20 1966.
1124 iv. Darin James King b. Oct 10 1969.
1125 v. Jonathan David King b. May 12 1978.

812. **Marjorie Ann**^{7} **KING** (528.Rita Theresa^{6} SMITH, 339.Frances Marie^{5} Arbogast, 142.Rush Arlington^{4}, 46.Michael^{3}, 6.Sophia^{2}, 1.Henry^{1}), b. Nov 23 1941.
Married Apr 30 1960, **David Robert Fisher**, b. Mar 25 1938. .

Children:

1126 i. Jeffrey Robert^{8} FISHER b. Nov 05 1960.
\+ 1127 ii. Scott Louis Fisher b. Apr 06 1962.
1128 iii. Mathew Allen Fisher b. Sep 17 1968.

813. **Deanna Rose**^{7} **SMITH** (529.Richard Joseph^{6}, 339.Frances Marie^{5} Arbogast, 142.Rush Arlington^{4}, 46.Michael^{3}, 6.Sophia^{2}, 1.Henry^{1}), b. Nov 24 1943.
Married Feb 02 1967, **Dennis Balmer**, b. Mar 02 1941.

Children:

1129 i. Darlene Ann^{8} Balmer b. Oct 13 1970.

814. **Allan Peter**^{7} **SMITH** (529.Richard Joseph^{6}, 339.Frances Marie^{5} Arbogast, 142.Rush Arlington^{4}, 46.Michael^{3}, 6.Sophia^{2}, 1.Henry^{1}), b. Jan 07 1945.

55555Married Jul 31 1965, **Janice M. Graham**, b. Oct 29 1941.

Children:

1130 i. Richard L.^{8} Smith b. Dec 30 1962.
1131 ii. Mary Louise Smith b. Apr 02 1968.
1132 iii. Victoria Marie Smith b. May 15 1969.
1133 iv. Tonia Margaret Smith b. Sep 01 1970.
1134 v. Leonard Allen Smith b. Jan 18 1974.
1135 vi. Alan Peter Smith b. May 14 1979.

815. **Alice Mary**^{7} **SMITH** (529.Richard Joseph^{6}, 339.Frances Marie^{5} Arbogast, 142.Rush Arlington^{4}, 46.Michael^{3}, 6.Sophia^{2}, 1.Henry^{1}), b. Feb 23 1949.
Married Sep 26 1970, **Dennis Teynor**, b. Sep 13 1947.

Children:

1136 i. Randall Scott^{8} Teynor b. Jul 30 1971.
1137 ii. Monica Anne Teynor b. Apr 30 1973.
1138 iii. Kevin Thomas Teynor b. Nov 12 1979.
1139 iv. Kathleen Marie Teynor.

816. **Jane Margaret^{7} SMITH** (529.Richard Joseph^{6}, 339.Frances Marie^{5} Arbogast, 142.Rush Arlington^{4}, 46.Michael^{3}, 6.Sophia^{2}, 1.Henry^{1}), b. Dec 30 1949.
Married Mar 16 1973, **Daniel Lee Ickes**, b. Dec 11 1953.

Children:

1140 i. Janelle Marie^{8} Ickes b. May 10 1980.
1141 ii. Joshua Paul Ickes b. Apr 01 1981.

817. **Gloria Jean^{7} Adams** (531.Marjorie Mary^{6} SMITH, 339.Frances Marie^{5} Arbogast, 142.Rush Arlington^{4}, 46.Michael^{3}, 6.Sophia^{2}, 1.Henry^{1}), b. Dec 11 1946.
She Married **Donald Miller**, b. Mar 16 1945.

Children:

1142 i. Mana Marie^{8} Miller b. Oct 16 1966.
1143 ii. Michael Edward Miller b. Sep 12 1967.
1144 iii. Chris Allen Miller b. Sep 26 1968.
1145 iv. Deborah Sue Miller b. Aug 20 1971.

819. **Gerald Edwards^{7} Adams** (531.Marjorie Mary^{6} SMITH, 339.Frances Marie^{5} Arbogast, 142.Rush Arlington^{4}, 46.Michael^{3}, 6.Sophia^{2}, 1.Henry^{1}), b. Feb 12 1954.
Married Jan 15 1972, **Arlene Stockmeister**.

Children:

1146 i. Jill Marie^{8} Adams b. Jun 14 1972.

820. **Cheryl Lajean^{7} SMITH** (532.Robert Eugene^{6}, 339.Frances Marie^{5} Arbogast, 142.Rush Arlington^{4}, 46.Michael^{3}, 6.Sophia^{2}, 1.Henry^{1}), b. Aug 27 1949.
Married Sep 20 1969, **Michael Grady**, b. Jun 09 1948.

Children:

1147 i. Eric Robert^{8} Grady b. Dec 14 1970.
1148 ii. Todd Michael Grady b. Sep 17 1973.

821. **Patricia Ann^{7} SMITH** (532.Robert Eugene^{6}, 339.Frances Marie^{5} Arbogast, 142.Rush Arlington^{4}, 46.Michael^{3}, 6.Sophia^{2}, 1.Henry^{1}), b. Nov 29 1954.

(1) She Married **George Harrison Dosh**, b. Oct 05 1947, d. Oct 26 1973.
(2) Married Jul 27 1976, **Michael Riedel**.

Children:

1149 i. Shane Michael^{8} Riedel b. Jul 12 1977.

822. **David Eugene^{7} HAMMER** (533.Helen Francis^{6} SMITH, 339.Frances Marie^{5} Arbogast, 142.Rush Arlington^{4}, 46.Michael^{3}, 6.Sophia^{2}, 1.Henry^{1}), b. Aug 21 1947.
Married Mar 21 1969, **Sandra West**.

Children:

1150 i. Scott Michael^{8} Hammer b. Oct 09 1972.
1151 ii. Brian Lee Hammer b. Apr 14 1976.

823. **Thomas Herbert^{7} HAMMER** (533.Helen Francis^{6} SMITH, 339.Frances Marie^{5} Arbogast, 142.Rush Arlington^{4}, 46.Michael^{3}, 6.Sophia^{2}, 1.Henry^{1}), b. Sep 13 1948.
Married Aug 09 1974, **Carol Mathias**, b. Jan 13 1954.

Children:

1152 i. Cory Thomas^{8} Hammer b. Jun 24 1975.
1153 ii. Malinda Lee Hammer.
1154 iii. Brett Hammer b. 1981.

824. **William Joseph^{7} HAMMER** (533.Helen Francis^{6} SMITH, 339.Frances Marie^{5} Arbogast, 142.Rush Arlington^{4}, 46.Michael^{3}, 6.Sophia^{2}, 1.Henry^{1}), b. Feb 11 1951.
He Married **Diane Marie Welty**, b. Jan 27 1949.

Children:

1155 i. Kristine Marie^{8} Hammer b. Nov 01 1972.
1156 ii. Daniel William Hammer b. Aug 01 1974.
1157 iii. Lori Ann Hammer b. Mar 29 1976.
1158 iv. Jeffery Richard Hammer b. Jan 30 1979.

825. **Donald Lee^{7} HAMMER** (533.Helen Francis^{6} SMITH, 339.Frances Marie^{5} Arbogast, 142.Rush Arlington^{4}, 46.Michael^{3}, 6.Sophia^{2}, 1.Henry^{1}), b. May 29 1953.
He Married **Mary Catherine Ray**, b. Apr 06 1951.

Children:

1159 i. Joseph Donald^{8} Hammer b. Jun 25 1977.
1160 ii. Regina Catherine Hammer b. Oct 01 1979.
1161 iii. Matthew Ray Hammer b. May 11 1981.
1162 iv. Bradley Charles Hammer b. May 11 1981.

826. **Kenneth Lewis^{7} HAMMER** (533.Helen Francis^{6} SMITH, 339.Frances Marie^{5} Arbogast, 142.Rush Arlington^{4}, 46.Michael^{3}, 6.Sophia^{2}, 1.Henry^{1}), b. May 29 1953.
(1) He Married **Denise Huth**, b. Oct 06 1955.

Children:

1163 i. Berry Alen^{8} Hammer b. Aug 06 1973.

(2) He Married **Geralyn Bloom**, b. Nov 07 1954.

Children:

1164 ii. Roberta Ann Hammer b. Oct 26 1975.
1165 iii. Andera Helen Hammer b. Mar 31 1977.

827. **Mary Alice^{7} HAMMER** (533.Helen Francis^{6} SMITH, 339.Frances Marie^{5} Arbogast, 142.Rush Arlington^{4}, 46.Michael^{3}, 6.Sophia^{2}, 1.Henry^{1}), b. Sep 02 1955.
She Married **Kenneth Baker**, b. Oct 27 1954.

Children:

1166 i. Kevin Ray^{8} Baker b. Feb 09 1976.
1167 ii. Kelly Francis Baker b. Dec 13 1977.
1168 iii. Keith Nicholas Baker b. Mar 24 1981.

828. **Eileen Marie^{7} HAMMER** (533.Helen Francis^{6} SMITH, 339.Frances Marie^{5} Arbogast, 142.Rush Arlington^{4}, 46.Michael^{3}, 6.Sophia^{2}, 1.Henry^{1}), b. Mar 16 1957.
She Married **John V. Hoover**, b. Jan 12 1957.

Children:

1169 i. Neil John^{8} Hoover b. Aug 29 1976.
1170 ii. Nicholas Allen Hoover b. Jul 15 1978.
1171 iii. Mark Steven Hoover b. Sep 03 1980.
+ 1172 iv. Elizabeth Marie Hoover b. Nov 16 1982.

829. **Roger Francis^{7} HAMMER** (533.Helen Francis^{6} SMITH, 339.Frances Marie^{5} Arbogast, 142.Rush Arlington^{4}, 46.Michael^{3}, 6.Sophia^{2}, 1.Henry^{1}), b. Sep 28 1958.
He Married **Debra Hill**, b. Apr 01 1958.

Children:

1173 i. Jessica Leah^{8} Hammer b. Jan 25 1980.
1174 ii. Nathaniel Richard Hammer b. Jun 01 1982.

835. **Jill Christine^{7} Smith** (534.Bernard Charles^{6}, 339.Frances Marie^{5} Arbogast, 142.Rush Arlington^{4}, 46.Michael^{3}, 6.Sophia^{2}, 1.Henry^{1}).
She Married **Douglas Hire**.

Children:

1175 i. Joseph Allen^{8} Hire b. Apr 21 1983.

839. **Edward Louis^{7} SMITH** (535.Leo Frederick^{6}, 339.Frances Marie^{5} Arbogast, 142.Rush Arlington^{4}, 46.Michael^{3}, 6.Sophia^{2}, 1.Henry^{1}).

He Married **Patricia Raitz**.

Children:

1176 i. Joshua Adam^8 Smith b. Mar 28 1983.
1177 ii. Sarah Elizabeth Smith b. Dec 21 1984.

Generation Eight

876. **Bradley Michael^8 Harper** (611.Vincent Bryson^7, 417.Mary Edith^6 Newman, 231.Myrtle^5 Waybright, 93.David Jasper^4, 24.Susannah^3 Lantz, 2.Eleanor^2 Arbogast, 1.Henry^1), b. Feb 2 1966.
Married Sep 21 1996, **April Dawn Wanless** (daughter of Richard Wanless and Judith Mann).

Children:

1178 i. Vincent Michael^9 Harper b. Sep 16 1997 in Elkins, Randolph Co., WV.
1179 ii. Bradley Isaac Harper b. Jan 19 1999 in Davis Memorial Hospital, Elkins, Randolph Co., WV.

890. **Lois Nadine^8 Hamilton** (628.Alma Joyce^7 Payne, 443.William Charles^6, 281.Mary^5 Morrison, 125.Sophia^4 Arbogast, 43.Jesse^3, 6.Sophia^2, 1.Henry^1), b. Dec 14 1936 in Delta Co., CO.
(1) Married Oct 04 1953 in Reno, Washoe Co., NV, **Richard Clinton Byerrum**, b. Nov 07 1936 in Montrose Co., CO.

Children:

1180 i. Richard Clinton^9 Byerrum b. Apr 25 1954 at Roseville, Placer Co., CA.
Married Oct 12 1985 in Yuba City, Sutter Co., CA, **Susan Ann Bell**.
1181 ii. Deborah Ann Byerrum b. Sep 11 1955 in Montrose Co., CO.
Married Jun 17 1977 in Yuba City, Sutter Co., CA, **Milton Lynn Greathouse**.
1182 iii. Sharalyn Sue Byerrum b. Sep 26 1957 in Roseville, Placer Co., CA.
1183 iv. Gregory Dean Byerrum b. Feb 27 1959 in Roseville, Placer Co., CA, d. Apr 13 1961 in Sacramento, Sacramento Co., CA.
1184 v. Judy Kay Byerrum b. Jun 20 1961 in Sacramento, Sacramento Co., CA.
Married Jul 07 1976, **Wayne Shamblin**.
1185 vi. Roy Craig Byerrum b. Sep 22 1962 in Stockton, San Joaquin Co., CA.
Married Jun 15 1985 in Yuba City, Sutter Co., CA, **Melody Fitzpatrick**.

(2) Married Dec 30 1975 in Reno, Washoe Co., NV, **Norman Clyde Phillips**.

893. **Charles Ronald^8 Robertson** (632.Marcia Roberta^7 Payne, 443.William Charles^6, 281.Mary^5 Morrison, 125.Sophia^4 Arbogast, 43.Jesse^3, 6.Sophia^2, 1.Henry^1), b. Jul 01 1941 in Delta Co., CO.
He Married **Judith Rachel Moraff**.

Children:

1186 i. Summer Suzette^9 Robertson b. Dec 25 1963 in Santa Cruz Co., CA.
1187 ii. Charles Ronald Robertson, Jr. b. Feb 04 1965 in Santa Cruz Co., CA.
1188 iii. Brittany Dawn Robertson b. Dec 08 1983 in Santa Cruz Co., CA.
1189 iv. Kylan Douglas Robertson b. Feb 14 1991 in Santa Cruz Co., CA.

895. **John Ralph^8 Robertson** (632.Marcia Roberta^7 Payne, 443.William Charles^6, 281.Mary^5 Morrison, 125.Sophia^4 Arbogast, 43.Jesse^3, 6.Sophia^2, 1.Henry^1), b. Mar 07 1952 in Santa Cruz Co., CA.
Married Apr 07 1971, **Patricia Sue Rosol**, b. in Pittsburgh, Allegheny Co., PA.

Children:

1190 i. Colin Ray^9 Robertson b. Jun 03 1971 in Santa Cruz Co., CA.
1191 ii. Clinton Heath Robertson b. Oct 25 1973 in Santa Cruz Co., CA.

901. **Donald Ralph^8 Woolerton** (636.Duane^7 Woolverton, 448.Harry^6, 285.Rose^5 Morrison, 125.Sophia^4 Arbogast, 43.Jesse^3, 6.Sophia^2, 1.Henry^1), b. Jul 20 1954 in Illinois.
Married Jun 08 1974, **Rhonda Hamm**.

Children:

1192 i. Jason Duane^9 Woolerton b. Aug 13 1976.
1193 ii. Stacey Dawn Woolerton b. Nov 19 1983.

935. **David Lee[8] Brewer** (660.Richard Gene[7], 464.Sarah Fern[6] Cozad, 301.Mae[5] Howard, 131.Sarah[4] Arbogast, 43.Jesse[3], 6.Sophia[2], 1.Henry[1]), b. Aug 13 1955 in Avon, Fulton Co., IL.
Married Jun 04 1977, **Debera Lee Palmer**, b. Oct 02 1955 in Princeton, Bureau Co., IL.

Children:

1194 i. Christopher David[9] Palmer b. Jul 06 1983 in Princeton, Bureau Co., IL.
1195 ii. Danial Edward Palmer b. Sep 30 1986 in Princeton, Bureau Co., IL.

936. **Donna Kay[8] Lawyer** (661.Barbara Mae[7] Black, 465.Faun Elizabeth[6] Cozad, 301.Mae[5] Howard, 131.Sarah[4] Arbogast, 43.Jesse[3], 6.Sophia[2], 1.Henry[1]), b. Apr 10 1945 in McComb, McDonough Co., IL.
She Married **Laverne McFadden**, b. May 02 1945 in Illinois.

Children:

1196 i. Torie Kaye[9] McFadden b. Oct 27 1968 in Champaign Co., IL.
Married Jul 04 1992, **Phillip Waterside**.
1197 ii. Chad Eric McFadden b. May 12 1971 in Champaign Co., IL.

937. **Linda Lou[8] Lawyer** (661.Barbara Mae[7] Black, 465.Faun Elizabeth[6] Cozad, 301.Mae[5] Howard, 131.Sarah[4] Arbogast, 43.Jesse[3], 6.Sophia[2], 1.Henry[1]), b. Mar 08 1950 in McComb, McDonough Co., IL.
She Married **John L. Partick**, b. Apr 30 1948.

Children:

1198 i. Lance Garrett[9] Partick b. Feb 15 1973 in McComb, McDonough Co., IL.
1199 ii. Grant Ashley Partick b. Jul 16 1975 in McComb, McDonough Co., IL.
1200 iii. Trenton Jay Partick b. Nov 19 1978 in McComb, McDonough Co., IL.

938. **William Authur[8] Black** (662.William Howard[7], 465.Faun Elizabeth[6] Cozad, 301.Mae[5] Howard, 131.Sarah[4] Arbogast, 43.Jesse[3], 6.Sophia[2], 1.Henry[1]), b. Dec 09 1947.
He Married **Kathy Rae Zander**, b. May 18 1952 in McComb, McDonough Co., IL.

Children:

1201 i. Eric William[9] Black b. May 20 1973 in McComb, McDonough Co., IL.
1202 ii. Craig Zander Black b. Nov 01 1975 in McComb, McDonough Co., IL.

939. **Susan Elizabeth[8] Black** (662.William Howard[7], 465.Faun Elizabeth[6] Cozad, 301.Mae[5] Howard, 131.Sarah[4] Arbogast, 43.Jesse[3], 6.Sophia[2], 1.Henry[1]), b. Sep 11 1948.
Married in Denver, Arapaho Co., CO, **Joe Dale Thomson**, b. Nov 30 1947.

Children:

1203 i. Christopher Allen[9] Thompson b. Mar 10 1970 in Denver, Arapaho Co., CO.
1204 ii. Edwards Aft, Cabrian Phillip Thompson b. Jan 28 1978.
1205 iii. Daniel Andrew Thompson b. in Pittsfield, Pike Co., IL.

940. **Rex Eugene[8] Black** (662.William Howard[7], 465.Faun Elizabeth[6] Cozad, 301.Mae[5] Howard, 131.Sarah[4] Arbogast, 43.Jesse[3], 6.Sophia[2], 1.Henry[1]), b. Jul 04 1950.
He Married **Carol Lynn Hughes**, b. Oct 27 1952.

Children:

1206 i. Scott Michael[9] Black b. Oct 27 1972 in McComb, McDonough Co., IL.
1207 ii. Aaron Paul Black b. Apr 11 1975 in Corinth, Alcorn Co., MS.
1208 iii. Elizabeth Kay Black b. Sep 09 1980 in Cedar Lake, Lake Co., IN.

944. **Harold William[8] Huston** (667.Kathryn Louise[7] Fox, 477.Keith Leroy[6], 310.Myrtle[5] Smith, 133.Frances[4] Arbogast, 43.Jesse[3], 6.Sophia[2], 1.Henry[1]), b. Jun 24 1959.
He Married **Kathryn Louise Slater-Frakes**, b. Mar 04 1958.

Children:

1209 i. Jordan Kelsey[9] Huston b. Dec 14 1987.
1210 ii. Morgan Taylor Hutson b. Nov 30 1993.

945. **Tracie Gaye[8] Fox** (668.Dean Edward[7], 477.Keith Leroy[6], 310.Myrtle[5] Smith, 133.Frances[4] Arbogast, 43.Jesse[3], 6.Sophia[2], 1.Henry[1]), b. Dec 03 1958.
She Married **George Kern**, b. Jan 03 1958.

Children:

1211 i. Heidi Elizabeth[9] Fox b. Jul 27 1983.
1212 ii. Michala Beth Fox b. Mar 01 1987.

946. **Dale Edward[8] Fox** (668.Dean Edward[7], 477.Keith Leroy[6], 310.Myrtle[5] Smith, 133.Frances[4] Arbogast, 43.Jesse[3], 6.Sophia[2], 1.Henry[1]), b. Sep 30 1967.
He Married **Stacy Ratcliff**, b. Apr 16 1969.

Children:

1213 i. Douglas Kieth[9] Fox b. Dec 27 1989.
1214 ii. Zachary Edward Fox b. Jul 09 1993.

947. **Amy Suzanne[8] Fox** (668.Dean Edward[7], 477.Keith Leroy[6], 310.Myrtle[5] Smith, 133.Frances[4] Arbogast, 43.Jesse[3], 6.Sophia[2], 1.Henry[1]).
Married Nov 28 1992, **Christopher Lackey**.

Children:

1215 i. Caleb Michael[9] Fox b. Apr 30 1993.

948. **Randy Joe[8] Schulte** (669.Carol Jean[7] Fox, 477.Keith Leroy[6], 310.Myrtle[5] Smith, 133.Frances[4] Arbogast, 43.Jesse[3], 6.Sophia[2], 1.Henry[1]), b. Jul 07 1957.
Married Jan 17 1981, **Terry Neer**, b. Aug 17 1959.

Children:

1216 i. Kristin Myrile[9] Schulte b. Oct 05 1982.
1217 ii. Ryan James Schulte b. Mar 25 1985.

955. **Barbara Jo[8] Clark** (672.Beverly Jane[7] Fox, 477.Keith Leroy[6], 310.Myrtle[5] Smith, 133.Frances[4] Arbogast, 43.Jesse[3], 6.Sophia[2], 1.Henry[1]), b. Jun 26 1961.
Married Jun 10 1983, **Ed McEwen**.

Children:

1218 i. Carolynn Irene[9] Clark b. Jun 15 1978.

956. **Linda Kay[8] Clark** (672.Beverly Jane[7] Fox, 477.Keith Leroy[6], 310.Myrtle[5] Smith, 133.Frances[4] Arbogast, 43.Jesse[3], 6.Sophia[2], 1.Henry[1]), b. May 15 1962.
Married Nov 05 1990, **Charles Wayne Lairson**.

Children:

1219 i. Brian Wayne[9] Clark b. Jan 11 1979.
1220 ii. Sherry Lee Tassara b. Mar 25 1981.
1221 iii. Mary Ann Tassara b. Jan 25 1983.

957. **Carol Ann[8] Clark** (672.Beverly Jane[7] Fox, 477.Keith Leroy[6], 310.Myrtle[5] Smith, 133.Frances[4] Arbogast, 43.Jesse[3], 6.Sophia[2], 1.Henry[1]), b. May 25 1963.
Married 1988, **Richard Lee Smith**, b. Jul 30 1962.

Children:

1222 i. Tyler Lee[9] Smith b. Mar 26 1990.
1223 ii. James Dale Smith b. Jan 11 1991, d. Jan 11 1991.
1224 iii. Kayla Mae Smith b. Feb 18 1993.

958. **Dorothy Elaine[8] Clark** (672.Beverly Jane[7] Fox, 477.Keith Leroy[6], 310.Myrtle[5] Smith, 133.Frances[4] Arbogast, 43.Jesse[3], 6.Sophia[2], 1.Henry[1]), b. Apr 28 1965.
Dorothy had a 3rd child, a boy, given up for adoption.
She Married **Curtis Devion Kimbrell**.

Children:

1225 i. Amy Marie[9] Kimbrell b. Dec 13 1980.
1226 ii. Casimur Devon Kimbrell b. Jun 1986.

972. **Donna Esther[8] Arbogast** (678.Richard Francis[7], 479.Theodore Fenton[6], 311.Clyde Stewart[5], 134.Stephen Aaron Douglas[4], 43.Jesse[3], 6.Sophia[2], 1.Henry[1]), b. Jan 08 1962 in Burley, Cassia Co., ID.
Married Nov 09 1979 in Burley, Cassia Co., ID, **Marshall Morris**, b. Jan 22 1961 in Burley, Cassia Co., ID.

Children:

1227 i. Raushanna Ann[9] Morris b. Nov 21 1980 in Burley, Cassia Co., ID.
1228 ii. Kayla Rose Morris b. Dec 27 1982 in Burley, Cassia Co., ID.
1229 iii. Trevor Scott Morris b. Jan 21 1985 in Burley, Cassia Co., ID.

973. **Richard Ray[8] Howard** (679.Patricia Ann[7] Arbogast, 479.Theodore Fenton[6], 311.Clyde Stewart[5], 134.Stephen Aaron Douglas[4], 43.Jesse[3], 6.Sophia[2], 1.Henry[1]), b. in Burley, Cassia Co., ID.
He Married **Susan Gay McCarty Lewis**, b. Jun 12 1959 in Burley, Cassia Co., ID.

Children:

1230 i. Whitney Nan[9] Howard b. Jun 13 1984 in Pocatello, Bannock Co., ID.

976. **Kathleen K.[8] Arbogast** (682.Theodore Clyde[7], 479.Theodore Fenton[6], 311.Clyde Stewart[5], 134.Stephen Aaron Douglas[4], 43.Jesse[3], 6.Sophia[2], 1.Henry[1]), b. Jun 19 1959 in Rupert, Hitchcock Co., NE.
Married Sep 16 1983 in Idaho Falls, Bonneville Co., ID, **Randy Keven Berksdale**, b. Nov 29 1959 in Rupert, Minidoka Co., ID.

Children:

1231 i. Larry Theodore[9] Berksdale b. Jul 23 1984 in Burley, Cassia Co., ID.
1232 ii. Laren Lynn Berksdale b. Jan 08 1987 in Twin Falls Co., ID.
1233 iii. Debra Michelle Berksdale b. Dec 30 1991 in Twin Falls Co., ID.

985. **Karen Diane[8] Arbogast** (685.Roland Allen[7], 482.Allen Sterart[6], 311.Clyde Stewart[5], 134.Stephen Aaron Douglas[4], 43.Jesse[3], 6.Sophia[2], 1.Henry[1]), b. Jan 18 1962 in Albany, Linn Co., OR.
Married Sep 08 1984 in Eugene, Lane Co., OR, **Joseph Nichols**, b. May 05 1960 in Eugene, Lane Co., OR.

Children:

1234 i. Bradley Joseph[9] Nichols b. Aug 17 1986 in Reno, Washoe Co., NV.
1235 ii. Brynna Katherine Nichols b. Nov 30 1988 in Springfield, Hampden Co., MA.

986. **Susan Lynn[8] Arbogast** (685.Roland Allen[7], 482.Allen Sterart[6], 311.Clyde Stewart[5], 134.Stephen Aaron Douglas[4], 43.Jesse[3], 6.Sophia[2], 1.Henry[1]), b. Jun 04 1963 in Salem, Marion Co., OR.
Married Nov 22 1986 in Eugene, Lane Co., OR, **Justin Wade Bradshaw**, b. Oct 10 1962.

Children:

1236 i. Tyler Wade[9] Bradshaw b. Mar 24 1991 in Chicago, Cook Co., IL.

1022. **Terri[8] Ritchie** (713.Patricia Leigh[7] Armour, 510.Gayl Jane[6] Arbogast, 333.James Michael[5], 141.Charles Sayers[4], 46.Michael[3], 6.Sophia[2], 1.Henry[1]).
She Married **Michael Hunka**.

Children:

1237 i. Michael Scott[9] Hunka.
1238 ii. Brian William Hunka.

1042. **Christina Rose[8] Sorg** (735.Jane[7] Arbogast, 516.Paul Joseph[6], 338.Charles Anthony[5], 142.Rush Arlington[4], 46.Michael[3], 6.Sophia[2], 1.Henry[1]), b. May 03 1969.
Married May 28 1988, **Eric Hughes**.

Children:

1239 i. Joshua Camerone[9] Hughes b. Mar 12 1988.

1127. **Scott Louis[8] FISHER** (812.Marjorie Ann[7] KING, 528.Rita Theresa[6] SMITH, 339.Frances Marie[5] Arbogast, 142.Rush Arlington[4], 46.Michael[3], 6.Sophia[2], 1.Henry[1]), b. Apr 06 1962.
Married Nov 08 1986, **Jennifer L. Fruth**, b. May 23 1961.

Children:

1240 i. Jaqueline Michelle[9] Fisher.

1172. **Elizabeth Marie[8] Hoover** (828.Eileen Marie[7] HAMMER, 533.Helen Francis[6] SMITH, 339.Frances Marie[5] Arbogast, 142.Rush Arlington[4], 46.Michael[3], 6.Sophia[2], 1.Henry[1]), b. Nov 16 1982.
She Married **Sherman Harrison Buzzard**.

Children:

\+ 1241 i. Cornelia Catherine[9] Buzzard b. Jan 15 1890.

Generation Nine

1241. **Cornelia Catherine^{9} Buzzard** (1172.Elizabeth Marie^{8} Hoover, 828.Eileen Marie^{7} HAMMER, 533.Helen Francis^{6} SMITH, 339.Frances Marie^{5} Arbogast, 142.Rush Arlington^{4}, 46.Michael^{3}, 6.Sophia^{2}, 1.Henry^{1}), b. Jan 15 1890 in Frost, Pocahontas Co., WV, d. Mar 21 1934 in Marlinton, Pocahontas Co., WV.
Married Mar 31 1920 in Marlinton, Pocahontas Co., WV, **Benjamin Franklin Hayes**, b. Jan 27 1879 in Jacox, Pocahontas Co., WV (son of Abraham Hayes and Margaret Jane Clutter), d. Dec 23 1932 in Marlinton, Pocahontas Co., WV.

Children:

1242 i. Frank Raymond^{10} Hayes b. Feb 9 1921, d. Feb 13 1986 in Harrisonburg, Rockingham Co., VA.
He Married **Betty Greer Hall**, b. Jan 19 1913 in Venire, Monroe Co., TN (daughter of James Nicholas Barksdale Hall and Margaret "Maggie" Henley), d. Jun 1 1999 in Collinsville, Hartford Co., CT.

Descendants of Peter Arbogast Seventh Child of Michael and Mary Elizabeth Samuels

Generation One

1. **Peter[1] Arbogast**, b. Aug 22 1770 in Augusta Co., VA (son of Michael Arbogast and Mary Elizabeth Samuels Amanapas), d. Nov 01 1842 in Pleasant Twp., Clark Co., OH, buried in Pleasant Hill Cem., Clark Co., OH.

   Peter and Henry were twins. Relocated to Champaign Co., OH (Clark Co. since 1818) about 1811 with brothers, David and Michael, Jr. by covered wagon. David went on to IN, about 1830. Grave is marked with a stone from which an inscription was copied, see Forbes and/or Hartmann records. Tombstone provides birth and death dates. Cemetery is about 1 1/2 mi. N/E of South Vienna, OH, on old Columbus Rd. Estate probated, Clark Co., OH, A-995, 1842.

   See Power of Attorney from Peter and his wife Sarah authorizing Cornelius Arbogast to dispose of their undivided share in real property in Crabbottom inherited from his father Michael. Pendleton Co. Court Records, Deed Book 11, Page 522. Names brothers John, Adam, Henry and George as well as his sister Dorothy, wife of Jacob Gum as co-inheritors of the property. Copy in file. Daughter Mary and spouse from letter to Patricia Bebernick from Amanda Arbogast Forbes, 1988, copy in file.

   Children list may not be complete and order of birth may not be correct.

   Family group records of 4th great granddaughter, Patricia Crissman Bebernick received 24 Sep 1992 giving day and month of birth for Peter and tracing her ancestry to Peter.

   Peter filed land claim 28 Jan. 1812 according to Patricia (Allen) McSherry who cites records at General Land Office, Cincinnati, OH. See patent on land, 31 May 1816, Clark Co., OH, Deed Book V, p. 85.

   Married ABT 00-___-1798 in Pendleton Co., WV, **Sarah Henderson**, b. ABT 00-___-1781 in Augusta Co., VA (daughter of Bennett Henderson and Elizabeth Lewis), d. Jul 18 1850 in Pleasant Twp., Clark Co., OH, buried in Pleasant Hill Cem., Clark Co., OH. **Sarah**: Information from Family Group Record of Patricia McSherry, New Orleans. LA. Documents include reference to A Standard History of Springfield and Clark Co., OH, 1922, Chicago and NY, Vol. II, pp.170-184; Pendleton Co., WV Records, Deed Book3, p. 8, 1797; Deed Book 6, pp. 221-222, 1814; Deed Book 11, p. 522, 1830; Mrs. Gay Darwin - Nebraska, 1987 and Iris Morley - Missouri. Notes that Champaign Co., OH formed 1808 and Clark Co. formed 1818 from Champaign Co.

   The above family group record includes 9 children, copy in file.

   The reference on page 182 of the History of Clark County that husband Peter was born and raised near Romney, WV may be an attempt to find the closest large settlement to the Crabbottom Section of then Augusta Co., VA and later Pendleton Co., VA/WV. It is well settled that Peter was born and raised in the Crabbottom which is near present-day Blue Grass, Highland Co., VA.

   Family group records from Patricia Crissman Bebernick on 25 Sept 1992 confirms above information and adds substantially more data including History of Pendleton Co., VA/WV p. 399 and reference to Clark Co., OH 1818 tax list ORPF, p. 109, vol. 9, #3. Also that Peter is on muster roll of Capt. Wm. Janes company of militia 6 Sep. 1794.

   Cemetery is located 1 1/2 mi. southeast of South Vienna, Ohio on Old Columbus Road. Birth and death from tombstone. Estate probated Clark Co., OH, A-521-621.

Children:

+ 2 i. Priscilla[2] Arbogast b. About 1800.
+ 3 ii. Rev. Cornelius Arbogast b. Oct 24 1801.
+ 4 iii. Otho Arbogast b. May 01 1803.
+ 5 iv. Mary Arbogast b. About 1806.
+ 6 v. Margaret Arbogast b. Jan 14 1808.
+ 7 vi. Susannah Arbogast b. About 1809.
+ 8 vii. Henry Arbogast b. Aug 19 1815.

9 viii. Lydia Arbogast, b. 1819 in Asbury, Pleasant Twp., Clark Co., OH, d. About 1889.
From family group record of Patricia McSherry. Clark Co. formed from Champaign Co. Confirmation from family group record of Patricia (Crissman) Bebernick and indicates day and month of marriage. Last known place of residence was Osceola, Iowa. Marriage record, Bk. 2, p. 239, Clark Co., OH. Marriage record indicates spouse as William Chaney of Green Co., OH.
Married Oct 24 1837 in Ohio, **William Cheney**, MD. (son of William C. Cheney and Elizabeth Kirkley), d. 1897.

+ 10 ix. Malinda "Linnie" Arbogast b. Oct 20 1822.
+ 11 x. Peter Arbogast Jr. b. About 1781.

Generation Two

2. **Priscilla[2] Arbogast** (1.Peter[1]), b. About 1800. From family group record of Patricia McSherry. Two sons and two daughters born to this marriage. Marriage record Bk. 1-B, p. 2, Clark Co., OH. From family group record of parents from Patricia (Crissman) Bebernick, confirmation of names and date of marriage, copy in file. From THE ROSEMARY SUMMERS PICKETT PAPERS citing "20th Century Springfield and Clark Co., Ohio" by Wm. A. Rockel, 1908, under Amos Smith, gr-grandson of Peter Arbogast, pp. 562-563. Jacob and Priscilla Arbogast Smith had two sons and two daughters only one of which is named, Eli Smith.
Married Apr 10 1821 in Clark Co., OH, **Jacob Amos Smith.** Jacob: Couple had 2 sons and 2 daughters, only one is named.

Children:

+ 12 i. Eli[3] Smith b. 1823.

3. **Rev. Cornelius[2] Arbogast** (1.Peter[1]), b. Oct 24 1801 in Pendleton Co., WV, d. Nov 04 1883 in Green Twp., Shelby Co., OH, buried Nov 09 1883 in Old Pioneer Cem., Plattsville, Shelby Co., OH. From family group record of Patricia McSherry. Two sons served in Civil War. Four sons and four daughters born to this marriage.
Memorial record of Shelby Co., OH, Old Pioneer - Plattsville Cem., p. 314.
Marriage - Clark Co., OH Marriages Book 1A, listed as 12 Mar 1821, Annacost, Cornelius & Davidson, Sarah, by W. Sailor, Justice of Peace.
Listed - ORPF Vol. 8, No. 3, p. 147

The Guthrie Papers indicate Cornelius was a minister of the Universalist Church and that he lived in Shelby Co., Green Twp. in 1851, moved to Clinton Twp. in 1858, returning to Green Twp. in 1865.

Marriage recorded, Clark Co., OH, Marriage Book 1-A, p. 77.

1850 census Pleasant, Clark, OH: Cornelius Arbogast, aged 49, farmer, real estate valued $4,000, OH; Sarah aged 49, OH; Jno aged 21; Elizabeth aged 19; Lewis aged 17; Allen aged 14; Ruth aged 11; female L. A. aged 8; Cornelius aged 3 -- all born OH; Margaret Davidson, aged 80 VA.

1870 census Green, Shelby, OH: Cornelius Arbogast, aged 68, real estate valued $6,500, personal estate $800, VA; Sarah aged 68, OH; Cornelius aged 22, OH. Living next door is their son John with family.

1880 census Greene, Shelby, OH: Albert G. Guthrie, aged 57, retired farmer, VA, both parents VA; Margaret aged 53, birth place OH, father VA, mother OH; father & mother-in-law, Cornelius Arbogast, aged 78, retired farmer, bp VA, both parents VA; Sarah Arbogast, aged 79, bp OH, father KY, mother VA.
Married Apr 12 1821 in Clark Co., OH, **Sarah Davidson**, b. Dec 19 1800 in Franklin Co., OH.

Children:

+ 13 i. Elizabeth P.[3] Arbogast b. Aug 01 1830.
+ 14 ii. Margaret May Arbogast b. May 13 1824.
+ 15 iii. John H. Arbogast b. Jul 08 1829.
+ 16 iv. Lewis Arbogast b. Jun 10 1833.
+ 17 v. Allen Arbogast b. Mar 11 1836.
+ 18 vi. Ruth Darletta Arbogast b. Apr 10 1838.
19 vii. Lydia Ann Arbogast b. Nov 20 1840 in Clark Co., OH. He Married **Daniel Leapley**.
+ 20 viii. Cornelius Arbogast, Jr. b. Mar 23 1847.
21 ix. Adaline Arbogast b. Dec 27 1824. Married in Clark Co., OH, **Joseph Watson**.

4. **Otho[2] Arbogast** (1.Peter[1]), b. May 01 1803 in Hampshire Co., WV, d. Mar 01 1875 in Mechanicsburg, Champaign Co., OH, buried in Nation Chapel, Pleasant Twp., Clark Co., OH.
From family records of Wilma M. (Mrs. Hugh R.) Guthrie with reference to Alvin Mullenax and Dean Davisson on Otho and Dorothy provides day and month of birth and counties of death and burial. These records will be referred to hereafter as The Guthrie Papers.

From merged computer records of Dean Davisson, birth is from tombstone, marriage from Clark Co., OH, Marriage Records, Book 1-B, p. 61, death from Champaign Co., OH, Death Records, Vol. 1, p. 62, # 12, Will from Champaign, Co., OH, Wills, Book D, p. 218, O-2932.

Married Dec 18 1823 in Clark Co., OH, **Dorothy Curl**, b. Nov 27 1802 in Mechanicsburg, Champaign Co., OH (daughter of Jerimiah Curl and Margaret Swisher), d. Jul 10 1881 in Pleasant Twp., Clark Co., OH.

Children:

+ 22 i. Margaret Ann[3] Arbogast b. Sep 06 1825.
+ 23 ii. Jackson Arbogast b. About 1830.
+ 24 iii. Eli M. Arbogast b. Dec 24 1834.

5. **Mary[2] Arbogast** (1.Peter[1]), b. About 1806 in Pendleton Co., WV.
From family group record of Patricia McSherry confirming data from Amanda Arbogast Forbes.
Married Dec 16 1824 in Clark Co., OH, **Jonathan William Hardman**, b. 1802 in Clarksburg, Harrison Co., VA (son of Peter Hartman and Margaret Hacker), d. 1876 in London, Madison Co., OH. **Jonathan**:.

Children:

25 i. Peter[3] Hardman. Peter died from injuries in the Civil War. He died after being brought home from Harpers Ferry. He Married **Lucia Lauman**.
26 ii. Sarah Hardman d. 1863.
27 iii. Charlotte Ann Hardman.
+ 28 iv. William H. Hardman b. Feb 28 1831.
29 v. Mary Hardman.
30 vi. Henderson Hardman.
+ 31 vii. Otho Hardman b. Dec 18 1856.
32 viii. Martha Hardman d. 1908.
33 ix. Wesley Hardman b. 1854.

6. **Margaret[2] Arbogast** (1.Peter[1]), b. Jan 14 1808 in Pendleton Co., WV, d. Sep 09 1889 in Cardington Twp., Morrow Co., OH, buried in Bethel Cem., Cardington Twp., Morrow Co., OH.
From family records of Wilma M. (Mrs. Hugh R.) Guthrie with reference to Alvin Mullenax as general source and Dean Davisson as source on Margaret and Otho provides birth and death date as well as place of death. These family records will be referred to hereafter as The Guthrie Papers. Marriage record, Bk. 1-B, p. 154, Clark Co., OH. Computer records merged with those of Dean Davisson.
See "Memorial Record of the Counties of Delaware, Union and Morrow, Ohio", Lewis Pub. Co., Chicago, 1895, p. 245; "born on the banks of the Potomac, in Virginia"; dau. of Peter & Sarah (Henderson) Arbogast. See also Marjorie Curl (1979), p.1.
Married Mar 01 1827 in Ohio, **William Curl**.

Children:

+ 34 i. Mary A.[3] Curl b. May 29 1837.
+ 35 ii. Isabella Jane Curl b. Jan 09 1828.
+ 36 iii. Henry William Curl b. Oct 21 1829.
+ 37 iv. Emily Curl b. Nov 11 1832.
+ 38 v. William Hayse Curl b. Aug 20 1834.

7. **Susannah[2] Arbogast** (1.Peter[1]), b. About 1809 in Pendleton Co., WV, d. Aug 20 1886 in Henry Co., OH.
Married Jul 08 1829 in Henry Co., OH, **John G. Wilkinson**, b. Feb 07 1806 in Harrison Co., VA (son of Asahel Wilkinson and Charity Ragen), d. Sep 26 1874 in Shelby Co., OH.

Children:

39 i. Martha E.[3] Wilkinson b. About 1830 in Champaign Co., OH. Married Feb 25 1851, **Astolphais Estlack**.
40 ii. Mary Wilkinson b. About 1833 in Marion Co., OH, d. About 1856.
41 iii. Henry N. Wilkinson b. 1835 in Marion Co., OH, d. 1856.
42 iv. Levi N. Wilkinson b. 1837 in Marion Co., OH, d. 1846.
+ 43 v. Margaret Jane Wilkinson b. Apr 16 1837.
+ 44 vi. John G. Wilkinson b. About 1842.
45 vii. Anna Eliza Wilkinson b. c1846 in Marion Co., OH. She Married **William Mitchell**.
46 viii. Laura C. Wilkinson b. About 1846 in Marrow Co., OH. She Married **Isaac Hoffman**..
47 ix. Sarah C. Wilkinson b. About 1850 in Marrow Co., OH. She Married Daniel Hoffman.
48 x. Newton Wilkinson b. About 1850 in Marrow Co., OH.

8. **Henry[2] Arbogast** (1.Peter[1]), b. Aug 19 1815 in Champaign Co., OH, d. Jan 26 1859 in Clark Co., OH, buried in Kirkwood Cem., London, Madison Co., OH.
Married Mar 25 1839 in Clark Co., OH, **Susan Clymer**, b. Feb 19 1816 in Ohio (daughter of Joseph Isaac Clymer and Elizabeth Alt), buried in Kirkwood Cem., London, Madison Co., OH, d. Nov 27 1894 in London, Madison Co., OH.

Children:

+ 49 i. Sarah Elizabeth[3] Arbogast b. Dec 05 1839.
+ 50 ii. Charles Rollin Arbogast b. Dec 09 1841.
+ 51 iii. James W. Arbogast b. Jan 12 1845.
+ 52 iv. Milton A. Arbogast b. Feb 06 1951.
53 v. Johanna Arbogast b. Jun 09 1857 in Clark Co., OH, d. 1945. She Married Charles Huffman.
+ 54 vi. Albert Arbogast b. Dec 04 1848.

10. **Malinda "Linnie"[2] Arbogast** (1.Peter[1]), b. Oct 20 1822 in Asbury, Pleasant Twp., Clark Co., OH, d. Jul 24 1886 in Clark Co., OH, buried in Nation Chapel, Pleasant Twp., Clark Co., OH.
(1) Married Dec 08 1839 in Ohio, **William Willis Clymer** (son of Joseph Isaac Clymer and Elizabeth Alt). .

Children by William Willis Clymer:

55 i. Miranda[3] Clymer b. About 1845 in Pleasant Twp., Clark Co., OH.
+ 56 ii. Mahalia Clymer b. Dec 15 1846.
57 iii. Mitilda Clymer b. About 1850 in Pleasant Twp., Clark Co., OH.
58 iv. Louis Clymer b. About 1851 in Pleasant Twp., Clark Co., OH.
59 v. Harriett Clymer b. About 1853 in Pleasant Twp., Clark Co., OH.
60 vi. Roxanna Clymer b. Apr 24 1856 in Pleasant Twp., Clark Co., OH, buried in Maple Grove Cem., Mechanicsburg, Champaign Co., OH, d. Mar 18 1940. Married Jan 08 1878 in Clark Co., OH, **Daniel Mathias Harmison**.
61 vii. Rollin Clymer b. Apr 24 1856 in Pleasant Twp., Clark Co., OH, buried in Maple Grove Cem., Mechanicsburg, Champaign Co., OH, d. May 21 1935.
62 viii. Laura Clymer b. About 1859 in Pleasant Twp., Clark Co., OH.
63 ix. William Clymer b. About 1863 in Pleasant Twp., Clark Co., OH.

(2) Married Feb 20 1842, **James Driscoll**

11. **Peter[2] Arbogast Jr.** (1.Peter[1]), d. Jun 09 1833 in Tiffin, Seneca Co., OH, b. About 1781 in Augusta Co., VA. Tombstone indicates death at 39 yrs. Centennial Biographical History of Seneca Co., OH indicates death in 1835. Same history lists children Phoebe, Christina, Jesse and Michael. "Peter Arbogast, who died in 1833, owned the west half of southwest quarter of Section 16, Township 2 north, Range 14 east He settled here in 1826. Mrs. Sophia Arbogast died in 1861. Michael Arbogast, born in Virginia in 1824, came here when two years old, and is now a resident of Seneca Township. Page 987, Michael Arbogast, farmer, P.O. Tiffin, was born in Virginia, 1 Aug 1824, a son of Peter and Sophia Arbogast, natives of Virginia, where they first settled; thence came to this county in 1826, locating in Hopewell Township, where they lived and died, the former in 1833, and the latter in 1861. Our subject (Michael, ed.) was united in marriage, 19Dec 1847, with **Jane Gedulting**, born in Frederick Co., MD, a daughter of Jacob and Elizabeth Gedulting. Mrs. Arbogast departed this life 6 Jan 1849 Married, 11 Mar 1852, for his second wife, Jane R. Stoner, born in Frederick Co., MD, 18 Jan 1825, a daughter of Henry and Sarah Stoner. Father of nine children, all named except an infant, as recorded, six living in 1886. Jane R. (Stoner) Arbogast died 23 Jun 1882. Our subject has met with fair success and now owns 300 acres of land". A photo of Michael appears therein. Peter is obviously a descendant of Michael Arbogast, unplaced at this time. On 1830 census, Seneca Co., OH, age 30-40 bracket. Also two males age 20-30 bracket unidentified.
Married Apr 16 1823 in Blue Grass, Highland Co., WV, **Sophia Arbogast**, b. About 1800 in Crabbottom, Highland Co., VA (daughter of Henry Arbogast and Sophia Wade), d. About 1861 in Tiffin, Seneca Co., OH. **Sophia**: References to Centennial Biographical History of Seneca Co., OH, p. 344 and Sophia named in father's will. .

Extracts from Seneca County Land Records and deeds, sent by Barbara Lawyer, indicate several real property transactions. One, a deed, from Christian Stoner and Anna Maria Stoner his wife, recorded on page 78, is of particular interest since Stoner and Arbogast families Married at least twice, Jesse Arbogast, to Susan Stoner and Michael Arbogast #3712, to Jane R. Stoner,.

In a civil action in Seneca Co., OH, Common Pleas Court, filed 31 Oct 1833, having to do with Peter's estate, Sophia represents that Jesse, Phebe, Christina, and Michael are her children and Peter's. Page 220 of court records.1830 census, Hopewell Twp., Seneca Co., OH, Sophia, age bracket 30-40, so her birth could be before 1800.

Children:

+ 64 i. Jesse[3] Arbogast b. Apr 01 1815.
65 ii. Phebe Arbogast b. About 1818 in Blue Grass, Highland Co., WV, d. in Ohio. She Married **Thomas J. Windsor**.
66 iii. Christina Arbogast b. About 1821 in Blue Grass, Highland Co., WV, d. About 1849 in Seneca Co., OH. She Married **Aaron Carr**.
+ 67 iv. Michael Arbogast b. Aug 01 1824.

Generation Three

12. **Eli[3] Smith** (2.Priscilla[2] Arbogast, 1.Peter[1]), b. 1823 in Clark Co., OH, d. Dec 22 1891.
Married 1846, **Minerva Shaw**, b. 1823, d. 1895.

Children:

+ 68	i.	Amos[4] Smith b. Jun 16 1848.
+ 69	ii.	Miranda E. Smith b. About 1850.
+ 70	iii.	Alice Smith b. Jul 03 1858.

13. **Elizabeth P.[3] Arbogast** (3.Rev. Cornelius[2], 1.Peter[1]), b. Aug 01 1830 in Clark Co., OH, buried to Plattsville, Shelby Co., OH, d. Sep 16 1902 in Sidney, Shelby Co., OH.
Married Dec 20 1850 in Urbana, Champaign Co., IL, **James David Latimer**, b. Aug 20 1815 in Clark Co., OH, buried in Coles Chapel Cem., Shelby Co., OH, d. Jun 24 1870 in Turtle Creek Twp., Shelby Co., OH.

Children:

+ 71	i.	Sarah E.[4] Latimer b. Sep 19 1851.
+ 72	ii.	Allen Latimer b. May 04 1853.
+ 73	iii.	Melissa Latimer b. Mar 23 1855.
+ 74	iv.	James C. Latimer b. Apr 02 1857.
+ 75	v.	Margaret Latimer b. 1859.
+ 76	vi.	David Latimer b. Mar 01 1861.
+ 77	vii.	Adaline Latimer b. Mar 01 1861.
+ 78	viii.	Gertrude Latimer b. Mar 15 1869.

14. **Margaret May[3] Arbogast** (3.Rev. Cornelius[2], 1.Peter[1]), b. May 13 1824 in Ohio, buried in Old Pioneer Cem., Plattsville, Shelby Co., OH, d. Jun 09 1881 in Plattsville, Shelby Co., OH.
She Married **Albert Gale Thorne Guthrie**, b. About 1822 in Virginia (son of John C. Guthrie and Nancy Jane Glass), buried in Old Pioneer Cem., Plattsville, Shelby Co., OH, d. Jan 05 1892 in Plattsville, Shelby Co., OH.

Children:

+ 79	i.	Cornelius Arbogast[4] Guthrie b. Nov 07 1846.
80	ii.	Arthur Guthrie b. Jan 15 1850 in Clark Co., OH. (1) Married Feb 19 1874 in Champaign Co., OH, **Sarah J. Shimer**. (2) Married Oct 31 1876 in Champaign Co., OH, **Ida S. Roberts**.
81	iii.	Louisa W. Guthrie b. Oct 27 1852, d. May 16 1877 in Plattsville, Shelby Co., OH.

15. **John H.[3] Arbogast** (3.Rev. Cornelius[2], 1.Peter[1]), b. Jul 08 1829 in Clark Co., OH, d. Jun 25 1885 in Plattsville, Shelby Co., OH.
Married Mar 04 1854 in Shelby Co., OH, **Martha Cunningham**, b. 1832, d. Aug 11 1919.

Children:

82	i.	Arthur H.[4] Arbogast b. About 1858 in Indiana.
83	ii.	Sarah J. Arbogast b. About 1862 in Ohio.
84	iii.	M. Ellen Arbogast b. About 1863 in Ohio.
85	iv.	Lewis B. Arbogast b. About 1867 in Ohio.
+ 86	v.	Neal Arbogast b. About 1969.

16. **Lewis[3] Arbogast** (3.Rev. Cornelius[2], 1.Peter[1]), b. Jun 10 1833 in Ohio, d. Apr 02 1898.
(1) Married Apr 30 1857 in Shelby Co., OH, **Sarah Margaret Chrisman**, b. Sep 08 1836, d. Mar 14 1870.

Children *by Sarah Margaret Chrisman:*

87	i.	Harriett E.[4] Arbogast b. May 08 1861, d. May 26 1930. She Married **Edward Shaw**.
88	ii.	Emma Arbogast b. Feb 14 1863, d. Aug 05 1919. She Married **Ruben Robertson**, b. 1861, d. Oct 15 1925.

(2) Married Sep 18 1870 in Shelby Co., OH, **Margaret M. Madras**, b. 1851 in Ohio, d. May 29 1930.

Children *by Margaret M. Madras:*

89	iii.	Daisy A. Arbogast b. Sep 07 1872, d. May 21 1923. She Married **Charles L. Windle**, b. Nov 16 1870, d. Nov 13 1941.
90	iv.	Ada Arbogast b. 1875.

17. **Allen[3] Arbogast** (3.Rev. Cornelius[2], 1.Peter[1]), b. Mar 11 1836 in Clark Co., OH, d. Aug 25 1899 in Plattsville, Shelby Co., OH.
Married Sep 03 1857 in Miami, Clermont Co., OH, **Lydia Scooby**, b. 1841 in Ohio, d. Sep 26 1905.

Children:

91 i. William L.[4] Arbogast b. About 1861. He Married **Libby Hart**.
92 ii. John A. Arbogast b. 1863, d. 1867.
+ 93 iii. Allen Johnson Arbogast b. About 1864.
94 iv. Alice A. Arbogast b. Sep 03 1865 in Ohio, d. Mar 03 1905.
+ 95 v. Etna A. Arbogast b. Jun 24 1867.
96 vi. Margaret L. Arbogast b. About 1870.
97 vii. Charles Francis Arbogast b. Nov 21 1871, d. Aug 03 1945. He Married **Nellie May Buchanan**, b. 1877, d. Feb 16 1901.
98 viii. Luther Arbogast b. Jul 05 1874.
99 ix. Dora Arbogast b. Oct 10 1876.
100 x. Mary Arbogast b. Aug 05 1879.
+ 101 xi. Roland Arbogast b. Jan 08 1882.

18. **Ruth Darletta[3] Arbogast** (3.Rev. Cornelius[2], 1.Peter[1]), b. Apr 10 1838 in Clark Co., OH. Married Jan 29 1857 in Shelby Co., OH, **Martin M. Comer**, b. 1830 in Millerstown, Champaign Co., OH. **Martin**: 1860 census Johnson, Champaign, OH: Isaac Corner, aged 27, farmer, bp OH; Amanda aged 20, bp VA; Martin Corner, aged 30, farmer, bp OH; Ruth Conner, gad 23, bp OH; T. J. Conner aged 2, bp OH
1900 census Payne, Paulding, OH: Martin Comer, aged 70, born Mar 1830, day laborer, bp OH, both parents OH; Ruth D. aged 62, born Jan 1838, Married 43 years, one child w/ one living, bp OH, both parents OH; son George W. Comer, aged 20, born Sep 1879, stave jointer, bp OH, both parents VA?

Children:

+ 102 i. Thomas Joseph[4] Comer b. Feb 12 1857.
103 ii. Sarah Comer b. About 1860 in Champaign Co., OH.
104 iii. Louisan Comer b. About 1863 in Champaign Co., OH.
105 iv. Mahalia M. Comer b. About 1855 in Champaign Co., OH.
106 v. Florrie Comer b. About 1873 in Champaign Co., OH.

20. **Cornelius[3] Arbogast, Jr.** (3.Rev. Cornelius[2], 1.Peter[1]), b. Mar 23 1847 in Clark Co., OH, d. 1880.
(1) Married May 26 1875 in Shelby Co., OH, **Frances M. Shotwell**, b. About 1858 in Iowa.

Children *by Frances M. Shotwell:*

107 i. Nannie[4] Arbogast b. About 1876.
108 ii. Grant Arbogast b. About 1878 in Kansas.

(2) Married Jun 15 1882, **Emma L. Powell Rhodehamel**.

22. **Margaret Ann[3] Arbogast** (4.Otho[2], 1.Peter[1]), b. Sep 06 1825 in Clark Co., OH, d. Apr 13 1910 in Mechanicsburg, Champaign Co., OH.
Married Dec 02 1843 in Clark Co., OH, **Joseph Frey Neer**, b. May 04 1819 in Clark Co., OH (son of Enos Neer), d. Jan 08 1898 in Champaign Co., OH.

Children:

109 i. Amy[4] Neer b. Jul 01 1846 in Pleasant Twp., Clark Co., OH, buried in Nation Chapel, Pleasant Twp., Clark Co., OH, d. Nov 03 1946 in Mechanicsburg, Champaign Co., OH.
110 ii. Sarah Catherine Neer b. May 05 1848 in Pleasant Twp., Clark Co., OH, buried in Nation Chapel, Pleasant Twp., Clark Co., OH, d. Nov 23 1860 in Mechanicsburg, Champaign Co., OH.
+ 111 iii. Dorothy Jane Neer b. Apr 14 1851.
+ 112 iv. Bruce Neer b. Aug 30 1857.
+ 113 v. William Brown Neer b. Dec 21 1862.
+ 114 vi. Grant Neer b. Dec 16 1984.

23. **Jackson[3] Arbogast** (4.Otho[2], 1.Peter[1]), b. About 1830, buried in Maple Grove Cem., Mechanicsburg, Champaign Co., OH, d. Apr 17 1900 in Champaign Co., OH.
He Married **Elizabeth Evens**, b. About 1830 in Ohio (daughter of Jesse Evans), buried in Maple Grove Cem., Mechanicsburg, Champaign Co., OH, d. Sep 16 1985 in Champaign Co., OH.

Children:

115 i. John W.[4] Arbogast b. About 1855 in Ohio.
+ 116 ii. Francis M. Arbogast b. About 1859.
+ 117 iii. Lovetta Arbogast b. c1862.

24. **Eli M.[3] Arbogast** (4.Otho[2], 1.Peter[1]), b. Dec 24 1834 in Champaign Co., OH, buried in Maple Grove Cem., Mechanicsburg, Champaign Co., OH, d. Feb 01 1916 in Champaign Co., OH.
Served with C Co., 110th OH Volunteer Infantry.
(1) Married Nov 13 1855 in Champaign Co., OH, **Mary Williams**, b. Mar 06 1837 in Champaign Co., OH, buried in Maple Grove Cem., Mechanicsburg, Champaign Co., OH, d. May 19 1918 in Somerford, Madison Co., OH. (

Children *by Mary Williams:*

+ 118 i. Laura A.[4] Arbogast b. Sep 05 1856.
+ 119 ii. Marion W. Arbogast b. Nov 15 1859.

2) Married Dec 29 1880, **Mrs. Anna E. Brodwell.**

28. **William H.[3] Hardman** (5.Mary[2] Arbogast, 1.Peter[1]), b. Feb 28 1831, d. 1908.
Married Oct 29 1856 in Clark Co., OH, **Margaret Ellen Bireley**, b. Mar 11 1838 in Maryland (daughter of Lewis Bireley), d. After 1908 in Pleasant Twp., Clark Co., OH. **Margaret**: Mr. Hartman was a sheep farmer in OH. He entered the Civil war, 176th Ohio Volunteer Infantry. While in camp in Ohio a man came to him with a note. It was from his partner in the sheep farming. The note said turn over your gun to this gentleman, who is Thomas Cartmell. His partner, J.R. Ware had arranged for Thomas to take is place, since he was unmarried. This is an example of the 'Rich man, poor man' name given the Civil War by folks like Mr. Cartmell.

Children:

+ 120 i. Minor W.[4] Hardman b. 1860.
+ 121 ii. Belle Hardman b. Aug 08 1867.
+ 122 iii. Eddie Hardman b. May 25 1877.
+ 123 iv. Ella Hardman b. May 25 1877.

31. **Otho[3] Hardman** (5.Mary[2] Arbogast, 1.Peter[1]), b. Dec 18 1856.
Married Jun 27 1937 in Clark Co., OH, **Eliza Weaver**, b. Jun 27 1837 in Clark Co., OH, d. Jan 17 1902.

Children:

124 i. Jennie[4] Hardman b. Nov 18 1957. Married Oct 04 1883, **William H Clark**.
125 ii. Ralph Hardman b. Jan 12 1861. Married Mar 11 1902, **Sarah C Smith**.
126 iii. Emma Hardman b. Feb 17 1863. Married Jan 14 1886, **William Harrison Harlen**, b. May 05 1856.
127 iv. Pearl Hardman b. Oct 18 1864.
128 v. Saile Hardman b. Jun 25 1869, d. Oct 11 1893. Married Apr 1890, **Zetta McDonald**.

34. **Mary A.[3] Curl** (6.Margaret[2] Arbogast, 1.Peter[1]), b. May 29 1837 in Cardington Twp., Morrow Co., OH, d. Oct 23 1915.
Married Oct 03 1858 in Ohio, **Enos Welsh**, b. Feb 02 1834 in Ohio, buried in Glendale, Cardington Twp., Morrow Co., OH, d. Jan 14 1915.

Children:

129 i. Nettie A.[4] Welsh b. 1861 in Cardington Twp., Morrow Co., OH, d. 1895.
130 ii. Saville A. Welsh b. 1866 in Cardington Twp., Morrow Co., OH, d. 1895.

35. **Isabella Jane[3] Curl** (6.Margaret[2] Arbogast, 1.Peter[1]), b. Jan 09 1828, buried in Glendale, Cardington Twp., Morrow Co., OH, d. Jan 23 1914 in Cardington Twp., Morrow Co., OH. Married Mar 27 1849 in Morrow Co., OH, **John Sellers**, b. Nov 01 1827 in Perry Co., OH, buried in Glendale, Cardington Twp., Morrow Co., OH, d. Sep 25 1912 in Cardington Twp., Morrow Co., OH.

Children:

131 i. A.[4] Sellers b. Sep 12 1850, buried in Glendale, Cardington Twp., Morrow Co., OH, d. Nov 20 1870.
+ 132 ii. Shelby Sellers b. Sep 21 1852.
+ 133 iii. Lucinda Sellers b. Nov 18 1854.
134 iv. Freeman Sellers b. Feb 17 1870, d. Jan 26 1871 in Glendale, Cardington Twp., Morrow Co., OH.
+ 135 v. Wilie Sellers.
+ 136 vi. Amanda Sellers b. About 1859.
137 vii. Isadora Sellers. She Married **George Van Shiver**.
+ 138 viii. Johnson Leamon Sellers b. Feb 1870.
+ 139 ix. Ross Sellers b. Feb 24 1868.
+ 140 x. Lovina Sellers b. About 1861.

36. **Henry William[3] Curl** (6.Margaret[2] Arbogast, 1.Peter[1]), b. Oct 21 1829 in Cardington Twp., Morrow Co., OH, buried in Bethel Cem., Cardington Twp., Morrow Co., OH, d. Mar 18 1893 in Cardington Twp., Morrow Co., OH.

(1) Married Oct 24 1850 in Morrow Co., OH, **Elizabeth Johnson**, b. Jul 04 1929 in Perry Co., OH, buried in Bethel Cem., Cardington Twp., Morrow Co., OH, d. Mar 11 1893 in Cardington Twp., Morrow Co., OH. (.

Children *by Elizabeth Johnson:*

+	141	i.	Elza S.[4] Curl b. Aug 22 1861.
+	142	ii.	Franklin M. Curl b. Aug 16 1853.
+	143	iii.	Cora A. Curl b. Mar 17 1857.
+	144	iv.	Haze D. Curl b. Jan 22 1860.
+	145	v.	Ida M. Curl b. Oct 03 1967.
	146	vi.	(infant) Curl b. Oct 03 1967, d. 1967.
+	147	vii.	Ada Blanche Curl b. Jan 17 1971.

(2) He Married **Alice Patterson**, d. After Mar 1896

37. **Emily[3] Curl** (6.Margaret[2] Arbogast, 1.Peter[1]), b. Nov 11 1832 in Pleasant Twp., Clark Co., OH, buried in Shawtown Cem., Westfield Twp., Morrow Co., OH, d. May 03 1919 in Westfield Twp., Marrow Co., OH.
(1) Married Oct 24 1848 in Morrow Co., OH, **Sylvester Shaw**, b. Apr 11 1828 in Westfield Twp., Marrow Co., OH, buried in Shawtown Cem., Westfield Twp., Morrow Co., OH, d. Dec 25 1852 in Marion Co., OH. (3) She Married **Ruben Aldrich**, b. May 15 1832 in Westfield Twp., Marrow Co., OH, d. Mar 31 1912 in Westfield Twp., Marrow Co., OH.

Children *by Sylvester Shaw:*

+	148	i.	Mary Jane[4] Shaw b. 1849.
+	149	ii.	Minerva Shaw b. Apr 02 1851.

(2) She Married **Leronzo Messinger**, b. Jan 01 1926 (son of Adonijah Messenger and Rache Burgess), buried in Shawtown Cem., Westfield Twp., Morrow Co., OH, d. Nov 17 1891 in Westfield Twp., Marrow Co., OH.

Children *by Leronzo Messinger:*

+	150	iii.	George Asa Messenger b. 16 Nov 1866.
	151	iv.	Eunice Messenger. She Married Henry Ault.

38. **William Hayse[3] Curl** (6.Margaret[2] Arbogast, 1.Peter[1]), b. Aug 20 1834 in Pleasant Twp., Clark Co., OH, d. Mar 01 1917, buried in Bethel Cem., Cardington Twp., Morrow Co., OH.
(1) Married Apr 27 1854, **Rebecca Johnson**, b. Feb 02 1832 in Cardington Twp., Morrow Co., OH (daughter of William Johnston and Catherine Fluckey), buried in Bethel Cem., Cardington Twp., Morrow Co., OH, d. Mar 01 1917 in Cardington Twp., Morrow Co., OH

Children *by Rebecca Johnson:*

+	152	i.	Perry N.[4] Curl b. Jan 30 1855.
	153	ii.	Sarah Lusena Curl b. Sep 11 1856 in Cardington Twp., Morrow Co., OH, d. Oct 27 1887. Married Mar 11 1879 in Cardington Twp., Morrow Co., OH, **Charles F. Ossing**.
+	154	iii.	Lemuel Otho Curl b. May 10 1958.

(2) Married Sep 14 1864 in Cardington Twp., Morrow Co., OH, **Susannah Shaw**, b. Feb 21 1841 in Marvin Twp., Delaware Co., OH (daughter of Jonathan Shaw, Jr. and Mary Ann Barry), buried in Bethel Cem., Cardington Twp., Morrow Co., OH, d. Jun 11 1920 in Cardington Twp., Morrow Co., OH.

Children *by Susannah Shaw:*

	155	iv.	Jonathan Shaw Curl b. Mar 22 1866 in Cardington Twp., Morrow Co., OH, buried in Bethel Cem., Cardington Twp., Morrow Co., OH, d. Sep 08 1877 in Cardington Twp., Morrow Co., OH.
	156	v.	William H. Curl b. May 29 1868 in Cardington Twp., Morrow Co., OH, d. May 10 1932 in Morrow Co., OH. (1) He Married **Lola B Schofield**. (2) He Married **Mary J. Carpenter**, d. Oct 11 1930 in Cardington Twp., Morrow Co., OH.
+	157	vi.	Margaret Ova Curl b. Mar 25 1873.
	158	vii.	Ellis Ray Curl b. Nov 26 1879 in Cardington Twp., Morrow Co., OH. (1) He Married **Imogene Clevenger**. (2) Married Mar 16 1821 in Cardington Twp., Morrow Co., OH, **Elva Henry**.
	159	viii.	Troy Walters Curl b. Sep 03 1881 in Cardington Twp., Morrow Co., OH. He Married **Rena Noble**, b. Jun 1809 in Ohio.
+	160	ix.	Stella Flossie Curl b. Mar 21 1885.

43. **Margaret Jane[3] Wilkinson** (7.Susannah[2] Arbogast, 1.Peter[1]), b. Apr 16 1837 in Carysville, Champaign Co., OH, d. Nov 02 1919 in Quincy, Champaign Co., OH.

Married Sep 04 1856, **David Coverstone**, b. Jan 08 1832 in Adams Twp., Champaign Co., OH, d. Jan 30 1918 in Quincy, Champaign Co., OH.

Children:

161 i. Allen Derastus[4] Coverstone b. Apr 16 1857 in Adams Twp., Champaign Co., OH, d. Jun 09 1942 in Sidney, Shelby Co., OH. He Married **Olive Harriet Williamson**, b. May 02 1874 in Union City, Randolph Co., IN, d. Jun 07 1939 in Quincy, Champaign Co., OH.
162 ii. Ellis Lehman Coverstone b. Jan 31 1860, d. Sep 17 1946. He Married **Sarah Wtatt**, b. 1862, d. 1945.
163 iii. Edgar McClelland Coverstone b. Feb 25 1863 in Adams Twp., Champaign Co., OH, d. Feb 01 1949.
\+ 164 iv. Elza Freeman Coverstone b. c1864.
\+ 165 v. Cora Melissa Coverstone b. Aug 27 1865.
166 vi. Selma Dora Coverstone b. 1869 in Adams Twp., Champaign Co., OH, d. 1956. Married Oct 20 1892 in Logan Co., OH, **James Kenton Cox**, b. 1865 in Logan Co., OH, d. 1939 in Logan Co., OH.
167 vii. Cary Sheridan Coverstone b. 1872 in Adams Twp., Champaign Co., OH. She Married **Ella Dresback**.

44. **John G.[3] Wilkinson** (7.Susannah[2] Arbogast, 1.Peter[1]), b. About 1842 in Marion Co., OH, d. May 31 1862 in Shiloh, Hardin Co., TN.
Died in battle of Shiloh, member of an Ohio regiment, under command or U.S. Grant.
Married 1858 in Logan Co., OH, **Elizabeth (Unknown)**.

Children:

\+ 168 i. George Washington[4] Wilkinson b. Mar 15 1859.
\+ 169 ii. John Nelson Wilkinson b. Mar 15 1859.

49. **Sarah Elizabeth[3] Arbogast** (8.Henry[2], 1.Peter[1]), b. Dec 05 1839 in Clark Co., OH, buried in Kirkwood Cem., London, Madison Co., OH, d. Nov 04 1894 in London, Madison Co., OH. Married Sep 22 1863 in Clark Co., OH, **Walter Chamberlan Henry**, b. 1834, d. 1913.

Children:

170 i. Caroline[4] Henry d. 1922.
171 ii. Carlton Henry d. 1922.
172 iii. May Estelle Henry d. After1922. She Married **Walter Jackson**.

50. **Charles Rollin[3] Arbogast** (8.Henry[2], 1.Peter[1]), b. Dec 09 1841, buried in Ferncliff Cem., Springfield, Clark Co., OH, d. Apr 18 1926 in Springfield, Gallia Co., OH.
Married Jan 07 1868 in Clark Co., OH, **Eliza Bierly**, b. May 24 1844 in Maryland, d. May 15 1933 in Ferncliff Cem., Springfield, Clark Co., OH. Served in the the Civil War.

Children:

173 i. Addie[4] Arbogast b. Jun 16 1872 in Clark Co., OH. She Married **Lewis Jones**.

51. **James W.[3] Arbogast** (8.Henry[2], 1.Peter[1]), b. Jan 12 1845 in Clark Co., OH, d. Aug 08 1935. Married Jun 01 1878, **Laura J. McConkey**, b. 1953, d. 1936.

Children:

174 i. Edna[4] Arbogast b. 1979, d. 1937.

52. **Milton A.[3] Arbogast** (8.Henry[2], 1.Peter[1]), b. Feb 06 1951 in Clark Co., OH, d. 1018.
Married Oct 14 1875, **Elizabeth J. McClennen**, b. 1843, d. 1930.

Children:

175 i. Ross Howard[4] Arbogast.
\+ 176 ii. Creston Willard Arbogast b. 1878.

54. **Albert[3] Arbogast** (8.Henry[2], 1.Peter[1]), b. Dec 04 1848 in Clark Co., OH, buried in Kirkwood Cem., London, Madison Co., OH, d. Aug 08 1935 in London, Madison Co., OH.
Married Jun 29 1876 in Madison Co., OH, **Mary Lurcretia Porter**, b. Oct 05 1855 in London, Madison Co., OH (daughter of Nehemiah Timmons and Catherine Carey), d. Feb 21 1939 in Kirkwood Cem., London, Madison Co., OH.

Children:

177 i. Ernest Gaylord[4] Arbogast b. May 18 1877, d. 1925.
\+ 178 ii. Ethel Kilbourne Arbogast b. Dec 18 1881.
179 iii. Lora S. Arbogast b. Dec 27 1884, d. 1974.
180 iv. Pearl G. Arbogast b. Jul 03 1881, d. 1951.

56. **Mahala[3] Clymer** (10.Malinda "Linnie"[2] Arbogast, 1.Peter[1]), b. Dec 15 1846 in Pleasant Twp., Clark Co., OH, d. Jun 17 1898. Married Jul 25 1872, **Perry Bumgardner**, b. Aug 10 1848, d. Mar 03 1921.

Children:

181 i. Sherwin[4] Bumgardner b. Aug 18 1873, buried in Asbury Cem., Clark Co., OH, d. 1946. Married Jan 06 1897, **Laura Belle Wingfield**, b. Dec 26 1968, buried in Asbury Cem., Clark Co., OH, d. Before 1942.
182 ii. Georgia Bumgardner b. Sep 18 1874.
183 iii. Foster Bumgardner b. Oct 03 1876.
184 iv. Lillian Bumgardner b. Jan 27 1879, d. Jan 24 1913.
\+ 185 v. Nellie Bumgardner b. Jan 31 1882.

64. **Jesse[3] Arbogast** (11.Peter[2], 1.Peter[1]), b. Apr 01 1815 in Harrison Co., WV, d. Sep 23 1874 in Bushnell, Walnut Grove Twp., McDonough Co., IL.
He Married **Susan Stoner**, b. Mar 05 1820 in Baltimore, Baltimore Co., MD, d. Nov 06 1891 in Bushnell, Walnut Grove Twp., McDonough Co., IL, buried in Prairie City Cem., Pierce Co., WA.

Children:

\+ 186 i. Sophia[4] Arbogast b. Jul 18 1838.
187 ii. Ann Eliza Arbogast b. About1842 in Wabash Co., IN, d. Jul 06 1920 in Prairie City, McDonough Co., IL. Married Apr 19 1856, **James Wilson**.
\+ 188 iii. Louis Peter Arbogast b. Jan 01 1844.
\+ 189 iv. Mary Jane Arbogast b. Jan 15 1845.
\+ 190 v. Henry S. Arbogast b. Mar 18 1847.
191 vi. Angeline Arbogast b. Abourt1849, d. About 1850.
\+ 192 vii. Sarah Arbogast b. Apr 23 1851.
\+ 193 viii. Cynthia Arbogast b. About 1853.
\+ 194 ix. Frances Arbogast b. Jul 20 1856.
\+ 195 x. Stephen Aaron Douglas Arbogast b. Jun 18 1859.
196 xi. Marion Arbogast b. ABOUT 1864 in Walnut Grove Twp., Knox Co., IL, d. in Grand Island, Hall Co., NE.

67. **Michael[3] Arbogast** (11.Peter[2], 1.Peter[1]), b. Aug 01 1824 in Seneca Co., OH, d. Oct 11 1902 in Seneca Co., OH.
(1) Married Mar 11 1852 in Seneca Co., OH, **Jane Stoner**, b. Jan 18 1825 in Frederick Co., MD, d. Aug 23 1882 in Seneca Co., OH. Michael Arbogast, the youngest child of Peter and Sophia Arbogast was only two years of age when brought by his parents to Seneca County, where he spent all the years of his childhood and manhood. He aided in the difficult task of clearing the farm and preparing the fields for cultivation, and when the land became arable he bore his part in the work of plowing, planting and harvesting. As his father died when he was only nine years of age, he and his mother carried on the work of the farm, with the aid of an ox team. It was in 1855 that he took up his abode upon the place where he would live out his life. On the 11th of March in1852, Michael was united in marriage to Miss Jane R. Stoner, a daughter of Henry and Sara (Reagan) Stoner. They were blessed with nine children before her death on June 23, 1882. They are: Alice, who Married Jacob Staib, is now deceased; John F. was a resident of Seneca township; Nettie became the wife of Robert E. Lutz, of Oklahoma; Lewis was a mechanic and resided in Tiffin; Charles resided near Bushnell, Illinois; Rush operated the homestead farm; and three sons passed away in childhood.

Mr. Arbogast put forth every effort to make a comfortable home for his family and to give his children the opportunity to prepare themselves for the practical and responsible duties of life. In 1854 he purchased one hundred and twenty-three acres of land, the improvements on which consisted of a log house and a log barn. He went in debt for the entire amount, $3690, and this was all paid in three years time. Fifty acres had been cleared and in the course of time his fields were green with the crops that promised golden harvests. As his financial resources increased he added to his landed possessions until the home farm comprised of two hundred acres. He also owned another farm, of one hundred acres, in Seneca township and had made excellent improvements on both. In 1875 he erected one of the most pretentious brick residences in the vicinity. He used the latest machinery for facilitating farm work and erected good barns and outbuildings for the shelter of grain and stock. His residence in the county covered more than three-quarters of acentury and the present generation cannot realize the changes which had occurred during this period.

Michael Arbogast remembered seeing many Indians in the locality and had driven through tiffin with an ox team many a time when the mud came up to the hubs of the wagon wheels. The flourishing city then contained only a few pioneer cabins and the county gave little promise of its present developments. However, the pioneers had laid broad and deep the foundations for its present progress, with Mr. Arbogast performing his full share in the work of citizenship. He favored reform and improvement, and his labors were effective in promoting the general welfare. Owing to his father's death he early had to take up the responsibilities of a business career, and industry, economy, and honest were salient features in his history, enabling him to advance steadily until he occupied a prominent place on the plane of affluence.

Children *by Jane Stoner:*

197 i. Warren D.[4] Arbogast b. May 11 1852, d. 1886.
+ 198 ii. Alice M. Arbogast b. Nov 30 1853.
+ 199 iii. John Franklin Arbogast b. Oct 18 1855.
+ 200 iv. Lewis Heenan Arbogast b. 1862.
+ 201 v. Annetta A. Arbogast.
+ 202 vi. Charles Sayers Arbogast b. Oct 13 1864.
+ 203 vii. Rush Arlington Arbogast b. Aug 15 1867.
204 viii. (infant) Arbogast.

(2) Married Dec 19 1847 in Frederick Co., MD, **Jane Gedulding**, b. Mar 21 1827 in Frederick Co., MD, d. Oct 11 1902 in Seneca Co., OH.

Children *by Jane Gedulding:*

205 ix. Henry W. Arbogast b. Jan 06 1849 in Seneca Co., OH, d. May 24 1949 in Seneca Co., OH.

Generation Four

68. **Amos[4] Smith** (12.Eli[3], 2.Priscilla[2] Arbogast, 1.Peter[1]), b. Jun 16 1848 in Clark Co., OH, d. 1908.
Amos was a well to do farmer and was credited with several patents of new farm equipment.
Married 1872, **Catherine Weit**, b. 1852.

Children:

206 i. Clifford[5] Smith b. Apr 07 1873, d. Dec 12 1898.
+ 207 ii. Sylvia Smith b. Nov 24 1875.
+ 208 iii. Leona Smith b. May 27 1883.
+ 209 iv. Nina Smith b. May 27 1883.
210 v. Fostoria Smith b. Mar 13 1891, d. After 1908.
211 vi. Kate Smith b. Jan 08 1893.

69. **Mianda E.[4] Smith** (12.Eli[3], 2.Priscilla[2] Arbogast, 1.Peter[1]), b. About 1850, d. 1891. She Married **J.W. Wright**.

Children:

212 i. Bertram[5] Wright b. 1869, d. 1870.
213 ii. Dellie Wright b. 1871, d. 1871.

70. **Alice[4] Smith** (12.Eli[3], 2.Priscilla[2] Arbogast, 1.Peter[1]), b. Jul 03 1858, d. About 1908. She Married **Oscar Runyan**.

Children:

214 i. Glennie[5] Runyan.

71. **Sarah E.[4] Latimer** (13.Elizabeth P.[3] Arbogast, 3.Rev. Cornelius[2], 1.Peter[1]), b. Sep 19 1851 in Ohio, d. May 24 1914.
Married Oct 14 1872, **David Allen Chrisman**, b. Mar 07 1843, d. Mar 16 1908.

Children:

215 i. Letha M.[5] Chrisman b. 1874, d. Jul 14 1958. She Married **John D. Partington**.
216 ii. Albert Earle Chrisman b. Sep 05 1877, d. Nov 15 1940. He Married **Mary Faye Clark**, b. Oct 03 1891, d. Jan 23 1944.
217 iii. Harriet Irene Chrisman b. Jan 13 1881, d. Jan 08 1943. She Married **Fred A. Hagman**, b. Jan 28 1880, d. Feb 22 1969.
218 iv. Joseph Clinton Chrisman b. Oct 24 1885, d. Oct 26 1941. He Married **Nina Mae Shipman**, b. Jul 11 1891, d. Feb 16 1973.

72. **Allen[4] Latimer** (13.Elizabeth P.[3] Arbogast, 3.Rev. Cornelius[2], 1.Peter[1]), b. May 04 1853, d. Jan 22 1919. He Married **Del Weatherhead**.

Children:

219 i. Lee[5] Latimer.

73. **Melissa[4] Latimer** (13.Elizabeth P.[3] Arbogast, 3.Rev. Cornelius[2], 1.Peter[1]), b. Mar 23 1855 in Port Jefferson, Champaign Co., OH, buried in Mendon, St. Joseph Co., MI, d. Jun 26 1936 in Quincy Twp., Branch Co., MI.
Married Oct 16 1877 in Sidney, Shelby Co., OH, **John Crissman**, b. Nov 10 1857 in West Carrolton, Montgomery Co., OH (son of Peter Jacon Crissman and Louisa Gieger), buried in Mendon, St. Joseph Co., MI, d. Jul 12 1929 in Mendon, St. Joseph Co., MI.

Children:

+ 220 i. Cornelius Eugene[5] Crissman b. Oct 06 1878.
 221 ii. Clarence C. Crissman b. Sep 11 1881 in Turtle Creek Twp., Shelby Co., OH, d. Apr 04 1957. He Married **Addie May Biddle**, b. Dec 16 1883, d. Oct 30 1956.
+ 222 iii. Ernest Raymond Crissman b. Mar 12 1889.

74. **James C.[4] Latimer** (13.Elizabeth P.[3] Arbogast, 3.Rev. Cornelius[2], 1.Peter[1]), b. Apr 02 1857 in Quincy, Champaign Co., OH, d. Jul 02 1929.
He Married **Ida McClellen**.

Children:

223 i. Cliffird[5] Latimer.
224 ii. Lavada Latimer.

75. **Margaret[4] Latimer** (13.Elizabeth P.[3] Arbogast, 3.Rev. Cornelius[2], 1.Peter[1]), b. 1859. She Married **Justin W. Huffman**, b. Jun 07 1854.

Children:

225 i. Lizzie[5] Huffman.
226 ii. Hattie Huffman.
227 iii. Arty G. Huffman.
228 iv. Jessie C. Huffman.
229 v. Lillian Huffman.
230 vi. Merrill Huffman.
231 vii. Tracy Huffman.

76. **David[4] Latimer** (13.Elizabeth P.[3] Arbogast, 3.Rev. Cornelius[2], 1.Peter[1]), b. Mar 01 1861, d. May 14 1944.
Married Mar 01 1861 in Ohio, **Edith L. Richards Huffman**, b. Sep 08 1870, d. Jul 22 1927.

Children:

232 i. M. Lester[5] Latimer b. Mar 18 1900, d. Nov 21 1961.
233 ii. Mary E. Latimer.
234 iii. Ethel G. Latimer.

77. **Adaline[4] Latimer** (13.Elizabeth P.[3] Arbogast, 3.Rev. Cornelius[2], 1.Peter[1]), b. Mar 01 1861, d. May 14 1944.
She Married **Nicholas G. Lauterbur**.

Children:

235 i. Clarence Orval[5] Lauterbur b. Oct 28 1888.
236 ii. Paul Lauterbur.
237 iii. Fred K. Lauterbur.
238 iv. Donna Lauterbur. She Married **Fred Brown**.

78. **Gertrude[4] Latimer** (13.Elizabeth P.[3] Arbogast, 3.Rev. Cornelius[2], 1.Peter[1]), b. Mar 15 1869, d. Mar 14 1939.
Married Dec 30 1888, **Stephen Ambrose Griffis**, b. Feb 03 1870, d. Feb 13 1949.

Children:

239 i. Emmitt E.[5] Griffis b. May 04 1889, d. May 11 1955. He Married **Margaret (Unknown),** b. 1898.
240 ii. Ralph Griffis.
241 iii. Carl Griffis.
242 iv. Cora Griffis.
243 v. Grace Griffis.
244 vi. Rowena Griffis.
245 vii. Leah Griffis.
246 viii. Evaline Griffis.

79. **Cornelius Arbogast[4] Guthrie** (14.Margaret May[3] Arbogast, 3.Rev. Cornelius[2], 1.Peter[1]), b. Nov 07 1846, buried in Graceland Cem., Sidney, Shelby Co., OH, d. Jul 25 1920 in Shelby Co., OH. Married Nov 07 1866 in Sidney, Shelby Co., OH, **Jane Elizabeth Young**, b. Apr 09 1948 in Shelby Co., OH (daughter of Samuel Young and Eliza Jane Johnson), buried in Graceland Cem., Sidney, Shelby Co., OH, d. Mar 27 1922 in Sidney, Shelby Co., OH.

***Children**:*

247 i. Albert Thomas[5] Guthrie b. Oct 02 1867 in Shelby Co., OH, buried in Plattsville, Shelby Co., OH, d. Aug 09 1878 in Shelby Co., OH.
248 ii. Samuel Cornelius Guthrie b. Aug 18 1869, d. May 27 1884.
249 iii. Lula Ada Guthrie b. Mar 13 1877 in Shelby Co., OH, buried in Plattsville, Shelby Co., OH, d. Jun 17 1877 in Shelby Co., OH.
\+ 250 iv. Brownie Frank Guthrie b. Jan 03 1883.
251 v. Fairy Mae Guthrie b. Jan 03 1883 in Christiansburg, Champaign Co., OH, d. Jan 20 1951 in Shelby Co., OH. Married Dec 27 1900 in Sidney, Shelby Co., OH, **Perry T. Develis**.

86. **Neal[4] Arbogast** (15.John H.[3], 3.Rev. Cornelius[2], 1.Peter[1]), b. About 1969 in Ohio.
He Married **Ella Briggs**.

***Children**:*

252 i. Lula Glendora[5] Arbogast b. Mar 15 1896 in Jackson Twp., Champaign Co., OH.

93. **Allen Johnson[4] Arbogast** (17.Allen[3], 3.Rev. Cornelius[2], 1.Peter[1]), b. About 1864, d. About 1923 in probably Preston Co., WV. Allen was an attorney in OH , later moved back to WV.
He Married **(unknown) Arbogast**.

***Children**:*

253 i. Hazel A.[5] Arbogast.
Married **Mr. Sarver**, living in Sidney, OH. Four children.
254 ii. Gladys A. Arbogast.
Married **Mr. Irvin**, one child, living in Kenore, OH
255 iii. Fred A. Arbogast.
Living in Aqueduct St., Akron, OH, two children.
256 iv. Doris Arbogast.
Teacher in Akron, OH; unmarried

95. **Etna A.[4] Arbogast** (17.Allen[3], 3.Rev. Cornelius[2], 1.Peter[1]), b. Jun 24 1867, d. Aug. 1937. She Married **Russell Pence**.

***Children**:*

257 i. Irma[5] Pence b. May 1888, d. Nov 1992.

101. **Roland[4] Arbogast** (17.Allen[3], 3.Rev. Cornelius[2], 1.Peter[1]), b. Jan 08 1882, d. About 1923. He Married **Georgie Rogers**, b. 1880.

***Children**:*

258 i. Roger[5] Arbogast b. Oct 02 1910, buried in Greenwood Cem., Clinton, DeWitt Co., IL, d. Jan 18 1911 in St. Louis, St. Louis Co., MO.
\+ 259 ii. Doris Arbogast b. May 18 1912.

102. **Thomas Joseph[4] Comer** (18.Ruth Darletta[3] Arbogast, 3.Rev. Cornelius[2], 1.Peter[1]), b. Feb 12 1857 in Champaign Co., OH, buried in Concord, Champaign Co., OH, d. Oct 06 1913 in Van Wert Co., OH.
(1) He Married **Sarah Catherine Zimmerman**, b. Mar 08 1868 in Concord, Champaign Co., OH (daughter of Isaac Zimmerman), d. Oct 04 1906 in Eris, Champaign Co., OH. (

***Children** by Sarah Catherine Zimmerman:*

\+ 260 i. Charles Wesley[5] Comer b. Oct 03 1885.
\+ 261 ii. Albert Lewis Comer b. About 1879.
262 iii. Elba Comer.

(2) He Married **Elizabeth Ann Greathouse**, b. May 08 1886 in Eris, Champaign Co., OH, buried in Concord, Champaign Co., OH, d. Jun 11 1978 in Russells Point, Logan Co., CO.

***Children** by Elizabeth Ann Greathouse:*

263 iv. Donald Comer b. Jun 17 1897 in Champaign Co., OH.

111. **Dorothy Jane[4] Neer** (22.Margaret Ann[3] Arbogast, 4.Otho[2], 1.Peter[1]), b. Apr 14 1851 in Pleasant Twp., Clark Co., OH, buried in Maple Grove Cem., Mechanicsburg, Champaign Co., OH, d. Jan 14 1924 in Mechanicsburg, Champaign Co., OH.
Married Sep 01 1869 in Clark Co., OH, **Elijah Lott Davisson**, b. Apr 12 1940 in Pleasant Twp., Clark Co., OH, buried in Maple Grove Cem., Mechanicsburg, Champaign Co., OH, d. Mar 29 1924 in Mechanicsburg, Champaign Co., OH.

Children:

+ 264 i. Charles Clifford[5] Davisson b. May 15 1871.
+ 265 ii. Clarence Weakley Davisson b. Aug 06 1878.
266 iii. Dr. Harry Lester Davisson b. Nov 29 1887, d. Feb 01 1944 in Yellow Springs, Greene Co., OH. (1) Married May 25 1935, Caroline **Lucille Scurry**, b. Mar 26 1907 in Columbus, Franklin Co., OH, buried in Maple Grove Cem., Mechanicsburg, Champaign Co., OH. (2) He Married **Lucille Wones**, d. Feb 01 1944 in Yellow Springs, Greene Co., OH.

112. **Bruce[4] Neer** (22.Margaret Ann[3] Arbogast, 4.Otho[2], 1.Peter[1]), b. Aug 30 1857 in Pleasant Twp., Clark Co., OH, buried in Maple Grove Cem., Mechanicsburg, Champaign Co., OH, d. Dec 16 1930.
Married Aug 31 1879 in Clark Co., OH, **Mary Elizabeth Wilkison**, b. Jan 12 1856, buried in Maple Grove Cem., Mechanicsburg, Champaign Co., OH, d. Dec 24 1929.

Children:

267 i. Esta B.[5] Neer b. Apr 05 1881, d. Feb 07 1971. Married Oct 10 1900 in Clark Co., OH, **Clarence West**, b. Jun 19 1877.
+ 268 ii. Cloice Edgar Neer b. Jun 13 1885.

113. **William Brown[4] Neer** (22.Margaret Ann[3] Arbogast, 4.Otho[2], 1.Peter[1]), b. Dec 21 1862, d. Aug 11 1946.
Married Oct 18 1888, **Anna May Kimble**, b. Sep 22 1868, buried at Maple Grove Cem., Mechanicsburg, Champaign Co., OH, d. Aug 11 1946 in Clark Co., OH.

Children:

269 i. Foster Madison[5] Neer b. Aug 11 1893, buried in Maple Grove Cem., Mechanicsburg, Champaign Co., OH, d. Feb 26 1973.
+ 270 ii. Florence Ruth Neer b. Aug 11 1893.
+ 271 iii. Milburn Theodore Neer b. Aug 01 1901.

114. **Grant[4] Neer** (22.Margaret Ann[3] Arbogast, 4.Otho[2], 1.Peter[1]), b. Dec 16 1984, d. Nov 09 1942 in Clark Co., OH.
Married Nov 10 1889 in Clark Co., OH, **Fannie Loveless**, b. Mar 09 1864, buried in Maple Grove Cem., Mechanicsburg, Champaign Co., OH, d. Dec 28 1956 in Mechanicsburg, Champaign Co., OH.

Children:

+ 272 i. Paul Joseph[5] Neer b. Sep 21 1893.

116. **Francis M.[4] Arbogast** (23.Jackson[3], 4.Otho[2], 1.Peter[1]), b. About 1859.
He Married **Sarah Ellen Smirh**.

Children:

273 i. Weldon[5] Arbogast.
+ 274 ii. Margaret J Arbogast.

117. **Lovetta[4] Arbogast** (23.Jackson[3], 4.Otho[2], 1.Peter[1]), b. c1862.
She Married **(unknown) Glenn**.

Children:

275 i. Archie[5] Glenn.
276 ii. Walter Glenn.
277 iii. Frank Glenn.

118. **Laura A.[4] Arbogast** (24.Eli M.[3], 4.Otho[2], 1.Peter[1]), b. Sep 05 1856.
Married Apr 04 1877, **Oscar Taylor**.

Children:

278 i. Marion[5] Taylor.
279 ii. Anna Taylor.

119. **Marion W.[4] Arbogast** (24.Eli M.[3], 4.Otho[2], 1.Peter[1]), b. Nov 15 1859, buried in Maple Grove Cem., Mechanicsburg, Champaign Co., OH, d. Jun 05 1951.

He Married **Minnie Belle Morris**, b. About 1970, buried in Maple Grove Cem., Mechanicsburg, Champaign Co., OH, d. Jun 02 1954.

Children:

+ 280 i. Morris Emerson[5] Arbogast b. Jul 31 1890.
  281 ii. Bertha Arbogast b. May 15 1893 in Pleasant Twp., Clark Co., OH.
+ 282 iii. Ruby Arbogast.
  283 iv. Ora Arbogast b. Jan 31 1897 in Pleasant Twp., Clark Co., OH.
  284 v. James Donel Arbogast b. Aug 10 1906 in Springfield, Clark Co., OH.
  285 vi. Elizabeth Arbogast b. Jul 24 1911 in Springfield, Clark Co., OH, buried in Maple Grove Cem., Mechanicsburg, Champaign Co., OH, d. Jun 12 1994 in Springfield, Clark Co., OH.

120. **Minor W.[4] Hardman** (28.William H.[3], 5.Mary[2] Arbogast, 1.Peter[1]), b. 1860 in 1938, buried in Asbury Cem., Clark Co., OH, d. 1927.
Married 1886, **Hattie Runyan**, b. May 29 1863, d. 1938 in Asbury Cem., Clark Co., OH.

Children:

  286 i. Omer[5] Hardman b. Nov 19 1882.
+ 287 ii. Anna Hardman b. Dec 1893.

121. **Belle[4] Hardman** (28.William H.[3], 5.Mary[2] Arbogast, 1.Peter[1]), b. Aug 08 1867.
She Married **Harry Milton Stipp**.

Children:

  288 i. Essie Carherine[5] Stipp b. Jan 03 1991.

122. **Eddie[4] Hardman** (28.William H.[3], 5.Mary[2] Arbogast, 1.Peter[1]), b. May 25 1877.
Married Nov 28 1906, **Effie Marsh**.

Children:

  289 i. William Marsh[5] Hartman b. May 10 1908.

123. **Ella[4] Hardman** (28.William H.[3], 5.Mary[2] Arbogast, 1.Peter[1]), b. May 25 1877.
Married Apr 07 1898, **P.m. Wilson**.

Children:

  290 i. William W.[5] Wilson b. Oct 12 1900.
  291 ii. Paul W. Wilson b. Dec 31 1902.
  292 iii. Orrin H. Wilson b. Aug 12 1905.

132. **Shelby[4] Sellers** (35.Isabella Jane[3] Curl, 6.Margaret[2] Arbogast, 1.Peter[1]), b. Sep 21 1852 in Cardington Twp., Morrow Co., OH, d. Jan 26 1911 in Cardington Twp., Morrow Co., OH. Married 3 Apr 1879 in Marion Co., OH, **Zenetta Nettie Barry**, b. Dec 1879 in Marion Co., OH, d. After 1911.

Children:

+ 293 i. Neva D.[5] Sellers b. Mar1881.
+ 294 ii. Samuel Arthur Sellers b. Nov 1883.
+ 295 iii. Elmer Hayse Sellers b. Sep 1886.
+ 296 iv. Lefa Mae Sellers b. May 1890.
  297 v. Clarence Sellers b. Apr 1988 in Cardington Twp., Morrow Co., OH.

133. **Lucinda[4] Sellers** (35.Isabella Jane[3] Curl, 6.Margaret[2] Arbogast, 1.Peter[1]), b. Nov 18 1854, d. Feb 21 1887 in Glendale, Cardington Twp., Morrow Co., OH.
She Married **Thomas C. Underhill**, b. About 1850 in Liberty, Union Co., OH (son of John Underhill).

Children:

+ 298 i. Charles Ross[5] Underhill b. 6 Dec 1875.
+ 299 ii. John Underhill.

135. **Wilie[4] Sellers** (35.Isabella Jane[3] Curl, 6.Margaret[2] Arbogast, 1.Peter[1]).
He Married **Weltha Rosella Schofield**, b. Jan 1882 in Cardington Twp., Morrow Co., OH.

Children:

+ 300 i. Bernice M.[5] Underhill b. 2 Jul 1884.

301 ii. Orlando Foid Underhill b. 31 Jul 1886 in Cardington Twp., Morrow Co., OH, d. Jun in Cardington Twp., Morrow Co., OH. Married About 1909, **Navada Dell Irwin**, b. 9 Dec 1889 in Cardington Twp., Morrow Co., OH (daughter of Frederick Irwin and Anna Wetherby).

136. **Amanda[4] Sellers** (35.Isabella Jane[3] Curl, 6.Margaret[2] Arbogast, 1.Peter[1]), b. About 1859 in Cardington Twp., Morrow Co., OH.
She Married **Thomas C. Underhill**, b. About 1850 in Liberty, Union Co., OH (son of John Underhill).

Children:

302 i. Ida Mae[5] Underhill b. About 1882 in Liberty, Union Co., OH, d. 8 Oct 1980 in Marysville, Union Co., OH.

138. **Johnson Leamon[4] Sellers** (35.Isabella Jane[3] Curl, 6.Margaret[2] Arbogast, 1.Peter[1]), b. Feb 1870 in Cardington Twp., Morrow Co., OH.
Married in Marion Co., OH, **Anne C. Key**, b. Apr 1873 in Cardington Twp., Morrow Co., OH.

Children:

303 i. Wesley T.[5] Sellars b. 26 Apr 1896 in Cardington Twp., Morrow Co., OH, d. Jan 1979 in Cardington Twp., Morrow Co., OH.
304 ii. Verna Inez Sellars b. Nov 1898 in Morrow Co., OH.
\+ 305 iii. Alta F. Sellars b. About 1903.

139. **Ross[4] Sellers** (35.Isabella Jane[3] Curl, 6.Margaret[2] Arbogast, 1.Peter[1]), b. Feb 24 1868 in Cardington Twp., Morrow Co., OH, buried in Glendale, Cardington Twp., Morrow Co., OH, d. Mar 18 1885 in Phoenix, Jackson Co., AZ.

Children:

\+ 306 i. Ross Randolph[5] Sellars b. 1 Mar 1898.
307 ii. Alice C. Sellars b. About 1906 in Phoenix, Maricopa Co., AZ.

140. **Lovina[4] Sellers** (35.Isabella Jane[3] Curl, 6.Margaret[2] Arbogast, 1.Peter[1]), b. About 1861 in Cardington Twp., Morrow Co., OH.
She Married **Samuel H. Paste**, b. 2 Jul 1858 in Cardington Twp., Morrow Co., OH, buried in Glendale Cem., Hamilton Co., OH, d. Aug 1936 in Cardington Twp., Morrow Co., OH.

Children:

\+ 308 i. M. Guy[5] Paste b. About 1892.

141. **Elza S.[4] Curl** (36.Henry William[3], 6.Margaret[2] Arbogast, 1.Peter[1]), b. Aug 22 1861 in Richland Twp., Marion Co., OH, buried in Glendale, Cardington Twp., Morrow Co., OH, d. May 28 1934 in Newark, Licking Co., OH.
He Married **Eliza S. Rose**, b. Mar 27 1858 in Lincoln Twp., Marion Co., OH, buried in Glendale, Cardington Twp., Morrow Co., OH, d. Dec 13 1927 in Newark, Licking Co., OH.

Children:

\+ 309 i. Lena Rose[5] Curl b. Mar 27 1978.

142. **Franklin M.[4] Curl** (36.Henry William[3], 6.Margaret[2] Arbogast, 1.Peter[1]), b. Aug 16 1853 in Richland Twp., Marion Co., OH, buried in Glendale, Cardington Twp., Morrow Co., OH, d. Nov 14 1932 in Cardington Twp., Morrow Co., OH.
Married Mar 07 1876 in Marrow Co., OH, **Ermina M. Bay**, b. Oct 09 1957 in Canaan Twp. Morrow Co., OH (daughter of Harrison Bay and Miranda J. Moore), buried in Glendale, Cardington Twp., Morrow Co., OH, d. Oct 25 1932 in Cardington Twp., Morrow Co., OH.

Children:

\+ 310 i. Alma Blanch[5] Curl b. Nov 12 1879.
\+ 311 ii. Henry Harrison Curl b. Dec 16 1891.

143. **Cora A.[4] Curl** (36.Henry William[3], 6.Margaret[2] Arbogast, 1.Peter[1]), b. Mar 17 1857 in Richland Twp., Marion Co., OH, d. Oct 04 1908.
Married Oct 13 1878, **George W. Jenkins**, b. Mar 16 1857 (son of Craven W. Jenkins and Hamutal Jackson), d. Aug 23 1933.

Children:

312 i. Lottie I.[5] Jenkins b. Sep 24 1881 in Cardington Twp., Morrow Co., OH, d. Feb 25 1959 in Morrow Co., OH. Married Sep 28 1904, **Arle Maxwell**, b. Dec 26 1876 in Cardington Twp., Morrow Co., OH (son of Robert R. Maxwell), d. Jul 01 1949 in Columbus, Franklin Co., OH.
313 ii. Iva Jenkins.

144. **Haze D.[4] Curl** (36.Henry William[3], 6.Margaret[2] Arbogast, 1.Peter[1]), b. Jan 22 1860, buried in Glendale, Cardington Twp., Morrow Co., OH, d. Jul 30 1923.
Married Apr 26 1900 in Cardington Twp., Morrow Co., OH, **Marie Mills**, b. Oct 14 1878 in Morrow Co., OH, buried in Glendale, Cardington Twp., Morrow Co., OH, d. Jan 01 1972.

***Children**:*

314 i. Elizabeth[5] Curl b. Dec 03 1901 in Cardington Twp., Morrow Co., OH, buried in Glendale, Cardington Twp., Morrow Co., OH, d. Feb 20 1940 in Cardington Twp., Morrow Co., OH.

145. **Ida M.[4] Curl** (36.Henry William[3], 6.Margaret[2] Arbogast, 1.Peter[1]), b. Oct 03 1967 in Cardington Twp., Morrow Co., OH, d. Sep 03 1922.
(1) Married Jun 23 1987, **Frank Sage**, b. Oct 22 1863, d. Jan 22 1908.

***Children** by Frank Sage:*

\+ 315 i. Bessie[5] Sage b. Mar 18 1888.
\+ 316 ii. Victor Sage b. Oct 13 1880.

(2) She Married **Walter Reed**, b. Sep 12 1855, d. Jan 18 1938.

147. **Ada Blanche[4] Curl** (36.Henry William[3], 6.Margaret[2] Arbogast, 1.Peter[1]), b. Jan 17 1971 in Cardington Twp., Morrow Co., OH, d. Nov 25 1954 in Chicago, Cook Co., IL.
Married 009261895, **George C. Miller**, b. Feb 14 1867, d. May 23 1939.

***Children**:*

\+ 317 i. Corinne[5] Miller b. Jan 11 1897.
\+ 318 ii. Robert H. Miller b. Aug 05 1901.

148. **Mary Jane[4] Shaw** (37.Emily[3] Curl, 6.Margaret[2] Arbogast, 1.Peter[1]), b. 1849.
Married Jan 01 1871 in Marrow Co., OH, **Robert A. Beatty**, b. Sep 24 1847 in Ohio, d. Dec 03 1926.

***Children**:*

319 i. Robert J.[5] Beatty b. Mar 13 1879.
320 ii. Samuel Ray Beatty b. Jul 01 1884. He Married **Georgia Miller**.
321 iii. Clifford Guy Beatty b. Mar 13 1886. He Married **Edna Grpscroft**.

149. **Minerva[4] Shaw** (37.Emily[3] Curl, 6.Margaret[2] Arbogast, 1.Peter[1]), b. Apr 02 1851 in Marion, Marion Co., OH.
Married Apr 02 1851 in Marion, Marion Co., OH, **Levi P. Dixon**, b. Sep 25 1843, d. Jan 08 1842.

***Children**:*

322 i. Oscar A.[5] Dixon b. Oct 02 1873, d. Sep 11 1894.
323 ii. Archibald Dixon b. Jul 31 1878, d. Sep 14 1878.
324 iii. John Smith Dixon b. May 08 1880, d. May -6 1956. He Married **Ola Ocker**.

150. **George Asa[4] Messenger** (37.Emily[3] Curl, 6.Margaret[2] Arbogast, 1.Peter[1]), b. 16 Nov 1866 in Westfield Twp., Marrow Co., OH, d. 16 Dec 1945 in Cardington Twp., Morrow Co., OH. Married 25 Dec 1890, **Addie May Schofield**, b. 1 May 1873 in Westfield Twp., Marrow Co., OH (daughter of Alpheus Schofield Jr. and Christiana Ann Kratt), buried in Glendale Cem., Hamilton Co., OH, d. 27 Mar 1938 in Cardington Twp., Morrow Co., OH.

***Children**:*

325 i. Eilene Isabel[5] Messenger b. in Cardington Twp., Morrow Co., OH. She Married **Hayes Delmore Ulrey**, b. Aug 1905 in Cardington Twp., Morrow Co., OH (son of Thomas Delmore Ulrey and Rosa E. Hayes), d. May 1980 in Cardington Twp., Morrow Co., OH.
\+ 326 ii. Cloise Hayes Messenger.

152. **Perry N.[4] Curl** (38.William Hayse[3], 6.Margaret[2] Arbogast, 1.Peter[1]), b. Jan 30 1855 in Cardington Twp., Morrow Co., OH, d. Mar 09 1864.
Married Jan 30 1855 in Cardington Twp., Morrow Co., OH, **Mollie A. McKibbin**, b. About 1853 in New Albany, Floyd Co., IN, d. Mar 27 1878 in Morrow Co., OH.

***Children**:*

327 i. Walter[5] Curl b. About 1881 in New Albany, Floyd Co., IN.
328 ii. Elma Curl b. About1890 in New Albany, Floyd Co., IN.
329 iii. Mayme Curl b. About 1890 in New Albany, Floyd Co., IN.

154. **Lemuel Otho⁴ Curl** (38.William Hayse³, 6.Margaret² Arbogast, 1.Peter¹), b. May 10 1958, buried in Glendale, Cardington Twp., Morrow Co., OH, d. Oct 14 1938 in Morrow Co., OH. Married Jul 31 1880 in Cardington Twp., Morrow Co., OH, **Eva L. Beatty**, b. 25 May 1861 in Cardington Twp., Morrow Co., OH (daughter of Samuel Beatty and Sarah Nichols), buried in Glendale, Cardington Twp., Morrow Co., OH, d. After 1950 in Cardington Twp., Morrow Co., OH.

***Children**:*

330 i. Arthur⁵ Curl b. About 1884 in Cardington Twp., Morrow Co., OH, buried in Glendale, Cardington Twp., Morrow Co., OH, d. About 1897.

331 ii. Sadie May Curl b. Jan 26 1883 in Cardington Twp., Morrow Co., OH. Married Jan 15 1902 in Cardington Twp., Morrow Co., OH, **Edson Aaron Rinehart**, b. Oct 13 1878 in Lincoln Twp., Marion Co., OH.

157. **Margaret Ova⁴ Curl** (38.William Hayse³, 6.Margaret² Arbogast, 1.Peter¹), b. Mar 25 1873 in Cardington Twp., Morrow Co., OH, d. Jun 17 1954 in Cleveland, Cuyahoga Co., OH. (1) Married Mar 25 1891 in Morrow Co., OH, **Charles W. Meyers**, d. 1895.

***Children** by Charles W. Meyers:*

332 i. Gilbert H.⁵ Myers b. 1895.

(2) She Married **Andrew L. Caton**.

160. **Stella Flossie⁴ Curl** (38.William Hayse³, 6.Margaret² Arbogast, 1.Peter¹), b. Mar 21 1885 in Cardington Twp., Morrow Co., OH, buried in Glendale Cem., Hamilton Co., OH, d. 02011910 in Mt. Gilead, Morrow Co., OH.
(1) Married Feb 01 1910 in Ohio, **Hartley Kirkpatrick**, b. Feb 01 1910.

***Children** by Hartley Kirkpatrick:*

333 i. Ruth⁵ Kirkpatrick. She Married **Corless Custer**.

334 ii. Doris Kirkpatrick. She Married **Clinton Beckley**.

(2) Married Jan 18 1953, **Howard Kunze**, d. 19 Mar 1970.

164. **Elza Freeman⁴ Coverstone** (43.Margaret Jane³ Wilkinson, 7.Susannah² Arbogast, 1.Peter¹), b. c1864 in Adams Twp., Champaign Co., OH.
He Married **Maria Wyatt**.

***Children**:*

335 i. Merl⁵ Coverstone.

336 ii. Chase Coverstone b. Sep 27 1882 in Shelby Co., OH. He Married **Elizabeth Frieschuler**.

337 iii. Oscar A Coverstone b. Apr 28 1887 in Shelby Co., OH, d. Jan 20 1958.

338 iv. Elza Coverstone b. Oct 25 1889, d. Sep 1964 in Ohio.

165. **Cora Melissa⁴ Coverstone** (43.Margaret Jane³ Wilkinson, 7.Susannah² Arbogast, 1.Peter¹), b. Aug 27 1865 in Adams Twp., Champaign Co., OH, d. Feb 01 1949 in Adams Twp., Champaign Co., OH.
Married Aug 11 1888, **Henry McKee**, b. May 06 1862 in Quincy, Champaign Co., OH, d. Dec 21 1945 in Lakeview, Logan Co., OH.

***Children**:*

339 i. Edgar Lloyd⁵ McKee.

340 ii. Ray McKee.

168. **George Washington⁴ Wilkinson** (44.John G.³, 7.Susannah² Arbogast, 1.Peter¹), b. Mar 15 1859 in Logan Co., OH, d. Jun 24 1939 in Willow, Wood Co., OH.
Married Nov 11 1885 in Wood Co., OH, **Ella Mayfield Thomas**, b. Apr 21 1868 in Brooklyn, Hennepin Co., MN (daughter of Alvah Curtis Thomas and Esther Elizabeth Manley), d. Jun 15 1940 in Wood Co., OH.

***Children**:*

\+ 341 i. Clair Whitman⁵ Wilkinson b. About 1887.

\+ 342 ii. Gerald Thomas Wilkinson b. Nov 14 1889.

343 iii. George Victor Wilkinson b. Aug 1900 in North Baltimore, Wood Co., OH, d. Sep 06 1902 in North Baltimore, Wood Co., OH.

344 iv. Marcus Alvah Wilkinson b. Oct 30 1903 in North Baltimore, Wood Co., OH, d. Aug 05 1995 in Las Vegas, Clark Co., NV. Married Jun 13 1934 in Pueblo, Pueblo Co., CO, **Theresa Kleomenis**, b. Dec 24 1912 in Pike View, Las Animas Co., CO (daughter of Efstratios Kleomenis and Irma Papp), d. Nov 21 2002 in Mesa, Maricopa Co., AZ. Theresa:

345 v. Elinor Elizabeth Wilkinson b. Aug 11 1905 in North Baltimore, Wood Co., OH, d. 1968. She Married **C.A. Beattie**.

346 vi. Robert Francis Wilkinson b. Oct 14 1907 in North Baltimore, Wood Co., OH, d. 1943. He Married **Audrey Blossom**.

347 vii. George Wayne Wilkinson b. May 10 1913 in North Baltimore, Wood Co., OH, d. Jan 19 1945. He Married **Gerelene Dick**.

169. **John Nelson[4] Wilkinson** (44.John G.[3], 7.Susannah[2] Arbogast, 1.Peter[1]), b. Mar 15 1859 in Logan Co., OH, d. About 1940 in Kenton, Harlan Co., OH.
He Married **Olive Lillian Wright.**, d. Jan 02 1918.

Children:

\+ 348 i. Geraldine[5] Wilkinson b. Nov 14 1889.
349 ii. Charles T Wilkinson d. About 1982 in Detroit, Wayne Co., MI.
350 iii. Charlotte Wilkinson d. About 1995 in Athens, Athens Co., OH.

176. **Creston Willard[4] Arbogast** (52.Milton A.[3], 8.Henry[2], 1.Peter[1]), b. 1878, d. 1969.
He Married **Edna Viola Harmison**, b. 1881, d. 1948.

Children:

351 i. Doris May[5] Arbogast b. 1905, d. 1987.
352 ii. Howard E. Arbogast b. 1907, d. 1926.
353 iii. Medelon Arbogast b. 1909, d. 1970.

178. **Ethel Kilbourne[4] Arbogast** (54.Albert[3], 8.Henry[2], 1.Peter[1]), b. Dec 18 1881 in London, Madison Co., OH.
Married May 27 1911 in Catlettsburg, Boyd Co., KY, **John Cleveland St. Clair**, b. Dec 29 1884 in Ansted, Fayette Co., WV, buried in Birchlawn Cem., Pearisburg, Giles Co., VA, d. Jul 17 1925.

Children:

\+ 354 i. Lilian Cary[5] St. Clair b. Feb 26 1912.
355 ii. John Craig St. Clair b. Mar 10 1915 in Charleston, Charleston Co., SC.
356 iii. Virginia Anne St. Clair b. Jul 02 1916 in London, Madison Co., OH.

185. **Nellie[4] Bumgardner** (56.Mahala[3] Clymer, 10.Malinda "Linnie"[2] Arbogast, 1.Peter[1]), b. Jan 31 1882, d. Aug 19 1936.
Married Dec 31 1902, **Howard Ritchie**, b. Jan 16 1882, d. Aug 19 1936.

Children:

357 i. Gwyneth[5] Ritchie b. Dec 10 1902, buried in Asbury Cem., Clark Co., OH, d. 1987. Married Aug 23 1927, Millard Allender, b. Aug 02 1905.

186. **Sophia[4] Arbogast** (64.Jesse[3], 11.Peter[2], 1.Peter[1]), b. Jul 18 1838 in Seneca Co., OH, d. Apr 30 1912 in Good Hope, Walnut Grove, Putnam Co., IL.
Married Aug 18 1858 in Rock Island, Rock Island Co., IL, **Josiah W Morrison**, b. 1836 in Pennsylvania, d. in McDonough Co., IL.

Children:

358 i. Catherine[5] Morrison b. 1853 in Good Hope, Walnut Grove, Putnam Co., IL.
\+ 359 ii. Mary Morrison b. Aug 01 1859.
360 iii. Warren Morrison b. 1862 in Good Hope, Walnut Grove, Putnam Co., IL.
361 iv. Margaret Morrison b. 1865 in Good Hope, Walnut Grove, Putnam Co., IL.
362 v. Charlotte Morrison b. 1867 in Good Hope, Walnut Grove, Putnam Co., IL.
\+ 363 vi. Rose Morrison b. Oct 18 1869.
364 vii. Rhoda Morrison b. Oct 10 1872 in Good Hope, Walnut Grove, Putnam Co., IL, d. May 19 1942. She Married **Elmer Ellaberry**.
\+ 365 viii. Ida Morrison b. 1875.

188. **Louis Peter[4] Arbogast** (64.Jesse[3], 11.Peter[2], 1.Peter[1]), b. Jan 01 1844 in Wabash Co., IN, d. Jul 13 1911 in Salem Twp., Knox Co., IL.
Married Feb 18 1875 in Galesburg, Knox Co., IL, **Easter E Potter**, b. in Salem Twp., Knox Co., IL.

Children:

366 i. Norman P[5] Arbogast b. Jun 18 1882 in Salem Twp., Knox Co., IL.

189. **Mary Jane^4 Arbogast** (64.Jesse^3, 11.Peter^2, 1.Peter^1), b. Jan 15 1845 in Wabash Co., IL, d. Nov 28 1927 in McComb, McDonough Co., IL.
Married Mar 03 1872 at St. Clair Co., IL, **Andrew Taylor Brown**, b. Aug 23 1843 in Caress, Braxton Co., VA, d. Sep 09 1891 in McComb, McDonough Co., IL.

Children:

- \+ 367 i. Amy^5 Brown b. Feb 06 1873.
- 368 ii. Carl Ivan Brown b. Jul 20 1874 in McComb, McDonough Co., IL, d. Jul 20 1916.
- \+ 369 iii. Ethel Clare Brown b. Sep 03 1875.
- 370 iv. Edith Nora Brown b. Nov 10 1876 in McComb, McDonough Co., IL, d. Jan 04 1962.
- \+ 371 v. Lois Irene Brown b. Feb 11 1880.
- 372 vi. Beatrice Brown b. Mar 17 1882 in McComb, McDonough Co., IL, d. Jan 05 1965. Married in Divorced, **Cliff Anderson**.
- \+ 373 vii. Mertice Loine Brown b. Oct 29 1886.
- 374 viii. Berdie Brown b. Aug 22 1889 in McComb, McDonough Co., IL, d. Feb 02 1980. Married in Divorced, **Alfred Homer**.

190. **Henry S.^{4} Arbogast** (64.Jesse^3, 11.Peter^2, 1.Peter^1), b. Mar 18 1847 in Wabash Co., IL, d. in Idaho. C Co., 151st IL during Civil War
Married Jan 01 1871 in Warren Co., IL, **Marietta Warden**, b. 1853 in Swan Lake, Warren Co., IL.

Children:

- 375 i. Marion S.^{5} Arbogast b. About 1877.
- 376 ii. Ira E. Arbogast b. About 1879.
- 377 iii. Donald E. Arbogast.

192. **Sarah^4 Arbogast** (64.Jesse^3, 11.Peter^2, 1.Peter^1), b. Apr 23 1851 in Wabash Co., IL, d. May 27 1927 in Scioto Twp., McDonough Co., IL.
Married Jul 30 1873, **Green Berry Howard**, b. Sep 15 1848 in Tompkinsville, Monroe Co., KY, d. May 30 1925 in Scioto Twp., McDonough Co., IL, buried in Macomb, McDonough Co., IL.

Children:

- 378 i. Hubert^5 Howard b. 1870. Married Oct 07 1891 in McComb, McDonough Co., IL, **Mary Cambell**, b. 1870.
- \+ 379 ii. Mae Howard b. May 01 1874.

193. **Cynthia^4 Arbogast** (64.Jesse^3, 11.Peter^2, 1.Peter^1), b. About 1853 in Terra Haute, Vigo Co., IN.
Married Oct 26 1887 in McDonough Co., IL, **Hugh Gilworth**, b. Apr 03 1857 in McComb, McDonough Co., IL, d. Aug 1946 in Duncan, Stephens Co., OK.

Children:

- 380 i. Edna M.^{5} Gilworth b. Apr 19 1891 in McComb, McDonough Co., IL, d. Apr 12 1955 in Duncan, Stephens Co., OK. She Married **Van Gaston Denman**, b. 1887, d. Jul 15 1946.
- 381 ii. Joseph Victory Gilworth b. Oct 14 1893 in Linn Co., MO, d. Nov 23 1918 in Camp Cody, Deming, Luna Co., NM.

194. **Frances^4 Arbogast** (64.Jesse^3, 11.Peter^2, 1.Peter^1), b. Jul 20 1856 in Walnut Grove Twp., Knox Co., IL, d. Jun 12 1909 in Walnut Grove Twp., Knox Co., IL.
She Married **Franklin King Smith**, b. 1853.

Children:

- \+ 382 i. Neil^5 Smith b. Dec 08 1877.
- \+ 383 ii. Emerson Eugene Smith.
- 384 iii. Charles Smith b. 1881 in Good Hope, Walnut Grove, Putnam Co., IL, d. 1936.
- \+ 385 iv. Jessie Smith.
- 386 v. Jesse N. Smith b. 1885 in Good Hope, Walnut Grove, Putnam Co., IL, d. 1956. He Married **Tessie N. Smith**.
- \+ 387 vi. June Smith b. Jun 1887.
- \+ 388 vii. Myrtle Smith b. Dec 17 1896.

195. **Stephen Aaron Douglas^4 Arbogast** (64.Jesse^3, 11.Peter^2, 1.Peter^1), b. Jun 18 1859 in Walnut Grove Twp., Knox Co., IL, d. Mar 21 1930 in Silver Creek, Merrick Co., NE.
Married Apr 04 1888, **Cora Maud Dille**, b. Jun 27 1872 in Lagrange Co., IN, d. Mar 21 1930 in Silver Creek, Merrick Co., NE.

Children:

+ 389 i. Clyde Stewart[5] Arbogast b. Feb 03 1891.
390 ii. George Dille Arbogast b. Apr 18 1894 in Rising City, Butler Co., NE, d. Apr 28 1950.
+ 391 iii. Nellie Millicent Arbogast b. Sep 22 1898.
+ 392 iv. Gladys Mary Arbogast b. May 18 1901.
+ 393 v. Harold Edson Arbogast b. Nov 30 1912.

198. **Alice M.[4] Arbogast** (67.Michael[3], 11.Peter[2], 1.Peter[1]), b. Nov 30 1853, d. Dec 11 1918. She Married **Jacob Staib**. .

Children:

394 i. Alverta[5] STAIB. She Married **Thomas Barclay**.
395 ii. Victor J. Staib. He Married **Mabel Gibbs**. .
+ 396 iii. Lorenzo Staib b. Feb 08 1892.
+ 397 iv. Nettie Staib.

199. **John Franklin[4] Arbogast** (67.Michael[3], 11.Peter[2], 1.Peter[1]), b. Oct 18 1855 in Seneca Co., OH, d. 1949 in Seneca Co., OH. He Married **Henrietta Calra Hiser**, b. 1861 in Seneca Co., OH, d. 1955 in Seneca Co., OH, buried in Tiffin, Seneca Co., OH. .

Children:

+ 398 i. Jessie L.[5] Arbogast b. Aug 20 1880.
399 ii. Franklin Seymore Arbogast b. 1883. He Married **Mary Weller**, b. 1889. .
400 iii. Ward Arbogast.

200. **Lewis Heenan[4] Arbogast** (67.Michael[3], 11.Peter[2], 1.Peter[1]), b. 1862, d. 1944 in Seneca Co., OH. He Married **Flora Caroline Sohn**, b. Jul 25 1864.

Children:

401 i. Hazel[5] Arbogast b. Apr 01 1888, d. c 1981. She Married **Robert Haskins**. .
402 ii. Russel Arbogast b. May 14 1892, d. Apr 29 1957. He Married **Jane Vanderstoop**. .
+ 403 iii. James Warren Arbogast b. Dec 29 1896.
404 iv. Herbert Arbogast. He Married **Garnet Warren**. .

201. **Annetta A.[4] Arbogast** (67.Michael[3], 11.Peter[2], 1.Peter[1]).
She Married **Robert Lutz**. .

Children:

405 i. Floyd[5] LUTZ.
406 ii. Hazel Lutz.
407 iii. Fern Lutz. She Married **Robert Brown**. .
408 iv. Ernest Lutz.
409 v. Ivy Lutz.
410 vi. Stanley Lutz.

202. **Charles Sayers[4] Arbogast** (67.Michael[3], 11.Peter[2], 1.Peter[1]), b. Oct 13 1864 in Seneca Co., OH, d. Oct 18 1931 in Calgary, Alberta.
He Married **Eva Maud Hudson**, b. Nov 01 1866 in Yates City, Knox Co., IL, d. Apr 20 1939 in Calgary, Alberta. .

Children:

+ 411 i. James Michael[5] Arbogast b. Dec 16 1887.
+ 412 ii. Alice Arbogast.
413 iii. Louise Arbogast. She Married **Percy McCarthy**. .
414 iv. Olind Ray Arbogast b. 1891, d. 1905.

203. **Rush Arlington[4] Arbogast** (67.Michael[3], 11.Peter[2], 1.Peter[1]), b. Aug 15 1867 in Seneca Co., OH, d. Apr 08 1965.
He Married **Clara Kingseed**. Rush Arbogast was born in a log cabin to Michael and Jane (Stoner) Arbogast. The log cabin was located where now, in 1986, are the grain handling facilities for Kingland Farms. He was their sixth child, having three older brothers and two sisters, plus three younger brothers who died in childhood. In 1875, when he was eight years old the family moved into their new large brick home which had been built several hundred feet northeast of the cabin. His mother passed away in June 1882. He resided with his father and in January 1892 he Married **Clara Kingseed** and they started housekeeping with his father. Rush and Clara were the parents of three children: Frances, who later Married **Louis Smith** and had 11 children; Charles, who Married Loretta Reinhart and had 11 children, one who died at birth; and Clarence, who Married **Aleta Talley** and had one son and one daughter. His father passed away in 1902. He continued to reside there and his wife passed away in 1938. About 1942 his son Clarence, with his wife Aleta and their two children, James and Naomi,

moved in to take over farming the 127-acre farm. His son Clarence passed away in January 1944. A short while later his daughter-in-law and her two children moved out leaving him to reside alone until his death in April 1965.

Children:

+ 415 i. Clarence James[5] Arbogast b. Jun-08-1904.
+ 416 ii. Charles Anthony Arbogast b. Sep-11-1900.
+ 417 iii. Frances Marie Arbogast b. Dec 28 1892.

Generation Five

207. **Sylvia[5] Smith** (68.Amos[4], 12.Eli[3], 2.Priscilla[2] Arbogast, 1.Peter[1]), b. Nov 24 1875, d. After 1908.
She Married **Noah Jones**.

Children:

418 i. Gladys[6] Jones b. Before 1908.

208. **Leona[5] Smith** (68.Amos[4], 12.Eli[3], 2.Priscilla[2] Arbogast, 1.Peter[1]), b. May 27 1883, d. After 1908.
Married 1899, **Charles Patterson**.

Children:

419 i. Robert[6] Patterson b. Before 1908.

209. **Nina[5] Smith** (68.Amos[4], 12.Eli[3], 2.Priscilla[2] Arbogast, 1.Peter[1]), b. May 27 1883, d. After 1908.
She Married **Dr. E. Dye**.

Children:

420 i. Max[6] Dye.
421 ii. Mildred Dye.

220. **Cornelius Eugene[5] Crissman** (73.Melissa[4] Latimer, 13.Elizabeth P.[3] Arbogast, 3.Rev. Cornelius[2], 1.Peter[1]), b. Oct 06 1878 in Turtle Creek Twp., Shelby Co., OH, d. Feb 10 1955 in Quincy Twp., Branch Co., MI.
Married Sep 06 1902, **Lilah Iva Gearhart**, b. Dec 21 1882 in Tipton, Mercer Co., OH, d. Apr 12 1968.

Children:

+ 422 i. Clara Loveda[6] Crissman b. Aug 22 1903.
423 ii. Vera Pauline Crissman b. Feb 08 1905.
+ 424 iii. John Dale Crissman b. May 01 1907.
+ 425 iv. Donald Leroy Crissman b. Nov 03 1908.
+ 426 v. Wanda Ruth Crissman b. Jul 09 1913.

222. **Ernest Raymond[5] Crissman** (73.Melissa[4] Latimer, 13.Elizabeth P.[3] Arbogast, 3.Rev. Cornelius[2], 1.Peter[1]), b. Mar 12 1889 in Latty, Paulding Co., OH, buried in Cornell Cem., Wexford Co., MI, d. 091411946 in Mesick, Wexford Co., MI.
Married Oct 12 1908 in Latty, Paulding Co., OH, **Bessie Mable Elliott**, b. Sep 14 1890 in Chictopia Twp., DeWitt Co., IL (daughter of Joseph Purley Elliott and Rose Ann Russell), buried in Cornell Cem., Wexford Co., MI, d. Jan 06 1984 in Traverse City, Grand Traverse Co., MI.

Children:

427 i. Harry Orval[6] Crissman b. Jul 23 1909 in Latty, Paulding Co., OH, d. Oct 23 1909.
+ 428 ii. Ellis Walter Crissman b. Jul 23 1910.
+ 429 iii. Hazel Melissa Crissman b. Dec 17 1912.
+ 430 iv. Clarence Eugene Crissman b. Jun 02 1915.
+ 431 v. Clyde Clifford Crissman b. Nov 10 1917.

250. **Brownie Frank[5] Guthrie** (79.Cornelius Arbogast[4], 14.Margaret May[3] Arbogast, 3.Rev. Cornelius[2], 1.Peter[1]), b. Jan 03 1883 in Shelby Co., OH, d. Jan 05 1954 in Eugene, Lane Co., OR.
Married Nov 09 1909, **Mary Gertrude Koverman**, b. Apr 21 1887 in Swanders, Shelby Co., OH (daughter of Henry Koverman and Mary Carolina Jacobs), buried in Mt. Calvary Cem., Eugene, Lane Co., OR, d. Oct 21 1961 in Eugene, Lane Co., OR.

Children:

432 i. Carolyn Elizabeth[6] Guthrie b. Nov 19 1911 in Sidney, Shelby Co., OH, d. Nov 19 1911 in Sidney, Shelby Co., OH.

433 ii. Henry Cornelius Guthrie b. Sep 21 1913 in Shelby Co., OH, d. Jan 20 1973 in Eugene, Lane Co., OR. Married Jun 06 1937, **Evelyn C. Martin**.
434 iii. Arthur William Guthrie b. Oct 14 1915 in Sidney, Shelby Co., OH, d. May 05 1989 in Portland, Multnomah Co., OR. Married Jan 04 1937 in Eugene, Lane Co., OR, **Elizabeth J. (Unknown).**
435 iv. Martha Juanita Guthrie b. 022219`8 in Sidney, Shelby Co., OH, d. Apr 27 1987 in Vida, Lane Co., OR. Married Nov 11 1941 in Eugene, Lane Co., OR, **Walter E. Evonuk**.
\+ 436 v. Hugh Robert Guthrie b. Apr 01 1920.
437 vi. George Francis Guthrie b. May 02 1922 in Eugene, Lane Co., OR. (1) He Married **Eva L. Frederick**. (2) He Married **Velda Dye**.

259. **Doris[5] Arbogast** (101.Roland[4], 17.Allen[3], 3.Rev. Cornelius[2], 1.Peter[1]), b. May 18 1912. Married Sep 14 1934 in Webster Grove, MO, **Henry Broewer**, b. 1908.

Children:

\+ 438 i. Jaqueline Georgia[6] Broewer b. Dec 23 1937.
\+ 439 ii. Henry B. Broewer b. Jul 31 1940.

260. **Charles Wesley[5] Comer** (102.Thomas Joseph[4], 18.Ruth Darletta[3] Arbogast, 3.Rev. Cornelius[2], 1.Peter[1]), b. Oct 03 1885 in Indiana, buried in Concord, Champaign Co., OH, d. Sep 10 1882 in Bellefontaine, Logan Co., CO.
Married Aug 24 1906 in Westville, Champaign Co., OH, **Elizabeth Ann Greathouse**, b. May 08 1886 in Eris, Champaign Co., OH, buried in Concord, Champaign Co., OH, d. Jun 11 1978 in Russells Point, Logan Co., CO.

Children:

440 i. Ruth[6] Comer d. About 1931. She Married **Richard Patrick**.

261. **Albert Lewis[5] Comer** (102.Thomas Joseph[4], 18.Ruth Darletta[3] Arbogast, 3.Rev. Cornelius[2], 1.Peter[1]), b. About 1879 in Ohio.
1930 census Union, Champaign, IL: Albert Comer, aged 50, farmer, bp OH, both parents OH; Cora aged 45, both first Married aged 27 & 23, respectively, bp OH, both parents OH; James aged 20; Blanche aged 19; Richard aged 17; Elsie aged 15; Lee aged 12; Reba aged 5 -- all born OH.
Married About 1906, **Cora Verna Greathouse**, b. Feb 05 1884 in Concord, Champaign Co., OH (daughter of Stephen E. Greathouse and Mary Samantha Neal).

Children:

441 i. Nellie[6] Comer b. About 1907 in Concord, Champaign Co., OH.
442 ii. James Comer b. About 1909 in Concord, Champaign Co., OH.
443 iii. Blanche Comer b. About 1912 in Concord, Champaign Co., OH.
444 iv. Richard Comer b. About 1913 in Concord, Champaign Co., OH.
445 v. Elsie Comer b. About 1917 in Concord, Champaign Co., OH.
446 vi. Lee Comer b. About 1919 in Concord, Champaign Co., OH.
447 vii. Reba Comer b. c1925 in Concord, Champaign Co., OH.

264. **Charles Clifford[5] Davisson** (111.Dorothy Jane[4] Neer, 22.Margaret Ann[3] Arbogast, 4.Otho[2], 1.Peter[1]), b. May 15 1871 in Pleasant Twp., Clark Co., OH, buried in Maple Grove Cem., Mechanicsburg, Champaign Co., OH, d. Jan 02 1956 in Mechanicsburg, Champaign Co., OH. Married Feb 05 1896 in New Moorefield, Clark Co., OH, **Nellie Belle Woodmancy**, b. Jan 19 1874 in Mansfield, Richland Co., OH, buried in Maple Grove Cem., Mechanicsburg, Champaign Co., OH, d. Dec 21 1957 in Urbana, Champaign Co., IL.

Children:

\+ 448 i. Floyd Lorain[6] Davisson b. Dec 13 1897.
\+ 449 ii. Bruce Raymond Davisson b. Nov 08 1903.
\+ 450 iii. Kenneth Elijah Davisson b. Mar 03 1907.
\+ 451 iv. Lt. Col. Dean Clifford Davisson b. Apr 13 1939.

265. **Clarence Weakley[5] Davisson** (111.Dorothy Jane[4] Neer, 22.Margaret Ann[3] Arbogast, 4.Otho[2], 1.Peter[1]), b. Aug 06 1878, d. Dec 02 1946 in Ferncliff Cem., Springfield, Clark Co., OH. (1) Married May 23 1990 in Clark Co., OH, **Lelia Dodson**, b. May 23 1881 in Clark Co., OH. .

***Children** by Lelia Dodson:*

\+ 452 i. Mable Corrine[6] Davisson b. Oct 08 1901.
453 ii. Marcienne Catherine Davisson b. Aug 26 1908, d. Jan 25 1940.

(2) He Married **Lillian Hall**, b. About 1890, buried in Clifton Cem., Greene Co., OH, d. About 1984

268. **Cloice Edgar^{5} Neer** (112.Bruce^{4}, 22.Margaret Ann^{3} Arbogast, 4.Otho^{2}, 1.Peter^{1}), b. Jun 13 1885, d. Aug 18 1922 in Maple Grove Cem., Mechanicsburg, Champaign Co., OH.
<u>Married</u> About 1907 in Clark Co., OH, **Bessie Everhart**, b. Feb 03 1887 in Pleasant Twp., Clark Co., OH, d. Jan 20 1951 in Maple Grove Cem., Mechanicsburg, Champaign Co., OH.

Children:

+ 454 i. Marvin Elwood^{6} Neer b. Jun 30 1908.
+ 455 ii. Ralph Everhart Neer b. Jul 13 1910.
456 iii. Mary Ella Neer b. Apr 28 1912, d. Jan 08 1972.
457 iv. Robert Neer b. Oct 18 1917, d. Sep 20 1950.

270. **Florence Rurth^{5} Neer** (113.William Brown^{4}, 22.Margaret Ann^{3} Arbogast, 4.Otho^{2}, 1.Peter^{1}), b. Aug 11 1893 in Pleasant Twp., Clark Co., OH, d. Jun 25 1977.
<u>Married</u> Aug 29 1918 in Clark Co., OH, **Jesse Earl McAdams**, b. Jul 15 1898 in Jeffersonville, Fayette Co., OH.

Children:

458 i. Virginia Ann^{6} McAdams b. Apr 01 1924, d. Apr 01 1924.
+ 459 ii. Annamae McAdams b. Dec 24 1926.

271. **Milburn Theodore^{5} Neer** (113.William Brown^{4}, 22.Margaret Ann^{3} Arbogast, 4.Otho^{2}, 1.Peter^{1}), b. Aug 01 1901, d. 1990.
<u>Married</u> Feb 08 1924, **Mary Brandy**, b. Apr 04 1905, d. Jul 30 1972.

Children:

+ 460 i. Theodore Grant^{6} Neer b. May 29 1928.
461 ii. Donald William Neer b. Jun 30 1931, d. Jan 27 1935.

272. **Paul Joseph^{5} Neer** (114.Grant^{4}, 22.Margaret Ann^{3} Arbogast, 4.Otho^{2}, 1.Peter^{1}), b. Sep 21 1893 in Nation Chapel, Pleasant Twp., Clark Co., OH, buried in Asbury Cem., Clark Co., OH, d. Apr 28 1952.
He <u>Married</u> **Grace B. Briggs**, b. Sep 17 1892 in Greenfield, Highland Co., OH, d. Mar 13 1970 in Asbury, Pleasant Twp., Clark Co., OH.

Children:

+ 462 i. F. Briggs^{6} Neer b. Apr 01 1915.
+ 463 ii. James Lowell Neer b. Apr 25 1919.

274. **Margaret J^{5} Arbogast** (116.Francis M.^{4}, 23.Jackson^{3}, 4.Otho^{2}, 1.Peter^{1}).
She <u>Married</u> **Oscar Gano**.

Children:

464 i. Margie Ann^{6} Gano.

280. **Morris Emerson^{5} Arbogast** (119.Marion W.^{4}, 24.Eli M.^{3}, 4.Otho^{2}, 1.Peter^{1}), b. Jul 31 1890 in Clark Co., OH.
He <u>Married</u> **Margaret Guisinger**, b. Oct 15 1896 in Mechanicsburg, Champaign Co., OH.

Children:

465 i. Harlan^{6} Arbogast b. May 15 1923.
He <u>Married</u> **Ethel Garden**.
466 ii. Robert Arbogast b. Apr 24 1927.
He <u>Married</u> **Olga Martin**.

282. **Ruby^{5} Arbogast** (119.Marion W.^{4}, 24.Eli M.^{3}, 4.Otho^{2}, 1.Peter^{1}).
She <u>Married</u> **Arthur F, Schwers**.

Children:

+ 467 i. Jane Ellen^{6} Schwers.
468 ii. William Schwers. He <u>Married</u> **Dorothy Donahue**.

287. **Anna^{5} Hardman** (120.Minor W.^{4}, 28.William H.^{3}, 5.Mary^{2} Arbogast, 1.Peter^{1}), b. Dec 1893, d. 1934. She <u>Married</u> **Willard Baumgardner**.

Children:

469 i. Robert^{6} Baumgardner b. 1916.
470 ii. Evelyn Baumgardner b. 1916.
471 iii. Betty Baumgardner b. 1917. She <u>Married</u> **John Goodfellow**.

293. **Neva D.[5] Sellers** (132.Shelby[4], 35.Isabella Jane[3] Curl, 6.Margaret[2] Arbogast, 1.Peter[1]), b. Mar1881 in Cardington Twp., Morrow Co., OH.
She Married **Charles Henry Burgraff**, b. Feb 14 1876 in Cardington Twp., Morrow Co., OH (son of Henry H. Burgraff and Henrietta Ossing), d. 1956.

***Children**:*

472 i. Edith[6] Burgraff b. in Cardington Twp., Morrow Co., OH.
473 ii. Estella Burgraff b. in Cardington Twp., Morrow Co., OH.
474 iii. Carl Henry Burgraff b. in Cardington Twp., Morrow Co., OH.

294. **Samuel Arthur[5] Sellers** (132.Shelby[4], 35.Isabella Jane[3] Curl, 6.Margaret[2] Arbogast, 1.Peter[1]), b. Nov 1883 in Cardington Twp., Morrow Co., OH.
He Married **Roma S. Gilson**, b. 4 Jun 1884 in Cardington Twp., Morrow Co., OH, d. Aug 1974 in Cardington Twp., Morrow Co., OH.

***Children**:*

475 i. Marjorie Ruth[6] Sellars b. 24 Feb 1912 in Cardington Twp., Morrow Co., OH, d. 12 Dec 2003 in Marion, Marion Co., OH.
Married 31 Dec 1936 in Mansfield, Richland Co., OH, **Donald O. Carpenter**.
476 ii. Lucile M. Sellars b. Apr 1915 in Cardington Twp., Morrow Co., OH.
Married Feb 1944 in Cardington Twp., Morrow Co., OH, Ivan W. Heacock, b. in Cardington Twp., Morrow Co., OH.

295. **Elmer Hayse[5] Sellers** (132.Shelby[4], 35.Isabella Jane[3] Curl, 6.Margaret[2] Arbogast, 1.Peter[1]), b. Sep 1886 in Cardington Twp., Morrow Co., OH, d. 26 Dec 1922 in Columbus, Franklin Co., OH.
Married 25 Dec 1910 in Cardington Twp., Morrow Co., OH, **Florence Estella Grover**, b. 12 May 1890 in Cardington Twp., Morrow Co., OH (daughter of Alpha A. Gruber and Mary Estella Maxwell).

***Children**:*

477 i. Leo Gilbert[6] Sellars b. 1 Apr 1912 in Cardington Twp., Morrow Co., OH, d. 2 Mar 1996 in Cardington Twp., Morrow Co., OH.
He Married **Ruth Hodge**.
478 ii. Earl Richard Sellars b. 16 May 1922 in Cardington Twp., Morrow Co., OH, d. 2 Feb 2004 in Bucyrus, Crawford Co., OH.
Married 24 Dec 1939, **Betty Mae Holt**.

296. **Lefa Mae[5] Sellers** (132.Shelby[4], 35.Isabella Jane[3] Curl, 6.Margaret[2] Arbogast, 1.Peter[1]), b. May 1890 in Cardington Twp., Morrow Co., OH, d. 12 Dec 1958 in Marion, Marion Co., OH. Married 12 Oct 1910, **Ernest L. Betts**, b. 11 Jun 1889 in Cardington Twp., Morrow Co., OH (son of Hubbard Betts and Annette 'Nettie' Henry), d. 7 Jan 1966 in Marion, Marion Co., OH.

***Children**:*

479 i. Howard R.[6] Betts b. 17 Mar 1912 in Cardington Twp., Morrow Co., OH, d. 8 Mar 1965 in Mount Gilead, Morrow Co., OH.
480 ii. Paul M. Betts b. 3 Apr 1915, d. 1 Aug 1999 in Cardington Twp., Morrow Co., OH. Married 25 Jun 1936, **Viola Kramer**, b. 26 Sep 1916 in Cardington Twp., Morrow Co., OH (daughter of David Augusta Kramer and Henrietta K. Beckel).
481 iii. Hilda L. Betts b. About 1918. She Married **Ralph A. Brake**, b. 26 Sep 1914 in Cardington Twp., Morrow Co., OH, d. 24 Jan 2001.
482 iv. Helen L. Betts b. About 1918. She Married **Ricky Sexton**.
483 v. Ruth Marie Betts b. 22 Sep 1920 in Cardington Twp., Morrow Co., OH, d. 24 May 1978 in Delaware Co., OH. She Married **Kenneth Weldon Smith**, b. 8 Feb 1914 at Cardington Twp., Morrow Co., OH (son of Forrest Wayne Smith and Orlena Pearl Ramsey).
484 vi. Warren G. Betts b. About 1923.
485 vii. Harold W. Betts b. Abour1926. He Married **Hazel Snyder**.
486 viii. Doris J. Betts b. About 1929. She Married **Thomas Campbell**.

298. **Charles Ross[5] Underhill** (133.Lucinda[4] Sellers, 35.Isabella Jane[3] Curl, 6.Margaret[2] Arbogast, 1.Peter[1]), b. 6 Dec 1875 in Liberty, Union Co., OH, buried in Raymond Cem., Liberty, Union Co., OH, d. 19 Oct 1947 in Essex, Union Co., OH.
(1) He Married **Grace F. Hicks**, b. Sep 1878 in Liberty Twp. Liberty Co., OH. (.

***Children** by Grace F. Hicks:*

\+ 487 i. Opal M.[6] Underhill b. May.

+ 488 ii. Florence Lucinda Underhill b. 7 Jul 1897.
+ 489 iii. Myrtle Underhill b. Aug 1899.
490 iv. Thomas Underhill b. About 1901 in Liberty, Union Co., OH.
491 v. Charles A. Underhill b. Abour1905 in Liberty, Union Co., OH.
492 vi. John M. Underhill b. About 1907 in Liberty, Union Co., OH.
493 vii. Erma Dell Underhill b. 28 May 1910 in Peoria, Union Co., OH, d. 10 Aug 1961 in Union Co., OH. Married 3 Sep 1927 in Lexington, Fayette Co., KY, **Clarence A. Shuler Sr**..
494 viii. Vada Underhill b. 21 Jun 1912 in Liberty, Union Co., OH, d. 2 Mar 1992 in Bay City, Bay Co., MI. (1) Married 1975, **Melvin Roy Chrisman**, b. 21 May 1923 in Bay City, Bay Co., MI. (2) She Married **(unknown) Herd**.
495 ix. Harry C. Underhill b. 6 Mar 1915 in Godwin Co., MI, d. 2 Jul 1966 in Marysville, Union Co., OH. Married 21 May 1933 in Raymond, Union Co., OH, **Sylvia McCarty**.
496 x. Daisy L. Underhill b. About 1917 in Liberty, Union Co., OH. She Married **Robert Cook**.
497 xi. Annabelle Underhill b. in Fairgrove, Tuscola Co., MI.

2) Married Jan 1934, **Emma Seaman**

299. **John[5] Underhill** (133.Lucinda[4] Sellers, 35.Isabella Jane[3] Curl, 6.Margaret[2] Arbogast, 1.Peter[1]), b. in Marion, Marion Co., OH.

Children:

+ 498 i. Thomas C.[6] Underhill b. About 1850.
+ 499 ii. Amanda Sellers b. About 1859.

300. **Bernice M.[5] Underhill** (135.Wilie[4] Sellers, 35.Isabella Jane[3] Curl, 6.Margaret[2] Arbogast, 1.Peter[1]), b. 2 Jul 1884 in Cardington Twp., Morrow Co., OH, d. Aug 1969.
Married in Cardington Twp., Morrow Co., OH, **Gladys Clabaugh**, b. 30 Mar 1891 in Clarinda, Page Co., IA (son of Charles Clabaugh and Sada Liggett), buried in Glendale, Cardington Twp., Morrow Co., OH, d. 24 Aug 1962 in Cardington Twp., Morrow Co., OH.

Children:

500 i. Hazel[6] Sellars b. 26 Feb 1911, d. Mar 1981 in Delaware Co., OH. She Married **Emmett Vanausdal**, b. 16 Jan 1909, d. 10 Dec 1993 in Delaware Co., OH.
501 ii. Mildred Sellars b. 24 Oct 1913, d. 13 Sep 1997 in Cardington Twp., Morrow Co., OH. She Married **Lowell Welch**, b. 24 May 1907, d. Mar 1984 in Cardington Twp., Morrow Co., OH.
502 iii. Louise Sellars b. 29 Aug 1917 in Cardington Twp., Morrow Co., OH, d. 28 Jun 1917 in Marion, Marion Co., OH.

305. **Alta F.[5] Sellars** (138.Johnson Leamon[4] Sellers, 35.Isabella Jane[3] Curl, 6.Margaret[2] Arbogast, 1.Peter[1]), b. About 1903 in Morrow Co., OH.

Children:

503 i. Thelma[6] Sellars b. About 1914 in Cardington Twp., Morrow Co., OH.

306. **Ross Randolph[5] Sellars** (139.Ross[4] Sellers, 35.Isabella Jane[3] Curl, 6.Margaret[2] Arbogast, 1.Peter[1]), b. 1 Mar 1898 in Phoenix, Maricopa Co., AZ, d. May 1985 in Tucson, Pima Co., AZ. He Married **Laura (unknown)**, b. About 1903 in Tucson, Pima Co., AZ.

Children:

504 i. Mildred[6] Sellars b. About 1924 in Tucson, Pima Co., AZ. She Married **Charles Pierre Mariotte**.
505 ii. Laura Lucille Sellars b. About 1927 in Tucson, Pima Co., AZ. Married Jun 1953, **Harry Glenn Page**.

308. **M. Guy[5] Paste** (140.Lovina[4] Sellers, 35.Isabella Jane[3] Curl, 6.Margaret[2] Arbogast, 1.Peter[1]), b. About 1892 in Cardington Twp., Morrow Co., OH. Married 1916, **Marie Wheeler**, b. About 1894, d. Dec 1977 in Cardington Twp., Morrow Co., OH.

Children:

506 i. Wesley[6] Paste.
507 ii. Inez Paste.
508 iii. Alta Paste.

309. **Lena Rose[5] Curl** (141.Elza S.[4], 36.Henry William[3], 6.Margaret[2] Arbogast, 1.Peter[1]), b. Mar 27 1978, d. Dec 11 1965.
She Married **R.E. Riley**, b. May 05 1870, d. Jan 12 1953.

Children:

+ 509 i. Dorothy[6] Riley b. Aug 01 1904.

310. **Alma Blanch[5] Curl** (142.Franklin M.[4], 36.Henry William[3], 6.Margaret[2] Arbogast, 1.Peter[1]), b. Nov 12 1879 in Canaan Twp. Morrow Co., OH, d. Dec 30 1957.
Married Nov 06 1901, **Cline Sherman**, b. Oct 10 1874, d. Dec 14 1945.

***Children*:**

+ 510 i. Harold[6] Sherman b. Dec 04 1902.
+ 511 ii. Frank Sherman b. Jul 29 1906.
+ 512 iii. Lois Sherman b. Nov 11 1908.
+ 513 iv. Lucille Sherman b. Aug 10 1915.

311. **Henry Harrison[5] Curl** (142.Franklin M.[4], 36.Henry William[3], 6.Margaret[2] Arbogast, 1.Peter[1]), b. Dec 16 1891, buried in Glendale, Cardington Twp., Morrow Co., OH, d. Dec 02 1950 in Cardington Twp., Morrow Co., OH.
(1) Married Dec 16 1917, **Gladys M. Newcomer**, b. Oct 25 1896, buried in Glendale, Cardington Twp., Morrow Co., OH, d. Jun 30 1919 in Cardington Twp., Morrow Co., OH. .

***Children** by Gladys M. Newcomer:*

+ 514 i. Jo Ann[6] Curl b. Jul 16 1928.
+ 515 ii. Kent Wayne Curl b. Aug 03 1930.
+ 516 iii. Franklin Dale Curl b. May 04 1935.
+ 517 iv. Dean Even Curl b. Oct 06 1937.

(2) He Married **Marjorie Copeland**, b. Aug 02 1903, buried in Glendale, Cardington Twp., Morrow Co., OH, d. Apr 20 1981 in Cardington Twp., Morrow Co., OH

315. **Bessie[5] Sage** (145.Ida M.[4] Curl, 36.Henry William[3], 6.Margaret[2] Arbogast, 1.Peter[1]), b. Mar 18 1888, d. Apr 15 1958 in 14 mi. south. (
1) Married Jun 05 1907, **Harry J. Butts**, b. Jun 05 1886, d. May 08 1940.

***Children** by Harry J. Butts:*

518 i. Francis[6] Butts b. Jul 03 1912, d. 1986. He Married Julie George.
+ 519 ii. Leroy Butts b. Sep 22 1916.

(2) She Married **Edward Casto**, b. Oct 04 1877, d. Jul 07 1971.

316. **Victor[5] Sage** (145.Ida M.[4] Curl, 36.Henry William[3], 6.Margaret[2] Arbogast, 1.Peter[1]), b. Oct 13 1880.

***Children*:**

520 i. Dorothy Ruth[6] Sage b. Oct 12 1917.

317. **Corinne[5] Miller** (147.Ada Blanche[4] Curl, 36.Henry William[3], 6.Margaret[2] Arbogast, 1.Peter[1]), b. Jan 11 1897.
Married Jul 20 1922, **Howard McMillion**, b. Nov 11 1897, d. May 01 1970.

***Children*:**

+ 521 i. Norman[6] McMillion b. Jun 07 1924.
+ 522 ii. Martha McMillion b. Oct 25 1926.
+ 523 iii. David McMillion b. Dec 03 1927.
+ 524 iv. Robert McMillion b. May 05 1936.

318. **Robert H.[5] Miller** (147.Ada Blanche[4] Curl, 36.Henry William[3], 6.Margaret[2] Arbogast, 1.Peter[1]), b. Aug 05 1901, d. Feb 29 1956.
Married Mar 04 1946, **Oneita McCauley**, b. Jan 24 1916.

***Children*:**

525 i. Margaret[6] Miller b. Jan 12 1947.
526 ii. Robert George Miller b. Oct 27 1948.

326. **Cloise Hayes[5] Messenger** (150.George Asa[4], 37.Emily[3] Curl, 6.Margaret[2] Arbogast, 1.Peter[1]). She Married **Varance L. Smith**, b. Oct 1898 in Westfield Twp., Marrow Co., OH (son of Archie Smith and Emma Maria Schorr).

***Children*:**

+ 527 i. Marie[6] Messenger.

341. **Clair Whitman^5 Wilkinson** (168.George Washington^4, 44.John G.^{3}, 7.Susannah^2 Arbogast, 1.Peter^1), b. About 1887 in North Baltimore, Wood Co., OH, d. Sep 23 1975 in Willard, Huron Co., OH.
Married Sep 01 1921 in Findlay, Hancock Co., OH, **Ruth Agnes House**, b. Apr 08 1893 in North Baltimore, Wood Co., OH, d. Mar 13 1976 in Willard, Huron Co., OH.

Children:

528 i. Jane^6 Wilkinson. She Married **Harold Herbert Slessman**. Harold: At the time this data was assembled this Family had 1 other child, who was unwed, and maybe living, that are not included here. Living children who are are listed, although data on them was limited.

529 ii. Bruce Windell Wilkinson. He Married Berdella Tonk. Berdella:

342. **Gerald Thomas^5 Wilkinson** (168.George Washington^4, 44.John G.^{3}, 7.Susannah^2 Arbogast, 1.Peter^1), b. Nov 14 1889 in North Baltimore, Wood Co., OH, d. Jan 1955. He Married **Geraldine Wilkinson**, b. Nov 14 1889 (daughter of John Nelson Wilkinson and Olive Lillian Wright.), d. 1977 in Athens, Athens Co., OH.

Children:

530 i. Phillip^6 Wilkinson.
He Married Jane Foote.

348. **Geraldine^5 Wilkinson** (169.John Nelson^4, 44.John G.^{3}, 7.Susannah^2 Arbogast, 1.Peter^1) (See marriage to number 342.)

354. **Lilian Cary^5 St. Clair** (178.Ethel Kilbourne^4 Arbogast, 54.Albert^3, 8.Henry^2, 1.Peter^1), b. Feb 26 1912 in Fayetteville, Fayette Co., WV. Married Apr 08 1941, **James Gaylord Blackford**, b. Jul 04 1906 in Richmond, Henrico Co., VA.

Children:

531 i. Gay^6 Blackford b. Feb 24 1942 in Wilmington, New Hanover Co., NC.

532 ii. Anne Courtenay Blackford b. Mar 29 1944 in Richmond, Henrico Co., VA.

359. **Mary^5 Morrison** (186.Sophia^4 Arbogast, 64.Jesse^3, 11.Peter^2, 1.Peter^1), b. Aug 01 1859 in Good Hope, Walnut Grove, Putnam Co., IL. (1) Married Dec 01 1876 in Monmouth, Warren Co., IL, **Edward Earl Payne**, b. Jul 15 1849 in Pleasant Valley, Scott Co., IA (son of Jeremiah E. Payne and Letitia Orr), d. Jan 01 1886 in Hannah, Henry Co., IL. (2) Married Aug 19 1890 in McComb, McDonough Co., IL, **Lafayette Powers**. **Lafayette**: Moved to Sedalia, MO 1n 1898.

***Children** by Edward Earl Payne:*

\+ 533 i. William Charles^6 Payne b. Feb 02 1878.

534 ii. Ida Mae Payne b. Feb 24 1879 in Good Hope, Walnut Grove, Putnam Co., IL, d. Feb 20 1902.
Died of tuberculosis.

535 iii. Ada Letitia Payne b. Aug 04 1882 in Good Hope, Walnut Grove, Putnam Co., IL, d. Oct 24 1902.
Died of tuberculosis.

536 iv. Leroy L Payne b. Oct 30 1882 in Good Hope, Walnut Grove, Putnam Co., IL, d. 1945. He Married Bessie E Stump.

537 v. Walter Scott Payne b. Jun 04 1884 in Good Hope, Walnut Grove, Putnam Co., IL, d. Jul 22 1906. Died of tuberculosis.

363. **Rose^5 Morrison** (186.Sophia^4 Arbogast, 64.Jesse^3, 11.Peter^2, 1.Peter^1), b. Oct 18 1869 in Good Hope, Walnut Grove, Putnam Co., IL, d. Oct 03 1954 in McComb, McDonough Co., IL. Married 1892, **Isaac Woolverton**.

Children:

\+ 538 i. Harry^6 Woolverton.

365. **Ida^5 Morrison** (186.Sophia^4 Arbogast, 64.Jesse^3, 11.Peter^2.Peter^1), b. 1875 in Good Hope, Walnut Grove, Putnam Co., IL. She Married **Ed Reipen**.

Children:

539 i. Helen^6 Reipen.

540 ii. Lottie Reipen.

367. **Amy^5 Brown** (189.Mary Jane^4 Arbogast, 64.Jesse^3, 11.Peter^2, 1.Peter^1), b. Feb 06 1873 in McComb, McDonough Co., IL, d. Jun 20 1947.
Married Dec 19 1900, **George Carl Clarke**, b. 1878.

Children:

\+ 541 i. Bernice^6 Clarke b. Jul 30 1912.

\+ 542 ii. Carl C Clarke b. Oct 04 1915.

369. **Ethel Clare[5] Brown** (189.Mary Jane[4] Arbogast, 64.Jesse[3], 11.Peter[2], 1.Peter[1]), b. Sep 03 1875 in McComb, McDonough Co., IL, d. Apr 30 1957.
Married Sep 19 1904, **Harold Mitchell**, b. 1877, d. 1961.

Children:

+ 543 i. R Taylor[6] Mitchell b. Nov 09 1908.

371. **Lois Irene[5] Brown** (189.Mary Jane[4] Arbogast, 64.Jesse[3], 11.Peter[2], 1.Peter[1]), b. Feb 11 1880 in McComb, McDonough Co., IL, d. Dec 08 1966.
Married Oct 13 1910, **Charles Frary**, b. Mar 15 1883, d. Apr 04 1966.

Children:

544 i. Robert Orlando[6] Frary b. Dec 11 1911. Married Jan 23 1944, **Delores Samuelson**.
+ 545 ii. Thelma Hannah Frary.
+ 546 iii. Alice Lucille Frary b. Jul 20 1914.
547 iv. Virginia Elizabeth Frary b. Oct 03 1916, d. Aug 20 1919.

373. **Mertice Loine[5] Brown** (189.Mary Jane[4] Arbogast, 64.Jesse[3], 11.Peter[2], 1.Peter[1]), b. Oct 29 1886 in McComb, McDonough Co., IL, d. Mar 19 1932.
She Married **Harry Mikesell**, b. Oct 12 1884, d. Oct 24 1954.

Children:

+ 548 i. Lewis[6] Mikesell b. Nov 14 1912.
+ 549 ii. Osmond Mikesell b. Feb 13 1914.
+ 550 iii. Weist Lamoine Mikesell b. May 15 1916.
+ 551 iv. Orth Arbogast Mikesell b. Nov 14 1919.
+ 552 v. Betty Lou Mikesell b. Jun 17 1921.
+ 553 vi. Erwin Claire Mikesell b. Apr 08 1924.

379. **Mae[5] Howard** (192.Sarah[4] Arbogast, 64.Jesse[3], 11.Peter[2], 1.Peter[1]), b. May 01 1874 in Scioto Twp., McDonough Co., IL, d. Dec 28 1932.
Married Feb 08 1898 in Good Hope, Walnut Grove, Putnam Co., IL, **William Oscar Cozad**, b. Jun 01 1868 in Ellisville, Fulton Co., IL, d. Jun 31 1949 in McComb, McDonough Co., IL.

Children:

+ 554 i. Sarah Fern[6] Cozad b. Jul 24 1899.
+ 555 ii. Faun Elizabeth Cozad b. Jun 12 1902.

382. **Neil[5] Smith** (194.Frances[4] Arbogast, 64.Jesse[3], 11.Peter[2], 1.Peter[1]), b. Dec 08 1877, d. Jan 03 1942 in Bayless, Pike Co., IL.
She Married **Thomas R. Askew**, b. Jan 19 1874, d. Oct 1952.

Children:

556 i. Wayne F[6] Askew b. Sep 12 1915 in Dahlgren, Hamilton Co., IL. Married Jun 01 1937, **Mary K. Johnson**.

383. **Emerson Eugene[5] Smith** (194.Frances[4] Arbogast, 64.Jesse[3], 11.Peter[2], 1.Peter[1]).
He Married **Aletha Bryan Morris**.

Children:

+ 557 i. Margaret[6] Smith b. Apr 06 1911.
558 ii. Caroline Smith b. May 31 1916. She Married **James Wicks**.
+ 559 iii. Russell Smith b. May 31 1916.

385. **Jessie[5] Smith** (194.Frances[4] Arbogast, 64.Jesse[3], 11.Peter[2], 1.Peter[1]).
She Married **Ezra Huffman**.

Children:

560 i. Irena[6] Huffman.
561 ii. Ruth Huffman.
562 iii. Glen Huffman.

387. **June[5] Smith** (194.Frances[4] Arbogast, 64.Jesse[3], 11.Peter[2], 1.Peter[1]), b. Jun 1887, d. Oct 31 1984.
Married Nov 21 1920, **Oscar Olson**, d. 1972.

Children:

563 i. Maxwell Terry[6] Olson.
564 ii. Francis Nels Olson.
565 iii. Marlyn Jean Olson.
566 iv. Oscar George Olson.

388. **Myrtle[5] Smith** (194.Frances[4] Arbogast, 64.Jesse[3], 11.Peter[2], 1.Peter[1]), b. Dec 17 1896, d. Dec 15 1982.
Married Oct 03 1909, **George Harold Fox**, b. Nov 10 1885, d. Jan 22 1961.

Children:

+ 567 i. Keith Leroy[6] Fox b. Oct 15 1911.
+ 568 ii. Ralth Wilton Fox b. May 01 1913.

389. **Clyde Stewart[5] Arbogast** (195.Stephen Aaron Douglas[4], 64.Jesse[3], 11.Peter[2], 1.Peter[1]), b. Feb 03 1891 in Rising City, Butler Co., NE, d. Aug 11 1965 in Burley, Cassia Co., ID.
Married Mar 24 1905, **Anta Marie Conkling**, b. Dec 18 1889 in Shelley, Bingham Co., ID, d. Jan 22 1927 in Maple Grove Cem., Rochester, Olmsted Co., MN.

Children:

+ 569 i. Theodore Fenton[6] Arbogast b. Sep 11 1905.
570 ii. Clare Eleanor Arbogast b. Nov 05 1910 in Silver Creek, Blaine Co., ID, d. Apr 01 1927.
+ 571 iii. Helen Elene Arbogast b. Aug 15 1912.
+ 572 iv. Allen Sterart Arbogast b. Jul 02 1914.
+ 573 v. Gladys Catherine Arbogast b. Aug 27 1917.
574 vi. Dorothy Dare Arbogast b. May 20 1920 in Burley, Cassia Co., ID, d. 1937.
+ 575 vii. Marilyn Inez Arbogast b. Jun 03 1924.

391. **Nellie Millicent[5] Arbogast** (195.Stephen Aaron Douglas[4], 64.Jesse[3], 11.Peter[2], 1.Peter[1]), b. Sep 22 1898 in Rising City, Butler Co., NE, d. Aug 16 1991 in Grand Island, Hall Co., NE. Married Nov 02 1920, **Gilfford E. Hutchison**, b. Dec 15 1896 in Ashland, Saunders Co., NE, d. Mar 11 1973 in Grand Island, Hall Co., NE.

Children:

+ 576 i. Carolyn Jean[6] Hutchison b. Aug 14 1921.
+ 577 ii. Betty Jane Hutchison b. Feb 04 1924.

392. **Gladys Mary[5] Arbogast** (195.Stephen Aaron Douglas[4], 64.Jesse[3], 11.Peter[2], 1.Peter[1]), b. May 18 1901 in Silver Creek, Merrick Co., NE.
She Married **John Gerber**.

Children:

+ 578 i. Marjorie Elaine[6] Gerber b. May 17 1921.
579 ii. Mary Lois Gerber b. Feb 24 1925 in Silver Creek, Merrick Co., NE, d. Aug 16 1977 in Chicago, Cook Co., IL. Married Oct 06 1944 in Florida, Emil Kupcik.

393. **Harold Edson[5] Arbogast** (195.Stephen Aaron Douglas[4], 64.Jesse[3], 11.Peter[2], 1.Peter[1]), b. Nov 30 1912 in Silver Creek, Merrick Co., NE, d. Oct 09 1963 in Nyssa, OR.
He Married **Nellie Hokanson**, b. Sep 26 1917 in Thayne, Lincoln Co., WY.

Children:

580 i. Patricia Ann[6] Arbogast b. Nov 29 1939 in Afton, Lincoln Co., WY. Married Jun 23 1955, **Brent J. Harrison**.
581 ii. Liola Arbogast b. Mar 20 1941 in Afton, Lincoln Co., WY. Married Oct 04 1957, **Rex N. Leavitt**.
582 iii. Gloria Arbogast b. Oct 26 1942 in Afton, Lincoln Co., WY. Married Jun 24 1958, **Edward Stumpp**.

396. **Lorenzo[5] STAIB** (198.Alice M.[4] Arbogast, 67.Michael[3], 11.Peter[2], 1.Peter[1]), b. Feb 08 1892, d. Sep 25 1970.
He Married **Mary Dartz**.

Children:

583 i. Lewis Victor[6] Staib.
584 ii. Alice Kay Staib. She Married Wilber Kenny.
585 iii. Jean Staib. She Married Charles Hughes.
586 iv. Paul Staib.
587 v. Helen Rose Staib.

397. **Nettie[5] STAIB** (198.Alice M.[4] Arbogast, 67.Michael[3], 11.Peter[2], 1.Peter[1]). She Married **Charles Kingseed**. .

Children:

588 i. Carl[6] Kingseed.

398. **Jessie L.[5] Arbogast** (199.John Franklin[4], 67.Michael[3], 11.Peter[2], 1.Peter[1]), b. Aug 20 1880 in Seneca Co., OH, d. Mar 13 1958 in Seneca Co., OH.
He Married **Etta Margaret Estep**, b. About 1881, d. About 1946, buried in Tacoma, Pierce Co., WA. .

Children:

589 i. Howard[6] Arbogast.
590 ii. Edgar Allen Arbogast b. Oct 24 1904, d. Nov 18 1980 in Tiffin, Seneca Co., OH.
591 iii. Merlin M. Arbogast b. About 1905, d. About 1937 in Tiffin, Seneca Co., OH.
592 iv. Neva Arbogast. She Married **Myron Tuttle**.
593 v. Annabelle Arbogast.
\+ 594 vi. Dwight Arbogast b. Jul 13 1911.
595 vii. Loris Arbogast b. About 1914 in Seneca Co., OH, d. About 1946 in Seneca Co., OH. He Married Mary **Lou Fosnaugh**.

403. **James Warren[5] Arbogast** (200.Lewis Heenan[4], 67.Michael[3], 11.Peter[2], 1.Peter[1]), b. Dec 29 1896, d. Jan 20 1981.
Married Oct 16 1920, **Milldred Hovis**. .

Children:

596 i. Ann[6] Arbogast.
597 ii. Sharlin Arbogast. She Married **Paul Troxell**.
598 iii. Joan Arbogast. She Married **Marion Miller**.

411. **James Michael[5] Arbogast** (202.Charles Sayers[4], 67.Michael[3], 11.Peter[2], 1.Peter[1]), b. Dec 16 1887 in Walnut Grove, Knox Co., IL, d. July 1965.
He Married **Tola Merle McGee**, b. Sep 11 1890. .

Children:

\+ 599 i. Lois Alberta[6] Arbogast.
\+ 600 ii. Gayl Jane Arbogast b. Oct 14 1921.
\+ 601 iii. Charles Sayers Arbogast b. Jul 29 1925.

412. **Alice[5] Arbogast** (202.Charles Sayers[4], 67.Michael[3], 11.Peter[2], 1.Peter[1]).
She Married **Chauncey Brewster Heath**. .

Children:

\+ 602 i. James Kenneth[6] Heath b. Jan 08 1913.
\+ 603 ii. Marion E. Heath b. Nov 18 1917.

415. **Clarence James[5] Arbogast** (203.Rush Arlington[4], 67.Michael[3], 11.Peter[2], 1.Peter[1]), b. Jun-08-1904, d. Jan-21-1904.
He Married **Aleta Talley**, b. 1902, d. 1976. .

Children:

\+ 604 i. James Clarence[6] Arbogast b. Mar 13 1927.
\+ 605 ii. Naomi Agnus Arbogast b. Jun 06 1938.

416. **Charles Anthony[5] Arbogast** (203.Rush Arlington[4], 67.Michael[3], 11.Peter[2], 1.Peter[1]), b. Sep-11-1900, d. 1171982 in Seneca Co., OH.
Married Nov-22-1921, **Loretta Rhinehart**, b. Sep-11-1900.

Children:

\+ 606 i. Paul Joseph[6] Arbogast b. Sep-06-1922.
\+ 607 ii. Lawrence Anselm Arbogast b. Dec-20-1924.
\+ 608 iii. Urban Anthony Arbogast b. Mar-20-1926.
\+ 609 iv. Eugene Jerome Arbogast b. Oct 24 1928.
\+ 610 v. Marion Victor Arbogast b. Apr 16 1930.
\+ 611 vi. Marguerite Elenora Arbogast b. Apr 30 1934.
\+ 612 vii. Harlan Clarence Arbogast b. Nov 24 1936.
\+ 613 viii. Lester Michael Arbogast b. Jul 21 1938.
\+ 614 ix. Rita Mae Arbogast b. Nov-26-1941.
\+ 615 x. Louis Cyril Arbogast b. Aug-01-1944.

616 xi. Joseph Arbogast b. Aug-01-1944, d. Aug-01-1944.

417. **Frances Marie^5 Arbogast** (203.Rush Arlington^4, 67.Michael^3, 11.Peter^2, 1.Peter^1), b. Dec 28 1892, d. Jan 29 1967. Married Jan 26 1915, **Louis Joseph Smith**. .

Children:

+ 617 i. Clarence Louis^6 SMITH b. Nov 17 1915.
+ 618 ii. Rita Theresa Smith b. Nov 07 1916.
+ 619 iii. Richard Joseph Smith b. Mar 12 1920.
620 iv. Dorothy Clara Smith b. Jul 29 1921, d. Jul 05 1950. Married Jan 16 1946, **Bernard Joseph Frankart**, b. Mar 22 1919, d. Feb 19 1980. .
+ 621 v. Marjorie Mary Smith b. Oct 17 1922.
+ 622 vi. Robert Eugene Smith b. Sep 19 1925.
+ 623 vii. Helen Francis Smith b. Sep 28 1927.
+ 624 viii. Bernard Charles Smith b. May 30 1929.
+ 625 ix. Leo Frederick Smith b. Feb 19 1931.
+ 626 x. Catherine Louise Smith b. Dec 20 1935.
+ 627 xi. Rosemary Smith b. Jan 22 1938.

Generation Six

422. **Clara Loveda^6 Crissman** (220.Cornelius Eugene^5, 73.Melissa^4 Latimer, 13.Elizabeth P.^{3} Arbogast, 3.Rev. Cornelius^2, 1.Peter^1), b. Aug 22 1903 in Payne, Paulding Co., OH, d. Jun 11 1960 in Coldwater, Branch Co., MI.
Married Oct 12 1925 in Quincy Twp., Branch Co., MI, **Chester Raymond McConnell**, b. Feb 08 1902 in Denver, Arapaho Co., CO, buried in Quincy Twp., Branch Co., MI.

Children:

+ 628 i. Max Ramon McConnell,^{7} b. Apr 04 1931.
+ 629 ii. Thomas Omar McConnell b. Jul 04 1934.
630 iii. Mary Diane McConnell b. Jul 16 1941 in Cold Water, Branch Co., MI.

424. **John Dale^6 Crissman** (220.Cornelius Eugene^5, 73.Melissa^4 Latimer, 13.Elizabeth P.^{3} Arbogast, 3.Rev. Cornelius^2, 1.Peter^1), b. May 01 1907.
He Married **Jane Reems**, b. Dec 26 1908.

Children:

631 i. John David^7 Crissman b. Feb 03 1939. He Married **Deborah Lynn Barnett**.
632 ii. Carol Ann Crissman b. Dec 04 1941. She Married **Donald Joseph Ardis**.

425. **Donald Leroy^6 Crissman** (220.Cornelius Eugene^5, 73.Melissa^4 Latimer, 13.Elizabeth P.^{3} Arbogast, 3.Rev. Cornelius^2, 1.Peter^1), b. Nov 03 1908.
He Married **Mary Postler**.

Children:

633 i. Sharon Ann^7 Crissman b. May 20 1940. She Married **James Carter**.
634 ii. Donald Anthony Crissman.
635 iii. Judith Crissman b. Feb 14 1941.

426. **Wanda Ruth^6 Crissman** (220.Cornelius Eugene^5, 73.Melissa^4 Latimer, 13.Elizabeth P.^{3} Arbogast, 3.Rev. Cornelius^2, 1.Peter^1), b. Jul 09 1913.
She Married **Clyde Robinson**, b. Oct 11 1916.

Children:

636 i. Nancy Ann^7 Robinson b. Mar 09 1934. He Married **Davis Swartz Bennett**.
637 ii. Patricia Lee Robinson b. Jun 01 1935. She Married **Leroy Wilson Morrell**.
638 iii. Jack Leroy Robinson b. Aug 27 1937. He Married **Elly Jones**.
639 iv. William Joseph Robinson b. Feb 26 1939. He Married **Janice Kay Weakly**, b. Jan 21 1939.

428. **Ellis Walter^6 Crissman** (222.Ernest Raymond^5, 73.Melissa^4 Latimer, 13.Elizabeth P.^{3} Arbogast, 3.Rev. Cornelius^2, 1.Peter^1), b. Jul 23 1910 in Bagnell, Miller Co., MI, d. Dec 18 1970.

Married Sep 01 1935, **Lela Myra Teall**, b. Feb 02 1913, d. Nov 29 1990.

***Children*:**

640 i. Lorraine Kay[7] Crissman b. Oct 12 1936. She Married **Richard Emil Asiala**, b. Feb 03 1934.
641 ii. Christina Gay Crissman b. Nov 10 1949. Married Nov 10 1949, **Danny Ray Allison**, b. Jul 21 1949.

429. **Hazel Melissa[6] Crissman** (222.Ernest Raymond[5], 73.Melissa[4] Latimer, 13.Elizabeth P.[3] Arbogast, 3.Rev. Cornelius[2], 1.Peter[1]), b. Dec 17 1912.
(1) Married Dec 23 1934, **William Allen Smith**, b. Feb 05 1900 in Bagnell, Miller Co., MI, d. Feb 11 1943. .

Children *by William Allen Smith:*

642 i. Donna Alice[7] Smith b. Feb 06 1936, d. Feb 20 1938.
643 ii. Neil Allen Smith b. Jun 30 1937, d. Sep 27 1988. (1) He Married **Patricia Follette**. (2) He Married **Margaret Morfitt**.

(2) She Married **Raymond Cletus Albaugh**, b. May 08 1908, d. Jun 20 1970

Children *by Raymond Cletus Albaugh:*

644 iii. Dianne Ray Albaugh b. Mar 29 1946. (1) She Married **Ronald Gorden** Davenport. (2) She Married Kerry Comerford.
645 iv. Charles Raymond Albaugh b. Oct 10 1950. (1) He Married Rebecca Sullins. (2) He Married **Cynthia Altemus**.

430. **Clarence Eugene[6] Crissman** (222.Ernest Raymond[5], 73.Melissa[4] Latimer, 13.Elizabeth P.[3] Arbogast, 3.Rev. Cornelius[2], 1.Peter[1]), b. Jun 02 1915 in Centerville, ST. Joseph Co., MI. Married Jan 23 1937 in Ann Arbor, Washtenaw Co., MI, **Marjorie Marie Adams**, b. Aug 19 1918 in Chemist, Wexford Co., MI (daughter of Wilber Frank Adams and Mary Margaret Crytzer), buried in Forest Lawn Cem., Detroit, Wayne Co., MI, d. Dec 23 1989 in East Lansing, Ingham Co., MI.

***Children*:**

\+ 646 i. Patricia Irene[7] Crissman b. Dec 07 1941.

431. **Clyde Clifford[6] Crissman** (222.Ernest Raymond[5], 73.Melissa[4] Latimer, 13.Elizabeth P.[3] Arbogast, 3.Rev. Cornelius[2], 1.Peter[1]), b. Nov 10 1917.
Married Nov 29 1945, **June Valencourt**, b. Jul 04 1924.

***Children*:**

647 i. Linda Elaine[7] Crissman b. Oct 25 1948. She Married **Derrell Ray Simmerson**, b. Aug 11 1948.
648 ii. Kathleen Joy Crissman b. Feb 22 1950. She Married **Joseph Edward Cudney**, b. Jan 14 1950.
649 iii. Kenneth Clyde Crissman b. Sep 30 1951.

436. **Hugh Robert[6] Guthrie** (250.Brownie Frank[5], 79.Cornelius Arbogast[4], 14.Margaret May[3] Arbogast, 3.Rev. Cornelius[2], 1.Peter[1]), b. Apr 01 1920 in Gooding, Gooding Co., CO.
Married Jan 12 1943 in Eugene, Lane Co., OR, **Wilma Marie Stien**, b. May 29 1922 in Eugene, Lane Co., OR (daughter of Albert Wright Stien and Nellie Agnus Hickey).

***Children*:**

650 i. Roger Hugh[7] Guthrie b. Jan 21 1943 in Eugene, Lane Co., OR. Married Oct 25 1969 in Urbana, Champaign Co., IL, **Doria A. Nelson**.
\+ 651 ii. Gayle Marie Guthrie b. Dec 16 1949.

438. **Jaqueline Georgia[6] Broewer** (259.Doris[5] Arbogast, 101.Roland[4], 17.Allen[3], 3.Rev. Cornelius[2], 1.Peter[1]), b. Dec 23 1937.
Married in Bentwood, St. Louis Co., MO, **Neil Hanks**, b. Sep 14 1928.

***Children*:**

652 i. Linda Ann[7] Hanks b. Oct 31 1963 in Richmond Height, St Louis, MO.
653 ii. Janet Lynn Hanks b. Mar 21 1968 in Chicago Hts., Will Co., IL.
654 iii. James Neil Hanks b. Jun 13 1969 in Chicago Hts., Will Co., IL.

439. **Henry B.[6] Broewer** (259.Doris[5] Arbogast, 101.Roland[4], 17.Allen[3], 3.Rev. Cornelius[2], 1.Peter[1]), b. Jul 31 1940.
Married Apr 14 1962 in Brentwood, St. Louis Co., MO, **Beverly Mark**, b. 1939.

***Children*:**

655 i. Christine[7] Broewer b. May 20 1965 in Kirkwood, St. Louis Co., MO.
656 ii. Joseph Broewer b. Dec 30 1966 in Kirksville, Adair Co., MO.
657 iii. John Broewer b. Jul 03 1970 in Kirksville, Adair Co., MO.
658 iv. Susanna Broewer b. Mar 03 1974 in Kirksville, Adair Co., MO.

448. **Floyd Lorain^{6} Davisson** (264.Charles Clifford^{5}, 111.Dorothy Jane^{4} Neer, 22.Margaret Ann^{3} Arbogast, 4.Otho^{2}, 1.Peter^{1}), b. Dec 13 1897 in Champaign Co., OH, d. May 14 1978.
(1) Married Jun 07 1918, **Lillian Turner**, b. Aug 08 1887 in Hemlock, Perry Co., OH, buried in Maple Grove Cem., Mechanicsburg, Champaign Co., OH, d. Dec 08 1918 in Columbus, Franklin Co., OH.

***Children** by Harriett Marie Shaw:*

\+ 659 i. Bonnie Nell^{7} Davidson b. Oct 19 1942.

(2) He Married **Harriett Marie Shaw**, b. May 31 1907 in Junction City, Perry Co., OH, buried in Xenia, Greene Co., OH, d. May 19 1968 in Florida.

449. **Bruce Raymond^{6} Davisson** (264.Charles Clifford^{5}, 111.Dorothy Jane^{4} Neer, 22.Margaret Ann^{3} Arbogast, 4.Otho^{2}, 1.Peter^{1}), b. Nov 08 1903 in Goshen Twp., Champaign Co., OH, buried in Oak Grove Cem., Delaware Co., OH, d. Jun 01 1982 in Liberty Twp. Liberty Co., OH.
Married Jun 29 1935 in Columbus, Franklin Co., OH, **Mable May Herbert**, b. Jan 06 1910 in Westfield Twp., Marrow Co., OH.

***Children**:*

\+ 660 i. David Herbert^{7} Davisson b. Nov 12 1936.
661 ii. Dean Clifford Davisson b. Apr 13 1939 in Seattle, King Co., WA.
\+ 662 iii. Dianne Sue Davisson b. Apr 06 1948.
\+ 663 iv. Daphne Jane Davisson b. Apr 06 1948.

450. **Kenneth Elijah^{6} Davisson** (264.Charles Clifford^{5}, 111.Dorothy Jane^{4} Neer, 22.Margaret Ann^{3} Arbogast, 4.Otho^{2}, 1.Peter^{1}), b. Mar 03 1907 in Pleasant Twp., Clark Co., OH.
(1) Married Dec 01 1934, **Von Cella Griffin**, b. Jun 12 1908, d. Mar 22 1980. (

***Children** by Von Cella Griffin:*

\+ 664 i. Deloris Ann^{7} Davisson b. Nov 22 1935.
665 ii. Raymond Davisson b. Jan 19 1937, buried in Maple Grove Cem., Mechanicsburg, Champaign Co., OH, d. Nov 28 1938.
\+ 666 iii. Carole Emily Davisson b. Sep 15 1940.
667 iv. Margaret Davisson b. Oct 31 1944, buried in Maple Grove Cem., Mechanicsburg, Champaign Co., OH, d. Sep 30 1945.
\+ 668 v. Donna Louise Davisson b. Aug 05 1947.

2) He Married **Betty Fell Damewood**, b. Nov 10 1910.

451. **Lt. Col. Dean Clifford^{6} Davisson** (264.Charles Clifford^{5}, 111.Dorothy Jane^{4} Neer, 22.Margaret Ann^{3} Arbogast, 4.Otho^{2}, 1.Peter^{1}), b. Apr 13 1939 in Columbus, Franklin Co., OH.
Married Sep 11 1960 in Marietta, Washington Co., OH, **Jan Foster Wheeler**, b. Feb 07 1939 in Gallipolis, Gallia Co., OH.

***Children**:*

\+ 669 i. David Craig^{7} Davisson b. Feb 17 1962.
\+ 670 ii. Robert Randell Davisson b. Jun 18 1964.
\+ 671 iii. Elizabeth Anne Davisson b. Jul 28 1969.

452. **Mable Corrine^{6} Davisson** (265.Clarence Weakley^{5}, 111.Dorothy Jane^{4} Neer, 22.Margaret Ann^{3} Arbogast, 4.Otho^{2}, 1.Peter^{1}), b. Oct 08 1901, d. Mar 11 1977.
Married Sep 18 1923, **Stanley Macrae Hanley**, b. Jun 13 1902, d. Mar 11 1977.

***Children**:*

\+ 672 i. John Franklin^{7} Hanley b. Apr 26 1916.

454. **Marvin Elwood^{6} Neer** (268.Cloice Edgar^{5}, 112.Bruce^{4}, 22.Margaret Ann^{3} Arbogast, 4.Otho^{2}, 1.Peter^{1}), b. Jun 30 1908, d. Jun 09 1982.
Married Mar 22 1929 at Clark Co., OH, **Rudy Roop**, b. Aug 28 1914, buried in McConkey Cem., Pleasant Twp., Clark Co., OH, d. Jun 09 1982.

***Children**:*

\+ 673 i. Clifford^{7} Neer b. Sep 27 1930.
\+ 674 ii. Elwood Neer b. Dec 16 1934.

+ 675 iii. Lawrence Neer b. Feb 24 1937.
+ 676 iv. Marion Neer b. Mar 21 1941.

455. **Ralph Everhart^6 Neer** (268.Cloice Edgar^5, 112.Bruce^4, 22.Margaret Ann^3 Arbogast, 4.Otho^2, 1.Peter^1), b. Jul 13 1910, d. Jun 02 1985.
Married Jun 05 1937, **Margaret Gridley**, b. Mar 12 1917.

Children:

+ 677 i. Carolyn Sue^7 Neer b. Mar 18 1939.
+ 678 ii. Elizabeth Gaye Neer b. Nov 11 1942.
+ 679 iii. Virginia Ann Neer b. Feb 17 1947.
+ 680 iv. Pamela Kay Neer b. Sep 14 1973.

459. **Annamae^6 McAdams** (270.Florence Rurth^5 Neer, 113.William Brown^4, 22.Margaret Ann^3 Arbogast, 4.Otho^2, 1.Peter^1), b. Dec 24 1926.
(1) Married May 28 1949, **Jack Ellsworth Mowery**, b. Jun 28 1925, d. Apr 20 1973.

***Children** by Jack Ellsworth Mowery:*

+ 681 i. Kathlene Ruth^7 Mowery b. Jan 27 1952.
+ 682 ii. Diane Kay Mowery.
683 iii. Michael Foster Mowery. Married Jul 20 1985, **Debbie Sue Parrott**, b. Aug 04 1961.
684 iv. Brian Arthur Mowery b. Sep 28 1960.

(2) Married Oct 28 1978, **Kenneth K. Kerting**, b. Dec 18 1924.

460. **Theodore Grant^6 Neer** (271.Milburn Theodore^5, 113.William Brown^4, 22.Margaret Ann^3 Arbogast, 4.Otho^2, 1.Peter^1), b. May 29 1928.
Married Nov 10 1956, **Patty Jo Bales**, b. Feb 27 1935.

Children:

+ 685 i. Lisa Denise^7 Neer b. Aug 02 1957.
686 ii. Amy Jo Neer b. Apr 30 1960.

462. **F. Briggs^6 Neer** (272.Paul Joseph^5, 114.Grant^4, 22.Margaret Ann^3 Arbogast, 4.Otho^2, 1.Peter^1), b. Apr 01 1915, buried in Asbury, Pleasant Twp., Clark Co., OH, d. Aug 12 1988.
He Married **Marguerite Yeazell**, b. Nov 17 1917 (daughter of William Curle Yeazell and Ida Wiet).

Children:

+ 687 i. Mary Kay^7 Neer b. Apr 02 1941.
+ 688 ii. Ruth Ann Neer b. Oct 03 1946.

463. **James Lowell^6 Neer** (272.Paul Joseph^5, 114.Grant^4, 22.Margaret Ann^3 Arbogast, 4.Otho^2, 1.Peter^1), b. Apr 25 1919.
Married Nov 22 1947, **Dorothy Miller**, b. Jan 18 1928.

Children:

+ 689 i. Keith Lowell^7 Neer b. Feb 18 1949.
+ 690 ii. Bart Frederick Neer b. Sep 29 1953.

467. **Jane Ellen^6 Schwers** (282.Ruby^5 Arbogast, 119.Marion W.^{4}, 24.Eli M.^{3}, 4.Otho^2, 1.Peter^1).
She Married **Raymond Ladd**.

Children:

691 i. Jane^7 Ladd.

487. **Opal M.^{6} Underhill** (298.Charles Ross^5, 133.Lucinda^4 Sellers, 35.Isabella Jane^3 Curl, 6.Margaret^2 Arbogast, 1.Peter^1), b. May in Liberty, Union Co., OH.
She Married **Harry Johnson**, b. About 1890 in Liberty, Union Co., OH.

Children:

692 i. Marie^7 Johnson b. About 1815 in Liberty, Union Co., OH.
693 ii. Evelyn Johnson b. About 1916 in Liberty, Union Co., OH.
694 iii. Ross T. Johnson b. About 1919 in Liberty, Union Co., OH.

488. **Florence Lucinda^6 Underhill** (298.Charles Ross^5, 133.Lucinda^4 Sellers, 35.Isabella Jane^3 Curl, 6.Margaret^2 Arbogast, 1.Peter^1), b. 7 Jul 1897 in Liberty, Union Co., OH, buried in Raymond Cem., Liberty, Union Co., OH, d. 10 Nov 1982 in Marysville, Union Co., OH.

(1) She Married **Brainard M. Drum**. . .

Children *by Brainard M. Drum:*

695 i. Junior^7 Drum.
696 ii. Clymena May Drum.

(2) She Married **Harry Paver Sr.**, b. About 1893 in Marysville, Union Co., OH

Children *by Harry Paver Sr.:*

697 iii. Harry 'Jake' Paver Jr. b. About1926 in Marysville, Union Co., OH, d. 31 Jan 2005. Married 26 Jun 1950 in Broadway, Union Co., OH**, Phyllis Ann Smith**, b. 6 Sep 1930 in Amlin, Franklin Co., OH (daughter of William Smith and Myrtle Underhill), buried in Raymond Cem., Liberty, Union Co., OH, d. 7 Dec 2005 in Marysville, Union Co., OH.

(3) Married 10 Feb 1915, **Earl F. Kreis**, b. c1891

Children *by Earl F. Kreis:*

698 iv. Charles Kreis b. About 1915 in Liberty, Union Co., OH.
699 v. Norma Kreis b. About 1917 in Liberty, Union Co., OH.
700 vi. John Kreis.

489. **Myrtle^6 Underhill** (298.Charles Ross^5, 133.Lucinda^4 Sellers, 35.Isabella Jane^3 Curl, 6.Margaret^2 Arbogast, 1.Peter^1), b. Aug 1899 in Liberty, Union Co., OH.

She Married **William Smith**.

Children:

701 i. Phyllis Ann^7 Smith b. 6 Sep 1930 in Amlin, Franklin Co., OH, buried in Raymond Cem., Liberty, Union Co., OH, d. 7 Dec 2005 in Marysville, Union Co., OH. Married 26 Jun 1950 in Broadway, Union Co., OH, **Harry 'Jake' Paver** Jr., b. About 1926 in Marysville, Union Co., OH (son of Harry Paver Sr. and Florence Lucinda Underhill), d. 31 Jan 2005.
702 ii. Harold Smith.

498. **Thomas C.^{6} Underhill** (299.John^5, 133.Lucinda^4 Sellers, 35.Isabella Jane^3 Curl, 6.Margaret^2 Arbogast, 1.Peter^1), b. About 1850 in Liberty, Union Co., OH.

(1) He Married **Lucinda Sellers** (See marriage to number 133)..

Children *by Lucinda Sellers:*

(See marriage to number 136)

(2) He Married **Amanda Sellers** (See marriage to number 499

499. **Amanda^6 Sellers** (35.Isabella Jane^5 Curl, 6.Margaret^4 Arbogast, 1.Peter^1) (See marriage to number 1498.)

509. **Dorothy^6 Riley** (309.Lena Rose^5 Curl, 141.Elza S.^{4}, 36.Henry William^3, 6.Margaret^2 Arbogast, 1.Peter^1), b. Aug 01 1904.

She Married **Royden W. Rader**, b. Jul 13 1902, d. Jan 16 1959.

Children:

\+ 703 i. Diane^7 Rader b. Dec 30 1930.
\+ 704 ii. John Rader b. Sep 29 1944.

510. **Harold^6 Sherman** (310.Alma Blanch^5 Curl, 142.Franklin M.^{4}, 36.Henry William^3, 6.Margaret^2 Arbogast, 1.Peter^1), b. Dec 04 1902, d. 1952.

Married Dec 25 1928, **Edna Inscho**, b. Nov 11 1904, d. Apr 29 1974.

Children:

\+ 705 i. Reita Jane^7 Sherman b. Dec 07 1930.

511. **Frank^6 Sherman** (310.Alma Blanch^5 Curl, 142.Franklin M.^{4}, 36.Henry William^3, 6.Margaret^2 Arbogast, 1.Peter^1), b. Jul 29 1906.

He Married **Margaret Smith**, b. Nov 26 1906.

Children:

706 i. Bonnie[7] Sherman b. Mar 06 1931, d. Feb 13 1940.
\+ 707 ii. Richard Sherman b. Oct 07 1932.
708 iii. Dana Sherman b. Nov 21 1938.
709 iv. Janice Gay Sherman b. Jan 01 1942, d. Jan 02 1942.
710 v. Judy Kay Sherman b. Jan 01 1942, d. Feb 21 1942.

512. **Lois[6] Sherman** (310.Alma Blanch[5] Curl, 142.Franklin M.[4], 36.Henry William[3], 6.Margaret[2] Arbogast, 1.Peter[1]), b. Nov 11 1908.
Married Nov 30 1933, **Walter McClaren**, b. Dec 11 1907.

Children:

711 i. Walda Lynn[7] McClaren b. Dec 31 1941. Married Jun 20 1964, **Nick Sapin**.
\+ 712 ii. Cheryl Dawn McClaren b. Dec 14 1944.

513. **Lucille[6] Sherman** (310.Alma Blanch[5] Curl, 142.Franklin M.[4], 36.Henry William[3], 6.Margaret[2] Arbogast, 1.Peter[1]), b. Aug 10 1915.
Married Jun 10 1939, **William Johnstone**, b. Aug 12 1913.

Children:

713 i. Gary[7] Johnstone b. Sep 27 1958.

514. **Jo Ann[6] Curl** (311.Henry Harrison[5], 142.Franklin M.[4], 36.Henry William[3], 6.Margaret[2] Arbogast, 1.Peter[1]), b. Jul 16 1928.
Married Dec 04 1953, **John Forbes**, b. Feb 10 1929.

Children:

\+ 714 i. Phyllis Lynn[7] Forbes b. Jun 12 1957.
715 ii. John Harrison Forbes b. Mar 11 1959, d. Mar 31 1981.

515. **Kent Wayne[6] Curl** (311.Henry Harrison[5], 142.Franklin M.[4], 36.Henry William[3], 6.Margaret[2] Arbogast, 1.Peter[1]), b. Aug 03 1930.
Married Oct 20 1956, **Shirley Arline Magden**, b. Oct 21 1935.

Children:

716 i. Kent Dewayne[7] Curl b. Oct 13 1957.
717 ii. Christopher Harting Curl b. Aug 30 1959.
718 iii. Tod Robert Curl b. Oct 25 1961.

516. **Franklin Dale[6] Curl** (311.Henry Harrison[5], 142.Franklin M.[4], 36.Henry William[3], 6.Margaret[2] Arbogast, 1.Peter[1]), b. May 04 1935.
Married Jun 15 1957, **Linda Gallagher**, b. Jan 27 1939.

Children:

719 i. Chauncey David[7] Curl b. Apr 19 1961.
720 ii. Rodney Alan Curl b. May 27 1963.
721 iii. Catharine Curl b. Feb 19 1966.

517. **Dean Even[6] Curl** (311.Henry Harrison[5], 142.Franklin M.[4], 36.Henry William[3], 6.Margaret[2] Arbogast, 1.Peter[1]), b. Oct 06 1937.
Married Apr 05 1963, **Carol Ann Kafer**, b. Dec 21 1939.

Children:

722 i. Bradley Dean[7] Curl b. Nov 05 1963.
723 ii. Cynthia Ann Curl b. Sep 22 1967.

519. **Leroy[6] Butts** (315.Bessie[5] Sage, 145.Ida M.[4] Curl, 36.Henry William[3], 6.Margaret[2] Arbogast, 1.Peter[1]), b. Sep 22 1916, d. Nov 18 1978.
He Married **Mary E. (Unknown)**.

Children:

724 i. Earl[7] Butts.

521. **Norman[6] McMillion** (317.Corinne[5] Miller, 147.Ada Blanche[4] Curl, 36.Henry William[3], 6.Margaret[2] Arbogast, 1.Peter[1]), b. Jun 07 1924, d. Jul 04 1972.
(1) Married Nov 19 1949, **Shirley Hammond**, b. Apr 20 1922, d. Jan 19 1965.

***Children** by Shirley Hammond:*

+ 725 i. Bonnie Sue[7] McMillion b. Aug 1952.
726 ii. Donald McMillion b. Jun 11 1954. Married Aug 02 1980, Julie Willner.
727 iii. Elizabeth Ann McMillion b. Mar 31 1961.

(2) Married Jul 17 1967, **Elizabeth Bengston**, b. Sep 03 1919.

522. **Martha[6] McMillion** (317.Corinne[5] Miller, 147.Ada Blanche[4] Curl, 36.Henry William[3], 6.Margaret[2] Arbogast, 1.Peter[1]), b. Oct 25 1926.
Married Aug 28 1947, **David C. Cull**.

Children:

+ 728 i. Merideth[7] Cull b. Jun 13 1952.
729 ii. Todd Cull b. Feb 01 1954. He Married **Diana Parish**.
+ 730 iii. Jeffery Cull b. Feb 29 1956.
731 iv. Andrew Cull b. Jan 28 1958.
732 v. Susan Cull b. Apr 22 1960.

523. **David[6] McMillion** (317.Corinne[5] Miller, 147.Ada Blanche[4] Curl, 36.Henry William[3], 6.Margaret[2] Arbogast, 1.Peter[1]), b. Dec 03 1927.
Married Nov 10 1951, **Mary Jane Billett**, b. Jan 07 1930.

Children:

733 i. Scott David[7] McMillion b. Jan 28 1955. He Married Kristine **Marie Joostana**.
734 ii. Martha Deann McMillion b. Feb 18 1959.
735 iii. Kathleen Mary McMillion b. Jun 12 1964.

524. **Robert[6] McMillion** (317.Corinne[5] Miller, 147.Ada Blanche[4] Curl, 36.Henry William[3], 6.Margaret[2] Arbogast, 1.Peter[1]), b. May 05 1936.
Married Aug 09 1958, **Edna Mae Hillner**, b. Dec 14 1937.

Children:

736 i. Douglass[7] McMillion b. Sep 20 1965.
737 ii. David Ellis McMillion b. Feb 17 1967.

527. **Marie[6] Messenger** (326.Cloise Hayes[5], 150.George Asa[4], 37.Emily[3] Curl, 6.Margaret[2] Arbogast, 1.Peter[1]).
She Married **A. Marlowe**.

Children:

738 i. Donald Andrew[7] Marlowe b. About Feb 1947, d. 31 May 1947 in Columbus, Franklin Co., OH.

533. **William Charles[6] Payne** (359.Mary[5] Morrison, 186.Sophia[4] Arbogast, 64.Jesse[3], 11.Peter[2], 1.Peter[1]), b. Feb 02 1878 in Prairie City, McDonough Co., IL, d. May 13 1957 in Delta Co., CO.
Married May 16 1901 in Oswego, Labette Co., KS, **Ida Mae Hail**, b. Jan 27 1882 in Keokuk, Lee Co., IA, d. Nov 17 1971 in Montrose Co., CO.

Children:

739 i. Grace[7] Payne b. Jul 24 1902 in Parsons, Labette Co., KS. Married Dec 15 1919, **Robert Willard Grant**.
740 ii. Djahlma Payne b. Feb 27 1904 in Parsons, Labette Co., KS, d. May 01 1979. He Married **Mary Owens**.
741 iii. Philman Earl Payne b. Jun 19 1908 in Gracemont, Caddo Co., OK, d. Jul 17 1984. Married Nov 08 1933, **Merle Ann Howard**.
+ 742 iv. Alma Joyce Payne b. Apr 10 1912.
743 v. Romala Payne b. in Gracemont, Caddo Co., OK. She Married **Arthur Davis**.
744 vi. Erma Ruth Payne b. Nov 14 1916 in Gracemont, Caddo Co., OK. Married Apr 21 1935, **Wilber Seath Adams**.
745 vii. Aletha Payne b. Aug 13 1919. Married Oct 20 1936, **George Ball**.
+ 746 viii. Marcia Roberta Payne b. May 16 1921.
+ 747 ix. Morris R Payne b. Aug 15 1923.
748 x. Loretta Blanch Payne b. Jan 19 1926 in Delta Co., CO. Married Jul 13 1946, **John Thomas Williams.**

538. **Harry[6] Woolverton** (363.Rose[5] Morrison, 186.Sophia[4] Arbogast, 64.Jesse[3], 11.Peter[2], 1.Peter[1]), d. Oct 19 1982 in McComb, McDonough Co., IL.
He Married **Alice Wright**, d. 1981.

Children:

749 i. Eloise^{7} Woolverton.
\+ 750 ii. Duane Woolverton b. May 11 1929.

541. **Bernice^{6} Clarke** (367.Amy^{5} Brown, 189.Mary Jane^{4} Arbogast, 64.Jesse^{3}, 11.Peter^{2}, 1.Peter^{1}), b. Jul 30 1912.
She Married **Glenn McMillian**, b. Jul 30 1912.

Children:

\+ 751 i. Marlin Glenn^{7} McMillian b. Feb 22 1934.
\+ 752 ii. Merrill Gene McMillian b. Jun 15 1935.

542. **Carl C^{6} Clarke** (367.Amy^{5} Brown, 189.Mary Jane^{4} Arbogast, 64.Jesse^{3}, 11.Peter^{2}, 1.Peter^{1}), b. Oct 04 1915.
He Married **Marjorie Taylor**, b. 1917 in McComb, McDonough Co., IL.

Children:

\+ 753 i. Terry^{7} Clarke b. 1944.
\+ 754 ii. Gary Taylor Clarke b. Jan 16 1949.
\+ 755 iii. Richard Allison Clarke b. Feb 23 1950.

543. **R Taylor^{6} Mitchell** (369.Ethel Clare^{5} Brown, 189.Mary Jane^{4} Arbogast, 64.Jesse^{3}, 11.Peter^{2}, 1.Peter^{1}), b. Nov 09 1908.
Married May 31 1938, **Carle Ivan**.

Children:

756 i. Liliam^{7} Mitchell b. 1940.
757 ii. Dan Gillin Mitchell b. Oct 13 1944. Married Nov 23 1966, **Margaret Sistler**, b. May 05 1944.

545. **Thelma Hannah^{6} Frary** (371.Lois Irene^{5} Brown, 189.Mary Jane^{4} Arbogast, 64.Jesse^{3}, 11.Peter^{2}, 1.Peter^{1}).
Married c 1931, **Homer Kincaid**, b. Nov 03 1909.

Children:

\+ 758 i. Jack Edward^{7} Kincaid b. Nov 27 1932.
\+ 759 ii. William Gerald Kincaid b. Sep 19 1934.
760 iii. Judith Alice Kincaid b. Mar 25 1936. She Married **Bill Carmichael**, b. Jan 21 1935.
\+ 761 iv. James Richard Kincaid b. Aug 09 1943.

546. **Alice Lucille^{6} Frary** (371.Lois Irene^{5} Brown, 189.Mary Jane^{4} Arbogast, 64.Jesse^{3}, 11.Peter^{2}, 1.Peter^{1}), b. Jul 20 1914.
She Married **Claude Miller**, b. Aug 11 1902.

Children:

\+ 762 i. Elizabeth Ann^{7} Miller b. Feb 19 1938.

548. **Lewis^{6} Mikesell** (373.Mertice Loine^{5} Brown, 189.Mary Jane^{4} Arbogast, 64.Jesse^{3}, 11.Peter^{2}, 1.Peter^{1}), b. Nov 14 1912, d. Jan 15 1980. He Married **Susan Bland**.

Children:

\+ 763 i. Jan Erwin^{7} Mikesell b. Feb 14 1943.

549. **Osmond^{6} Mikesell** (373.Mertice Loine^{5} Brown, 189.Mary Jane^{4} Arbogast, 64.Jesse^{3}, 11.Peter^{2}, 1.Peter^{1}), b. Feb 13 1914, d. Dec 19 1969.
He Married **Mary Barnes**.

Children:

\+ 764 i. Norma Jean^{7} Mikesell b. Mar 01 1936.
765 ii. Betty Lou Mikesell b. Nov 22 1937. She Married **Thomas Dillon**.

550. **Weist Lamoine^{6} Mikesell** (373.Mertice Loine^{5} Brown, 189.Mary Jane^{4} Arbogast, 64.Jesse^{3}, 11.Peter^{2}, 1.Peter^{1}), b. May 15 1916.
He Married **Louise Bubb**, b. Jun 17 1917.

Children:

\+ 766 i. Ralph^{7} Mikesell b. Dec 04 1936.
\+ 767 ii. Herbert Mikesell b. Jul 20 1938.

551. **Orth Arbogast^{6} Mikesell** (373.Mertice Loine^{5} Brown, 189.Mary Jane^{4} Arbogast, 64.Jesse^{3}, 11.Peter^{2}, 1.Peter^{1}), b. Nov 14 1919.
Married Nov 21 1940, **Delores Stenger**, b. May 07 1922.

Children:

768 i. Gary Lewis^{7} Mikesell b. Jan 03 1943, d. Jun 10 1944.
\+ 769 ii. Gayle Lynn Mikesell b. May 17 1945.
770 iii. Gloria Kay Mikesell b. Jul 15 1948. Married Dec 31 1972, **Connie Watt, Jr.**.

552. **Betty Lou^{6} Mikesell** (373.Mertice Loine^{5} Brown, 189.Mary Jane^{4} Arbogast, 64.Jesse^{3}, 11.Peter^{2}, 1.Peter^{1}), b. Jun 17 1921. She Married **Robert E Moore**, b. Jul 06 1920, d. Jan 14 1979.

Children:

771 i. Thomas^{7} Moore b. Jun 21 1955.

553. **Erwin Claire^{6} Mikesell** (373.Mertice Loine^{5} Brown, 189.Mary Jane^{4} Arbogast, 64.Jesse^{3}, 11.Peter^{2}, 1.Peter^{1}), b. Apr 08 1924. Married Apr 23 1955, **Grace Pawlicki**, b. Mar 03 1928.

Children:

772 i. Erwin Claire^{7} Mikesell, Jr. b. May 30 1959.
773 ii. Chis John Mikesell.

554. **Sarah Fern^{6} Cozad** (379.Mae^{5} Howard, 192.Sarah^{4} Arbogast, 64.Jesse^{3}, 11.Peter^{2}, 1.Peter^{1}), b. Jul 24 1899 in Roseville, Warren Co., IL, d. Mar 28 1991 in McComb, McDonough Co., IL. She Married **Alva Brewer**, b. in Bushnell, Walnut Grove Twp., McDonough Co., IL, d. Feb 06 1986 in McComb, McDonough Co., IL.

Children:

\+ 774 i. Richard Gene^{7} Brewer b. Jul 07 1930.

555. **Farn Elizabeth^{6} Cozad** (379.Mae^{5} Howard, 192.Sarah^{4} Arbogast, 64.Jesse^{3}, 11.Peter^{2}, 1.Peter^{1}), b. Jun 12 1902 in Roseville, Warren Co., IL, d. Mar 07 1983.
Married Sep 17 1919 in Quincy, Adams Co., IL, **Harold Black**, b. Nov 27 1899, d. 1987.

Children:

\+ 775 i. Barbara Mae^{7} Black b. Oct 07 1922.
\+ 776 ii. William Howard Black b. May 19 1925.

557. **Margaret^{6} Smith** (383.Emerson Eugene^{5}, 194.Frances^{4} Arbogast, 64.Jesse^{3}, 11.Peter^{2}, 1.Peter^{1}), b. Apr 06 1911. She Married **Robert Maxey**.

Children:

777 i. Joan^{7} Maxey.
778 ii. Susan Maxey.
779 iii. Charles Eugene Maxey.

559. **Russell^{6} Smith** (383.Emerson Eugene^{5}, 194.Frances^{4} Arbogast, 64.Jesse^{3}, 11.Peter^{2}, 1.Peter^{1}), b. May 31 1916 in Good Hope, Walnut Grove, Putnam Co., IL.
Married Dec 31 1939, **Lois Penvarvis**, b. Mar 1918.

Children:

\+ 780 i. Judy^{7} Smith.

567. **Keith Leroy^{6} Fox** (388.Myrtle^{5} Smith, 194.Frances^{4} Arbogast, 64.Jesse^{3}, 11.Peter^{2}, 1.Peter^{1}), b. Oct 15 1911, d. Oct 16 1991. Married Jul 20 1933 in Divorced, **Elsie Pauline Herchenroder**, b. Feb 02 1915.

Children:

\+ 781 i. Kathryn Louise^{7} Fox b. Oct 10 1934.
\+ 782 ii. Dean Edward Fox b. Oct 08 1935.
\+ 783 iii. Carol Jean Fox b. Mar 23 1938.
784 iv. Marylyn Kay Fox b. Aug 24 1939. Married Jun 22 1957, **Gerald Cole**, b. May 22 1935.
\+ 785 v. George Leroy Fox b. Jun 27 1941.
\+ 786 vi. Beverly Jane Fox b. Dec 23 1942.
\+ 787 vii. James Keith Fox b. Mar 16 1944.
\+ 788 viii. Kenneth Lee Fox b. Jul 15 1949.

568. **Ralth Wilton^{6} Fox** (388.Myrtle^{5} Smith, 194.Frances^{4} Arbogast, 64.Jesse^{3}, 11.Peter^{2}, 1.Peter^{1}), b. May 01 1913. Married Mar 25 1955, **Mildred Welty**, b. Sep 03 1924.

Children:

+ 789 i. David Bruce[7] Fox b. Sep 19 1956.
+ 790 ii. Joni Sue Fox b. Feb 04 1959.
791 iii. Cheryl Ann Fox b. Feb 20 1962. Married Aug 12 1989, **William Michael Barrett.**

569. **Theodore Fenton[6] Arbogast** (389.Clyde Stewart[5], 195.Stephen Aaron Douglas[4], 64.Jesse[3], 11.Peter[2], 1.Peter[1]), b. Sep 11 1905 in Silver Creek, Merrick Co., NE, d. Jun 28 1980 in Twin Falls Co., ID.
Married Aug 13 1932 in Blaire, Washington Co., NE, **Esther Wilhelmina Lallman**, b. Apr 16 1912 in Arlington, Washington Co., NE, d. Nov 23 1993 in Idaho Falls, Bonneville Co., ID.

***Children**:*

+ 792 i. Richard Francis[7] Arbogast b. Feb 10 1934.
+ 793 ii. Patricia Ann Arbogast b. May 28 1935.
794 iii. Nancy Lou Arbogast b. Dec 03 1936.
+ 795 iv. Gerald Lee Arbogast b. Apr 13 1936.
+ 796 v. Theodore Clyde Arbogast b. Dec 31 1937.

571. **Helen Elene[6] Arbogast** (389.Clyde Stewart[5], 195.Stephen Aaron Douglas[4], 64.Jesse[3], 11.Peter[2], 1.Peter[1]), b. Aug 15 1912 in Silver Creek, Blaine Co.,
ID. She Married **Arndt Andrew Oscar Chelberg**, b. Feb 16 1910 in Malmo, Saunders Co., NE.

***Children**:*

+ 797 i. Larry Arndt[7] Chelberg b. Mar 13 1938.
+ 798 ii. Gary Allen Chelberg b. Nov 13 1939.

572. **Allen Sterart[6] Arbogast** (389.Clyde Stewart[5], 195.Stephen Aaron Douglas[4], 64.Jesse[3], 11.Peter[2], 1.Peter[1]), b. Jul 02 1914 in Silver Creek, Merrick Co., NE, d. Apr 08 1994 in Eugene, Lane Co., OR.
Married Apr 21 1940 in Rupert, Minidoka Co., ID, **Ilene Johnson**, b. Apr 13 1923 in Burley, Cassia Co., ID.

***Children**:*

+ 799 i. Roland Allen[7] Arbogast b. Nov 19 1940.
+ 800 ii. Calvin Stewart Arbogast b. Jun 04 1942.
+ 801 iii. Sherry Lorraine Arbogast b. Apr 21 1944.
+ 802 iv. Leland G. Arbogast b. Mar 06 1946.
+ 803 v. Darrell Ray Arbogast b. Jan 28 1948.

573. **Gladys Catherine[6] Arbogast** (389.Clyde Stewart[5], 195.Stephen Aaron Douglas[4], 64.Jesse[3], 11.Peter[2], 1.Peter[1]), b. Aug 27 1917 in Cedar Bluffs, Saunders Co., NE.
(1) Married Mar 19 1934, **John H. Holmes**, b. Feb 03 1908 in Elgin, Kane Co., IL, d. Jul 01 1936 in Burley, Cassia Co., ID. (.

***Children** by John H. Holmes:*

+ 804 i. John Stewart[7] Holmes b. Oct 13 1934.

2) She Married **Milford Milton Coons**, b. in Canton, McPherson Co., KS, d. May 14 1989 in Chico, Butte Co., CA

***Children** by Milford Milton Coons:*

+ 805 ii. David Coons b. Sep 22 1951.

575. **Marilyn Inez[6] Arbogast** (389.Clyde Stewart[5], 195.Stephen Aaron Douglas[4], 64.Jesse[3], 11.Peter[2], 1.Peter[1]), b. Jun 03 1924 in Cedar Bluffs, Saunders Co., NE.
(1) She Married **Robert Allen Sagarra**. .

***Children** by Robert Allen Sagarra:*

806 i. Robert Craig[7] Sagarra b. Feb 15 1948 in Los Angeles, Los Angeles Co., CA.
+ 807 ii. Karen Sue Sagarra b. Feb 17 1951.
808 iii. Diane Lyn Sagarra b. Jun 04 1962 in Los Altos, Santa Clara Co., CA. She Married **Jeff Sanders**.

(2) Married Aug 17 1968, **Anthony Janulis**

576. **Carolyn Jean[6] Hutchison** (391.Nellie Millicent[5] Arbogast, 195.Stephen Aaron Douglas[4], 64.Jesse[3], 11.Peter[2], 1.Peter[1]), b. Aug 14 1921 in Silver Creek, Merrick Co., NE, d. May 19 1989 in Kearney, Buffalo Co., NE.
Married Jun 14 1942 in Yuma Co., AZ, **Richard A. House**, b. May 21 1921 in Silver Creek, Merrick Co., NE.

***Children**:*

809 i. Andra Kay[7] House b. Apr 13 1945 in Stormberg, Polk Co., NE. She Married **Cohn Cobb**.

810 ii. Cinda Rea House b. Mar 05 1949 in Grand Island, Hall Co., NE. Married Apr 23 1971, **Gale Bertrand**.
811 iii. Belinda Jane House b. Jul 24 1951 in Grand Island, Hall Co., NE. Married Apr 03 1971, **Gilbert Rude**.
812 iv. Marcia Lynn House b. Sep 10 1952 in Grand Island, Hall Co., NE. Married Nov 23 1971, **Larry Trompke**.
813 v. Patti Jean House b. Jul 31 1956 in Grand Island, Hall Co., NE. She Married **David Swift**, b. Feb 07 1976.
814 vi. Richard Gary House b. May 27 1960 in Sioux Falls, Minnehaha Co., SD.

577. **Betty Jane[6] Hutchison** (391.Nellie Millicent[5] Arbogast, 195.Stephen Aaron Douglas[4], 64.Jesse[3], 11.Peter[2], 1.Peter[1]), b. Feb 04 1924 in Silver Creek, Merrick Co., NE.
She Married **George I. Slone**, b. Aug 04 1922.

Children:

815 i. Donald Lynn[7] Slone b. Dec 14 1949 in Lincoln, Lancaster Co., NE. Married Jul 18 1971 in Colorado Springs, El Paso Co., CO, **Charlene Taylor**.
816 ii. Robert Dean Slone b. Feb 06 1952 in Syracuse, Otoe Co., NE. Married Aug 26 1981 in Seattle, King Co., WA, **Julianna Uerling**.
817 iii. Gregg Ivan Slone b. Jun 19 1953 in Neligh, Antelope Co., NE. Married in Glenwood Springs, Garfield Co., CO, **Susan Richards**.
818 iv. Bryan Eugene Slone b. Jul 28 1957 in Wayne Co., NE. Married Oct 29 1984 in Lincoln, Lancaster Co., NE, **Leslie Shaner**.

578. **Marjorie Elaine[6] Gerber** (392.Gladys Mary[5] Arbogast, 195.Stephen Aaron Douglas[4], 64.Jesse[3], 11.Peter[2], 1.Peter[1]), b. May 17 1921 in Silver Creek, Merrick Co., NE, d. Aug 1959 in Denver, Arapaho Co., CO.
She Married **Lambert Bukacek**.

Children:

819 i. Darrell Gene[7] Bukacek.
820 ii. Jerry Dean Bukacek.
821 iii. Jody Ann Bukacek.

594. **Dwight[6] Arbogast** (398.Jessie L.[5], 199.John Franklin[4], 67.Michael[3], 11.Peter[2], 1.Peter[1]), b. Jul 13 1911.
He Married **Helen Louise Shely**.

Children:

\+ 822 i. John Allen[7] Arbogast.
\+ 823 ii. Carol Jean Arbogast.
\+ 824 iii. Rual Arbogast.

599. **Lois Alberta[6] Arbogast** (411.James Michael[5], 202.Charles Sayers[4], 67.Michael[3], 11.Peter[2], 1.Peter[1]), b. in Richdale, Alberta, CA.
Married Jan 12 1941, **Douglas Earl Slater**.

Children:

\+ 825 i. Brian Earl[7] Slater b. Nov 02 1946.
\+ 826 ii. Lynn Marie Slater b. Oct 10 1948.

600. **Gayl Jane[6] Arbogast** (411.James Michael[5], 202.Charles Sayers[4], 67.Michael[3], 11.Peter[2], 1.Peter[1]), b. Oct 14 1921, d. Nov 27 1967.
She Married **Charles Arthur Armour**.

Children:

\+ 827 i. Patricia Leigh[7] Armour b. Jan 24 1943.
828 ii. Arthur Glenn Armour b. Dec 15 1944, d. Jun 04 1969.
829 iii. Myrna Rea Armour b. Aug 03 1946.

601. **Charles Sayers[6] Arbogast** (411.James Michael[5], 202.Charles Sayers[4], 67.Michael[3], 11.Peter[2], 1.Peter[1]), b. Jul 29 1925, d. Feb 04 1992.
He Married **Ruth Pedersen**.

Children:

830 i. Carol Annetta[7] Arbogast b. May 07 1954. She Married **Ivor Oberholtzer**.
831 ii. Craig Sayers Arbogast b. Sep 28 1955, d. Dec 21 1973.
832 iii. Dale Scott Arbogast b. Nov 29 1958. He Married **Wanda Gorman**.

602. **James Kenneth^{6} Heath** (412.Alice^{5} Arbogast, 202.Charles Sayers^{4}, 67.Michael^{3}, 11.Peter^{2}, 1.Peter^{1}), b. Jan 08 1913 in Canada, d. Jan 02 1988 in Good Hope, Walnut Grove, Putnam Co., IL.
He Married **Josephine Bobrick**, b. Nov 18 1913 in Van Meter, Westmoreland Co., PA.

Children:

+ 833 i. John^{7} Heath b. Jul 05 1946.
834 ii. Joseph Heath b. Jun 15 1949 in McComb, McDonough Co., IL. He Married **Shirley Lensch**.
+ 835 iii. Susan Heath b. Dec 08 1952.

603. **Marion E.^{6} Heath** (412.Alice^{5} Arbogast, 202.Charles Sayers^{4}, 67.Michael^{3}, 11.Peter^{2}, 1.Peter^{1}), b. Nov 18 1917.
(1) She Married **Charles Thomas Buell**, b. Jul 1917

***Children** by Newburn Bates:*

+ 836 i. Danial Claude^{7} Bates b. Jan 20 1946.
+ 837 ii. Donna Ruth Bates b. Nov 21 1949.

(2) She Married **Newburn Bates**, b. Apr 04 1919 at Eva, Morgan Co., AL, d. Jul 07 1960 in Peoria, Peoria Co., IL.

604. **James Clarence^{6} Arbogast** (415.Clarence James^{5}, 203.Rush Arlington^{4}, 67.Michael^{3}, 11.Peter^{2}, 1.Peter^{1}), b. Mar 13 1927 in Seneca Co., OH, d. Jul 1 1982 in Tiffin, Seneca Co., OH, buried in St. Mary's Cem., Tiffin, Seneca Co., OH.
Married Oct 25 1947 in Tiffin, Seneca Co., OH, **Margery Louise Shaull**, b. Jan 25 1929.**Margery**:
.

Children:

+ 838 i. Suzanne Marie^{7} Arbogast b. Nov 2 0052.
+ 839 ii. Teresa Kay Arbogast b. May 6 0055.
840 iii. Michael James Arbogast b. Jun 1 0058 in Tiffin, Seneca Co., OH. Married May 29 1981, **Rosann Kessler**, b. May 15 1960.
+ 841 iv. Gregory Charles Arbogast b. Mar 1 0062.
842 v. Brett Arbogast b. May 22 0065 in Tiffin, Seneca Co., OH.
843 vi. Karen Ann Arbogast b. Oct 21 1948. Married Sep 03 1971**, James Lynn Mars**, b. Mar 12 1949.
+ 844 vii. Anita Louise Arbogast b. Aug 14 1960.
845 viii. Laura Jenne Arbogast b. May 01 1962.
This Family has 4 living children as of 2005.
Married Aug 25 1984, **Randal W. Brickner**, b. Sep 19 1960.

605. **Naomi Agnus^{6} Arbogast** (415.Clarence James^{5}, 203.Rush Arlington^{4}, 67.Michael^{3}, 11.Peter^{2}, 1.Peter^{1}), b. Jun 06 1938.
Married Sep 05 1959, **Peter Eugene Hankish**, b. Feb 10 1932. **Peter**: Nickname:<NICK> Gene
.

Children:

846 i. Deborah Sue^{7} Hankish b. Nov 16 1960.
847 ii. Steven Michael Hankish b. Apr 01 1963.
848 iii. Timothy Joseph Hankish b. Jul 17 1966.

606. **Paul Joseph^{6} Arbogast** (416.Charles Anthony^{5}, 203.Rush Arlington^{4}, 67.Michael^{3}, 11.Peter^{2}, 1.Peter^{1}), b. Sep-06-1922.
He Married **Florence Clouse**. .

Children:

+ 849 i. Jane^{7} Arbogast.
+ 850 ii. Dean Lawrence Arbogast.
+ 851 iii. Ruth Ann Arbogast.
+ 852 iv. Judith Carol Arbogast.
853 v. Carl Arbogast.
+ 854 vi. Mark Anthony Arbogast b. Sep 30 1963.

607. **Lawrence Anselm^{6} Arbogast** (416.Charles Anthony^{5}, 203.Rush Arlington^{4}, 67.Michael^{3}, 11.Peter^{2}, 1.Peter^{1}), b. Dec-20-1924.
He Married **Marion Schullenburger**. .

Children:

+ 855 i. Daria^{7} Arbogast b. Apr 29 1953.
856 ii. Lydia Ann Arbogast b. Oct 15 1954.
857 iii. Clara Ellen Arbogast b. Jan 07 1956.

+ 858 iv. Paula Louise Arbogast b. Sep 15 1958.
859 v. Peter Eugene Arbogast b. Mar 26 1966. Married Jun 06 1978, **Carol Sue Kimbell**.
860 vi. Mariea Rose Arbogast b. Mar 28 1968.
861 vii. Elmer Lester Arbogast b. Mar 31 1971.
862 viii. Anita Arbogast b. Sep 05 1974.

608. **Urban Anthony^{6} Arbogast** (416.Charles Anthony^{5}, 203.Rush Arlington^{4}, 67.Michael^{3}, 11.Peter^{2}, 1.Peter^{1}), b. Mar-20-1926. Married Oct 16 1948 in Seneca Co., OH, **Dorothy Ann Daniels**, b. Jun 05 1928 in Seneca Co., OH. .

Children:

+ 863 i. Virginia Ann^{7} Arbogast b. Oct 11 1949.
+ 864 ii. Alice Rose Arbogast b. Sep 10 1950.
+ 865 iii. Pauline Mary Arbogast b. Sep 06 1951.
+ 866 iv. Helen Lucille Arbogast b. Mar 16 1953.
+ 867 v. Susan Theresa Arbogast b. Mar 29 1953.
+ 868 vi. Doris Mae Arbogast b. May 04 1955.
+ 869 vii. Angela Marie Arbogast b. May 21 1956.
+ 870 viii. Janice Eileen Arbogast b. May 17 1958.
+ 871 ix. Patricia Louise Arbogast b. May 05 1960.
+ 872 x. June Ellen Arbogast b. Jun 04 1961.
+ 873 xi. Linda Kay Arbogast b. Oct 27 1966.
874 xii. Betty Jean Arbogast b. Aug 13 1968. Married Jun 05 1992, **James Basset**, b. Jan 03 1961.
875 xiii. David Anthony Arbogast b. Jun 25 1971, d. Aug 15 1971.

609. **Eugene Jerome^{6} Arbogast** (416.Charles Anthony^{5}, 203.Rush Arlington^{4}, 67.Michael^{3}, 11.Peter^{2}, 1.Peter^{1}), b. Oct 24 1928. Married Mar 17 1952, **Eileen Wagner**, b. Dec 25 1932, d. Oct 16 1966. .

Children:

+ 876 i. Marilyn Ann^{7} Arbogast b. Dec 05 1952.
877 ii. Ronald Marion Arbogast b. Jan 23 1954. Married Aug 24 1985, **Brenda Nique**, b. Apr 04 1961.
+ 878 iii. Barbara Jean Arbogast b. Nov 27 1957.
+ 879 iv. Kenneth Arbogast b. Mar 30 1959.
880 v. Gary Arbogast b. Sep 15 1960.
+ 881 vi. Lois Marie Arbogast b. Jul 05 1962.

610. **Marion Victor^{6} Arbogast** (416.Charles Anthony^{5}, 203.Rush Arlington^{4}, 67.Michael^{3}, 11.Peter^{2}, 1.Peter^{1}), b. Apr 16 1930. Married Jun 18 1955, **Kathleen Marie Wilhelm**, b. Nov 27 1931.

Children:

+ 882 i. Diane Ruth^{7} Arbogast b. Jan 10 1956.
883 ii. Roxanne Marguerite Arbogast b. Feb 25 1957. She Married **Timothy Ferrell**.
884 iii. Nancy Eileen Arbogast b. Aug 02 1958.
885 iv. Norma Mae Arbogast b. Dec 27 1959, d. Apr 22 1962.
886 v. Sharon Marie Arbogast b. May 02 1961. Married May 05 1984, **Daniel Eugene George**, b. Jan 21 1957.

611. **Marguerite Elenora^{6} Arbogast** (416.Charles Anthony^{5}, 203.Rush Arlington^{4}, 67.Michael^{3}, 11.Peter^{2}, 1.Peter^{1}), b. Apr 30 1934. She Married **Eugene Boes**. .

Children:

+ 887 i. Theresa Marie^{7} Boes b. Jun 15 1954.
888 ii. Michael Eugene Boes b. Sep 06 1957. Married Apr 14 1984, **Sandra Watson**.
889 iii. John Charles Boes b. Aug 26 1959.
890 iv. Donald Marion Boes b. Oct 05 1961.
891 v. Mary Irene Boes b. Aug 26 1965. Married Sep 13 1986, **Gregory Scott Bussing**.

612. **Harlan Clarence^{6} Arbogast** (416.Charles Anthony^{5}, 203.Rush Arlington^{4}, 67.Michael^{3}, 11.Peter^{2}, 1.Peter^{1}), b. Nov 24 1936. Married Jan 31 1959, **Rosemary Schriner**, b. Feb 07 1940. .

Children:

+ 892 i. Mary Catherine^{7} Arbogast b. Aug 17 1959.
+ 893 ii. Carol Sue Arbogast b. Sep 10 1960.
+ 894 iii. Sandra Marie Arbogast b. May 23 1962.
895 iv. Steven Joseph Arbogast b. Jun 08 1963. Married Jun 08 1985, **Yvonne Haubert**.

896 v. Phillis Jean Arbogast. Married Jul 30 1988, **Brian Ream**.
897 vi. James Lester Arbogast b. Jun 23 1965.
898 vii. Tina Rose Arbogast b. Nov 11 1967.
899 viii. Roger Urban Arbogast b. Feb 04 1969. Married May 07 1988, **Lori Bigley**.
\+ 900 ix. Wanda Ann Arbogast b. Jun 23 1970.
901 x. Joanna Mary Arbogast b. Feb 25 1972.
902 xi. Justin Lee Arbogast b. Mar 10 1973.
903 xii. Dennis Larry Arbogast b. Mar 20 1975.
904 xiii. Melissa Ann Arbogast b. Jul 27 1976.
905 xiv. Bruce Dean Arbogast b. Jul 27 1976.
906 xv. Douglas Ronald Arbogast b. Aug 07 1978.
907 xvi. Jessica Lynn Arbogast b. Oct 01 1980.

613. **Lester Michael[6] Arbogast** (416.Charles Anthony[5], 203.Rush Arlington[4], 67.Michael[3], 11.Peter[2], 1.Peter[1]), b. Jul 21 1938. Married Sep-26-1942, **Eloise Marie Piper**, b. Sep 26 1942.

Children:

908 i. Kevin Michael[7] Arbogast b. Sep 23 1963.
909 ii. Brian James Arbogast b. Mar 08 1965. He Married **Dawn Marie Kuhn**.
910 iii. Randel Louis Arbogast b. Mar 19 1969.
911 iv. Laura Marie Arbogast b. Jun 14 1973.

614. **Rita Mae[6] Arbogast** (416.Charles Anthony[5], 203.Rush Arlington[4], 67.Michael[3], 11.Peter[2], 1.Peter[1]), b. Nov-26-1941. She Married **Robert Joseph Kelbley**. .

Children:

912 i. Deborah Louise[7] Kelbley b. Mar 13 1961.
913 ii. Lynn Edward Kelbley b. Jun 02 1962. Married Jul 12 1986, **Rebecca J. Smith**.
914 iii. Pamala Jane Kelbley b. May 07 1964.
\+ 915 iv. Neil Eugene Kelbley b. Jun 07 1965.

615. **Louis Cyril[6] Arbogast** (416.Charles Anthony[5], 203.Rush Arlington[4], 67.Michael[3], 11.Peter[2], 1.Peter[1]), b. Aug-01-1944. Married Jul 22 1967, **Jennette An Hammer**, b. Apr 11 1947.

Children:

916 i. Leonard Michael[7] Arbogast b. May 12 1968.
917 ii. Amy Jo Arbogast b. May 02 1969.
918 iii. Karen Ann Arbogast b. Jun 24 1970. Married Nov 19 1988, **James McNulty**, b. Apr 18 1960.
919 iv. Gene Blaser Arbogast b. Oct 13 1972.
920 v. Eli Victor Arbogast b. Feb 26 1973.

617. **Clarence Louis[6] SMITH** (417.Frances Marie[5] Arbogast, 203.Rush Arlington[4], 67.Michael[3], 11.Peter[2], 1.Peter[1]), b. Nov 17 1915.
Married May 13 1938, **Rita Margaret Sendelbach**. .

Children:

\+ 921 i. Elmo Harold[7] SMITH b. Jan 25 1941.
\+ 922 ii. Norman Paul Smith b. Sep 27 1943.
\+ 923 iii. Nancy Smith b. Feb 13 1945.
\+ 924 iv. Ramona Teresita Smith b. Jan 07 1950.

618. **Rita Theresa[6] SMITH** (417.Frances Marie[5] Arbogast, 203.Rush Arlington[4], 67.Michael[3], 11.Peter[2], 1.Peter[1]), b. Nov 07 1916. Married Nov 25 1937, **James Allen King**, b. Aug 21 1910, d. Mar 15 1979. .

Children:

\+ 925 i. Louis James[7] KING b. Dec 04 1938.
\+ 926 ii. Marjorie Ann King b. Nov 23 1941.

619. **Richard Joseph[6] SMITH** (417.Frances Marie[5] Arbogast, 203.Rush Arlington[4], 67.Michael[3], 11.Peter[2], 1.Peter[1]), b. Mar 12 1920.
Married Feb 02 1943, **Margaret Dorothy Sloma**, b. Aug 04 1921. .

Children:

+ 927 i. Deanna Rose[7] SMITH b. Nov 24 1943.
+ 928 ii. Allan Peter Smith b. Jan 07 1945.
+ 929 iii. Alice Mary Smith b. Feb 23 1949.
+ 930 iv. Jane Margaret Smith b. Dec 30 1949.

621. **Marjorie Mary[6] SMITH** (417.Frances Marie[5] Arbogast, 203.Rush Arlington[4], 67.Michael[3], 11.Peter[2], 1.Peter[1]), b. Oct 17 1922.
She Married **Calvin James Adams**, b. Apr 17 1921. .

Children:

+ 931 i. Gloria Jean[7] Adams b. Dec 11 1946.
932 ii. Carol Ann Adams b. Aug 19 1948. She Married **Gary Wilson**.
+ 933 iii. Gerald Edwards Adams b. Feb 12 1954.

622. **Robert Eugene[6] SMITH** (417.Frances Marie[5] Arbogast, 203.Rush Arlington[4], 67.Michael[3], 11.Peter[2], 1.Peter[1]), b. Sep 19 1925.
Married Aug 28 1947, **Clarice M. Keller**, b. Dec 17 1925. .

Children:

+ 934 i. Cheryl Lajean[7] SMITH b. Aug 27 1949.
+ 935 ii. Patricia Ann Smith b. Nov 29 1954.

623. **Helen Francis[6] SMITH** (417.Frances Marie[5] Arbogast, 203.Rush Arlington[4], 67.Michael[3], 11.Peter[2], 1.Peter[1]), b. Sep 28 1927, d. Sep 29 1959.
She Married **Herbert Hammer**. .

Children:

+ 936 i. David Eugene[7] HAMMER b. Aug 21 1947.
+ 937 ii. Thomas Herbert Hammer b. Sep 13 1948.
+ 938 iii. William Joseph Hammer b. Feb 11 1951.
+ 939 iv. Donald Lee Hammer b. May 29 1953.
+ 940 v. Kenneth Lewis Hammer b. May 29 1953.
+ 941 vi. Mary Alice Hammer b. Sep 02 1955.
+ 942 vii. Eileen Marie Hammer b. Mar 16 1957.
+ 943 viii. Roger Francis Hammer b. Sep 28 1958.
944 ix. Michael Paul Hammer b. Sep 29 1959. He Married **Judith Ann Bonham**.

624. **Bernard Charles[6] SMITH** (417.Frances Marie[5] Arbogast, 203.Rush Arlington[4], 67.Michael[3], 11.Peter[2], 1.Peter[1]), b. May 30 1929.
He Married **Carolyn Smith**. .

Children:

945 i. Michael Lynn[7] SMITH b. Oct 13 1953. He Married **Victoria Kersch**.
946 ii. Joseph Lynn Smith b. Oct 28 1954. He Married **Jean Brickner**.
947 iii. Lorraine Ann Smith b. Feb 26 1956.
948 iv. Steven Patrick Smith b. Sep 18 1957. He Married **Linda Elchert**.
+ 949 v. Jill Christine Smith.
950 vi. John Damian Smith b. Feb 23 1964.
951 vii. Michelle Marie Smith b. Sep 05 1967.

625. **Leo Frederick[6] SMITH** (417.Frances Marie[5] Arbogast, 203.Rush Arlington[4], 67.Michael[3], 11.Peter[2], 1.Peter[1]), b. Feb 19 1931.
He Married **Elizabeth Zole**. .

Children:

952 i. Thomas Joseph[7] SMITH b. Apr 09 1957.
+ 953 ii. Edward Louis Smith.
954 iii. Virginia Marie Smith b. Jan 07 1963.
955 iv. Christopher Lee Smith b. Apr 24 1964.
956 v. Deborah Sue Smith b. Feb 02 1966.
957 vi. Donna Jean Smith b. Apr 24 1968.
958 vii. Jude Ann Smith b. Oct 14 1980.

626. **Catherine Louise^6 SMITH** (417.Frances Marie^5 Arbogast, 203.Rush Arlington^4, 67.Michael^3, 11.Peter^2, 1.Peter^1), b. Dec 20 1935.
She Married **Frederick Tiell**. .

Children:

959 i. Steven Joseph^7 Tiell b. Jul 14 1961.
960 ii. Susan Lynn Tiell b. Sep 13 1969.

627. **Rosemary^6 SMITH** (417.Frances Marie^5 Arbogast, 203.Rush Arlington^4, 67.Michael^3, 11.Peter^2, 1.Peter^1), b. Jan 22 1938.
She Married **Thomas Widmam**, b. Apr 17 1933. .

Children:

961 i. Mark Thomas^7 Widmam b. Feb 12 1961.
962 ii. Jean Marie Widman b. Jun 20 1963.
963 iii. Sharon Rose Widman b. Sep 08 1965.
964 iv. Anna Kristin Widman b. Mar 10 1970.

Generation Seven

628. **Max Ramon McConnell,^{7} DDS** (422.Clara Loveda^6 Crissman, 220.Cornelius Eugene^5, 73.Melissa^4 Latimer, 13.Elizabeth P.^{3} Arbogast, 3.Rev. Cornelius^2, 1.Peter^1), b. Apr 04 1931 in Three Rivers, St. Joseph Co., MI.
(1) Married Dec 23 1953, **Susan E. Button**

Children *by Susan E. Button:*

965 i. Mark Raynold^8 McConnell b. Mar 16 1955 in Ann Arbor, Washtenaw Co., MI.
966 ii. Kimberly Ann McConnell b. Mar 16 1957 in Ann Arbor, Washtenaw Co., MI. Married Nov 29 1986 in Dallas, Dallas Co., TX, **Larry Masters**.
\+ 967 iii. Scott Douglas McConnell b. Aug 02 1958.
968 iv. Jay Michael McConnell b. Nov 28 1960 in Tampa, Pasco Co., FL.

. (2) He Married **Judith L. Reed**, b. Mar 12 1950. (3) He Married **Marjorie J. Houston**.

629. **Thomas Omar^7 McConnell** (422.Clara Loveda^6 Crissman, 220.Cornelius Eugene^5, 73.Melissa^4 Latimer, 13.Elizabeth P.^{3} Arbogast, 3.Rev. Cornelius^2, 1.Peter^1), b. Jul 04 1934 in Cold Water, Branch Co., MI.
(1) Married Aug 27 1960 in Tampa, Pasco Co., FL, **Sharon Barnes Strong**. (

Children *by Sharon Barnes Strong:*

\+ 969 i. Troy Len^8 McConnell b. May 12 1962.
970 ii. Stephen Michael McConnell b. May 04 1965 in Fort Myers, Lee Co., FL. Married Nov 28 1992 in Jacksonville, Duval Co., FL, **Tracy Renee Riley.**

3) He Married **Darlene Hammond**.
(4) He Married **Barbara Evens**.

646. **Patricia Irene^7 Crissman** (430.Clarence Eugene^6, 222.Ernest Raymond^5, 73.Melissa^4 Latimer, 13.Elizabeth P.^{3} Arbogast, 3.Rev. Cornelius^2, 1.Peter^1), b. Dec 07 1941 in Mt. Clemens, Macomb Co., MI.
(1) Married Sep 02 1961, **Charles Curtiss Solmon**, b. Jun 20 1941.

Children *by Charles Curtiss Solmon:*

971 i. Debora Kay^8 Salmon b. Apr 04 1963 in Mt. Clemens, Macomb Co., MI. Married Aug 03 1985, William Becker.
972 ii. Donna Kim Salmon b. Oct 28 1964 in Mt. Clemens, Macomb Co., MI. Married Oct 19 1985, Curtiss Hargrove.

(2) Married Dec 29 1979, **Gerald Leroy Bebernick**, b. Feb 05 1944 in Detroit, Wayne Co., MI (son of Erwin J. Bebernick and Helen Fedorka).

651. **Gayle Marie^7 Guthrie** (436.Hugh Robert^6, 250.Brownie Frank^5, 79.Cornelius Arbogast^4, 14.Margaret May^3 Arbogast, 3.Rev. Cornelius^2, 1.Peter^1), b. Dec 16 1949 in Eugene, Lane Co., OR.
Married May 13 1972 in Eugene, Lane Co., OR, **Daniel Tracy Aldridge**, b. Feb 06 1944 in Sacramento, Sacramento Co., CA (son of Clifford Earl Aldridge and Helen Elizabeth Sawyer).

Children:

973 i. Natalie Machelle[8] Aldridge b. Sep 22 1975 in Eugene, Lane Co., OR.
974 ii. Stephany Marie Aldridge b. Feb 14 1978 in Eugene, Lane Co., OR.

659. **Bonnie Nell[7] Davidson** (448.Floyd Lorain[6] Davisson, 264.Charles Clifford[5], 111.Dorothy Jane[4] Neer, 22.Margaret Ann[3] Arbogast, 4.Otho[2], 1.Peter[1]), b. Oct 19 1942.
(1) She Married **Richard Crossley**. .

Children *by Richard Crossley:*

975 i. Truman B.[8] Crossley b. Jun 29 1964.
976 ii. Mark L. Crossley b. Oct 09

(2) She Married **Benjamin P. Lockwood, Sr.**.

Children *by Benjamin P. Lockwood, Sr.:*

977 iii. Benjamin P. Lockwood, Jr. b. Dec 24 1970.

660. **David Herbert[7] Davisson** (449.Bruce Raymond[6], 264.Charles Clifford[5], 111.Dorothy Jane[4] Neer, 22.Margaret Ann[3] Arbogast, 4.Otho[2], 1.Peter[1]), b. Nov 12 1936 in Columbus, Franklin Co., OH.
Married Dec 14 1958 in Delaware Co., OH, **Jane Louise Miller**, b. May 23 1938.

Children:

978 i. Douglas Raymond[8] Davisson b. Aug 14 1972.
\+ 979 ii. Denise Louise Davisson b. Dec 21 1960.
980 iii. Deborah Jane Davisson b. Aug 23 1967 in Columbus, Franklin Co., OH. Married Oct 09 1993 in Spartanburg Co., SC, **Thomas Lee Chapps, Jr.**.

662. **Dianne Sue[7] Davisson** (449.Bruce Raymond[6], 264.Charles Clifford[5], 111.Dorothy Jane[4] Neer, 22.Margaret Ann[3] Arbogast, 4.Otho[2], 1.Peter[1]), b. Apr 06 1948 in Columbus, Franklin Co., OH.
Married Jun 11 1967 in Liberty Church, Delaware Co., OH, **Ralph Edward Williamson**, b. 1948.

Children:

981 i. Brian Kier[8] Williamson b. Dec 04 1967.
982 ii. Megan Miranda Williamson b. Jul 07 1973.

663. **Daphne Jane[7] Davisson** (449.Bruce Raymond[6], 264.Charles Clifford[5], 111.Dorothy Jane[4] Neer, 22.Margaret Ann[3] Arbogast, 4.Otho[2], 1.Peter[1]), b. Apr 06 1948 in Columbus, Franklin Co., OH.
Married Dec 19 1970, **Paul Edwin Magnusson**, b. Jul 06 1945.

Children:

983 i. Michael Brandon[8] Magnusson b. May 05 1972.
984 ii. Laura Louise Magnusson b. Mar 19 1974.

664. **Deloris Ann[7] Davisson** (450.Kenneth Elijah[6], 264.Charles Clifford[5], 111.Dorothy Jane[4] Neer, 22.Margaret Ann[3] Arbogast, 4.Otho[2], 1.Peter[1]), b. Nov 22 1935 in Clark Co., OH.
Married Jul 06 1957, **Robert Baird**, b. Feb 17 1935.

Children:

\+ 985 i. Robert Mark[8] Baird b. Jul 18 1959.
986 ii. Tamara Lynn Baird b. Jun 05 1962. Married Nov 07 1987 in Troy, Greene Co., OH, **Allan Ganley**, b. Dec 28 1960 in Cleveland, Cuyahoga Co., OH.
987 iii. Brent Allen Baird b. Aug 23 1966.

666. **Carole Emily[7] Davisson** (450.Kenneth Elijah[6], 264.Charles Clifford[5], 111.Dorothy Jane[4] Neer, 22.Margaret Ann[3] Arbogast, 4.Otho[2], 1.Peter[1]), b. Sep 15 1940.
Married May 11 1963, **Glen Allen Long**, b. Oct 01 1939.

Children:

988 i. Jeremy Andrew[8] Long b. Dec 13 1963.
\+ 989 ii. Eric Michael Long b. Jul 13 1965. Married Sep 14 1968, **Gary Van Winkle**, b. Oct 12 1942.

Children:

990 i. Darren[8] Van Winkle b. Mar 12 1969.

669. **David Craig[7] Davisson** (451.Lt. Col. Dean Clifford[6], 264.Charles Clifford[5], 111.Dorothy Jane[4] Neer, 22.Margaret Ann[3] Arbogast, 4.Otho[2], 1.Peter[1]), b. Feb 17 1962 in Marietta, Washington Co., OH.

Married 0907191 in Columbus, Franklin Co., OH, **Carrie Jo Fabbro**, b. Aug 14 1968 in Columbus, Franklin Co., OH.

Children:

991 i. James Fabbro[8] Davisson b. 1993.

670. **Robert Randell[7] Davisson** (451.Lt. Col. Dean Clifford[6], 264.Charles Clifford[5], 111.Dorothy Jane[4] Neer, 22.Margaret Ann[3] Arbogast, 4.Otho[2], 1.Peter[1]), b. Jun 18 1964 in Griffins AFB, Rome, Oneida Co., NY.
Married Nov 24 1984 in Altenburg, Castle, Bamberg, Germany, **Bridget Marie Metzner**, b. Dec 20 1964 in Bamberg, Batavia, Germany.

Children:

992 i. Christian Werner[8] Davisson b. Apr 10 1981.
993 ii. Tamara Savannah Davisson.

671. **Elizabeth Anne[7] Davisson** (451.Lt. Col. Dean Clifford[6], 264.Charles Clifford[5], 111.Dorothy Jane[4] Neer, 22.Margaret Ann[3] Arbogast, 4.Otho[2], 1.Peter[1]), b. Jul 28 1969.
Married Aug 19 1989 in Fairborn, Greene Co., OH, **James Sayaang Brantley**, b. Oct 13 1969.

Children:

994 i. Sarah Elizabeth[8] Johnson b. Jun 26 1988 in Dayton, Montgomery Co., OH.
995 ii. Jennifer Pearl Brantley b. Aug 12 1990 in Cherry Point, Havelock Co., NC.

672. **John Franklin[7] Hanley** (452.Mable Corrine[6] Davisson, 265.Clarence Weakley[5], 111.Dorothy Jane[4] Neer, 22.Margaret Ann[3] Arbogast, 4.Otho[2], 1.Peter[1]), b. Apr 26 1916.
Married Jan 03 1954, **Clarie Francis Campbell**, b. Jul 12 1978.

Children:

996 i. Paul Campbell[8] Hanley b. Feb 01 1957.
\+ 997 ii. Norma June Hanley b. Jun 26 1935.

673. **Clifford[7] Neer** (454.Marvin Elwood[6], 268.Cloice Edgar[5], 112.Bruce[4], 22.Margaret Ann[3] Arbogast, 4.Otho[2], 1.Peter[1]), b. Sep 27 1930.
(1) Married Jan 28 1952, **Marvene Louise Davis**, b. Aug 16 1932.

***Children** by Marvene Louise Davis:*

998 i. Teresa Faye[8] Neer b. Sep 28 1952.
999 ii. Marvin Jay Neer b. Jun 05 1954.
1000 iii. Russell Dwayne Neer b. May 07 1956.
1001 iv. Dana Neer b. Nov 05 1957.
1002 v. Nancy Ann Neer b. Mar 10 1963.

(2) He Married **Diane Coutee**, b. Mar 22 1942.

***Children** by Diane Coutee:*

1003 vi. Jeffery Todd Neer b. Nov 18 1970.
1004 vii. Lisa Neer b. Jul 23 1961.
1005 viii. Mitzi Neer b. Nov 07 1962.

674. **Elwood[7] Neer** (454.Marvin Elwood[6], 268.Cloice Edgar[5], 112.Bruce[4], 22.Margaret Ann[3] Arbogast, 4.Otho[2], 1.Peter[1]), b. Dec 16 1934.
Married Oct 31 1953, **Viola Howington**, b. Oct 16 1934.

Children:

1006 i. Deborah Suzanne[8] Neer b. Sep 04 1954. She Married **Harry L. Rixey**, b. Mar 23 1978.
1007 ii. Robert Elwood b. Aug 11 1955.
1008 iii. Michael Steven Neer b. Dec 18 1957.

675. **Lawrence[7] Neer** (454.Marvin Elwood[6], 268.Cloice Edgar[5], 112.Bruce[4], 22.Margaret Ann[3] Arbogast, 4.Otho[2], 1.Peter[1]), b. Feb 24 1937.
Married Jul 10 1959, **Ruth Ann Shade**, b. Mar 04 1940.

Children:

1009 i. Gary Lee[8] Neer b. Jan 11 1960. Married Oct 30 1986, **Tammy Walker**.
1010 ii. Douglas Alan Neer b. Jun 16 1961.
1011 iii. Gregory David Neer b. Dec 07 1970.

676. **Marion**^{7} **Neer** (454.Marvin Elwood^{6}, 268.Cloice Edgar^{5}, 112.Bruce^{4}, 22.Margaret Ann^{3} Arbogast, 4.Otho^{2}, 1.Peter^{1}), b. Mar 21 1941.
Married Jun 06 1970, **Aneta Carol Evilsizor**, b. 101141947.

***Children**:*

1012 i. Stephanie Denise^{8} Neer b. Jun 22 1072.
1013 ii. Chad Andrew Neer b. Sep 08 1974.

677. **Carolyn Sue**^{7} **Neer** (455.Ralph Everhart^{6}, 268.Cloice Edgar^{5}, 112.Bruce^{4}, 22.Margaret Ann^{3} Arbogast, 4.Otho^{2}, 1.Peter^{1}), b. Mar 18 1939.
(1) Married Aug 31 1958, **Fred L. Channell**, b. Jan 19 1940.

***Children** by Fred L. Channell:*

1014 i. Melissa Kay^{8} Channell b. Oct 03 1963.
1015 ii. Melinda Sue Channell b. Oct 10 1965.
1016 iii. David Franklin Channell b. Mar 02 1971.

(2) She Married **Roy Teixeira**.
(3) She Married **Jon Pensyl**.

678. **Elizabeth Gaye**^{7} **Neer** (455.Ralph Everhart^{6}, 268.Cloice Edgar^{5}, 112.Bruce^{4}, 22.Margaret Ann^{3} Arbogast, 4.Otho^{2}, 1.Peter^{1}), b. Nov 11 1942.
Married May 18 1963, **Robert Franklin Hurd**, b. Oct 23 1941.

***Children**:*

1017 i. Brian Robert^{8} Hurd b. Nov 22 1963.
1018 ii. Beth Ann Hurd b. Oct 30 1965.

679. **Virginia Ann**^{7} **Neer** (455.Ralph Everhart^{6}, 268.Cloice Edgar^{5}, 112.Bruce^{4}, 22.Margaret Ann^{3} Arbogast, 4.Otho^{2}, 1.Peter^{1}), b. Feb 17 1947.
Married Aug 28 1966, **Daniel McBride**, b. Jul 05 1946.

***Children**:*

\+ 1019 i. Shawn Patrick^{8} McBride b. Feb 16 1967.
1020 ii. Alisa Michelle McBride b. Jul 20 1971.
1021 iii. Christopher Michael McBride b. Feb 20 1976.

680. **Pamela Kay**^{7} **Neer** (455.Ralph Everhart^{6}, 268.Cloice Edgar^{5}, 112.Bruce^{4}, 22.Margaret Ann^{3} Arbogast, 4.Otho^{2}, 1.Peter^{1}), b. Sep 14 1973.
She Married **David Sheman**.

***Children**:*

1022 i. Zachary Neer^{8} Sheman b. Aug 30 1984.
1023 ii. Emily Neer Sheman b. Aug 18 1986.

681. **Kathlene Ruth**^{7} **Mowery** (459.Annamae^{6} McAdams, 270.Florence Rurth^{5} Neer, 113.William Brown^{4}, 22.Margaret Ann^{3} Arbogast, 4.Otho^{2}, 1.Peter^{1}), b. Jan 27 1952.
Married Jun 21 1975, **Dewaune Martis Dodds**, b. Jan 25 1951.

***Children**:*

1024 i. Nathan Michael^{8} Dodds b. Mar 12 1977.
1025 ii. Christopher Ketring Dodds b. Sep 18 1980.
1026 iii. Jonathan Patrick Dodds b. Mar 22 1983.

682. **Diane Kay**^{7} **Mowery** (459.Annamae^{6} McAdams, 270.Florence Rurth^{5} Neer, 113.William Brown^{4}, 22.Margaret Ann^{3} Arbogast, 4.Otho^{2}, 1.Peter^{1}).
Married Aug 26 1978, **James Brian Halpin**, b. Jan 26 1953.

***Children**:*

1027 i. Tiffany Anne^{8} Halpin b. Feb 12 1981.

685. **Lisa Denise**^{7} **Neer** (460.Theodore Grant^{6}, 271.Milburn Theodore^{5}, 113.William Brown^{4}, 22.Margaret Ann^{3} Arbogast, 4.Otho^{2}, 1.Peter^{1}), b. Aug 02 1957.

Married Apr 03 1976, **Terry Lee Kidder**, b. Feb 24 1958.

Children:

1028 i. Douglas Theodore^{8} Kidder b. Feb 12 1981.

687. **Mary Kay^{7} Neer** (462.F. Briggs^{6}, 272.Paul Joseph^{5}, 114.Grant^{4}, 22.Margaret Ann^{3} Arbogast, 4.Otho^{2}, 1.Peter^{1}), b. Apr 02 1941.
Married Dec 15 1962, **Michael E. Russell**, b. Jul 31 1940.

Children:

1029 i. Andrew Wesley^{8} Russell b. Nov 13 1968.
1030 ii. Amy Michelle Russell b. Apr 15 1972.

688. **Ruth Ann^{7} Neer** (462.F. Briggs^{6}, 272.Paul Joseph^{5}, 114.Grant^{4}, 22.Margaret Ann^{3} Arbogast, 4.Otho^{2}, 1.Peter^{1}), b. Oct 03 1946.
Married Aug 09 1969, **Benny Herbert George**, b. Oct 04 1942.

Children:

1031 i. Molly Beth^{8} George b. Oct 25 1975.

689. **Keith Lowell^{7} Neer** (463.James Lowell^{6}, 272.Paul Joseph^{5}, 114.Grant^{4}, 22.Margaret Ann^{3} Arbogast, 4.Otho^{2}, 1.Peter^{1}), b. Feb 18 1949.
Married 081151971, **Regina Kay Snyder**, b. Jul 07 1949.

Children:

1032 i. Michelle Denise^{8} Neer b. Jan 17 1978.
1033 ii. Brent Erman Neer b. Oct 15 1979.
1034 iii. Jennifer Diane Neer b. Nov 15 1982.

690. **Bart Frederick^{7} Neer** (463.James Lowell^{6}, 272.Paul Joseph^{5}, 114.Grant^{4}, 22.Margaret Ann^{3} Arbogast, 4.Otho^{2}, 1.Peter^{1}), b. Sep 29 1953.
Married Mar 12 1977, **Karen Lynn Spencer**, b. Mar 27 1956.

Children:

1035 i. Julie Lynn^{8} Neer b. May 14 1981.
1036 ii. Eric James Neer b. Nov 23 1982.

703. **Diane^{7} Rader** (509.Dorothy^{6} Riley, 309.Lena Rose^{5} Curl, 141.Elza S.^{4}, 36.Henry William^{3}, 6.Margaret^{2} Arbogast, 1.Peter^{1}), b. Dec 30 1930.
Married Jun 13 1952, **Harold Scott**, b. Oct 21 1930.

Children:

1037 i. John Kevin^{8} Scott b. Jul 10 1958.
1038 ii. Randolph Shawn Scott b. Jan 21 1960.
1039 iii. Christopher Scott b. Oct 21 1964.

704. **John^{7} Rader** (509.Dorothy^{6} Riley, 309.Lena Rose^{5} Curl, 141.Elza S.^{4}, 36.Henry William^{3}, 6.Margaret^{2} Arbogast, 1.Peter^{1}), b. Sep 29 1944.
(1) He Married **Sheri Johnson**. .

***Children** by Sheri Johnson:*

1040 i. Renee^{8} Rader b. Aug 23 1967.
1041 ii. Shannon Rader b. Jan 05 1969.

(2) He Married **Linda Smith**, b. 1941

705. **Reita Jane^{7} Sherman** (510.Harold^{6}, 310.Alma Blanch^{5} Curl, 142.Franklin M.^{4}, 36.Henry William^{3}, 6.Margaret^{2} Arbogast, 1.Peter^{1}), b. Dec 07 1930.
Married Jan 25 1952, **Robert Stebbins**, b. Aug 30 1929.

Children:

1042 i. Connie^{8} Stebbins b. Sep 13 1952.
1043 ii. Dawn Ann Stebbins b. Sep 24 1953.
1044 iii. Rebecca Lee Stebbins b. Apr 15 1955.
1045 iv. Reita Kay Stebbins b. Nov 29 1956.
1046 v. Robert Lee Stebbins b. Aug 12 1958.
1047 vi. William Sherman Stebbins b. Nov 16 1961.

1048 vii. Edward Scott Stebbins b. Oct 07 1964.

707. **Richard^7 Sherman** (511.Frank^6, 310.Alma Blanch^5 Curl, 142.Franklin M.^{4}, 36.Henry William^3, 6.Margaret^2 Arbogast, 1.Peter^1), b. Oct 07 1932. (
1) He Married **Gay Johnson**. .

Children *by Gay Johnson:*

1049 i. Donna^8 Sherman b. May 12 1961.

(2) Married Oct 23 1965, **Diana Main**

Children *by Diana Main:*

1050 ii. Douglas Sherman b. Apr 10 1967.
1051 iii. Denise Sherman b. Oct 01 1969.

712. **Cheryl Dawn^7 McClaren** (512.Lois^6 Sherman, 310.Alma Blanch^5 Curl, 142.Franklin M.^{4}, 36.Henry William^3, 6.Margaret^2 Arbogast, 1.Peter^1), b. Dec 14 1944.
Married Jun 13 1970, **Gerald Porter**.

Children:

1052 i. Grant^8 Porter b. Apr 13 1971.

714. **Phyllis Lynn^7 Forbes** (514.Jo Ann^6 Curl, 311.Henry Harrison^5, 142.Franklin M.^{4}, 36.Henry William^3, 6.Margaret^2 Arbogast, 1.Peter^1), b. Jun 12 1957.
She Married **Dennis Grounds**.

Children:

1053 i. John Forbes^8 Grounds b. Sep 02 1991.
1054 ii. Rose Ira Grounds b. Sep 02 1991.

725. **Bonnie Sue^7 McMillion** (521.Norman^6, 317.Corinne^5 Miller, 147.Ada Blanche^4 Curl, 36.Henry William^3, 6.Margaret^2 Arbogast, 1.Peter^1), b. Aug 1952.
She Married **David Slobodiem**.

Children:

1055 i. Anna Macmillion^8 Slobodiem b. May 03 1980.

728. **Merideth^7 Cull** (522.Martha^6 McMillion, 317.Corinne^5 Miller, 147.Ada Blanche^4 Curl, 36.Henry William^3, 6.Margaret^2 Arbogast, 1.Peter^1), b. Jun 13 1952. She
Married **Don Fair**.

Children:

1056 i. Kelly Corinne^8 Fair b. Aug 27 1979.

730. **Jeffery^7 Cull** (522.Martha^6 McMillion, 317.Corinne^5 Miller, 147.Ada Blanche^4 Curl, 36.Henry William^3, 6.Margaret^2 Arbogast, 1.Peter^1), b. Feb 29 1956. He Married **Martha Elston**.

Children:

1057 i. Garrett Ekow^8 Cull b. Oct 13 1980.

742. **Alma Joyce^7 Payne** (533.William Charles^6, 359.Mary^5 Morrison, 186.Sophia^4 Arbogast, 64.Jesse^3, 11.Peter^2, 1.Peter^1), b. Apr 10 1912 in Gracemont, Caddo Co., OK.
Married Nov 09 1930 in Montrose Co., CO, **Isham Reese Hamilton**, b. Mar 24 1909 in Kearney, Buffalo Co., NE, d. Jan 13 1977 in Montrose Co., CO.

Children:

1058 i. Glen Dean^8 Hamilton b. Aug 06 1931 in Delta Co., CO. He Married **Norma Campbell**, b. Jun 06 1960 in Grand Junction, Mesa Co., CO.
1059 ii. Eddie Lee Hamilton b. Jun 23 1934 in Delta Co., CO. Married Jun 09 1968 in Montrose Co., CO, **Lila David**.
\+ 1060 iii. Lois Nadine Hamilton b. Dec 14 1936.
1061 iv. Kit J Hamilton b. Jan 21 1938 in Delta Co., CO. She Married **Sue Dickerson**, b. Sep 29 1973 in New York City, NY.
1062 v. Corliss Ann Hamilton b. Feb 07 1940 in Delta Co., CO. (1) Married Dec 24 1958 in Divorced, **William Fredricks**. (2) Married May 62 1967, **George Butler**, d. Jun 24 1973. (3) Married Apr 11 1977, **Seebert Smith**.

746. **Marcia Roberta^{7} Payne** (533.William Charles^{6}, 359.Mary^{5} Morrison, 186.Sophia^{4} Arbogast, 64.Jesse^{3}, 11.Peter^{2}, 1.Peter^{1}), b. May 16 1921 in Gracemont, Caddo Co., OK.
Married Jun 09 1939 in Delta Co., CO, **Charles Russell Robertson**, b. Jan 37 1914 in Denison, Grayson Co., TX.

Children:

+ 1063 i. Charles Ronald^{8} Robertson b. Jul 01 1941.
1064 ii. Jay Douglas Robertson b. Oct 24 1943 in Eugene, Lane Co., OR, d. May 26 1974 in Scotts Valley, Santa Cruz Co., CA. He Married **Brenda Sue Mayberry**.
+ 1065 iii. John Ralph Robertson b. Mar 07 1952.

747. **Morris R^{7} Payne** (533.William Charles^{6}, 359.Mary^{5} Morrison, 186.Sophia^{4} Arbogast, 64.Jesse^{3}, 11.Peter^{2}, 1.Peter^{1}), b. Aug 15 1923.
Married Jun 09 1946 in Ouray, Ouray Co., CO, **Dema Mae Bullock**, b. Mar 10 1926 in Maple City, Cowley Co., KS.

Children:

1066 i. Mary Ann^{8} Payne b. Jul 26 1949 in Alameda, Alameda Co., CA.
1067 ii. Richard Charles Payne b. Feb 01 1956 in Alameda, Alameda Co., CA.
1068 iii. Kenneth Bernard Payne b. Mar 29 1960 in Alameda, Alameda Co., CA.

750. **Duane^{7} Woolverton** (538.Harry^{6}, 363.Rose^{5} Morrison, 186.Sophia^{4} Arbogast, 64.Jesse^{3}, 11.Peter^{2}, 1.Peter^{1}), b. May 11 1929.
He Married **Ann Lou Harl**, b. Jul 13 1928.

Children:

1069 i. Wayne Harl^{8} Woolverton b. Dec 31 1950 in Illinois.
1070 ii. Gary Allen Woolerton b. May 13 1953 in Illinois.
+ 1071 iii. Donald Ralph Woolerton b. Jul 20 1954.
1072 iv. Ned Wayne Woolerton b. Jun 25 1958.

751. **Marlin Glenn^{7} McMillian** (541.Bernice^{6} Clarke, 367.Amy^{5} Brown, 189.Mary Jane^{4} Arbogast, 64.Jesse^{3}, 11.Peter^{2}, 1.Peter^{1}), b. Feb 22 1934.
He Married **Carol Peterson**.

Children:

1073 i. Norman Wayne^{8} McMillian.
1074 ii. Michael Kevin McMillian b. Aug 10 1957.
1075 iii. Kim Reese McMillian b. 1959.

752. **Merrill Gene^{7} McMillian** (541.Bernice^{6} Clarke, 367.Amy^{5} Brown, 189.Mary Jane^{4} Arbogast, 64.Jesse^{3}, 11.Peter^{2}, 1.Peter^{1}), b. Jun 15 1935.
He Married **Wanda Bush**.

Children:

1076 i. Shelby^{8} McMillian b. Jul 24 1958.
1077 ii. Mitchell Glenn McMillian b. Dec 07 1960.
1078 iii. Stacey Diane McMillian b. Feb 20 1969.

753. **Terry^{7} Clarke** (542.Carl C^{6}, 367.Amy^{5} Brown, 189.Mary Jane^{4} Arbogast, 64.Jesse^{3}, 11.Peter^{2}, 1.Peter^{1}), b. 1944.
Married Jan 16 1964, **Jayne Coddington**, b. 1945.

Children:

1079 i. Del^{8} Clarke b. 1965.
1080 ii. Penny Jane Clarke b. Feb 08 1970.

754. **Gary Taylor^{7} Clarke** (542.Carl C^{6}, 367.Amy^{5} Brown, 189.Mary Jane^{4} Arbogast, 64.Jesse^{3}, 11.Peter^{2}, 1.Peter^{1}), b. Jan 16 1949.
Married Apr 14 1970, **Sally Wright**.

Children:

1081 i. Jason Carl^{8} Clarke.

755. **Richard Allison^{7} Clarke** (542.Carl C^{6}, 367.Amy^{5} Brown, 189.Mary Jane^{4} Arbogast, 64.Jesse^{3}, 11.Peter^{2}, 1.Peter^{1}), b. Feb 23 1950.
He Married **Becky Creek**, b. Nov 28 1946.

Children:

1082 i. Jason Parrish^{8} Clarke b. May 06 1973.

758. **Jack Edward[7] Kincaid** (545.Thelma Hannah[6] Frary, 371.Lois Irene[5] Brown, 189.Mary Jane[4] Arbogast, 64.Jesse[3], 11.Peter[2], 1.Peter[1]), b. Nov 27 1932.
Married May 11 1959, **Sandra Wagader**.

Children:

1083 i. John Edward[8] Kincaid b. Aug 01 1961.
1084 ii. Susan Jean Kincaid b. May 07 1964.

759. **William Gerald[7] Kincaid** (545.Thelma Hannah[6] Frary, 371.Lois Irene[5] Brown, 189.Mary Jane[4] Arbogast, 64.Jesse[3], 11.Peter[2], 1.Peter[1]), b. Sep 19 1934.
He Married **Patricia Fabricia**, b. Aug 12 1933.

Children:

1085 i. Craig William[8] Kincaid b. Feb 27 1961.

761. **James Richard[7] Kincaid** (545.Thelma Hannah[6] Frary, 371.Lois Irene[5] Brown, 189.Mary Jane[4] Arbogast, 64.Jesse[3], 11.Peter[2], 1.Peter[1]), b. Aug 09 1943.
He Married **Deana Rusk**.

Children:

1086 i. Brian Richard[8] Kincaid b. Mar 20 1961.

762. **Elizabeth Ann[7] Miller** (546.Alice Lucille[6] Frary, 371.Lois Irene[5] Brown, 189.Mary Jane[4] Arbogast, 64.Jesse[3], 11.Peter[2], 1.Peter[1]), b. Feb 19 1938.
She Married **Wendell Meyer**, b. Feb 13 1936.

Children:

1087 i. Mark Allen[8] Meyer b. Apr 25 1958.
1088 ii. Sandra Meyer b. Dec 29 1961.
1089 iii. Lisa Meyer b. Feb 17 1963.

763. **Jan Erwin[7] Mikesell** (548.Lewis[6], 373.Mertice Loine[5] Brown, 189.Mary Jane[4] Arbogast, 64.Jesse[3], 11.Peter[2], 1.Peter[1]), b. Feb 14 1943.
He Married **Pamela Priestwood**.

Children:

1090 i. Shalee[8] Mikesell.
1091 ii. Doni Mikesell.

764. **Norma Jean[7] Mikesell** (549.Osmond[6], 373.Mertice Loine[5] Brown, 189.Mary Jane[4] Arbogast, 64.Jesse[3], 11.Peter[2], 1.Peter[1]), b. Mar 01 1936.
Married in Divorced, **Stanley Creech**.

Children:

1092 i. Sharon Deane[8] Creech b. Mar 30 1962.
1093 ii. Steven David Creech b. Mar 30 1962.

766. **Ralph[7] Mikesell** (550.Weist Lamoine[6], 373.Mertice Loine[5] Brown, 189.Mary Jane[4] Arbogast, 64.Jesse[3], 11.Peter[2], 1.Peter[1]), b. Dec 04 1936.
He Married **Nancy Mathers**, b. Apr 17 1937.

Children:

1094 i. Victoria[8] Mikesell b. Jul 30 1956.
1095 ii. Steven Mikesell b. Apr 06 1958.
1096 iii. Christopher Mikesell b. Oct 21 1959.
1097 iv. Timothy Mikesell b. Aug 08 1961.
1098 v. David Mikesell b. Mar 12 1962, d. Nov 10 1976.

767. **Herbert[7] Mikesell** (550.Weist Lamoine[6], 373.Mertice Loine[5] Brown, 189.Mary Jane[4] Arbogast, 64.Jesse[3], 11.Peter[2], 1.Peter[1]), b. Jul 20 1938.
He Married **Elizabeth Cosello**, b. Nov 28 1938.

Children:

1099 i. Joel Eugene[8] Mikesell b. Jan 16 1966.

1100 ii. Mary Elizabeth Mikesell b. Apr 08 1971.

769. **Gayle Lynn[7] Mikesell** (551.Orth Arbogast[6], 373.Mertice Loine[5] Brown, 189.Mary Jane[4] Arbogast, 64.Jesse[3], 11.Peter[2], 1.Peter[1]), b. May 17 1945.
Married Aug 30 1964, **Jim Garrison**, b. Mar 21 1945.

Children:

1101 i. Angela Lynn[8] Garrison b. Jul 14 1970.
1102 ii. Todd James Garrison b. Jun 26 1972.
1103 iii. Melanie Ann Garrison b. Apr 12 1978.

774. **Richard Gene[7] Brewer** (554.Sarah Fern[6] Cozad, 379.Mae[5] Howard, 192.Sarah[4] Arbogast, 64.Jesse[3], 11.Peter[2], 1.Peter[1]), b. Jul 07 1930.
Married Sep 09 1950, **Carolyn May Mochel**, b. Apr 30 1930 in Downers Grove, DuPage Co., IL.

Children:

1104 i. Dennis Gene[8] Brewer b. May 09 1953 in Avon, Fulton Co., IL.
+ 1105 ii. David Lee Brewer b. Aug 13 1955.

775. **Barbara Mae[7] Black** (555.Faun Elizabeth[6] Cozad, 379.Mae[5] Howard, 192.Sarah[4] Arbogast, 64.Jesse[3], 11.Peter[2], 1.Peter[1]), b. Oct 07 1922 in Colchester, McDonough Co., IL.
Married Dec 24 1941, **Donovan Kinkade Lawyer**, b. Jan 23 1921 in Industry, McDonough Co., IL, d. May 24 1991 in McComb, McDonough Co., IL.

Children:

+ 1106 i. Donna Kay[8] Lawyer b. Apr 10 1945.
+ 1107 ii. Linda Lou Lawyer b. Mar 08 1950.

776. **William Howard[7] Black** (555.Faun Elizabeth[6] Cozad, 379.Mae[5] Howard, 192.Sarah[4] Arbogast, 64.Jesse[3], 11.Peter[2], 1.Peter[1]), b. May 19 1925 in Good Hope, Walnut Grove, Putnam Co., IL. He Married **Nita Orlayne Toland**, b. Apr 19 1926 in Industry, McDonough Co., IL.

Children:

+ 1108 i. William Authur[8] Black b. Dec 09 1947.
+ 1109 ii. Susan Elizabeth Black b. Sep 11 1948.
+ 1110 iii. Rex Eugene Black b. Jul 04 1950.
1111 iv. Scott Black b. Oct 01 1952.

780. **Judy[7] Smith** (559.Russell[6], 383.Emerson Eugene[5], 194.Frances[4] Arbogast, 64.Jesse[3], 11.Peter[2], 1.Peter[1]), b. in McComb, McDonough Co., IL.
She Married **Robert Worman**.

Children:

1112 i. Emma[8] Worman. She Married **Kent Poulter**.
1113 ii. Kate Worman.

781. **Kathryn Louise[7] Fox** (567.Keith Leroy[6], 388.Myrtle[5] Smith, 194.Frances[4] Arbogast, 64.Jesse[3], 11.Peter[2], 1.Peter[1]), b. Oct 10 1934 in Ellisville, Fulton Co., IL.
She Married **Marion Frank Huston**, b. Jul 08 1928 in McDonough Co., IL.

Children:

+ 1114 i. Harold William[8] Huston b. Jun 24 1959.

782. **Dean Edward[7] Fox** (567.Keith Leroy[6], 388.Myrtle[5] Smith, 194.Frances[4] Arbogast, 64.Jesse[3], 11.Peter[2], 1.Peter[1]), b. Oct 08 1935 in Hartsburg, Logan Co., IL.
He Married **Maxine Starkley**, b. Mar 01 1935.

Children:

+ 1115 i. Tracie Gaye[8] Fox b. Dec 03 1958.
+ 1116 ii. Dale Edward Fox b. Sep 30 1967.
+ 1117 iii. Amy Suzanne Fox.

783. **Carol Jean[7] Fox** (567.Keith Leroy[6], 388.Myrtle[5] Smith, 194.Frances[4] Arbogast, 64.Jesse[3], 11.Peter[2], 1.Peter[1]), b. Mar 23 1938.
Married Mar 23 1957 in Divorced, **James Joseph Schulte**, b. Dec 01 1935.

Children:

\+ 1118 i. Randy Joe^{8} Schulte b. Jul 07 1957.

1119 ii. James Kent Schulte b. May 23 1959, d. Dec 01 1984. Married Aug 09 1980, **Wendy Woodward**, b. Sep 28 1959.

1120 iii. Matthew Schulte b. Apr 06 1960, d. Apr 06 1960.

1121 iv. Mark Schulte b. Apr 06 1960, d. Apr 06 1960.

1122 v. Kelly Jean Schulte b. Sep 04 1962. Married Sep 10 1983 in Divorced, **Gary Tueschmann**.

785. **George Leroy^{7} Fox** (567.Keith Leroy^{6}, 388.Myrtle^{5} Smith, 194.Frances^{4} Arbogast, 64.Jesse^{3}, 11.Peter^{2}, 1.Peter^{1}), b. Jun 27 1941.
Married in Divorced, **Victoria Ann Woerly**, b. Aug 02 1944.

Children:

1123 i. Tori Lynn^{8} Fox b. May 06 1967. She Married **Robert Sumter**, b. Apr 14 1990.

1124 ii. Michael George Fox b. Sep 10 1970.

786. **Beverly Jane^{7} Fox** (567.Keith Leroy^{6}, 388.Myrtle^{5} Smith, 194.Frances^{4} Arbogast, 64.Jesse^{3}, 11.Peter^{2}, 1.Peter^{1}), b. Dec 23 1942.
Married Nov 17 1960 in Divorced, **William Clark**, b. Feb 06 1943.

Children:

\+ 1125 i. Barbara Jo^{8} Clark b. Jun 26 1961.

\+ 1126 ii. Linda Kay Clark b. May 15 1962.

\+ 1127 iii. Carol Ann Clark b. May 25 1963.

\+ 1128 iv. Dorothy Elaine Clark b. Apr 28 1965.

787. **James Keith^{7} Fox** (567.Keith Leroy^{6}, 388.Myrtle^{5} Smith, 194.Frances^{4} Arbogast, 64.Jesse^{3}, 11.Peter^{2}, 1.Peter^{1}), b. Mar 16 1944.
James married twice, divorced each time.
(1) Married Apr 18 1964, **Kathy (Unknown).Kathy**: One child to this marriage.

***Children** by Kathy (Unknown):*

1129 i. James Todd^{8} Fox b. Feb 13 1966.

(2) Married in Divorced, **Tannie Wilson**.

***Children** by Tannie Wilson:*

1130 ii. Brian Keith Fox b. Jul 17 1972.

788. **Kenneth Lee^{7} Fox** (567.Keith Leroy^{6}, 388.Myrtle^{5} Smith, 194.Frances^{4} Arbogast, 64.Jesse^{3}, 11.Peter^{2}, 1.Peter^{1}), b. Jul 15 1949.
He Married **Shirley Ann Sauvageau**.

Children:

1131 i. Sandra Jane^{8} Fox b. Feb 07 1972.

1132 ii. Carrie Lynn Fox b. May 08 1975.

1133 iii. Lori Ann Fox b. Oct 24 1976.

1134 iv. Kristy Loleen Fox b. Jun 30 1978.

1135 v. Norleen Lynette Fox b. Apr 01 1980.

789. **David Bruce^{7} Fox** (568.Ralth Wilton^{6}, 388.Myrtle^{5} Smith, 194.Frances^{4} Arbogast, 64.Jesse^{3}, 11.Peter^{2}, 1.Peter^{1}), b. Sep 19 1956.
Married in Divorced 1988, **Lori Sears**, b. Jun 11 1961.

Children:

1136 i. Cassandra June^{8} Fox b. Nov 07 1982.

1137 ii. Mallary Erin Fox b. Jul 23 1985.

790. **Joni Sue^{7} Fox** (568.Ralth Wilton^{6}, 388.Myrtle^{5} Smith, 194.Frances^{4} Arbogast, 64.Jesse^{3}, 11.Peter^{2}, 1.Peter^{1}), b. Feb 04 1959.
She Married **James Calvin Poisel, Jr.**.

Children:

1138 i. Heather^{8} Poisel b. Sep 21 1982.

1139 ii. Jessica Dawn Poisel b. Oct 30 1984.

1140 iii. Jenna Rose Poisel b. Jun 21 1989.

1141 iv. Janelle Christine Poisel b. Mar 20 1991.

792. **Richard Francis[7] Arbogast** (569.Theodore Fenton[6], 389.Clyde Stewart[5], 195.Stephen Aaron Douglas[4], 64.Jesse[3], 11.Peter[2], 1.Peter[1]), b. Feb 10 1934 in Silver Creek, Merrick Co., NE. Married Nov 10 1960 in Burley, Cassia Co., ID, **Donna Hutchinson Williams**, b. Mar 01 1920 in Evanston, Uinta Co., WY.

Children:

+ 1142 i. Donna Esther[8] Arbogast b. Jan 08 1962.

793. **Patricia Ann[7] Arbogast** (569.Theodore Fenton[6], 389.Clyde Stewart[5], 195.Stephen Aaron Douglas[4], 64.Jesse[3], 11.Peter[2], 1.Peter[1]), b. May 28 1935 in Burley, Cassia Co., ID.
Married Aug 23 1955 in Elko, Elko Co., NV, **Price Ray Howard**, b. Apr 14 1935 in Lewisburg, Greenbrier Co., WV.

Children:

+ 1143 i. Richard Ray[8] Howard.

795. **Gerald Lee[7] Arbogast** (569.Theodore Fenton[6], 389.Clyde Stewart[5], 195.Stephen Aaron Douglas[4], 64.Jesse[3], 11.Peter[2], 1.Peter[1]), b. Apr 13 1936 in Burley, Cassia Co., ID.
Married Apr 16 1966 in Rupert, Minidoka Co., ID, **Sandra Kay Dozer**, b. Oct 17 1947.

Children:

1144 i. Nicole Ann[8] Arbogast b. Nov 28 1969 in Oxnard, Ventura Co., CA. Married Sep 11 1992, **Clyde Lay**.
1145 ii. Rebecca Ann Arbogast b. Aug 26 1971 in Burley, Cassia Co., ID.

796. **Theodore Clyde[7] Arbogast** (569.Theodore Fenton[6], 389.Clyde Stewart[5], 195.Stephen Aaron Douglas[4], 64.Jesse[3], 11.Peter[2], 1.Peter[1]), b. Dec 31 1937 in Burley, Cassia Co., ID.
Married Jun 19 1958 in Rupert, Minidoka Co., ID, **Lorna Karen Rasmussen**, b. Dec 31 1937.

Children:

+ 1146 i. Kathleen K.[8] Arbogast b. Jun 19 1959.
1147 ii. Jeffery C. Arbogast b. Nov 20 1961. Married Oct 25 1986, **Kathy Shipuro**.
1148 iii. Gregory T. Arbogast b. Feb 19 1964. Married Jun 04 1994, **Sherry Risa Lee Hooper**.

797. **Larry Arndt[7] Chelberg** (571.Helen Elene[6] Arbogast, 389.Clyde Stewart[5], 195.Stephen Aaron Douglas[4], 64.Jesse[3], 11.Peter[2], 1.Peter[1]), b. Mar 13 1938 in Wahoo, Saunders Co., NE.
Married Jan 31 1959 in Wahoo, Saunders Co., NE, **Mary Kay Kacirck**.

Children:

1149 i. Craig Allen[8] Chelberg b. Jul 13 1959 in Omaha, Douglas Co., NE.
1150 ii. Leann Chelberg b. Aug 19 1960 in Omaha, Douglas Co., NE.
1151 iii. Steven Michael Chelberg b. Dec 31 1961 in Omaha, Douglas Co., NE.
1152 iv. Mark Lee Chelberg b. Apr 27 1965 in Omaha, Douglas Co., NE. Married Jun 14 1989, **Penny Heidt**.

798. **Gary Allen[7] Chelberg** (571.Helen Elene[6] Arbogast, 389.Clyde Stewart[5], 195.Stephen Aaron Douglas[4], 64.Jesse[3], 11.Peter[2], 1.Peter[1]), b. Nov 13 1939 in Neligh, Antelope Co., NE.
Married Dec 28 1960 in Wahoo, Saunders Co., NE, **Jean Berry**.

Children:

1153 i. Pamela Renae[8] Chelberg b. May 30 1961. Married Apr 30 1983, **Les Kotera**.
1154 ii. Scott Allen Chelberg b. Sep 18 1962 in David City, Butler Co., NE. Married Oct 14 1989, **Barbara Jean Lewsin**.

799. **Roland Allen[7] Arbogast** (572.Allen Sterart[6], 389.Clyde Stewart[5], 195.Stephen Aaron Douglas[4], 64.Jesse[3], 11.Peter[2], 1.Peter[1]), b. Nov 19 1940 in Burley, Cassia Co., ID.
Married Apr 28 1961 in Caldwell, Canyon Co., ID, **Judith Marie Reynolds**, b. Jul 20 1941 in Denver, Arapaho Co., CO.

Children:

+ 1155 i. Karen Diane[8] Arbogast b. Jan 18 1962.
+ 1156 ii. Susan Lynn Arbogast b. Jun 04 1963.
1157 iii. Nancy Anne Arbogast b. May 11 1965. Married Feb 25 1989 in Eugene, Lane Co., OR, Bradley Zakes.
1158 iv. Janet Kay Arbogast b. Jul 09 1968 in Portland, Multnomah Co., OR.
1159 v. Steven Craig Arbogast b. Oct 03 1975 in Portland, Multnomah Co., OR.

800. **Calvin Stewart[7] Arbogast** (572.Allen Sterart[6], 389.Clyde Stewart[5], 195.Stephen Aaron Douglas[4], 64.Jesse[3], 11.Peter[2], 1.Peter[1]), b. Jun 04 1942.
(1) Married Sep 16 1962 in Lebanon, Linn Co., OR, **Leona May Stenberg**, b. Jan 21 1943.

Children *by Leona May Stenberg:*

1160 i. Dawn Deann[8] Arbogast b. Feb 28 1969 in Cottage Grove. Lane Co., OR.

(2) Married Aug 04 1978 in Salem, Marion Co., OR, **Leila May Corrasco**, b. Aug 25 1949 in Cotabato, Philippines.

Children *by Leila May Corrasco:*

1161 ii. Brent Tyler Arbogast b. Nov 25 1988 in Kent, King Co., WA.
1162 iii. Bryce Taylor Arbogast b. Nov 25 1988 in Kent, King Co., WA.

801. **Sherry Lorraine[7] Arbogast** (572.Allen Sterart[6], 389.Clyde Stewart[5], 195.Stephen Aaron Douglas[4], 64.Jesse[3], 11.Peter[2], 1.Peter[1]), b. Apr 21 1944 in Burley, Cassia Co., ID.
Married Jan 25 1963 in Albany, Linn Co., OR, **James Jordon May**, b. Mar 22 1943.

Children:

1163 i. Nathan James[8] May b. Aug 11 1963 in Lebanon, Linn Co., OR.
1164 ii. Jordon Michael May b. May 21 1966 in Lebanon, Linn Co., OR.
1165 iii. Lewis Vandiver May b. Nov 02 1968 in Kenie, AR.
1166 iv. Leland George May b. Jul 21 1971 in Soldotna, Kenai Peninsula Borough, AK.

802. **Leland G.[7] Arbogast** (572.Allen Sterart[6], 389.Clyde Stewart[5], 195.Stephen Aaron Douglas[4], 64.Jesse[3], 11.Peter[2], 1.Peter[1]), b. Mar 06 1946.
He Married **Diane Alice Beck**, b. Jan 09 1945 in Lebanon, Linn Co., OR.

Children:

1167 i. Jason Allen[8] Arbogast b. May 06 1970 in Cottage Grove. Lane Co., OR.
1168 ii. Justin Lee Arbogast b. Jul 01 1973 in Cottage Grove. Lane Co., OR.

803. **Darrell Ray[7] Arbogast** (572.Allen Sterart[6], 389.Clyde Stewart[5], 195.Stephen Aaron Douglas[4], 64.Jesse[3], 11.Peter[2], 1.Peter[1]), b. Jan 28 1948 in Burley, Cassia Co., ID.
Married Apr 08 1972 in Corvallis, Benton Co., OR, **Janet Louise Stiles**, b. Aug 13 1950 in Tacoma, Pierce Co., WA.

Children:

1169 i. Alicia Dawn[8] Arbogast b. Nov 03 1974 in Albany, Linn Co., OR.
1170 ii. Brian Loren Arbogast b. Dec 30 1976 in Springfield, Lane Co., OR.
1171 iii. Kristin Ilene Arbogast b. Dec 28 1978 in Eugene, Lane Co., OR.

804. **John Stewart[7] Holmes** (573.Gladys Catherine[6] Arbogast, 389.Clyde Stewart[5], 195.Stephen Aaron Douglas[4], 64.Jesse[3], 11.Peter[2], 1.Peter[1]), b. Oct 13 1934 in Lincoln, Lancaster Co., NE. Married Oct 30 1955 in Lincoln, Lancaster Co., NE, **Janice Rae Street**.

Children:

1172 i. Jeffery[8] Holmes b. Nov 02 1957 in Santa Monica, Los Angeles Co., CA.
1173 ii. Kristin Holmes b. Jan 01 1961 in Santa Monica, Los Angeles Co., CA. Married May 30 1987, **Jeffery Fafara**.
1174 iii. John Steven Holmes b. Aug 26 1964 in Santa Monica, Los Angeles Co., CA.

805. **David[7] Coons** (573.Gladys Catherine[6] Arbogast, 389.Clyde Stewart[5], 195.Stephen Aaron Douglas[4], 64.Jesse[3], 11.Peter[2], 1.Peter[1]), b. Sep 22 1951 in Lincoln, Lancaster Co., NE. He Married **Pamela Elaine Johnston**, b. Nov 04 1954 in Ft. Worth, Tarrant Co., TX.

Children:

1175 i. Rachel Leigh[8] Coons b. Jul 09 1986 in Lubbock, Lubbock Co., TX.

807. **Karen Sue[7] Sagarra** (575.Marilyn Inez[6] Arbogast, 389.Clyde Stewart[5], 195.Stephen Aaron Douglas[4], 64.Jesse[3], 11.Peter[2], 1.Peter[1]), b. Feb 17 1951 in Los Angeles, Los Angeles Co., CA. She Married **Steven Knorpp**.

Children:

1176 i. Benjamin S[8] Knorpp b. Mar 25 1971.

822. **John Allen[7] Arbogast** (594.Dwight[6], 398.Jessie L.[5], 199.John Franklin[4], 67.Michael[3], 11.Peter[2], 1.Peter[1]).
He Married **Sue Mitten**.

Children:

1177 i. Jo[8] Arbogast. She Married **Albert Schank**.
1178 ii. Steve Arbogast. He Married **Carol Fleetwood**.
1179 iii. John Arbogast. He Married **Kerry Fredericks**.
1180 iv. James Arbogast.
1181 v. Susan Arbogast. She Married **Peter Galipeau**.

823. **Carol Jean[7] Arbogast** (594.Dwight[6], 398.Jessie L.[5], 199.John Franklin[4], 67.Michael[3], 11.Peter[2], 1.Peter[1]). She Married **Joseph Engle**.

Children:

1182 i. Melissa[8] Engle.
1183 ii. Louise Engle.
1184 iii. James Engle.

824. **Rual[7] Arbogast** (594.Dwight[6], 398.Jessie L.[5], 199.John Franklin[4], 67.Michael[3], 11.Peter[2], 1.Peter[1]), d. Nov 22 1978. Married Jun 12 1837, **Walter Hill**, b. Jun 05 1808, d. Dec 25 1883.

Children:

1185 i. Patricia[8] Hill. She Married **Raymond Scherger**.
1186 ii. Bill Hill.

825. **Brian Earl[7] Slater** (599.Lois Alberta[6] Arbogast, 411.James Michael[5], 202.Charles Sayers[4], 67.Michael[3], 11.Peter[2], 1.Peter[1]), b. Nov 02 1946.
He Married **Sharon Rose Maddess**.

Children:

1187 i. Kari Rose[8] Slater b. Aug 26 1978.
1188 ii. Curtis Earl Slater b. Mar 22 1980.

826. **Lynn Marie[7] Slater** (599.Lois Alberta[6] Arbogast, 411.James Michael[5], 202.Charles Sayers[4], 67.Michael[3], 11.Peter[2], 1.Peter[1]), b. Oct 10 1948.
She Married **Lorne Adamschek**.

Children:

1189 i. Jodi Lynn[8] Adamschek b. Aug 07 1981.
1190 ii. Lisa Marie Adamschek b. Mar 14 1983.
1191 iii. Douglas Adamschek b. Jun 18 1985.

827. **Patricia Leigh[7] Armour** (600.Gayl Jane[6] Arbogast, 411.James Michael[5], 202.Charles Sayers[4], 67.Michael[3], 11.Peter[2], 1.Peter[1]), b. Jan 24 1943.
She Married **Gary Ritchie**.

Children:

\+ 1192 i. Terri[8] Ritchie.
1193 ii. Todd Arthur Ritchie.
1194 iii. James Ritchie.

833. **John[7] Heath** (602.James Kenneth[6], 412.Alice[5] Arbogast, 202.Charles Sayers[4], 67.Michael[3], 11.Peter[2], 1.Peter[1]), b. Jul 05 1946. He Married **Maxine Spicker**.

Children:

1195 i. Jason[8] Heath.
1196 ii. Ryan Heath.
1197 iii. Jeremy Heath.

835. **Susan[7] Heath** (602.James Kenneth[6], 412.Alice[5] Arbogast, 202.Charles Sayers[4], 67.Michael[3], 11.Peter[2], 1.Peter[1]), b. Dec 08 1952 in McComb, McDonough Co., IL. She Married **J Greg Hummel**.

Children:

1198 i. J. Chris[8] Hummel.
1199 ii. Cara Hummel.
1200 iii. Cortney Hummel.

836. **Danial Claude^{7} Bates** (603.Marion E.^{6} Heath, 412.Alice^{5} Arbogast, 202.Charles Sayers^{4}, 67.Michael^{3}, 11.Peter^{2}, 1.Peter^{1}), b. Jan 20 1946.
He Married **Susan Lee Miler**.

***Children**:*

1201 i. Brian Michael^{8} Heath.

837. **Donna Ruth^{7} Bates** (603.Marion E.^{6} Heath, 412.Alice^{5} Arbogast, 202.Charles Sayers^{4}, 67.Michael^{3}, 11.Peter^{2}, 1.Peter^{1}), b. Nov 21 1949.
She Married **Wayne Thomas Inman**, b. Nov 25 1943 in Wyandotte, Wayne Co., MI.

***Children**:*

1202 i. Thomas D.^{8} Inman b. Nov 11 1982 in Peoria, Peoria Co., IL.

838. **Suzanne Marie^{7} Arbogast** (604.James Clarence^{6}, 415.Clarence James^{5}, 203.Rush Arlington^{4}, 67.Michael^{3}, 11.Peter^{2}, 1.Peter^{1}), b. Nov 2 0052.
She Married **David Curlis**. .

***Children**:*

1203 i. Trisha Lee^{8} CURLIS b. Jan 17 1980.
1204 ii. Adrienne Curlis b. Oct 09 1985.

839. **Teresa Kay^{7} Arbogast** (604.James Clarence^{6}, 415.Clarence James^{5}, 203.Rush Arlington^{4}, 67.Michael^{3}, 11.Peter^{2}, 1.Peter^{1}), b. May 6 0055 in Tiffin, Seneca Co., OH.
Married Nov 25 1977, **Richard Burkett**, b. Nov 15 1953. .

***Children**:*

1205 i. Benjamin^{8} BURKETT.
1206 ii. Katherine Burkett.

841. **Gregory Charles^{7} Arbogast** (604.James Clarence^{6}, 415.Clarence James^{5}, 203.Rush Arlington^{4}, 67.Michael^{3}, 11.Peter^{2}, 1.Peter^{1}), b. Mar 1 0062 in Tiffin, Seneca Co., OH.
He Married **Diane Louise Kessler**. .

***Children**:*

1207 i. Brandy Rose^{8} Arbogast b. Oct 12 1984 in Tiffin, Seneca Co., OH.
1208 ii. Haili Nicole Arbogast b. in Tiffin, Seneca Co., OH.
1209 iii. Eric Gregory Arbogast b. in Tiffin, Seneca Co., OH.

844. **Anita Louise^{7} Arbogast** (604.James Clarence^{6}, 415.Clarence James^{5}, 203.Rush Arlington^{4}, 67.Michael^{3}, 11.Peter^{2}, 1.Peter^{1}), b. Aug 14 1960.
Married Jun 08 1979, **Joseph Gosche**, b. Jun 30 1958.

***Children**:*

1210 i. Heather Jo^{8} Gosche b. Dec 08 1982.
1211 ii. Nicholas James Gosche b. Jun 07 1985.

849. **Jane^{7} Arbogast** (606.Paul Joseph^{6}, 416.Charles Anthony^{5}, 203.Rush Arlington^{4}, 67.Michael^{3}, 11.Peter^{2}, 1.Peter^{1}).
(1) She Married **Lawrence Sorg**, b. Dec 20 1946.

***Children** by Lawrence Sorg:*

\+ 1212 i. Christina Rose^{8} Sorg b. May 03 1969.
1213 ii. Kelley Eugene Sorg b. Mar 30 1972.
1214 iii. Randy Alexander Sorg b. Feb 23 1975.

(2) She Married **Dan Gildermister**.

850. **Dean Larwence^{7} Arbogast** (606.Paul Joseph^{6}, 416.Charles Anthony^{5}, 203.Rush Arlington^{4}, 67.Michael^{3}, 11.Peter^{2}, 1.Peter^{1}).
Married Feb 12 1972, **Mary Edith Lumberjack**.

***Children**:*

1215 i. Wendy Ann^{8} Arbogast b. Mar 06 1973.
1216 ii. Chad Anthony Arbogast b. Apr 10 1975.
1217 iii. Denise Ellen Arbogast.
1218 iv. Kimberley Kay Arbogast b. Jun 05 1981.

851. **Ruth Ann^{7} Arbogast** (606.Paul Joseph^{6}, 416.Charles Anthony^{5}, 203.Rush Arlington^{4}, 67.Michael^{3}, 11.Peter^{2}, 1.Peter^{1}).
Married Nov 07 1970, **Gary Lynn Hawk**.

***Children*:**

1219 i. Victoria Lynn^{8} Hawk b. Jun 03 1971.
1220 ii. Matthew Glen Hawk b. Sep 25 1975.
1221 iii. Debra Ann Hawk b. May 17 1979.

852. **Judith Carol^{7} Arbogast** (606.Paul Joseph^{6}, 416.Charles Anthony^{5}, 203.Rush Arlington^{4}, 67.Michael^{3}, 11.Peter^{2}, 1.Peter^{1}).
(1) Married Jan 12 1974, **Donald Staats**, d. Jan 07 1984. .

Children *by Donald Staats:*

1222 i. Stephanie Carol^{8} Staats b. May 11 1974.
1223 ii. Donald Christopher Staats b. Apr 20 1977.
1224 iii. Jenifer Renee Staats b. Jun 06 1980.

(2) She Married **Ralph Stearn**

854. **Mark Anthony^{7} Arbogast** (606.Paul Joseph^{6}, 416.Charles Anthony^{5}, 203.Rush Arlington^{4}, 67.Michael^{3}, 11.Peter^{2}, 1.Peter^{1}), b. Sep 30 1963.
Married Feb 28 1987, **Dorette Reguiti**.

***Children*:**

1225 i. Ryan Anthony^{8} Arbogast b. Jan 20 1989.

855. **Daria^{7} Arbogast** (607.Lawrence Anselm^{6}, 416.Charles Anthony^{5}, 203.Rush Arlington^{4}, 67.Michael^{3}, 11.Peter^{2}, 1.Peter^{1}), b. Apr 29 1953.
Married 1982, **Pat Walsh**.

***Children*:**

1226 i. Edmund Anthony^{8} Walsh b. Aug 29 1983.

858. **Paula Louise^{7} Arbogast** (607.Lawrence Anselm^{6}, 416.Charles Anthony^{5}, 203.Rush Arlington^{4}, 67.Michael^{3}, 11.Peter^{2}, 1.Peter^{1}), b. Sep 15 1958.
Married Dec 22 1979, **Martin Karlin**.

***Children*:**

1227 i. James Francis^{8} Karlin b. Apr 14 1982.
1228 ii. Melissa Francine Karlin b. Dec 03 1983.
1229 iii. Virginia Winfred Karlin b. Mar 11 1985.

863. **Virginia Ann^{7} Arbogast** (608.Urban Anthony^{6}, 416.Charles Anthony^{5}, 203.Rush Arlington^{4}, 67.Michael^{3}, 11.Peter^{2}, 1.Peter^{1}), b. Oct 11 1949.
Married Oct 26 1968, **Larry Charles Shock**, b. Mar 06 1947 in Seneca Co., OH.

***Children*:**

1230 i. Denise Marie^{8} Shock b. Jul 19 1969.
1231 ii. Anthony Charles Shock b. Nov 10 1973.

864. **Alice Rose^{7} Arbogast** (608.Urban Anthony^{6}, 416.Charles Anthony^{5}, 203.Rush Arlington^{4}, 67.Michael^{3}, 11.Peter^{2}, 1.Peter^{1}), b. Sep 10 1950.
Married Apr 04 1970, **Christopher Oscar Mugrage**.

***Children*:**

1232 i. Phillip Anthony^{8} Mugrage b. Dec 26 1972.
1233 ii. Jason Michael Mugrage b. Jul 05 1974.

865. **Pauline Mary^{7} Arbogast** (608.Urban Anthony^{6}, 416.Charles Anthony^{5}, 203.Rush Arlington^{4}, 67.Michael^{3}, 11.Peter^{2}, 1.Peter^{1}), b. Sep 06 1951.
(1) She Married **Samuel Fey**, b. Apr 01 1963. (.

Children *by Samuel Fey:*

1234 i. Samantha^{8} Fey b. Jul 22 1986.
1235 ii. Dolly Fey b. Jan 20 1988.

(2) She Married **Michael Sparkman**, b. Feb 08 1952

Children *by Michael Sparkman:*

1236 iii. Honey Marie Sparkman b. May 25 1973.
1237 iv. Michael David Sparkman b. May 02 1976.

866. **Helen Lucille**^{7} **Arbogast** (608.Urban Anthony^{6}, 416.Charles Anthony^{5}, 203.Rush Arlington^{4}, 67.Michael^{3}, 11.Peter^{2}, 1.Peter^{1}), b. Mar 16 1953.
Married Apr 28 1972, **James Lemmerman**, b. Feb 18 1950.

Children:

1238 i. Jami Jo^{8} Lemmerman b. Oct 21 1972.
1239 ii. Joshua David Lemmerman b. Feb 19 1977.

867. **Susan Theresa**^{7} **Arbogast** (608.Urban Anthony^{6}, 416.Charles Anthony^{5}, 203.Rush Arlington^{4}, 67.Michael^{3}, 11.Peter^{2}, 1.Peter^{1}), b. Mar 29 1953.
Married May 05 1973 in St. Aloysius Church, Mercer Co., OH, **David Lewis Robison**, b. Dec 29 1933.

Children:

1240 i. Toby David^{8} Robison b. May 29 1975.
1241 ii. Christopher Shawn Robison b. Nov 29 1976.

868. **Doris Mae**^{7} **Arbogast** (608.Urban Anthony^{6}, 416.Charles Anthony^{5}, 203.Rush Arlington^{4}, 67.Michael^{3}, 11.Peter^{2}, 1.Peter^{1}), b. May 04 1955.
Married Jul 12 1974, **Bruce Lambert**, b. Oct 20 1955.

Children:

1242 i. Melissa Ann^{8} Lambert b. Sep 07 1978.
1243 ii. Laura Mae Lambert b. Nov 03 1979.
1244 iii. Matthew Paul Lambert b. Jul 27 1981.
1245 iv. Sheene Marie Lambert b. Jan 12 1983.

869. **Angela Marie**^{7} **Arbogast** (608.Urban Anthony^{6}, 416.Charles Anthony^{5}, 203.Rush Arlington^{4}, 67.Michael^{3}, 11.Peter^{2}, 1.Peter^{1}), b. May 21 1956.
Married Jun 20 1975, **Dennis A. Roush**, b. Mar 11 1954.

Children:

1246 i. Eric David^{8} Roush b. Dec 19 1979.
1247 ii. Aaron Patrick Roush b. Sep 21 1981.

870. **Janice Eileen**^{7} **Arbogast** (608.Urban Anthony^{6}, 416.Charles Anthony^{5}, 203.Rush Arlington^{4}, 67.Michael^{3}, 11.Peter^{2}, 1.Peter^{1}), b. May 17 1958.

(1) Married Aug 20 1978, **Ronald Roush**, b. Sep 27 1957. .

Children *by Ronald Roush:*

1248 i. Rhyn William^{8} Roush b. Jun 01 1981.

(2) Married Aug 03 1983, **Kenneth Miller**, b. Aug 17 1954

Children *by Kenneth Miller:*

1249 ii. Christa Miller b. Aug 21 1975.
1250 iii. Bradley Alan Miller b. Jul 30 1986.
1251 iv. Timothy Joseph Miller b. Dec 15 1987.

871. **Patricia Louise**^{7} **Arbogast** (608.Urban Anthony^{6}, 416.Charles Anthony^{5}, 203.Rush Arlington^{4}, 67.Michael^{3}, 11.Peter^{2}, 1.Peter^{1}), b. May 05 1960.
Married Oct 12 1984, **Stanley Tolbert**, b. Aug 10 1960.

Children:

1252 i. Cory Maurice^{8} Tolbert b. Nov 02 1987.
1253 ii. Catrina Tolbert b. Apr 24 1989.

872. **June Ellen**^{7} **Arbogast** (608.Urban Anthony^{6} Arbogast, 416.Charles Anthony^{5}, 203.Rush Arlington^{4}, 67.Michael^{3}, 11.Peter^{2}, 1.Peter^{1}), b. Jun 04 1961.

(1) Married Aug 20 1978, **Joseph Conrad**. (2) Married Dec 22 1987,

Children *by Joseph Conrad:*

1254 i. Kendall Owen^{8} Conrad b. Oct 18 1981.

Donald Eveland, b. Sep 13 1959.

Children *by Donald Eveland:*

1255 ii. Nicole Eveland b. May 12 1993.

873. **Linda Kay^{7} Arbogast** (608.Urban Anthony^{6}, 416.Charles Anthony^{5}, 203.Rush Arlington^{4}, 67.Michael^{3}, 11.Peter^{2}, 1.Peter^{1}), b. Oct 27 1966.

Married Nov 28 1987, **Christopher Barger**, b. Nov 07 1964.

Children*:*

1256 i. Amanda^{8} Barger b. Sep 03 1993.

876. **Marilyn Ann^{7} Arbogast** (609.Eugene Jerome^{6}, 416.Charles Anthony^{5}, 203.Rush Arlington^{4}, 67.Michael^{3}, 11.Peter^{2}, 1.Peter^{1}), b. Dec 05 1952.

Married Jun 18 1976, **John Gagen**.

Children*:*

1257 i. Jason Robert^{8} Gagen b. Jan 04 1978.

878. **Barbara Jean^{7} Arbogast** (609.Eugene Jerome^{6}, 416.Charles Anthony^{5}, 203.Rush Arlington^{4}, 67.Michael^{3}, 11.Peter^{2}, 1.Peter^{1}), b. Nov 27 1957.

Married Oct 14 1977, **Clifton Hicklin**.

Children*:*

1258 i. Christopher Lane^{8} Hicklin b. Feb 27 1978.
1259 ii. Charles Andrew Hicklin b. Aug 01 1979.
1260 iii. Jeffery Wayne Hicklin b. May 02 1981.
1261 iv. Jermey Scott Hicklin b. Sep 02 1983.

879. **Kenneth^{7} Arbogast** (609.Eugene Jerome^{6}, 416.Charles Anthony^{5}, 203.Rush Arlington^{4}, 67.Michael^{3}, 11.Peter^{2}, 1.Peter^{1}), b. Mar 30 1959.

Married Apr 27 1984, **Lori Schroeder**.

Children*:*

1262 i. Michelle Renee^{8} Arbogast b. Jul 24 1984.
1263 ii. Brent Michael Arbogast b. Jun 18 1986.
1264 iii. Rachel Ann Arbogast b. Mar 18 1988.

881. **Lois Marie^{7} Arbogast** (609.Eugene Jerome^{6}, 416.Charles Anthony^{5}, 203.Rush Arlington^{4}, 67.Michael^{3}, 11.Peter^{2}, 1.Peter^{1}), b. Jul 05 1962.

Married Aug 08 1981, **Dave McQuiston**.

Children*:*

1265 i. Kristin Eileen^{8} McQuiston b. Dec 12 1981.

882. **Diane Ruth^{7} Arbogast** (610.Marion Victor^{6}, 416.Charles Anthony^{5}, 203.Rush Arlington^{4}, 67.Michael^{3}, 11.Peter^{2}, 1.Peter^{1}), b. Jan 10 1956.

Married Aug 06 1976, **Michael Girdler**.

Children*:*

1266 i. Douglas Michael^{8} Girdler b. Oct 22 1977.
1267 ii. Matthew Scot Girdler b. Apr 02 1981.
1268 iii. Steven Girdler b. Mar 13 1985.

887. **Theresa Marie^{7} Boes** (611.Marguerite Elenora^{6} Arbogast, 416.Charles Anthony^{5}, 203.Rush Arlington^{4}, 67.Michael^{3}, 11.Peter^{2}, 1.Peter^{1}), b. Jun 15 1954.

Married Feb 04 1984, **Jerry Barrett**.

Children*:*

1269 i. Alicia Marie^{8} Boes b. Jul 09 1984.

892. **Mary Catherine⁷ Arbogast** (612.Harlan Clarence[6], 416.Charles Anthony[5], 203.Rush Arlington[4], 67.Michael[3], 11.Peter[2], 1.Peter[1]), b. Aug 17 1959.
Married Apr 29 1978, **Dennis Pierce**.

***Children**:*

1270 i. Christopher Jason[8] Pierce b. Dec 01 1979.

893. **Carol Sue[7] Arbogast** (612.Harlan Clarence[6], 416.Charles Anthony[5], 203.Rush Arlington[4], 67.Michael[3], 11.Peter[2], 1.Peter[1]), b. Sep 10 1960.
Married Sep 25 1982, **Dennis Lofat**.

***Children**:*

1271 i. Nathan Carl[8] Lofat b. Aug 15 1983.
1272 ii. Andrea Rose Lofay b. Jan 24 1986.

894. **Sandra Marie[7] Arbogast** (612.Harlan Clarence[6], 416.Charles Anthony[5], 203.Rush Arlington[4], 67.Michael[3], 11.Peter[2], 1.Peter[1]), b. May 23 1962.
Married Aug 14 1986, **Mark Sexton**.

***Children**:*

1273 i. Allab Thomas[8] Sexton b. Nov 27 1984.
1274 ii. Renee Marie Sexton b. Aug 25 1986.

900. **Wanda Ann[7] Arbogast** (612.Harlan Clarence[6], 416.Charles Anthony[5], 203.Rush Arlington[4], 67.Michael[3], 11.Peter[2], 1.Peter[1]), b. Jun 23 1970.

***Children**:*

1275 i. Amanda Marie[8] Arbogast b. Dec 14 1988.

915. **Neil Eugene[7] Kelbley** (614.Rita Mae[6] Arbogast, 416.Charles Anthony[5], 203.Rush Arlington[4], 67.Michael[3], 11.Peter[2], 1.Peter[1]), b. Jun 07 1965.
Married Sep 21 1985, **Brenda Haubert**, b. Dec 18 1966.

***Children**:*

1276 i. Ashley Rose[8] Kelbley b. May 30 1984.
1277 ii. Andrew Jonathan Kelbley b. Dec 20 1986.

921. **Elmo Harold[7] SMITH** (617.Clarence Louis[6], 417.Frances Marie[5] Arbogast, 203.Rush Arlington[4], 67.Michael[3], 11.Peter[2], 1.Peter[1]), b. Jan 25 1941.
(1) He Married **Bernice Stromme**. .

***Children** by Bernice Stromme:*

1278 i. Brent Stromme[8] Smith b. Apr 02 1967.
1279 ii. Dena Stromme Smith b. May 07 1968.

(2) He Married **Jennett Mac Daniel**, b. Jun 09 1945, d. Sep 28 1974

***Children** by Jennett Mac Daniel:*

1280 iii. Geoffery Quinton Smith b. Apr 27 1964.
1281 iv. Michele Renee Smith.
1282 v. Jennifer Ann Smith b. Jun 09 1972.

922. **Norman Paul[7] SMITH** (617.Clarence Louis[6], 417.Frances Marie[5] Arbogast, 203.Rush Arlington[4], 67.Michael[3], 11.Peter[2], 1.Peter[1]), b. Sep 27 1943.
He Married **Jean Marie Nienberg**, b. Nov 25 1945.

***Children**:*

1283 i. Teresa Lynn[8] Smith b. Jun 07 1966.
1284 ii. Todd Smith b. May 08 1967.
1285 iii. Matt Ross Smith b. Feb 26 1969.
1286 iv. Melinda Marie Smith b. May 29 1971.

923. **Nancy[7] SMITH** (617.Clarence Louis[6], 417.Frances Marie[5] Arbogast, 203.Rush Arlington[4], 67.Michael[3], 11.Peter[2], 1.Peter[1]), b. Feb 13 1945.
Married Aug 10 1968, **Richard Neile Heebsh**, b. Dec 17 1941.

***Children*:**

1287 i. Brian William^{8} Heebsh b. Dec 29 1969.
1288 ii. Kevin Markwood Heebsh b. Jul 23 1971.

924. **Ramona Tereista^{7} SMITH** (617.Clarence Louis^{6}, 417.Frances Marie^{5} Arbogast, 203.Rush Arlington^{4}, 67.Michael^{3}, 11.Peter^{2}, 1.Peter^{1}), b. Jan 07 1950. Married May 02 1970, **Richard Peter Cleary**, b. Aug 19 1949.

***Children*:**

1289 i. Christopher Sean^{8} Cleary b. Sep 10 1970.
1290 ii. April Joan Cleary b. Apr 12 1973.

925. **Louis James^{7} KING** (618.Rita Theresa^{6} SMITH, 417.Frances Marie^{5} Arbogast, 203.Rush Arlington^{4}, 67.Michael^{3}, 11.Peter^{2}, 1.Peter^{1}), b. Dec 04 1938. Married Jun 24 1962, **Joanne Kent**, b. Dec 23 1939. .

***Children*:**

1291 i. Randall Joseph^{8} KING b. Apr 02 1962.
1292 ii. Lucenda Marie King b. Oct 25 1963.
1293 iii. Melissa Beth King b. Jul 20 1966.
1294 iv. Darin James King b. Oct 10 1969.
1295 v. Jonathan David King b. May 12 1978.

926. **Marjorie Ann^{7} KING** (618.Rita Theresa^{6} SMITH, 417.Frances Marie^{5} Arbogast, 203.Rush Arlington^{4}, 67.Michael^{3}, 11.Peter^{2}, 1.Peter^{1}), b. Nov 23 1941. Married Apr 30 1960, **David Robert Fisher**, b. Mar 25 1938. .

***Children*:**

1296 i. Jeffrey Robert^{8} FISHER b. Nov 05 1960.
\+ 1297 ii. Scott Louis Fisher b. Apr 06 1962.
1298 iii. Mathew Allen Fisher b. Sep 17 1968.

927. **Deanna Rose^{7} SMITH** (619.Richard Joseph^{6}, 417.Frances Marie^{5} Arbogast, 203.Rush Arlington^{4}, 67.Michael^{3}, 11.Peter^{2}, 1.Peter^{1}), b. Nov 24 1943. Married Feb 02 1967, **Dennis Balmer**, b. Mar 02 1941.

***Children*:**

1299 i. Darlene Ann^{8} Balmer b. Oct 13 1970.

928. **Allan Peter^{7} SMITH** (619.Richard Joseph^{6}, 417.Frances Marie^{5} Arbogast, 203.Rush Arlington^{4}, 67.Michael^{3}, 11.Peter^{2}, 1.Peter^{1}), b. Jan 07 1945. Married Jul 31 1965, **Janice M. Graham**, b. Oct 29 1941.

***Children*:**

1300 i. Richard L.^{8} Smith b. Dec 30 1962.
1301 ii. Mary Louise Smith b. Apr 02 1968.
1302 iii. Victoria Marie Smith b. May 15 1969.
1303 iv. Tonia Margaret Smith b. Sep 01 1970.
1304 v. Leonard Allen Smith b. Jan 18 1974.
1305 vi. Alan Peter Smith b. May 14 1979.

929. **Alice Mary^{7} SMITH** (619.Richard Joseph^{6}, 417.Frances Marie^{5} Arbogast, 203.Rush Arlington^{4}, 67.Michael^{3}, 11.Peter^{2}, 1.Peter^{1}), b. Feb 23 1949. Married Sep 26 1970, **Dennis Teynor**, b. Sep 13 1947.

***Children*:**

1306 i. Randall Scott^{8} Teynor b. Jul 30 1971.
1307 ii. Monica Anne Teynor b. Apr 30 1973.
1308 iii. Kevin Thomas Teynor b. Nov 12 1979.
1309 iv. Kathleen Marie Teynor.

930. **Jane Margaret^{7} SMITH** (619.Richard Joseph^{6}, 417.Frances Marie^{5} Arbogast, 203.Rush Arlington^{4}, 67.Michael^{3}, 11.Peter^{2}, 1.Peter^{1}), b. Dec 30 1949.
Married Mar 16 1973, **Daniel Lee Ickes**, b. Dec 11 1953.

***Children*:**

1310 i. Jenelle Marie^{8} Ickes b. May 10 1980.
1311 ii. Joshua Paul Ickes b. Apr 01 1981.

931. **Gloria Jean[7] Adams** (621.Marjorie Mary[6] SMITH, 417.Frances Marie[5] Arbogast, 203.Rush Arlington[4], 67.Michael[3], 11.Peter[2], 1.Peter[1]), b. Dec 11 1946.
She Married **Donald Miller**, b. Mar 16 1945.

***Children**:*

1312 i. Mana Marie[8] Miller b. Oct 16 1966.
1313 ii. Michael Edward Miller b. Sep 12 1967.
1314 iii. Chris Allen Miller b. Sep 26 1968.
1315 iv. Deborah Sue Miller b. Aug 20 1971.

933. **Gerald Edwards[7] Adams** (621.Marjorie Mary[6] SMITH, 417.Frances Marie[5] Arbogast, 203.Rush Arlington[4], 67.Michael[3], 11.Peter[2], 1.Peter[1]), b. Feb 12 1954.
Married Jan 15 1972, **Arlene Stockmeister**.

***Children**:*

1316 i. Jill Marie[8] Adams b. Jun 14 1972.

934. **Cheryl Lajean[7] SMITH** (622.Robert Eugene[6], 417.Frances Marie[5] Arbogast, 203.Rush Arlington[4], 67.Michael[3], 11.Peter[2], 1.Peter[1]), b. Aug 27 1949.
Married Sep 20 1969, **Michael Grady**, b. Jun 09 1948.

***Children**:*

1317 i. Eric Robert[8] Grady b. Dec 14 1970.
1318 ii. Todd Michael Grady b. Sep 17 1973.

935. **Patricia Ann[7] SMITH** (622.Robert Eugene[6], 417.Frances Marie[5] Arbogast, 203.Rush Arlington[4], 67.Michael[3], 11.Peter[2], 1.Peter[1]), b. Nov 29 1954.
(1) She Married **George Harrison Dosh**, b. Oct 05 1947, d. Oct 26 1973.

***Children** by Michael Riedel:*

1319 i. Shane Michael[8] Riedel b. Jul 12 1977.

(2) Married Jul 27 1976, **Michael Riedel**.

936. **David Eugene[7] HAMMER** (623.Helen Francis[6] SMITH, 417.Frances Marie[5] Arbogast, 203.Rush Arlington[4], 67.Michael[3], 11.Peter[2], 1.Peter[1]), b. Aug 21 1947.
Married Mar 21 1969, **Sandra West**.

***Children**:*

1320 i. Scott Michael[8] Hammer b. Oct 09 1972.
1321 ii. Brian Lee Hammer b. Apr 14 1976.

937. **Thomas Herbert[7] HAMMER** (623.Helen Francis[6] SMITH, 417.Frances Marie[5] Arbogast, 203.Rush Arlington[4], 67.Michael[3], 11.Peter[2], 1.Peter[1]), b. Sep 13 1948.
Married Aug 09 1974, **Carol Mathias**, b. Jan 13 1954.

***Children**:*

1322 i. Cory Thomas[8] Hammer b. Jun 24 1975.
1323 ii. Malinda Lee Hammer.
1324 iii. Brett Hammer b. 1981.

938. **William Joseph[7] HAMMER** (623.Helen Francis[6] SMITH, 417.Frances Marie[5] Arbogast, 203.Rush Arlington[4], 67.Michael[3], 11.Peter[2], 1.Peter[1]), b. Feb 11 1951.
He Married **Diane Marie Welty**, b. Jan 27 1949.

***Children**:*

1325 i. Kristine Marie[8] Hammer b. Nov 01 1972.
1326 ii. Daniel William Hammer b. Aug 01 1974.
1327 iii. Lori Ann Hammer b. Mar 29 1976.
1328 iv. Jeffery Richard Hammer b. Jan 30 1979.

939. **Donald Lee[7] HAMMER** (623.Helen Francis[6] SMITH, 417.Frances Marie[5] Arbogast, 203.Rush Arlington[4], 67.Michael[3], 11.Peter[2], 1.Peter[1]), b. May 29 1953.
He Married **Mary Catherine Ray**, b. Apr 06 1951.

***Children**:*

1329 i. Joseph Donald[8] Hammer b. Jun 25 1977.
1330 ii. Regina Catherine Hammer b. Oct 01 1979.
1331 iii. Matthew Ray Hammer b. May 11 1981.
1332 iv. Bradley Charles Hammer b. May 11 1981.

940. **Kenneth Lewis[7] HAMMER** (623.Helen Francis[6] SMITH, 417.Frances Marie[5] Arbogast, 203.Rush Arlington[4], 67.Michael[3], 11.Peter[2], 1.Peter[1]), b. May 29 1953.
1) He Married **Denise Huth**, b. Oct 06 1955.

***Children** by Denise Huth:*

1333 i. Berry Alen[8] Hammer b. Aug 06 1973.

(2) He Married **Geralyn Bloom**, b. Nov 07 1954.

***Children** by Geralyn Bloom:*

1334 ii. Roberta Ann Hammer b. Oct 26 1975.
1335 iii. Andera Helen Hammer b. Mar 31 1977.

941. **Mary Alice[7] HAMMER** (623.Helen Francis[6] SMITH, 417.Frances Marie[5] Arbogast, 203.Rush Arlington[4], 67.Michael[3], 11.Peter[2], 1.Peter[1]), b. Sep 02 1955.
She Married **Kenneth Baker**, b. Oct 27 1954.

***Children**:*

1336 i. Kevin Ray[8] Baker b. Feb 09 1976.
1337 ii. Kelly Francis Baker b. Dec 13 1977.
1338 iii. Keith Nicholas Baker b. Mar 24 1981.

942. **Eileen Marie[7] HAMMER** (623.Helen Francis[6] SMITH, 417.Frances Marie[5] Arbogast, 203.Rush Arlington[4], 67.Michael[3], 11.Peter[2], 1.Peter[1]), b. Mar 16 1957.
She Married **John V. Hoover**, b. Jan 12 1957.

***Children**:*

1339 i. Neil John[8] Hoover b. Aug 29 1976.
1340 ii. Nicholas Allen Hoover b. Jul 15 1978.
1341 iii. Mark Steven Hoover b. Sep 03 1980.
\+ 1342 iv. Elizabeth Marie Hoover b. Nov 16 1982.

943. **Roger Francis[7] HAMMER** (623.Helen Francis[6] SMITH, 417.Frances Marie[5] Arbogast, 203.Rush Arlington[4], 67.Michael[3], 11.Peter[2], 1.Peter[1]), b. Sep 28 1958.
He Married **Debra Hill**, b. Apr 01 1958.

***Children**:*

1343 i. Jessica Leah[8] Hammer b. Jan 25 1980.
1344 ii. Nathaniel Richard Hammer b. Jun 01 1982.

949. **Jill Christine[7] Smith** (624.Bernard Charles[6], 417.Frances Marie[5] Arbogast, 203.Rush Arlington[4], 67.Michael[3], 11.Peter[2], 1.Peter[1]).
She Married **Douglas Hire**.

***Children**:*

1345 i. Joseph Allen[8] Hire b. Apr 21 1983.

953. **Edward Louis[7] SMITH** (625.Leo Frederick[6], 417.Frances Marie[5] Arbogast, 203.Rush Arlington[4], 67.Michael[3], 11.Peter[2], 1.Peter[1]).
He Married **Patricia Raitz**.

***Children**:*

1346 i. Joshua Adam[8] Smith b. Mar 28 1983.
1347 ii. Sarah Elizabeth Smith b. Dec 21 1984.

Generation Eight

967. **Scott Douglas⁸ McConnell** (628.Max Ramon McConnell,[7] DDS, 422.Clara Loveda[6] Crissman, 220.Cornelius Eugene[5], 73.Melissa[4] Latimer, 13.Elizabeth P.[3] Arbogast, 3.Rev. Cornelius[2], 1.Peter[1]), b. Aug 02 1958 in Ft. Meade, Anne Arundel Co., MD.
Married Oct 25 1986, **Debbie Staar**.

***Children*:**

1348 i. Scott Douglas[9] McConnell, Jr. b. Sep 28 1987 in Naples, Collier Co., FL.

969. **Troy Len[8] McConnell** (629.Thomas Omar[7], 422.Clara Loveda[6] Crissman, 220.Cornelius Eugene[5], 73.Melissa[4] Latimer, 13.Elizabeth P.[3] Arbogast, 3.Rev. Cornelius[2], 1.Peter[1]), b. May 12 1962 in Tampa, Pasco Co., FL.
Married Feb 09 1990 in Atlanta, Fulton Co., GA, **Michel Lucille Mouton**.

***Children*:**

1349 i. Adam Thomas[9] McConnell b. Jul 14 1990 in Atlanta, Fulton Co., GA.

979. **Denise Louise[8] Davisson** (660.David Herbert[7], 449.Bruce Raymond[6], 264.Charles Clifford[5], 111.Dorothy Jane[4] Neer, 22.Margaret Ann[3] Arbogast, 4.Otho[2], 1.Peter[1]), b. Dec 21 1960 in Seattle, King Co., WA.
Married Jun 19 1981 in Woodruff, Spartanburg Co., SC, **Robin Brown**, b. Oct 27 1960.

***Children*:**

1350 i. Zachary Alan[9] Brown b. May 30 1985.
1351 ii. Bethany Miranda Brown b. Dec 28 1987.
1352 iii. Kaitlin Rebekah Brown b. Jan 19 1992.

985. **Robert Mark[8] Baird** (664.Deloris Ann[7] Davisson, 450.Kenneth Elijah[6], 264.Charles Clifford[5], 111.Dorothy Jane[4] Neer, 22.Margaret Ann[3] Arbogast, 4.Otho[2], 1.Peter[1]), b. Jul 18 1959. Married Jun 24 1960, **Carol Sue Harter**, b. Jun 24 1960.

***Children*:**

1353 i. Carly[9] Baird.
1354 ii. Matthew Baird.

989. **Eric Michael[8] Long** (666.Carole Emily[7] Davisson, 450.Kenneth Elijah[6], 264.Charles Clifford[5], 111.Dorothy Jane[4] Neer, 22.Margaret Ann[3] Arbogast, 4.Otho[2], 1.Peter[1]), b. Jul 13 1965. He Married **Sagunya (Unknown)**.

***Children*:**

1355 i. Mali[9] Long.

997. **Norma June[8] Hanley** (672.John Franklin[7], 452.Mable Corrine[6] Davisson, 265.Clarence Weakley[5], 111.Dorothy Jane[4] Neer, 22.Margaret Ann[3] Arbogast, 4.Otho[2], 1.Peter[1]), b. Jun 26 1935.
Married May 23 1959, **John Luther Zimmerman, III**, b. Aug 09 1933.

***Children*:**

1356 i. Laura Leigh[9] Zimmerman b. Apr 17 1961.
1357 ii. Jennifer Lynn Zimmerman b. Jul 23 1965.

1019. **Shawn Patrick[8] McBride** (679.Virginia Ann[7] Neer, 455.Ralph Everhart[6], 268.Cloice Edgar[5], 112.Bruce[4], 22.Margaret Ann[3] Arbogast, 4.Otho[2], 1.Peter[1]), b. Feb 16 1967.
He Married **Megan Phelp**, b. Feb 08 1966.

***Children*:**

1358 i. Joshua Partick[9] McBride b. Feb 11 1987.

1060. **Lois Nadine[8] Hamilton** (742.Alma Joyce[7] Payne, 533.William Charles[6], 359.Mary[5] Morrison, 186.Sophia[4] Arbogast, 64.Jesse[3], 11.Peter[2], 1.Peter[1]), b. Dec 14 1936 in Delta Co., CO.
(1) Married Oct 04 1953 in Reno, Washoe Co., NV, **Richard Clinton Byerrum**, b. Nov 07 1936 in Montrose Co., CO.

***Children** by Richard Clinton Byerrum:*

1359 i. Richard Clinton[9] Byerrum b. Apr 25 1954 at Roseville, Placer Co., CA. Married Oct 12 1985 in Yuba City, Sutter Co., CA, **Susan Ann Bell**.
1360 ii. Deborah Ann Byerrum b. Sep 11 1955 in Montrose Co., CO. Married Jun 17 1977 in Yuba City, Sutter Co., CA, **Milton Lynn Greathouse**.
1361 iii. Sharalyn Sue Byerrum b. Sep 26 1957 in Roseville, Placer Co., CA.

1362 iv. Gregory Dean Byerrum b. Feb 27 1959 in Roseville, Placer Co., CA, d. Apr 13 1961 in Sacramento, Sacramento Co., CA.
1363 v. Judy Kay Byerrum b. Jun 20 1961 in Sacramento, Sacramento Co., CA. Married Jul 07 1976, **Wayne Shamblin**.
1364 vi. Roy Craig Byerrum b. Sep 22 1962 in Stockton, San Joaquin Co., CA. Married Jun 15 1985 in Yuba City, Sutter Co., CA, **Melody Fitzpatrick**.

(2) Married Dec 30 1975 in Reno, Washoe Co., NV, **Norman Clyde Phillips**.

1063. **Charles Ronald[8] Robertson** (746.Marcia Roberta[7] Payne, 533.William Charles[6], 359.Mary[5] Morrison, 186.Sophia[4] Arbogast, 64.Jesse[3], 11.Peter[2], 1.Peter[1]), b. Jul 01 1941 in Delta Co., CO.
He Married **Judith Rachel Moraff**.

Children:

1365 i. Summer Suzette[9] Robertson b. Dec 25 1963 in Santa Cruz Co., CA.
1366 ii. Charles Ronald Robertson, Jr. b. Feb 04 1965 in Santa Cruz Co., CA.
1367 iii. Brittany Dawn Robertson b. Dec 08 1983 in Santa Cruz Co., CA.
1368 iv. Kylan Douglas Robertson b. Feb 14 1991 in Santa Cruz Co., CA.

1065. **John Ralph[8] Robertson** (746.Marcia Roberta[7] Payne, 533.William Charles[6], 359.Mary[5] Morrison, 186.Sophia[4] Arbogast, 64.Jesse[3], 11.Peter[2], 1.Peter[1]), b. Mar 07 1952 in Santa Cruz Co., CA.
Married Apr 07 1971, **Patricia Sue Rosol**, b. in Pittsburgh, Allegheny Co., PA.

Children:

1369 i. Colin Ray[9] Robertson b. Jun 03 1971 in Santa Cruz Co., CA.
1370 ii. Clinton Heath Robertson b. Oct 25 1973 in Santa Cruz Co., CA.

1071. **Donald Ralph[8] Woolerton** (750.Duane[7] Woolverton, 538.Harry[6], 363.Rose[5] Morrison, 186.Sophia[4] Arbogast, 64.Jesse[3], 11.Peter[2], 1.Peter[1]), b. Jul 20 1954 in Illinois.
Married Jun 08 1974, **Rhonda Hamm**.

Children:

1371 i. Jason Duane[9] Woolerton b. Aug 13 1976.
1372 ii. Stacey Dawn Woolerton b. Nov 19 1983.

1105. **David Lee[8] Brewer** (774.Richard Gene[7], 554.Sarah Fern[6] Cozad, 379.Mae[5] Howard, 192.Sarah[4] Arbogast, 64.Jesse[3], 11.Peter[2], 1.Peter[1]), b. Aug 13 1955 in Avon, Fulton Co., IL. Married Jun 04 1977, **Debera Lee Palmer**, b. Oct 02 1955 in Princeton, Bureau Co., IL.

Children:

1373 i. Christopher David[9] Palmer b. Jul 06 1983 in Princeton, Bureau Co., IL.
1374 ii. Danial Edward Palmer b. Sep 30 1986 in Princeton, Bureau Co., IL.

1106. **Donna Kay[8] Lawyer** (775.Barbara Mae[7] Black, 555.Faun Elizabeth[6] Cozad, 379.Mae[5] Howard, 192.Sarah[4] Arbogast, 64.Jesse[3], 11.Peter[2], 1.Peter[1]), b. Apr 10 1945 in McComb, McDonough Co., IL.
She Married **Laverne McFadden**, b. May 02 1945 in Illinois.

Children:

1375 i. Torie Kaye[9] McFadden b. Oct 27 1968 in Champaign Co., IL. Married Jul 04 1992, **Phillip Waterside**.
1376 ii. Chad Eric McFadden b. May 12 1971 in Champaign Co., IL.

1107. **Linda Lou[8] Lawyer** (775.Barbara Mae[7] Black, 555.Faun Elizabeth[6] Cozad, 379.Mae[5] Howard, 192.Sarah[4] Arbogast, 64.Jesse[3], 11.Peter[2], 1.Peter[1]), b. Mar 08 1950 in McComb, McDonough Co., IL.
She Married **John L. Partick**, b. Apr 30 1948.

Children:

1377 i. Lance Garrett[9] Partick b. Feb 15 1973 in McComb, McDonough Co., IL.
1378 ii. Grant Ashley Partick b. Jul 16 1975 in McComb, McDonough Co., IL.
1379 iii. Trenton Jay Partick b. Nov 19 1978 in McComb, McDonough Co., IL.

1108. **William Authur[8] Black** (776.William Howard[7], 555.Faun Elizabeth[6] Cozad, 379.Mae[5] Howard, 192.Sarah[4] Arbogast, 64.Jesse[3], 11.Peter[2], 1.Peter[1]), b. Dec 09 1947.
He Married **Kathy Rae Zander**, b. May 18 1952 in McComb, McDonough Co., IL.

Children:

1380 i. Eric William[9] Black b. May 20 1973 in McComb, McDonough Co., IL.
1381 ii. Craig Zander Black b. Nov 01 1975 in McComb, McDonough Co., IL.

1109. **Susan Elizabeth[8] Black** (776.William Howard[7], 555.Faun Elizabeth[6] Cozad, 379.Mae[5] Howard, 192.Sarah[4] Arbogast, 64.Jesse[3], 11.Peter[2], 1.Peter[1]), b. Sep 11 1948.
Married in Denver, Arapaho Co., CO, **Joe Dale Thomson**, b. Nov 30 1947.

Children:

1382 i. Christopher Allen[9] Thompson b. Mar 10 1970 in Denver, Arapaho Co., CO.
1383 ii. Edwards Aft, Cabrian Phillip Thompson b. Jan 28 1978.
1384 iii. Daniel Andrew Thompson b. in Pittsfield, Pike Co., IL.

1110. **Rex Eugene[8] Black** (776.William Howard[7], 555.Faun Elizabeth[6] Cozad, 379.Mae[5] Howard, 192.Sarah[4] Arbogast, 64.Jesse[3], 11.Peter[2], 1.Peter[1]), b. Jul 04 1950.
He Married **Carol Lynn Hughes**, b. Oct 27 1952.

Children:

1385 i. Scott Michael[9] Black b. Oct 27 1972 in McComb, McDonough Co., IL.
1386 ii. Aaron Paul Black b. Apr 11 1975 in Corinth, Alcorn Co., MS.
1387 iii. Elizabeth Kay Black b. Sep 09 1980 in Cedar Lake, Lake Co., IN.

1114. **Harold William[8] Huston** (781.Kathryn Louise[7] Fox, 567.Keith Leroy[6], 388.Myrtle[5] Smith, 194.Frances[4] Arbogast, 64.Jesse[3], 11.Peter[2], 1.Peter[1]), b. Jun 24 1959.
He Married **Kathryn Louise Slater-Frakes**, b. Mar 04 1958.

Children:

1388 i. Jordan Kelsey[9] Huston b. Dec 14 1987.
1389 ii. Morgan Taylor Hutson b. Nov 30 1993.

1115. **Tracie Gaye[8] Fox** (782.Dean Edward[7], 567.Keith Leroy[6], 388.Myrtle[5] Smith, 194.Frances[4] Arbogast, 64.Jesse[3], 11.Peter[2], 1.Peter[1]), b. Dec 03 1958.
She Married **George Kern**, b. Jan 03 1958.

Children:

1390 i. Heidi Elizabeth[9] Fox b. Jul 27 1983.
1391 ii. Michala Beth Fox b. Mar 01 1987.

1116. **Dale Edward[8] Fox** (782.Dean Edward[7], 567.Keith Leroy[6], 388.Myrtle[5] Smith, 194.Frances[4] Arbogast, 64.Jesse[3], 11.Peter[2], 1.Peter[1]), b. Sep 30 1967.
He Married **Stacy Ratcliff**, b. Apr 16 1969.

Children:

1392 i. Douglas Kieth[9] Fox b. Dec 27 1989.
1393 ii. Zachary Edward Fox b. Jul 09 1993.

1117. **Amy Suzanne[8] Fox** (782.Dean Edward[7], 567.Keith Leroy[6], 388.Myrtle[5] Smith, 194.Frances[4] Arbogast, 64.Jesse[3], 11.Peter[2], 1.Peter[1]).
Married Nov 28 1992, **Christopher Lackey**.

Children:

1394 i. Caleb Michael[9] Fox b. Apr 30 1993.

1118. **Randy Joe[8] Schulte** (783.Carol Jean[7] Fox, 567.Keith Leroy[6], 388.Myrtle[5] Smith, 194.Frances[4] Arbogast, 64.Jesse[3], 11.Peter[2], 1.Peter[1]), b. Jul 07 1957.
Married Jan 17 1981, **Terry Neer**, b. Aug 17 1959.

Children:

1395 i. Kristin Myrile[9] Schulte b. Oct 05 1982.
1396 ii. Ryan James Schulte b. Mar 25 1985.

1125. **Barbara Jo[8] Clark** (786.Beverly Jane[7] Fox, 567.Keith Leroy[6], 388.Myrtle[5] Smith, 194.Frances[4] Arbogast, 64.Jesse[3], 11.Peter[2], 1.Peter[1]), b. Jun 26 1961.
Married Jun 10 1983, **Ed McEwen**.

Children:

1397 i. Carolynn Irene^{9} Clark b. Jun 15 1978.

1126. **Linda Kay^{8} Clark** (786.Beverly Jane^{7} Fox, 567.Keith Leroy^{6}, 388.Myrtle^{5} Smith, 194.Frances^{4} Arbogast, 64.Jesse^{3}, 11.Peter^{2}, 1.Peter^{1}), b. May 15 1962.
Married Nov 05 1990, **Charles Wayne Lairson**.

Children:

1398 i. Brian Wayne^{9} Clark b. Jan 11 1979.
1399 ii. Sherry Lee Tassara b. Mar 25 1981.
1400 iii. Mary Ann Tassara b. Jan 25 1983.

1127. **Carol Ann^{8} Clark** (786.Beverly Jane^{7} Fox, 567.Keith Leroy^{6}, 388.Myrtle^{5} Smith, 194.Frances^{4} Arbogast, 64.Jesse^{3}, 11.Peter^{2}, 1.Peter^{1}), b. May 25 1963.
Married 1988, **Richard Lee Smith**, b. Jul 30 1962.

Children:

1401 i. Tyler Lee^{9} Smith b. Mar 26 1990.
1402 ii. James Dale Smith b. Jan 11 1991, d. Jan 11 1991.
1403 iii. Kayla Mae Smith b. Feb 18 1993.

1128. **Dorothy Elaine^{8} Clark** (786.Beverly Jane^{7} Fox, 567.Keith Leroy^{6}, 388.Myrtle^{5} Smith, 194.Frances^{4} Arbogast, 64.Jesse^{3}, 11.Peter^{2}, 1.Peter^{1}), b. Apr 28 1965.
Dorothy had a 3rd child, a boy, given up for adoption.
She Married **Curtis Devion Kimbrell**.

Children:

1404 i. Amy Marie^{9} Kimbrell b. Dec 13 1980.
1405 ii. Casimur Devon Kimbrell b. Jun 1986.

1142. **Donna Esther^{8} Arbogast** (792.Richard Francis^{7}, 569.Theodore Fenton^{6}, 389.Clyde Stewart^{5}, 195.Stephen Aaron Douglas^{4}, 64.Jesse^{3}, 11.Peter^{2}, 1.Peter^{1}), b. Jan 08 1962 in Burley, Cassia Co., ID.
Married Nov 09 1979 in Burley, Cassia Co., ID, **Marshall Morris**, b. Jan 22 1961 in Burley, Cassia Co., ID.

Children:

1406 i. Raushanna Ann^{9} Morris b. Nov 21 1980 in Burley, Cassia Co., ID.
1407 ii. Kayla Rose Morris b. Dec 27 1982 in Burley, Cassia Co., ID.
1408 iii. Trevor Scott Morris b. Jan 21 1985 in Burley, Cassia Co., ID.

1143. **Richard Ray^{8} Howard** (793.Patricia Ann^{7} Arbogast, 569.Theodore Fenton^{6}, 389.Clyde Stewart^{5}, 195.Stephen Aaron Douglas^{4}, 64.Jesse^{3}, 11.Peter^{2}, 1.Peter^{1}), b. in Burley, Cassia Co., ID.
He Married **Susan Gay McCarty Lewis**, b. Jun 12 1959 in Burley, Cassia Co., ID.

Children:

1409 i. Whitney Nan^{9} Howard b. Jun 13 1984 in Pocatello, Bannock Co., ID.

1146. **Kathleen K.^{8} Arbogast** (796.Theodore Clyde^{7}, 569.Theodore Fenton^{6}, 389.Clyde Stewart^{5}, 195.Stephen Aaron Douglas^{4}, 64.Jesse^{3}, 11.Peter^{2}, 1.Peter^{1}), b. Jun 19 1959 in Rupert, Hitchcock Co., NE.
Married Sep 16 1983 in Idaho Falls, Bonneville Co., ID, **Randy Keven Berksdale**, b. Nov 29 1959 in Rupert, Minidoka Co., ID.

Children:

1410 i. Larry Theodore^{9} Berksdale b. Jul 23 1984 in Burley, Cassia Co., ID.
1411 ii. Laren Lynn Berksdale b. Jan 08 1987 in Twin Falls Co., ID.
1412 iii. Debra Michelle Berksdale b. Dec 30 1991 in Twin Falls Co., ID.

1155. **Karen Diane^{8} Arbogast** (799.Roland Allen^{7}, 572.Allen Sterart^{6}, 389.Clyde Stewart^{5}, 195.Stephen Aaron Douglas^{4}, 64.Jesse^{3}, 11.Peter^{2}, 1.Peter^{1}), b. Jan 18 1962 in Albany, Linn Co., OR.
Married Sep 08 1984 in Eugene, Lane Co., OR, **Joseph Nicholas**, b. May 05 1960 in Eugene, Lane Co., OR.

Children:

1413 i. Bradley Joseph^{9} Nichols b. Aug 17 1986 in Reno, Washoe Co., NV.
1414 ii. Brynna Katherine Nichols b. Nov 30 1988 in Springfield, Hampden Co., MA.

1156. **Susan Lynn^{8} Arbogast** (799.Roland Allen^{7}, 572.Allen Sterart^{6}, 389.Clyde Stewart^{5}, 195.Stephen Aaron Douglas^{4}, 64.Jesse^{3}, 11.Peter^{2}, 1.Peter^{1}), b. Jun 04 1963 in Salem, Marion Co., OR.
Married Nov 22 1986 in Eugene, Lane Co., OR, **Justin Wade Bradshaw**, b. Oct 10 1962.

Children:

1415 i. Tyler Wade^{9} Bradshaw b. Mar 24 1991 in Chicago, Cook Co., IL.

1192. **Terri^{8} Ritchie** (827.Patricia Leigh^{7} Armour, 600.Gayl Jane^{6} Arbogast, 411.James Michael^{5}, 202.Charles Sayers^{4}, 67.Michael^{3}, 11.Peter^{2}, 1.Peter^{1}).
She Married **Michael Hunka**.

Children:

1416 i. Michael Scott^{9} Hunka.
1417 ii. Brian William Hunka.

1212. **Christina Rose^{8} Sorg** (849.Jane^{7} Arbogast, 606.Paul Joseph^{6}, 416.Charles Anthony^{5}, 203.Rush Arlington^{4}, 67.Michael^{3}, 11.Peter^{2}, 1.Peter^{1}), b. May 03 1969.
Married May 28 1988, **Eric Hughes**.

Children:

1418 i. Joshua Camerone^{9} Hughes b. Mar 12 1988.

1297. **Scott Louis^{8} FISHER** (926.Marjorie Ann^{7} KING, 618.Rita Theresa^{6} SMITH, 417.Frances Marie^{5} Arbogast, 203.Rush Arlington^{4}, 67.Michael^{3}, 11.Peter^{2}, 1.Peter^{1}), b. Apr 06 1962. Married Nov 08 1986, **Jennifer L. Fruth**, b. May 23 1961.

Children:

1419 i. Jaqueline Michelle^{9} Fisher.

1342. **Elizabeth Marie^{8} Hoover** (942.Eileen Marie^{7} HAMMER, 623.Helen Francis^{6} SMITH, 417.Frances Marie^{5} Arbogast, 203.Rush Arlington^{4}, 67.Michael^{3}, 11.Peter^{2}, 1.Peter^{1}), b. Nov 16 1982.
She Married **Sherman Harrison Buzzard**.

Children:

\+ 1420 i. Cornelia Catherine^{9} Buzzard b. Jan 15 1890.

Descendants of John Arbogast Eight Child of Michael and Mary Elizabeth Samuels

Generation One

1. **John C.[1] Arbogast**, b. About 1771 in Frederick or, Augusta Co., VA (son of Michael Arbogast and Mary Elizabeth Samuels), d. About 1821 in Churchville, Pendleton Co., WV. BIRTH: Estimated from census cited and 1787 Personal Property Tax List for Augusta Co., VA. John listed as over 21 years of age. Born in Frederick or Augusta Co., VA. MARRIAGE: Date estimated but must have been before 1790. DEATH: Will dated 20 Dec., 1820, proven on 3 Apr., 1821. Will Book 4, Page 49, Pendleton Co., VA/WV; lists children. Also see CENSUS: 1810 and 1820, Pendleton Co., VA.

   DEEDS: See deed from John Arbogast heirs and George Arbogast and his wife, Katherine, to Henry Arbogast. Deed Book 14, pages 173 & 174, Pendleton Co. Court Records, 1838. John in will of his father, Michael, in Pendleton Co.

   HOMESTEAD: Near Circleville, across the mountain from his parents. His children Married into families from the Circleville area.

   MILITARY: Private, Capt. Peter Hull's Company, 2nd Bn, Augusta Militia, 1779, page148, "Virginia Militia in the Revolutionary War", by McAllister. Pages 22 and 93, Company in battles during the Yorktown Campaign, 1781. On D.A.R. List of Patriots from Augusta Co., VA, DAR Index, Supplement 1982, p. 3.

   TRANSCRIPT OF JOHN Arbogast's WILL

   From Will Book 4, Page 49, Pendleton County, Virginia In the name of God Amen - I John Arbogast of the County of Pendleton and State of Virginia, weak in body, but of a perfect sound mind and memory, calling to mind the mortalities of all flesh, do make and ordain this my last will and testament. First of all I will and recommend my soul into the hands of God who gave it, and my body to the earth from whence it was taken, to be buried in a Christian Like Manner, nothing doubting but in the general resurrection of the last day when I shall receive it again. And as touching these worldly goods, where with it has pleased God to bless me with in this life, I will and bequeath of the same in the following manner. That is to say I principally and firstly will that all my lawful debts and demands be justly paid out of my estate, and first of all my funeral charges. And amongst my living heirs, I divide my estate as follows. First, I will and bequeath unto my beloved wife, Hannah Arbogast, the plantation that I now live on, and all the movables on the plantation, all my household and kitchen furniture, as long as shelves, except one sorrel mare, one new rifle gun and two three year old heifers. I will and bequeath them unto my son, John. And I will and desire that my son, Jonathan, is to have the possession of the land that he now lives on as long as his mother lives. I also will and bequeath unto my wife, Hannah, five notes on the following men, one on Henry and George Arbogast, one on Benjamin Swecker, one on Ruben Buzzard, one on Benjamin Flesher, and one on Mathias Waybright. And I will and bequeath unto my son, Michael Arbogast, one twenty pound note on John Henkle due on the 16th of January 1821.

   And I will unto my son, Jonathan, one twenty pound note o John Henkle due January the 16th 1822. I likewise will unto my son Joseph a note of twenty pounds on John Henkle which was due January the 16th 1820. I will unto my son Moses one twenty pound note on John Henkle due the 16th of January 1824. I will and bequeath unto my son Adam one twenty pound note on John Henkle due January the 16th 1827. I will and bequeath to my son John one twenty pound note on John Henkle due January 16 1828. I will and bequeath unto my daughter Rachel one twenty pound not on John Henkle due January the 16th 1826. I also will unto my daughter Rachel twenty acres of land adjoining the land that Daniel Wibright now lives on on the east side of his plantation. I will and bequeath unto my daughter Rebekah o twenty pound note on John Henkle due January the 16th 1823. I also will and bequeath unto my daughter Rebekah my part of the land that she now lives on, and unto my daughter Mary I will and bequeath unto her one twenty pound note on John Henkle due January the 16th 1825 and it is my will and desire that after my death t wife Hannah is to pay all my just debts and it is also my will and desire that after my wife's death that my plantation is to be sold and all the property that she holds at the time of her death be sold likewise and be equally divided amongst my heirs exce. Michael and Adam. I will unto them ten pounds each to be paid out of the land or movables and Jonathan to come in equal with the res of my heirs all to five pounds which he has received, and lastly I ordain and appoint Adam

Gum and George Colar executors of this m last will and testament. In witness were of I have hereunto set my hand and seal this 20th day of December 1820. Signed sealed and acknowledged in the presence of

John X Arbogast

mark -seal-

Jonas Lantz
George Arbogast
Henry Arbogast
At a court held for Pendleton County the 3rd day of April 1821 - This last will and testament of John Arbogast, deceased, was presented in Court and proved by the oaths of Jonas Lantz and Henry Arbogast, two of the subscribing witnesses thereto and ordered to be Recorded and Exam.

Teste - L. Dyer C.P.C.
49, Pendleton Co., VA/WV; lists children.

CENSUS: 1810 and 1820, Pendleton Co., VA/WV.

DEEDS: See deed from John Arbogast heirs and George Arbogast and his wife, Katherine, to Henry Arbogast. Deed Book 14, pages 173 & 174, Pendleton Co. Court Records, 1838. John in will of his father, Michael, in Pendleton Co.

HOMESTEAD: Near Circleville, across the mountain from his parents. His children Married into families from the Circleville area.

MILITARY: Private, Capt. Peter Hull's Company, 2nd Bn, Augusta Militia, 1779, page148, "Virginia Militia in the Revolutionary War", by McAllister. Pages 22 and 93, Company in battles during the Yorktown Campaign, 1781. On D.A.R. List of Patriots from Augusta Co., VA, DAR Index, Supplement 1982, p. 3.
Married About 1789 in Pendleton Co., WV, **Hannah Davis**, b. About 1775 in Augusta Memorial Park Cem., Augusta Co., VA (daughter of John Davis), d. About 1830 in Pendleton Co., WV. **Hannah**: BIRTH: Estimated from 1810, 20 and 30 census, Augusta Co., VA, later Pendleton Co., VA/WV. DEATH: Living on 1830 census, not on 1840 census or deed from heirs, 1838. Deed Book 14, Pages 171-174, Pendleton Co. PARENTS: Unknown, maiden name from Morton's histories of Pendleton and Highland.

***Children*:**

2 i. Jonathan[2] Arbogast, b. About 1789 in Crabbottom, Highland Co., VA, d. Jul 30 1861 in Straight Creek, Pendleton/Highland Co., VA.
From research of AAF RIN # 440, copy in file. Records f or determining birth vary considerably. 1850 census of Highland Co., VA indicate age as 61; 1860 census, age 83 and obviously incorrect; age was indicated as 66 on his death record. The 1850 census age is used. Death record filed in Highland Co., VA indicates 30 Jul 1861. Will filed in

Highland Co., VA, Will Book 2, p.30, dated 19 Sep 1859 and probated Sept. 1861. Marriage recorded in Pendleton Co., VA/WV.

From his will it is most probable that Jonathan did not have any children.
Beneficiaries named were Cain and Phoebe Wimer, and Wm. Baker. At the time of his will his place of residence was at the mouth of Strait Creek.

Jonathan named in will of father, John Arbogast, and on the deed of heirs in 1838.
Married 1813, **Katherine Wimer**.

\+ 3 ii. Michael Arbogast b. 1790/94.
\+ 4 iii. Rachel Arbogast b. 1791.
\+ 5 iv. Rebecca Arbogast b. 1792.
\+ 6 v. Joseph E. Arbogast b. 1795.
\+ 7 vi. Moses Arbogast b. Nov 30 1799.
\+ 8 vii. Adam Sr. Arbogast b. 1799.
\+ 9 viii. Mary Ann Arbogast b. Jan 13 1800.

+ 10 ix. John C. Arbogast, Jr. b. 1804.

Generation Two

3. **Michael[2] Arbogast** (1.John C.[1]), b. 1790/94 in Pendleton Co., WV, d. ABT 00-___-1832 in Pendleton Co., WV.
Listed on census as living in Timber Ridge Section of Pendleton Co. 1820, 30, 40, 50 and 60 census, Pendleton Co. No will found in Pendleton Co. See will of his father, John, Pendleton Co., VA, Will Book 4, page 49. Pendleton Co. birth, death and marriage records.
He Married **Edith Ketterman**, b. Abt 1799 (daughter of George F. Ketterman and Mary Magdalena Henkle), d. Oct 28, 1879, buried in Old Livingood Cm, Numa, Ia. Edith: https://www.wikitree.com/wiki/Ketterman-29

***Children**:*

+ 11 i. Emily[3] Arbogast b. 1822.
+ 12 ii. George Washington Arbogast.
+ 13 iii. Mary Magdalene. Arbogast.
+ 14 iv. Christina Arbogast b. About 1825.
+ 15 v. Nichodemus Arbogast b. Oct 12, 1826.
+ 16 vi. Michael Arbogast, Jr. b. Oct 16 1827.

4. **Rachel[2] Arbogast** (1.John C.[1]), b. 1791 in Pendleton Co., WV, d. Feb 1879 in Pendleton Co., WV, buried in Pendleton Co., WV.
Married Dec 6 1813 in Pendleton Co., WV, **Daniel Waybright**, b. 1787 in Adams Co., PA (son of Johann Martin Waybright and Elizabeth Ammer Amman), d. Jan 7 1852 in Crabbottom, Highland Co., VA.

***Children**:*

17 i. Mary[3] Waybright b. 1812 in Pendleton Co., WV. Married Aug 9 1832, **George Halterman** (son of Adam Halterman and Sarah Peck).
+ 18 ii. Jemima Maria Waybright b. Apr 17 1814.
+ 19 iii. Jesse Waybright b. 1817.
20 iv. John Waybright b. 1818 in Pendleton Co., WV. Married Apr 8 1843, **Elizabeth Ann Ketterman**.
+ 21 v. Daniel Waybright, Jr. b. 1823.
+ 22 vi. Nathan Waybright b. Apr 10 1828.
+ 23 vii. Elizabeth Waybright b. 1828.
+ 24 viii. Levi Waybright b. 1829.
+ 25 ix. Miles Waybright.
+ 26 x. Martha Ann Waybright b. May 30 1830.

5. **Rebecca[2] Arbogast** (1.John C.[1]), b. 1792 in Pendleton Co., WV, d. Jul 1 1878 in Pendleton Co., WV, buried Jul 3 1878 in Waybright Cem., Pendleton Co., WV.
Married Dec 16 1813 in Pendleton Co., WV, **Mathias Waybright**, b. 1790 in Pendleton Co., WV.

***Children**:*

+ 27 i. Cyrus[3] Waybright b. 1819.
+ 28 ii. Alice Waybright b. 1824.
+ 29 iii. Sidney Waybright b. 1825.
+ 30 iv. Adam Waybright b. May 16 1826.
31 v. Susanna Waybright b. About 1827 in Pendleton Co., WV. Married Aug 03 1844, **Solomon Harold** (son of Andrew Harold and Barbara Rexrode).
+ 32 vi. Elijah Waybright b. 1831.
33 vii. Benjamin Waybright b. About 1831, d. About 1865.
+ 34 viii. Catherine Elizabeth Waybright b. Sep 12 1832.
+ 35 ix. Morgan Waybright b. 1835.
+ 36 x. Miles Waybright b. 1835.
37 xi. Jesse Waybright b. 1839 in Pendleton Co., WV, d. 1864 in Camp Chase, Franklin Co., OH. Died During and because of Civil War, details unknown.
38 xii. Elsie Waybright. Married Jan 28 1847, **Essau A Ketterman**, b. May 20 1822 in North Fork, Pendleton Co., VA (son of Jacob D. Ketterman and Mary Ann Arbogast), d. 1863 in Civil War.

6. **Joseph E.[2] Arbogast** (1.John C.[1]), b. 1795 in Pendleton Co., WV, d. February 8, 1884 in Churchville, Pendleton Co., WV.

Married Jan 24 1820, **Sarah Ketterman** (daughter of George F. Ketterman and Mary Magdalena Henkle).

***Children*:**

+ 39 i. Cain[3] Arbogast b. October 1819.
+ 40 ii. Lemuel Arbogast b. 1820.
41 iii. Eliel Arbogast b. 1825.
+ 42 iv. Joseph Elili Arbogast, Jr. b. 1826.
+ 43 v. Sidney Dean Arbogast b. 1830.
44 vi. George W. Arbogast b. 1832 or 1833.
+ 45 vii. Sylvanus Arbogast.
46 viii. Hannah C. Arbogast b. 1836 or 1837.
47 ix. Mary Polly Arbogast b. 1838 or 1839.
48 x. Jacob Arbogast b. 1840 or 1841.
49 xi. Sarah A. Arbogast b. 1842 or 1843.
50 xii. Susan Arbogast b. 1844 or 1845, d. 1860.

7. **Moses[2] Arbogast** (1.John C.[1]), b. Nov 30 1799 in Circleville, Pendleton Co., WV, d. Mar 26 1869 in Valley Head, Randolph Co., WV, buried in Maple Cem., Conley Run, Randolph Co., WV. Comments written by Martha Neighnors.
Moses moved from Pendleton County to Randolph County some time between 1820 and 1830. Records indicate he had numerous children with numerous women. Some while Married to another. Moses was married four times, fathered eleven children and was a step-father to nineteen children.
His first wife was Sara Elizabeth Zickafoose. Moses and Sara were Married 24 Oct 1819 in Pendleton Co, Virginia and had four children, Hannah, Priscilla, Allen and Nancy before she died about 1833.
His second marriage was to Margaret Wamsley 25 Oct 1834 in Randolph Co, Virginia. This was her first marriage. They had a total of seven children, Martha, Jefferson, Rachel, Daniel, Sarah, Moses and John. Martha died in 1853 at the age of 44.
Moses third marriage was to Matilda Ware who was 49 and widowed. Malilda's first husband was William Ware (no relation) and they had six children. This was Moses third marriage and Matilda's second. They had no children together. Matilda died in 1864 at the age of 58.
Moses fourth marriage was to Matilda's niece, Eleanor Elizabeth (Ware) Channell. He was 66 and she was 33 and widowed. They were Married 11 Sep 1865 in Randolph Co, West Virginia. Eleanor's first husband was Jesse Channell and they had eight children. Moses and Eleanor had no children together.
(1) Married Oct. 4 1818 in Pendleton Co., WV, **Sara Elizabeth Zickafoose**, b. BEF 1800 in Pendleton Co., WV, d. in Randolph Co., WV.

Children *by Sara Elizabeth Zickafoose:*

+ 51 i. Hannah V.[3] Arbogast b. ABT 1823.
+ 52 ii. Allen Arbogast b. ABT 1824.
53 iii. Priscilla Arbogast b. ABT 1824 in Pendleton Co., WV.
+ 54 iv. Ailcey (Elsey) Arbogast b. ABT 1828.

(2) He Married **Eleanor Elizabeth Ware** (daughter of Hiram Ware and Mary Brady). .

(3) Married Oct 25 1834 in Randolph Co., WV, **Margaret Wamsley**, b. ABT 1809 in Virginia, (daughter of Joseph Wamsley and Martha Patsy Jamison), d. Dec 11 1853 in Randolph Co., WV, buried in Maple Cem., Conley Run, Randolph Co., WV.

Children *by Margaret Wamsley:*

55 v. Martha Arbogast b. ABT 1836 in Randolph Co., WV. She Married Curtis Taylor, b. ABT 1832.
56 vi. Jefferson Arbogast b. ABT 1838 in Randolph Co., WV, d. 1864 in Civil War Battle, Bloody Angle, Spotsylvania, VA.
+ 57 vii. Rachel E. Arbogast b. 1840.
58 viii. Daniel W. Arbogast b. 1842 in Randolph Co., WV, d. Sep 1 1861 in Randolph Co., WV.
+ 59 ix. Sarah Elizabeth Arbogast b. Aug 16 1844.
+ 60 x. Moses Wamsley Arbogast b. 1847.
+ 61 xi. John B. (Jack) Arbogast b. 1849.

(4) Married 1854, **Matilda Ware**, b. Jan 4 1805 in Virginia, (daughter of Richard Ware and Mary Polly Wilson), b. ABT 1806 in Virginia, d. Jan 8 1864, d. AFT 1850 in Randolph Co., WV

8. **Adam Sr.[2] Arbogast** (1.John C.[1]), b. 1799 in Pendleton Co., WV, d. Oct 6 1857 in Pocahontas Co., WV.
Married May 30 1823 in Pendleton Co., WV, **Mary Davis**, b. Abt 1804 in Pendleton Co., WV, d. Abt 1851 in Highland Co., VA.

***Children*:**

62 i. Caroline[3] Arbogast b. Abt 1823 in Pendleton Co., WV.
\+ 63 ii. Adam Jr. Arbogast b. 1825.
64 iii. Jesse Arbogast b. May 1829 in Straight Creek, Pendleton/Highland Co., VA, d. Aft 1900 in Highland Co., VA.
65 iv. Daniel Arbogast b. Abt 1834 in Hightown, Pendleton Co., WV, d. Aft 1900 in Lewis Co., WV.
\+ 66 v. Peter William Arbogast b. June 2, 1836.
67 vi. James Arbogast b. Jan 15 1840 in Straight Creek, Pendleton/Highland Co., VA, d. Dec 30 1900 in Peck's Run, Upshur Co., WV, buried in Mt. Zion Cem. Peck's Run U B Church, Upshur Co., WV.
68 vii. Sarah (Sally) Arbogast b. Mar 8 1841, d. Nov 11 1900.
69 viii. Ephraim Arbogast b. Abt 1842 in Straight Creek, Pendleton/Highland Co., VA, d. Aft 1860.

9. **Mary Ann[2] Arbogast** (1.John C.[1]), b. Jan 13 1800 in Pendleton Co., WV, d. Aft 11 Aug 1870 in Pendleton Co., WV. Married Jan 13 1820, **Jacob D. Ketterman**, b. 1797 in Hardy Co., WV (son of George F. Ketterman and Mary Magdalena Henkle), d. Jan 4 1869 in Pendleton Co., WV, buried in Dorcas Grant Co., WV.

Children:

70 i. Sabina M.[3] Ketterman b. Jan 17 1820 in North Fork, Pendleton Co., VA. Married Jun 19 1844, **Abraham Flinn**.
71 ii. Essau A Ketterman b. May 20 1822 in North Fork, Pendleton Co., VA, d. 1863 in Civil War. Married Jan 28 1847, **Elsie Waybright** (daughter of Mathias Waybright and Rebecca Arbogast).
\+ 72 iii. Esau Lacey Ketterman b. May 20 1822.
73 iv. Salem S. Ketterman b. Dec 21 1826 in Seneca Creek, Pendleton Co., VA/WV, d. May 15 1910. Married Oct 28 1847, **Mary Bennett**, b. Dec 21 1824 (daughter of Elijah Bennett and Barbara Bible).
74 v. Miles Ketterman b. Dec 6 1828 in Seneca Creek, Pendleton Co., VA/WV.
75 vi. Hannah Ketterman b. Jan 3 1831 in Seneca Creek, Pendleton Co., VA/WV. Married Nov 15 1845, **Silas Miller** (son of John Taylor Miller and Susannah Hedrick).
\+ 76 vii. Leah Ketterman b. Dec 8 1834.
77 viii. Rebecca Ketterman b. Apr 29 1837 in Seneca Creek, Pendleton Co., VA/WV. Married Oct 25 1856, **George F Day**.
\+ 78 ix. Nicholas Harper Ketterman b. Jul 12 1839.
\+ 79 x. John George Ketterman.
80 xi. Joseph Ketterman b. Jul 11 1841 in Seneca Creek, Pendleton Co., VA/WV, d. Jan 2 1863.
\+ 81 xii. Sarah Ketterman b. Apr 1843.

10. **John C.[2] Arbogast, Jr.** (1.John C.[1]), b. 1804 in Pendleton Co., WV, d. After 1880 in Mingo Area, Randolph Co., WV. Information from Amanda Arbogast Forbes research record # 21 copy in file. On 1870 census, Randolph Co., age 66; 1880 census Randolph Co., age 75 according to records of Beverly Kenny (Mrs. Donald) Pensacola, FL. John and wife Mary assign their interest in 160ac. of land in Pendleton Co., VA, 21 Feb. 1831. See Deed Book 11, p. 30.

49, Pendleton Co., VA/WV; lists children.

CENSUS: 1810 and 1820, Pendleton Co., VA/WV.

DEEDS: See deed from John Arbogast heirs and George Arbogast and his wife, Katherine, to Henry Arbogast. Deed Book 14, pages 173 & 174, Pendleton Co. Court Records, 1838. John in will of his father, Michael, in Pendleton Co.

HOMESTEAD: Near Circleville, across the mountain from his parents. His children Married into families from the Circleville area.

MILITARY: Private, Capt. Peter Hull's Company, 2nd Bn, Augusta Militia, 1779, page148, "Virginia Militia in the Revolutionary War", by McAllister. Pages 22 and 93, Company in battles during the Yorktown Campaign, 1781. On D.A.R. List of Patriots from Augusta Co., VA, DAR Index, Supplement 1982, p. 3.
Married Jan 15 1824 in Pendleton Co., WV, **Mary A. Wood**, b. 1796 in Pendleton Co., WV.

Children:

\+ 82 i. Solomon[3] Arbogast b. Dec 07 1820.
83 ii. Mary Arbogast.
\+ 84 iii. George Washington Arbogast b. 1825.
85 iv. Priscilla Arbogast.
86 v. Elizabeth Arbogast.
87 vi. Martha Jane Arbogast.

Generation Three

11. **Emily[3] Arbogast** (3.Michael[2], 1.John C.[1]), b. 1822 in Pendleton Co., WV, d. Bef 1849 in Pendleton Co., WV.
(1) Married Mar 17 1849, **Joshua Teter**. (

Children *by Cyrus Waybright:*

+	88	i.	Christina[4] Waybright b. 1842.
	89	ii.	Amos C. Waybright b. 1844 in Pendleton Co., WV.
	90	iii.	Cyrus Waybright b. 1846 in Pendleton Co., WV, d. Jul 6 1864 in Winchester, Frederick Co., VA.

2) Married Dec 6 1838 in Pendleton Co., WV, **Cyrus Waybright**, b. 1819 in Pendleton Co., WV (son of Mathias Waybright and Rebecca Arbogast).

12. **George Washington[3] Arbogast** (3.Michael[2], 1.John C.[1]).
Married Mar 05 1842 in Pendleton Co., WV, **Mary Reed**.

Children:

	91	i.	Michael[4] Arbogast b. About 1843. MILITARY: Enlistment record indicates age 19 at September 15, 1961, Charleston, WV. Union army, 3yrs., K Co., 7th Rgt-, WV Cavalry. June, 1862, wounded at Battle of Cross Keys, under Surgeons care. July, 1862, sick at Cumberland Hospital. 28 Feb., 1863, promoted to Sergeant 31 Dec., 1863, absent, detached -for service of recruiting. 24 Jul., 1864, run, deserted before enemy at Cherry Run. 26 Jan., 1865, appears on Company Muster Roll Out. No pension record found. No record of imprisonment at Andersonville according to Oliver Arbogast who has checked records and has videotape of old prison and burial site of Charles U. Arbogast, Pvt., 1st Rgt., UV Lt. Artery. Died 11 Aug 1864. Enlisted at Beverly, UV, Randolph Co. He was son of Solomon Arbogast and Nottingham, grandson of Benjamin Arbogast, Sr. and great grandson of Adam Arbogast. Michael Arbogast is believed to have died as a result of the war. No Pension record found.
+	92	ii.	Francis M. Arbogast b. 1847.
+	93	iii.	George Washington Arbogast, Jr. b. Jan 29 1849.
	94	iv.	Christina Arbogast b. 1853, d. Dec 09 1873.
	95	v.	Ferdinand Arbogast b. 1855, d. Dec 23 1873.
	96	vi.	Gracy Arbogast b. 1855, d. Dec 25 1873.
+	97	vii.	Nichodemus Arbogast b. About 1857.
+	98	viii.	Amos Cyrus Arbogast b. Jan 27 1862.
	99	ix.	Levi Arbogast b. 1866, d. Dec 25 1873.
	100	x.	Noah Arbogast b. May 13 1871, d. May 05 1875.

13. **Mary Magdalene.[3] Arbogast** (3.Michael[2], 1.John C.[1]).
She Married **Amos Shreve**, b. 1810 in Smoke Holes, Grant Co., WV (son of John Shreve and Frances Eliza Platt).

Children:

+	101	i.	Nicodemus[4] Shreve b. 1843.
+	102	ii.	Benjamin "Little Ben" Shreve b. 1845.
+	103	iii.	Edith Jane Shreve b. 1849.
	104	iv.	Jesse D. Shreve b. 1851.
	105	v.	Ann Rebecca Shreve b. 1854.
	106	vi.	Becky Shreve.

14. **Christina[3] Arbogast** (3.Michael[2], 1.John C.[1]), b. About 1825, d. Apr 27 1854.
Married 1843, **Jesse Davis**, b. 1819 (son of James Davis and Margaret Bland).

Children:

+	107	i.	Jethro[4] Davis b. 1842.
	108	ii.	Lucy Davis b. About 1844.
+	109	iii.	Miles Davis b. About 1846.
+	110	iv.	Michael Davis b. About 1847.
	111	v.	Cornelius Davis b. About 1850.

112 vi. Nicholas Davis. He Married **Margaret Hedrick**.
113 vii. Emily Davis.

15. **Nichodemus[3] Arbogast** (3.Michael[2], 1.John C.[1]), b. Oct 12, 1826, d. July 2, 1915.
(1) Married Abt 1848, **Mary Simmons**, b. Abt 1828 (daughter of Jacob R. Simmons and Mary Magdalen), d. Aug 31, 1870.

***Children** by Mary Simmons:*

\+ 114 i. Edith[4] Arbogast b. About 1849.
115 ii. Margaret Arbogast b. About 1853 in Nicholas Co., WV, d. 1870 in Nicholas Co., WV.
116 iii. America Arbogast b. 1855 in Nicholas Co., WV, d. 1889 in Nicholas Co., WV.
\+ 117 iv. Sarah D. Arbogast b. 1855.
\+ 118 v. Rocksena Arbogast b. About 1856.
\+ 119 vi. George Franklin Arbogast b. Feb 28 1857.
120 vii. Lemuel Arbogast b. May 01 1859.
\+ 121 viii. Thomas Arbogast b. 1862.
122 ix. Francis Marion Arbogast b. About 1867, d. 1945.
123 x. Watson Ketterman Arbogast b. May 20 1868, d. Mar 23 1952.

(2) He Married **Margaret Jeffers**, b. 1847 in Virginia.

***Children** by Margaret Jeffers:*

124 xi. Michael Arbogast b. 1876.
125 xii. Shilonah Arbogast b. About 1878.
126 xiii. Tecumptas Arbogast b. Jun 15 1880.

16. **Michael[3] Arbogast Jr.** (3.Michael[2], 1.John C.[1]), b. Oct 16 1827 in Pendleton Co., WV, d. Jan 25 1917 in Numa, Appanoose Co., IA.
Married Oct 14 1847 in Franklin Co., WV, **Mary Ann Pierce**, b. Jul 29 1827 in Numa, Appanoose Co., IA, d. Mar 05 1909.

***Children**:*

127 i. Francis J.[4] Arbogast b. About 1848 in Virginia.
\+ 128 ii. Emily Catharine Arbogast b. Oct 29 1849.
129 iii. George Washington Arbogast b. About 1853 in Iowa.
130 iv. Martha E. Arbogast b. About 1856 in Iowa.
\+ 131 v. Stephen Douglas Arbogast b. Aug 13 1860.
132 vi. John Breckenridge Arbogast. Married Aug 28 1879 in Appanoose Co., IA, **Isabella Keller**, b. Jun 23 1855 in Pendleton Co., WV (daughter of Adam H. Keller and Sarah Catharine Harper), d. Mar 20 1931.
133 vii. James Arbogast.
134 viii. Elsworth Arbogast.
135 ix. Columbus Arbogast.
136 x. Charles Arbogast.
137 xi. Eddy Arbogast.
138 xii. Mary Arbogast.

18. **Jemima Maria[3] Waybright** (4.Rachel[2] Arbogast, 1.John C.[1]), b. Apr 17 1814 in Pendleton Co., WV, d. Nov 15 1859 in Lewis Co., WV, buried in Lewis Co., WV.
Married Feb 13 1834 in Pendleton Co., WV, **William Sponaugle**, b. Mar 17 1815 in Hunting Ground, Pendleton Co., (W)VA (son of Balsor Sponaugle and Sarah White), d. Feb 9 1888 in Yorktown, Page Co., IA, buried in Baker Cem., Page Co., IA.

***Children**:*

139 i. Catherine[4] Sponaugle b. Sep 19 1834 in Pendleton Co., WV, d. Oct 23 1868 in Middlebury, Elkhart Co., IN, buried in Middlebury, Elkhart Co., IN. Married Sep 30 1856, **Jeremiah Sampsell Anawalt**, b. Oct 29 1835 in Somerset Co., PA, d. Aug 1915 in Oklahoma.
140 ii. Jacob Sponaugle b. Dec 14 1835 in Pendleton Co., WV, d. 1864 in Page Co., IA. He **married (unknown) Bachlor**, b. 1839 in Lewis Co., WV.
141 iii. Maria S. Sponaugle b. Jun 6 1837 in Pendleton Co., WV, d. in Page Co., IA. (1) She Married **David E. Vient**, b. 1833 in Pendleton Co., WV. (2) She Married **John Sprigg**, b. 1834 in Pendleton Co., WV.
142 iv. Mary Sponaugle b. Aug 10 1838 in Pendleton Co., WV, d. Aft 1873. Married Jan 4 1855, John D. Sprigg.
143 v. William Jackson Sponaugle b. Jan 10 1840 in Pendleton Co., WV, d. Oct 4 1909 in Clarinda, Page Co., IA, buried Oct 8 1909 in Summers Cem., Clarinda, Page Co., IA. (1) Married May 25 1897 in Clarinda, Page Co., IA, **Mary Weidner**. (2) Married Jan 12 1865 in Illinois, **Mary Angeline Gillson**. (3) Married May 15 1885 in Clarinda, Page Co., IA, **Anna M. Markel**. (4) Married Jun 8 1909 in Clarinda, Page Co., IA, **Pearl Stewart**.

144 vi. Martha Jane Sponaugle b. Apr 10 1842 in Pendleton Co., WV. She Married **Edward Halterman**.
+ 145 vii. Daniel Sponaugle b. Apr 10 1844.
146 viii. Levi Sponaugle b. Aug 10 1847 in Lewis Co., WV, d. Sep 18 1934 in Barnes, Washington Co., KS. Married Mar 13 1869 in Galesburg, Knox Co., IL, **Elizabeth Jane Gillson**, b. 1851 in Lewis Co., WV.
147 ix. John Sponaugle b. Feb 1 1849 in Lewis Co., WV, d. May 3 1918 in Howard, Elk Co., KA. Married Jun 1873 in Page Co., IA, **Christina A. Thompson**, b. 1853 in Lewis Co., WV.
148 x. Henry Sponaugle b. May 15 1850 in Lewis Co., WV, d. Jul 29 1927 in Page Co., IA. He Married **Catherine O'Day**, b. 1854.
149 xi. Elizabeth Jane Sponaugle b. Aug 22 1855 in Lewis Co., WV, d. Bef 1930 in Page Co., IA. She Married **Jasper Newton Johnson**, b. 1851 in Lewis Co., WV.

19. **Jesse[3] Waybright** (4.Rachel[2] Arbogast, 1.John C.[1]), b. 1817 in Pendleton Co., WV, d. 1864 in Pendleton Co., WV, buried in Warner Cem., Hunting Ground, Pendleton Co., VA/WV.
(1) Married Nov 15 1849 in Pendleton Co., WV, **Nancy Jane Bland**, b. 1826 in Pendleton Co., WV (daughter of Enoch Bland and Amy Naomi Terer), d. Jun 16 1899 in Pendleton Co., WV, buried in Warner Cem., Hunting Ground, Pendleton Co., VA/WV..

See #3973 for marriage and son, Henry T. Waybright.

Children *by Nancy Jane Bland:*

+ 150 i. Isaac P[4] Waybright b. Sep 1851.
+ 151 ii. James Bud Waybright b. Jan 16 1853.
+ 152 iii. Alvah C. Waybright b. Feb 17 1855.
153 iv. Carietta Waybright b. in Pendleton Co., WV.
154 v. Susan A. Waybright b. Jan 1857 in Pendleton Co., WV.
+ 155 vi. Mary Elizabeth Waybright b. Dec 25 1863.

(2) He Married **Hester Arbogast**, b. About 1823 in Crabbottom, Highland Co., VA (daughter of Henry Arbogast and Elizabeth Seybert), d. BEF NOV-1844 in Crabbottom, Highland Co., VA. **Hester**: Source is AAF research with references to; not found on census records so dates are estimated, probably died before 1849 when husband remarried and may have had one child born about 1845. From, Teter Descendants, by Eva A. Winfield, Ridgeley, WV, Hester was his first wife, Jane Bland his second. He had a son with Hester, Henry T. Waybright. Jesse was ambushed outside his home during the Civil War

Children *by Hester Arbogast:*

156 vii. Henry Teter Waybright b. 1844 or prior to. in Pendleton Co., WV.

21. **Daniel[3] Waybright Jr.** (4.Rachel[2] Arbogast, 1.John C.[1]), b. 1823 in Pendleton Co., WV, d. 1879 in Pendleton Co., WV.
(1) Married Aug 17 1848 in Pendleton Co., WV, **Christina Mullenax**, b. May 6 1830 in Pendleton Co., WV (daughter of William Mullenax and Christina Vance), d. Dec 16 1905 in Pendleton Co., WV, buried in Butchers Cem., Onego, Pendleton Co., WV.

Children *by Christina Mullenax:*

+ 157 i. Abraham[4] Waybright b. May 5 1850.
+ 158 ii. Mary Margaret Waybright b. Jan 14 1856.
+ 159 iii. William Washington Waybright b. Apr 1857.
160 iv. Henry Clay Waybright b. Feb 2 1864 in Pendleton Co., WV, d. Nov 5 1922.
+ 161 v. Isaac Perry Waybright b. Mar 20 1866.
+ 162 vi. Cordelia Waybright b. Jul 6 1869.
163 vii. Lettie S. Waybright b. Aug 22 1873 in Crabbottom, Highland Co., VA, d. 20 Jan. Married Aug 24 1899, **James P. Davis**.
+ 164 viii. John Edward Waybright b. Mar 16 1875.

(2) Married Nov 24 1842, **Martha Mullenax** (daughter of George Mullenax and Elizabeth Lambert).

Children *by Martha Mullenax:*

+ 165 ix. Columbus P. Waybright b. Jul 1845.
+ 166 x. Mary Jane Waybright b. 1847.
+ 167 xi. Albert Waybright b. May 1848.

22. **Nathan[3] Waybright** (4.Rachel[2] Arbogast, 1.John C.[1]), b. Apr 10 1828 in Pendleton Co., WV, d. Sep 16 1904 in Omaha, Douglas Co., NE, buried Sep 18 1904 in Forest Lawn Cem., Omaha, Douglas Co., NE.
He Married **Leah Ketterman**, b. Dec 8 1834 in Seneca Creek, Pendleton Co., VA/WV (daughter of Jacob D. Ketterman and Mary Ann Arbogast), d. Aft 10 Jun 1885.

Children:

+ 168 i. Andrew Jackson[4] Waybright b. Jan 23 1851.
+ 169 ii. Adam Harness Waybright b. Feb 1855.
+ 170 iii. Martha Jane Waybright b. Mar 1 1859.
+ 171 iv. Mary Catherine Waybright b. Jan 15 1865.
172 v. John Waybright b. May 1872 in Omaha, Douglas Co., NE, d. Jul 16 1904 in Omaha, Douglas Co., NE, buried Jul 18 1904 in Forest Lawn Cem., Omaha, Douglas Co., NE. Married Jun 9 1891, **Agnes Fox**.
173 vi. Edward M. Waybright b. Mar 1874 in Plattsmouth Cass Co., NE, d. Bef 1928. Married Oct 22 1891, Margaret Smith.

23. **Elizabeth[3] Waybright** (4.Rachel[2] Arbogast, 1.John C.[1]), b. 1828 in Virginia.
Married Dec 26 1844, **Nicholas Rexroad**, b. 1825 (son of Conrad Rexrode and Catharine Harper). **Nicholas**: He was son of Conrad Rexroad and Catherine Harper.

Children:

174 i. Sarah J[4] Rexroad b. About 1846 in Pendleton Co., WV.
175 ii. Samuel C Rexroad b. About 1848. Married Jun 11 1867, **Martha J. Fox**. Martha: Child of William H. Fox and Margaret Hodge.
+ 176 iii. Amby Rexroad b. Oct 10 1851.
+ 177 iv. Jefferson D Rexroad b. About 1862.

24. **Levi[3] Waybright** (4.Rachel[2] Arbogast, 1.John C.[1]), b. 1829 in Pendleton Co., WV, d. Feb 7 1863 in Camp Washington, VA, buried in Braxton Co., VA. was a private Co. G 62nd Va. Cavalry
was a slave owner no name female born Jan 1854 mother Elizabeth, LeMaster Stephenson father David born 28 Sep 185 5Maddison 25 Nov 1857 William 9 Apr 185 7 female died Jan 1854 (6 days old) buried Braxton Co. VA. LeMaster Stephenson i
Married May 16 1854 in Braxton Co., WV, **Maryann Jane Evans**, b. 1827 in Braxton Co., WV.

Children:

178 i. John[4] Waybright b. 1845 in Braxton Co., WV.
179 ii. Edna Waybright b. 1847 in Braxton Co., WV.
180 iii. James Waybright b. in Braxton Co., WV.
+ 181 iv. Clark W. Waybright b. 1855.
182 v. Andrew Jenkins Waybright b. 1857 in Braxton Co., WV.
+ 183 vi. Sarah Amanda Waybright b. May 22 1860.

25. **Miles[3] Waybright** (4.Rachel[2] Arbogast, 1.John C.[1]), b. in Pendleton Co., WV, d. Nov 13 1903 in Omaha, Douglas Co., NE, buried Nov 15 1903 in Forest Lawn Cem., Omaha, Douglas Co., NE. (1) He Married **Ann Rebecca Nicholas**, b. 1825 in Pendleton Co., WV, d. Bef 1874 in Lexington, McLean Co., IL. (

Children *by Ann Rebecca Nicholas:*

184 i. Louise[4] Waybright b. About 1846.
185 ii. Mary Waybright b. About 1849.
186 iii. Amos Waybright b. About 1852.

(2) Married Nov 30 1882 in Douglas Co., KA, **Isa Dora Gilbert**, b. 1865 in Iroquois Co., IL.

Children *by Isa Dora Gilbert:*

187 iv. Edith Waybright.
188 v. Rosa Waybright.

26. **Martha Ann[3] Waybright** (4.Rachel[2] Arbogast, 1.John C.[1]), b. May 30 1830 in Pendleton Co., WV, d. Nov 7 1883, buried in Dry Run Cem., Cherry Grove, Pendleton Co., WV.
Married Sep 14 1847 in Highland Co., VA, **William Hinkle**, b. May 1826 in Pendleton Co., WV (son of Solomon Hinkle and Phoebe (Susan) Calhoun), d. 1907, buried in Dry Run Cem., Cherry Grove, Pendleton Co., WV.

Children:

+ 189 i. Elbridge L.[4] Hinkle b. Jul 1848.
+ 190 ii. Susan Hinkle b. Mar 25 1853.
+ 191 iii. Elizabeth C Hinkle b. Mar 1855.
+ 192 iv. Eliza Ann Hinkle b. Oct 31 1856.
+ 193 v. Catherine Beam Hinkle b. 1859.

\+ 194 vi. Isaac Harness Hinkle b. 1862.
195 vii. Jasper Triplett Hinkle b. Mar 18 1865 in Dry Run, Pendleton Co., WV. He Married **Florence Warner**, b. Jun 15 1883 in Riverton, Pendleton Co., WV.
196 viii. Leonard Harper Hinkle b. 1867 in Dry Run, Pendleton Co., WV. He Married **Sarah Catherine Hammer**, b. Mar 16 1875, d. Jul 04 1950. Sarah: Child of Leonard Hammer and Sarah Trimble.
197 ix. (unknown) Hinkle b. May 1870 in Dry Run, Pendleton Co., WV.
198 x. Pauline Hinkle b. 1873 in Dry Run, Pendleton Co., WV. She Married **Philip M. Hinkle**, b. 1874.

27. **Cyrus[3] Waybright** (5.Rebecca[2] Arbogast, 1.John C.[1]) (See marriage to number 11.)

28. **Alice[3] Waybright** (5.Rebecca[2] Arbogast, 1.John C.[1]), b. 1824 in Pendleton Co., WV, d. Bef 1900.
(1) Married Jan 28 1847 in Pendleton Co., WV, **Esau Lacey Ketterman**, b. May 20 1822 in Pendleton Co., WV (son of Jacob D. Ketterman and Mary Ann Arbogast).

***Children** by Esau Lacey Ketterman:*

\+ 199 i. Roseann[4] Ketterman b. 1848.
\+ 200 ii. Solomon W. Ketterman b. Dec 1851.
201 iii. Bud O. Ketterman b. 1852 in Pendleton Co., WV.
202 iv. Amanda Ketterman b. Oct 12 1853 in Pendleton Co., WV.
203 v. Malvina Ketterman b. Oct 12 1853 in Pendleton Co., WV.
\+ 204 vi. Ann Rebecca Ketterman b. Nov 24 1855.
\+ 205 vii. Susan P. Ketterman b. Mar 17 1858.
206 viii. (infant) Ketterman b. Aug 29 1859 in Pendleton Co., WV, d. Aug 29 1859 in Pendleton Co., WV.
207 ix. Flora A. Ketterman b. 1864 in Pendleton Co., WV, d. Apr 23 1864 in Pendleton Co., WV.

(2) Married in Pendleton Co., WV, **John R. Allen**, b. 1819 in Pendleton Co., WV.

***Children** by John R. Allen:*

\+ 208 x. Churchill Waybright b. Aug 3 1844.

29. **Sidney[3] Waybright** (5.Rebecca[2] Arbogast, 1.John C.[1]), b. 1825 in Pendleton Co., WV.
Married Nov 30 1853 in Pendleton Co., WV, **Emanuel Wimer**, b. Dec 16 1830 in Randolph Co., WV (son of George Wimer and Christina Rexrode), d. Feb 3 1873. **Emanuel**: Son of George Wimer and Christina Rexroad.

***Children**:*

\+ 209 i. Millie Amelia[4] Wimer b. Feb 2 1855.
210 ii. Margaret Ann Wimer b. Aug 5 1855 in Pendleton Co., WV. Married Dec 30 1880, **William A Rexrode**, b. 1856.
\+ 211 iii. George Wesley Wimer b. 1858.
\+ 212 iv. Jeremiah Emanuel Wimer b. Dec 28 1860.
\+ 213 v. Jennie Wimer b. 1864.
\+ 214 vi. Ephraim A. Wimer b. 1866.
\+ 215 vii. Alexander Wimer b. 1870.

30. **Adam[3] Waybright** (5.Rebecca[2] Arbogast, 1.John C.[1]), b. May 16 1826 in Pendleton Co., WV, d. 1900.
(1) Married Sep 22 1847 in Pendleton Co., WV, **Amilia Wicks**, b. in Shenandoah Co., VA, d. 1880.

***Children** by Alice Colaw:*

216 i. Leslie[4] Waybright.
217 ii. Walter D. Waybright b. May 22 1890, d. Jul 1965.
218 iii. James Adam Waybright b. Dec 2 1891, d. Jan 1968 in Downs, Mclean Co., IL. He Married **Jewel Clark**.

(2) Married Mar 5 1885 in Lincoln Co., MO, **Alice Colaw**, b. 1853 in Lewis Co., WV.

32. **Elijah[3] Waybright** (5.Rebecca[2] Arbogast, 1.John C.[1]), b. 1831, d. Jun 7 1882, buried Jun 10 1882 in Green Bank, Pocahontas Co., WV.
Married Mar 28 1851, **Catherine Helmick**, b. 1836 in Pendleton Co., WV (daughter of Miles Helmick and Elizabeth Vandevender), d. Mar 17 1895, buried in Waybright Cem., Pendleton Co., WV.

***Children**:*

\+ 219 i. Ann Rebecca Elizabeth[4] Waybright b. Jan 2 1853.
220 ii. (unknown) Waybright b. May 1854 in Pendleton Co., WV, d. May 1854 in Pendleton Co., WV, buried in Waybright Cem., Pendleton Co., WV.
\+ 221 iii. Sarah Anne Waybright b. Jul 7 1855.

222	iv.	William C. Waybright b. Jan 1857 in Pendleton Co., WV, d. Jan 4 1874.
+ 223	v.	Margaret Ann Waybright b. Feb 7 1858.
+ 224	vi.	George Washington Waybright b. Nov 1 1859.
+ 225	vii.	Phoebe Jane Waybright b. 1861.
226	viii.	James B. Waybright b. Mar 31 1865 in Pendleton Co., WV.

34. **Catherine Elizabeth[3] Waybright** (5.Rebecca[2] Arbogast, 1.John C.[1]), b. Sep 12 1832 in Pendleton Co., WV, d. Jul 16 1907 in Pendleton Co., WV, buried in Blue Grass Cem., Highland Co., VA.
Married Jan 11 1849 in Pendleton Co., WV, **Miles Harold**, b. Aug 7 1830 (son of Daniel Harold and Elizabeth Holloway), d. Jan 31 1897, buried in Blue Grass Cem., Highland Co., VA.

Children:

+ 227	i.	Martha Ellen[4] Harold b. May 13 1850.
+ 228	ii.	Barbara Elizabeth Harold b. Apr 1 1852.
229	iii.	Alexander P. Harold b. Jan 11 1855 in Pendleton Co., WV.
230	iv.	Florence C. Harold b. Mar 6 1859 in Pendleton Co., WV.
+ 231	v.	Loring Ashby Harold b. Dec 16 1861.
232	vi.	Dora B Harold b. About 1866. She Married **James S Judy**, b. 1864 in Pendleton Co., WV.
233	vii.	Pauline D Harold b. About 1866. She Married **Harrison Teter**, b. 1861 in Pendleton Co., WV (son of Balaam Teter and Mary J Warner).
234	viii.	Jasper Norris Harold b. About 1871.

35. **Morgan[3] Waybright** (5.Rebecca[2] Arbogast, 1.John C.[1]), b. 1835 in Pendleton Co., WV, d. Abt 1878 in Pendleton Co., WV.
Married Oct 1 1857 in Pendleton Co., WV, **Lucinda Arbogast**, b. May 1 1840 in Churchville, Pendleton Co., WV (daughter of Lemuel Arbogast and Susan Bennett), d. Mar 31 1913 in Blue Grass, Highland Co., WV.

Children:

235	i.	Isaac S.[4] Waybright b. in Pendleton Co., WV, d. 1929.
+ 236	ii.	Lemuel Benjamin Waybright b. May 27 1859.
+ 237	iii.	Rebecca Susan Waybright b. 1866.
238	iv.	Catherine Waybright b. 1868 in Highland Co., VA.
+ 239	v.	Miles Adam Waybright b. Oct 22 1869.
+ 240	vi.	Morgan Edward Waybright b. Jan 1875.

36. **Miles[3] Waybright** (5.Rebecca[2] Arbogast, 1.John C.[1]), b. 1835 in Pendleton Co., WV.
Married Oct 18 1852 in Pendleton Co., WV, **Mahala Rexrode**, b. 1832 in Pendleton Co., WV (daughter of Conrad Rexrode and Catharine Harper).

Children:

+ 241	i.	Nicholas[4] Waybright b. 1854.
+ 242	ii.	Ann Elizabeth Waybright b. Sep 11 1855.
+ 243	iii.	George W. Waybright b. Oct 25 1857.
244	iv.	Ephraim Waybright b. Sep 6 1863 in Pendleton Co., WV. He Married **Martha Ellen Moyer**.

39. **Cain[3] Arbogast** (6.Joseph E.[2], 1.John C.[1]), b. October 1819 in Churchville, Pendleton Co., WV, d. October 1900 in Cherry Grove, Pendleton Co., WV.
Married August 9, 1843 in Pendleton Co., WV, **Mary Ann Teter Arbogast**, b. June 1826 in Pendleton Co., WV.

Children:

245	i.	Martha Jane[4] Arbogast b. 1845 in Pendleton Co., WV.
246	ii.	John W Arbogast b. 1846 in Pendleton Co., WV.
+ 247	iii.	Isaac N. Arbogast b. 1849.
248	iv.	Mary Elizabeth Arbogast b. 1851 in Pendleton Co., WV, d. 1877.
249	v.	Catherine Arbogast b. 1853 in Pendleton Co., WV.
250	vi.	Margaret Arbogast b. 1855 in Pendleton Co., WV.
251	vii.	Lucinda Arbogast b. 1 May 1840 in Circleville Pendleton Co., WV, d. 31 Mar 1913 in Highland Co., VA.
+ 252	viii.	Sidney Ellen Arbogast b. Aug 1859.
+ 253	ix.	Hannah Susan Gertrude Arbogast b. Oct 1862.
254	x.	Sarah Dean Arbogast b. 1864 in Pendleton Co., WV.
255	xi.	Jacob Arbogast b. March 18, 1868 in Pendleton Co., WV, d. January 20, 1895.
256	xii.	Esau Arbogast b. March 18, 1868 in Pendleton Co., WV, d. January 3, 1951.

40. **Lemuel[3] Arbogast** (6.Joseph E.[2], 1.John C.[1]), b. 1820 in Pendleton Co., WV, d. 1903 in Pendleton Co., WV.
Married March 2, 1841 in Pendleton Co., WV, **Susan Bennett**, b. 1824 (daughter of Josiah Bennett and Mary Catherine Bennett), d. 1880 in Pendleton Co., WV.

***Children**:*

+ 257 i. Lucinda[4] Arbogast b. May 1 1840.
258 ii. Isaac N. Arbogast b. 1840 or 1842 in Churchville, Pendleton Co., WV, d. 1898. Married May 27 1864 in Alleghany Co., MD, **Rachel Duckworth**, b. in Alleghany Co., MD.
+ 259 iii. Martin Van Buren Arbogast b. July 15, 1844.
260 iv. Agnes T. Arbogast b. October 6, 1846, d. June 20, 1922.
261 v. William J. Arbogast b. April 16, 1849, d. May 24, 1934.
262 vi. Lemuel Jefferson Arbogast b. July 1850 or 1851 in Pendleton Co., WV, d. November 26, 1935. Died of Influenza.
263 vii. George Wesley Arbogast b. January 2, 1854, d. October 16, 1929.
264 viii. Adam L. Arbogast b. December 10, 1855, d. December 19, 1860.
265 ix. James C. Arbogast b. October 1856, d. 1932.
266 x. Mary S. Arbogast b. May 16, 1859, d. 1932.
+ 267 xi. Jacob A. Arbogast b. May 4, 1864.
268 xii. Rachel Ellen Arbogast b. 1867, d. 1898.
+ 269 xiii. Alfred T. Arbogast b. April 30, 1869.

42. **Joseph Elili[3] Arbogast Jr.** (6.Joseph E.[2], 1.John C.[1]), b. 1826.
Married Oct 21 1847 in Pendleton Co., WV, **Prudence Nelson**, b. 1826 in Pendleton Co., WV (daughter of Isaac Nelson, Sr. and Catherine Pennington), d. c 1910 in Pendleton Co., WV.

***Children**:*

+ 270 i. Hannah Elizabeth[4] Arbogast b. Dec 30 1856.
271 ii. Amanda C. Arbogast b. 1856 in Pendleton Co., WV, d. May 18 1933 in Pendleton Co., WV.
+ 272 iii. Mary Jane Arbogast b. April 1856.
+ 273 iv. Ruth Ellen Arbogast b. Apr 1 1862.
+ 274 v. Elijah J. Arbogast b. Feb 14 1865.

43. **Sidney Dean[3] Arbogast** (6.Joseph E.[2], 1.John C.[1]), b. 1830 in Cherry Grove, Pendleton Co., WV, d. AFT 1900.
Notes for Sidney Dean Arbogast:
Source is research of Glenn Huffman. In 1900 widow, living in separated welling on same farm as son, minor and family. Born 1830, 9 chil, 7living.
Married Nov 20 1846 in Pendleton Co., WV, **Martin T. Bennett**, b. 1824 in Cherry Grove, Pendleton Co., WV, (son of Joseph Bennett and Phoebe Cunningham), d. WFT Est. 1868-1916. [cal5.FTW]
Notes for Martin T. Bennett: son of Joseph and Phoebe (Cunningham) Bennett per Glenn Huffman research.

. ***Children**:*

+ 275 i. Hannah Catharine[4] Bennett b. Feb 1 1852.

45. **Sylvenus[3] Arbogast** (6.Joseph E.[2], 1.John C.[1]).
(1) He Married **Susan S Murphy** (daughter of John Murphy and Elizabeth Jordan).

***Children** by Jemima S Bennett:*

276 i. Henry Lee[4] Arbogast b. About 1864.
277 ii. Susan Arbogast.
278 iii. Abbie Arbogast b. About 1868 in Pendleton Co., WV.
+ 279 iv. Christina Arbogast b. About 1870.
280 v. Naomi Arbogast.
281 vi. James Howard Arbogast b. About 1871, d. 1901.
282 vii. Sarah Ida Arbogast b. About 1875.
283 viii. Phoebe Arbogast b. About 1877.
284 ix. Emma Arbogast b. About 1879.
+ 285 x. Nettie Arbogast b. Nov 30 1880.
286 xi. Paul Arbogast b. About 1885.

(2) He Married **Jemima S Bennett**, b. About 1845 (daughter of Henry Bennett and Naomi Williams Helmick). **Jemima**: Daughter of Henry Bennett.

51. **Hannah V.[3] Arbogast** (7.Moses[2], 1.John C.[1]), b. ABT 1823 in Pendleton Co., WV, d. Sep 18 1854 in Barbour Co., WV.
Died in childbed. Married by D. Thompson, J.P., Barbour County.
She Married **Adam Kerr**, b. May 22 1820 in Pocahontas Co., WV (son of Robert Dunlap Kerr and Elizabeth Ann Arbogast), d. May 2 1901 in Barbour Co., WV. **Adam**:

Children:

287 i. Ezra[4] Kerr b. 1847 in Barbour Co., WV.
See Amanda Arbogast record 388. A twin
\+ 288 ii. William Bailey Kerr b. 1847.
289 iii. Isabela E. Kerr b. 1851 in Barbour Co., WV.
See Amanda Arbogast record 388.
290 iv. Enoch Kerr b. Sep 18 1854 in Barbour Co., WV.
See Amanda Arbogast record 388. Twin to fifth child. A twin
291 v. (infant) Kerr b. Sep 18 1854 in Barbour Co., WV, d. Sep 18 1854 in Barbour Co., WV. See AAF record 388

52. **Allen[3] Arbogast** (7.Moses[2], 1.John C.[1]), b. ABT 1824 in Pendleton Co., WV, d. AFT 1880 in Randolph Co., WV,
Married Mar 6 1854 in Randolph Co., WV, **Frances Fannie Riffle**, b . in Randolph Co., WV, d. AFT 1880,

Children:

292 i. Susan[4] Arbogast b. JUL 1854 in Randolph Co., WV, b. JUL 1854 in Randolph Co., WV,
293 ii. Priscilla Arbogast b. ABT 1856 in Randolph Co., WV,
294 iii. Charlotte Adinah Arbogast b. ABT 1859 in Randolph Co., WV,
295 iv. Adena Arbogast b. Jan 17 1859 in Randolph Co., WV, d. Feb 27 1943,
296 v. David H. Arbogast b. ABT 1861 in Randolph Co., WV, d. AFT 1900 in Randolph Co., WV,
297 vi. Tabitha Arbogast b. Nov 27 1866 in Randolph Co., WV, b. Nov 27 1866 in Randolph Co., WV, d. BEF 1901,
298 vii. Elias E. Arbogast b. ABT 1872 in Randolph Co., WV,
299 viii. Mary Arbogast b. Jun 30 1873 in Randolph Co., WV,
300 ix. William Arbogast b. ABT 1878 in Randolph Co., WV,

54. **Ailcey (Elsey)[3] Arbogast** (7.Moses[2], 1.John C.[1]), b. ABT 1828 in Randolph Co., WV, d. in Randolph Co., WV, Married Jan 15 1847 in Randolph Co., WV, **Peter Conrad**, b. ABT 1826 in Randolph Co., WV.

Children:

301 i. Justus Milton[4] Conrad b. ABT 1847 in Randolph Co., WV.
302 ii. Lloyd Conrad b. 1848 in Randolph Co., WV.
303 iii. Serena Conrad b. Sep 23 1850 in Randolph Co., WV, d. ABT 1940, buried in Cowger Cem., Monterville, Randolph Co., WV.
304 iv. Jeremiah C. Conrad b. 1852 in Randolph Co., WV.
305 v. John Conrad b. ABT 1854 in Randolph Co., WV.
306 vi. Mary Conrad b. Oct 2 1854 in Randolph Co., WV, buried in Stalnaker Cem., Monterville, Randolph Co., WV.
307 vii. Ann Conrad b. Aug 2 1856 in Randolph Co., WV.
308 viii. Jenny Conrad b. ABT 1858 in Randolph Co., WV.
309 ix. Priscilla Conrad b. ABT 1860 in Randolph Co., WV.
310 x. Mariah Conrad b. Jan 15 1860 in Randolph Co., WV, d. Mar 6 1925, buried in Cowger Cem., Monterville, Randolph Co., WV.
311 xi. Eda Conrad b. Aug 4 1862 in Randolph Co., WV, d. Jul 2 1930 in Valley Head, Randolph Co., WV, buried in Maple Cem., Conley Run, Randolph Co., WV.

57. **Rachel E.[3] Arbogast** (7.Moses[2], 1.John C.[1]), b. 1840, b. ABT 1839 in Randolph Co., WV, d. 1913, She Married **John Richard Ware**, b. 1839, d. 1907.

Children:

312 i. Richard Lee[4] Ware b. MAR 1863.
313 ii. Stuart Ware b. Oct 8 1865, d. Sep 28 1883.
314 iii. Caroline Ware b. 1867.
\+ 315 iv. Jacob G. Ware b. Oct 5 1869.
316 v. Wade Howard Ware b. OCT 1872.

59. **Sarah Elizabeth[3] Arbogast** (7.Moses[2], 1.John C.[1]), b. Aug 16 1844 in Randolph Co., WV, b. Aug 16 1844, d. Jul 2 1906 in Randolph Co., WV, d. Jul 2 1906, buried in Simmons Family Cem., Valley Head, Randolph Co., WV,
Married Feb 22 1865 in Pocahontas Co., WV, **Chesley Simmons**, b. Jul 18 1840 in Pendleton Co., WV, b. Jul 18 1840, d. Feb 18 1925 in Randolph Co., WV, d. 1925, buried in Simmons Family Cem., Valley Head, Randolph Co., WV.

Children:

317 i. Valentine[4] Simmons b. Nov 24 1865 in Randolph Co., WV, d. Dec 31 1924 in Randolph Co., WV, buried in Simmons Family Cem., Valley Head, Randolph Co., WV. Married Jul 18 1888, **Elverda B. Ware**.
318 ii. Samuel G. Simmons b. JAN 1868 in Randolph Co., WV.
319 iii. Lethia Belle Simmons b. Mar 18 1871 in Randolph Co., WV, d. Apr 29 1948.
320 iv. Alexander Simmons b. Aug 9 1873 in Randolph Co., WV, d. Feb 3 1957.
321 v. Jacob G. Simmons b. MAY 1880 in Randolph Co., WV, d. Feb 15 1934.
+ 322 vi. Thomas J. Simmons b. 1881.
323 vii. Lilly M. Simmons b. MAY 1882 in Randolph Co., WV.
324 viii. Althea I. Simmons.

60. **Moses Wamsley[3] Arbogast** (7.Moses[2], 1.John C.[1]), b. 1847 in Randolph Co., WV, d. Feb 2 1902 in Valley Head, Randolph Co., WV.
Married Apr 27 1874 in Beverly, Randolph Co., WV, **Margaret Eleanor Channell**, b. 1857 in Randolph Co., WV, (daughter of Eleanor Elizabeth Ware), b. 1857, d. Apr 23 1882 in Valley Head, Randolph Co., WV.

Children:

325 i. Ida Mae[4] Arbogast b. Sep 8 1873 in Randolph Co., WV, d. in Washington State.
+ 326 ii. Eva Jane Arbogast b. Apr 3 1875.
327 iii. Arvis N. Arbogast b. MAR 1877 in Randolph Co., WV.
328 iv. Rachel Ann Arbogast b. 1879 in Randolph Co., WV.
329 v. Margaret Alice Arbogast b. Apr 23 1882 in Randolph Co., WV.

61. **John B. (Jack)[3] Arbogast** (7.Moses[2], 1.John C.[1]), b. 1849 in Mingo Area, Randolph Co., WV, d. 1933 in Randolph Co., WV, buried in Old Brick Church, Cem., Huttonsville, Randolph Co., WV.
Married ABT 1885, **Othelia Ann Ramsey**, b. JUN 1850 in Randolph Co., WV, d. AFT 1900 in Randolph Co., WV.

Children:

+ 330 i. Samuel Henry[4] Arbogast b. Aug 2 1881.
331 ii. Elisha W. Arbogast b. APR 1889 in Randolph Co., WV.
332 iii. Charles W. Arbogast b. NOV 1890 in Randolph Co., WV.

63. **Adam Jr.[3] Arbogast** (8.Adam Sr.[2], 1.John C.[1]), b. 1825 in Straight Creek, Pendleton/Highland Co., VA, d. After 1900 in Weston, Lewis Co., WV.
Their children per 1880 Lewis Co. census (13 children, 4 girls, 9 boys) The children's marriages confirmed by Lewis Co. marriage records 1881-1937.
Married Mar 8 1853 in Highland Co., VA, **Elizabeth Peck**, b. Mar 1836 in Virginia, d. Aft 1900.

Children:

+ 333 i. Francis M[4] Arbogast b. May 26 1854.
334 ii. Andrew Jackson Arbogast b. Abt 1856. Married Jun 8 1882 in Lewis Co., WV, **Dora Alice Bond**, b. Aug 1865. Dora: See Arbogast genealogy for children.
335 iii. William Morgan Arbogast b. Abt 1858. Married Oct 2 1888 in Lewis Co., WV, **Anna Hoar**, b. Abt 1858.
+ 336 iv. Mary Susan Arbogast b. 1859-1860.
337 v. John Letcher Arbogast b. Abt 1862.
338 vi. Jeremiah W. Arbogast b. Abt 1865.
339 vii. Jacob M. Arbogast b. Abt 1866.
340 viii. Peter A. Arbogast b. Abt 1868.
341 ix. Amanda Ellen Arbogast b. 1872 in Lewis Co., WV. Married Apr 18 1892 in Lewis Co., WV, **James William Halterman**, b. Abt 1868, d. Jun 20 1921 in Camden, Lewis Co., WV, buried in Family Cem. near home, Lewis Co., WV. James: Per his obit in (Ind. Wed. 06 Jul 1921) he was survived by his widow, 2 sons, and 4 daughters. Death record found in Lewis Co. Obits, Vol 4.
342 x. Henry Arbogast b. Jun 29 1873 in Lewis Co., WV.
343 xi. Martha M. Arbogast b. Abt 1875. Married Jan 3 1896 in Lewis Co., WV, **William Sprouse**, b. Abt 1875.
344 xii. Josephine Arbogast b. Abt 1877.
345 xiii. Thomas D. Arbogast b. Abt 1879. Married Dec 24 1912 in Lewis Co., WV, **Anna Ervine**, b. Abt 1879.

66. **Peter William[3] Arbogast** (8.Adam Sr.[2], 1.John C.[1]), b. June 2, 1836, d. after 1900 in Grant County, WV. MARRIAGE: Filed in Pendleton Co., WV.
PARENTS: From marriage record and census reports. Marriage records lists Almira's parents as S. & P. Pennington but on 1850 census she is listed as age

13 and under family of Sampson and Mary Pennington.
DEATH: Not followed after 1900 census. No Cemetery records found in Highland Co., VA or Pendleton Co., WV.
A Peter Arbogast listed as a Confederate soldier, C. Co., 62nd VA, living in Grant Co. March 1, 1900 per Morton's History of Pendleton (Highland Co., VA) County, WV, p.402.
Married February 08, 1820 to Grant Co., WV, **Almira Pennington**, b. January 1834 (daughter of Sampson Pennington, Sr. and Mary Montanye).

***Children*:**

346 i. Mary E.[4] Arbogast b. About 1861, d. After 1880.
+ 347 ii. Saulsbury Arbogast b. Mar 1865.
+ 348 iii. Kenton Arbogast b. December 21, 1867.
349 iv. Willie F. Arbogast b. About 1877 in West Virginia.
350 v. Harman Arbogast b. Jan 1880.
351 vi. unknown Arbogast b. October 16, 1873, d. October 17, 1873.

72. **Esau Lacey[3] Ketterman** (9.Mary Ann[2] Arbogast, 1.John C.[1]) (See marriage to number 28.)

76. **Leah[3] Ketterman** (9.Mary Ann[2] Arbogast, 1.John C.[1]), b. Dec 8 1834 in Seneca Creek, Pendleton Co., VA/WV, d. Aft 10 Jun 1885.
(1) Married 1884, **John Harter**.

(2) She Married **Nathan Waybright** (See marriage to number 22).

Children *by Nathan Waybright:*
(See marriage to number 22)

78. **Nicholas Harper[3] Ketterman** (9.Mary Ann[2] Arbogast, 1.John C.[1]), b. Jul 12 1839 in Seneca Creek, Pendleton Co., VA/WV, d. Mar 14 1904, buried in Hopewell Cem., Downs Co., IL.
War of 1861, Union Army, Company D., 6th Civil War Veteran, Regiment of the Iowa Volunteer Infantry. Also, with Company K., 26th Infantry, Illinois Volunteer Infantry.
Married Feb 4 1864 in McLean Co., IL, **Elizabeth Teter**, b. Oct 1 1844 in Pendleton Co., WV (daughter of Benjamin Teter and Mary Hartman), d. Jan 4 1878 in Illinois.

***Children*:**

+ 352 i. Tecumseh Sherman[4] Ketterman b. Apr 17 1866.
+ 353 ii. Lena Leona Ketterman b. Dec 13 1868.
354 iii. Lilly Ketterman b. March 1870 in Illinois, d. 4 Apr 1942. She Married **Clark Johnson.**
+ 355 iv. Bertha Viola Ketterman b. Dec 30 1874.
+ 356 v. Paul Ketterman b. Dec 26 1876.

79. **John George[3] Ketterman** (9.Mary Ann[2] Arbogast, 1.John C.[1]), d. 1884.
Married Aug 18 1845, **Malinda Full** (daughter of George Full and Margaret Judy).

***Children*:**

+ 357 i. Hannah J.[4] Ketterman.

81. **Sarah[3] Ketterman** (9.Mary Ann[2] Arbogast, 1.John C.[1]), b. Apr 1843 in Pendleton Co., WV, d. in Churchville, Pendleton Co., WV.
Tis couple may have been divorced by 1900.
Married Jan 14 1889, **Marcellus Bennett**, d. Oct 20 1930.

***Children*:**

+ 358 i. Ida V.[4] Ketterman b. Oct 1864.

82. **Solomon[3] Arbogast** (10.John C.[2], 1.John C.[1]), b. Dec 07 1820 in Pendleton Co., WV. He Married **Emily M. Anderson** (daughter of William Anderson and Mary Madeline Rhodes).

***Children*:**

359 i. William H[4] Arbogast b. Aug 3- 1854.
360 ii. Rebecca Jane Arbogast.
361 iii. Charles Arbogast.

362 iv. Drucilla Arbogast b. born 11-29-1855.
363 v. Jefferson Davis Arbogast b. 11-21-1869 in Webster Co., WV, d. 10-4-1944 in Valley Head, Randolph Co., WV.
364 vi. George Washington Arbogast.
365 vii. Emelee Arbogast.
366 viii. Albert J Arbogast.
367 ix. Jasper Arbogast.
368 x. Melvina E Arbogast.
369 xi. William W Arbogast b. 7-17-1877.
370 xii. Randolph Cleaterson Arbogast.

84. **George Washington[3] Arbogast** (10.John C.[2], 1.John C.[1]), b. 1825 in Randolph Co., WV, d. May 18 1864 in Meadows Bluff, Greenbrier Co., WV.
He died while serving in the Union Army Military Service.
Married Jun 07 1855 in Barbour Co., WV, **Margaret Mace**, b. 1835 in Barbour Co., WV.

Children:

371 i. Melvina J.[4] Arbogast b. Jun 03 1856, d. Dec 06 1865.
+ 372 ii. Washington Sherman Arbogast.
373 iii. Caroline Arbogast b. Mar 16 1858, d. Dec 15 1865.
374 iv. Allena Arbogast b. Jun 06 1860, d. Dec 23 1865.
+ 375 v. George McClelland Arbogast b. Oct 1861.

Generation Four

88. **Christina[4] Waybright** (11.Emily[3] Arbogast, 3.Michael[2], 1.John C.[1]), b. 1842 in Pendleton Co., WV, d. Bef 1900.
Married 1860, **Mayberry Christopher C. Hedrick**, b. Aug 1839.

Children:

+ 376 i. Amos C.[5] Hedrick b. 1862.
377 ii. Adam Hedrick b. 1866.
+ 378 iii. George Washington Hedrick b. 1868.
379 iv. James P. Hedrick.
380 v. Amby Hedrick b. 1870, d. 1958.
381 vi. Lettie T. Hedrick b. 1872.
382 vii. Henry J. Hedrick b. 1876.
383 viii. William Hedrick b. 1879.
384 ix. Sarah F. Hedrick b. 1886.

92. **Francis M.[4] Arbogast** (12.George Washington[3], 3.Michael[2], 1.John C.[1]), b. 1847, d. May 16 1868. MILITARY: Enlistment record at 1 Dec., 1862, Coolsniouth, indicates age 18, K
Co., 7th UV Cavalry. Also saw service as Sgt., 8th UV In-f. May, 1864, sick at Government Hospital, Grafton. 1 Aug., 1865, muster out, Charleston, UV. Premium and bounty paid.
Pension record, widow, Elvira J. Shaw and minor, Elvira J. Williams, 19 Apr.,1879-
DEATH: Certificate by father indicates he was born in 1847, not 1844 as indicated to Army at enlistment. Died of tuberculosis at 20 yrs., 11 mos.
Wife, Elvira Schoonover remarried after his death. Marriage record, 6 Oct.,
1869 to Wm. Williams. On 1870 census, Wm. Williams lists Francis E. Arbogast, age 3 yrs.
He Married **Elvira J. Scoonover**.

Children:

385 i. Francis[5] E. Arbogast b. May 14 1867 in Clay Co., WV.

93. **George Washington[4] Arbogast, Jr.** (12.George Washington[3], 3.Michael[2], 1.John C.[1]), b. Jan 29 1849 in Sycamore, Calhoun Co., WV, d. 1925. MILITARY: Enlistment record at 1 Dec., 1862, Coolsniouth, indicates age 18, K Co., 7th UV Cavalry. Also saw service as Sgt., 8th UV In-f.
May, 1864, sick at Government Hospital, Grafton. 1 Aug., 1865, muster out, Charleston, UV. Premium and bounty paid. Pension record, widow, Elvira J. Shaw and minor, Elvira J. Williams, 19 April 1879- DEATH: Certificate by father indicates he was born in 1847, not 1844 as indicated to Army at enlistment. Died of tuberculosis at 20 yrs., 11 mos.

Wife, Elvira Schoonover remarried after his death. Marriage record, 6 Oct.1869 to Wm. Williams. On 1870 census, Wm. Williams lists Francis E. Arbogast,

(1) Married Sep 11 1873 in Clay Co., VA, **Martha Scoonover**, b. 1857 in Clay Co., VA, d. Sep 11 1873 in Clay Co., WV. (., b. 1866 in Clay Co., VA. .

Children *by Sarah Ellen Scoonover:*

386 i. Calvin P[5] Arbogast b. Sep 1876. Married Sep 20 1900, Ocie Danials.
387 ii. Daniel Arbogast b. Apr 1884.
388 iii. James Austin Arbogast.
389 iv. William Everett Arbogast.
390 v. Glenna May Arbogast.
391 vi. George Arbogast b. Sep 19 1890.
392 vii. (infant) Arbogast d. Oct 1892.

2) He Married **Sarah Ellen Scoonover**

(3) He Married **Mary Riffle**

Children *by Mary Riffle:*

393 viii. Sarah Arbogast b. 1905. She Married Curt May.

(4) He Married **Rose Ann Holcomb**

Children *by Rose Ann Holcomb:*

\+ 394 ix. Floyd Holcomb.

97. **Nichodemus[4] Arbogast** (12.George Washington[3], 3.Michael[2], 1.John C.[1]), b. About 1857, d. About 1915.

(1) He Married **Caroline Simmons**, b. 1863.

Children *by Caroline Simmons:*

395 i. George F[5] Arbogast b. Feb 23 1884, d. Jun 28 1896.
396 ii. Robert C. Arbogast b. Sep 15 1892.
397 iii. America Arbogast b. Nov 05 1892.
398 iv. Ford Arbogast.
399 v. Mary C Arbogast.
\+ 400 vi. Americas Deborah Arbogast b. Nov 25 1892.

. (2) He Married **Sarah Igo**, b. 1887 in Clay Co., WV.

98. **Amos Cyrus[4] Arbogast** (12.George Washington[3], 3.Michael[2], 1.John C.[1]), b. Jan 27 1862, d. May 10 1950.

Family homestead and cemetery is on Big Sycamore Creek about 5 miles from its confluence with the Elk River, near Indore, Pleasant Twp., Clay Co., WV. County road # 12 traverses Big Sycamore Creek many times from Indore down to the Elk River, then down the Elk along the old B&O railroad track, past the old train station to Little Sycamore Creek, then up Little Sycamore Creek past war-field to County Road # 1 near Indore. Eldorado is at the mouth of Big Sycamore Creek. County Road # 12-1 runs from Uarfield to near the Homestead on County Road # 12, completing the circle of roads # 12 and # 12-1. Supplies were shipped from Charleston up the Elk River on the B&O railroad to the train station and then by wagon up road # 12 to the homestead. Some supplies were purchased at war-field, the nearest settlement, and at Indore, a larger settlement but somewhat further away. The road to Indore was better than the road to War-field. Information from uncle Joseph Monroe Arbogast by conversation and Letters. The roads through this area are not improved. Many are now only logging, gas pipeline and other utility maintenance roads.

Deputy Sheriff of Clay Co. for brother, George Washington Arbogast, Jr., "Wash", Sheriff. Farming was primary occupation. As Deputy, a member of posse to arrest Jesse James type gang. Shoot-out resulted in arrests, several wounded, one member of gang killed.

Substantial research and records on the Amos Cyrus Arbogast and other Arbogast families in West Virginia, Virginia and other states has been done by Amanda Crawford Arbogast Forbes of Silver Spring, MD. Amanda is descended from George Arbogast, son of Michael Arbogast, the pioneer.

Raised a foster child as one of their own, Walter Stewart. Photo in file of Walter with Naomi holding granddaughter, Joyce Cant ley, daughter of Lucy Esta (Arbogast) and Dewey Cantley. Photo taken about 1928. Walter was only 3 mos. of age when they took him to raise.

Headstone indicates date of birth as 10 Dec 1867, date of death as 17 Jan 1937.

Married in Lizemores, Clay Co., WV, **Naomi Neal**, b. Dec 10 1868 in Indora, Kanawha Co., WV, d. Jan 15 1935 in Indora, Kanawha Co., WV. **Naomi**: Daughter of Alex Neal and Sarah Rogers.

Children:

401 i. Grace[5] Arbogast b. 1882 in Indora, Kanawha Co., WV, d. Feb 01 1894.
402 ii. James Preston Arbogast b. May 11 1888 in Indora, Kanawha Co., WV, d. May 02 1958 in Family Cem., Indore, Clay Co., WV.
403 iii. Francis M. Arbogast b. Dec 16 1889, d. 1918 in World War II.
404 iv. Emmeretta Arbogast b. May 29 1891 in Indora, Kanawha Co., WV, d. 1924 in Family Cem., Indore, Clay Co., WV.
\+ 405 v. Minnie May Arbogast b. Jan 20 1894.
406 vi. George Alexander Arbogast b. Nov 2 1896, d. Dec 10 1917.
Sgt. Machine gun Co., 7th Inf.
\+ 407 vii. Mary Arbogast b. Jun 7 1898.
\+ 408 viii. Glendora Arbogast b. Mar 23 1899.
\+ 409 ix. Faye Elvira Arbogast b. Apr 3 1901.
\+ 410 x. Jessie Sarah Arbogast b. Mar 03 1903.
\+ 411 xi. Joseph Monroe Arbogast b. Jul 8 1906.
\+ 412 xii. Lucy Esta Arbogast b. Apr 06 1911.

101. **Nicodemus[4] Shreve** (13.Mary Magdalene.[3] Arbogast, 3.Michael[2], 1.John C.[1]), b. 1843.
Married Apr 07 1864, **Sarah Catherine Huffman**.

Children:

413 i. Julie[5] Shreve.
414 ii. Phebe Shreve.
415 iii. Ida Shreve.
416 iv. Etta Shreve.
417 v. Magdalena Shreve.
418 vi. Asberry Shreve.
419 vii. John Newton Shreve.
420 viii. George Shreve.

102. **Benjamin "Little Ben"[4] Shreve** (13.Mary Magdalene.[3] Arbogast, 3.Michael[2], 1.John C.[1]), b. 1845 in Smoke Holes, Grant Co., WV.
Married Aug 14 1864, **Hannah J. Ketterman** (daughter of John George Ketterman and Malinda Full).

Children:

\+ 421 i. Joanna[5] Shreve b. 1874.
422 ii. Branson Shreve.
423 iii. Solomon Shreve.
424 iv. Gibe Shreve.
425 v. Walter Shreve.
426 vi. Linda Shreve.
427 vii. Hulda Shreve.
428 viii. Roxy Shreve.

103. **Edith Jane[4] Shreve** (13.Mary Magdalene.[3] Arbogast, 3.Michael[2], 1.John C.[1]), b. 1849. She Married **Adam Fisher Helmick**.

Children:

429 i. Amby[5] Helmick.
430 ii. Lavene Helmick.
431 iii. Ecky Helmick.
432 iv. Mary Magdalene Helmick.
433 v. George Helmick.
434 vi. Alice Helmick.
\+ 435 vii. Anna Helmick.

107. **Jethro[4] Davis** (14.Christina[3] Arbogast, 3.Michael[2], 1.John C.[1]), b. 1842.
He Married **Phoebe J (Unknown)**.

Children:

436 i. Elizabeth[5] Davis b. 1866.
437 ii. John A Davis b. 1868.
438 iii. Effa A Davis b. 1870.

439 iv. Nenevah Davis b. About 1873.
440 v. James P Davis b. 1877.
\+ 441 vi. Rumsey Smithson Davis b. Apr 1880.

109. **Miles[4] Davis** (14.Christina[3] Arbogast, 3.Michael[2], 1.John C.[1]), b. About 1846.
He Married **Martha Susan Lambert**, b. 1854.

Children:

442 i. George Amos[5] Davis b. 1870.
443 ii. Kenny E Davis b. 1877.
444 iii. (infant) Davis b. Mar 1880.

110. **Michael[4] Davis** (14.Christina[3] Arbogast, 3.Michael[2], 1.John C.[1]), b. About 1847.
He Married **Jane Thompson**.

Children:

445 i. Edward[5] Davis b. 1875.
446 ii. Lottie Davis b. 1878. She Married Amos Davis.

114. **Edith[4] Arbogast** (15.Nichodemus[3], 3.Michael[2], 1.John C.[1]), b. About 1849 in Nicholas County VA, d. 1925 in Oklahoma.
She Married **Lester Pease**.

Children:

447 i. Nick[5] Arbogast.
448 ii. Lewis Arbogast.

117. **Sarah D.[4] Arbogast** (15.Nichodemus[3], 3.Michael[2], 1.John C.[1]), b. 1855, d. 1889. She Married **Samuel Wetzel Markle**, b. in Pennsylvania, d. Sep 01 1930 in Elkhurst, Clay Co., WV.

Children:

449 i. Jacob Albert[5] Markle b. Aug 30 1881 in Elkhurst, Clay Co., WV, d. Feb 25 1969.
\+ 450 ii. Acinith Lieuticia Markle b. Sep 08 1883.
451 iii. Elvira May Markle b. Nov 25 1885, d. Feb 04 1973. She Married **Windfield Pierson.**
452 iv. Lon Jimerson Markle b. Mar 11 1888 in Elkhurst, Clay Co., WV, d. Mar 18 1973.

118. **Rocksena[4] Arbogast** (15.Nichodemus[3], 3.Michael[2], 1.John C.[1]), b. About 1856.
She Married **Albert L Jefferies**, b. c 1855.

Children:

453 i. Lyda[5] Jefferies.
454 ii. Vick Jefferies.
455 iii. Olah Jefferies.
456 iv. Sarah Jefferies.

119. **George Franklin[4] Arbogast** (15.Nichodemus[3], 3.Michael[2], 1.John C.[1]), b. Feb 28 1857 in Nicholas Co., WV, d. Mar 08 1912.
Married Mar 22 1878, **Lucy Estella Morton**, b. Feb 13 1866, d. Dec 01 1953 in Clay Co., WV.

Children:

\+ 457 i. Watson A[5] Arbogast b. Sep 17 1884.
458 ii. David L Arbogast b. c 1888. He Married **Nora Marks**.
\+ 459 iii. Albert Lee Arbogast b. Mar 27 1889.
\+ 460 iv. Joseph Martin Arbogast b. Jun 27 1890.
461 v. Howard Arbogast b. Apr 02 1893, d. Apr 28 1988.
\+ 462 vi. Sarah Alice Arbogast b. May 22 1896.
463 vii. Rossel Arbogast b. c 1898.
464 viii. Minnie Arbogast b. May 16 1901, d. Aug 17 1921. She Married **Austin Jones**.
465 ix. Richard Arbogast b. Oct 07 1903, d. Aug 28 1919.
466 x. John Lloyd Arbogast b. c 1905, d. Nov 25 1969 in Charleston, Kanawha Co., WV.
\+ 467 xi. Leona Estelle Arbogast b. 1910.

121. **Thomas[4] Arbogast** (15.Nichodemus[3], 3.Michael[2], 1.John C.[1]), b. 1862 in Nicholas Co., WV, d. Mar 16 1937 in Blue Creek, Kanawha Co., WV.
(1) He Married **Linda V. Jeffers**, b. 1868, d. 1892..

Children *by Linda V. Jeffers:*

+ 468 i. Fred Lee[5] Arbogast b. May 25 1890.
+ 469 ii. Robert L. Arbogast b. Feb 16, 1916.

(2) Married c 1892, **Hallie Jane Young**, b. 1877 in Kanawha Co., WV, d. Mar 10 1943

Children *by Hallie Jane Young:*

470 iii. Bessie Edna Arbogast b. Dec 06 1894, d. Dec 10 1979.
471 iv. Maggie Gertrude Arbogast b. Mar 18 1897, d. Oct 11 1981.
472 v. Nannie Myrtle Arbogast b. May 23 1899, d. Jan 19 1970.
473 vi. Elsie Mae Arbogast b. Oct 20 1902, d. Mar 20 1979.
474 vii. Thurman Arbogast b. About 1902, d. May 28 1977.
475 viii. Estol Harry Arbogast b. Nov 28 1913, d. Aug 17 1987.
476 ix. Robert L Arbogast b. Jan 16 1916, d. Feb 25 1979.

128. **Emily Catharine[4] Arbogast** (16.Michael[3], 3.Michael[2], 1.John C.[1]), b. Oct 29 1849, d. Jul 7 1902.
Married Apr 10 1887 in Appanoose Co., IA, **Philip Keller**, b. About 1843 in Pendleton Co., WV (son of Adam H. Keller and Sarah Catharine Harper).

Children:

+ 477 i. Harvey[5] Keller b. Jan 27 1868.
478 ii. George Keller b. Feb 14 1870 in Iowa, d. Oct 26 1895 in Waldo, Russell Co., KS.
+ 479 iii. William Thomas Keller b. Aug 2 1874.
480 iv. Mary E. Keller b. Sep 9 1876 in Iowa, d. Nov 7 1895 in Waldo, Russell Co., KS.
481 v. Joseph Keller b. About 1880.
+ 482 vi. Leander Frank Keller.
483 vii. Pearl Keller b. About 1880 in Kansas.
484 viii. Nettie Mae Keller b. May 28 1880, d. Nov -1 1895 in Waldo, Russell Co., KS.
485 ix. Adam H. Keller b. Apr 17 1882 in Iowa, d. Nov 2 1895.
486 x. Sadie B. Keller b. Aug 11 1883, d. Sep 25 1895.
+ 487 xi. Glen Elmer Keller b. Aug 19 1888.

131. **Stephen Douglas[4] Arbogast** (16.Michael[3], 3.Michael[2], 1.John C.[1]), b. Aug 13 1860 in Leon, Decatur Co., IA, d. Nov 20 1897 in Leon, Decatur Co., IA.
Married Oct 25 1883 in Leon, Decatur Co., IA, **Catherine Melvina Gammon**, b. Mar 28 1863 in Leon, Decatur Co., IA (daughter of James Wilkenson Gammon and Armilda Eliza Myers), d. May 21 1916 in Los Angeles, Los Angeles Co., CA.

Children:

+ 488 i. Glen Elvin[5] Arbogast b. Aug 31 1884.
489 ii. Ona Leonard Arbogast b. Jul 5 1886 in Leon, Decatur Co., IA, d. Jan 5 1967 in Los Angeles, Los Angeles Co., CA. He Married **Angela McLaughlin**.
+ 490 iii. Daisy Arbogast b. Apr 25 1889.
+ 491 iv. Armilda D. "Fairy" Arbogast b. 1896.

145. **Daniel[4] Sponaugle** (18.Jemima Maria[3] Waybright, 4.Rachel[2] Arbogast, 1.John C.[1]), b. Apr 10 1844 in Lewis Co., WV, d. Feb 23 1932.
(1) Married Feb 13 1866 in Monmouth, McDonough Co., IL, **Lucinda Mead**, b. 1849.

Children *by Ursula Belle Boyle:*

492 i. Ida Mable[5] Sponaugle b. Nov 3 1892, d. May 9 1965.
493 ii. Dorothea Emeline Sponaugle b. Dec 25 1895, d. Jul 21 1896.
+ 494 iii. Bertha Jane Sponaugle b. Mar 28 1899.
495 iv. Charles Ralph Sponaugle b. Feb 17 1904.
496 v. Mattie Ann Sponaugle b. Jan 26 1909, d. Sep 25 1909.

(2) Married Apr 6 1892, **Ursula Belle Boyle**, b. Mar 10 1864, d. Feb 18 1943.

150. **Isaac P[4] Waybright** (19.Jesse[3], 4.Rachel[2] Arbogast, 1.John C.[1]), b. Sep 1851 in Pendleton Co., WV.
(1) Married Nov 28 1877, **Mary Elizabeth Mullenax**, b. 1855..

(2) He Married **Sidney Ellen Arbogast**, b. Aug 1859 in Pendleton Co., WV (daughter of Cain Arbogast and Mary Ann Teter Arbogast)

***Children** by Sidney Ellen Arbogast:*

497 i. Faith Anna[5] Waybright b. Mar 1882 in Tucker Co., WV. She Married **Charles Judy**.
498 ii. Barbara Waybright b. Oct 1883 in Tucker Co., WV.
499 iii. Lena Waybright b. Apr 23 1885 in Tucker Co., WV. She Married **Oley Rhodes**.
500 iv. Hiner Waybright b. May 7 1887 in Tucker Co., WV, d. Jun 1963. He Married **Anna (Unknown)**.
\+ 501 v. Don Waybright b. Oct 2 1888.
502 vi. Catherine Waybright b. May 1892 in Tucker Co., WV.
503 vii. Luther Waybright b. Oct 1893 in Tucker Co., WV.
\+ 504 viii. Zula Waybright.
\+ 505 ix. Moses Randolph Waybright b. Mar 8 1897.

151. **James Bud[4] Waybright** (19.Jesse[3], 4.Rachel[2] Arbogast, 1.John C.[1]), b. Jan 16 1853 in Pendleton Co., WV, d. Dec 10 1935 in Pendleton Co., WV, buried in Waybright Cem., Pendleton Co., WV.
Married Mar 4 1877 in Pocahontas Co., WV, **Louisa Virginia Murphy**, b. Jan 24 1857, d. Sep 18 1935, buried in Waybright Cem., Pendleton Co., WV.

***Children**:*

\+ 506 i. Ollie W.[5] Waybright b. Feb 13 1877.
\+ 507 ii. Anna Elizabeth Waybright b. Mar 21 1879.
\+ 508 iii. Ira Waybright b. Nov 3 1880.
\+ 509 iv. Michael Waybright b. Mar 25 1883.
\+ 510 v. Esther Waybright b. Apr 1 1885.
\+ 511 vi. Jesse Waybright b. Jan 22 1887.
\+ 512 vii. Sarah Waybright b. Oct 1889.
\+ 513 viii. Nancy Jane Waybright b. Jul 18 1890.
514 ix. Sadie Waybright b. Apr 1893 in Pendleton Co., WV. She Married **Edward Moyers**.

152. **Alvah C.[4] Waybright** (19.Jesse[3], 4.Rachel[2] Arbogast, 1.John C.[1]), b. Feb 17 1855 in Pendleton Co., WV, d. May 26 1933 in Pendleton Co., WV, buried in Waybright Cem., Pendleton Co., WV.
Married Nov 4 1883, **Hannah Susan Gertrude Arbogast**, b. Oct 1862 in Pendleton Co., WV (daughter of Cain Arbogast and Mary Ann Teter Arbogast), d. Dec 7 1903 in Pendleton Co., WV, buried in Waybright Cem., Pendleton Co., WV.

***Children**:*

\+ 515 i. Sophia[5] Waybright b. 1884.
\+ 516 ii. Theodore Waybright b. May 6 1886.
\+ 517 iii. Troy Waybright b. Nov 27 1887.
\+ 518 iv. Clarence Waybright b. Jan 10 1891.
\+ 519 v. Amy Waybright b. Feb 18 1893.
520 vi. Sudie Waybright b. Mar 9 1894 in Pendleton Co., WV, d. Apr 18 1976 in Blue Grass Cem., Highland Co., VA.
521 vii. Elsie Waybright b. May 14 1900 in Pendleton Co., WV, d. Nov 7 1985. She Married **Jesse Thompson**.
522 viii. Marian Waybright b. Oct 1901 in Pendleton Co., WV, d. Aug 20 1902 in Pendleton Co., WV, buried in Pendleton Co., WV.
523 ix. Susan Mae Waybright b. Dec 15 1902 in Pendleton Co., WV, d. Jun 1969, buried in Waybright Cem., Pendleton Co., WV. Married Sep 21 1940 in Moyers, Pendleton Co., WV, **Bruce Rexrode**, b. Nov 22 1918, d. Aug 15 1987. Bruce: At the time this data was assembled this Family may have 5 living, unwed children (child), that are not included here.
524 x. (unknown) Waybright b. Dec 7 1903 in Pendleton Co., WV, d. Dec 7 1903 in Pendleton Co., WV, buried in Pendleton Co., WV.

155. **Mary Elizabeth[4] Waybright** (19.Jesse[3], 4.Rachel[2] Arbogast, 1.John C.[1]), b. Dec 25 1863 in Pendleton Co., WV, d. May 8 1944, buried in Headwaters Cem., Highland Co., VA.
Mary was common law wife of Minor.
(1) She Married **Minor Vandevender**, b. Apr 8 1854 in Pendleton Co., WV, d. Bef 1894

***Children** by Minor Vandevender:*

\+ 525 i. Lenora Jane[5] Waybright b. Apr 5 1889.

***Children** by Floyd Calhoun:*

526 ii. Lenora Jane Calhoun b. Apr 5 1886 in Boyer, Pocahontas Co., WV, d. May 2 1951.
527 iii. Grace Lou Calhoun b. Dec 30 1896 in Boyer, Pocahontas Co., WV, d. May 6 1926, buried in Headwaters Cem., Highland Co., VA. Married Dec 7 1913 in Boyer, Pocahontas Co., WV, **Edward Carrington Hodge**, b. Mar 29 1893, d. Jan 12 1973, buried in Headwaters Cem., Highland Co., VA.

528 iv. Zola M. Calhoun b. Mar 14 1900 in Boyer, Pocahontas Co., WV.
+ 529 v. Estella Calhoun b. Sep 13 1901.

(2) Married May 4 1894 in Pendleton Co., WV, **Floyd Calhoun**, b. Sep 1871 in Pendleton Co., WV. (3) She Married **(unknown) Armgash**, b. Dec 25 1860 in Pendleton Co., WV, d. in Pendleton Co., WV.

157. **Abraham[4] Waybright** (21.Daniel[3], 4.Rachel[2] Arbogast, 1.John C.[1]), b. May 5 1850 in Pendleton Co., WV, d. Apr 10 1885. He Married **Sarah Christina Wratchford**, b. Nov 8 1847, d. May 25 1930, buried in Waybright Cem., Pendleton Co., WV.

Children:

530 i. Mary J[5] Waybright b. 1872.
531 ii. Abraham Waybright b. 1874.
+ 532 iii. Mary Christina Waybright b. Apr 23 1874.
533 iv. Rosetta Waybright b. May 18 1876, d. Jun 9 1892 in Randolph Co., WV, buried in Waybright Cem., Pendleton Co., WV. She Married **Henry Harrison Clayton**, b. Oct 17 1867 in Pendleton Co., WV, d. Jan 29 1937 in Randolph Co., WV.
534 v. Luther Waybright b. Jun 19 1878, d. Oct 15 1894, buried in Waybright Cem., Pendleton Co., WV.
535 vi. Verna Waybright b. Oct 18 1885, d. Jan 1982 in Parsons, Tucker Co., WV. Married 1903, **Walter W. Lambert**.

158. **Mary Margaret[4] Waybright** (21.Daniel[3], 4.Rachel[2] Arbogast, 1.John C.[1]), b. Jan 14 1856 in Onego, Pendleton Co., WV, d. Nov 18 1932 in Whipped, ID.
Mary never Married but lived with 4 different men
(1) She Married **David Huffman**, b. 1850 in Pendleton Co., WV, buried in Reed Cem., Pendleton Co., WV.

***Children** by David Huffman:*

536 i. Marian A.[5] Huffman b. About 1875.
+ 537 ii. Mary Marcella Huffman b. Aug 27 1879.
+ 538 iii. Eve Frances Waybright b. Sep 24 1880.
+ 539 iv. Thaddeus Waybright b. Apr 12 1892.
540 v. Ica Chloe Waybright b. May 12 1894 in Onego, Pendleton Co., WV, d. Jun 28 1948 in Lewiston, Nez Perez Co., ID. Married Dec 1913, Hetzel (John) Jordan, b. May 20 1886 in Job, Randolph Co., WV, d. Feb 9 1964 in Lewiston, Nez Perez Co., ID.

(2) She Married **Simeon Harper**. (3) She Married **Henry Cunningham**. (4) She Married **John Sites**.

159. **William Washington[4] Waybright** (21.Daniel[3], 4.Rachel[2] Arbogast, 1.John C.[1]), b. Apr 1857 in Pendleton Co., WV, d. Aft 1930 in Logan, Fayette Co., WV, buried in Chauncey, Logan Co., WV.
Married Jan 4 1885 in Pendleton Co., WV, **Mary A. Lewis**, b. Apr 1867 in Pendleton Co., WV.

Children:

+ 541 i. Oscar Blaine[5] Waybright b. Oct 7 1887.
542 ii. Walter C. Waybright b. May 22 1890 in Pendleton Co., WV, d. Dec 1963. He Married **Fransina (Unknown)**.
+ 543 iii. Rettia C. Waybright b. Jul 1892.

161. **Isaac Perry[4] Waybright** (21.Daniel[3], 4.Rachel[2] Arbogast, 1.John C.[1]), b. Mar 20 1866 in Pendleton Co., WV, d. Oct 5 1908 in Tucker Co., WV.
Isaac was a carpenter
Married Jul 28 1893 in Randolph Co., WV, **Arthena Cunningham**, b. Apr 19 1873 in Pendleton Co., WV, d. Nov 9 1948.

Children:

+ 544 i. Solomon Robert[5] Waybright b. Apr 11 1894.
545 ii. Silva Gladys Waybright b. Feb 14 1897 in Randolph Co., WV.
546 iii. Oliver Waybright b. Jan 19 1899 in Randolph Co., WV, d. May 22 1899 in Randolph Co., WV.
547 iv. Cecil Waybright b. Dec 8 1899 in Randolph Co., WV, d. 26 Jan in Randolph Co., WV.
548 v. Mary Jane Waybright b. Mar 22 1904 in Hendricks, Tucker Co., WV, d. Jul 28 1964. She Married **Joseph Bragg**.

162. **Cordelia[4] Waybright** (21.Daniel[3], 4.Rachel[2] Arbogast, 1.John C.[1]), b. Jul 6 1869 in Crabbottom, Highland Co., VA, d. Jan 20 1955 in Parsons, Tucker Co., WV, buried in Parsons, Tucker Co., WV.
Married Dec 6 1899, **Samuel Henry Arbogast**, b. Aug 2 1881 in Pendleton Co., WV (son of John B. (Jack) Arbogast and Othelia Ann Ramsey), d. Feb 22 1920 in Pendleton Co., WV, buried in Arbogast Cem., Roaring Creek Pendleton Co., WV.

Children:

+ 549 i. Perlie[5] Arbogast b. Jun 16 1900.
+ 550 ii. Wilbur Arbogast b. Jun 2 1901.
551 iii. Jasper Arbogast b. Jan 24 1903 in Pendleton Co., WV, d. Apr 1984 in Dilliner, Greene Co., PA. He Married **Gladys Roy.**
552 iv. Henry Clay Arbogast b. Jun 9 1905 in Pendleton Co., WV, d. Sep 28 1985 in Elkins, Randolph Co., WV, buried in Mountain State Memorial Gardens Elkins Randolph Co., WV. Married 1923, **Gertrude Ellen Teter**, d. Jul 19 1970 in Elkins, Randolph Co., WV, buried in Parsons, Tucker Co., WV.
553 v. Chloe Arbogast b. Jul 7 1907 in Pendleton Co., WV. She Married **Allen Isner**.
554 vi. Mary Susan Arbogast b. Aug 6 1909 in Pendleton Co., WV, d. Feb 10 1990 in Akron, Summit Co., OH, buried in Crown Hill Cem., Twinsburg, OH. Married Jun 21 1929, **Wilbur Gay Loughry**.
555 vii. Hazel Mae Arbogast b. Feb 16 1911 in Pendleton Co., WV, d. Jul 10 1978 in Randolph Co., WV, buried in Tucker Co., WV. She Married **Arthur B Parsons**, b. Oct 15 1904 in Slip Hill, Kanawha Co., WV, d. Aug 25 1965 in Toms River, Ocean Co., NJ.

164. **John Edward[4] Waybright** (21.Daniel[3], 4.Rachel[2] Arbogast, 1.John C.[1]), b. Mar 16 1875 in Dry Fork, Randolph Co., WV, d. Jan 29 1958 in Laurel Run, South Parsons, Tucker Co., WV, buried Feb 1958 in Parsons, Tucker Co., WV.
Married Mar 7 1898 in Pendleton Co., WV, **Sophia Catherine Clayton**, b. Oct 15 1881 in Job, Randolph Co., WV, d. Oct 1973 in Parsons, Tucker Co., WV, buried in Parsons, Tucker Co., WV.

Children:

+ 556 i. Clifton Mason[5] Waybright b. Jul 28 1899.
+ 557 ii. Guy Daniel Waybright b. Dec 5 1901.
+ 558 iii. Burley McCoy Waybright b. Oct 30 1904.
+ 559 iv. Edna Margaret Waybright b. Apr 23 1907.
560 v. Martha Elizabeth Waybright b. Feb 16 1910 in Onego, Pendleton Co., WV, d. Mar 23 1991. She Married **Walter Hedrick**, b. Mar 5 1904 in West Virginia, d. Jul 1980 in Buckhannon, Upshur Co., WV, buried Jul 1980 in Buckhannon, Upshur Co., WV. Walter: .
561 vi. James Albert Waybright b. Sep 19 1912 in Onego, Pendleton Co., WV, d. Apr 18 1989. He Married **Philope Humphrey.**
562 vii. Jessie Susan Waybright b. Oct 2 1915 in Dry Fork, Randolph Co., WV, d. Nov 1987 in Parsons, Tucker Co., WV. She Married **Roy Hottle**. Roy: .
563 viii. Ethel Virginia Waybright b. Jul 7 1919 in Davis, Tucker Co., WV.
Married Oct 5 1940 in West Virginia, Vincent Carr. Vincent: At the time this data was assembled this Family may have 3 living, unwed children (child), that are not included here.
.564
ix. Virgil Lee Waybright b. Aug 16 1922 in Montrose, Randolph Co., WV. Married Aug 17 1940, Mary Belle McClintic, b. Aug 4 1923.
565 x. Edger Roy Waybright b. Apr 23 1925 in Montrose, Randolph Co., WV.
.

165. **Columbus P.[4] Waybright** (21.Daniel[3], 4.Rachel[2] Arbogast, 1.John C.[1]), b. Jul 1845 in Pendleton Co., WV, d. in Huntington, Cabell Co., WV.
Married Dec 7 1865, **Phoebe Jane Huffman**, b. 1848 in Pendleton Co., WV.

Children:

566 i. Mona[5] Waybright.
567 ii. (infant) Waybright b. Jul 27 1860 in Pendleton Co., WV.
568 iii. Mary Bella Waybright b. 1867 in Pendleton Co., WV.
569 iv. Martha J. Waybright b. Aug 1870 in Pendleton Co., WV.

166. **Mary Jane[4] Waybright** (21.Daniel[3], 4.Rachel[2] Arbogast, 1.John C.[1]), b. 1847.
She Married **Perry Vance**, b. 1843.

Children:

570 i. Phoebe C.[5] Vance b. About 1866.
571 ii. Martha E Vance b. About 1868.
572 iii. Sarah Vance b. About 1869.
573 iv. Mary J Vance b. About 1869.

167. **Albert[4] Waybright** (21.Daniel[3], 4.Rachel[2] Arbogast, 1.John C.[1]), b. May 1848 in Whitmer, Randolph Co., WV, d. Feb 27 1909, buried in Seneca Creek, Pendleton Co., VA/WV.

Married Oct 20 1876 in Pendleton Co., WV, **Dorothy Dolly**, b. Apr 16 1858 in Pendleton Co., WV, d. Oct 29 1904, buried in Waybright Cem., Pendleton Co., WV.

Children:

574 i. Lloyd[5] Waybright b. Jan 1878 in Pendleton Co., WV.
575 ii. Rosie Waybright b. May 1882 in Pendleton Co., WV.
576 iii. Jasper Waybright b. Oct 3 1884 in Pendleton Co., WV, d. Feb 18 1904 in Onego, Pendleton Co., WV, buried in Seneca Creek, Pendleton Co., VA/WV. He Married **Rachel Turner**.
577 iv. Henry V. Waybright b. Sep 1887 in Pendleton Co., WV.
\+ 578 v. Bert Waybright b. Oct 1890.
579 vi. Myrtle Waybright b. Aug 1893.
580 vii. Martha Jane Waybright b. Aug 1895 in Pendleton Co., WV. She Married **Frank Huffman**.
581 viii. Arthur Waybright b. Apr 1897 in Pendleton Co., WV.

168. **Andrew Jackson[4] Waybright** (22.Nathan[3], 4.Rachel[2] Arbogast, 1.John C.[1]), b. Jan 23 1851 in Pendleton Co., WV, d. Oct 26 1937 in Redondo Beach, Los Angeles Co., CA, buried Oct 28 1937 in Pacific Crest Cem., Redondo Beach, Los Angele Co., CA.
Married Sep 4 1870 in Monterey, Highland Co., VA, **Margaret Ann Simmons**, b. Apr 11 1848 in Crabbottom, Highland Co., VA, d. May 25 1936 in Redondo Beach, Los Angeles Co., CA, buried May 28 1936 in Pacific Crest Cem., Redondo Beach, Los Angele Co., CA.

Children:

582 i. Mary[5] Waybright b. in Monterey, Highland Co., VA, d. Feb 23 1959, buried Feb 26 1959 in Richmond, Henrico Co., VA. Married 1905, **Edward Ford**.
583 ii. John Samuel Waybright b. Sep 4 1871 in Monterey, Highland Co., VA, d. Oct 23 1957 in South Laguna Orange Co., CA, buried Oct 24 1957 in Fairhaven Memorial Park, Orange Co., CA. He Married **Lenore Whitmore**, b. Jun 28 1882 in Minnesota, d. Jan 25 1963 in New Port, Orange Co., CA, buried Jan 28 1963 in Fairhaven Memorial Park, Orange Co., CA.
\+ 584 iii. William Pearl Waybright b. Jan 3 1874.
585 iv. Charles Pinkney Waybright b. Apr 23 1878 in Monterey, Highland Co., VA, d. Nov 7 1950 in Monterey, Highland Co., VA, buried in Monterey, Highland Co., VA. Married Oct 17 1906, **Annie Laurie Blagg**, b. Aug 31 1888 in Highland Co., VA, d. Aug 1 1974.
\+ 586 v. Wilbur Glen Waybright b. Nov 12 1882.
587 vi. Hannah Cornelia Waybright b. Sep 27 1886 in Monterey, Highland Co., VA, d. Jun 12 1943 in Redondo Beach, Los Angeles Co., CA, buried in Pacific Crest Cem., Redondo Beach, Los Angele Co., CA. Married Aug 31 1903, **Jesse Booker Botkin**, d. in Redondo Beach, Los Angeles Co., CA, buried in Pacific Crest Cem., Redondo Beach, Los Angele Co., CA.
588 vii. (infant) Waybright b. Sep 27 1886 in Monterey, Highland Co., VA, d. Sep 27 1886 in Monterey, Highland Co., VA, buried Sep 28 1886 in Monterey, Highland Co., VA.

169. **Adam Harness[4] Waybright** (22.Nathan[3], 4.Rachel[2] Arbogast, 1.John C.[1]), b. Feb 1855, d. Sep 8 1924 in Omaha, Douglas Co., NE, buried Sep 10 1924 in Laurl Hill Cem., Omaha, Douglas Co., NE.
Maybe born in Richmond Henrico County, VA
(1) Married Oct 12 1893, **Sarah Johnson**, b. Jun 1870.

(2) Married Mar 13 1886 in Omaha, Douglas Co., NE, **Betty Frank**, b. 1863 in Sweden, d. in Omaha, Douglas Co., NE, buried in Omaha, Douglas Co., NE.

***Children** by Betty Frank:*

\+ 589 i. Frank Adam[5] Waybright b. Mar 12 1886.
\+ 590 ii. Grover Cleveland Waybright b. Nov 5 1888.

170. **Martha Jane[4] Waybright** (22.Nathan[3], 4.Rachel[2] Arbogast, 1.John C.[1]), b. Mar 1 1859 in Crabbottom, Highland Co., VA, d. Jan 6 1923 in Omaha, Douglas Co., NE, buried Jan 10 1923 in Forest Lawn Cem., Omaha, Douglas Co., NE.
Married Feb 11 1881 in Omaha, Douglas Co., NE, **Michael Bushey**, b. 1856 in Michigan, d. Bef 1910 in Omaha, Douglas Co., NE.

Children:

591 i. Frank N[5] Bushey b. in Omaha, Douglas Co., NE.
592 ii. Edward Bushey b. in Omaha, Douglas Co., NE.
593 iii. Harry H. Bushey b. Aug 18 1877 in Omaha, Douglas Co., NE, d. Oct 1962. He Married **Alma (Unknown).**
594 iv. Lottie Bushey b. 1879 in Omaha, Douglas Co., NE.

595 v. Fred H Bushey b. Sep 15 1889 in Omaha, Douglas Co., NE, d. Jan 19 1971 in San Jose, Santa Clara Co., CA. He Married **Betty (Unknown).**

171. **Mary Catherine[4] Waybright** (22.Nathan[3], 4.Rachel[2] Arbogast, 1.John C.[1]), b. Jan 15 1865 in Highland Co., VA, d. Nov 30 1928 in Omaha, Douglas Co., NE, buried Dec 3 1928 in Forest Lawn Cem., Omaha, Douglas Co., NE.
Married Jul 2 1879 in Omaha, Douglas Co., NE, **William Henery Norton**, b. Jan 1864 in Iowa, d. Bef 1928.

Children:

596 i. Mable[5] Norton b. in Omaha, Douglas Co., NE. She Married **Everett L. Baveyart**.
597 ii. William Norton b. in Omaha, Douglas Co., NE. He Married **Lillian (Unknown).**
598 iii. Adam Norton b. in Omaha, Douglas Co., NE.
599 iv. John Norton b. in Omaha, Douglas Co., NE.
600 v. Nathan Norton b. in Omaha, Douglas Co., NE.
601 vi. Ralph Norton b. in Omaha, Douglas Co., NE.
602 vii. Parnell Norton b. in Omaha, Douglas Co., NE. He Married **Elsie (Unknown).**
603 viii. Lena Norton b. 1883 in Omaha, Douglas Co., NE. She Married **Michael Stonesypher**.
604 ix. Philip Norton b. Apr 1884 in Omaha, Douglas Co., NE.

176. **Amby[4] Rexroad** (23.Elizabeth[3] Waybright, 4.Rachel[2] Arbogast, 1.John C.[1]), b. Oct 10 1851, d. Jun 21 1925.
He Married **Martha Jane Colaw**, b. Apr 14 1859. **Martha**: Daughter of Ephraim Colaw and Angeline Helmick.

Children:

\+ 605 i. Hilbert[5] Rexroad b. About 1872.
606 ii. Kenny Rexroad b. About 1873.
607 iii. Maggie A Rexroad b. About 1877.
608 iv. Abbie Rexroad b. Oct 06 1878, d. Jan 27 1923, buried in Snowy Mtn., Pendleton Co., WV. She Married **Arthur Fox**, b. Apr 1872.
609 v. Clara Rexroad b. About 1894.
610 vi. Margie Rexroad b. About 1903.
611 vii. Catherine Rexroad.

177. **Jefferson D[4] Rexroad** (23.Elizabeth[3] Waybright, 4.Rachel[2] Arbogast, 1.John C.[1]), b. About 1862 in Dry Fork, Randolph Co., WV.
Married 1879, **Elizabeth S Mullenax**, b. May 1858 (daughter of Edward Mullenax and Winifred Calhoun).

Children:

\+ 612 i. Kemper D[5] Rexroad b. June 1881.
613 ii. Arthur Rexroad b. Apr 1883.
614 iii. Clinton D Rexroad b. 1884.
615 iv. Forrest Rexroad b. Mar 1888.
616 v. Lena Rexroad b. Apr1889. She Married **Ira H Rexroad**, b. 1892 in Highland Co., VA (son of Benjamin Rexroad and Delia Weese).
617 vi. Grace Rexroad b. 1894, d. 1918, buried in Blue Grass Cem., Highland Co., VA. She Married **William Hover**, b. About 1893 in Pocahontas Co., WV.
618 vii. Robert Rexroad b. June 1896.
619 viii. Mary E Rexroad b. July 1899.

181. **Clark W.[4] Waybright** (24.Levi[3], 4.Rachel[2] Arbogast, 1.John C.[1]), b. 1855 in Braxton Co., WV, d. 1904 in West Virginia.
Married Oct 14 1883 in Braxton Co., WV, **Sarah S. Starrett**, b. Abt 1855 in Braxton Co., WV, d. Abt 1904 in Braxton Co., WV, buried Abt 1904 in Braxton Co., WV.

Children:

\+ 620 i. Erma Creigh[5] Waybright.
621 ii. Georgia Waybright b. Oct 1 1884 in Braxton Co., WV, d. Jul 1975. She Married **William C. King**.
622 iii. William Roy Waybright b. Feb 14 1887 in Braxton Co., WV, d. May 1973.
623 iv. Fredrick Lewis Waybright b. 1888 in Braxton Co., WV, d. 1933. He Married **Beulah McCarty.**
624 v. Lenora W. Waybright b. 1889 in Braxton Co., WV, d. 1936. She Married **Harry Johnstone.**
\+ 625 vi. Walter Wade Waybright b. Apr 5 1893.
626 vii. Mary E. Waybright b. 1895 in Braxton Co., WV, d. 1895.

183. **Sarah Amanda[4] Waybright** (24.Levi[3], 4.Rachel[2] Arbogast, 1.John C.[1]), b. May 22 1860 in Braxton Co., WV, d. Nov 2 1936.

Married Feb 14 1878 in Braxton Co., WV, **Asa Lee Shaver**, b. Oct 16 1849 in Braxton Co., WV, d. Dec 18 1908 in Braxton Co., WV, buried in Flatwoods, Braxton Co., WV.

Children:

627 i. Olen Burr[5] Shaver b. Aug 26 1880 in Flatwoods, Braxton Co., WV, d. Jul 29 1940 in Wheaton Montgomery Co., MD, buried in Fort Lincoln Cem., Bladensburg, Prince George's Co., MD. Married Sep 27 1911, **Anna Caroline Mollohan**, b. May 17 1885 in Sutton, Braxton Co., WV, d. Dec 28 1975 in Hagerstown, Washington Co., MD, buried in Fort Lincoln Cem., Bladensburg, Prince George's Co., MD.

628 ii. Charles Shaver b. Jun 1 1884 in Flatwoods, Braxton Co., WV, d. Jun 15 1885.

629 iii. Melvin Russell Shaver b. Jul 27 1887 in Flatwoods, Braxton Co., WV.

630 iv. Lucille Rhea Shaver b. Apr 4 1890 in Flatwoods, Braxton Co., WV, d. Apr 2 1922. Married Oct 19 1909, **Charles A. Orrahood**.

189. **Elbridge L.[4] Hinkle** (26.Martha Ann[3] Waybright, 4.Rachel[2] Arbogast, 1.John C.[1]), b. Jul 1848 in Dry Run, Pendleton Co., WV, d. Aug 1924 in Crabbottom, Highland Co., VA.
He Married **Sarah S Nelson**, b. 1845. **Sarah**: Child of Absolon Nelson and Susannah Calhoun.

Children:

631 i. Clara[5] Hinkle b. About 1873.

\+ 632 ii. Fannie May Hinkle b. May 27 1877.

190. **Susan[4] Hinkle** (26.Martha Ann[3] Waybright, 4.Rachel[2] Arbogast, 1.John C.[1]), b. Mar 25 1853 in Dry Run, Pendleton Co., WV, d. Jan 25 1916 in Dry Run, Pendleton Co., WV.
Married Feb 4 1877, **Jacob Harper Rymer**, b. Aug 30 1858, d. Feb 15 1940 in Dry Run, Pendleton Co., WV. **Jacob**: Son of George W. Rymer and Margaret Harper.

Children:

633 i. Mattie[5] Rymer b. Jun 25 1879, d. May 02 1914. She Married **Will Simmons**.

\+ 634 ii. Clyde Rymer b. Mar 30 1881.

\+ 635 iii. Sudie R Rymer b. Feb 12 1886.

191. **Elizabeth C[4] Hinkle** (26.Martha Ann[3] Waybright, 4.Rachel[2] Arbogast, 1.John C.[1]), b. Mar 1855 in Dry Run, Pendleton Co., WV, d. Jan 20 1928.
She Married **Elijah Mullenax**, b. Aug 30 1853 in Dry Run, Pendleton Co., WV (son of William Isaac Mullenax and Elizabeth Nelson), d. Jan 20 1928, buried in Elk Mt. Cem., Pendleton. Co., WV.

Children:

\+ 636 i. Dolly[5] Mullenax b. Mar 04 1879.

\+ 637 ii. Lura Mullenax b. Jun 28 1881.

\+ 638 iii. McClelland Mullenax b. Oct 25 1883.

\+ 639 iv. Martha Ellen Mullenax b. Feb 1891.

\+ 640 v. Betty Alice Mullenax b. Feb 28 1891.

192. **Eliza Ann[4] Hinkle** (26.Martha Ann[3] Waybright, 4.Rachel[2] Arbogast, 1.John C.[1]), b. Oct 31 1856 in Dry Run, Pendleton Co., WV, d. Mar 5 1926 in Pendleton Co., WV.
Married Apr 1883 in Pendleton Co., WV, **Benjamin B. Phares**, b. May 1858 in Churchville, Pendleton Co., WV, d. Apr 1917 in Pendleton Co., WV. **Benjamin**: Son of Benjamin Phares and Catherine Bennett.

Children:

\+ 641 i. Cleat[5] Phares b. Sep 19 1884.

642 ii. Martha Phares b. 1890.

643 iii. Bulah Phares b. Sep 1894.

193. **Catherine Beam[4] Hinkle** (26.Martha Ann[3] Waybright, 4.Rachel[2] Arbogast, 1.John C.[1]), b. 1859 in Dry Run, Pendleton Co., WV.
She Married **Abraham Lantz Cunningham**, b. Abt 1854 in Dry Run, Pendleton Co., WV.

Children:

644 i. Zena[5] Cunningham.

645 ii. Willie Cunningham.

646 iii. Hinkle Cunningham.

647 iv. Chloe Cunningham.

648 v. Vella J Cunningham.

194. **Isaac Harness[4] Hinkle** (26.Martha Ann[3] Waybright, 4.Rachel[2] Arbogast, 1.John C.[1]), b. 1862 in Dry Run, Pendleton Co., WV, d. 1950, buried in Blue Grass Cem., Highland Co., VA.
Married Jun 17 1901 in Highland Co., VA, **Phoebe J Stone Nicholas**, b. 1864.

Children:

649 i. Isaac Harness[5] Hinkle, Jr. b. Mar 12 1893.
650 ii. Salma Hinkle.
\+ 651 iii. Martha Ann Hinkle b. May 11 1902.

199. **Roseann[4] Ketterman** (28.Alice[3] Waybright, 5.Rebecca[2] Arbogast, 1.John C.[1]), b. 1848 in Pendleton Co., WV, buried in Sponaugle Family Cem., Hunting Grounds Pendleton County WV.
She Married **Jacob Sponaugle, Jr.**, b. 1841 in Pendleton Co., WV, (son of Jacob Phillip Sponaugle and Elizabeth L. Arbogast), d. Sep 13 1880 in Pendleton Co., WV.

Children:

\+ 652 i. Ashby[5] Sponaugle b. 1868.
\+ 653 ii. Gilbert Kenton Sponaugle b. Jan 2 1870.
654 iii. Eli Perry Sponaugle b. Jan 28 1871 in Hunting Ground, Pendleton Co., (W)VA, d. Jan 15 1893.
655 iv. Flora Anna Sponaugle b. JUN 1874 in Hunting Ground, Pendleton Co., (W)VA, d. Dec 26 1947, buried in Sponaugle Family Cem., Hunting Grounds Pendleton County WV.
\+ 656 v. William Letcher Sponaugle b. Sep 16 1875.
\+ 657 vi. Herman Henry Sponaugle b. Jan 13 1877.

200. **Solomon W.[4] Ketterman** (28.Alice[3] Waybright, 5.Rebecca[2] Arbogast, 1.John C.[1]), b. Dec 1851, d. 1922 in Paw Paw Morgan Co., WV.
Married Aug 3 1871 in Pendleton Co., WV, **Francis Tabitha Harold**, b. Oct 10 1856 in Pendleton Co., WV, d. 1941 in West Virginia.

Children:

658 i. Dora[5] Ketterman b. in Pendleton Co., WV, d. in Paw Paw Morgan Co., WV. She Married **Jerry O. Patterson**, b. Dec 16 1876, d. Nov 1964 in Paw Paw Morgan Co., WV.
659 ii. Elmer P. Ketterman b. 1873 in Pendleton Co., WV, d. 1918 in Ohio. He Married Minnie Nelson.
660 iii. Louise J. Ketterman b. Aug 6 1878 in Pendleton Co., WV, d. Feb 14 1904. She Married **Howard Homan**.
661 iv. Earlie Austin Ketterman b. Jun 15 1879 in Pendleton Co., WV, d. Oct 25 1918 in Kempton, Garrett Co., MD. Married Sep 2 1902, **Martha Thompson**, b. Jun 2 1879 in Pendleton Co., WV, d. Sep 1 1957 in Whitmer, Randolph Co., WV.
662 v. Lorine Ketterman b. 1880 in Pendleton Co., WV.
663 vi. Leta M. Ketterman b. Apr 1887 in Pendleton Co., WV, d. in Elkins, Randolph Co., WV. She Married **Cad Gilmore**.
\+ 664 vii. Katie Ketterman b. Aug 1893.
665 viii. Andrew Salem Ketterman b. Nov 1897 in Pendleton Co., WV. Married Jul 25 1921 in Randolph Co., WV, **Datha McCroby**.

204. **Ann Rebecca[4] Ketterman** (28.Alice[3] Waybright, 5.Rebecca[2] Arbogast, 1.John C.[1]), b. Nov 24 1855 in Pendleton Co., WV, d. Jun 17 1892 in Pendleton Co., WV.
(1) Married Dec 20 1876 in Pendleton Co., WV, **Adam Sponaugle**..

Children *by Dyer Pennington:*

\+ 666 i. Louella[5] Pennington b. Apr 25 1880.
667 ii. Ostella Pennington b. Feb 28 1882 in Pendleton Co., WV, d. 1943. (1) She Married **Robert B Bennett**, b. 1871, d. 1924. (2) She Married **Walter S Dunkle**, b. 1875, d. 1951.
668 iii. Oley S Pennington b. Jan 19 1884 in Pendleton Co., WV, d. 1930. He Married **Otie Kate Judy**, b. 1884, d. 1972.

(2) Married Apr 17 1882 in Pendleton Co., WV, **Dyer Pennington**, b. Feb 20 1858 in Pendleton Co., WV, d. o3311947 in Pendleton Co., WV

205. **Susan P.[4] Ketterman** (28.Alice[3] Waybright, 5.Rebecca[2] Arbogast, 1.John C.[1]), b. Mar 17 1858 in Pendleton Co., WV, d. in Glady, WV.
(1) Married Nov-15-1874, **Jacob McKendry Strauder**, b. Mar-25-1854 in Hunting Ground, Pendleton Co., (W)VA, d. 1930 in Glady, Randolph Co., WV.

Children *by Jacob McKendry Strauder:*

+ 669 i. Melissa Francis[5] Strauder b. Aug-19-1975.
+ 670 ii. Fleetwood Strauder b. Jun-23-1877.
671 iii. William Phillip Strauder b. Feb-14-1849, d. Aug-05-1945. Married Dec-27-1900, **Did Bennett** (daughter of George Bennett and Martha Arbogast).
672 iv. Edward G. Strauder b. Oct 1880. He Married **Madie Bessie Bennett**.
+ 673 v. Molley Strauder b. Sep 1894.
+ 674 vi. Ora Clifton Strauder b. Mar 1886.
675 vii. Jacob Floyd Strauder b. Apr-12-1888, d. Oct-16-1919.
+ 676 viii. Mayberry Strauder b. May-10-1890.

(2) Married Mar-17-1858, **Jacob McKendry Strawder**, b. Mar 25 1854 in Hunting Ground, Pendleton Co., (W)VA, (son of William Strawder and Mary Elizabeth Sponaugle), d. 1930 in Randolph Co., WV

208. **Churchill[4] Waybright** (28.Alice[3], 5.Rebecca[2] Arbogast, 1.John C.[1]), b. Aug 3 1844 in Blue Grass, Highland Co., WV, d. Jul 11 1911 in Thornwood, Pocahontas Co., WV, buried in Bartow, Pocahontas Co., WV. Allen took his mothers maiden name
Married Jun 15 1868 in Churchville, Pendleton Co., WV, **Mary Permelia Catherine Mullenax**, b. Aug 7 1848 in Dry Run, Pendleton Co., WV (daughter of William Isaac Mullenax and Elizabeth Nelson), d. Apr 16 1932 in Pocahontas Co., WV, buried Apr 18 1932 in Thornwood, Pocahontas Co., WV.

Children:

677 i. Sarah P[5] Waybright b. About 1867.
+ 678 ii. Wilber Allen Waybright b. Jul 8 1869.
679 iii. Clara Ann Waybright b. May 15 1871 in Dry Run, Pendleton Co., WV. Married 1912, **Minor Mullenax**.
+ 680 iv. Amby Stanton Waybright b. Sep 30 1873.
681 v. James Buckhannan Waybright b. Apr 10 1875 in Dry Run, Pendleton Co., WV, d. Apr 9 1950. Married Mar 4 1897 in Back Mt. Cem., Pocahontas Co., WV, **Louise Murphy.**
+ 682 vi. Fransina Lee Waybright b. Mar 28 1877.

209. **Millie Amelia[4] Wimer** (29.Sidney[3] Waybright, 5.Rebecca[2] Arbogast, 1.John C.[1]), b. Feb 2 1855 in Pendleton Co., WV, d. Sep 3 1917.
Married Jun 5 1906, **Charles W. Botkin**.

Children:

683 i. Audie Glenn[5] Wimer b. About 1878.

211. **George Wesley[4] Wimer** (29.Sidney[3] Waybright, 5.Rebecca[2] Arbogast, 1.John C.[1]), b. 1858 in Pendleton Co., WV.
Married Jun 26 1885, **Alice Weese**.

Children:

684 i. Almeda Amanda[5] Wimer b. 1888. Married 1915, **Cameron Lloyd Rexroad**, b. 1887, d. 1968.
685 ii. Christina Ethel Wimer b. 1889, d. 1941. She Married **Charles A Beverage**.

212. **Jeremiah Emanuel[4] Wimer** (29.Sidney[3] Waybright, 5.Rebecca[2] Arbogast, 1.John C.[1]), b. Dec 28 1860 in Pendleton Co., WV, d. Mar 8 1950.
Married Oct 5 1884, **Ellen Catherine Rexrode**, b. Oct 1862, d. Dec 6 1944, buried in Middle Mount High Co., VA home farm.

Children:

+ 686 i. Arbelia[5] Wimer b. 1886.
687 ii. Alfred Glenn Wimer b. 1888, d. 1972. She Married **Effie Florence Sponaugle**, b. 1889, d. 1981.
+ 688 iii. Mary Ellen Wimer b. Aug 27 1892.
689 iv. Paul E Wimer b. 1895, d. 1979. He Married **Elsie Grace Barkley,** b. 1906.
690 v. Edward Brown Wimer b. 1897, d. 1985. (1) He Married **Ollie Barkley**. (2) He Married **Lulu Jarrells**.
691 vi. John Richard Wimer b. 1900, d. 1995. He Married **Arzola Lambert**.
692 vii. Goldie Wimer b. 1902, d. 1976. She Married **Dennis Brown Fleisher**, b. 1895, d. 1983.
693 viii. Eva Wimer b. 1904. She Married **Arlie Wimer.**

213. **Jennie[4] Wimer** (29.Sidney[3] Waybright, 5.Rebecca[2] Arbogast, 1.John C.[1]), b. 1864 in Pendleton Co., WV.
Married May 10 1885, **Mayberry F. Harold**.

Children:

694 i. (unknown)[5] Harold b. Mar 20 1886, d. May 27 1886.

695 ii. Alva M Harold. Married 1906 in Highland Co., VA, **Elizabeth Botkin**.
696 iii. Bonnie Maude Harold b. 1890. She Married **Charles Bodkin**.
\+ 697 iv. Ida H Harold b. 1902.

214. **Ephraim A.[4] Wimer** (29.Sidney[3] Waybright, 5.Rebecca[2] Arbogast, 1.John C.[1]), b. 1866 in Pendleton Co., WV, d. 1945, buried in Wimer Family Cem., Pendleton Co., WV. Married Jan 29 1888, **Malinda F. Propst**.

Children:

698 i. Lewis Andrew[5] Wimer b. 1888, d. 1988. (1) Married 1910 in Highland Co., VA, **Almeda Mae Sponaugle**, b. 1893, d. 1972. (2) He Married **Lona May**.
699 ii. Lloyd Wimer b. 1890, d. 1971. Married 1913 in Highland Co., VA, **Lela Sponaugle**, b. 1890, d. 1983.
700 iii. Lillie May Wimer b. 1895, d. 1982. Married 1910 in Highland Co., VA, **Floyd W Rexroad**, b. 1885, d. 1965.
701 iv. Lura Este Wimer b. 1900, d. 1970. Married 1920, **Arlie Martin Jack**, b. 1895, d. 1965.
702 v. Ray W Wimer. He Married **Neta Grace Simmons**, b. 1914, d. 1991.

215. **Alexander[4] Wimer** (29.Sidney[3] Waybright, 5.Rebecca[2] Arbogast, 1.John C.[1]), b. 1870 in Pendleton Co., WV. Married Jul 23 1893, **Martha P. Helmick**.

Children:

703 i. Clarence Eldridre[5] Helmick b. 1894, d. 1967.
704 ii. Arlie Phillip Helmick b. 1898, d. 1977. Married 1921, **Ida Mae Barkley**, b. 1900, d. 1971.

219. **Ann Rebecca Elizabeth[4] Waybright** (32.Elijah[3], 5.Rebecca[2] Arbogast, 1.John C.[1]), b. Jan 2 1853 in Pendleton Co., WV, d. Jan 19 1922.
Married Sep 28 1873 in Pendleton Co., WV, **George W Grady**, b. 1849 in Pendleton Co., WV. **George**: Son of Strother Grady and Sarah Leahy.

Children:

\+ 705 i. Luticia S[5] Grady b. 1879.
\+ 706 ii. James Pearl Grady b. 1885.
\+ 707 iii. Cora A. Grady b. Nov 30 1886.
\+ 708 iv. Ora Francis Grady b. 1886.
\+ 709 v. Sallie Odessa Grady b. 1889.
710 vi. Edward W Grady b. 1890. He Married **Sallie E Harman**, b. 1881, d. 1920.
711 vii. Rosa Grady b. 1893, d. 1993.

221. **Sarah Anne[4] Waybright** (32.Elijah[3], 5.Rebecca[2] Arbogast, 1.John C.[1]), b. Jul 7 1855 in Pendleton Co., WV, d. Jan 1 1914. Married Feb 8 1874, **Isaac N. Arbogast**, b. 1849 in Pendleton Co., WV (son of Cain Arbogast and Mary Ann Teter Arbogast), d. Aft 1910.

Children:

712 i. Abraham[5] Arbogast b. 1875 in Pendleton Co., WV. Married Jan 14 1894 in Pendleton Co., WV, **Effie Lambert**.
713 ii. Balam Arbogast b. 1876 in Pendleton Co., WV. Married Feb 24 1896 in Pendleton Co., WV, **Hannah Bennett**.
714 iii. Abel Arbogast b. 1877 in Pendleton Co., WV. Married Nov 5 1896 in Pendleton Co., WV, **Ella C. May**.
715 iv. Elijah W Arbogast b. 1880 in Pendleton Co., WV. Married Oct 24 1897 in Pendleton Co., WV, **Orvisa Lambert**.

223. **Margaret Ann[4] Waybright** (32.Elijah[3], 5.Rebecca[2] Arbogast, 1.John C.[1]), b. Feb 7 1858 in Pendleton Co., WV, d. 1916, buried in Maple Springs Cem., Eglon, Preston Co., WV.
(1) Married Aug 27 1876 in Pendleton Co., WV, **Reuben H. Hedrick**, b. Jul 1 1854 in Pendleton Co., WV.

Children *by Reuben H. Hedrick:*

716 i. Mary[5] Hedrick b. 1873 in Pendleton Co., WV.
717 ii. Annie Elizabeth Hedrick b. 1875 in Riverton, Pendleton Co., WV. Married 1897, **Adam C Vandevander**.
718 iii. Phoebe Hedrick b. 1878 in Pendleton Co., WV. Married 1903, **Patrick Vandevender.**
719 iv. Able Hedrick b. Aug 12 1884 in Pendleton Co., WV. He Married **Elizabeth Catherine Nelson**, b. Jan 1867.
720 v. James Hedrick b. Mar 20 1886 in Riverton, Pendleton Co., WV.
721 vi. Jesse Hedrick b. Aug 1895 in Riverton, Pendleton Co., WV.

(2) She Married **William Isaac Mullenax**, b. Jul 5 1825 in Dry Run, Pendleton Co., WV (son of James W. Mullenax and Permelia Murphy), d. Sep 8 1901 in Elk Mountain, Pocahontas Co., WV, buried in Pocahontas Co., WV.

Children *by William Isaac Mullenax:*

722 vii. William Benny Mullenax b. Jul 4 1883, d. Feb 22 1979 in Memorial General Hospital, Elkins, Randolph Co., WV. He Married **Susan Martin (Unknown).**
723 viii. Arthur Mullenax b. 1891.
724 ix. Jesse Mullenax b. Jun 7 1895, d. Jan 1977 in Iowa.
725 x. Dora Mullenax b. 1899.
726 xi. Willie Mullenax b. 1894.
ROOTS IN TUCKER CO. 1979, P. 30, tells of a William Benny Mullenax b. 7/4/1884, son of William Isaac Mullenax and Margaret Ann Waybright , Married **Susan Millie Martin** b. 1890. Other comments makes Millie fit this family.

224. **George Washington[4] Waybright** (32.Elijah[3], 5.Rebecca[2] Arbogast, 1.John C.[1]), b. Nov 1 1859 in Pendleton Co., WV, d. Nov 4 1934, buried in Maple Springs Cem., Eglon, Preston Co., WV. (1) Married Nov 1 1925, **Mintie Belle Wimer Arbogast**, b. 1879 in West Virginia, d. 1959.

Children *by Mintie Belle Wimer Arbogast:*

727 i. Elizabeth Catherine[5] Waybright b. Apr 3 1927 in West Virginia. (1) She Married Frank Simmons. (2) She Married **Alfred Stemple**.

(2) Married Jun 2 1878 in Pendleton Co., WV, **Elizabeth Catherine Zickafoose**, b. Mar 27 1858 in Pendleton Co., WV, d. Bef 1925 in Preston Co., WV, buried in Maple Springs Cem., Eglon, Preston Co., WV. **Elizabeth**: Child of George Zickefoose and Elizabeth Wimer.

Children *by Elizabeth Catherine Zickafoose:*

\+ 728 ii. Abel Washington Waybright b. Feb 6 1880.
729 iii. Achin Cline Waybright b. May 4 1882 in Pendleton Co., WV, d. Mar 29 1947, buried in Accident Cem., Preston Co., WV.
(1) He Married **Elva Ann Harsh**, b. Apr 26 1900 in Eglon, Preston Co., WV, d. Jan 6 1983, buried in Accident Cem., Preston Co., WV.
(2) Married Nov 1 1903, **Sarah C. Teter**, b. 1874, d. 1942, buried in Accident Cem., Preston Co., WV.
\+ 730 iv. Luther Lee Waybright b. Jun 16 1883.
\+ 731 v. Hendricks Cleveland Waybright b. Apr 16 1886.
\+ 732 vi. Surrilda Florence Waybright b. Aug 28 1887.
\+ 733 vii. Martha Anne Waybright b. Dec 24 1889.

225. **Phoebe Jane[4] Waybright** (32.Elijah[3], 5.Rebecca[2] Arbogast, 1.John C.[1]), b. 1861 in Pendleton Co., WV, d. Jul 10 1898, buried in Sugarland Tucker Co., WV.
Married Nov 2 1882 in Tucker Co., WV, **John W. Helmick**, b. 1861, d. 1891, buried in Sugarland Tucker Co., WV.

Children*:*

734 i. Fannie[5] Helmick.
She Married **John Moreland**.
735 ii. Lana Helmick.
She Married **Arthur Moreland**.
736 iii. Jenny Helmick.
She Married **Milford Glass**.
737 iv. Cora Helmick.
She Married **Edward Lipson**.
738 v. Esta Helmick d. 1957.
She Married **James P. Bennett**, b. Jul 20 1898 in Pendleton Co., WV, d. Jan 15 1983 in United Hospital Center, Pendleton Co., VA.
739 vi. Silas Helmick.
740 vii. James Helmick.
741 viii. Soloma Catherine Helmick b. Aug 5 1883 in Grant Co., WV, d. Mar 16 1927 in Bismarck, Grant Co., WV.
Married Dec 25 1900 in Garrett Co., MD, **Joseph Robert Cosner**, b. Sep 20 1876 in Bismarck, Grant Co., WV, d. Oct 11 1951 in Bismarck, Grant Co., WV.

227. **Martha Ellen[4] Harold** (34.Catherine Elizabeth[3] Waybright, 5.Rebecca[2] Arbogast, 1.John C.[1]), b. May 13 1850 in Pendleton Co., WV, d. Aug 4 1913.
She Married **Ephraim Wimer**, b. July 1834, d. Feb 26 1910. **Ephraim**: This dude was a 2nd Lt. in the 1st co, 62nd VA Inf. Captured, in battle of Fisher Hill in prison at Fort McHenry, MD.

Children*:*

742 i. Alexander Lee[5] Wimer b. Jun 1869, d. Mar 07 1944. Married Dec 03 1893 in Pendleton Co., WV, **Ida Hinkle**.
743 ii. Emory Newton Wimer b. Mar 07 1870, d. Aug 19 1943. Married Oct 25 1891 in Highland Co., VA, **Mary Jeanette Moyers**, b. 1871.
744 iii. William Kemper Wimer b. May 11 1873, d. Apr 15 1952. Married Apr 07 1895 in Highland Co., VA, **Dottie Lillian Colaw**.
745 iv. Mary Alice Wimer b. Feb 14 1876, d. Mar 30 1944. She Married **J Fremont Colaw**.
746 v. Lelia M Wimer b. Jan 1879, d. Nov 1883.
\+ 747 vi. Franklin Cameron Wimer b. Nov 14 1881.

228. **Barbara Elizabeth[4] Harold** (34.Catherine Elizabeth[3] Waybright, 5.Rebecca[2] Arbogast, 1.John C.[1]), b. Apr 1 1852 in Pendleton Co., WV, d. Jan 2 1930 in Long Beach, Los Angeles Co., CA.
Married Jan 16 1870 in Crabbottom, Highland Co., VA, **Asgil Stevenson Will**, b. Apr 23 1848 in Crabbottom, Highland Co., VA, d. Feb 22 1939 in Hennessy, Kingfisher Co., OK.

***Children*:**

748 i. Jasper W.[5] Will.
749 ii. Blanche Dora Will. She Married **(unknown) Spangler**.
750 iii. Minnie Lena Will. She Married **Wade William Windham**.
751 iv. Thomas Jefferson Will.
752 v. Grover Will.
753 vi. Frances Will.
754 vii. Robert S. Will.
755 viii. Fredrick Stuart Will b. Jun 28 1871 in Crabbottom, Highland Co., VA, d. Mar 7 1950 in Oklahoma City, Oklahoma Co., OK. Married Feb 27 1895 in Cass Co., NE, **Nellie Satchell**.

231. **Loring Ashby[4] Harold** (34.Catherine Elizabeth[3] Waybright, 5.Rebecca[2] Arbogast, 1.John C.[1]), b. Dec 16 1861, d. Mar 04 1905.
Killed digging well.
Married Jan 18 1885, **Hannah Margaret Colaw**, b. Apr 28 1865 in Crabbottom, Highland Co., VA.

***Children*:**

756 i. Lorwing W[5] Harold b. Mar 1881.
757 ii. William M Harold b. Dec 1886.
758 iii. Virgil M Harold b. Aug 1888.
759 iv. Meade F Harold b. Feb 1895.
760 v. Sarah K Harold b. Jan 1899.
761 vi. Myrtle Colaw Harold b. Oct 13 1901.
762 vii. Mable Lou Harold b. Oct 03 1904.
Family moved to Kansas in 1903.

236. **Lemuel Benjamin[4] Waybright** (35.Morgan[3], 5.Rebecca[2] Arbogast, 1.John C.[1]), b. May 27 1859 in Pendleton Co., WV, d. Nov 18 1913.
(1) Married Dec 12 1894, **Lucy B. Mullenax**.

***Children** by Lucy B. Mullenax:*

763 i. Margie B[5] Waybright b. Jul 1895.

(2) Married Mar 1 1904 in Highland Co., VA, **Emmet Bartlett Wimer**, b. Jan 22 1876 in Missouri (daughter of James Polk Wimer and Elizabeth Ellen Chipman), d. 11-14-1904.

237. **Rebecca Susan[4] Waybright** (35.Morgan[3], 5.Rebecca[2] Arbogast, 1.John C.[1]), b. 1866 in Pendleton Co., WV.
Married Nov 30 1898, **John Haymond Weese**, b. Jul 1874.

***Children*:**

764 i. Arlie[5] Weese b. Mar 1895.
765 ii. Ray Weese b. June 1899.

239. **Miles Adam[4] Waybright** (35.Morgan[3], 5.Rebecca[2] Arbogast, 1.John C.[1]), b. Oct 22 1869 in Highland Co., VA, d. Oct 1 1945, buried in Union Cem., Churchville, Pendleton Co., WV.
(1) Married Jun 25 1892, **Delphia Weese**, b. 1870 in Blue Grass Cem., Highland Co., VA, d. in Dartmone, Butler Co., WV, buried in Thornrose Cem., Staunton, Augusta Co., VA. (

***Children** by Delphia Weese:*

+ 766 i. Fredrick Cleveland[5] Waybright b. Feb 7 1893.
767 ii. Pearlie Waybright b. 1899 in Blue Grass Cem., Highland Co., VA.
768 iii. William Waybright b. Jul 7 1901 in Blue Grass Cem., Highland Co., VA, d. Dec 8 1983.
769 iv. Cloe Waybright b. Jul 7 1901 in Blue Grass Cem., Highland Co., VA.
770 v. Elsie Waybright b. Jul 7 1905 in Blue Grass Cem., Highland Co., VA.

2) He Married **Cora Nelson**.

240. **Morgan Edward[4] Waybright** (35.Morgan[3], 5.Rebecca[2] Arbogast, 1.John C.[1]), b. Jan 1875 in Highland Co., VA, d. 1958, buried in Blue Grass Cem., Highland Co., VA.
Married Nov 16 1898 in Highland Co., VA, **Flora Belle Wimer**, b. Jan 31 1871 in Highland Co., VA, d. Feb 22 1944, buried in Blue Grass Cem., Highland Co., VA.

Children:

771 i. Luther B.[5] Waybright b. Sep 1899.
772 ii. Evelyn Waybright b. 1901.
773 iii. Beulah Waybright b. 1905.
774 iv. Andrew M. Waybright b. 1908, d. 1952.

241. **Nicholas[4] Waybright** (36.Miles[3], 5.Rebecca[2] Arbogast, 1.John C.[1]), b. 1854 in Pendleton Co., WV. He Married **Mary Ellen Nelson**, b. 1859.

Children:

775 i. Ann[5] Waybright. She Married **(unknown) Wagoner**.
+ 776 ii. William Garrett Waybright b. Jan 7 1879.

242. **Ann Elizabeth[4] Waybright** (36.Miles[3], 5.Rebecca[2] Arbogast, 1.John C.[1]), b. Sep 11 1855 in Pendleton Co., WV, d. Jun 23 1920.
Married Nov 20 1877, **Henry Markwood Moyers**, b. Aug 26 1855 in Hunting Ground, Pendleton Co., (W)VA, d. Aug 23 1942 in Canton, Stark Co., OH, buried in Bartow, Pocahontas Co., WV.

Children:

777 i. Carrie E.[5] Moyers b. Jul 20 1878 in West Virginia.
778 ii. S. Florence Moyers b. Feb 24 1880 in West Virginia. She Married **Hiram Kisner**.
779 iii. Harry McClelland Moyers b. Nov 10 1881 in Churchville, Pendleton Co., WV, d. Oct 17 1972 in Carroll Co., OH, buried in New Harrisburg Cem., Carroll Co., OH. (1) Married May 20 1950, **Lillie Jane Rose Martin**, b. May 18 1889 in Wetzel Co., WV, d. Dec 19 1959, buried in Leavittsville Cem., Carroll Co., OH. (2) Married Oct 13 1960, **Emma Withrow**, b. Sep 21 1893 in North Beaver, Lawrence Co., PA, d. Jun 11 1972, buried in Hillside Memorial Park Cem., Akron Summit Co., OH. (3) Married Mar 23 1904, **Lura Bennett**, b. Apr 27 1882 in Pendleton Co., WV, d. Oct 3 1948, buried in New Harrisburg Cem., Carroll Co., OH.
780 iv. Walter G. Moyers b. Mar 3 1883 in West Virginia, d. Jan 29 1964. Married May 14 1905, **Dora Mae Harper**.
781 v. Thomas Dice Moyers b. Feb 1 1885 in Cove Hancock Co., WV, d. Jun 9 1947 in Canton, Stark Co., OH, buried in Forest Hill Cem., Canton, Stark Co., OH.
Married Dec 3 1904, **Anna Bennett**, b. Oct 25 1888 in Cherry Grove, Pendleton Co., WV, d. Jun 17 1958 in Aultman, buried in Forest Hill Cem., Canton, Stark Co., OH.
782 vi. Levie Lillian Moyers b. Jan 22 1888, d. Oct 10 1926. She Married **Harness Sponaugle**.
783 vii. Zernia Moyers b. Jun 30 1890 in West Virginia, d. Jul 21 1968, buried in Forest Hill Cem., Canton, Stark Co., OH. Married Sep 1914, **Miner J. Rexrode**, b. 1889 in Blue Grass Cem., Highland Co., VA, d. Oct 20 1981.
784 viii. Grover Cleveland Moyers b. Sep 5 1891 in Franklin Co., WV, d. Feb 10 1983, buried in Pleasant Valley Cem., Dennison, Tuscarawas Co., OH. (1) Married May 9 1974, **Maggie White**. (2) Married Mar 8 1919, **Cleo Catherine Stark**, b. Oct 11 1899, d. Jul 28 1973, buried in Pleasant Valley Cem., Dennison, Tuscarawas Co., OH.
785 ix. Homer Snowden Moyers b. Jan 10 1894 in West Virginia, d. Mar 1894 in West Virginia.
786 x. Bertha C. Moyers b. Jan 25 1895 in West Virginia, d. Aug 1980. She Married **Arlie Armstrong,** b. Apr 14 1899, d. May 1984.
787 xi. Lillian N. Moyers b. Jul 4 1898 in West Virginia.
+ 788 xii. Levi Lillian Moyers.

243. **George W.[4] Waybright** (36.Miles[3], 5.Rebecca[2] Arbogast, 1.John C.[1]), b. Oct 25 1857 in Pendleton Co., WV, d. Oct 12 1921.
Married Jan 12 1887, **Loretta Florence Hevener**.

Children:

789 i. Mildred[5] Waybright d. 1993.

247. **Isaac N.[4] Arbogast** (39.Cain[3], 6.Joseph E.[2], 1.John C.[1]) (See marriage to number 221.)

252. **Sidney Ellen[4] Arbogast** (39.Cain[3], 6.Joseph E.[2], 1.John C.[1]) (See marriage to number 150.)

253. **Hannah Susan Gertrude[4] Arbogast** (39.Cain[3], 6.Joseph E.[2], 1.John C.[1]) (See marriage to number 152.)

257. **Lucinda[4] Arbogast** (40.Lemuel[3], 6.Joseph E.[2], 1.John C.[1]), b. May 1 1840 in Churchville, Pendleton Co., WV, d. Mar 31 1913 in Blue Grass, Highland Co., WV. (1) Married Oct 1 1857 in Pendleton Co., WV, **Morgan Waybright** (See marriage to number 35). (2) She Married **George E. M. Chew**, b. About 1841 in Crabbottom, Highland Co., VA (son of Joseph L. Chew and Mary "Polly" Arbogast), d. in Crabbottom, Highland Co., VA.

Children *by Morgan Waybright:*
(See marriage to number 35)

Children *by George E. M. Chew:*

\+ 790 vii. Saulsberry N Chew b. Dec 1879.
\+ 791 viii. Lillie May Chew b. Nov 09 1882.

259. **Martin Van Buren[4] Arbogast** (40.Lemuel[3], 6.Joseph E.[2], 1.John C.[1]), b. July 15, 1844, d. June 1928.
(1) Married Dec 08 1864 in Pendleton Co., WV, **Martha Turner**, b. 1848/1850 in Pendleton Co., WV, d. Jul 15 1890 in Pendleton Co., WV.

Children *by Martha Turner:*

\+ 792 i. Lettie Susan[5] Arbogast b. Feb 22 1871.
\+ 793 ii. Mary Jane Arbogast b. Mar 1873.
\+ 794 iii. Robert Calvin Arbogast b. Jan 01 1876.
795 iv. Adam Lorrington Arbogast b. Jun 02 1884, d. Mar 1975.

(2) He Married **Martha Ellen Helmick**. **Martha**: Daughter of Joseph Helmick and Amanda Melvina Wilfong.

Children *by Martha Ellen Helmick:*

\+ 796 v. Roberta Arbogast b. Feb 02 1892.
797 vi. Bessie Arbogast b. Apr 01 1893 in Pendleton Co., WV, d. Dec 22 1967.
798 vii. Virginia C. Arbogast b. Apr 29 1894 in Pendleton Co., WV.
799 viii. James W Arbogast b. Apr 23 1895 in Pendleton Co., WV.
800 ix. Benjamin H Arbogast b. Jun 01 1896 in Pendleton Co., WV, d. Feb 17 1939.
801 x. Nada Ann Arbogast b. Sep 16 1897 in Pendleton Co., WV.
802 xi. Ada May Arbogast b. Feb 02 1899 in Pendleton Co., WV.
803 xii. Odie Arbogast b. Feb 02 1899 in Pendleton Co., WV.
804 xiii. Walter J Arbogast b. Apr 14 1900 in Pendleton Co., WV.
805 xiv. Lemuel J Arbogast b. Apr 07 1902 in Pendleton Co., WV, d. Aug 26 1965.
806 xv. Rosa Lee Arbogast b. Dec 07 1903 in Pendleton Co., WV.
807 xvi. Herbert R Arbogast b. Oct 27 1907 in Pendleton Co., WV.
808 xvii. Peachie S Arbogast b. Jan 06 1911 in Pendleton Co., WV.
809 xviii. Martin V Arbogast b. Dec 10 1915 in Pendleton Co., WV, d. Apr 16 1971.
810 xix. Ellen T Arbogast b. Dec 10 1915 in Pendleton Co., WV, d. Apr 16 1971.
\+ 811 xx. Bess Ann Arbogast.

267. **Jacob A.[4] Arbogast** (40.Lemuel[3], 6.Joseph E.[2], 1.John C.[1]), b. May 4, 1864, d. October 14, 1932.
He Married **Louella F. Warner Arbogast**.

Children*:*

812 i. Essa[5] Arbogast b. March 8, 1888, d. September 10, 1902.
813 ii. Don N. Arbogast b. April 25, 1890, d. December 7, 1893.
\+ 814 iii. Samuel Arbogast b. May 7, 1903.

269. **Alfred T.[4] Arbogast** (40.Lemuel[3], 6.Joseph E.[2], 1.John C.[1]), b. April 30, 1869, d. March 29, 1956.
Married November 17, 1892, **Sarah E. Wyant Arbogast**, b. October 17, 1873, d. January 18, 1853.

Children*:*

815 i. Chloe[5] Arbogast b. September 10, 1893, d. September 7, 1978.

No children.
She Married **Don Bennett**, b. Sep 1888, d. May 20 1941.

+ 816 ii. Don Arbogast b. December 21, 1894.
+ 817 iii. Grace Arbogast b. September 6, 1901.
818 iv. Marlin Arbogast b. October 6, 1904, d. 1989.
+ 819 v. Argie Arbogast b. April 22, 1908.
820 vi. Bonnie Arbogast b. May 24, 1918, d. December 27, 1924.
+ 821 vii. Marlin Arbogast b. Oct-06-1904.

270. **Hannah Elizabeth[4] Arbogast** (42.Joseph Elili[3], 6.Joseph E.[2], 1.John C.[1]), b. Dec 30 1856 in Pendleton Co., WV, d. May 18 1933 in Pendleton Co., WV.
Married Oct 27 1891 in Pendleton Co., WV, **Norval Luther Johnston**, b. Sept 1843.

Children:

+ 822 i. Ada M.[5] Arbogast.
823 ii. Katie S. Arbogast b. About 1906.

272. **Mary Jane[4] Arbogast** (42.Joseph Elili[3], 6.Joseph E.[2], 1.John C.[1]), b. April 1856 in Pendleton Co., WV.
Married Sep 8 1883 in Pendleton Co., WV, **Matthew Helmick**, b. 1844.

Children:

+ 824 i. Tallahassee[5] Helmick.

273. **Ruth Ellen[4] Arbogast** (42.Joseph Elili[3], 6.Joseph E.[2], 1.John C.[1]), b. Apr 1 1862 in Pendleton Co., WV, d. Jun 20 1956 in Pendleton Co., WV.
She Married **Adam H. Vandevender**.

Children:

825 i. Lula Kate[5] Vandevender b. About 1883.
+ 826 ii. Wayne Sylvester Vandevender b. About 1885.
827 iii. Betty Alice Vandevender b. Oct 1888.
828 iv. Jacob Jay Vandevender b. May 1892.
829 v. Jesse James Vandevender b. Oct 7 1898 in Pendleton Co., WV, d. Jun 10 1987 in Pendleton Co., WV.

274. **Elijah J.[4] Arbogast** (42.Joseph Elili[3], 6.Joseph E.[2], 1.John C.[1]), b. Feb 14 1865 in Pendleton Co., WV, d. Jul 12 1954 in Pendleton Co., WV.
Married Mar 31 1887 in Pendleton Co., WV, **Roberta Prudence Arbaugh**, b. Dec 25 1868 in Pendleton Co., WV (daughter of Jacob Arbaugh and Susan Tingler Kimble), d. May 9 1945 in Pendleton Co., WV.

Children:

+ 830 i. Lula[5] Arbogast b. May 15 1891.
+ 831 ii. Truman Arbogast b. May 15 1891.
+ 832 iii. Bertie Kate Arbogast b. Jun 1 1893.
+ 833 iv. Leona Arbogast b. Aug 18 1899.
834 v. John M. Arbogast b. Apr 1 1901 in Pendleton Co., WV, d. Feb 7 1982 in Pendleton Co., WV. Married Aug 23 1939 in Pendleton Co., WV, **Nora Belle Mullenax,** b. May 9 1895 in Pendleton Co., WV, d. Feb 26 1976 in Pendleton Co., WV.
+ 835 vi. Richard Vosler Arbogast b. Sep 9 1903.
836 vii. Boyd Leo Arbogast b. Nov 2 1906 in Pendleton Co., WV, d. Dec 29 1953 in Pendleton Co., WV. Married May 8 1940 in Pendleton Co., WV, **Wanda Lee Vandevander**, b. Jan 20 1923 in Pendleton Co., WV, d. Jun 29 1991 in Randolph Co., WV.
+ 837 viii. Anna Arbogast b. Sep 15 1909.
838 ix. Russell Arbogast b. Nov 5 1912 in Pendleton Co., WV, d. Jan 13 1920 in Pendleton Co., WV.

275. **Hannah Catharine[4] Bennett** (43.Sidney Dean[3] Arbogast, 6.Joseph E.[2], 1.John C.[1]), b. Feb 1 1852 in Pendleton Co., WV, b. Feb 1 1852 in Pendleton Co., WV, d. Feb 5 1915 in Upper Tract, Pendleton Co., WV, d. Feb 5 1915 in Upper Tract, Pendleton Co., WV.
. 12 children. Married ABT 1877 in Pendleton Co., WV,
Married, **Winfield Scott Calhoun**, b. Aug 16 1852 in Pendleton Co., WV, b, d. Nov 12 1914 in Upper Tract, Pendleton Co., WV, d..

Children:

+ 839 i. William Cecil[5] Calhoun b. DEC 1871.

840	ii.	Martin Dow Calhoun b. Jul 31 1873 in Pendleton Co., WV, d. May 17 1961 in Kline, Pendleton Co., WV. Married Oct 21 1896 in Pendleton Co., WV, **Rachel Ann Graham**.
841	iii.	Dora D Calhoun b. Jan 31 1875 in Pendleton Co., WV, d. Nov 6 1885 in Pendleton Co., WV.
+ 842	iv.	Nina Beth Calhoun b. Jan 12 1877.
843	v.	Carrol F Calhoun b. Dec 12 1878 in Pendleton Co., WV, d. Dec 14 1878 in Pendleton Co., WV.
844	vi.	Ethel G Calhoun b. Dec 31 1879 in Pendleton Co., WV, d. Oct 10 1880 in Pendleton Co., WV.
845	vii.	Eddie Kate Calhoun b. Sep 2 1881 in Kline, Pendleton Co., WV, d. Feb 21 1906 in Kline, Pendleton Co., WV. Married Nov 20 1897 in Kline, Pendleton Co., WV, **John Harmon**.
846	viii.	Ruby W Calhoun b. Feb 22 1884 in Pendleton Co., WV, d. Feb 24 1884 in Pendleton Co., WV.
847	ix.	Fredrick Clinton Calhoun b. Aug 7 1885 in Kline, Pendleton Co., WV, d. Feb 27 1963 in Oswayo, Potter Co., PA. Married Oct 3 1907 in West Virginia, **Mary Elizabeth Helmick**.
848	x.	Ernest Click Calhoun Calhoun b. Feb 28 1887 in Mozer, Pendleton Co., WV, d. Oct 15 1943 in Friendship, Allegany Co., NY. Married Jun 14 1911 in Pendleton Co., WV, **Myrtle Jane Armentrout**.
849	xi.	Summers Ford Calhoun b. Jun 15 1888 in Pendleton Co., WV.
850	xii.	Orion Otteniton Calhoun b. Aug 21 1895 in Pendleton Co., WV.

279. **Christina[4] Arbogast** (45.Sylvenus[3], 6.Joseph E.[2], 1.John C.[1]), b. About 1870.
She Married **Charles Kemper Mauzy**.

Children:

+ 851	i.	William Whitfield[5] Mauzy b. Sep 12 1903.
+ 852	ii.	Mary Geneva Mauzy b. Apr 14 1905.
+ 853	iii.	Roscoe Mauzy b. Jan 26 1907.

285. **Nettie[4] Arbogast** (45.Sylvenus[3], 6.Joseph E.[2], 1.John C.[1]), b. Nov 30 1880 in Churchville, Pendleton Co., WV, d. Feb 17 1973 in Harrisonburg, Rockingham Co., VA.
She Married **Harry Crigler**, b. in Churchville, Pendleton Co., WV, d. May 04 1956 in Harrisonburg, Rockingham Co., VA.

Children:

854	i.	Golda[5] Crigler.
855	ii.	Virgil Crigler.
856	iii.	Edgar Crigler.
857	iv.	Harry Crigler.
858	v.	Richard Crigler.

288. **William Bailey[4] Kerr** (51.Hannah V.[3] Arbogast, 7.Moses[2], 1.John C.[1]), b. 1847 in Barbour Co., WV, d. May 14 1918 in Randolph Co., WV.
Middle name and date of death and marriage from family records of Betty Jane Lewis of Beverly, WV, in Allegheny Regional Family History Society Ancestor Charts.
Married by Rev. John Rexroad.
Ref: Randolph 1991: 94; information from great granddaughter, Margaret (Kerr) Beckwith.
Married May 31 1872 in Barbour Co., WV, **Mary Elizabeth Burner**, b. Mar 4 1849 in Barbour Co., WV (daughter of Morgan Burner and Sarah Baker), d. May 8 1898 in Elkins, Randolph Co., WV. Source is family records of Betty Jane (Kerr) Lewis of Beverly, WV. Daughter of Morgan H. and Sarah Ann (Baker) Burner.
Ref: Names of parents from granddaughter Betty Jane Kerr Lewis
.

Children:

859	i.	Anna Valina[5] Kerr b. 1873 in Barbour Co., WV. She Married **(unknown) Weese.**
860	ii.	Alden Ernest Kerr b. 1874 in Barbour Co., WV.
861	iii.	Luda Jane Kerr b. 1877 in Barbour Co., WV. She Married **(unknown) Maxon**.
+ 862	iv.	Orville Erry Kerr b. Dec 15 1880.
863	v.	Grover William Kerr b. 1881.
864	vi.	Walter Thurman Kerr b. 1888.

315. **Jacob G.[4] Ware** (57.Rachel E.[3] Arbogast, 7.Moses[2], 1.John C.[1]), b. Oct 5 1869, d. Nov 3 1947.
He Married **Sarah M Hamrick**, b. Oct 7 1873, d. SEP 1969.

Children:

865	i.	Spencer[5] Ware.

866 ii. Walker Gay Ware b. Apr 2 1901, d. Apr 10 1970. He Married Ora Lee Ware.
867 iii. Herbert P. Ware.
868 iv. Roy Ware. He Married **Retha Waybright** (daughter of Bricel Waybright and Dollie Vorden Fansler).

322. **Thomas J.[4] Simmons** (59.Sarah Elizabeth[3] Arbogast, 7.Moses[2], 1.John C.[1]), b. 1881 in Randolph Co., WV.
He Married **Mary Simmons**.

Children:

869 i. Robert[5] Simmons.
870 ii. Mae Simmons.
871 iii. Clarence Simmons.
872 iv. Arson Clinton Simmons b. Aug 27 1898, d. Aug 22 1983. Married Dec 30 1922,

326. **Eva Jane[4] Arbogast** (60.Moses Wamsley[3], 7.Moses[2], 1.John C.[1]), b. Apr 3 1875 in Valley Head, Randolph Co., WV, b. Apr 3 1875, d. Feb 23 1964 in Valley Bend, Randolph Co., WV, buried Feb 25 1964 in Valley Head, Randolph Co., WV.
She Married **Spencer Dorfice Channell**, b. May 19 1874, d. Feb 15 1942.

Children:

\+ 873 i. Birdie Cleo[5] Channell b. Feb 18 1902.

330. **Samuel Henry[4] Arbogast** (61.John B. (Jack)[3], 7.Moses[2], 1.John C.[1]) (See marriage to number 162.)

333. **Francis M[4] Arbogast** (63.Adam Jr.[3], 8.Adam Sr.[2], 1.John C.[1]), b. May 26 1854 in Highland Co., VA, d. Aft 1932. Per 1860-1880 Lewis Co. census. (1st of 13 children). Maybe died in OH
Married Nov 23 1876 in Lewis Co., WV, **Josephine Cawthon**, b. Apr 1860 in Pendleton or Lewis Co., VA, d. Aft 1935.**Josephine**: 1900 Lewis Co census reflect Married 23 yrs, 10 children, 10 living, Nee Josephine Cawthon. HH 194/195 Court House District 60 . In 1930 lived in PA per her brothers Obit. In 1935 lived in OH per her sister, Mary's obit.

Children:

\+ 874 i. Louisa May[5] Arbogast b. May 29 1877.
875 ii. Lucy Ellen Arbogast b. Dec 1878 in Lewis Co., WV.
876 iii. Watson Arbogast b. Sep 1881 in Lewis Co., WV.
\+ 877 iv. Elizabeth Ann Arbogast b. Sep 1884.
878 v. Ella Lucile (Eller) Arbogast b. Oct 1886 in Lewis Co., WV. Married Oct 26 1904 in Lewis Co., WV, **James Stewart Johnson**, b. 1878 in Kanawha Co., WV.
879 vi. Bessie Arbogast b. Jul 22 1888 in Lewis Co., WV.
880 vii. Earl Arbogast b. Sep 1890 in Lewis Co., WV.
881 viii. Jessie Arbogast b. Nov 1892 in Lewis Co., WV.
882 ix. Ora Arbogast b. May 11 1895 in Lewis Co., WV.
883 x. Grace Arbogast b. Jul 1897 in Lewis Co., WV.
884 xi. Oswald Arbogast b. Jul 4 1901 in Lewis Co., WV.
885 xii. Thelma Arbogast b. Jul 20 1903 in Lewis Co., WV.

336. **Mary Susan[4] Arbogast** (63.Adam Jr.[3], 8.Adam Sr.[2], 1.John C.[1]), b. 1859-1860 in Highland Co., VA, d. 1946 in Glenville, Gilmer Co., WV, buried in Union Turner Cem. Gilmer Co., WV.
At time of her death she lived with son, Elmer, in Glenville, WV.
Married Mar 24 1881 in Lewis Co., WV, **William Howard Cawthon**, b. 1858-1859 in Pendleton Co., WV, d. Jan 1919 in Hardman, Gilmer Co., WV, buried in Union Turner Cem. Gilmer Co., WV.

Children:

\+ 886 i. Luty (Lutie) Ester[5] Cawthon b. Feb 19 1882.
\+ 887 ii. Oleva (Levy) Alice Cawthon b. Mar 3 1885.
\+ 888 iii. Burna (Berna) Mary Cawthon b. Apr 11 1886.
\+ 889 iv. John Florent Cawthon b. Mar 5 1888.
\+ 890 v. Anna Susan (Bridget) Cawthon b. Nov 11 1889.
\+ 891 vi. Elmer Ray Cawthon b. Mar 16 1892.
\+ 892 vii. Elbert Clay Cawthon b. Mar 16 1892.
\+ 893 viii. Lona Elizabeth Cawthon b. Mar 6 1898.
894 ix. Myrtle Edith Cawthon b. Jul 6 1902 in Lewis Co., WV, d. Oct 1936 in Letter Gap, Gilmer Co., WV, buried in Union Turner Cem. Gilmer Co., WV.

Obit in (Ind. Wed. 28 Oct 1936). "Miss Myrtle Cawthon of Letter Gap died several days ago. Sister of Mrs. Berna O'Hara and Elbert Cawthon of this city". Have picture.

347. **Saulsbury[4] Arbogast** (66.Peter William[3], 8.Adam Sr.[2], 1.John C.[1]), b. Mar 1865 in Pendleton Co., WV, d. Aft 1900 in Grant Co., WV.
Married February 29, 1892 in Grant Co., WV, **Mary Burgess**, b. Aug 1856, d. Aft 1900.

Children:

895 i. (unknown)[5] Arbogast b. Feb 05 1892.
896 ii. Claude Arbogast b. May 01 1895, d. Dec 1975 in Elkins, Randolph Co., WV.
897 iii. May Arbogast b. May 1898.

348. **Kenton[4] Arbogast** (66.Peter William[3], 8.Adam Sr.[2], 1.John C.[1]), b. December 21, 1867. He Married **Sarah M. Rohrbaugh**, b. February 27, 1870.

Children:

898 i. Mary A.[5] Arbogast b. Jan 1887.
899 ii. Peter Christian Arbogast b. Mar 28 1890, d. Jul 1967 in Petersburg, Grant Co., WV.
He Married Estella Susan Turner, b. Aug 03 1885, d. Oct 30 1948.
\+ 900 iii. Dollie Ethel Arbogast b. November 24, 1898.

352. **Tecumseh Sherman[4] Ketterman** (78.Nicholas Harper[3], 9.Mary Ann[2] Arbogast, 1.John C.[1]), b. Apr 17 1866, d. July, 1955.
He Married **Emma Kirby**, b. in Summer Twp., Kankakee Co., IL, d. May 1909.

Children:

\+ 901 i. Daffel[5] Ketterman b. 28 Jun 1892.
902 ii. Bessie Elizabeth Ketterman b. 6 Mar 1894, d. Apr 1965.
They have six children, mostly living.
She Married **Marion Hobbs**.
903 iii. Earl Ketterman b. 27 Mar 1897, d. 1914.
904 iv. Mildred Ketterman b. 17 Sep 1900.
\+ 905 v. Miles Ketterman b. 19 Jan 1904.
\+ 906 vi. Rudy Ketterman b. 17 Mar 1906.
907 vii. Keith Ketterman b. 2 May 1909, d. 1919.
908 viii. Kenneth Ketterman b. 2 May 1909, d. 2 May 1909.

353. **Lena Leona[4] Ketterman** (78.Nicholas Harper[3], 9.Mary Ann[2] Arbogast, 1.John C.[1]), b. Dec 13 1868 in McLean Co., IL, d. Apr 24 1958 in Richmond Beach, King Co., WA.
She Married **George Allen Colaw**, b. 23 Nov 1867 in McLean Co., IL, d. 22 Apr 1950 in McLean Co., IL.

Children:

\+ 909 i. Harvey William[5] Colaw b. 7 Jul 1888.
\+ 910 ii. Hazel Dell Colaw b. 16 Aug 1892.

355. **Bertha Viola[4] Ketterman** (78.Nicholas Harper[3], 9.Mary Ann[2] Arbogast, 1.John C.[1]), b. Dec 30 1874, d. Apr 4 1942.
/ She Married **Alphorus Colaw**, b. Sep 19 1868 in Illinois (son of Dyer W Colaw and Mary Jane Garr), d. 1939.

Children:

\+ 911 i. Wayne[5] Colaw b. Jan 28 1897.
\+ 912 ii. Grace Colaw.
\+ 913 iii. Glen Dyer Colaw b. Apr 20 1907.
\+ 914 iv. Merle C. Colaw b. Apr 20 1907.
915 v. Dorothy Colaw b. Jan 19 1909, d. Jul 30 1984. Married Nov 1947 in Las Vegas, Clark Co., NV, **Don Jeneves**.
\+ 916 vi. Thornton Colaw b. May 19 1914.

356. **Paul[4] Ketterman** (78.Nicholas Harper[3], 9.Mary Ann[2] Arbogast, 1.John C.[1]), b. Dec 26 1876 in Illinois, d. Aug 13 1958 in Seattle, King Co., WA.
He Married **Mary Ellen Hopkins**, b. 12 Apr 1870, d. 26 Jul 1961.

Children:

917 i. Anthony Hugh[5] Ketterman b. 26 Oct 1900 in Carrington, Foster Co., ND.
918 ii. Paul Leo Ketterman b. 17 Jul 1902 in Carrington, Foster Co., ND, d. 23 Aug 1920.

919	iii.	Mary Isabelle Ketterman b. 26 Jul 1904 in Carrington, Foster Co., ND.
+ 920	iv.	Merle Nicholas Ketterman b. 16 Oct 1906.
921	v.	Lucile Elizabeth Ketterman b. 26 Nov 1910 in Wahpeton, Richland Co., ND, d. 26 Feb 1970 in Seattle, King Co., WA.
922	vi.	Helen Bridget Ketterman b. Aug 7 1906 in Wapetin, ND.
923	vii.	Bertha Victoria Ketterman b. Jul 26 1914 in St Paul, MN, Married. Married in Sunnyside, WA, J. M. Berg.

357. **Hannah J.[4] Ketterman** (79.John George[3], 9.Mary Ann[2] Arbogast, 1.John C.[1]) (See marriage to number 102.)

358. **Ida V.[4] Ketterman** (81.Sarah[3], 9.Mary Ann[2] Arbogast, 1.John C.[1]), b. Oct 1864.
This couple may have been divorced by 1900. There is no explanation why their children are not Sponaugle or why one is Harman.
Married 1907 in Rockingham Co., VA, **Jacob Sponaugle**.

Children:

924	i.	Benjamin[5] Katterman b. 1883.
925	ii.	Blaine Ketterman b. 1886.
926	iii.	Bertha Harman b. 1894.
927	iv.	Grace Ketterman b. June 1898. Married Apr 12 1921, **Lester Landis**, b. About 1892 in Grant Co., WV.

372. **Washington Sherman[4] Arbogast** (84.George Washington[3], 10.John C.[2], 1.John C.[1]).
Married Mar 4- 1888, **Roxannie Rosy Row**.

Children:

+ 928	i.	Viola Belle[5] Arbogast b. 2-27-1890.
929	ii.	Allena Arbogast b. About 1893.
+ 930	iii.	Leslie Herman Arbogast b. About 1895.
+ 931	iv.	Arley Arbogast b. About 1904.
932	v.	George W Arbogast b. About 1905, d. 1994.
933	vi.	Margaret Edna Arbogast b. About 1911.
934	vii.	Porter Arbogast.

375. **George McClelland[4] Arbogast** (84.George Washington[3], 10.John C.[2], 1.John C.[1]), b. Oct 1861, d. Feb 18 1945 in Barbour Co., WV. He
Married **Rachel Matthews**, b. Sep 21 1860.

Children:

+ 935	i.	Roscoe[5] Arbogast b. June 1885.
936	ii.	Lona Georgia Arbogast b. Nov 1886 in Barbour Co., WV.
+ 937	iii.	Ralph Arbogast b. Feb 1888.
+ 938	iv.	Vannie Arbogast b. Aug 1890.
+ 939	v.	Margaret Arbogast b. Apr 13 1893.
+ 940	vi.	Hannah Arbogast b. Jan 1897.
+ 941	vii.	Jennie Arbogast b. Oct 1899.

Generation Five

376. **Amos C.[5] Hedrick** (88.Christina[4] Waybright, 11.Emily[3] Arbogast, 3.Michael[2], 1.John C.[1]), b. 1862. He Married **Annie Lough**.

Children:

942	i.	Denver[6] Hedrick b. 1897.
943	ii.	Ethel Hedrick b. 1904.

378. **George Washington[5] Hedrick** (88.Christina[4] Waybright, 11.Emily[3] Arbogast, 3.Michael[2], 1.John C.[1]), b. 1868.
Married 1891, **Rosetta Burns**.

Children:

944	i.	Jullia[6] Hedrick b. 1892.
945	ii.	Sarah Alice Hedrick b. 1893.
946	iii.	Arson George Hedrick b. About 1895.

947 iv. (infant) Hedrick.
\+ 948 v. Ottie Jane Hedrick b. About 1901.
949 vi. Emmie K, Hedrick b. About 1905.
950 vii. Elva M Hedrick b. About 1907.
951 viii. Zola Hedrick b. About 1909, d. About 1952.

394. **Floyd[5] Holcomb** (93.George Washington[4] Arbogast, Jr., 12.George Washington[3], 3.Michael[2], 1.John C.[1]).
He Married **Arabell Jones**.

Children:

952 i. Mamie[6] Holcomb. She Married **William Jennings Arbogast**.

400. **Americas Deborah[5] Arbogast** (97.Nichodemus[4], 12.George Washington[3], 3.Michael[2], 1.John C.[1]), b. Nov 25 1892 in Clay Co., WV, d. Dec 31 1921 in Clay Co., WV.
Married Aug 19 1923, **Marcellus Elmore Morrison**, b. Jul 10 1885 in Corley, Braxton Co., WV (daughter of Benjamin Wesley Morrison and Francis Adeline Delaney), d. Jul 19 1962 in Gassaway, Braxton Co., WV.

Children:

953 i. Harriet[6] Morrison b. c1911 in West Virginia.
954 ii. Glen Chadwick Morrison b. c1915 in West Virginia, d. in Clendenin, Kanawha Co., WV.

405. **Minnie May[5] Arbogast** (98.Amos Cyrus[4], 12.George Washington[3], 3.Michael[2], 1.John C.[1]), b. Jan 20 1894, d. 1953.
She Married **James Garfield Smith**, d. 1935.

Children:

\+ 955 i. James Elloitt[6] Smith b. May 27 1922.
\+ 956 ii. Wilbur Amos Smith b. May 05 1923.
\+ 957 iii. Wavie Smith b. Feb 16 1925.
\+ 958 iv. Oliver Irvin Smith b. May 31 1927.
959 v. Alcha Smith. She Married **Ervin Samples**.
\+ 960 vi. Robert Q Smith.
\+ 961 vii. Alpha Smith.

407. **Mary[5] Arbogast** (98.Amos Cyrus[4], 12.George Washington[3], 3.Michael[2], 1.John C.[1]), b. Jun 7 1898, d. Feb 15 1971.
She Married **Ace A. Hughes**, b. Apr 22 1882 in Vaughn, Nicholas Co., WV. **Ace**: Son of Thomas Hughes.

Children:

\+ 962 i. Juanita[6] Hughes b. Apr 01 1923.
\+ 963 ii. Amos Hughes b. Mar 11 1924.
964 iii. Cellia Hughes b. Aug 24 1926.
965 iv. Minnie Hughes b. Mar 25 1928, d. Oct 1972.
\+ 966 v. Ethel Hughes b. Feb 03 1931.
\+ 967 vi. William Thomas Hughes b. Mar 14 1933.
\+ 968 vii. Magie Hughes b. May 05 1936.
969 viii. Berenice Hughes b. Aug 21 1937.

408. **Glendora[5] Arbogast** (98.Amos Cyrus[4], 12.George Washington[3], 3.Michael[2], 1.John C.[1]), b. Mar 23 1899, d. Aug 1987.
Married 1922, **Odie J. Turner**, d. 1958.

Children:

970 i. Odie[6] Turner, Jr..
971 ii. Melvin Turner.
972 iii. Calvin Turner.
973 iv. Crystal Turner. She Married **John Holcomb**.
974 v. Naomi Turner. She Married **Robert Hewitt**.
975 vi. Sylvia Turner.
976 vii. Paul Turner.
977 viii. Roy Turner.
\+ 978 ix. James Turner.

409. **Faye Elvira[5] Arbogast** (98.Amos Cyrus[4], 12.George Washington[3], 3.Michael[2], 1.John C.[1]), b. Apr 3 1901, d. Oct 02 1935 in Cincinnati, Hamilton Co., OH, buried in Baltimore Park Cem., Sect 7 #321,Cincinnati, OH. (

1) She Married **William Robert Eades**, b. Apr 07 1889 in Saratoga Co., NY, d. Jan 19 1940 in Cincinnati, Hamilton Co., OH. **William**: Son of William Robert Edas and Eliza Marie Williams.

***Children** by William Robert Eades:*

+ 979 i. Charles Joseph[6] Eades b. Jul 02 1929.
+ 980 ii. Amos Cyrus Eades b. Feb 27 1931.

(2) She Married **Eugene Price**.

***Children** by Eugene Price:*

+ 981 iii. William Leonard Arbogast.

410. **Jessie Sarah[5] Arbogast** (98.Amos Cyrus[4], 12.George Washington[3], 3.Michael[2], 1.John C.[1]), b. Mar 03 1903, d. Mar 16 1929. She Married **Okey Berton Neal**, b. 1898 in Vaughn, Nicholas Co., WV, d. Dec 11 1958 in Logan, Fayette Co., WV. **Okey**: Son of John Neal and Catherine C. Brown.

***Children**:*

+ 982 i. Denver McDonald[6] Neal b. Jun 11 1920.
+ 983 ii. Violet Gustava Neal b. Sep 14 1921.
+ 984 iii. Johnny R. Neal b. Mar 30 1923.
+ 985 iv. Oprha Naomi Neal b. Aug 11 1925.
986 v. Ruth Pauline Neal b. Feb 23 1927 in Bickmore, Clay Co., WV, d. Jul 23 1958.

411. **Joseph Monroe[5] Arbogast** (98.Amos Cyrus[4], 12.George Washington[3], 3.Michael[2], 1.John C.[1]), b. Jul 8 1906, d. Jun 18 1994. Married Oct 19 1930, **Verbe Gladys Samples**, b. in Paxton, Clay Co., WV, d. May 22 1993 in Precious, Clay Co., WV. **Verbe**: Daughter of Abner John Samples and Laura Alice Dodd.

***Children**:*

+ 987 i. Oliver Wendell[6] Arbogast b. Oct 23 1931.
+ 988 ii. Addie Ramona Arbogast b. Oct 23 1931.
+ 989 iii. Anna May Arbogast b. Jun 05 1935.

412. **Lucy Esta[5] Arbogast** (98.Amos Cyrus[4], 12.George Washington[3], 3.Michael[2], 1.John C.[1]), b. Apr 06 1911 in Indora, Kanawha Co., WV, d. After 1949 in Beckley, Raleigh Co., WV. She Married **Dewey W Cantley**.

***Children**:*

+ 990 i. Joyce[6] Cantley b. Apr 01 1927.
+ 991 ii. Jack Cantley b. Mar 31 1928.
992 iii. Dewey W Cantley, Jr. b. Feb 25 1929 in Big Sycamore, Clay Co., WV, d. Jun 19 1932 in Indora, Kanawha Co., WV.
+ 993 iv. Naomi Rose Cantley b. Jun 15 1937.
+ 994 v. Carolyn Cantley b. Feb 14 1946.
+ 995 vi. Brenda Cantley b. Sep 04 1947.

421. **Joanna[5] Shreve** (102.Benjamin "Little Ben"[4], 13.Mary Magdalene.[3] Arbogast, 3.Michael[2], 1.John C.[1]), b. 1874, d. 1963. She Married **Andrew Berkley Shreves**, b. 1868.

***Children**:*

+ 996 i. Orpha Gladys[6] Shreves b. Nov 11 1901.
997 ii. Austin Shreves.
998 iii. Emma Florence Shreves.
999 iv. Roda Shreves.
1000 v. Lucy Shreves.
1001 vi. Ethel Shreves.
1002 vii. Ottis Shreves.
1003 viii. Ona Shreves.
1004 ix. Andy Shreves.

435. **Anna[5] Helmick** (103.Edith Jane[4] Shreve, 13.Mary Magdalene.[3] Arbogast, 3.Michael[2], 1.John C.[1]). She Married **Joe Kimble**.

***Children**:*

1005 i. Mary Jane[6] Kimble. She Married **Homar Propst**.
1006 ii. Victor Kimble.

1007 iii. Margie Kimble. She Married **Jake Hinkle**.

441. **Rumsey Smithson**[5] **Davis** (107.Jethro[4], 14.Christina[3] Arbogast, 3.Michael[2], 1.John C.[1]), b. Apr 1880. He Married **Rosa C. Pennington**.

Children:

\+ 1008 i. Nellie[6] Davis b. Apr 26 1910.

450. **Acinith Lieuticia**[5] **Markle** (117.Sarah D.[4] Arbogast, 15.Nichodemus[3], 3.Michael[2], 1.John C.[1]), b. Sep 08 1883 in Elkhurst, Clay Co., WV, d. Jan 18 1979 in Medina, Medina Co., OH. Married Dec 30 1904, **Luther Aras Reedy**, b. Feb 26 1880 in Nicholas Co., WV, d. Feb 23 1961 in Elkhurst, Clay Co., WV.

Children:

\+ 1009 i. Mabel Perl[6] Reedy b. Aug 26 1903.

1010 ii. Estella Freda Reedy b. Mar 01 1906 in Indora, Kanawha Co., WV, d. Sep 12. She Married **Cecil Westfall**, d. Feb 22 1962.

1011 iii. Agnus Beatrice Reedy b. Mar 02 1908. She Married **Harold Jefferies**, d. Aug 04 1969.

\+ 1012 iv. Donnie Fern Reedy b. Sep 08 1908.

1013 v. William Herman Reedy b. Mar 21 1912, d. Aug 06 1966. He Married **Iva Woods** Legg, d. Oct 31 1988.

1014 vi. Opal Mae Reedy b. Feb 12 1914. Married Jun 16 1935, **Leonard Moore**, d. Oct 07 1977.

1015 vii. (infant) Reedy b. 1916, d. 1916.

1016 viii. Zelma Zela Reedy b. Aug 26 1918, d. Apr 22 1963. She Married G**randville Montgomery.**

\+ 1017 ix. Olive Doris Reedy b. Jan 05 1927.

457. **Watson A**[5] **Arbogast** (119.George Franklin[4], 15.Nichodemus[3], 3.Michael[2], 1.John C.[1]), b. Sep 17 1884 in Clay Co., WV, d. Nov 26 1949.
He Married **Martha Justice**.

Children:

\+ 1018 i. Inez[6] Arbogast.

459. **Albert Lee**[5] **Arbogast** (119.George Franklin[4], 15.Nichodemus[3], 3.Michael[2], 1.John C.[1]), b. Mar 27 1889 in Logan, Fayette Co., WV, d. Oct 29 1968.
Married Dec 02 1916, **Harriet Bumpus**, b. Apr 10 1898, d. Feb 12 1972 in Charleston, Kanawha Co., WV.

Children:

\+ 1019 i. Alberta Maxine[6] Arbogast b. Jan 20 1921.

\+ 1020 ii. Donald R Arbogast b. Oct 03 1924.

\+ 1021 iii. Lois Jean Arbogast b. Oct 15 1927.

\+ 1022 iv. William Bert Arbogast b. 1930.

460. **Joseph Martin**[5] **Arbogast** (119.George Franklin[4], 15.Nichodemus[3], 3.Michael[2], 1.John C.[1]), b. Jun 27 1890 in Clay Co., WV, d. Jun 08 1973 in Brooksville, Hernando Co., FL.
He Married **Hattie Ethel Adkins**, b. Mar 30 1892 in Roane Co., WV, d. Jun 12 1973 in Tampa, Pasco Co., FL.

Children:

1023 i. Herbert[6] Arbogast b. 1914, d. 1916.

\+ 1024 ii. Milton Brown Arbogast b. Aug 11 1916.

\+ 1025 iii. Francis Vivian Arbogast b. Dec 08 1917.

\+ 1026 iv. Masel Arbogast b. 1919.

1027 v. Emma Opal Arbogast b. Jul 21 1921, d. Apr 11 1987 in Port Clinton, Ottawa Co., OH. She Married **Richard Paul Cooper**.

\+ 1028 vi. Maggie Jo Arbogast b. 1926.

\+ 1029 vii. Ethel Malinda Arbogast b. Apr 12 1927.

\+ 1030 viii. Ralph Martin Arbogast b. Feb 17 1929.

\+ 1031 ix. Clarissa Velma Arbogast b. Mar 17 1931.

\+ 1032 x. George Lee Arbogast b. Feb 10 1939.

462. **Sarah Alice**[5] **Arbogast** (119.George Franklin[4], 15.Nichodemus[3], 3.Michael[2], 1.John C.[1]), b. May 22 1896, d. Aug 23 1959, buried in Arbogast Cem., Beech Ridge, Clay Co., WV. She Married **John Berton Perkins**, b. Oct 11 1898, d. Aug 08 1969 in Charleston, Kanawha Co., WV, buried in Arbogast Cem., Beech Ridge, Clay Co., WV. **John**: Son of David Perkins and Mary E. Gillespie.

Children:

1033 i. James Leanord^{6} Perkins b. Nov 18 1924 in Charleston, Kanawha Co., WV. He Married **Nadine Dye**. Daughter of Everett S. Dye and Georgia Robison.

\+ 1034 ii. Lucy Kathryn Perkins b. Oct 02 1926.

467. **Leona Estelle^{5} Arbogast** (119.George Franklin^{4}, 15.Nichodemus^{3}, 3.Michael^{2}, 1.John C.^{1}), b. 1910 in Elkhurst, Clay Co., WV. Married 1936, **Bernard G Conner**, b. 1909 in Charleston, Kanawha Co., WV, d. 1992 in Columbus, Franklin Co., OH.

Children:

1035 i. Beverly Kay^{6} Conner b. Mar 26 1939 in Charleston, Kanawha Co., WV.

1036 ii. Bernard Lee Conner b. Jun 10 1946 in Charleston, Kanawha Co., WV.

468. **Fred Lee^{5} Arbogast** (121.Thomas^{4} Arbogast, 15.Nichodemus^{3}, 3.Michael^{2}, 1.John C.^{1}), b. May 25 1890, d. Feb 09 1972. Married Nov 18 1912, **Martha Mae Hilton Seibert**, b. Apr 16 1891, d. Aug 29 1976.

Children:

\+ 1037 i. Louella Francis^{6} Arbogast b. Dec 28 1913.

\+ 1038 ii. Florence Doris Arbogast b. Sep 05 1915.

\+ 1039 iii. Samuel Roy Arbogast b. Apr 09 1918.

\+ 1040 iv. Bernard Fredrick Arbogast b. Jan 20 1920.

\+ 1041 v. Stewart Franklin Arbogast b. Dec 01 1922.

1042 vi. Maggie Madeline Arbogast b. Jul 01 1925.

1043 vii. Paul Raymond Arbogast b. Nov 28 1929.

469. **Robert L.^{5} Arbogast** (121.Thomas^{4}, 15.Nichodemus^{3}, 3.Michael^{2}, 1.John C.^{1}), b. Feb 16, 1916 in Blue Creek, Kanawha Co., WV, d. Feb 27, 1977 in Linwood, Delaware Co., PA.
Married June 14, 1946 in Charleston, Kanawha Co., WV, **Virginia Goldie Burgess**, b. 3/12/1924 in Sanderson, Kanawha Co., WV.

Children:

\+ 1044 i. Ginger Lynn^{6} Arbogast b. Apr 18 1947.

1045 ii. Victoria Susan Arbogast b. Dec 26, 1949 in Blue Creek, Kanawha Co., WV, d. Sept 1990 in Newark, New Castle Co., DE.

1046 iii. Sandra Rea Arbogast b. Jun 14 1951.

\+ 1047 iv. Venisa Robina Arbogast b. May 16 1954.

1048 v. Jody Caroline Arbogast b. Jun 05 1965.

477. **Harvey^{5} Keller** (128.Emily Catharine^{4} Arbogast, 16.Michael^{3}, 3.Michael^{2}, 1.John C.^{1}), b. Jan 27 1868, d. Jun 13 1918. Married Jan 12 1893 in Waldo, Russell Co., KS, **Nora Bell Reitzel**, b. Jan 2 1875 in Hendricks Co., IN, d. Nov 10 1959.

Children:

\+ 1049 i. Roy Everett^{6} Keller b. Oct 18 1896.

1050 ii. Ray B. Keller b. Sep 12 1899 in Kansas, d. Jan 1 1989.

1051 iii. Oren G. Keller b. Jun 12 1904, d. Feb 11 1990. He Married **Rosalie Senesac.**

479. **Willias Thomas^{5} Keller** (128.Emily Catharine^{4} Arbogast, 16.Michael^{3}, 3.Michael^{2}, 1.John C.^{1}), b. Aug 2 1874 in Numa, Appanoose Co., IA, d. Jun 1 1950 in Coeur d'Alene, Kootenai Co., ID. Married Oct 11 1900 in Kansas, **Bertha Blagrave**.

Children:

1052 i. Ada^{6} Keller b. Sep 12 1905 in Idaho, d. Jun 6 1920.

\+ 1053 ii. Willis Leroy Keller b. Jul 27 1914.

1054 iii. Clara Keller.

1055 iv. Lester Keller b. in Kansas. Married Apr 20 1904 in Coeur d'Alene, Kootenai Co., ID, **Neita C. Anderson**.

482. **Leander Frank^{5} Keller** (128.Emily Catharine^{4} Arbogast, 16.Michael^{3}, 3.Michael^{2}, 1.John C.^{1}), b. in Kansas. He Married **Lenora (Unknown)**, b. c 1872.

Children:

\+ 1056 i. Opel J.^{6} Keller.

487. **Glen Elmer^{5} Keller** (128.Emily Catharine^{4} Arbogast, 16.Michael^{3}, 3.Michael^{2}, 1.John C.^{1}), b. Aug 19 1888, d. Feb 8 1959. Married Nov 19 1920, **Gertie Ortina Russom**, b. Mar 5 1904, d. Mar 8 1990.

Children:

1057 i. Marie Jane[6] Keller b. Sep 16 1921, d. May 20 1997.
1058 ii. Cecil Wesley Keller b. Nov 22 1922, d. Jan 7 1945.
1059 iii. Lois Elizabeth Keller b. Jul 14 1924, d. Mar 12 1980.
1060 iv. Glen Elmer Keller b. Jan 14 1926, d. Feb 25 1972.
1061 v. Doris Irene Keller.
1062 vi. Rena Mae Keller b. Aug 4 1932, d. Feb 7 1991.

488. **Glen Elvin[5] Arbogast** (131.Stephen Douglas[4], 16.Michael[3], 3.Michael[2], 1.John C.[1]), b. Aug 31 1884 in Leon, Decatur Co., IA, d. Aug 24 1961 in Los Angeles, Los Angeles Co., CA.
Married 1908, **Emerald Lucy Barman**, b. May 30 1887 in Washington, d. Aug 3 1975 in Los Angeles, Los Angeles Co., CA.

Children:

1063 i. Wanda E.[6] Arbogast.
1064 ii. Juanita L. Arbogast.
1065 iii. Richard Elven Arbogast b. Sep 3 1912 in Los Angeles, Los Angeles Co., CA, d. Apr 17 1989 in Los Angeles, Los Angeles Co., CA.
1066 iv. Woodrow W. Arbogast.
1067 v. Dorothy M. Arbogast.
1068 vi. Grant E. Arbogast b. Aug 3 1924 in Los Angeles, Los Angeles Co., CA, d. Jul 19 1984 in Los Angeles, Los Angeles Co., CA.

490. **Daisy[5] Arbogast** (131.Stephen Douglas[4], 16.Michael[3], 3.Michael[2], 1.John C.[1]), b. Apr 25 1889 in Leon, Decatur Co., IA, d. Jul 23 1985 in Stanislaus Co., CA.
Married Jul 21 1910, **Andrew E. Hartman**, b. Jan 25 1886 in Illinois, d. Jun 24 1955 in Glendale, Los Angeles Co., CA.

Children:

1069 i. Marion[6] Hartman.
1070 ii. Ruby Jewel Hartman. She Married **Colon T. Greenlaw**.
1071 iii. Joyce May Hartman.

491. **Armilda D. "Fairy"[5] Arbogast** (131.Stephen Douglas[4], 16.Michael[3], 3.Michael[2], 1.John C.[1]), b. 1896 in Leon, Decatur Co., IA.
Married Apr 11 1918, **Marion James Skinner**, b. Jun 23 1897 in Missouri, d. Feb 5 1957 in Los Angeles, Los Angeles Co., CA.

Children:

1072 i. Melvin J.[6] Skinner.
1073 ii. Robert G. Skinner.

494. **Bertha Jane[5] Sponaugle** (145.Daniel[4], 18.Jemima Maria[3] Waybright, 4.Rachel[2] Arbogast, 1.John C.[1]), b. Mar 28 1899 in Collinsville, Rogers Co., OK.
Married Sep 16 1920, **James Elmer Finley**, b. May 25 1896 in Chetopa, Labette Co., KA, d. Sep 28 1963 in Chetopa, Labette Co., KA, buried in Oak Hill Cem., Chetopa, Labette Co., KS.

Children:

1074 i. Vernon Donald[6] Finley.
1075 ii. Irene Imogene Finley.
1076 iii. Warren Luther Finley b. 28 Sep.
1077 iv. Fredrick Lee Finley b. 28 Sep.
1078 v. Herbert Allen Finley b. Jan 2 1922.
1079 vi. Leota Nadine Finley b. Jan 26 1922 in Chetopa, Labette Co., KA.
1080 vii. Peggy Marie Finley b. Mar 26 1928.
1081 viii. Shirley Mae Finley b. Apr 22 1935 in Chetopa, Labette Co., KA, d. Sep 4 1994 in Colorado Springs, El Paso Co., CO, buried in Oak Hill Cem., Chetopa, Labette Co., KS.

501. **Don[5] Waybright** (150.Isaac P[4], 19.Jesse[3], 4.Rachel[2] Arbogast, 1.John C.[1]), b. Oct 2 1888 in Tucker Co., WV, d. Apr 1963 in Elkins, Randolph Co., WV, buried in Red Creek, Tucker Co., WV.
Married Dec 10 1909 in Garrett Co., MD, **Izabelle Teter**, b. Jun 18 1891 in Tucker Co., WV (daughter of Andrew Teter and Rachel Ann Tusing), d. 1958 in Tucker Co., WV, buried in Red Creek, Tucker Co., WV.

Children:

1082 i. Eva Pearl[6] Waybright b. Sep 9 1911 in Osceola Randolph Co., WV. She Married **Ivan Eye**.
1083 ii. Carl Waybright b. 1915 in Osceola Randolph Co., WV.

1084 iii. Jesse Willard Waybright b. Mar 26 1917 in Osceola Randolph Co., WV, d. Oct 1975, buried in Flanagan Hill Cem., Tucker Co., WV. He Married **Savannah White.**

1085 iv. Cornelia Ruth Waybright b. Jan 9 1919 in Osceola Randolph Co., WV, d. 1971.

1086 v. Alma Helen Waybright b. Jun 1919 in Osceola Randolph Co., WV.

1087 vi. Sturl Robert Waybright b. Feb 9 1921 in Osceola Randolph Co., WV. (2) He Married **Ruth Thomson**.

1088 vii. Freddie Rachel Waybright b. Jan 6 1923 in Osceola Randolph Co., WV. Married Dec 10 1945, **Thomas Lindsy Bonner**. Thomas: At the time this data was assembled this Family may have 3 living, unwed children (child), that are not included here.

1089 viii. Earl Donald Waybright b. Oct 20 1925 in Tucker Co., WV, d. 1951.

1090 ix. Erma Gertrude Waybright b. Aug 6 1927 in Tucker Co., WV. She Married **Blair Gordon.**

1091 x. Andrew Jerald Waybright b. Jun 19 1929 in Shavers Mountain, Tucker Co., WV.

504. **Zula[5] Waybright** (150.Isaac P[4], 19.Jesse[3], 4.Rachel[2] Arbogast, 1.John C.[1]), b. in Tucker Co., WV.
(1) She Married **Bill Gilmer**.
(2) She Married **Harrison Roy**.

Children *by Harrison Roy:*

1092 i. Isaac Lee[6] Roy b. Apr 21 1916, d. Sep 19 1986. He Married Pearl Marie Bright.

505. **Moses Randolph[5] Waybright** (150.Isaac P[4], 19.Jesse[3], 4.Rachel[2] Arbogast, 1.John C.[1]), b. Mar 8 1897 in Tucker Co., WV, d. Jan 20 1976. U.S. Army 2 Sep 1918----13 Dec 1918 Private Camp Lee Virginia Honorable discharge. Mose & Zelma Married 25 Jan 1927 at Webster Springs WV. Serenaded at Sarah Hamricks after wedding Cake Pop And Candy were served. Married Jan 25 1927 in Webster Springs, Webster Co., WV, **Mary Zelma Hamrick**, b. Sep 14 1909 in Webster Springs, Webster Co., WV, d. Jan. **Mary**: went by her Stepfathers name :

Children*:*

\+ 1093 i. Aluna Jean[6] Waybright b. Feb 4 1928.

506. **Ollie W.[5] Waybright** (151.James Bud[4], 19.Jesse[3], 4.Rachel[2] Arbogast, 1.John C.[1]), b. Feb 13 1877 in Pendleton Co., WV. Married Jan 2 1895 in Dry Run, Pendleton Co., WV, **Floyd Warner**, b. in Dry Run, Pendleton Co., WV, d. 1946, buried in Pendleton Co., WV.

Children*:*

\+ 1094 i. Rhoda[6] Warner b. Jan 14 1896.

1095 ii. Arlie Warner b. Jun 14 1898 in Dry Run, Pendleton Co., WV, d. Feb 13 1940 in Pendleton Co., WV, buried in Joseph Warner Cem., Pendleton Co., WV. He Married **Leona (Unknown).**

1096 iii. Royal Warner b. Jun 22 1900 in Dry Run, Pendleton Co., WV, d. Nov 1966 in Franklin Co., WV.

1097 iv. Robert J Warner b. May 24 1902 in Dry Run, Pendleton Co., WV, d. Jan 26 1995 in Red House, Putnam Co., WV.

1098 v. Verlie Warner b. Nov 25 1904 in Pendleton Co., WV, d. Jul 1969 in Franklin Co., WV.

1099 vi. Virgil Warner b. May 8 1907 in Pendleton Co., WV, d. Dec 1976.

1100 vii. Frank Warner b. 1910 in Pendleton Co., WV.

1101 viii. Russell Warner. He Married **Gretta May Waybright**, b. Oct 6 1916 in Cherry Grove, Pendleton Co., WV (daughter of Michael Waybright and Frances Warner).

507. **Anna Elizabeth[5] Waybright** (151.James Bud[4], 19.Jesse[3], 4.Rachel[2] Arbogast, 1.John C.[1]), b. Mar 21 1879 in Cherry Grove, Pendleton Co., WV, d. Oct 23 1956, buried in Bud Waybright Cem., Pendleton Co., VA/WV.
Married Jan 14 1897 in Pendleton Co., WV, **William Jackson Mullenax**, b. Jun 1 1860 in Buffalo Hills Putnam Co., WV, d. Jan 11 1936, buried in Bud Waybright Cem., Pendleton Co., VA/WV.

Children*:*

1102 i. Ruth[6] Mullenax b. in Cherry Grove, Pendleton Co., WV. She Married **Richard Warner.**

1103 ii. Violet Mullenax b. in Cherry Grove, Pendleton Co., WV.

\+ 1104 iii. Edna Mullenax b. 1899.

\+ 1105 iv. James Edward Mullenax b. Feb 13 1900.

\+ 1106 v. Judith Mullenax b. Sep 20 1901.

1107 vi. Luella Mullenax b. 1903 in Cherry Grove, Pendleton Co., WV, buried in Bud Waybright Cem., Pendleton Co., VA/WV.

1108 vii. Jared Mullenax b. Apr 11 1905 in Cherry Grove, Pendleton Co., WV.

\+ 1109 viii. Elva Mullenax b. Apr 1907.

\+ 1110 ix. Audrey Mabel Mullenax b. May 26 1909.

1111 x. John M Mullenax b. Sep 16 1913 in Pendleton Co., WV. He Married **Dorothy Dolf' Waybright,** b. Jun 17 1921 in Pendleton Co., WV (daughter of Troy Waybright and Katie Warner), d. May 20 1994.

1112 xi. Irene Jean Mullenax b. 1917 in Cherry Grove, Pendleton Co., WV. Married 1938, **Owen Jacob Raines**, b. 1913, d. 1995.

508. **Ira^{5} Waybright** (151.James Bud^{4}, 19.Jesse^{3}, 4.Rachel^{2} Arbogast, 1.John C.^{1}), b. Nov 3 1880 in Pendleton Co., WV, d. Feb 1964, buried in Puffenbarger Cem. Monterey Highland Co., VA. Married Feb 22 1903, **Mary Ettie Rexrode**, b. 1886 in Pendleton Co., WV, d. 1967, buried in Puffenbarger Cem. Monterey Highland Co., VA.

***Children**:*

1113 i. Laura^{6} Waybright b. in Pendleton Co., WV.

\+ 1114 ii. Ray Waybright b. Nov 28 1905.

\+ 1115 iii. Beulah Waybright b. Jan 5 1907.

1116 iv. Rita W. Waybright b. Jan 20 1914 in Pendleton Co., WV, d. Dec 25 1997, buried in Puffenbarger Cem. Monterey Highland Co., VA.
She Married **Ocie Rohrbaugh**.

1117 v. Amby Waybright b. Sep 14 1916 in Pendleton Co., WV, d. Jun 29 1989 in Moyers, Pendleton Co., WV, buried in Waybright Cem., Pendleton Co., WV. Married Dec 21 1942, **Margaret Virginia Whisman**.

1118 vi. Elmer James Waybright b. Feb 11 1919 in Pendleton Co., WV, d. Nov 14 1985.

1119 vii. Carl Waybright b. Sep 18 1924 in Pendleton Co., WV, d. Nov 8 1996, buried in Puffenbarger Cem. Monterey Highland Co., VA. He Married **Vadia Judy.**

509. **Michael^{5} Waybright** (151.James Bud^{4}, 19.Jesse^{3}, 4.Rachel^{2} Arbogast, 1.John C.^{1}), b. Mar 25 1883 in Pendleton Co., WV, d. Jun 19 1976 in Pendleton Co., WV, buried in Cedar Hill Cem., Pendleton Co., WV. (
1) He Married **Pauline Elza Eye**.
(2) Married Jan 14 1904 in Pendleton Co., WV, **Frances Warner**, b. Dec 14 1886 in Pendleton Co., WV, d. 1963 in Pendleton Co., WV, buried in Cedar Hill Cem., Pendleton Co., WV.

***Children** by Frances Warner:*

1120 i. Dora Evelyn^{6} Waybright b. Feb 7 1907 in Cherry Grove, Pendleton Co., WV, d. Jan 1985. Married Nov 25 1927, **Roy Refin Rexrode**, b. Jan 8 1907 in Pennsylvania, d. Jan 1973 in Hershey, Dauphin Co., PA. Roy: .

1121 ii. Emily Ethel Waybright b. Sep 26 1908 in Cherry Grove, Pendleton Co., WV, d. May 12 1985. She Married **(unknown) Colaw**.

1122 iii. Dwight Moody Waybright b. Aug 15 1910 in Cherry Grove, Pendleton Co., WV, d. Jun 13 1994 in Hershey, Dauphin Co., PA. He Married **Martha (Unknown)**.

1123 iv. Nora Marie Waybright b. Jun 16 1912 in Cherry Grove, Pendleton Co., WV, d. Mar 16 1918.

1124 v. Gretta May Waybright b. Oct 6 1916 in Cherry Grove, Pendleton Co., WV. She Married **Russell Warner** (son of Floyd Warner and Ollie W. Waybright).

1125 vi. Gaitha Gay Waybright b. Aug 6 1920 in Cherry Grove, Pendleton Co., WV. She Married **Lloyd Edwin Bell**.

1126 vii. Junior Mike Waybright b. Feb 23 1922 in Cherry Grove, Pendleton Co., WV. Married Jun 1946, **Jean Grace Stehman**.

1127 viii. Joseph James Waybright b. Jan 14 1925 in Cherry Grove, Pendleton Co., WV. He Married **Martha Elizabeth Heisey**.

\+ 1128 ix. Jason Paschal Waybright b. Sep 21 1929.

510. **Esther^{5} Waybright** (151.James Bud^{4}, 19.Jesse^{3}, 4.Rachel^{2} Arbogast, 1.John C.^{1}), b. Apr 1 1885 in Pendleton Co., WV, d. Oct 15 1955 in Highland Co., VA, buried in Blue Grass Cem., Highland Co., VA.
Married Feb 22 1904 in Pendleton Co., WV, **Luther Hammer**, b. Jul 30 1880 in Pendleton Co., WV, d. Jul 12 1949 in Blue Grass Cem., Highland Co., VA, buried in Blue Grass Cem., Highland Co., VA.

***Children**:*

\+ 1129 i. Glen^{6} Hammer b. Apr 23 1903.

1130 ii. Robert Hammer b. Dec 3 1904 in Crabbottom, Highland Co., VA, d. Dec 17 1912 in Blue Grass Cem., Highland Co., VA, buried in Blue Grass Cem., Highland Co., VA.

1131 iii. John Forest Hammer b. Aug 2 1906 in Crabbottom, Highland Co., VA, d. Jan 6 1982. Married Jul 18 1928 in Monterey, Highland Co., VA, **Rizpah Hevener**, b. Sep 5 1904, d. Aug 20 1989. Rizpah: Child of William Hevener and Laura Mae Mullenax.

1132 iv. Marie Hammer b. Jan 25 1908 in Crabbottom, Highland Co., VA, d. Dec 23 1997. Married 1926, **Walter Vernon Newman**, b. 1905, d. 1974.

1133 v. Leonard Harper Hammer b. Mar 10 1912 in Crabbottom, Highland Co., VA, d. Nov 10 1978 in Blue Grass Cem., Highland Co., VA, buried in Blue Grass Cem., Highland Co., VA. Married 1932, **Virginia Dare Wimer**, b. Jan 1914.

1134 vi. Gladys Ferguson Hammer b. in Crabbottom, Highland Co., VA, d. Jan 25 1992. Married Jun 26 1920, **William Jason Newman**, b. Aug 2 1900, d. Sep 25 1979.

1135 vii. Leona Hammer b. Jan 20 1915 in Crabbottom, Highland Co., VA, d. Mar 6 1994. Married Apr 27 1940 in Augusta Co., VA, **Andrew Dean Gutshall**, b. Apr 1915.

1136 viii. Elmer Cyrus Hammer b. Jul 18 1916. (1) Married Aug 10 1937 in McDowell, Highland Co., VA, **Virginia Brock**, b. Dec 1915. (2) Married Sep 5 1959, **Dixie Lou Byrd**.

1137 ix. Virginia Phoebe Hammer b. Jul 22 1919 in Crabbottom, Highland Co., VA. Married Jan 29 1938 in Cumberland, Alleghany Co., MD, **William Ralph Rexrode**, b. Mar 1915.

1138 x. Luther Hammer, Jr. b. Nov 9 1921 in Crabbottom, Highland Co., VA, d. Jan 1 1986 in Harrisburg, Raleigh Co., VA, buried Jan 4 1986 in Crabbottom, Highland Co., VA. Married 1945, **Martha Swadley Simmons**, b. May 10 1922 in Crabbottom, Highland Co., VA.

1139 xi. James Burtner Hammer b. Nov 23 1923 in Crabbottom, Highland Co., VA. Married 1949 in Richmond, Henrico Co., VA, **Mildred Eugene Stanley**.

1140 xii. William Curtis Hammer b. Oct 29 1927 in Crabbottom, Highland Co., VA. Married Jul 15 1948, **Martha Lynn Marshall.**

511. **Jesse[5] Waybright** (151.James Bud[4], 19.Jesse[3], 4.Rachel[2] Arbogast, 1.John C.[1]), b. Jan 22 1887 in Pendleton Co., WV, d. Jul 29 1967 in Staunton, Augusta Co., VA, buried in Arbovale Cem., Arbovale, Pocahontas Co., WV.
Married Jan 17 1904, **Attie Bessie Rexrode**, b. Jun 5 1886 in Pendleton Co., WV, d. Dec 24 1973 in Staunton, Augusta Co., VA, buried Dec 27 1973 in Arbovale Cem., Arbovale, Pocahontas Co., WV.

Children:

\+ 1141 i. Kenny[6] Waybright b. Jul 26 1904.

1142 ii. Archie Waybright b. Jun 5 1908 in Cherry Grove, Pendleton Co., WV, d. Nov 25 1980 in Lewisburg, Greenbrier Co., WV.

\+ 1143 iii. Martha Jane Waybright b. Jan 5 1910.

\+ 1144 iv. Erma Lillian Waybright b. Jan 10 1912.

1145 v. Ralph William Waybright b. Mar 28 1914 in Cherry Grove, Pendleton Co., WV, d. Jun 2 1980 in Memorial Division Cam., Charleston, Kanawha Co., WV, buried in Arbovale Cem., Arbovale, Pocahontas Co., WV. Married Jul 4 1938, **Nellie Burr Pugh**, b. Nov 3 1921 in Arbovale Cem., Arbovale, Pocahontas Co., WV.

1146 vi. Hiner Waybright b. Feb 28 1917 in Cherry Grove, Pendleton Co., WV, d. Nov 16 1999 in Alleghany Regional Hospital, Low Moor, Alleghany Co., VA, buried Nov 20 1999 in Arbovale Cem., Arbovale, Pocahontas Co., WV.
Member of the Men's organization. Army Veteran of ww2 and a cook from
Western State Hospital i n Staunton Va.
He Married **Edith Pearl Bennett**, b. May 22 1919 in Hot Springs, Bath Co., VA.

1147 vii. Agnes Waybright b. Jan 7 1918 in Cherry Grove, Pendleton Co., WV. Married Jun 5 1935, John Adams Raines, b. in Cherry Grove, Pendleton Co., WV. John: .

1148 viii. Roy Waybright b. Jun 12 1922 in Cherry Grove, Pendleton Co., WV, d. Dec 31 1977 in University of Virginia Medical Center, Charlottesville, VA, buried Jan 2 1978 in Oak Lawn Gardens Staunton Augusta Co., VA.
.
(1) He Married **Irene Eye.** (2) He Married **Helen Brown**.

1149 ix. Jesse Waybright b. Jun 28 1925 in Cherry Grove, Pendleton Co., WV, d. Jul 16 1990 in Charleston, Kanawha Co., WV.
At the time this data was assembled this Family may have 5 living, unwed children (child), that are not included here.
Married Aug 6 1946 in Monterey, Highland Co., VA, **Litha Carol Mullenax**, b. in Arbovale Cem., Arbovale, Pocahontas Co., WV.

1150 x. Katherine Virginia Waybright b. Jul 23 1927 in Cherry Grove, Pendleton Co., WV, d. May 9 1986 in Fort Wayne, Allen Co., IN, buried in Indiana. Married Mar 9 1946, **Charles J. Grogg**, b. in Durbin, Pocahontas Co., WV. Charles: At the time this data was assembled this Family may have 3 living, unwed children (child), that are not included here.

512. **Sarah[5] Waybright** (151.James Bud[4], 19.Jesse[3], 4.Rachel[2] Arbogast, 1.John C.[1]), b. Oct 1889 in Pendleton Co., WV, d. in Hightown, Pendleton Co., WV, buried in Bud Waybright Cem., Pendleton Co., VA/WV.
(1) She Married **James Killiam**, buried in Bud Waybright Cem., Pendleton Co., VA/WV. (

Children *by James Killiam:*

1151 i. Blanchard[6] Killiam.
1152 ii. Jennings Killiam. He Married Dorothy Stephenson.
1153 iii. Walter Killiam.
1154 iv. Wayne Killiam.

2) She Married **John Hammer**. lived with John but never Married.

Children *by John Hammer:*

\+ 1155 v. Jay Hammer b. Nov 9 1909.

513. **Nancy Jane[5] Waybright** (151.James Bud[4], 19.Jesse[3], 4.Rachel[2] Arbogast, 1.John C.[1]), b. Jul 18 1890 in Pendleton Co., WV, d. Mar 10 1968, buried in Butchers Cem., Onego, Pendleton Co., WV.
Married Apr 26 1909, **Paul Nelson**, b. Mar 25 1888, d. Apr 1 1955, buried in Butchers Cem., Onego, Pendleton Co., WV.

Children:

1156 i. Harding[6] Nelson. He Married **Virginia Judy**.
1157 ii. Homan Nelson b. 1910. He Married **Beulah Bennett**.
1158 iii. Ola R. Nelson b. 1912. She Married **Pete Smith**.
1159 iv. Mildred Nelson b. 1914. She Married **Amos Lambert.**
1160 v. Catherine V. Nelson b. 1918.

515. **Sophia[5] Waybright** (152.Alvah C.[4], 19.Jesse[3], 4.Rachel[2] Arbogast, 1.John C.[1]), b. 1884 in Pendleton Co., WV, d. 1971.
She Married **Ezra Hinkle**, b. 1881.

Children:

1161 i. Ed[6] Hinkle.
1162 ii. Ide Hinkle.
1163 iii. Loren Hinkle d. 1945 in World War II.
1164 iv. Roland Hinkle.
1165 v. Marvin Hinkle.
\+ 1166 vi. Sophie Grace Hinkle b. 1910.

516. **Theodore[5] Waybright** (152.Alvah C.[4], 19.Jesse[3], 4.Rachel[2] Arbogast, 1.John C.[1]), b. May 6 1886 in Pendleton Co., WV, d. Jun 14 1962.
He Married **Delphia Florence Propst**, b. Oct 2 1891 in Blue Grass, Highland Co., WV, d. Feb 17 1986 in Pendleton Nurse home Franklin Co., WV, buried in Waybright Cem., Pendleton Co., WV.

Children:

\+ 1167 i. Reva[6] Waybright b. Feb 18 1912.
1168 ii. Raymond Waybright b. Oct 11 1914, d. Feb 13 1931.
1169 iii. Clarice Waybright b. Mar 28 1917. She Married **(unknown) Bliss**. (unknown): .
1170 iv. Leah Waybright b. Oct 10 1918. She Married **Marlin Murphy**.
1171 v. June Waybright b. Sep 11 1922.
1172 vi. Thelma Waybright b. Nov 2 1925.
1173 vii. Marie Waybright b. Feb 28 1928. She Married **(unknown) Reeves**.

517. **Troy[5] Waybright** (152.Alvah C.[4], 19.Jesse[3], 4.Rachel[2] Arbogast, 1.John C.[1]), b. Nov 27 1887 in Pendleton Co., WV, d. Nov 22 1971 in North Fork of South Branch, WV., buried Nov 25 1971 in Blue Grass Cem., Highland Co., VA.
Married Mar 27 1910 in West Virginia, **Katie Warner**, b. Dec 6 1892 in West Virginia, d. Oct 18 1976 in Rockingham Memorial Hospital, Harrisonburg Rockingham Co., VA, buried in Blue Grass Cem., Highland Co., VA.

Children:

\+ 1174 i. Vivin Richard[6] Waybright b. Jan 6 1910.
\+ 1175 ii. Gertrude Lee Waybright b. Mar 7 1911.
1176 iii. Norma Waybright b. Mar 26 1912 in Pendleton Co., WV, d. May 1912 in Pendleton Co., WV, buried in Family Cem., Alveys Home, Pendleton Co., WV.
1177 iv. Thomas Jefferson Waybright b. Apr 16 1913 in Pendleton Co., WV, d. Jul 25 1981 in Blacksburg, Montgomery Co., VA. He Married **Martha Pasco**.
1178 v. Warner Everett Waybright b. Feb 12 1915 in Pendleton Co., WV, d. Feb 20 1984 in Clinton Prince George Co., MD, buried in Bethel Cem., Old Field, Hardy Co., WV.

At the time this data was assembled this Family may have 4 living, unwed children (child), that are not included here.
(1) He Married Sylvia Lambert, d. 1949. (2) He Married **Bertha Lynn (Unknown)**.

1179 vi. Theresa O. Waybright b. Jun 24 1917 in Dry Run, Pendleton Co., WV. Married Apr 3 1936, **Joseph Cannon Lambert**, d. May 1975.

1180 vii. Gwendolyn Waybright b. Jun 18 1919 in Dry Run, Pendleton Co., WV. Married Oct 12 1940 in Elkton, Cecil Co., MD, **Joseph Day**, b. Jul 6 1915 in Tamworth England.

1181 viii. Dorothy 'Dolf' Waybright b. Jun 17 1921 in Pendleton Co., WV, d. May 20 1994. (1) She Married **Berrett Heise**. (2) She Married **John M Mullenax**, b. Sep 16 1913 in Pendleton Co., WV (son of William Jackson Mullenax and Anna Elizabeth Waybright).

1182 ix. Connie Waybright b. Jun 2 1923 in Pendleton Co., WV, d. Jan 23 1989 in Blue Grass Cem., Highland Co., VA. Married Jul 18 1941 in Blue Grass Highland Co., VA, **Robert Lee Marshall**, b. May 11 1915 in Blue Grass Cem., Highland Co., VA.

1183 x. Ishmel Waybright b. Aug 3 1925 in Pendleton Co., WV, d. Jun 11 1928 in Pendleton Co., WV, buried in Family Cem., Alveys Home, Pendleton Co., WV.

1184 xi. Troy Waybright b. Jul 5 1928 in Cherry Grove, Pendleton Co., WV.

518. **Clarence[5] Waybright** (152.Alvah C.[4], 19.Jesse[3], 4.Rachel[2] Arbogast, 1.John C.[1]), b. Jan 10 1891 in Pendleton Co., WV, d. May 1 1955.
He Married **Mary Ellen Wimer**, b. Aug 27 1892 in Middle Mountain Tyler Co., WV (daughter of Jeremiah Emanuel Wimer and Ellen Catherine Rexrode), d. Feb 23 1978 in Lower Thorne Creek Pendleton Co., WV, buried in Wimer Family Cem., Middle Mountain, Tyler Co., WV.

Children:

\+ 1185 i. Delbert[6] Waybright b. Jun 3 1920.

1186 ii. Susan Mae Waybright b. Mar 17 1922 in Highland Co., VA. She Married **Bruce Rexrode.**

1187 iii. Bessie Elizabeth Waybright b. Aug 30 1923 in Highland Co., VA. Married in Pendleton Co., WV, **Harry Olin Hoover**, b. Sep 20 1918 in Lower Thorne Creek Pendleton Co., WV. Harry:

1888 iv. Myrtle Catherine Waybright b. Oct 23 1925 in Highland Co., VA. Married Mar 1948, **Ollie Rexrode**, b. May 8 1923, d. Apr 29 1987. Ollie: At the time this data was assembled this Family may have 5 living, unwed children (child), that are not included here.

1189 v. Martin Jerry Waybright b. Aug 10 1927 in Highland Co., VA.

1190 vi. Alvy Melvin Waybright b. Jun 21 1930 in Highland Co., VA, d. Aug 11 1994 in Bartow, Pocahontas Co., WV.

519. **Amy[5] Waybright** (152.Alvah C.[4], 19.Jesse[3], 4.Rachel[2] Arbogast, 1.John C.[1]), b. Feb 18 1893 in Pendleton Co., WV, d. Jun 1 1988 in Waynesboro Community Hospital, Waynesboro, Augusta Co., VA, buried in Rexrode Family Cem., Blue Grass Highland Co., VA.
She Married **Eddie B. Rexrode**, d. Aug 1970.

Children:

1191 i. Arval[6] Rexrode. He Married **Bernice Beckner.**

525. **Lenora Jane[5] Waybright** (155.Mary Elizabeth[4], 19.Jesse[3], 4.Rachel[2] Arbogast, 1.John C.[1]), b. Apr 5 1889 in Boyer, Pocahontas Co., WV, d. May 23 1951.
Married May 14 1904, **Snowden Talbott Tracy**, b. Jul 29 1881 in Pocahontas Co., WV, d. Feb 25 1970 in Pendleton Co., WV.

Children:

1192 i. Hazel[6] Tracy.

1193 ii. Pearl Tracy.

\+ 1194 iii. Leonard Lee Tracy.

\+ 1195 iv. Glenn Parker Tracy b. Sep 28 1906.

529. **Estella[5] Calhoun** (155.Mary Elizabeth[4] Waybright, 19.Jesse[3], 4.Rachel[2] Arbogast, 1.John C.[1]), b. Sep 13 1901 in Boyer, Pocahontas Co., WV, d. Nov 1984.
Married Mar 7 1927, **Charles Bellard Varner**, b. Apr 9 1876 (son of John Phillip Varner and Dianah V. Nottingham).
Charles: From Wm. C. Varner.

Children:

1196 i. Arnold Richard[6] Varner b. Jun 27 1927.
Married, has 5 children.

1197 ii. Mary Ann Varner b. Mar 18 1929.
Married **Mr. Sponaugle**, have two daughters.

She Married **(unknown) Sponaugle**.
1198 iii. Catherine Varner b. Mar 4 1930.
Married **Mr. Mc Crea**, has a daughter.
1199 iv. Robert Lee Varner b. Oct 1 1932.
Married, has four children.
+ 1200 v. Louise Varner b. Nov 6 1934.
+ 1201 vi. Retha Lucille Varner b. Mar 20 1937.
1202 vii. Guy Varner.

532. **Mary Christina[5] Waybright** (157.Abraham[4], 21.Daniel[3], 4.Rachel[2] Arbogast, 1.John C.[1]), b. Apr 23 1874 in Pendleton Co., WV, d. Jun 3 1960, buried in Waybright Cem., Pendleton Co., WV.
Married Jan 3 1893 in Harman, Randolph Co., WV, **John Robert Adamson**, b. Aug 26 1867 in Pendleton Co., WV, d. Feb 21 1943, buried in Joseph Adamson Cem., Pendleton Co., WV.

Children:

1203 i. Nellie C.[6] Adamson b. May 1894 in Pendleton Co., WV.
1204 ii. Rosa N. Adamson b. Oct 3 1894 in Pendleton Co., WV, d. Feb 16 1973. She Married **(unknown) Malberg**.
1205 iii. Fred A. Adamson b. Oct 31 1896 in Pendleton Co., WV, d. Apr 1972.
1206 iv. Glenn Adamson b. Apr 3 1899 in Pendleton Co., WV, d. Sep 28 1968.
1207 v. Verner C. Adamson b. 1902 in Pendleton Co., WV.
1208 vi. Albert C Adamson b. Apr 10 1903 in Pendleton Co., WV, d. Aug 1986.
1209 vii. Rula K. Adamson b. 1907 in Pendleton Co., WV.

537. **Mary Marcella[5] Huffman** (158.Mary Margaret[4] Waybright, 21.Daniel[3], 4.Rachel[2] Arbogast, 1.John C.[1]), b. Aug 27 1879 in Onego, Pendleton Co., WV, d. Mar 11 1950 in Lewiston, Nez Perez Co., ID. Married Aug 27 1906, **Fleet Jordan**, b. Jan 14 1875 in Churchville, Pendleton Co., WV, d. Dec 22 1965 in Lewiston, Nez Perez Co., ID.

Children:

1210 i. Glen Weed[6] Jordan b. May 16 1902 in Whitmer, Randolph Co., WV, d. Apr 5 1978 in Lewiston, Nez Perez Co., ID. Married Mar 29 1928, **Florna Jane Carr**.

538. **Eve Frances[5] Waybright** (158.Mary Margaret[4], 21.Daniel[3], 4.Rachel[2] Arbogast, 1.John C.[1]), b. Sep 24 1880 in Onego, Pendleton Co., WV, d. Aug 1 1961 in Wayne, Ashtabula Co., OH, buried in Wayne, Ashtabula Co., OH.
Married Jun 14 1897 in Onego, Pendleton Co., WV, **Hayes Wheeler Kisamore**, b. May 19 1876 in Onego, Pendleton Co., WV, d. Mar 24 1983 in Morgan, Ashtabula Co., OH, buried in Wayne, Ashtabula Co., OH.

Children:

1211 i. Ethel May[6] Kisamore b. Aug 27 1898 in Onego, Pendleton Co., WV, d. Nov 12 1984. Married 24 Aug, **Thomas Roach**.
1212 ii. Marjorie Ettie Kisamore b. Oct 21 1900 in Onego, Pendleton Co., WV, d. Jul 13 1901.
1213 iii. Zernie Kisamore b. Jul 7 1902 in Onego, Pendleton Co., WV. She Married **Allie Winch.**
1214 iv. Byron Stanley Kisamore b. Jun 22 1904 in Onego, Pendleton Co., WV, d. May 2 1982. Married Sep 27 1928, **Patsey Ethel Farence**.
1215 v. Elaine Kisamore b. Aug 13 1906 in Onego, Pendleton Co., WV, d. Mar 28 1913.
1216 vi. Gola Kisamore b. Dec 11 1908 in Onego, Pendleton Co., WV, d. Feb 18 1966. She Married **Fredwin Holcomb**.
1217 vii. Mary Frances Kisamore b. Jul 24 1912 in Onego, Pendleton Co., WV, d. Feb 9 1981. Married May 25 1946, **Vern Niles Birdette**.
1218 viii. Nina Elizabeth Kisamore b. Feb 14 1916 in Unus, Greenbrier Co., WV, d. Dec 12 1994. She Married **Harold V Heath**.
1219 ix. Ruth Virginia Kisamore b. Apr 1 1918 in Falling Springs, Greenbrier Co., WV. She Married **William Heath**.
1220 x. Oliver Wayne Kisamore b. Mar 30 1922 in Wayne, Ashtabula Co., OH, d. Aug 13 1944.

539. **Thaddeus[5] Waybright** (158.Mary Margaret[4], 21.Daniel[3], 4.Rachel[2] Arbogast, 1.John C.[1]), b. Apr 12 1892 in Onego, Pendleton Co., WV, d. Jan 22 1977 in West Virginia.
Married Oct 27 1917 in Onego, Pendleton Co., WV, **Alpha Hollie Elza**, b. Sep 25 1899 in Whitmer, Randolph Co., WV, d. Mar 1987.

Children:

1221 i. Mary Margaret[6] Waybright b. Sep 12 1919 in Whitmer, Randolph Co., WV. Married Dec 5 1942, Earl Frederick Kerr.
+ 1222 ii. Mary Waybright b. 1920.
1223 iii. Paul Waybright b. Dec 13 1923 in Whitmer, Randolph Co., WV, d. Jan 11 1925.

1224 iv. Leonard Thaddeus Waybright b. Apr 22 1926 in Whitmer, Randolph Co., WV, d. May 23 1999 in Clarksburg, Harrison Co., WV, buried May 27 1999 in WV National Cem., Grafton, Taylor Co., WV.
U.S. Navy S2C
Married Dec 20 1945, **Betty Loraine Tolliver**.

1225 v. James Herman Waybright b. Aug 17 1929 in Whitmer, Randolph Co., WV.
James H. PFC Infantry 14 th Inf. Regt 25th div. wounded 12 Mar 1952
North Korea by missile, returned to duty

541. **Oscar Blaine[5] Waybright** (159.William Washington[4], 21.Daniel[3], 4.Rachel[2] Arbogast, 1.John C.[1]), b. Oct 7 1887 in Pendleton Co., WV, d. Mar 15 1926 in Barnabas, Logan Co., WV, buried in Cham Cem., Barnabas Logan Co., WV.
Married Jul 9 1908, **Rosa Lee Loughrey**, b. 1891, d. Feb 10 1919 in Tucker Co., WV, buried in Tucker Co., WV.

Children:

1226 i. Verlin[6] Waybright d. 1921.
1227 ii. Dove Waybright b. 1910 in Parsons, Tucker Co., WV. She Married **Filmore Neace**, b. Aug 6 1906, d. Jun 1957.
\+ 1228 iii. Darl Blaine Waybright b. Jun 16 1913.

543. **Rettia C.[5] Waybright** (159.William Washington[4], 21.Daniel[3], 4.Rachel[2] Arbogast, 1.John C.[1]), b. Jul 1892 in Pendleton Co., WV, d. 1950.
Married in Tucker Co., WV, **Nathan Andrew Warren Loughrey**, b. 1887, d. in Hendricks, Tucker Co., WV.

Children:

1229 i. Viola[6] Loughrey b. Aug 28 1908 in Hendricks, Tucker Co., WV, d. Feb 6 1996 in Maryland. She Married **Andrew Brewster**.
1230 ii. Georgia Virginia Loughrey b. 1912. Married Jul 12 1933 in Tucker Co., WV, **William Shirley McDonald.**
1231 iii. Rosalie Loughrey b. Aug 18 1913 in Hendricks, Tucker Co., WV, d. Feb 17 1989 in Fairview Memorial Hospital, Elmhurst, Moscow, PA. She Married **Willard James Scheitlin.**
1232 iv. James Patrick Loughrey b. Feb 24 1919 in Hendricks, Tucker Co., WV, d. Apr 1980 in Fairview Memorial Hospital, Elmhurst, Moscow, PA. He Married **Mildred Barb**.

544. **Solomon Robert[5] Waybright** (161.Isaac Perry[4], 21.Daniel[3], 4.Rachel[2] Arbogast, 1.John C.[1]), b. Apr 11 1894 in Randolph Co., WV, d. Mar 9 1967 in Detroit, Wayne Co., MI, buried in Woodlawn Cem., Detroit Wayne Co., MI.
Married Aug 11 1923 in Detroit, Wayne Co., MI, **Erma Blanche Gennette**, b. Dec 13 1900 in Hancock Houghton Co., MI, d. Feb 10 1982 in Monroe, Monroe Co., MI, buried Feb 13 1982 in St. Joseph Catholic, Monroe City, Monroe Co., MI.

Children:

1233 i. Donald Henry[6] Waybright b. May 13 1929 in Detroit, Wayne Co., MI.

549. **Perlie[5] Arbogast** (162.Cordelia[4] Waybright, 21.Daniel[3], 4.Rachel[2] Arbogast, 1.John C.[1]), b. Jun 16 1900 in Pendleton Co., WV, d. Deceased in Baltimore, Baltimore Co., MD.
(1) She Married **Gary Kisamore**.

Children *by Gary Kisamore:*

1234 i. Harry[6] Kisamore b. 1918, d. 1918.
\+ 1235 ii. Margie Kisamore b. Jul 27 1919.
1236 iii. Grace Kisamore.
\+ 1237 iv. Troy Kisamore.
\+ 1238 v. Glen Kisamore b. Oct 13 1927.
1239 vi. Goldie Kisamore b. Oct 13 1927.
\+ 1240 vii. Guy Kisamore b. Jan 18 1934.
1241 viii. Ralph Hugh Kisamore b. Jan 18 1934, d. Dec 24 1978.
1242 ix. Valley Kisamore.

(2) She Married **John Nestor**.
(3) She Married **Okey Kittle**, b. Feb 06 1900.

550. **Wilbur[5] Arbogast** (162.Cordelia[4] Waybright, 21.Daniel[3], 4.Rachel[2] Arbogast, 1.John C.[1]), b. Jun 2 1901 in Pendleton Co., WV, d. Oct 16 1977 in Akron, Summit Co., OH, buried in Crown Hill Cem., Akron, Summit Co., OH.
Married May 23 1926 in Parsons, Tucker Co., WV, **Effie May Hardy**, b. Aug 02 1908 in Hendricks, Tucker Co., WV, buried in Tucker Co., WV. **Effie**: Daughter of Ed Hardy and Jean Hawkins.

Children:

1243 i. Rose Joy[6] Arbogast b. Apr 05 1927, d. Apr 05 1927.

\+ 1244 ii. Samuel Henry Arbogast b. Jul 10 1928.
\+ 1245 iii. Lovie May Arbogast b. Aug 18 1929.
\+ 1246 iv. Wilbur Junior Arbogast b. Jun 21 1932.
1247 v. Margaret Arbogast.
1248 vi. Betty Virginia Arbogast b. Mar 12 1936 in Montrose, Randolph Co., WV, d. Apr 06 1994 in Garrard's Fort, Greene Co., PA. Married Dec 18 1954 in Waynesburg, Greene Co., PA, **Kramer Darr**, b. Jun 14 1921 in Waynesburg, Greene Co., PA, d. May 14 1976 in Waynesburg, Greene Co., PA.
1249 vii. Ruby Jane Arbogast b. Nov 22 1937.
1250 viii. Pauline Faye Arbogast b. Sep 10 1939.
1251 ix. Roselee Arbogast b. Apr 16 1941.
1252 x. Carl Lee Arbogast b. Nov 1943, d. Nov 1943.

556. **Clifton Mason[5] Waybright** (164.John Edward[4], 21.Daniel[3], 4.Rachel[2] Arbogast, 1.John C.[1]), b. Jul 28 1899 in Onego, Pendleton Co., WV, d. Mar 23 1960 in Cassity Cem., Cassity, Randolph Co., WV, buried in Maplewood Cem., Elkins, Randolph Co., WV. Married Sep 10 1918, **Mary Elizabeth Bennett**, b. Oct 18 1903 in Dry Run, Pendleton Co., WV, d. May 14 1973 in Elkins, Randolph Co., WV.

Children:

1253 i. Gerald Mason[6] Waybright b. Sep 22 1919 in Parsons, Tucker Co., WV, d. Jan 10 1987 in Baltimore, Baltimore Co., MD.
Married Sep 8 1940 in Red House, Garrett Co., MD, **Wila Jenieva Hart**, b. May 7 1918 in Karens, Tucker Co., WV, d. Nov 1997 in Baltimore, Baltimore Co., MD.
1254 ii. Elmer Lewis Waybright b. Nov 10 1921, d. 1936.
1255 iii. Harold Burton Waybright b. Apr 22 1924 in Kerens, Randolph Co., WV, d. Aug 4 1991 in Elkins, Randolph Co., WV.
1256 iv. Katheryn Mary Waybright b. May 20 1926 in Randolph Co., WV. She Married **Edward Earl Flemming**, b. 1921, d. May 1 1997 in Illinois, buried in River Bend Cem., Will Co., IL. Edward: At the time this data was assembled this Family may have 3 living, unwed children (child), that are not included here.
1257 v. Clarice June Waybright b. Jun 21 1929 in Randolph Co., WV. She Married **Bernard Thomas.**
1258 vi. Betty Jean Waybright b. Aug 23 1932 in Clover, Roane Co., WV, d. Mar 2 1995. Married Mar 11 1953 in Cold Water, Branch Co., MI, **Carl Thomas Ash**, b. Mar 21 1930 in Cold Water, Branch Co., MI, d. Mar 2 1995 in Cold Water, Branch Co., MI, buried Mar 5 1995 in Oak Grove Cem., Coldwater Branch Co., MI.

557. **Guy Daniel[5] Waybright** (164.John Edward[4], 21.Daniel[3], 4.Rachel[2] Arbogast, 1.John C.[1]), b. Dec 5 1901 in Onego, Pendleton Co., WV, d. Nov 29 1965 in Cuyahoga Falls Summit Co., OH. He Married **Toy Helen Bennett**, b. Apr 22 1908 in Dry Fork, Randolph Co., WV.

Children:

1259 i. Stanley Guy[6] Waybright b. Jan 2 1923 in Montrose, Randolph Co., WV.
Married Dec 22 1946, **Kitty Lou Rhodes**.
1260 ii. Robert Lewis Waybright b. Aug 22 1924 in Montrose, Randolph Co., WV.
Married Dec 19 1944, Wilma Gatewood, b. 1926 (daughter of Willie Nathen Gatewood and **Hassie Blanche Wimer**).
1261 iii. Glenn McCoy Waybright b. Aug 9 1926 in Montrose, Randolph Co., WV. Married Jul 31 1947 in Oakland, Garrett Co., MD, Cora **Eleanor Toothman**, b. Mar 20 1928 in Pennsburg, Ritchie Co., WV.

558. **Burley McCoy[5] Waybright** (164.John Edward[4], 21.Daniel[3], 4.Rachel[2] Arbogast, 1.John C.[1]), b. Oct 30 1904 in Dry Fork, Randolph Co., WV, d. May 16 1967.
Married Feb 22 1930 in Porterwood Tucker Co., WV, **Violet Elizabeth Miller**, b. May 18 1912 in Hambleton Tucker Co., WV, d. Feb 10 1964 in Mount Pifer Cem., Tucker Co., WV.

Children:

1262 i. June Elizabeth[6] Waybright b. Jan 7 1931 in Porterwood Tucker Co., WV, d. Oct 24 1985 in St. Frances Cabini Hospital, Alexandria, Rapides Co., LA, buried Oct 27 1985 in Alexandria Rapides Co., Louisiana. Married May 22 1948, **William Russell Clingerman. William:**
1263 ii. Grace Marie Waybright b. Oct 17 1933 in Porterwood Tucker Co., WV, d. Jul 17 1979, buried in Mount Pifer Cem., Tucker Co., WV. She Married **Nobel Edward Auvil**.
1264 iii. Ella Catherine Waybright b. Aug 13 1934 in Kearns WV, d. Apr 21 1939.
1265 iv. Vavil Virginia Waybright b. Apr 10 1936 in Kerens, Randolph Co., WV, d. Nov 8 1994.
\+ 1266 v. Ellis Paul Waybright b. Mar 12 1941.

559. **Edna Margaret[5] Waybright** (164.John Edward[4], 21.Daniel[3], 4.Rachel[2] Arbogast, 1.John C.[1]), b. Apr 23 1907 in Onego, Pendleton Co., WV, d. Dec 30 1990.
She Married **Odes Botkin**, b. Oct 17 1905 in West Virginia, d. Apr 1982 in Elkins, Randolph Co., WV.

***Children*:**

1267 i. John[6] Botkin. He Married **Josephine Pennington**.
1268 ii. Wanda Botkin.
1269 iii. Margaret Botkin.
1270 iv. Thomas Botkin.
1271 v. Susan Botkin.
1272 vi. Jack Botkin b. 23 May in West Virginia.
1273 vii. Odes Botkin b. Aug 15 1926 in West Virginia, d. Dec 6 1992.
1274 viii. James Botkin b. May 22 1932 in West Virginia, d. Jan 21 1965 in Korea.

578. **Bert[5] Waybright** (167.Albert[4], 21.Daniel[3], 4.Rachel[2] Arbogast, 1.John C.[1]), b. Oct 1890 in Pendleton Co., WV.
(1) He Married **Minnie V. (Unknown)**, b. Oct 3 1891, d. Jan 1981 in Alleghany Co., MD.

Children *by Minnie V. (Unknown):*

1275 i. Ruth V.[6] Waybright.
1276 ii. (unknown) Waybright.
1277 iii. (unknown) Waybright.
1278 iv. Edsel Waybright b. Jul 24 1919.
1279 v. Gerald Waybright b. Jul 10 1922.

(2) He Married **Artie Dolly Hedrick**, b. May 10 1894, d. Jan 15 1968 in Elkins, Randolph Co., WV.

Children *by Artie Dolly Hedrick:*

\+ 1280 vi. Bricel Waybright b. Dec 13 1911.

584. **William Pearl[5] Waybright** (168.Andrew Jackson[4], 22.Nathan[3], 4.Rachel[2] Arbogast, 1.John C.[1]), b. Jan 3 1874 in Monterey, Highland Co., VA, d. Dec 14 1956 in Redondo Beach, Los Angeles Co., CA, buried Dec 17 1956 in Pacific Crest Cem., Redondo Beach, Los Angele Co., CA.
He Married **Phoebe Katherine Blagg**, b. Mar 13 1874 in Crabbottom, Highland Co., VA, d. Jun 16 1956 in Redondo Beach, Los Angeles Co., CA, buried Jun 19 1956 in Pacific Crest Cem., Redondo Beach, Los Angele Co., CA.

***Children*:**

\+ 1281 i. Walter Lee[6] Blagg b. Jun 5 1895.
\+ 1282 ii. Merrill Frithoff Waybright b. Jun 13 1902.
\+ 1283 iii. Mabel Virginia Waybright b. Sep 28 1904.
1284 iv. William Ward Waybright b. Jul 16 1906 in Monterey, Highland Co., VA, d. Oct 15 1973 in Redondo Beach, Los Angeles Co., CA, buried in Pacific Crest Cem., Redondo Beach, Los Angele Co., CA. Married Feb 20 1965**,** **Neva Lucille Scott**, b. Sep 13 1913 in Missouri, d. Sep 3 1995 in Los Angeles, Los Angeles Co., CA.
\+ 1285 v. Thomas Mead Waybright b. Mar 21 1909.
1286 vi. Benny Andrew Waybright b. Aug 18 1911 in Durbin, Pocahontas Co., WV, d. Jan 27 1988 in Galena, Otis Co., KS. Married May 11 1959, **Ollie Leona Bledsoe**, d. in Galena, Otis Co., KS.
1287 vii. Clara Marie Waybright b. Oct 24 1913 in Pico Rivera, Los Angeles Co., CA, d. Jan 12 1991 in Lawndale, Los Angeles Co., CA, buried in Pacific Crest Cem., Redondo Beach, Los Angele Co., CA. (1) Married Sep 9 1937, **Verde Alvin Wenzel**. (2) Married Sep 9 1937 in Redondo Beach, Los Angeles Co., CA, **Verde Alvin Wenzel**, b. Oct 22 1917 in Hermosa Beach, Los Angeles Co., CA, d. Sep 27 1968, buried in Manteca, San Juaquin Co., CA.

586. **Wilbur Glen[5] Waybright** (168.Andrew Jackson[4], 22.Nathan[3], 4.Rachel[2] Arbogast, 1.John C.[1]), b. Nov 12 1882 in Monterey, Highland Co., VA, d. Jul 27 1933 in Elkins, Randolph Co., WV, buried in Grafton, Taylor Co., WV. Married, **Hazel Simmons**.

***Children*:**

1288 i. (unknown)[6] Waybright.
1289 ii. (unknown) Waybright.

589. **Frank Adam[5] Waybright** (169.Adam Harness[4], 22.Nathan[3], 4.Rachel[2] Arbogast, 1.John C.[1]), b. Mar 12 1886 in Omaha, Douglas Co., NE, d. Nov 11 1971 in Long Beach, Los Angeles Co., CA. Married Jul 2 1912 in Omaha, Douglas Co., NE, **Clara May Scott**, b. May 14 1893 in Council Bluffs, Pottawattamie Co., IA, d. Dec 15 1986 in Long Beach, Los Angeles Co., CA.

Children:

1290 i. Alvin Oscar[6] Waybright b. Mar 9 1913 in Omaha, Douglas Co., NE, d. Aug 4 1997 in Bakersfield, Kern Co., CA.
1291 ii. Roy Willis Waybright b. Feb 25 1917 in Omaha, Douglas Co., NE. He Married **Janice M. Jackley**, b. Jan 3 1917 in Kansas, d. Dec 18 1990 in San Francisco, CA.
1292 iii. Robert Franklin Waybright b. Apr 19 1922 in Omaha, Douglas Co., NE, d. Jul 29 1992 in Bakersfield, Kern Co., CA. Married 1942, **Ermgard Helene Schnecke**, b. 1922 in Germany.

590. **Grover Cleveland[5] Waybright** (169.Adam Harness[4], 22.Nathan[3], 4.Rachel[2] Arbogast, 1.John C.[1]), b. Nov 5 1888 in Omaha, Douglas Co., NE, d. Feb 14 1975 in Long Beach, Los Angeles Co., CA, buried in Medford. Middlesex Co., MA.
Married 1926 in Omaha, Douglas Co., NE, **Grace Davies Wiley**, b. Jul 8 1897 in Dorchester, Suffolk Co., MA, d. Jul 11 1962.

Children:

1293 i. Bruce Wiley[6] Waybright b. Jul 23 1927 in Medford. Middlesex Co., MA, d. Jan 16 1991.
1294 ii. Douglas Giles Waybright b. Nov 27 1928 in Winthrop, Suffolk's Co., MA, d. Nov 2 1965 in Saugus, Essex Co., MA.. the School was named after Douglas Waybright a great football player for Saugus High school, Graduated from Notre Dame.

605. **Hilbert[5] Rexroad** (176.Amby[4], 23.Elizabeth[3] Waybright, 4.Rachel[2] Arbogast, 1.John C.[1]), b. About 1872.
Married About 1892, **Sally T (Unknown)**.

Children:

1295 i. Emma Lillie[6] Rexroad b. About 1896.
1296 ii. Ida B Rexroad b. About 1898.
1297 iii. Myron S Rexroad b. About 1905.

612. **Kemper D[5] Rexroad** (177.Jefferson D[4], 23.Elizabeth[3] Waybright, 4.Rachel[2] Arbogast, 1.John C.[1]), b. June 1881.
Married Jan 14 1907 in Highland Co., VA, **Linnie M Newman**, b. About 1882. **Linnie**: Child of Salisbury Newman and Phebe Rymer.

Children:

1298 i. Edwin C[6] Rexroad b. About 1910.

620. **Erma Creigh[5] Waybright** (181.Clark W.[4], 24.Levi[3], 4.Rachel[2] Arbogast, 1.John C.[1]), b. in Braxton Co., WV.
She Married **James B Jackson**.

Children:

1299 i. Frances M.[6] Jackson.
1300 ii. Margaret Jackson.

625. **Walter Wade[5] Waybright** (181.Clark W.[4], 24.Levi[3], 4.Rachel[2] Arbogast, 1.John C.[1]), b. Apr 5 1893 in Braxton Co., WV, d. Jul 1965.
He Married **Margaret Cottrill**.

Children:

1301 i. James Franklin[6] Waybright.
1302 ii. John Robert Waybright.
1303 iii. Betty Lee Waybright.
1304 iv. Walter Roy Waybright.

632. **Fannie May[5] Hinkle** (189.Elbridge L.[4], 26.Martha Ann[3] Waybright, 4.Rachel[2] Arbogast, 1.John C.[1]), b. May 27 1877, d. Jan 10 1933.
Married Jun 12 1899 in Highland Co., VA, **Albert Simmons**, b. Feb 09 1872, d. Jul 08 1934, buried in Blue Grass Cem., Highland Co., VA.

Children:

1305 i. Ethel S[6] Simmons b. April 1900.
\+ 1306 ii. Ralph Scott Simmons b. Jan 18 1903.
1307 iii. Elbridge H Simmons b. 1904.
1308 iv. Roxie Simmons b. 1906.
1309 v. Roy Simmons b. 1906.
1310 vi. Sylvia H Simmons b. 1912.

634. **Clyde[5] Rymer** (190.Susan[4] Hinkle, 26.Martha Ann[3] Waybright, 4.Rachel[2] Arbogast, 1.John C.[1]), b. Mar 30 1881, d. Mar 22 1956.
He Married **Sallie Cook**, b. Oct 13 1885, d. Dec 11 1970.

Children:

	1311	i.	Mary[6] Rymer b. 1908.
+	1312	ii.	Virgil Rymer b. Nov 03 1908.

635. **Sudie R[5] Rymer** (190.Susan[4] Hinkle, 26.Martha Ann[3] Waybright, 4.Rachel[2] Arbogast, 1.John C.[1]), b. Feb 12 1886, d. Jun 29 1966.
Married c 1907, **Charlie N Bennett**, b. Sep 24 1885, d. Sep 25 1941.

Children:

	1313	i.	John[6] Bennett.
	1314	ii.	Ada Bennett.

636. **Dolly[5] Mullenax** (191.Elizabeth C[4] Hinkle, 26.Martha Ann[3] Waybright, 4.Rachel[2] Arbogast, 1.John C.[1]), b. Mar 04 1879 in Pendleton Co., WV, d. Jul 10 1957 in Arbovale Cem., Arbovale, Pocahontas Co., WV.
(1) Married Nov 22 1894, **Solomon Harvey Johnston**, b. Jan 01 1871, d. Aug 26 1962 in Arbovale Cem., Arbovale, Pocahontas Co., WV. (.

Children *by Solomon Harvey Johnston:*

	1315	i.	Mona[6] Johnston b. Feb 10 1896. She Married **Lacy Bowling**.
	1316	ii.	Otis Johnston b. Jul 7 1897, d. Jun 20 1920.
+	1317	iii.	Cletis Johnston b. Jul 31 1902.
	1318	iv.	William Johnston b. Oct 26 1904. He Married **Elizabeth Matheney**.
+	1319	v.	Jesse Johnston b. Jul 2 1907.
	1320	vi.	Judith Johnston b. Sep 25 1909 in Bartow, Pocahontas Co., WV, d. Jul 26 1990. Married Jun 26 1939, **Paul Lowell Bennett**, d. Nov 25 1981.
+	1321	vii.	Georgia Ellen Johnston b. Oct 01 1911.
	1322	viii.	Mildred Johnston b. Dec 30 1913, d. 1992. She Married **W. I. Willey**.
	1323	ix.	Virginia Johnston b. Oct 27 1916. She Married Carl Mallow.
	1324	x.	Merle Johnston b. Sep 9 1922. He Married **Mary Musser**.
	1325	xi.	CLETUS Johnston. She Married **Ollice C Warner**, b. Mar-01-1915 (son of Charles Warner and Maryellen Wimer).

(2) She Married **Solomon Johnson**

637. **Lura[5] Mullenax** (191.Elizabeth C[4] Hinkle, 26.Martha Ann[3] Waybright, 4.Rachel[2] Arbogast, 1.John C.[1]), b. Jun 28 1881, d. Dec 11 1961.
She Married **Pet Warner**, b. Sep 29 1877, d. Sep 22 1952 in Warner Cem., Hunting Ground, Pendleton Co., VA/WV.

Children:

	1326	i.	Jenna[6] Warner b. Sep 18 1902. Married Mar 10 1951, **Otha Lambert**, d. 1968.
+	1327	ii.	Verlie Warner b. Dec 27 1903.
	1328	iii.	Evelyn Warner b. Jan 23 1907. She Married **Richard Phares**.
+	1329	iv.	Betty Warner b. Jul 26 1913.
+	1330	v.	Judith Warner b. Dec 18 1915.
	1331	vi.	Argle Warner b. Feb 26 1922.

638. **Mcclelland[5] Mullenax** (191.Elizabeth C[4] Hinkle, 26.Martha Ann[3] Waybright, 4.Rachel[2] Arbogast, 1.John C.[1]), b. Oct 25 1883, d. 1961.
He Married **Anna B. Cummingham**, b. 1882, d. 1943.

Children:

+	1332	i.	Brooks Burdette[6] Mullenax b. Apr 23 1918.

639. **Martha Ellen[5] Mullenax** (191.Elizabeth C[4] Hinkle, 26.Martha Ann[3] Waybright, 4.Rachel[2] Arbogast, 1.John C.[1]), b. Feb 1891.
She Married **Otha Lambert**, d. 1968.

Children:

+	1333	i.	Harlan[6] Mullenax b. May 11 1912.
+	1334	ii.	Halcie Mullenax.

640. **Betty Alice[5] Mullenax** (191.Elizabeth C[4] Hinkle, 26.Martha Ann[3] Waybright, 4.Rachel[2] Arbogast, 1.John C.[1]), b. Feb 28 1891 in Churchville, Pendleton Co., WV, d. Sep 09 1941 in Beverly, Randolph Co., WV.
Married Apr 25 1938, **David Frederick Hulver**.

Children:

1335 i. Hinkle[6] Hulver.
1336 ii. Mildred Hulver. She Married **George Fencemaker**.
1337 iii. Irene Hulver.
Died in teens, accident top Allegany Mnt.

641. **Cleat[5] Phares** (192.Eliza Ann[4] Hinkle, 26.Martha Ann[3] Waybright, 4.Rachel[2] Arbogast, 1.John C.[1]), b. Sep 19 1884, d. May 22 1938.
He Married **Edith C Hammer**, b. May 22 1884, d. Oct 10 1937.

Children:

\+ 1338 i. Elmer P.[6] Phares b. 1908.
1339 ii. Myrtle K Phares b. Apr 16 1911, d. Dec 26 1980. She Married **Ramsey Teter**, b. Apr 09 1910. Ramsey: Son of Ambrose Teter and Ann Rebecca Warner.

651. **Martha Ann[5] Hinkle** (194.Isaac Harness[4], 26.Martha Ann[3] Waybright, 4.Rachel[2] Arbogast, 1.John C.[1]), b. May 11 1902, d. Oct 12 1992.
She Married **Charles A Warner**.

Children:

1340 i. Genevieve[6] Warner.
1341 ii. Ann Warner.
1342 iii. Harold Warner.
1343 iv. Jack T Warner.
1344 v. Charles J Warner.
1345 vi. John Edward Warner.

652. **Ashby[5] Sponaugle** (199.Roseann[4] Ketterman, 28.Alice[3] Waybright, 5.Rebecca[2] Arbogast, 1.John C.[1]), b. 1868 in Hunting Ground, Pendleton Co., (W)VA, d. Feb 24 1945.
Married Feb-12-1889 in Randolph County, WV, **Mary Catherine Mullenax**.

Children:

1346 i. Glenn[6] Sponaugle.

653. **Gilbert Kenton[5] Sponaugle** (199.Roseann[4] Ketterman, 28.Alice[3] Waybright, 5.Rebecca[2] Arbogast, 1.John C.[1]), b. Jan 2 1870 in Hunting Ground, Pendleton Co., (W)VA, d. Dec 30 1924, buried in Sponaugle Family Cem., Hunting Grounds Pendleton County WV.
He Married **Annie Pressie Mallow**, b. Nov-14-1986 in Circleville Pendleton Co., WV (daughter of Benjamin Franklin Mallow and Roxanna Nelson), buried in Sponaugle, Circleville, WV, d. Dec-27-1982 in Elkins, Randolph Co., WV. **Annie**: She had been Married twice. After her first husband, **Gilbert Sponaugle**, died in 1925, she Married **Bead Sponaugle**. DEC 1982 in Randolph Co., WV Pendleton Times Obituary

Children:

1347 i. Shirley Arlene[6] Sponaugle b. Jan 13 1914 in Pendleton Co., WV, d. Apr 19 1974 in Springville, Utah Co., UT. (1) Married Sep 9 1933 in Pendleton Co., WV, **William Guy Johnston,** b. Mar 17 1913 in Pendleton Co., WV (son of Robert Boyd Johnston and Bertie Kate Arbogast), d. Jul 13 2003 in Provo, Utah Co., UT. (2) She Married **Thomas Lynn Johnston**, b. Dec 18 1954 in Randolph Co., WV, d. Oct 8 1980 in Boise, Ada Co., ID.
\+ 1348 ii. Ethel Mae Sponaugle b. Aug-06-1906.
1349 iii. Zallie Sponaugle b. 1908, d. 1910.
\+ 1350 iv. Brison Jay Sponaugle b. Apr 03 1911.
1351 v. Benjamin Franklin Sponaugle b. Jun-06-1916 in Pendleton Co., WV, d. Sep-28-1999. He Married **Ruthenia Marie Vanaman Blankenship**, b. Jul-23-1927 (daughter of Charles Isaac Vanaman and Minnie Belle Bishop), buried in Arlington, Arlington VA, d. Feb-13-1974.
1352 vi. John Eber Sponaugle b. Jun-07-1918 in Hunting Ground, Pendleton Co. WV, buried in Sponaugle Cem., Smith Creek, Pendleton Co., WV, d. Sep-21-1940 in Hunting Ground, Pendleton Co. WV. Informant, Isaac Mallow - cause of death, Suicide (gun shot in right side of head - place of death, School Ground

1353 vii. Mary Wilda Sponaugle b. Jun-14-1922 in Hunting Ground, Pendleton Co. WV, d. Dec-16-2012 in Cuyahoga Co., OH. She Married **Lloyd E Bennett**, b. Jan-18-1925, buried in Sponaugle Family Cem., Hunting Grounds Pendleton County WV, d. May-28-1901.

656. **William Letcher[5] Sponaugle** (199.Roseann[4] Ketterman, 28.Alice[3] Waybright, 5.Rebecca[2] Arbogast, 1.John C.[1]), b. Sep 16 1875 in Hunting Ground, Pendleton Co., (W)VA, d. May 21 1960. He Married **Leona Arbogast**, b. Aug 18 1899 in Pendleton Co., WV (daughter of Elijah J. Arbogast and Roberta Prudence Arbaugh), d. Aug 27 1992 in Harrisburg, Raleigh Co., VA.

Children:

+ 1354 i. Herbert Charles[6] Sponaugle b. Sep 1 1913.
+ 1355 ii. Nola Lee Sponaugle b. Jan 21 1916.
1356 iii. Olin Raymond Sponaugle b. Jan 15 1918 in Cherry Grove, Pendleton Co., WV, d. May 10 1992 in Hunting Ground, Pendleton Co., (W)VA.
1357 iv. Sudie Sponaugle b. Nov 29 1919 in Cherry Grove, Pendleton Co., WV, d. Aug 16 1932.
1358 v. Thelma Sponaugle b. Sep 4 1921 in Cherry Grove, Pendleton Co., WV. She Married **James William Sponaugle**, b. May 17 1914 in Pendleton Co., WV, d. Nov 30 1996 in Raleigh Co., NC.
1359 vi. Jacob Cenior Sponaugle b. Apr 20 1923 in Pendleton Co., WV. Married Jul 8 1949, **Emma Lee Wilson**, b. Feb 14 1928.
+ 1360 vii. Roche Elijah Sponaugle b. Mar 1 1925.
1361 viii. Merlie Sponaugle b. Dec 14 1926 in Pendleton Co., WV.
+ 1362 ix. Rosie Zona Sponaugle b. Jul 20 1928.

657. **Herman Henry[5] Sponaugle** (199.Roseann[4] Ketterman, 28.Alice[3] Waybright, 5.Rebecca[2] Arbogast, 1.John C.[1]), b. Jan 13 1877 in Hunting Ground, Pendleton Co. WV, d. Sep 25 1953 in Pendleton Co., WV.
Married Jun-08-1902, **Etta Beulah Warner**.

Children:

+ 1363 i. Marvin Luther[6] Sponaugle b. Jun-08-1903.
+ 1364 ii. Beulah Sponaugle b. Jul-26-1901.
+ 1365 iii. Raymond Sponaugle b. Mar-09-1905.
+ 1366 iv. Alpha Cynyhia Sponaugle b. Dec-18-1907.
+ 1367 v. Myrtle M Sponaugle b. Dec-13-1908.
1368 vi. Elsie Mildred Sponaugle b. Apr-17-1919. She Married **Stanley White**.
1369 vii. Kitty Belle Sponaugle b. Apr 24 1912 in Churchville, Pendleton Co., WV. Married in Franklin Co., WV, **Morris Waybright**, b. Sep 30 1905 in Rich Mountain, Pendleton Co., WV (son of Wilber Allen Waybright and Sena White).
+ 1370 viii. Mary Kerlin Sponaugle b. Mar-07-1914.
+ 1371 ix. Levern Sponaugle b. Dec-16-1919.
+ 1372 x. Roscoe Sponaugle b. May-10-1921.
1373 xi. Idelta Rebecca Sponaugle b. Nov-01-1925.
1374 xii. Jacob Sponaugle.
1375 xiii. Clifford Sponaugle.
+ 1376 xiv. Ruth Sponaugle b. May-18-1918.

664. **Katie[5] Ketterman** (200.Solomon W.[4], 28.Alice[3] Waybright, 5.Rebecca[2] Arbogast, 1.John C.[1]), b. Aug 1893 in Pendleton Co., WV, d. in Paw Paw Morgan Co., WV.
She Married **Merley Waybright**, b. Aug 1893, d. in Paw Paw Morgan Co., WV.

Children:

1377 i. William[6] Waybright d. in Paw Paw Morgan Co., WV.
1378 ii. Francis Waybright d. in Paw Paw Morgan Co., WV.
1379 iii. Andrew Waybright d. in Paw Paw Morgan Co., WV.
1380 iv. (unknown) Waybright d. in Paw Paw Morgan Co., WV.
1381 v. Robert Waybright d. in Paw Paw Morgan Co., WV.
1382 vi. Elizabeth Waybright d. in Paw Paw Morgan Co., WV.

666. **Louella[5] Pennington** (204.Ann Rebecca[4] Ketterman, 28.Alice[3] Waybright, 5.Rebecca[2] Arbogast, 1.John C.[1]), b. Apr 25 1880 in Pendleton Co., WV, d. Jan 6 1964 in Flintstone, Allegheny Co., MD.
(1) She Married **James May**, b. Jan 1875, d. Jun 11 1904 in Randolph Co., WV.

Children *by James May:*

1383 i. Leslie Jane[6] May b. Apr 21 1901 in Pendleton Co., WV, d. Sep 26 1971 in Kanawha, Kanawha Co., WV. Married May 11 1922 in Pendleton Co., WV, **Albert Thompson**, b. Apr 19 1896 in Riverton, Pendleton Co., WV, d. Feb 18 1982 in Charleston, Kanawha Co., WV, buried in Cunningham Memorial Park, St Albans, Kanawha Co., WV.

1384 ii. Jesse Jay May b. About 1905.

(2) Married c 1907, **George Arbaugh**, b. Aug 9 1870 in Pendleton Co., WV, d. Jun 18 1963 in Flintstone, Allegheny Co., MD.

Children *by George Arbaugh:*

1385 iii. Lillian Arbaugh b. Feb 6 1907 in Pendleton Co., WV, d. Nov 28 1988 in Rockville, Montgomery Co., MD. Married Jun 11 1928, **John Murphy**.

\+ 1386 iv. Karl Janson Arbaugh b. Jul 06 1909.

1387 v. Ruby Kate Arbaugh b. Sep 14 1911 in Pendleton Co., WV, d. Sep 1989 in Anne Arundel Co., MD.

1388 vi. Nona Virginia Arbaugh b. Dec 19 1913 in Pendleton Co., WV, d. Feb 17 1981 in Cumberland, Alleghany Co., MD.

1389 vii. Marjorie Arbaugh b. Aug 30 1918 in Pendleton Co., WV, d. Mar 30 1990.

1390 viii. Rebecca Anna Arbaugh b. Dec 14 1920 in Pendleton Co., WV, d. Feb 22 1987.

1391 ix. Ollie N Arbaugh b. Jul 28 1923 in Pendleton Co., WV, d. Jul 30 1990.

669. **Melissa Francis[5] Strauder** (205.Susan P.[4] Ketterman, 28.Alice[3] Waybright, 5.Rebecca[2] Arbogast, 1.John C.[1]), b. Aug-19-1975, d. Aug-27-1939. (

1) Married Aug-18-1975, **Eli Louk** (son of Andrew Louk and Rachel Louk). (.

Children *by Eli Louk:*

1392 i. Eli[6] Louk b. c 1901.

2) Married Sep-01-1916 in Randolph Co., WV, **Ed Johnson**

670. **Fleetwood[5] Strauder** (205.Susan P.[4] Ketterman, 28.Alice[3] Waybright, 5.Rebecca[2] Arbogast, 1.John C.[1]), b. Jun-23-1877, d. Jul-17-1949.

He Married **Sally Bennett**, b. 1883.

Children:

1393 i. Lillie[6] Bennett b. 1918, d. 1921.

673. **Molley[5] Strauder** (205.Susan P.[4] Ketterman, 28.Alice[3] Waybright, 5.Rebecca[2] Arbogast, 1.John C.[1]), b. Sep 1894.

(1) She Married **James Vest**, b. c1893.

Children *by James Vest:*

1394 i. Helen[6] Vest b. c 1904.

1395 ii. Ernest Vest b. 1908.

\+ 1396 iii. Virginia C. Vest b. 1910.

(2) Married Apr-12-1923 in Randolph Co., WV, **Henry Weese**, b. in Barbour Co., WV.

674. **Ora Clifton[5] Strauder** (205.Susan P.[4] Ketterman, 28.Alice[3] Waybright, 5.Rebecca[2] Arbogast, 1.John C.[1]), b. Mar 1886.

He Married **Roberta Arbogast**, b. Feb 02 1892 in Pendleton Co., WV (daughter of Martin Van Buren Arbogast and Martha Ellen Helmick), d. Dec 22 1968.

Children:

1397 i. Cecil[6] Strauder b. 1910.

1398 ii. Gilbert Strauder.

1399 iii. Delmar Strauder.

1400 iv. Ora Strauder.

1401 v. Delbert Strauder b. 1918, d. 1994. He Married **Ella Davis**.

1402 vi. Elmer Strauder b. 1927, d. 1932.

676. **Mayberry[5] Strauder** (205.Susan P.[4] Ketterman, 28.Alice[3] Waybright, 5.Rebecca[2] Arbogast, 1.John C.[1]), b. May-10-1890, d. Aug-30-1974.

Matberry had a child with Mary Artie Hedrick, Mason Strawser, born 1908 and Married Georgie Vandevender born 1915.

She Married **Verna May**, b. 1896.

Children:

1403 i. Russie[6] Strauder. She Married **Clifford Harr**.
1404 ii. Raymond Strauder. He Married **Alma Kearns.**

678. **Wilber Allen[5] Waybright** (208.Churchill[4], 28.Alice[3], 5.Rebecca[2] Arbogast, 1.John C.[1]), b. Jul 8 1869 in Dry Run, Pendleton Co., WV, d. Jun 2 1958 in Elkins, Randolph Co., WV, buried in Old Fellows Cem., Elkins, Randolph Co., WV.
Married 1893, **Sena White**, b. Mar 8 1875 in Dry Run, Pendleton Co., WV, d. Apr 12 1963 in Canton, Stark Co., OH, buried in Old Fellows Cem., Elkins, Randolph Co., WV.

Children:

\+ 1405 i. Iona Patrica[6] Waybright b. Apr 24 1894.
1406 ii. Morris Waybright b. Sep 30 1905 in Rich Mountain, Pendleton Co., WV. Married in Franklin Co., WV, Kitty **Belle Sponaugle**, b. Apr 24 1912 in Churchville, Pendleton Co., WV (daughter of Herman Henry Sponaugle and Etta Beulah Warner).

680. **Amby Stanton[5] Waybright** (208.Churchill[4], 28.Alice[3], 5.Rebecca[2] Arbogast, 1.John C.[1]), b. Sep 30 1873 in Dry Run, Pendleton Co., WV, d. Jul 12 1935 in Thornwood, Pocahontas Co., WV, buried in Thornwood, Pocahontas Co., WV.
Married Sep 30 1902 in Cumberland, Alleghany Co., MD, **Charlotte Nelson**, b. Apr 17 1883 in Pendleton Co., WV, d. Dec 27 1980, buried in Arbovale Cem., Arbovale, Pocahontas Co., WV.

Children:

\+ 1407 i. Ollie Katherine[6] Waybright b. Sep 30 1903.
\+ 1408 ii. Grace Elizabeth Waybright b. Jun 16 1905.
\+ 1409 iii. Gertrude Lee Waybright b. Dec 2 1907.
\+ 1410 iv. Rella K Waybright b. Sep 29 1908.
1411 v. Emery Henry Waybright b. Jun 1 1910 in Pocahontas Co., WV, d. Apr 3 1989 in Bartow, Pocahontas Co., WV. He Married **Margie K Varner**, b. May 23 1911 in Pocahontas Co., WV, d. Feb 7 1985 in Randolph Co., WV, buried in Arbovale Cem., Arbovale, Pocahontas Co., WV.
\+ 1412 vi. Edna Alice Waybright b. Mar 27 1912.

682. **Fransina Lee[5] Waybright** (208.Churchill[4], 28.Alice[3], 5.Rebecca[2] Arbogast, 1.John C.[1]), b. Mar 28 1877 in Dry Run, Pendleton Co., WV, d. Apr 25 1929 in Pocahontas Co., WV, buried in Warner Cem., Hunting Ground, Pendleton Co., VA/WV.
Married 1897 in Pendleton Co., WV, **John W. Warner**, b. May 15 1874 in Pendleton Co., WV, d. Sep 5 1960, buried in Warner Cem., Hunting Ground, Pendleton Co., VA/WV.

Children:

\+ 1413 i. Bertie Catherine[6] Warner b. Jul 9 1903.
1414 ii. Myrtle R. Warner b. Nov 25 1907 in Churchville, Pendleton Co., WV. (1) Married Dec 3 1924, **Robert C. Bennett**, b. Apr 1904. (2) She Married **Bead Sponaugle**, b. Apr 1908.
1415 iii. Emory J. Warner b. Jan 9 1913 in Churchville, Pendleton Co., WV, d. Apr 19 1994. He Married **Tina Judy** (daughter of Olie Judy and Tina Warner).

686. **Arbelia[5] Wimer** (212.Jeremiah Emanuel[4], 29.Sidney[3] Waybright, 5.Rebecca[2] Arbogast, 1.John C.[1]), b. 1886.
She Married **Aaron C. Mullenax**, b. Wft Est. 1858-1885 (son of Henry Clay Mullenax and Elizabeth Susan Calhoun), d. Wft Est. 1878-1964.

Children:

\+ 1416 i. Ollie Elizabeth[6] Mullenax b. Mar 2 1905.
1417 ii. Elva Mullenax.
1418 iii. Lester Mullenax.
1419 iv. Calhoun Mullenax b. 1910, d. 1989. He Married **Haxel Mullenax**.
1420 v. Merle Mullenax b. 1915.
\+ 1421 vi. Nellie Susan Mullenax b. Jun 6 1912.

688. **Mary Ellen[5] Wimer** (212.Jeremiah Emanuel[4], 29.Sidney[3] Waybright, 5.Rebecca[2] Arbogast, 1.John C.[1]) (See marriage to number 518.)

697. **Ida H[5] Harold** (213.Jennie[4] Wimer, 29.Sidney[3] Waybright, 5.Rebecca[2] Arbogast, 1.John C.[1]), b. 1902, d. 1966. M
Married 1919, **Zellie Bryan Moyers**, b. 1897, d. 1960.

Children:

1422 i. Stella[6] Moyers. She Married **Raymond Eye**.
1423 ii. Rubie Moyers. She Married **Guy Turley**.
1424 iii. Ray Moyers.

1425 iv. Raymonds Moyers.

705. **Luticia S^5 Grady** (219.Ann Rebecca Elizabeth^4 Waybright, 32.Elijah^3, 5.Rebecca^2 Arbogast, 1.John C.^{1}), b. 1879. She Married **Joseph Thompson**, b. 1867, d. 1926. **Joseph**: There may have bee one of 2 more children.

Children:

1426 i. Don A^6 Thompson b. 1897, d. 1911.
1427 ii. Marvin Thompson b. 1900.
1428 iii. Margie Thompson b. 1903.
1429 iv. Harry G Thompson b. 1905.
1430 v. Fay Thompson b. 1907.
1431 vi. Grace Thompson b. 1909.

706. **James Pearl^5 Grady** (219.Ann Rebecca Elizabeth^4 Waybright, 32.Elijah^3, 5.Rebecca^2 Arbogast, 1.John C.^{1}), b. 1885. Married 1905, **Stella S George**.

Children:

1432 i. Orpha^6 Grady b. 1910.
1433 ii. Delmar Grady b. 1920.

707. **Cora A.^{5} Grady** (219.Ann Rebecca Elizabeth^4 Waybright, 32.Elijah^3, 5.Rebecca^2 Arbogast, 1.John C.^{1}), b. Nov 30 1886 in Churchville, Pendleton Co., WV.
Married Dec 28 1902 in Pendleton Co., WV, **Tirah McCullen Phares**, b. Aug 28 1877 in Churchville, Pendleton Co., WV.

Children:

1434 i. Bessie L^6 Phares b. 1905. She Married **Otto Seymour**.
1435 ii. Roy H Phares b. 1907. He Married **Marie Daukman**.
1436 iii. Massell Marie Phares b. 1911, d. 1990. He Married **Henry Burrell Lambert**, b. 1905, d. 1984.
1437 iv. Lee Phares.

708. **Ora Francis^5 Grady** (219.Ann Rebecca Elizabeth^4 Waybright, 32.Elijah^3, 5.Rebecca^2 Arbogast, 1.John C.^{1}), b. 1886, d. 1972. He Married **Maude Kee Hedrick**.

Children:

1438 i. William Tennyson^6 Grady b. 1911, d. 1911.
1439 ii. Leta Marie Grady b. 1912, d. 1916.
1440 iii. Herbert Brille Grady b. 1914. He Married **Lillie Belle Long**.
1441 iv. Woodrow Wilson Grady b. 1918. He Married **Tejlma Alene Cololan**, b. 1925.
1442 v. Freda Lucille Grady b. 1920. Married 1937, **Roy Otis Thompson**, b. 1913.
1443 vi. Ora Francis Grady, Jr. b. 1922. He Married **Jessie Alt.**
1444 vii. Mary Violet Grady b. 1923, d. 1932.
1445 viii. (infant) Grady b. 1928, d. 1928.

709. **Sallie Odessa^5 Grady** (219.Ann Rebecca Elizabeth^4 Waybright, 32.Elijah^3, 5.Rebecca^2 Arbogast, 1.John C.^{1}), b. 1889, d. 1961. She Married **Charles B Smith, Sr.**.

Children:

1446 i. Mable C^6 Smith.
1447 ii. Guy E Smith b. 1910.

728. **Abel Washington^5 Waybright** (224.George Washington^4, 32.Elijah^3, 5.Rebecca^2 Arbogast, 1.John C.^{1}), b. Feb 6 1880 in Spruce Mountain Pendleton Co., WV, d. Nov 28 1958 in Fellowsville, Preston Co., WV, buried in Mount Israel Methodist Church Fellowsville, Preston Co., WV.
(1) Married Oct 2 1901 in Pendleton Co., WV, **Hannah Elizabeth Bennett**, b. Jan 29 1875 in Pendleton Co., WV, d. Feb 22 1922 in Eglon, Preston Co., WV, buried in Maple Springs Cem., Eglon, Preston Co., WV.

***Children** by Hannah Elizabeth Bennett:*

\+ 1448 i. Noah Washington^6 Waybright b. May 12 1902.
\+ 1449 ii. Josiah Waybright b. Mar 6 1905.
\+ 1450 iii. John Waybright b. Jun 10 1907.
1451 iv. Ettie Waybright b. Jan 21 1911 in Accident Cem., Preston Co., WV. (1) Married Jul 13 1978 in Oakland, Garrett Co., MD, **Lyle Mitter**, b. Sep 30 1921 in New Bern, Craven Co., NC. (2) Married Jul 17 1935 in Kingwood,

Preston Co., WV, **Joseph Ezra Loughridge**, b. Jul 27 1881, d. Apr 15 1973 in Kingwood, Preston Co., WV. (3) She Married **Wait Hershman**.

1452 v. Margaret Waybright d. Feb 3 1997 in Accident Cem., Preston Co., WV, buried in Mount Zion Church Cem., Marques, Hampshire Co., WV. (1) Married Oct 12 1931 in Sinclair Preston Co., WV, **Joseph G. Holyfield**, b. Sep 25 1867 in Sinclair Preston Co., WV, d. Apr 1 1943 in Stevensburg, Culpeper Co., WV, buried in Mount Zion Church Cem., Marques, Hampshire Co., WV. (2) Married Oct 31 1944 in Oakland, Garrett Co., MD, **John Maurice Ridenour**, b. Nov 23 1897 in Flag Run Preston Co., WV, d. Jun 12 1980, buried in Flag Chapel Cem., Preston Co., WV.

1453 vi. Anabelle Waybright b. Feb 22 1919 in Erwin, Preston Co., WV, d. Mar 30 1987, buried in Mount Israel Methodist Church Fellowsville, Preston Co., WV. Married Sep 24 1938 in Kingwood, Preston Co., WV, **Neal Howard Hershman**, b. Jun 20 1913 in Kasson, Preston Co., WV.

(2) Married Sep 30 1925 in Pendleton Co., WV, **Zula Bennett**, b. Apr 6 1894, d. Feb 28 1963, buried in Mount Israel Methodist Church Fellowsville, Preston Co., WV.

Children *by Zula Bennett:*

1454 vii. Myrtle Bennett b. Aug 20 1906 in Churchville, Pendleton Co., WV.
Father said to be Hendricks Waybright
Married Oct 15 1927 in Pierce, Tucker Co., WV, **James Andrew Ketterman**.

1455 viii. Roy Bennett b. Mar 25 1914 in Eglon, Preston Co., WV.
Roy's father said to be Abel Waybright
Married Aug 1 1942 in Oakland, Garrett Co., MD, **Martha Hester Nethken**.

1456 ix. Elsie Waybright b. Jun 5 1924 in Erwin, Preston Co., WV, d. Dec 25 1994 in Webster Springs, Webster Co., WV, buried in Wood Dale Memorial Park, Pruntytown, Grafton, Taylor Co., WV. Married Mar 30 1942 in Oakland, Garrett Co., MD, **Andrew Jay Mitchell**, b. Apr 2 1911 in Clemtown, Barbour Co., WV, d. Nov 7 1999 in Riverside Regional Hospital, Newport News, VA, buried in Wood Dale Memorial Park, Pruntytown, Grafton, Taylor Co., WV. Andrew: Was in the U.S. Army.

1457 x. Ida Waybright b. Aug 22 1926 in Pierce, Tucker Co., WV. Married Aug 27 1948 in Oakland, Garrett Co., MD, **Ray Edward Simon**, b. Jul 31 1928 in Kingwood, Preston Co., WV. Ray: .

1458 xi. Ernest Waybright b. Feb 12 1929 in Etam, Preston Co., WV.

730. **Luther Lee[5] Waybright** (224.George Washington[4], 32.Elijah[3], 5.Rebecca[2] Arbogast, 1.John C.[1]), b. Jun 16 1883 in Rowlesburg, Preston Co., WV.

(1) He Married **Myrtle L. Owens**.

(2) He Married **Pallie Susan Summerfield**.

Children *by Pallie Susan Summerfield:*

1459 i. Mary C.[6] Waybright b. May 8 1905 in Pendleton Co., WV.

\+ 1460 ii. Ethel Florence Waybright b. Mar 12 1907.

1461 iii. Burgess Lee Waybright b. Jan 22 1909 in Pendleton Co., WV, d. May 7 1978, buried in Mount Olive Cem., Lantz Ridge Road, Preston Co., WV. Married Aug 5 1932, **Myrtle G. Nice**, b. May 30 1913 in Rowlesburg, Preston Co., WV.

\+ 1462 iv. Sadie Annie Waybright b. Dec 11 1910.

1463 v. Monnie Dove Waybright b. Dec 2 1912 in Pendleton Co., WV.
She Married **Linwood Andrew Mann**, b. Oct 20 1909 in Hampton, VA, d. Mar 1980.

1464 vi. Henry Clay Waybright b. May 15 1914 in Pendleton Co., WV, d. Oct 22 1969, buried in Limestone Cem. He Married **Florence Virginia James**.

1465 vii. Glespa George Waybright b. Aug 17 1915 in Pendleton Co., WV, d. Nov 29 1916 in Pendleton Co., WV.

(3) He Married **Sarah Ellen Streets**, b. Apr 17 1907 in Tucker Co., WV, d. Mar 11 1963 in Tucker Co., WV, buried Mar 14 1963 in Nestor Cem., Bull Run, St. George, Tucker Co., WV.

Children *by Sarah Ellen Streets:*

1466 viii. Bonnie Virginia Mae Waybright b. Mar 23 1926 in Rowlesburg, Preston Co., WV, d. Oct 26 1926 in Rowlesburg, Preston Co., WV, buried in Nestor Cem., Bull Run, St. George, Tucker Co., WV.

1467 ix. Carl Esron Waybright b. May 9 1927 in Rowlesburg, Preston Co., WV.

1468 x. Kenneth Ray Waybright b. Dec 9 1935 in Rowlesburg, Preston Co., WV, d. Jun 28 1973 in Tarrant Co., TX.

1469 xi. James Burl Waybright b. Oct 11 1945 in Rowlesburg, Preston Co., WV, d. Nov 20 1977 in Parsons, Tucker Co., WV.

731. **Hendricks Cleveland[5] Waybright** (224.George Washington[4], 32.Elijah[3], 5.Rebecca[2] Arbogast, 1.John C.[1]), b. Apr 16 1886 in Rowlesburg, Preston Co., WV, d. Oct 23 1951, buried in Warner Cem., Hunting Ground, Pendleton Co., VA/WV. Died from cancer.
Married Mar 13 1918 in Oakland, Garrett Co., MD, **Vesta Odas Knotts**, b. Dec 12 1902 in Rowlesburg, Preston Co., WV, d. Aug 15 1931, buried in Knotts Cem., Aurora, Preston Co., WV. **Vesta**: had epilepsy died from it.

Children:

+ 1470 i. George William[6] Waybright b. Apr 28 1919.
1471 ii. Woodrow Wilson Waybright b. Feb 22 1921, d. Aug 16 1943.
Killed by Lightning charring an Ax in woods
1472 iii. Elijah Edward Waybright b. Jan 3 1923, d. Feb 21 1970, buried Feb 25 1970 in Culpeper National Cem., Culpeper Co., VA. He Married **(unknown) Moats**.
1473 iv. Mary Virginia Waybright b. May 23 1926. She Married **Ira Bolyard**.
1474 v. Martha Catherine Waybright b. May 23 1926, d. Nov 16 1926.
died from whooping cough

732. **Surrilda Florence[5] Waybright** (224.George Washington[4], 32.Elijah[3], 5.Rebecca[2] Arbogast, 1.John C.[1]), b. Aug 28 1887 in Hunting Ground, Pendleton Co., (W)VA, d. Sep 13 1962, buried in Warner Cem., Hunting Ground, Pendleton Co., VA/WV.
Married Apr 3 1910, **Amby H. Warner**, b. Jun 20 1868 in Hunting Ground, Pendleton Co., (W)VA, d. Jun 19 1955, buried in Warner Cem., Hunting Ground, Pendleton Co., VA/WV.

Children:

1475 i. Samuel[6] Warner b. Jul 12 1909 in West Virginia, d. Sep 7 1984. (1) He Married **Ona Bell Teter**. (2) Married May 1 1930, **Ethel M. Bennett**, b. Jul 30 1910.
+ 1476 ii. Leota M. Warner b. Feb 11 1912.
1477 iii. Noah Warner b. Jul 4 1914 in West Virginia. Married Jul 27 1940, **Flornie Bennett**, b. Jun 19 1919.
+ 1478 iv. Peachie N. Warner b. Jun 29 1916.
1479 v. Opal V. Warner b. Oct 30 1921 in West Virginia. Married Jan 26 1946 in Riverton, Pendleton Co., WV, **Maxwell H. Bennett**, b. Mar 15 1922.
1480 vi. Bessie R Warner b. Dec 2 1924 in West Virginia. She Married **Curtis R. Warner**, b. Jun 16 1904 (son of Amby H. Warner and Debby Jane Sponaugle), d. Jul 9 1980.

733. **Martha Anne[5] Waybright** (224.George Washington[4], 32.Elijah[3], 5.Rebecca[2] Arbogast, 1.John C.[1]), b. Dec 24 1889 in Spruce Mountain Pendleton Co., WV, d. Dec 31 1972 in Oakland, Garrett Co., MD, buried in Accident Cem., Preston Co., WV.
Married Nov 5 1906, **Mcclelland Bennett**, b. Jan 1881.

Children:

1481 i. Clara[6] Bennett b. Aug 10 1908, d. Aug 23 1908.
1482 ii. Jennie Bennett b. Nov 3 1909, d. Jul 4 1996. She Married **Randall Garrett**, b. Oct 23 1906, d. Feb 7 1985.
1483 iii. Wesley Bennett b. Jan 8 1912, d. Mar 5 1990. He Married **Minnie Sophia Simmons**, b. Feb 20 1905, d. Sep 6 1990, buried in Accident Cem., Preston Co., WV.
1484 iv. Mary Catherine Bennett b. May 28 1914, d. Dec 4 1994, buried in Horse Shoe Run, Pendleton Co., WV.
1485 v. Maggie May Bennett b. Jun 15 1916. She Married **John Finley Pennington**.
1486 vi. Mabel Josephine Bennett b. Sep 12 1918. She Married **Jack Kenneth Cassidy**.
1487 vii. Leona Bennett b. Nov 27 1920. Married Jan 9 1939, **Russell Hanlon**, b. Jul 14 1920, d. Oct 16 1976.
1488 viii. Henry Robert Bennett b. Jun 3 1923, d. Aug 1961.
1489 ix. Alta Waybright Bennett b. Jun 9 1925. Married Apr 27 1943, **Arthur Junior Slaubaugh**, b. Sep 5 1924.
1490 x. Ada Bennett b. Jun 9 1925. She Married **Cecil Slaubaugh**, b. May 26 1916 in Horse Shoe Run, Pendleton Co., WV, d. Oct 17 1984 in Montrose, Randolph Co., WV.
1491 xi. Frank Eldon Bennett b. Nov 14 1933, d. Oct 21 1934.
1492 xii. George Adam Bennett d. Sep 6 1992.

747. **Franklin Cameron[5] Wimer** (227.Martha Ellen[4] Harold, 34.Catherine Elizabeth[3] Waybright, 5.Rebecca[2] Arbogast, 1.John C.[1]), b. Nov 14 1881, d. Oct 07 1941. Married Dec 27 1905 in Highland Co., VA, **Bonnie Kate Wimer**, b. 1885, d. 1972.

Children:

+ 1493 i. Eugene[6] Wimer b. Jan 24 1921.

766. **Fredrick Cleveland[5] Waybright** (239.Miles Adam[4], 35.Morgan[3], 5.Rebecca[2] Arbogast, 1.John C.[1]), b. Feb 7 1893 in Blue Grass Cem., Highland Co., VA, d. Dec 1972 in Ripley, Jackson Co., WV, buried in Union Cem., Churchville, Pendleton Co., WV.

Married Sep 3 1912 in Blue Grass, Highland Co., WV, **Laura Alice Lantz**, b. Dec 28 1896 in Blue Grass Cem., Highland Co., VA, d. Oct 11 1980 in Hagerstown, Washington Co., MD, buried in Union Cem., Churchville, Pendleton Co., WV.

Children:

1494 i. Dennis Cleo[6] Waybright b. Dec 31 1915 in Highland Co., VA, d. Jul 9 1935.
1495 ii. Stella Grace Waybright b. Mar 2 1916 in Highland Co., VA, d. Jan 14 1998 in Lyndhurst Waynesboro WV. She Married **Ray Burns**.
1496 iii. Paul Lee Waybright b. Apr 11 1918 in Highland Co., VA, d. Jan 24 1919 in Highland Co., VA.
1497 iv. Berlie Fredrick Waybright b. Dec 28 1919 in Highland Co., VA, d. Oct 1985.
1498 v. Roy Adam Waybright b. Dec 15 1922 in Middlebrook Augusta Co., VA, d. Nov 2 1999 in Richmond, Henrico Co., VA. Married Jul 12 1940, **Ruby Wolfe (Unknown)**.
1499 vi. Virginia May Waybright b. Jun 22 1925 in Highland Co., VA. Married Aug 19 1944, **James Mohler**.
1500 vii. Laura Madeline Waybright b. Jul 8 1928 in Highland Co., VA, d. Nov 3 1928 in Highland Co., VA.
1501 viii. Edna Maxine Waybright b. Oct 13 1929 in Augusta Co., VA. Married Jan 12 1948, Daniel Duff.
1502 ix. Homer Hyde Waybright b. Aug 17 1935 in Augusta Co., VA, d. Sep 21 1935 in Augusta Co., VA.

776. **William Garrett[5] Waybright** (241.Nicholas[4], 36.Miles[3], 5.Rebecca[2] Arbogast, 1.John C.[1]), b. Jan 7 1879 in Churchville, Pendleton Co., WV, d. Dec 23 1953 in Bath County Community Hospital, Hot Springs, VA, buried Dec 26 1953 in Waybright Cem., Blue Grass, Highland Co., VA.

(1) Married Jan 8 1905 in Highland Co., VA, **Lucinda Jane Helmick**, b. Aug 1886 in Monterey, Highland Co., VA, d. Jun 18 1927 in Blue Grass Cem., Highland Co., VA, buried Jun 21 1927 in Waybright Cem., Blue Grass, Highland Co., VA

***Children** by Lucinda Jane Helmick:*

\+ 1503 i. Rizpah Florence[6] Waybright b. Oct 4 1914.
\+ 1504 ii. Alda Christine Waybright b. Sep 19 1917.
1505 iii. Alleen Elizabeth Waybright b. Feb 14 1920 in Blue Grass Cem., Highland Co., VA, d. Feb 10 2000 in University of Virginia Medical Center, Charlottesville, VA, buried Feb 13 2000 in Waybright Cem., Blue Grass, Highland Co., VA. Married Jun 13 1934 in Churchville, Pendleton Co., WV, **James Vandevender**. _Divorce.
1506 iv. William Garnett Waybright b. May 21 1922 in Blue Grass Cem., Highland Co., VA, d. Oct 8 1988 in Rockingham Memorial Hospital, Harrisonburg Rockingham Co., VA, buried Oct 11 1988 in Mount Pleasant Church Cem., Harrisonburg Shenandoah Co., VA.
Married in Highland Co., VA, **Dora Blanch Hedrick**, b. Dec 18 1924 in Highland Co., VA.
1507 v. Cathern Almede Waybright b. Sep 12 1923 in Blue Grass, Highland Co., WV, d. Nov 1 1999 in Grant County Memorial Hospital Petersburg VA, buried Nov 4 1999 in North Fork, Pendleton Co., VA. Married Nov 11 1945 in Riverton, Pendleton Co., WV, **Edward Ervine Vandevender**. Edward: .

(2) He Married **Sarah Ellen Streets**, b. Apr 17 1907 in Tucker Co., WV, d. Mar 11 1963 in Tucker Co., WV, buried Mar 14 1963 in Nestor Cem., Bull Run, St. George, Tucker Co., WV.

788. **Levi Lillian[5] Moyers** (242.Ann Elizabeth[4] Waybright, 36.Miles[3], 5.Rebecca[2] Arbogast, 1.John C.[1]). She Married **Adam Harness Sponaugle**, b. Mar 12 1878 in Hunting Ground, Pendleton Co., (W)VA (son of George Washington Sponaugle and Ursula Thompson), d. Oct 27 1968 in Cherry Grove, Pendleton Co., WV.

Children:

\+ 1508 i. Omar Wilson[6] Sponaugle b. May 21 1921.

790. **Saulsberry N[5] Chew** (257.Lucinda[4] Arbogast, 40.Lemuel[3], 6.Joseph E.[2], 1.John C.[1]), b. Dec 1879. He Married **Edith Catherine Lambert**, b. Apr 06 1881, d. Aug 17 1965.

Children:

\+ 1509 i. George B.[6] Crew b. Aug 07 1904.

791. **Lillie May[5] Chew** (257.Lucinda[4] Arbogast, 40.Lemuel[3], 6.Joseph E.[2], 1.John C.[1]), b. Nov 09 1882, d. Sep 06 1936. Married Dec 21 1902 in Highland Co., VA, **George Washington Wimer**, b. Dec 03 1874, d. Nov 30 1950.

Children:

1510 i. Alvenza Morgan[6] Wimer b. 1904.
1511 ii. Louisanna Wimer b. 1906.
1512 iii. Lora Wimer b. 1908.
1513 iv. Claricy Wimer b. 1910.
1514 v. Lona Wimer b. 1914.
1515 vi. Vernon Wimer b. 1917.
1516 vii. Luther Harold Wimer b. 1920.

792. **Lettie Susan^5 Arbogast** (259.Martin Van Buren^4, 40.Lemuel^3, 6.Joseph E.^{2}, 1.John C.^{1}), b. Feb 22 1871, d. Nov 22 1930. She Married **Martin Michael Bell**, b. May 05 1867, d. Feb 04 1948.

Children:

1517 i. Annie^6 Bell.
\+ 1518 ii. Martin Boston Bell.
1519 iii. Minor Bell.
1520 iv. Dovie Bell.
1521 v. Coy Bell.
1522 vi. Thomas Bell.
1523 vii. Dora Bell.
1524 viii. Rachel Bell.
1525 ix. Cletus Bell.
1526 x. Garfield Bell.
1527 xi. Lula Bell.

793. **Mary Jane^5 Arbogast** (259.Martin Van Buren^4, 40.Lemuel^3, 6.Joseph E.^{2}, 1.John C.^{1}), b. Mar 1873. Married Feb 04 1914, **Cain Morral**, b. Jan 30 1868 in Pendleton Co., WV.

Children:

1528 i. Melvin^6 Morral b. Jan 1892.
\+ 1529 ii. Wineberg Morral b. Apr 1895.
1530 iii. Floda Morral b. Dec 1896.
1531 iv. Florence Morral b. Jan 1899, d. 1964.
\+ 1532 v. Arthur Morral b. Jun 10 1902.
1533 vi. Bertha C. Morral.
1534 vii. Delmar Morral b. May 05 1910 in Elkins, Randolph Co., WV, d. Mar 15 1995. She Married **Josia Lona Raines**, b. Jan 14 1903 in Horton, Randolph Co., WV, d. Apr 04 1994 in Elkins, Randolph Co., WV, buried in Riverton, Pendleton Co., WV. Daughter of William Jacton Taines and Sally Agnus Bland.
1535 viii. Grace Morral.

794. **Robert Calvin^5 Arbogast** (259.Martin Van Buren^4, 40.Lemuel^3, 6.Joseph E.^{2}, 1.John C.^{1}), b. Jan 01 1876 in Roaring Creek, Randolph Co., WV, d. Apr 02 1920.
Married Oct 25 1898 in Oakland, Garrett Co., MD, **Delphia Mae Vance**, b. May 22 1880 in Owego, Tioga Co., NY, d. Apr 09 1968 in Bridgewater, Rockingham Co., VA.

Children:

1536 i. Denver Lynn^6 Arbogast b. Aug 05 1899 in Pendleton Co., WV, d. Oct 16 1925 in Pendleton Co., WV.
\+ 1537 ii. Bertha Catherine Arbogast b. May 30 1903.
1538 iii. Earl Calvin Arbogast b. Jul 16 1905, d. Jul 24 1949.
1539 iv. Olie Martin Arbogast b. May 31 1910.
1540 v. Alta Gae Arbogast b. Jul 15 1915.
\+ 1541 vi. Blanche Ann Arbogast b. Jan 31 1918.

796. **Roberta^5 Arbogast** (259.Martin Van Buren^4, 40.Lemuel^3, 6.Joseph E.^{2}, 1.John C.^{1}) (See marriage to number 674.)

811. **Bess Ann^5 Arbogast** (259.Martin Van Buren^4, 40.Lemuel^3, 6.Joseph E.^{2}, 1.John C.^{1}).
She Married **Charles Walter Sponaugle**, b. Mar 04 1876 (son of Eli Perry Sponaugle and Anna Rebecca Kile), d. Nov 28 1949.

Children:

1542 i. Helen^6 Sponaugle.

814. **Samual^5 Arbogast** (267.Jacob A.^{4}, 40.Lemuel^3, 6.Joseph E.^{2}, 1.John C.^{1}), b. May 7, 1903, d. February 23, 1959.
Married December 27, 1927, **Pearl E. Bowers Arbogast**.

Children:

1543 i. Alline^6 Arbogast b. Mar 12 1927 in Randolph Co., WV, d. 1927 in Randolph Co., WV.
\+ 1544 ii. Allen Arbogast b. Mar 12 1927.
\+ 1545 iii. Audrey Maxine Arbogast b. Apr 14 1928.
\+ 1546 iv. Betty Jean Arbogast b. Aug 01 1929.
\+ 1547 v. Jeff Jake Arbogast b. Oct 31 1930.

1548 vi. Charlotte Bernice Arbogast b. Oct 28 1931 in Randolph Co., WV, d. Sep 05 1932 in Randolph Co., WV.
1549 vii. (infant) Arbogast b. Oct 28 1931 in Randolph Co., WV, d. Oct 28 1931 in Randolph Co., WV.
1550 viii. Loretta Arbogast b. Nov 13 1932 in Randolph Co., WV.
+ 1551 ix. John Mutt Arbogast b. February 4, 1934.
+ 1552 x. Mary Bessie Arbogast b. Jan 25 1936.
1553 xi. (infant) Arbogast b. Jan 25 1936 in Randolph Co., WV.
+ 1554 xii. Donald Lee Arbogast b. Jun 22 1937.
+ 1555 xiii. Lois Ann Arbogast b. Jun 22 1937.
1556 xiv. Amenthia Mae Arbogast b. Aug 31 1939 in Randolph Co., WV.
1557 xv. Ira Sam Arbogast b. Oct 08 1940 in Randolph Co., WV.
1558 xvi. Claude Denver Arbogast b. May 21 1941 in Randolph Co., WV.
1559 xvii. Jerry Joe Arbogast b. Oct 20 1942 in Randolph Co., WV.
1560 xviii. Robert William Arbogast b. Apr 18 1944 in Randolph Co., WV.
1561 xix. James Lewis Arbogast b. Apr 28 1946 in Randolph Co., WV, d. Apr 30 1946 in Randolph Co., WV.
1562 xx. David Richard Arbogast b. Aug 31 1947 in Randolph Co., WV.
1563 xxi. Phillip Dale Arbogast b. Apr 21 1950 in Randolph Co., WV.

816. **Don[5] Arbogast** (269.Alfred T.[4], 40.Lemuel[3], 6.Joseph E.[2], 1.John C.[1]), b. December 21, 1894 in Cherry Grove, Pendleton Co., WV, d. December 21, 1963, buried in Franklin, Pendleton Co., WV. He Married **Icie Grace Teter**, b. March 21, 1897 in Teter Gap, Circleville, Pendleton Co., WV, d. December 10, 1984 in Cherry Grove, Pendleton Co., WV.

***Children**:*

1564 i. Delbert[6] Arbogast b. April 30, 1915.
1565 ii. Elva Arbogast b. April 27, 1918, d. June 21, 1984.
1566 iii. William Hoy Arbogast b. July 30, 1920, d. October 17, 1983.
1567 iv. Cynthia Arbogast b. December 30, 1921.
1568 v. Alva Dreamish Arbogast b. December 1, 1923.
1569 vi. Betty Jean Arbogast b. December 11, 1925.
1570 vii. Rosa Lee Arbogast b. January 10, 1928.
1571 viii. Coy Arbogast b. November 12, 1929.
1572 ix. Guy Arbogast.
1573 x. Carl Arbogast.
1574 xi. Earl Arbogast.
1575 xii. Bonnie Arbogast.

817. **Grace[5] Arbogast** (269.Alfred T.[4], 40.Lemuel[3], 6.Joseph E.[2], 1.John C.[1]), b. September 6, 1901, d. 1939. She Married **(unknown) Ewick**.

***Children**:*

1576 i. Bonnie[6] Ewick b. 1918.
1577 ii. Gladys Ewick.
1578 iii. Betty Jean Ewick.

819. **Argie[5] Arbogast** (269.Alfred T.[4], 40.Lemuel[3], 6.Joseph E.[2], 1.John C.[1]), b. April 22, 1908, d. 1934. She Married **Charles Edward Nicholas**, b. February 26, 1898, d. January 14, 1961.

***Children**:*

1579 i. Paul[6] Nicholas b. September 27, 1925, d. August 18, 1995.
He Married **Leona Jea Wimer,** b. Sep-08-1928 (daughter of Charles Amos Wimer and Zoe Etta Thompson).
1580 ii. Patsy Ruth Nicholas McDonald b. April 14, 1927 in Churchville, Pendleton Co., WV.
Married October 22, 1943 in Washington, D.C., **Mack Daniel McDonald**, b. June 14, 1915 in Key, Pendleton Co., WV. Mack: Places lived: East Capitol Street, Washington, SC; 18th Street Washington, SC; College Park, MD; Riverdale, MD; & Arlington, VA: 1007 S. Taylor Street (Virginia Gardens). 5009 S. 8th Road and 5011 S. 8th Road.
1581 iii. Betty Lou Nicholas b. May 17, 1928.
(1) She **Married Lou Summers**, b. March 11, 1916. Lou:
. (2) She Married **Calin Alimanestianu**, b. December 29, 1922. Calin:

821. **Marlin[5] Arbogast** (269.Alfred T.[4], 40.Lemuel[3], 6.Joseph E.[2], 1.John C.[1]), b. Oct-06-1904, buried in Rest Haven Mem Gar, Harrisonburg VA.

Married Mar-11-1992, **Ethel Mae Sponaugle**, b. Aug-06-1906 (daughter of Gilbert Kenton Sponaugle and Annie Pressie Mallow), d. Oct-29-1992.

Children:

1582 i. Mike[6] Arbogast b. Mar-11-1926 in Glady, Randolph Co., WV, d. Jan-05-1998 in Harrisonburg, Rockingham Co., VA. He Married **Charlotte Swecker**, d. Aug-02-1987 in Harrisonburg, Rockingham Co., VA.

1583 ii. Merl Arbogast b. Nov-18-1929, d. Dec-06-2014 in Flagler County, FL. He Married **Carmela Ida Arbogast**, b. Mar-27-1926, d. Aug-15-1999.

1584 iii. Cam Arbogast b. Sep-28-1927 in Circleville Pendleton Co., WV, d. May-01-2014 in Harrisonburg, Rockingham Co., VA.

822. **Ada M.[5] Arbogast** (270.Hannah Elizabeth[4], 42.Joseph Elili[3], 6.Joseph E.[2], 1.John C.[1]). Married Jun 27 1898 in Pendleton Co., WV, **Lafayette Bennett**, b. Jul 28 1875 in Randolph Co., WV, d. Nov 10 1954 in Randolph Co., WV.

Children:

\+ 1585 i. Monna[6] Bennett b. Apr 14 1898.
\+ 1586 ii. John B. Bennett b. May 3 1901.
\+ 1587 iii. Kate Sadie Bennett b. 1905.
\+ 1588 iv. Ethel Bennett b. Jul 30 1910.

824. **Tallahassee[5] Helmick** (272.Mary Jane[4] Arbogast, 42.Joseph Elili[3], 6.Joseph E.[2], 1.John C.[1]).
She Married **James Richmond**.

Children:

1589 i. Carrie[6] Richmond b. 1904.
1590 ii. Ida Richmond b. 1906.
1591 iii. Eston Richmond b. 1909.
1592 iv. Mary J. Richmond b. 1911.
1593 v. Willard Richmond b. 1914.
1594 vi. Dierie Richmond b. 1917.

826. **Wayne Sylvester[5] Vandevender** (273.Ruth Ellen[4] Arbogast, 42.Joseph Elili[3], 6.Joseph E.[2], 1.John C.[1]), b. About 1885.
He Married **Lena Tingler**, b. Aug 26 1883, (daughter of Zebulon Tingler and Sarah Sponaugle), d. May 5 1962. **Lena**:.

Children:

1595 i. Adam[6] Vandevender.
1596 ii. Joseph Vandevender.
\+ 1597 iii. Mary Dessie Vandevender.
1598 iv. Sylvia Mae Vandevender b. Oct 12 1910 in Pendleton Co., WV, d. Jun 16 2003 in Pendleton Co., WV. She Married **Mason Thompson**, b. 1906, d. Apr 29 1968 in Pendleton Co., WV.
1599 v. Willie Vandevender b. Apr 6 1914 in Pendleton Co., WV, d. May 21 1999 in Pendleton Co., WV. He Married **Grethal Lee Lambert,** b. Oct 30 1913 in Cherry Grove, Pendleton Co., WV, d. Mar 6 2005 in Elkins, Randolph Co., WV.
1600 vi. Betty Vandevender b. About 1918.
1601 vii. Belva Vandevender b. About 1921.
\+ 1602 viii. Virgil Vandevender.

830. **Lula[5] Arbogast** (274.Elijah J.[4], 42.Joseph Elili[3], 6.Joseph E.[2], 1.John C.[1]), b. May 15 1891 in Pendleton Co., WV, d. Sep 8 1974 in Preston Co., WV.
Married Jan 11 1910 in Pendleton Co., WV, **Donald Byrd Hinkle**, b. Dec 15 1890 in Pendleton Co., WV (son of Adam Jay Hinkle and Amanda Simmons), d. Apr 5 1987 in Preston Co., WV.

Children:

1603 i. Ola[6] Hinkle b. Nov 7 1910 in Pendleton Co., WV, d. Jan 19 1998. She Married **John Stanko Selepeck,** b. Jun 8 1905 in Jenner, Somerset Co., PA, d. July 1965 in Morgantown, Monongalia Co., WV.
1604 ii. Roy B. Hinkle b. Dec 14 1913 in Pendleton Co., WV, d. Feb 25 1918 in Pendleton Co., WV.
1605 iii. Marie Hinkle b. About 1914 in Pendleton Co., WV.
1606 iv. Leta Mae Hinkle b. Aug 30 1915 in Pendleton Co., WV, d. Mar 10 2001 in Clinton, Prince George's Co., MD. He Married **Vernon G Hoffman**.
1607 v. Zola Hinkle b. About 1917 in Pendleton Co., WV.
1608 vi. Lester Hinkle b. May 3 1919 in Pendleton Co., WV, d. Nov 5 1953 in Monongalia Co., WV.
1609 vii. Sylvia Hinkle.

831. **Truman[5] Arbogast** (274.Elijah J.[4], 42.Joseph Elili[3], 6.Joseph E.[2], 1.John C.[1]), b. May 15 1891 in Pendleton Co., WV, d. Apr 5 1992 in Crystal Springs, Randolph Co., WV.
Married Oct 3 1914 in Pendleton Co., WV, **Eva Mae Simmons**, b. May 7 1894 in Pendleton Co., WV, d. Oct 16 1963.

Children:

\+ 1610 i. Irma Mae[6] Arbogast b. Sep 27 1915.
1611 ii. Robert Paul Arbogast b. 1918. He Married **Izetta Canfield**.
1612 iii. Mary Elouise Arbogast b. 1920. (1) She Married **Paul Harper**. (2) Married Mar 23 1940 in Highland Co., VA, **Roy T. Judy**, b. Oct 14 1919, d. Jun 11 1985.
1613 iv. Nila Violet Arbogast b. 1923. She Married **Hugh Good**.
1614 v. James Price Arbogast b. Jun 5 1928 in Pendleton Co., WV, d. Nov 17 2005 in Pendleton Co., WV.

832. **Bertie Kate[5] Arbogast** (274.Elijah J.[4], 42.Joseph Elili[3], 6.Joseph E.[2], 1.John C.[1]), b. Jun 1 1893 in Pendleton Co., WV, d. Nov 26 1972 in Pendleton Co., WV.
Married May 29 1912 in Pendleton Co., WV, **Robert Boyd Johnston**, b. May 21 1886 in Pendleton Co., WV (son of James William Johnston and Sarah Catherine Phares), d. Jun 11 1965 in Pendleton Co., WV.

Children:

1615 i. William Guy[6] Johnston b. Mar 17 1913 in Pendleton Co., WV, d. Jul 13 2003 in Provo, Utah Co., UT. Married Sep 9 1933 in Pendleton Co., WV, **Shirley Arlene Sponaugle**, b. Jan 13 1914 in Pendleton Co., WV (daughter of Gilbert Kenton Sponaugle and Annie Pressie Mallow), d. Apr 19 1974 in Springville, Utah Co., UT.
1616 ii. Mary Kathleen Johnston b. Dec 20 1914 in Pendleton Co., WV, d. Sep 10 1973. She Married **Joseph Kemp Baber**, b. May 21 1939 in Spencer, Rhone Co., WV.
\+ 1617 iii. Woodrow Richard Johnson b. Apr 2 1917.
1618 iv. Constance May Johnston b. Sep 29 1922 in Pendleton Co., WV, d. Nov 7 1985 in Charlottesville, Albemarle Co., VA. Married Feb 4 1956, **Morris Foster Woods**.
1619 v. Norma J Johnston b. Apr 30 1925 in Pendleton Co., WV, d. Jan 13 2004 in Petersburg, Grant Co., WV. She Married **Wayne Edward Colaw**.
1620 vi. Jack Lynn Johnston b. Oct 12 1933 in Pendleton Co., WV, d. Mar 27 1991 in Charleston, Kanawha Co., WV.

833. **Leona[5] Arbogast** (274.Elijah J.[4], 42.Joseph Elili[3], 6.Joseph E.[2], 1.John C.[1]) (See marriage to number 656.)

835. **Richard Vosler[5] Arbogast** (274.Elijah J.[4], 42.Joseph Elili[3], 6.Joseph E.[2], 1.John C.[1]), b. Sep 9 1903 in Pendleton Co., WV, d. May 19 1978 in Harrisonburg, Rockingham Co., VA.
Married Jan 31 1928 in Pendleton Co., WV, **Erma Mary Cook**, b. Jul 22 1911 in Pendleton Co., WV, d. Feb 1 2002 in Harrisonburg, Rockingham Co., VA.

Children:

1621 i. Wanda Lee[6] Arbogast. She Married **Everette Grimes**.

837. **Anna[5] Arbogast** (274.Elijah J.[4], 42.Joseph Elili[3], 6.Joseph E.[2], 1.John C.[1]), b. Sep 15 1909 in Pendleton Co., WV, d. Jan 16 1995 in Pendleton Co., WV.
(1) She Married **Russell Paul Nelson**, b. Nov 29 1903 in Pendleton Co., WV, d. Aug 23 1988 in Pendleton Co., WV.
(2) Married Jan 23 1926 in Pendleton Co., WV, **Lester Mauzy**, b. Mar 23 1901 in Pendleton Co., WV, d. Mar 29 1926 in Pendleton Co., WV.

***Children** by Lester Mauzy:*

1622 i. Lester[6] Mauzy b. About 1927, d. Mar 27 1947 in Pendleton Co., WV.

839. **William Cecil[5] Calhoun** (275.Hannah Catharine[4] Bennett, 43.Sidney Dean[3] Arbogast, 6.Joseph E.[2], 1.John C.[1]), b. DEC 1871 in Pendleton Co., WV, d. WFT Est. 1888-1961.
Married Jun 27 1897 in West Virginia, **Emma Susan Graham**.

Children:

\+ 1623 i. Nora Gustava[6] Calhoun b. Feb 28 1915.

842. **Nina Beth[5] Calhoun** (275.Hannah Catharine[4] Bennett, 43.Sidney Dean[3] Arbogast, 6.Joseph E.[2], 1.John C.[1]), b. Jan 12 1877 in Pendleton Co., WV, d. Oct 9 1918 in Pendleton Co., WV.
Married DEC 1892, **George William Lough**, b. WFT Est. 1842-1884, d. 1918.

Children:

1624 i. Artie Emma[6] Lough b. 1893, d. 1967. He Married **Carson W Fitzwater**, b. Private, d. 1961.
1625 ii. Ethel Magdalene Lough b. 1896, d. 1972. She Married **George Stiffe**,.

1626 iii. William Carl Lough b. 1898, d. 1941. He Married **Ann Lewens**.
1627 iv. Edward Scott Lough b. 1900, d. 1919.
+ 1628 v. Lula Pauline Lough b. 1902.
1629 vi. Viola Freddie Lough b. 1906, d. 1975. She Married **Edward S Eckard**, b. 1905, d. 1977.
1630 vii. Raymond Rufus Lough b. 1909. Married 1929, **Iris D Stewart**, b. 1912.
1631 viii. Erma Lough b. 1912. She Married **John Alvin Owens**, b. 1910, d. 1977.
1632 ix. Erma Olett Lough b. 1912. Married 1936, **John Alvin Owens**, b. 1910, d. 1977.
1633 x. Paul Lough.

851. **William Whitfield[5] Mauzy** (279.Christina[4] Arbogast, 45.Sylvenus[3], 6.Joseph E.[2], 1.John C.[1]), b. Sep 12 1903 in Hightown, Highland Co., VA, d. Nov 21 1990 in Franklin Co., WV.
Married Jan 23 1933, **Grace Harper**, d. Nov 21 1986.

Children:

1634 i. Betty[6] Mauzy.
1635 ii. Mary Mauzy.
1636 iii. Charles Mauzy.
1637 iv. Robert Mauzy.
1638 v. Jack Mauzy.
1639 vi. John Mauzy.

852. **Mary Geneva[5] Mauzy** (279.Christina[4] Arbogast, 45.Sylvenus[3], 6.Joseph E.[2], 1.John C.[1]), b. Apr 14 1905 in Hightown, Highland Co., VA, d. Dec 07 1979 in Staunton, Augusta Co., VA. S
he Married **Howard Puffenbarger**.

Children:

1640 i. Dareld[6] Puffenbarger.

853. **Roscoe[5] Mauzy** (279.Christina[4] Arbogast, 45.Sylvenus[3], 6.Joseph E.[2], 1.John C.[1]), b. Jan 26 1907, d. Feb 23 1985 in University of Virginia Medical Center, Charlottesville, VA.
He Married **Nola B. (Unknown)**.

Children:

1641 i. Charlotte[6] Mauzy.
1642 ii. Julie Ann Mauzy.
1643 iii. William L Mauzy.
1644 iv. Larry D Mauzy.
1645 v. Michael Mauzy.

862. **Orville Erry[5] Kerr** (288.William Bailey[4], 51.Hannah V.[3] Arbogast, 7.Moses[2], 1.John C.[1]), b. Dec 15 1880 in Barbour Co., WV, d. Nov 26 1956 in Spencer, Rhone Co., WV.
Source is family records of Betty Jane (Kerr) Lewis of Beverly, WV. Same person as #7736 in line of Michael Arbogast's son, George.
Married Nov 26 1906 in Randolph Co., WV, **Jessie Lucy Louk**, b. Jan 17 1892 in Glady, Randolph Co., WV (daughter of John Francis Louk and Elizabeth Jane Sponaugle), d. Apr 06 1962 in Weston, Lewis Co., WV.

Children:

1646 i. Martha Elizabeth[6] Kerr b. Dec 21 1907 in Randolph Co., WV, d. Apr 25 1989. Married Nov 15 1926 in Randolph Co., WV, **Gordon Atkins Ricketts**.
+ 1647 ii. Oscar William Kerr b. Oct 10 1909.
+ 1648 iii. Eunice Kerr b. Jan 14 1912.
1649 iv. Rita Irene Kerr b. 1914 in Randolph Co., WV. She Married **Edward I. Roberts**.
1650 v. Dorothy Bernice Kerr b. Dec 14 1916 in Randolph Co., WV, d. Sep 10 1981. She Married **Bruce Haden White**.
+ 1651 vi. Earl Frederick Kerr b. Sep 18 1918.
1652 vii. Alfred Lee Kerr b. Sep 18 1920 in Randolph Co., WV, d. Sep 23 1987. He Married **Freda Bennett**.
1653 viii. Hilda Helen Kerr b. Mar 7 1923 in Randolph Co., WV, d. Jun 9 1979. She Married **Creed Runner**.
+ 1654 ix. Betty Jane Kerr b. Jan 10 1925.
1655 x. Kenneth Kermit Kerr b. Sep 13 1926 in Randolph Co., WV, d. Sep 2 1962.
(1) He Married **Patricia Johnson**. (2) He Married **Carolyn Sutton**.
1656 xi. Raymond Harold Kerr b. Aug 7 1928 in Randolph Co., WV, d. May 31 1977. (1) He Married **Dawn Sherman**. (2) He Married **Alma Everson**.

1657 xii. Mary Lourean Kerr b. Dec 31 1930 in Randolph Co., WV, d. Nov 12 1991. (1) She Married **Elza Lambert**, b. Apr 16 1923. (2) She Married **John Elza**.

873. **Birdie Cleo[5] Channell** (326.Eva Jane[4] Arbogast, 60.Moses Wamsley[3], 7.Moses[2], 1.John C.[1]), b. Feb 18 1902 in Randolph Co., WV, d. Oct 6 1986.
D/o Spencer Dorfice and Eva Jane (Arbogast) Channell. Birdie is the same person as #6229, a descendant of John Arbogast; see Volume I for her ancestry. Birdie also Married **Cecil Barb**.
Married Nov 5 1923 in Unsure, **Stanley Stalnaker**, b. 1898 (son of Floyd Reese Stalnaker and Delphia Wamsley).

***Children*:**

+ 1658 i. Calvin William[6] Stalnaker b. Feb 20 1924.
1659 ii. Joseph Stalnaker. Lived only a couple years.

874. **Louisa May[5] Arbogast** (333.Francis M[4], 63.Adam Jr.[3], 8.Adam Sr.[2], 1.John C.[1]), b. May 29 1877 in Lewis Co., WV, d. 1965.
Married Mar 28 1894 in Lewis Co., WV, **George Hamilton Ballard**, b. Jan 28 1871 in Lewis Co., WV, d. May 1945 in Lewis Co., WV. **George**: May be other children, names unknown.

***Children*:**

1660 i. Harry[6] Ballard b. Jan 1 1901 in Lewis Co., WV, d. Nov 8 1979 in Morgantown, Monongalia Co., WV, buried in Masonic Cem., Weston, Lewis Co., WV. Married 1929 in Weston, Lewis Co., WV, **Lena H. Martin**, b. Oct 8 1905 in Lewis Co., WV, d. Dec 6 1985, buried in Masonic Cem., Weston, Lewis Co., WV.
1661 ii. Beatrice Ballard b. May 23 1915 in Lewis Co., WV.
Confirmed per birth record in Lewis Co.

877. **Elizabeth Ann[5] Arbogast** (333.Francis M[4], 63.Adam Jr.[3], 8.Adam Sr.[2], 1.John C.[1]), b. Sep 1884 in Lewis Co., WV.
Married Mar 2 1904 in Lewis Co., WV, **Charles Cecil Bailey**, b. Abt 1877.

***Children*:**

1662 i. Raymond D.[6] Bailey b. Mar 9 1907 in Lewis Co., WV.
Child confirmed per birth record, Lewis Co.

886. **Luty (Lutie) Ester[5] Cawthon** (336.Mary Susan[4] Arbogast, 63.Adam Jr.[3], 8.Adam Sr.[2], 1.John C.[1]), b. Feb 19 1882, d. Bf 1927 in Gilmer Co., WV.
Oscar: Married **Rocena (Cincy) Brown**, on 22 Jun 1927 in Gilmer Co. after the death of Lutie, per Gilmer Co. marriage records.
Married Mar 4 1901 in Gilmer Co., WV, **Oscar J. Young**, b. Abt 1877 in Gilmer Co., WV.

***Children*:**

1663 i. Odie[6] Young b. Abt 1905.
1664 ii. Pearl B. Young b. Abt 1907 in Gilmer Co., WV.
Married Apr 19 1925 in Gilmer Co., WV, **Maise Furr**, b. 1901 in Gilmer Co., WV.

887. **Oleva (Levy) Alice[5] Cawthon** (336.Mary Susan[4] Arbogast, 63.Adam Jr.[3], 8.Adam Sr.[2], 1.John C.[1]), b. Mar 3 1885 in Lewis Co., WV, d. 1955 in Gilmer Co., WV, buried in Union Turner Cem. Gilmer Co., WV.
(1) Married Sep 6 1909 in Gilmer Co., WV, **Jacob Stout**, b. Abt 1840 in Virginia.

Children *by Jacob Stout:*

+ 1665 i. Monnie Irene[6] Stout b. Sep 26 1911.

(2) Married Abt 1914, **Asbury Smith**, b. Abt 1884.

888. **Burna (Berna) Mary[5] Cawthon** (336.Mary Susan[4] Arbogast, 63.Adam Jr.[3], 8.Adam Sr.[2], 1.John C.[1]), b. Apr 11 1886 in Lewis Co., WV. Births of Weston Lewis Co. WV Book 2 pg. 74 line 32. Has mother middle initial Mary E. Cawthon (BK):
(1) Married Jan 25 1911 in Lewis Co., WV, **Elijah F. O'Hara**, b. Jul 4 1855 in Jackson Co., WV, d. Jul 13 1939 in Weston, Lewis Co., WV, buried in Masonic Cem., Weston, Lewis Co., WV. July 19, 1939). Date of birth per 1860 Roane Co. census..

Children *by Elijah F. O'Hara:*

1666 i. James "Jackie"[6] O'Hara b. Abt 1913, buried in Masonic Cem., Weston, Lewis Co., WV.
Name James confirmed by Father's obit. James maybe buried in Masonic Cem., Lewis Co. per veterans buried in Lewis Co. list.

(2) Married Abt 1925, **Judd Ocheltree**, b. Abt 1886

889. **John Florent[5] Cawthon** (336.Mary Susan[4] Arbogast, 63.Adam Jr.[3], 8.Adam Sr.[2], 1.John C.[1]), b. Mar 5 1888 in Lewis Co., WV, d. 1949 in Lewis Co., WV, buried in Waldeck Cem., Waldeck, Lewis Co., WV Sec D. Married Dec 26 1910 in Lewis Co., WV, **Georgia Dodson**, b. Abt 1891 in Lewis Co., WV, d. 1987 in Lewis Co., WV, buried in Waldeck Cem., Waldeck, Lewis Co., WV Sec D.

***Children**:*

1667 i. Aaron[6] Cawthon b. Jul 4 1913 in Lewis Co., WV, d. in Lewis Co., WV, buried in Waldeck Cem., Waldeck, Lewis Co., WV Sec D.

1668 ii. John H. Ross Cawthon b. Abt 1915 in Lewis Co., WV. Married Aug 22 1936 in Lewis Co., WV, **Kathryn Irene Duvall**, b. Abt 1918 in Lewis Co., WV.

1669 iii. Earl Royce Cawthon b. Nov 5 1918 in Alum Bridge, Lewis Co., WV.

1670 iv. Margaret T. Cawthon b. Jan 31 1920 in Lewis Co., WV.

1671 v. Mary Lillian Cawthon b. Aug 19 1929 in FC District.

1672 vi. Carole Ann Cawthon b. 1940 in Lewis Co., WV, d. 1944 in Lewis Co., WV, buried in Waldeck Cem., Waldeck, Lewis Co., WV Sec D.
May be a granddaughter ??

890. **Anna Susan (Bridget)[5] Cawthon** (336.Mary Susan[4] Arbogast, 63.Adam Jr.[3], 8.Adam Sr.[2], 1.John C.[1]), b. Nov 11 1889 in Lewis Co., WV, d. 1967 in Illinois.
One story is that she rode a donkey as a traveling nurse in eastern KY.
After the death of James in 1937 she returned to work as a private duty nurse for a time. She lived in a retirement home at the time of her death.
Married Abt 1918, **Dr. James Theodore Redwine**, b. Feb 29 1876 in Randolph Co., AR, d. 1937 in Michigan. **Dr.**: 1st wife, Ivy Shamel, d Abt 1910, had 1 child (d 1965), Possible he was raised by James and 2nd wife Anna. Have photo of Dr. James w/his family. Worked in Fairmont, WV where he met Anna. Dr. at Weston State Hosp. for short time. Supt in Epilepsy Hosp in MI. Also practiced in MO and KY.

***Children**:*

1673 i. Jack T.[6] Redwine b. Jul 1 1919 in Michigan.
In Jul 2000 still living in Evanston, IL per telephone call. He grew up in various Insane Hospitals where his father worked. Graduated Law School in MI. Went to work for Quaker Oats Co in their Legal Dept, retired in 1981 at age of 62.

Married Abt 1944 in Illinois, **Avis Ann Foege**, b. Abt 1921.

891. **Elmer Ray[5] Cawthon** (336.Mary Susan[4] Arbogast, 63.Adam Jr.[3], 8.Adam Sr.[2], 1.John C.[1]), b. Mar 16 1892 in Lewis Co., WV, d. 1953 in Glenville, Gilmer Co., WV, buried in Union Turner Cem. Gilmer Co., WV.
Married Nov 18 1917 in Gilmer Co., WV, **Ruth Frashure**, b. 1898, d. 1981 in Glenville, Gilmer Co., WV, buried in Union Turner Cem. Gilmer Co., WV.

***Children**:*

1674 i. Elmer Ray Jr.[6] Cawthon b. Aug 17 1920 in Gilmer Co., WV, d. Apr 1 1943, buried in Union Turner Cem. Gilmer Co., WV.
1st Lt. Army Air Corps, 386 Bomb Squadron. WWII.

892. **Elbert Clay[5] Cawthon** (336.Mary Susan[4] Arbogast, 63.Adam Jr.[3], 8.Adam Sr.[2], 1.John C.[1]), b. Mar 16 1892 in Lewis Co., WV.
(
1) Married Feb 25 1914 in Lewis Co., WV, **Nellie May Steerman**, b. Abt 1895 in Lewis Co., WV.

***Children** by Nellie May Steerman:*

1675 i. Nona[6] Cawthon b. Abt 1915.
Married to a photographer and lived in Clendenin, WV.
Husbands name
maybe Steve per WB.

1676 ii. Virginia Cawthon b. Abt 1918.
(Rumor- not confirmed. After her Mother's death, she was adopted OUT to a Catholic family.

(2) Married Abt 1920, **Virginia Cawthon**, b. Abt 1892.

893. **Lona Elizabeth[5] CAWTHON** (336.Mary Susan[4] Arbogast, 63.Adam Jr.[3], 8.Adam Sr.[2], 1.John C.[1]), b. Mar 6 1898 in Little Ellis, Lewis Co., WV., d. May 18 1963 in Parkersburg, Wood Co., WV, buried in Evergreen South Cem., Wood Co., WV. Married Nov 24 1917 in Gilmer Co., WV, **Arbie Hill Kuhl**, b. Mar 16 1896 in Gilmer Co., WV, d. Dec 22 1991 in Parkersburg, Wood Co., WV, buried Evergreen So. in Parkersburg, Wood Co., WV. **Arbie**: In later life adopted their granddaughter, Patricia Diane Kuhl.

Children:

+ 1677 i. Ermal Lenore Cawthon[6] KUHL b. Mar 10 1916.
+ 1678 ii. Edith Murl Kuhl b. 14 Oct. 1919.
1679 iii. Mary Pearl Kuhl b. May 10 1922 in Gilmer Co., WV, d. Dec 24 1993 in Vienna, Wood Co., WV, buried in Evergreen South Cem., Wood Co., WV.
(1) Married Abt 1955, **Johnny O'Curran**, b. Abt 1922. (2) Married Abt 1946, **Neal J. McVey**, b. Abt 1925. Neal:. (3) Married Feb 21 1961, **Paul Alexander Livingston**, b. Jan 13 1919 in York Co., NY, d. Feb 5 1991 in Wood Co., WV, buried in Evergreen South Cem., Wood Co., WV.
1680 iv. Staunton Hill Kuhl b. May 22 1924 in Burnsville, Braxton Co., WV, d. Jan 7 1945 in Belgium, buried in Luxembourg, France.
Enlisted in military in Apr 1943. Qualified as glider man in Jan 1944.
Qualified as parachutist in Jun 1944, went overseas in Aug 1944. He was killed in action during the Battle of the Bulge. WWII.
+ 1681 v. Winifred Elaine Kuhl b. Aug 20 1926.

900. **Dollie Ethel[5] Arbogast** (348.Kenton[4], 66.Peter William[3], 8.Adam Sr.[2], 1.John C.[1]), b. November 24, 1898, d. January 23, 1985. She Married **John Evers Evans**, b. September 15,1894, d. June 20, 1961.

Children:

1682 i. Helen Viola[6] Evans. She Married **Ivan Loy Teter**, b. December 1915, d. January 23, 1998 in Elkins, Randolph Co., WV.

901. **Daffel[5] Ketterman** (352.Tecumseh Sherman[4], 78.Nicholas Harper[3], 9.Mary Ann[2] Arbogast, 1.John C.[1]), b. 28 Jun 1892, d. 20 Oct 1985. (
1) She Married **Orville Bailey**. .

***Children** by Orville Bailey:*

1683 i. Thelma[6] Bailey.
1684 ii. Neal Bailey.
1685 iii. Durward Bailey.

***Children** by Renzo Hobbs:*

(2) She Married **Renzo Hobbs**
1686 iv. Sherman Hobbs.

905. **Miles[5] Ketterman** (352.Tecumseh Sherman[4], 78.Nicholas Harper[3], 9.Mary Ann[2] Arbogast, 1.John C.[1]), b. 19 Jan 1904, d. 18 Oct 1973.
He Married **Irene Rhiel**.

Children:

1687 i. Donald[6] Ketterman b. 27 Jun 1930. He Married **Lois Tucker**, b. f.

906. **Rudy[5] Ketterman** (352.Tecumseh Sherman[4], 78.Nicholas Harper[3], 9.Mary Ann[2] Arbogast, 1.John C.[1]), b. 17 Mar 1906.
He Married **Virgie Carter**, b. 26 Oct 1907 in Shelby Co., IL.

Children:

1688 i. Lenor A.[6] Ketterman.
1689 ii. Harry Ketterman.
1690 iii. Keith A. Ketterman.

909. **Harvey William[5] Colaw** (353.Lena Leona[4] Ketterman, 78.Nicholas Harper[3], 9.Mary Ann[2] Arbogast, 1.John C.[1]), b. 7 Jul 1888 in Downs, Mclean Co., IL, d. 14 Jul 1914.
He Married **Minnie Barret**.

Children:

1691 i. Ewell[6] Colaw b. 31 May 1912.

910. **Hazel Dell[5] Colaw** (353.Lena Leona[4] Ketterman, 78.Nicholas Harper[3], 9.Mary Ann[2] Arbogast, 1.John C.[1]), b. 16 Aug 1892 in Downs, Mclean Co., IL, d. 22 Feb 1939.
She Married **Homer Kelly**.

Children:

1692 i. Ray[6] Kelly buried in Hopewell Cem., Downs Co., IL, d. in Died at 8 years old.
1693 ii. Roy Allen Kelly b. 7 Jun 1918, d. 25 Mar 1969. Sgt., U.S. Army, WW II.

911. **Wayne[5] Colaw** (355.Bertha Viola[4] Ketterman, 78.Nicholas Harper[3], 9.Mary Ann[2] Arbogast, 1.John C.[1]), b. Jan 28 1897, d. July 1971.
He Married **Bertha Wilson**.

Children:

1694 i. Betty[6] Colaw.
1695 ii. Donald Colaw.

912. **Grace[5] Colaw** (355.Bertha Viola[4] Ketterman, 78.Nicholas Harper[3], 9.Mary Ann[2] Arbogast, 1.John C.[1]).
She Married **(unknown) Weaver**.

Children:

1696 i. Darrell[6] Weaver.

913. **Glen Dyer[5] Colaw** (355.Bertha Viola[4] Ketterman, 78.Nicholas Harper[3], 9.Mary Ann[2] Arbogast, 1.John C.[1]), b. Apr 20 1907, d. May 1980.
He Married **Leal Manahan**.

Children:

\+ 1697 i. Russell G.[6] Colaw b. Mar 28 1941.

914. **Merle C.[5] Colaw** (355.Bertha Viola[4] Ketterman, 78.Nicholas Harper[3], 9.Mary Ann[2] Arbogast, 1.John C.[1]), b. Apr 20 1907, d. May, 1980.
He Married **Lois Lee**.

Children:

1698 i. Lee[6] Colaw.

916. **Thornton[5] Colaw** (355.Bertha Viola[4] Ketterman, 78.Nicholas Harper[3], 9.Mary Ann[2] Arbogast, 1.John C.[1]), b. May 19 1914, d. Jan 1984.
He Married **Bessie Compton**.

Children:

1699 i. Sandra[6] Colaw.
1700 ii. Suzanne Colaw.

920. **Merle Nicholas[5] Ketterman** (356.Paul[4], 78.Nicholas Harper[3], 9.Mary Ann[2] Arbogast, 1.John C.[1]), b. 16 Oct 1906 in Fargo, Cass Co., ND.
He Married **Vivian Frederick**, b. May 26 1914 in Coalgate, Sask. Canada, d. Dec 13 2008 in Plentywood, MT.

Children:

\+ 1701 i. Leo Dwain[6] Ketterman b. Jan 17 1937.

928. **Viola Belle[5] Arbogast** (372.Washington Sherman[4], 84.George Washington[3], 10.John C.[2], 1.John C.[1]), b. 2-27-1890, d. 2-20-1973.
She Married **George Amos Moore**, b. 7-16-1888, d. 5-22-1977.

Children:

1702 i. Nellie[6] Moore b. 1909.
1703 ii. Madeline Moore b. 1910.
1704 iii. Virginia Moore b. 1912.
1705 iv. Dorothy Moore b. 1914, d. 1978.
1706 v. Phillis Moore b. 1918.

930. **Leslie Herman[5] Arbogast** (372.Washington Sherman[4], 84.George Washington[3], 10.John C.[2], 1.John C.[1]), b. About 1895. At the time this data was assembled this Family has 3 other children, who were unwed, and maybe living, that are not included here.
He Married **Mary Estaline Valentine**.

***Children**:*

1707 i. Helen[6] Arbogast.
1708 ii. Charles Leslie Arbogast b. Jan 8- 1923 in Junior, Barbour Co., WV, d. 6-24-1994 in Davis Memorial Hospital, Elkins, Randolph Co., WV.
1709 iii. Lois Arbogast. She Married **Jasper Emery Farris**.
1710 iv. Robert Arbogast.
1711 v. Jack Arbogast b. 1929.

931. **Arley[5] Arbogast** (372.Washington Sherman[4], 84.George Washington[3], 10.John C.[2], 1.John C.[1]), b. About 1904, d. 1995.
He Married **Adis Kittle**, b. 1889.

***Children**:*

1712 i. Constance[6] Arbogast b. Feb 1929.
1713 ii. Joe Arbogast.

935. **Roscoe[5] Arbogast** (375.George McClelland[4], 84.George Washington[3], 10.John C.[2], 1.John C.[1]), b. June 1885 in Barbour Co., WV.
He Married **Birdie Williams**, b. About 1893.

***Children**:*

1714 i. Earl[6] Arbogast b. About 1908.
1715 ii. Madge Arbogast b. About 1911.
1716 iii. Roy Arbogast b. About 1913.
1717 iv. Thamer Ray Arbogast b. Jul 8- 1917 in Junior, Barbour Co., WV, d. 5-26-2000.

937. **Ralph[5] Arbogast** (375.George McClelland[4], 84.George Washington[3], 10.John C.[2], 1.John C.[1]), b. Feb 1888 in Barbour Co., WV.
He Married **Evalena (Unknown)**.

***Children**:*

1718 i. Pete[6] Arbogast.
1719 ii. Londa Arbogast b. About 1912.
1720 iii. Melford Arbogast b. About 1913.

938. **Vannie[5] Arbogast** (375.George McClelland[4], 84.George Washington[3], 10.John C.[2], 1.John C.[1]), b. Aug 1890 in Barbour Co., WV, d. Mar 02 1954 in Belington, Barbour Co., WV.
She Married **Dick Myers**.

***Children**:*

1721 i. Edyth[6] Myers.
1722 ii. Arley Myers.

939. **Margaret[5] Arbogast** (375.George McClelland[4], 84.George Washington[3], 10.John C.[2], 1.John C.[1]), b. Apr 13 1893 in Barbour Co., WV, d. May 08 1995 in South Carolina.
(1) Married May 29 1920 in Barbour Co., WV, **Albert Shomo**, b. Feb 02 1889.

***Children** by Albert Shomo:*

\+ 1723 i. Mabel[6] Shomo b. Aug 06 1912.
1724 ii. Willard Alton Shomo b. Jun 01 1914 in Barbour Co., WV.

2) She Married **Noah Francis Robinson**, b. Nov 14 1889.

940. **Hannah[5] Arbogast** (375.George McClelland[4], 84.George Washington[3], 10.John C.[2], 1.John C.[1]), b. Jan 1897 in Barbour Co., WV. (1) Married Apr 05 1911, **Albert Flaherty**.

***Children** by Albert Flaherty:*

1725 i. Wilma[6] Flaherty b. 11-9-1913.
1726 ii. Alton Flaherty b. 3-22-1915, d. 3-13-1941.
1727 iii. Agnes Flaherty b. 5-22-1917.

1728 iv. Leslie Flaherty b. Sep 9- 1918.
1729 v. Ronald Flaherty b. 4-21-1921.

(2) She Married **Martin Moreno**.

Children *by Martin Moreno:*

1730 vi. Kathleen Moreno b. in Junior, Barbour Co., WV.

941. **Jennie⁵ Arbogast** (375.George McClelland⁴, 84.George Washington³, 10.John C.², 1.John C.¹), b. Oct 1899 in Barbour Co., WV, d. in Smithtown, Monongalia Co., WV.
She Married **Dallas Herron**, b. 1894.

Children:

1731 i. Leo Herron.⁶ .
1732 ii. Byron Herron b. 1919.

Generation Six

948. **Ottie Jane⁶ Hedrick** (378.George Washington⁵, 88.Christina⁴ Waybright, 11.Emily³ Arbogast, 3.Michael², 1.John C.¹), b. About 1901.
Married May 3 1924, **John Alton Wooddell**, b. Sep 6 1904 in Green Bank, Pocahontas Co., WV (son of Adam Arbogast Wooddell and Lucinda Margaret Simms), d. Nov 19 1968.

Children:

1733 i. Fredrick L.⁷ Wooddell b. Apr 21 1921 in Cass, Pocahontas Co., WV, d. Jan 2 1980 in Pocahontas Co., WV. (1) He Married **Elva Potter**, b. Dec 16 1926 in Buckeye, Pocahontas Co., WV, d. Oct 19 1999 in New Martinsville, Wetzel Co., WV. (2) Married Nov 14 1945, **Pearl Davis**.
1734 ii. Lucinda Helen Wooddell b. May 12 1925. She Married **(unknown) Workman**.

955. **James Elloitt⁶ Smith** (405.Minnie May⁵ Arbogast, 98.Amos Cyrus⁴, 12.George Washington³, 3.Michael², 1.John C.¹), b. May 27 1922, d. Jun 17 1985.
He Married **Alice Marie Browning**.

Children:

1735 i. Nancy Sue⁷ Smith b. Jan 29 1949.
1736 ii. Carol Sue Smith b. Jul 30 1953.

956. **Wilbur Amos⁶ Smith** (405.Minnie May⁵ Arbogast, 98.Amos Cyrus⁴, 12.George Washington³, 3.Michael², 1.John C.¹), b. May 05 1923, d. Mar 02 1983.
Married Oct 09 1940, **Mary E. Rogers**.

Children:

1737 i. Carol May⁷ Smith b. Feb 28 1941, d. Mar 01 1941.
1738 ii. Wilber Allen Smith b. Jan 08 1948, d. Jun 02 1969.
Wilber died 06021969 in Vietnam.
1739 iii. Stella Lee Smith b. Jan 07 1950. Married Jul 06 1984, **Paul Lee Jerrett**.
\+ 1740 iv. Shelby Ruth Smith b. Jun 17 1953.

957. **Wavie⁶ Smith** (405.Minnie May⁵ Arbogast, 98.Amos Cyrus⁴, 12.George Washington³, 3.Michael², 1.John C.¹), b. Feb 16 1925, d. Jul 07 1992.
She Married **Waener Samples**, d. Jul 02 1992 in Charleston, Kanawha Co., WV, buried in Bomont, Clay Co., WV.

Children:

1741 i. Jerry⁷ Samples.
1742 ii. Mike Samples.
1743 iii. Doug Samples.
1744 iv. Thomas Samples.
\+ 1745 v. Kathy Samples.
1746 vi. Phillip Samples.
1747 vii. James Samples.

958. **Oliver Irvin[6] Smith** (405.Minnie May[5] Arbogast, 98.Amos Cyrus[4], 12.George Washington[3], 3.Michael[2], 1.John C.[1]), b. May 31 1927 in Queen Shoals, Kanawha Co., WV.
He Married **Virginia Louise Rogers**. **Virginia**:

Children:

+ 1748 i. Michael Irving[7] Smith b. May 13 1955.
1749 ii. David Darrell Smith b. Nov 23 1956. (1) He Married B. (2) He Married **Elizabeth Townsend.**
+ 1750 iii. Edward Allen Smith b. Mar 07 1958.

960. **Robert Q[6] Smith** (405.Minnie May[5] Arbogast, 98.Amos Cyrus[4], 12.George Washington[3], 3.Michael[2], 1.John C.[1]).
He Married **Rachel Irena Belcher**.

Children:

1751 i. Linda[7] Smith.
1752 ii. Dottie Smith.
1753 iii. Cheri Smith.
1754 iv. Robert Smith.

961. **Alpha[6] Smith** (405.Minnie May[5] Arbogast, 98.Amos Cyrus[4], 12.George Washington[3], 3.Michael[2], 1.John C.[1]).
She Married **Joseph Engle**.

Children:

1755 i. Ronnie[7] Engle.
1756 ii. Rex Engle.
1757 iii. Jim Engle.

962. **Juanita[6] Hughes** (407.Mary[5] Arbogast, 98.Amos Cyrus[4], 12.George Washington[3], 3.Michael[2], 1.John C.[1]), b. Apr 01 1923.
She Married **Basil Pawley**.

Children:

1758 i. Drema[7] Pawley.
1759 ii. Dena Pawley.
1760 iii. Richard Pawley.

963. **Amos[6] Hughes** (407.Mary[5] Arbogast, 98.Amos Cyrus[4], 12.George Washington[3], 3.Michael[2], 1.John C.[1]), b. Mar 11 1924.
Married 050719690 in Pearisburg, Giles Co., VA, **Nora Perry**, b. May 26 1926 in Mammoth, Kanawha Co., WV.

Children:

1761 i. Charolette[7] Hughes b. May 08 1956.
+ 1762 ii. Mary Hughes b. Sep 02 1957.
1763 iii. William Hughes b. Dec 30 1964.

966. **Ethel[6] Hughes** (407.Mary[5] Arbogast, 98.Amos Cyrus[4], 12.George Washington[3], 3.Michael[2], 1.John C.[1]), b. Feb 03 1931, d. Jan 23 1990.
She Married **Harold Tate**.

Children:

1764 i. Tom[7] Tate.
1765 ii. Gary Tate.

967. **William Thomas[6] Hughes** (407.Mary[5] Arbogast, 98.Amos Cyrus[4], 12.George Washington[3], 3.Michael[2], 1.John C.[1]), b. Mar 14 1933, d. Jun 16 1973.
He Married **Mavis Houchins**.

Children:

1766 i. David[7] Hughes.
1767 ii. Danny Thomas Hughes.
1768 iii. Donna Hughes.

968. **Magie[6] Hughes** (407.Mary[5] Arbogast, 98.Amos Cyrus[4], 12.George Washington[3], 3.Michael[2], 1.John C.[1]), b. May 05 1936.
She Married **James Cook**.

Children:

1769 i. Kim[7] Cook.
1770 ii. Bruce Cook.

1771 iii. Mary Cook.

978. **James[6] Turner** (408.Glendora[5] Arbogast, 98.Amos Cyrus[4], 12.George Washington[3], 3.Michael[2], 1.John C.[1]).
He Married **Dorothy Estelle Wilfong**, b. Nov 29 1931 (daughter of James Clarence Wilfong and Anna Lee Dilley).

Children:

1772 i. Gerald A.[7] Turner.
1773 ii. Charles D. Turner.
1774 iii. Randall L. Turner.

979. **Charles Joseph[6] Eades** (409.Faye Elvira[5] Arbogast, 98.Amos Cyrus[4], 12.George Washington[3], 3.Michael[2], 1.John C.[1]), b. Jul 02 1929 in Cincinnati, Hamilton Co., OH.
Charles was author of multiple volumes of research on the Michael Arbogast family and all of his children. Much of the Arbogast data in this database came fro this source,
President, TN Insurance Co., and Affiliated Companies 1979 - 1990 and Vice president Ingram Ind. Nashville, TN 1978 - 1990. Retired.
Married Sep 06 1947 in Newport, Campbell Co., KY, **Doris Lee Grimm**, b. Dec 03 1929.**Doris**: Daughter of Elmer Harold Grimm and Alma Ernestine Schmidt.

Children:

1775 i. Kathy Lynn[7] Eades b. Jan 28 1948 in Cincinnati, Hamilton Co., OH.
1776 ii. Charles Joseph Eades, Jr. b. Dec 31 1951.
1777 iii. David Douglas Eades b. Jan 06 1964.

980. **Amos Cyrus[6] Eades** (409.Faye Elvira[5] Arbogast, 98.Amos Cyrus[4], 12.George Washington[3], 3.Michael[2], 1.John C.[1]), b. Feb 27 1931.
Married Dec 27 1949, **Janet Lee Burton**, b. Sep 28 1932 in Pleasant Plain, Warren Co., OH. **Janet**: Daughter of Henry Burton and Norma Lucille Snowhill.

Children:

\+ 1778 i. Phillip Brett[7] Eades b. Feb 12 1952.
1779 ii. Jeffery Allen Eades b. Jun 20 1955 in Mariemont, Hamilton Co., OH. Married Nov 05 1990, **Susan Wallace**, b. Jan 27 1954.
\+ 1780 iii. Kerrilou Eades b. Sep 27 1960.

981. **William Leanord[6] Arbogast** (409.Faye Elvira[5], 98.Amos Cyrus[4], 12.George Washington[3], 3.Michael[2], 1.John C.[1]).
Married Nov 22 1952 in Bremerhaven, Germany, **Waltraud Kuehne**, b. Mar 27 1929 in Wilhelmshaven, Germany.

Children:

\+ 1781 i. Hertha Velma[7] Arbogast b. Feb 01 1952.
\+ 1782 ii. Beverley Arbogast b. Jan 12 1954.
\+ 1783 iii. Leonard Warren Arbogast b. Nov 05 1957.

982. **Denver McDonald[6] Neal** (410.Jessie Sarah[5] Arbogast, 98.Amos Cyrus[4], 12.George Washington[3], 3.Michael[2], 1.John C.[1]), b. Jun 11 1920 in Bickmore, Clay Co., WV, d. Oct 24 1987 in Beckley, Raleigh Co., WV. (1
) He Married **Gertrude Hopkins**.

***Children** by Gertrude Hopkins:*

1784 i. Betty Jean[7] Neal.

(2) He Married **Helen Pettit**.

***Children** by Helen Pettit:*

1785 ii. Denver Douglas Neal b. Oct 06 1950. He Married **Kum So**, b. Sep 17 1950 in Seoul, Korea.
\+ 1786 iii. Paul Joseph Neal b. Feb 18 1954.

983. **Violet Gustava[6] Neal** (410.Jessie Sarah[5] Arbogast, 98.Amos Cyrus[4], 12.George Washington[3], 3.Michael[2], 1.John C.[1]), b. Sep 14 1921.
Married Apr 13 1941 in Bickmore, Clay Co., WV, **Jesse A. Samples, Jr**, b. Oct 06 1918 in Precious, Clay Co., WV, d. Mar 09 1985 in Bickmore, Clay Co., WV. **Jesse**: Son of Jesse A. Samples and Fannie Corbett.

Children:

\+ 1787 i. Edna[7] Samples b. Dec 19 1942.
1788 ii. Jesse A Samples, III b. Jan 11 1945. He Married **Billie Budua,** b. Apr 17 1939.

+ 1789 iii. Linda Fay Samples b. Sep 14 1947.
1790 iv. Leslie Frank Samples b. Feb 17 1949, d. May 14 1977.
+ 1791 v. Easter Susan Samples b. Apr 12 1954.
+ 1792 vi. Kenneth Richard Samples b. Jun 03 1958.

984. **Johnny R.[6] Neal** (410.Jessie Sarah[5] Arbogast, 98.Amos Cyrus[4], 12.George Washington[3], 3.Michael[2], 1.John C.[1]), b. Mar 30 1923 in Bickmore, Clay Co., WV.
Married 1951, **Betty Schoonover**.

Children:

1793 i. Christine[7] Neal. She Married **Richard McLaughlan**.

985. **Oprha Naomi[6] Neal** (410.Jessie Sarah[5] Arbogast, 98.Amos Cyrus[4], 12.George Washington[3], 3.Michael[2], 1.John C.[1]), b. Aug 11 1925 in Bickmore, Clay Co., WV. S
he Married **Russell R. Burnette**, b. 1913 in Paxton, Clay Co., WV, d. Aug 23 1976.

Children:

1794 i. Russell R.[7] Burnette, Jr. b. Aug 26 1944. Married Dec 25 1961 in Glen, Marshall Co., WV, **Karen P. Hinkle**, b. Aug 1944.

987. **Oliver Wendell[6] Arbogast** (411.Joseph Monroe[5], 98.Amos Cyrus[4], 12.George Washington[3], 3.Michael[2], 1.John C.[1]), b. Oct 23 1931 in Precious, Clay Co., WV.
He Married **Myrtle Belle Brown**, b. Nov 04 1935 in Ovapa, Clay Co., WV.

Children:

1795 i. Oliver Wendell[7] Arbogast, Jr. b. Jun 04 1954 in Charleston, Kanawha Co., WV.
+ 1796 ii. Berry Andrew Arbogast b. May 11 1957.
1797 iii. Cindy Leigh Arbogast b. Mar 11 1963 in Charleston, Kanawha Co., WV. She Married **Stephen Mariani**.

988. **Addie Ramona[6] Arbogast** (411.Joseph Monroe[5], 98.Amos Cyrus[4], 12.George Washington[3], 3.Michael[2], 1.John C.[1]), b. Oct 23 1931 in Precious, Clay Co.,
WV. Married Sep 07 1951 in Spencer, Rhone Co., WV, **Gorden Lee Samples**, b. Dec 24 1931 in Opapa, WV.

Children:

+ 1798 i. Betsy Lynn[7] Samples b. Feb 10 1953.
1799 ii. Nancy Ann Samples b. Oct 18 1954.
1800 iii. Mary Louise Samples b. Nov 26 1965 in Charleston, Kanawha Co., WV.

989. **Anna May[6] Arbogast** (411.Joseph Monroe[5], 98.Amos Cyrus[4], 12.George Washington[3], 3.Michael[2], 1.John C.[1]), b. Jun 05 1935, d. Oct 19 1976.
Married Jul 21 1956 in Charleston, Kanawha Co., WV, **Peter J. Adams**, b. Apr 28 1929 in Breslau, Germany, d. Oct 19 1976 in Niagara Falls, Ontario, Canada.

Children:

+ 1801 i. Carolyn Elizabeth[7] Adams b. May 11 1957.
+ 1802 ii. John Michael Adams b. Jul 24 1958.
1803 iii. Paul Rogers Adams b. May 13 1961 in Jersey City, Jersey City NJ. Married 1983 in Detroit, Wayne Co., MI, **Deborah Stump**.
1804 iv. Susan Jean Adams b. Mar 04 1965 in Jersey City, Jersey City NJ. Married Oct 01 1994 in Niagara Falls, Ontario, Canada, **Robert Glenn**.

990. **Joyce[6] Cantley** (412.Lucy Esta[5] Arbogast, 98.Amos Cyrus[4], 12.George Washington[3], 3.Michael[2], 1.John C.[1]), b. Apr 01 1927 in Mullins, Wyoming Co., WV.
Married Jan 17 1946 in Catlettsburg, Boyd Co., KY, **Elizia H Meadows**, b. May 03 1924 in Mabscott, Raleigh Co., WV, d. Dec 14 1976 in Beckley, Raleigh Co., WV.

Children:

+ 1805 i. Harold Lloyd[7] Meadows b. Oct 16 1946.

991. **Jack[6] Cantley** (412.Lucy Esta[5] Arbogast, 98.Amos Cyrus[4], 12.George Washington[3], 3.Michael[2], 1.John C.[1]), b. Mar 31 1928 in Beckley, Raleigh Co., WV.
Married May 18 1947 in Beckley, Raleigh Co., WV, **Shirley Barbour**, b. Sep 27 1929 in Beckley, Raleigh Co., WV.

Children:

+ 1806 i. Jacquenlin^7 Cantley b. Dec 19 1947.
+ 1807 ii. Clair Cantley b. Jun 30 1952.
+ 1808 iii. Steven Cantley b. Dec 08 1953.

993. **Naomi Rose^6 Cantley** (412.Lucy Esta^5 Arbogast, 98.Amos Cyrus^4, 12.George Washington^3, 3.Michael^2, 1.John C.^{1}), b. Jun 15 1937 in Beckley, Raleigh Co., WV.
Married Dec 05 1951 in Catlettsburg, Boyd Co., KY, **John William Jones**, b. Jan 01 1932 in Atkins, Boone Co., WV.

***Children*:**

+ 1809 i. Mary Esta^7 Jones b. Aug 24 1952.
+ 1810 ii. Kathy Ann Jones b. Jul 07 1953.
+ 1811 iii. John William Jones, Jr. b. Mar 23 1955.

994. **Carolyn^6 Cantley** (412.Lucy Esta^5 Arbogast, 98.Amos Cyrus^4, 12.George Washington^3, 3.Michael^2, 1.John C.^{1}), b. Feb 14 1946.
She Married **Kenneth Calhoun**, b. Aug 19 1944 in Anawalt, McDowell Co., WV.

***Children*:**

+ 1812 i. Lesa^7 Calhoun b. Mar 08 1965.
1813 ii. Kera Calhoun b. Sep 30 1968 in Cheverly, Prince George Co., MD.

995. **Brenda^6 Cantley** (412.Lucy Esta^5 Arbogast, 98.Amos Cyrus^4, 12.George Washington^3, 3.Michael^2, 1.John C.^{1}), b. Sep 04 1947.
(1) She Married **Frankie Slate**, b. 1946.

Children *by Frankie Slate:*

1814 i. Tammy^7 Slate b. Jan 07 1967.

(2) She Married **Edsil Delp**, b. Oct 04 1933 in Josephine, Raleigh Co., WV.

996. **Orpha Gladys^6 Shreves** (421.Joanna^5 Shreve, 102.Benjamin "Little Ben"^{4}, 13.Mary Magdalene.^{3} Arbogast, 3.Michael^2, 1.John C.^{1}), b. Nov 11 1901, d. Jun 10 1976 in Petersburg, Grant Co., WV.
Married Jul 26 1918, **Osa Clemon Judy**, b. Jun 29 1900, d. Apr 14 1977.

***Children*:**

+ 1815 i. Denver Henry^7 Judy b. Aug 24 1924.
1816 ii. Goldie Judy.
1817 iii. Verda Ethel Judy.

1008. **Nellie^6 Davis** (441.Rumsey Smithson^5, 107.Jethro^4, 14.Christina^3 Arbogast, 3.Michael^2, 1.John C.^{1}), b. Apr 26 1910 in Randolph Co., WV, d. Dec 30 1988 in Randolph Co., WV.
Married May 21 1929 in Randolph Co., WV, **John B. Bennett**, b. May 3 1901 in Pendleton Co., WV (son of Lafayette Bennett and Ada M. Arbogast), d. Oct 17 1980 in Randolph Co., WV.

***Children*:**

1818 i. Ray^7 Bennett.
1819 ii. Denver Bennett.
1820 iii. Josie Bennett.
1821 iv. Nellie Bennett. She Married **William McCallister**.
1822 v. Roselee Bennett b. Nov 2 1929. She Married **Thomas Howard Gibson**, b. 1947, d. Aug 25 1986.
1823 vi. Keith Bennett b. Jan 21 1931, d. Apr 25 2002.
1824 vii. Richard Davis Bennett b. Jul 30 1934, d. Apr 4 1995.

1009. **Mabel Perl^6 Reedy** (450.Acinith Lieuticia^5 Markle, 117.Sarah D.^{4} Arbogast, 15.Nichodemus^3, 3.Michael^2, 1.John C.^{1}), b. Aug 26 1903 in Elkhurst, Clay Co., WV, d. Feb 11.
Married 1920, **Lee Okey Woods**, d. Dec 19 1983.

***Children*:**

+ 1825 i. Madeline^7 Woods b. Aug 13 1923.

1012. **Donnie Fern^6 Reedy** (450.Acinith Lieuticia^5 Markle, 117.Sarah D.^{4} Arbogast, 15.Nichodemus^3, 3.Michael^2, 1.John C.^{1}), b. Sep 08 1908.
Married Sep 08 1934, **Robert J Legg**, b. Sep 13 1902 in Indora, Kanawha Co., WV.

***Children*:**

1826 i. Jo Ann[7] Legg b. Jan 11 1932 in Charleston, Kanawha Co., WV. She Married **Roger K Reed.**
1827 ii. Alton O Legg b. Aug 23 1934 in Indora, Kanawha Co., WV.
1828 iii. Kline A Legg b. Jul 19 1937. He Married **Fannie Wilson**.

1017. **Olive Doris[6] Reedy** (450.Acinith Lieuticia[5] Markle, 117.Sarah D.[4] Arbogast, 15.Nichodemus[3], 3.Michael[2], 1.John C.[1]), b. Jan 05 1927.
Married Sep 06 1946, **Lawrence Delmar Wriston**, b. Jul 09 1925 in Keith, Boone Co., WV.

***Children*:**

\+ 1829 i. Roger Lee[7] Wriston b. Feb 14 1949.

1018. **Inez[6] Arbogast** (457.Watson A[5], 119.George Franklin[4], 15.Nichodemus[3], 3.Michael[2], 1.John C.[1]). She Married **R. Everett Trent**, b. c 1910, d. Feb 03 1995 in Ashland, Boyd Co., KY.

***Children*:**

1830 i. Marcine[7] Trent.
1831 ii. Racine Trent.
1832 iii. Jo Trent.
1833 iv. Roy Trent.

1019. **Alberta Maxine[6] Arbogast** (459.Albert Lee[5], 119.George Franklin[4], 15.Nichodemus[3], 3.Michael[2], 1.John C.[1]), b. Jan 20 1921, d. Aug 21 1989 in Gainesville, Alachua Co., FL, buried in Charleston, Kanawha Co., WV.
(1) Married July 1938, **William Braden**.

***Children** by William Braden:*

1834 i. Edward Lee[7] Braden b. May 30 1940.
1835 ii. John Ray Breden b. May 09 1942. He Married Virginia June Ellis, b. Jun 02 1937, d. Nov 13 1992.

(2) She Married **Carlton Watson Stallworth**, b. Feb 16 1924 in Meriwether, Co., GA.

***Children** by Carlton Watson Stallworth:*

\+ 1836 iii. Carlton Watson Stallworth b. Aug 30 1947.

1020. **Donald R[6] Arbogast** (459.Albert Lee[5], 119.George Franklin[4], 15.Nichodemus[3], 3.Michael[2], 1.John C.[1]), b. Oct 03 1924, d. Nov 03 1948 in Glossop, Derby, England, buried in Charleston, Kanawha Co., WV. (1) He Married **Reva Hunt**. (2) He Married **Patricia Edens**.

***Children** by Patricia Edens:*

1837 i. Donna Kay[7] Stallworth.
1838 ii. Janet Rae Stallworth.

1021. **Lois Jean[6] Arbogast** (459.Albert Lee[5], 119.George Franklin[4], 15.Nichodemus[3], 3.Michael[2], 1.John C.[1]), b. Oct 15 1927, d. Jul 12 1983.
Married Jun 18 1948 in Charleston, Kanawha Co., WV, **Kendell Sebert Perry**, b. Nov 12 1926 in Boone Co., WV, d. Jan 13 1981 in Charleston, Kanawha Co., WV.

***Children*:**

\+ 1839 i. Janet Gail[7] Perry b. Mar 11 1956.
1840 ii. Donald Kent Perry b. Apr 21 1958 in Kanawha Co., WV. Married 1980, **Sandra Rhodes.**

1022. **William Bert[6] Arbogast** (459.Albert Lee[5], 119.George Franklin[4], 15.Nichodemus[3], 3.Michael[2], 1.John C.[1]), b. 1930, d. Mar 08 1959.
He Married **Isobel Vance**.

***Children*:**

\+ 1841 i. Diana Sue[7] Arbogast b. Oct 19 1947.
1842 ii. Deborah Sue Arbogast.

1024. **Milton Brown[6] Arbogast** (460.Joseph Martin[5], 119.George Franklin[4], 15.Nichodemus[3], 3.Michael[2], 1.John C.[1]), b. Aug 11 1916.
He Married **Maxine (Unknown)**.

***Children*:**

1843 i. Gordon[7] Arbogast.
1844 ii. James Arbogast.

1025. **Francis Vivian^{6} Arbogast** (460.Joseph Martin^{5}, 119.George Franklin^{4}, 15.Nichodemus^{3}, 3.Michael^{2}, 1.John C.^{1}), b. Dec 08 1917 in Breathitt Co., KY, d. Apr 27 1990 in Marion Co., OH. (1) She Married **George L Hughes**, b. Nov 17 1894 in Mobile, Mobile Co., AL, d. Mar 26 1980 in Dayton, Montgomery Co., OH. (

Children *by George L Hughes:*

+ 1845 i. Patsy Jo^{7} Hughes b. Feb 24 1939.
+ 1846 ii. George Hughes b. Feb 14 1941.

2) She Married **Edward Lloyd Carter**
. (3) She Married **Austin Jack Martin**.

Children *by Austin Jack Martin:*

1847 iii. Austin Jack Martin II b. About 1952 in Chillicothe, Ross Co., OH.
+ 1848 iv. Nancy Martin b. About 1954.

1026. **Masel^{6} Arbogast** (460.Joseph Martin^{5}, 119.George Franklin^{4}, 15.Nichodemus^{3}, 3.Michael^{2}, 1.John C.^{1}), b. 1919. Married in Divorced, **Levi Collins**.

Children:

+ 1849 i. William Levi^{7} Collins b. Sep 05 1939.
1850 ii. Alexandria Collins.

1028. **Maggie Jo^{6} Arbogast** (460.Joseph Martin^{5}, 119.George Franklin^{4}, 15.Nichodemus^{3}, 3.Michael^{2}, 1.John C.^{1}), b. 1926. Married in Divorced, **Collins Woodruff**.

Children:

+ 1851 i. Earl^{7} Woodruff b. Oct 02 1942.
+ 1852 ii. Joyce Woodruff b. Nov 08 1944.
1853 iii. Sharon Woodruff b. Jul 26 1946.

1029. **Ethel Malinda^{6} Arbogast** (460.Joseph Martin^{5}, 119.George Franklin^{4}, 15.Nichodemus^{3}, 3.Michael^{2}, 1.John C.^{1}), b. Apr 12 1927 in Clarksburg, Harrison Co., WV, d. Dec 09 1990 in Columbus, Franklin Co., OH.
(1) Married Oct 02 1942, **Everett Bishop**.
2) She Married **Edwin Chrystal**.

Children *by Edwin Chrystal:*

+ 1854 i. Tamara^{7} Chrystal.

1030. **Ralph Martin^{6} Arbogast** (460.Joseph Martin^{5}, 119.George Franklin^{4}, 15.Nichodemus^{3}, 3.Michael^{2}, 1.John C.^{1}), b. Feb 17 1929.
Married Jul 05 1946 in Greenup Co., KY, **Laura Epple**.

Children:

1855 i. Martin^{7} Arbogast b. Feb 21 1949.
+ 1856 ii. Mary Lou Arbogast.

1031. **Clarissa Velma^{6} Arbogast** (460.Joseph Martin^{5}, 119.George Franklin^{4}, 15.Nichodemus^{3}, 3.Michael^{2}, 1.John C.^{1}), b. Mar 17 1931.
Married Aug 08 1946 in Greenup Co., KY, **Donald Wesley Collins**.

Children:

+ 1857 i. Donald Wesley^{7} Collins, II b. Jun 10 1947.
+ 1858 ii. Temara Jo Collins b. Apr 14 1958.

1032. **George Lee^{6} Arbogast** (460.Joseph Martin^{5}, 119.George Franklin^{4}, 15.Nichodemus^{3}, 3.Michael^{2}, 1.John C.^{1}), b. Feb 10 1939 in Chillicothe, Ross Co., OH.
Married Mar 30 1958, **Norma Jean Ward**, b. Jul 17 1939 in Columbus, Franklin Co., OH.

Children:

+ 1859 i. George Lee^{7} Arbogast b. Aug 07 1960.
+ 1860 ii. Robert Larwence Arbogast.

1034. **Lucy Kathryn^{6} Perkins** (462.Sarah Alice^{5} Arbogast, 119.George Franklin^{4}, 15.Nichodemus^{3}, 3.Michael^{2}, 1.John C.^{1}), b. Oct 02 1926 in Charleston, Kanawha Co., WV.

She Married **Clarence Harold Hart**, b. Aug 24 1924.

Children:

+ 1861 i. John Edward^7 Hart b. Dec 03 1949.
+ 1862 ii. Teresa Yvonne Hart b. Mar 28 1955.

1037. **Louella Francis^6 Arbogast** (468.Fred Lee^5 Arbogast, 121.Thomas^4 Arbogast, 15.Nichodemus^3, 3.Michael^2, 1.John C.^{1}), b. Dec 28 1913 in West Virginia, d. May 22 1984 in Dunbar, Kanawha Co., WV.

(1) Married Oct 20 1930, **Wilson C Lanham**, b. Dec 01 1913, d. May 26 1978..

***Children** by Wilson C Lanham:*

+ 1863 i. Donald Wilson^7 Lanham b. Aug 29 1934.

(2) Married 1942 in Kanawha Co., WV, **Rameo Freer Casto**, b. Nov 10 1897 in Jackson Co., WV (son of William Richard Casto and Hannah Margaret Little), d. Nov 30 1968 in Dunbar, Kanawha Co., WV

***Children** by Rameo Freer Casto:*

+ 1864 ii. Bobby Lee Casto b. Jul 25 1947.

1038. **Florence Doris^6 Arbogast** (468.Fred Lee^5 Arbogast, 121.Thomas^4 Arbogast, 15.Nichodemus^3, 3.Michael^2, 1.John C.^{1}), b. Sep 05 1915.

Married Apr 29 1935, **Rex R White**, b. Jun 13 1913 in Blue Creek, Kanawha Co., WV.

Children:

+ 1865 i. Olga^7 White b. Oct 31 1936.

1039. **Samuel Roy^6 Arbogast** (468.Fred Lee^5 Arbogast, 121.Thomas^4 Arbogast, 15.Nichodemus^3, 3.Michael^2, 1.John C.^{1}), b. Apr 09 1918.

Married Apr 24 1953, **Nina Jean Belcher**, b. Jul 25 1935.

Children:

+ 1866 i. Sheree Joan^7 Arbogast b. Jun 23 1954.
+ 1867 ii. Steven Samuel Arbogast b. Oct 15 1958.
+ 1868 iii. Sheldon Douglas Arbogast b. Dec 02 1960.
+ 1869 iv. Sheila Francis Arbogast b. Mar 12 1963.

1040. **Bernard Fredrick^6 Arbogast** (468.Fred Lee^5 Arbogast, 121.Thomas^4 Arbogast, 15.Nichodemus^3, 3.Michael^2, 1.John C.^{1}), b. Jan 20 1920, d. Sep 27 1989.

Married Oct 02 1943, **Ellen Mae Hall**, b. Jun 23 1918, d. Sep 27 1989.

Children:

+ 1870 i. Bradford Edward^7 Arbogast b. Jul 12 1944.
+ 1871 ii. Jack Ray Arbogast b. Dec 04 1947.
+ 1872 iii. Ronald Allen Arbogast b. Sep 20 1950.

1041. **Stewart Franklin^6 Arbogast** (468.Fred Lee^5 Arbogast, 121.Thomas^4 Arbogast, 15.Nichodemus^3, 3.Michael^2, 1.John C.^{1}), b. Dec 01 1922.

Married Apr 29 1944, **Dorothy Geraldine Blackshire**, b. Aug 06 1926, d. Mar 27 1979.

Children:

1873 i. Connie Lou^7 Arbogast b. Jun 30 1946.
1874 ii. Larry Franklin Arbogast b. Nov 04 1947.
1875 iii. Robert Owen Arbogast b. Nov 23 1950.
1876 iv. Freddie Lee Arbogast b. Jun 30 1953.
1877 v. Clifton Daniel Arbogast b. Dec 08 1957.

1044. **Ginger Lynn^6 Arbogast** (469.Robert L.^{5}, 121.Thomas^4, 15.Nichodemus^3, 3.Michael^2, 1.John C.^{1}), b. Apr 18 1947.

She Married **Frank Constantini**, b. Nov 19 1944.

Children:

+ 1878 i. Theresa Lynn^7 Constantini b. Aug 22 1964.
1879 ii. Linda Marie Constantini b. Aug 20 1965.
1880 iii. David Francis Constantini b. Dec 31 1968.
1881 iv. Josie Lynn Constantini b. May 24 1972.
1882 v. Rebecca Lynn Constantini b. Jan 18 1974.

1047. **Venisa Robina[6] Arbogast** (469.Robert L.[5], 121.Thomas[4], 15.Nichodemus[3], 3.Michael[2], 1.John C.[1]), b. May 16 1954. She Married **Andrew Joseph Sullivan**, b. Sept 27, 1946 in Chester Co., PA, d. Nov 1999 in Elkton, Cecil Co., MD.

Children:

1883 i. Venisa Robina[7] Sullivan b. Jun 05 1975.
1884 ii. Michelle Lee Sullivan b. Dec 05 1976.
1885 iii. Brooke Beth Sullivan b. Jun 03 1979.

1049. **Roy Everett[6] Keller** (477.Harvey[5], 128.Emily Catharine[4] Arbogast, 16.Michael[3], 3.Michael[2], 1.John C.[1]), b. Oct 18 1896 in Osborne Co., KS, d. Apr 7 1969 in Russell, Lucas Co., IA.
Married Jul 20 1918 in Osborne Co., KS, **Jessie Rosa Luder**, b. Mar 9 1897 in Waldo, Russell Co., KS (daughter of Jacob Luder and Rosa Henning), d. Jan 26 1981 in Osborne Co., KS.

Children:

\+ 1886 i. Majorie[7] Keller.
1887 ii. Everett Keller. He Married **Edith Tabler**.
1888 iii. Rosalie Keller b. Dec 3 1926 in Waldo, Russell Co., KS, d. Sep 24 1941 in Luray, Page Co., VA.

1053. **Willis Leroy[6] Keller** (479.Willias Thomas[5], 128.Emily Catharine[4] Arbogast, 16.Michael[3], 3.Michael[2], 1.John C.[1]), b. Jul 27 1914 in Coeur d'Alene, Kootenai Co., ID, d. Oct 1960 in Spokane, Spokane Co., WA.
He Married **June Lavine Stearns**.

Children:

1889 i. Linda Lee[7] Keller b. Aug 19 1947 in Spokane, Spokane Co., WA, d. Jul 21 2001 in Palmdale, Los Angeles Co., CA.

1056. **Opel J.[6] Keller** (482.Leander Frank[5], 128.Emily Catharine[4] Arbogast, 16.Michael[3], 3.Michael[2], 1.John C.[1]).
She Married **(unknown) Wilkerson**.

Children:

1890 i. Wayne[7] Wilkerson.

1093. **Aluna Jean[6] Waybright** (505.Moses Randolph[5], 150.Isaac P[4], 19.Jesse[3], 4.Rachel[2] Arbogast, 1.John C.[1]), b. Feb 4 1928 in Webster Springs, Webster Co., WV.
Married Dec 5 1945 in Elkins, Randolph Co., WV, **Lyle Chester Ware**, b. Feb 27 1922 in Valley Head, Randolph Co., WV.

Children:

1891 i. Judith Ann[7] Ware b. Nov 15 1947 in Elkins, Randolph Co., WV, d. Mar 10 1956, buried in Valley Head, Randolph Co., WV.

1094. **Rhoda[6] Warner** (506.Ollie W.[5] Waybright, 151.James Bud[4], 19.Jesse[3], 4.Rachel[2] Arbogast, 1.John C.[1]), b. Jan 14 1896 in Dry Run, Pendleton Co., WV, d. Sep 22 1984 in Sun City, Maricopa Co., AZ. Married Feb 28 1915, **James Lester Thompson**, b. May 5 1892, d. Dec 27 1976.

Children:

\+ 1892 i. Mary Ollie[7] Thompson.
\+ 1893 ii. James Ralph Thompson.
\+ 1894 iii. Robert Isaac Thompson.
\+ 1895 iv. Wilmer Thompson.
\+ 1896 v. Leona Catherine Thompson.
1897 vi. Martha Alice Thompson b. May 14 1921, d. 1928.
1898 vii. Jacob H. Thompson b. Dec 5 1923, d. Nov 13 1990. He Married **Mary Wimer**.

1104. **Edna[6] Mullenax** (507.Anna Elizabeth[5] Waybright, 151.James Bud[4], 19.Jesse[3], 4.Rachel[2] Arbogast, 1.John C.[1]), b. 1899 in Cherry Grove, Pendleton Co., WV.
She
Married **Dick Lambert** (son of Bean Lambert and Phoebe Moyers). **Dick**: Parents were Bean Lambert and Phoebe Moyers.

Children:

1899 i. Sherman O.[7] Lambert.
1900 ii. Shirley L. Lambert b. 1922, d. 1994. She Married **Omer Sponaugle**.

1105. **James Edward^{6} Mullenax** (507.Anna Elizabeth^{5} Waybright, 151.James Bud^{4}, 19.Jesse^{3}, 4.Rachel^{2} Arbogast, 1.John C.^{1}), b. Feb 13 1900 in Cherry Grove, Pendleton Co., WV, d. Jul 12 1989 in Blue Grass Cem., Highland Co., VA, buried Jul 16 1989 in Blue Grass Cem., Highland Co., VA.
Married Aug 5 1926, **Gertrude Lee Waybright**, b. Mar 7 1911 in Pendleton Co., WV (daughter of Troy Waybright and Katie Warner), d. Dec 24 1998 in Rockingham Memorial Hospital, Harrisonburg Rockingham Co., VA, buried Dec 28 1998 in Blue Grass Cem., Highland Co., VA.

Children:

+ 1901 i. Brooks^{7} Mullenax b. Jul 17 1927.
1902 ii. Avis Theresa Mullenax b. Jun 15 1929.
1903 iii. Grace Irene Mullenax b. May 02 1931. She Married **Curtis Donald Smith**, b. Jan 11 1926.
1904 iv. Owen Edward Mullenax b. Sep 16 1938.
1905 v. Glenna Ann Mullenax b. Feb 06 1942. She Married **Ronald Wilson Moyers**, b. May 4 1940, d. Jan 11 1997.
1906 vi. Nancy Marie Mullenax b. Dec 24 1946.
1907 vii. Linda Lee Mullenax b. Oct 25 1952.

1106. **Judith^{6} Mullenax** (507.Anna Elizabeth^{5} Waybright, 151.James Bud^{4}, 19.Jesse^{3}, 4.Rachel^{2} Arbogast, 1.John C.^{1}), b. Sep 20 1901 in Cherry Grove, Pendleton Co., WV, d. Aug 10 1985 in Pendleton Co., WV.
Married Oct 6 1920, **Lee Moyers**, b. Feb 1 1899 in Deer Run, Pendleton Co., WV, d. Jul 13 1971 in Pendleton Co., WV.

Children:

1908 i. Sally^{7} Moyers.
1909 ii. Roselee Moyers.
1910 iii. Glenn Moyers.
1911 iv. Ada. V Moyers.
1912 v. Dorothy M Moyers.
1913 vi. Melvin E Moyers.
1914 vii. Bobby L Moyers.
1915 viii. Charles E Moyers.

1109. **Elva^{6} Mullenax** (507.Anna Elizabeth^{5} Waybright, 151.James Bud^{4}, 19.Jesse^{3}, 4.Rachel^{2} Arbogast, 1.John C.^{1}), b. Apr 1907, d. Sep 1984.
She Married **Raymond B Nelson**, b. Apr 03 1902, d. May 14 1982 in Highland Co., VA.

Children:

1916 i. Jennings Bryan^{7} Nelson.
1917 ii. Anna Nelson.
+ 1918 iii. Irene Nelson.
1919 iv. Francis Nelson.
1920 v. William Nelson.
1921 vi. Raymond Nelson.
1922 vii. Wilson Nelson.

1110. **Audrey Mabel^{6} Mullenax** (507.Anna Elizabeth^{5} Waybright, 151.James Bud^{4}, 19.Jesse^{3}, 4.Rachel^{2} Arbogast, 1.John C.^{1}), b. May 26 1909 in Cherry Grove, Pendleton Co., WV.
She Married **Virgil Nelson**, b. Feb 28 1902 in Riverton, Pendleton Co., WV, d. Apr 11 1982 in Petersburg, Grant Co., WV, buried in Riverton, Pendleton Co., WV. **Virgil**: Child of John Nelson and Susan Dice.

Children:

1923 i. Sylvia^{7} Nelson.
1924 ii. Freddy Nelson.
1925 iii. Berlie Nelson.

1114. **Ray^{6} Waybright** (508.Ira^{5}, 151.James Bud^{4}, 19.Jesse^{3}, 4.Rachel^{2} Arbogast, 1.John C.^{1}), b. Nov 28 1905 in Straight Creek, Pendleton/Highland Co., VA, d. Dec 28 1959 in Highland Co., VA, buried in Puffenbarger Cem. Monterey Highland Co., VA.

(1) He Married **Nellie Susan Mullenax**, b. Jun 6 1912 in Highland Co., VA (daughter of Aaron C. Mullenax and Arbelia Wimer), buried in Puffenbarger Cem. Monterey Highland Co., VA, d. Dec 4 1959 in Highland Co., VA.

***Children** by Nellie Susan Mullenax:*

1926 i. Randolph Ray^{7} Waybright b. Sep 14 1931 in Cave, Pendleton Co., WV, d. Nov 24 1993.
1927 ii. Ocie Aaron Waybright b. Dec 24 1944 in Cave, Pendleton Co., WV, d. Nov 23 1967, buried in Rohrbaugh Farm, Highland Co., VA.

1115. **Beulah[6] Waybright** (508.Ira[5], 151.James Bud[4], 19.Jesse[3], 4.Rachel[2] Arbogast, 1.John C.[1]), b. Jan 5 1907 in Rich Mountain, Pendleton Co., WV, d. Aug 29 1996, buried in Staunton, Augusta Co., VA. She Married **Algie R Tichenor**, b. Jan 20 1907, d. Aug 1963.

Children:

1928 i. Leroy Junior[7] Tichenor b. Jan 2 1930 in Blue Grass Cem., Highland Co., VA, d. Apr 17 1986 in Staunton, Augusta Co., VA, buried in Augusta Memorial Park Cem., Augusta Co., VA.
1929 ii. Charles Berlie Tichenor b. Jan 17 1934 in Staunton, Augusta Co., VA, d. Jan 20 1996.
1930 iii. Kenneth Guy Tichenor b. Jun 18 1937 in Cherry Grove, Pendleton Co., WV, d. Mar 22 1988.

1128. **Jason Paschal[6] Waybright** (509.Michael[5], 151.James Bud[4], 19.Jesse[3], 4.Rachel[2] Arbogast, 1.John C.[1]), b. Sep 21 1929 in Cherry Grove, Pendleton Co., WV, d. Nov 28 1988.
He Married **(unknown) Clements**.

Children:

1931 i. Danny J.[7] Waybright b. May 27 1957 in Pennsylvania, d. Oct 11 1992 in Lebanon, Lebanon Co., PA.
was a machinist a member of Rod and Gun Club and a avid outdoorsman.

1129. **Glen[6] Hammer** (510.Esther[5] Waybright, 151.James Bud[4], 19.Jesse[3], 4.Rachel[2] Arbogast, 1.John C.[1]), b. Apr 23 1903 in Crabbottom, Highland Co., VA, d. Mar 5 1995 in Augusta Co., VA, buried Mar 8 1995 in Monterey Cem., Monterey, Highland Co., VA.
Married Feb 28 1922 in Crabbottom, Highland Co., VA, **Monna Lee Mullenax**, b. Aug 31 1901 (daughter of Henry Walter Mullenax and Mamie Katherine Collins), d. Jan 24 1993. **Monna**: Child of Henry Walter Mullenax and Mamie Collins.

Children:

1932 i. Robert G.[7] Hammer.
1933 ii. C. E. Hammer.

1141. **Kenny[6] Waybright** (511.Jesse[5], 151.James Bud[4], 19.Jesse[3], 4.Rachel[2] Arbogast, 1.John C.[1]), b. Jul 26 1904 in Cherry Grove, Pendleton Co., WV, d. Oct 28 1990 in Staunton, Augusta Co., VA, buried in Arbovale Cem., Arbovale, Pocahontas Co., WV.
Married Apr 19 1924 in Crabbottom, Highland Co., VA, **Ollie Elizabeth Mullenax**, b. Mar 2 1905 in Blue Grass Cem., Highland Co., VA (daughter of Aaron C. Mullenax and Arbelia Wimer), d. Jun 11 1998 in Churchville, Pendleton Co., WV.

Children:

\+ 1934 i. William Nevin[7] Waybright b. Jan 25 1925.
1935 ii. Lucille Mae Waybright b. Apr 27 1927 in Blue Grass Cem., Highland Co., VA. Married May 10 1947 in Churchville, Pendleton Co., WV, **Stanley Miller Back**, b. Aug 23 1925 in Churchville, Pendleton Co., WV. Stanley:
\+ 1936 iii. George Samuel Waybright, Sr..
\+ 1937 iv. Dollie Elizabeth Waybright.
1938 v. George Samuel Waybright.
S/o Kennie and Ollie (Mullenax) Waybright. Both Kennie and Ollie were descendants of John Arbogast, Volume I. Kennie is #22073 and Ollie's mother Arbelia (Wimer) Mullenax is #23236. The marriage to Naomi Wenger was George's second marriage.
Married Apr 1 1976 in Staunton, Augusta Co., VA, **Naomi Gay Wenger**, b. Feb 8 1932 (daughter of Leonard C. Wenger and Maudie Dolin).Naomi: Ref: Pocahontas 1981: 482.

1143. **Martha Jane[6] Waybright** (511.Jesse[5], 151.James Bud[4], 19.Jesse[3], 4.Rachel[2] Arbogast, 1.John C.[1]), b. Jan 5 1910 in Blue Grass Cem., Highland Co., VA, d. Jun 12 1983 in Waynesboro Community Hospital, Waynesboro, Augusta Co., VA, buried in Augusta Memorial Park Waynesboro, Franklin Co.,, VA. She
Married **Marshall Raines** (son of Stewart Raines and Elizabeth A. Lambert).

Children:

1939 i. Delbert[7] Raines.
1940 ii. Russell Raines b. 1926.
1941 iii. Una Raines b. Jul 6 1930, d. Nov 30 1993. She Married **Camon Wolfe**.

1144. **Erma Lillian[6] Waybright** (511.Jesse[5], 151.James Bud[4], 19.Jesse[3], 4.Rachel[2] Arbogast, 1.John C.[1]), b. Jan 10 1912 in Cherry Grove, Pendleton Co., WV, d. Nov 9 1986 in Waynesboro, Augusta Co., VA, buried in Blue Grass Cem., Highland Co., VA. She Married **Ralph Scott Simmons**, b. Jan 18 1903 in Blue Grass Cem., Highland Co., VA (son of Albert Simmons and Fannie May Hinkle), d. Feb 27 1970.

***Children**:*

1942 i. Joy Lou^{7} Simmons b. Nov 5 1933 in Virginia, d. Aug 13 1963. She Married **Thomas L. Mitchell**.

1155. **Jay^{6} Hammer** (512.Sarah^{5} Waybright, 151.James Bud^{4}, 19.Jesse^{3}, 4.Rachel^{2} Arbogast, 1.John C.^{1}), b. Nov 9 1909, d. Mar 27 1983, buried in Monterey Cem., Monterey, Highland Co., VA. He Married **Sallie K. Rexrode**, b. Nov 3 1912, buried in Monterey Cem., Monterey, Highland Co., VA.

***Children**:*

1943 i. Randolph E.^{7} Hammer b. Sep 11 1935, d. Feb 4 1936.

1166. **Sophie Grace^{6} Hinkle** (515.Sophia^{5} Waybright, 152.Alvah C.^{4}, 19.Jesse^{3}, 4.Rachel^{2} Arbogast, 1.John C.^{1}), b. 1910. Married Nov 13 1927, **Reon Howard Kline**, b. Apr 1 1906 in Churchville, Pendleton Co., WV, d. May 17 1993. **Reon**: .

***Children**:*

1944 i. Waldo E.^{7} Kline.

1167. **Reva^{6} Waybright** (516.Theodore^{5}, 152.Alvah C.^{4}, 19.Jesse^{3}, 4.Rachel^{2} Arbogast, 1.John C.^{1}), b. Feb 18 1912, d. Sep 9 1970, buried in Puffenbarger Cem. Monterey Highland Co., VA. She
Married **Richard Arthur Varner**, b. Jun 20 1906, d. Jun 7 1981, buried in Puffenbarger Cem. Monterey Highland Co., VA

***Children**:*

1945 i. Arthur Junior^{7} Varner b. Sep 15 1941 in Monterey, Highland Co., VA, d. Nov 5 1982 in Richmond, Henrico Co., VA, buried in Puffenbarger Cem. Monterey Highland Co., VA.

1174. **Vivin Richard^{6} Waybright** (517.Troy^{5}, 152.Alvah C.^{4}, 19.Jesse^{3}, 4.Rachel^{2} Arbogast, 1.John C.^{1}), b. Jan 6 1910 in Cherry Grove, Pendleton Co., WV, d. May 6 1981 in Loudoun Mem. Hospital, Leesburg, Loudoun, County VA, buried in Blue Grass Cem., Highland Co., VA.
(1) He Married **Iris Geneva Ratcliff**, b. Dec 1 1920 in Ratford, Montgomery Co., VA, d. Dec 5 1995 in Colonial Beach, Westmoreland Co., VA. .

***Children** by Iris Geneva Ratcliff:*

1946 i. Roy B^{7} Waybright.
1947 ii. Larry Waybright.
1948 iii. Ona Jean Waybright. She Married **(unknown) Armentrout**.
1949 iv. Danial D Waybright.
1950 v. Larry L Waybright.

(2) He Married **Erma Lambert**

1175. **Gertrude Lee^{6} Waybright** (517.Troy^{5}, 152.Alvah C.^{4}, 19.Jesse^{3}, 4.Rachel^{2} Arbogast, 1.John C.^{1}) (See marriage to number 1105.)

1185. **Delbert^{6} Waybright** (518.Clarence^{5}, 152.Alvah C.^{4}, 19.Jesse^{3}, 4.Rachel^{2} Arbogast, 1.John C.^{1}), b. Jun 3 1920 in Highland Co., VA.
Married Sep 30 1933, **Sherron Virginia Calhoun**, b. Aug 28 1915 (daughter of Virgil McQuain Calhoun and Nellie Mae Mullenax).

***Children**:*

\+ 1951 i. Ralph David^{7} Waybright b. Apr 19 1949.

1194. **Leonard Lee^{6} Tracy** (525.Lenora Jane^{5} Waybright, 155.Mary Elizabeth^{4}, 19.Jesse^{3}, 4.Rachel^{2} Arbogast, 1.John C.^{1}). He Married **(unknown) Spouse**.

***Children**:*

\+ 1952 i. Donna^{7} Tracy.
1953 ii. Lee L. Tracy.

1195. **Glenn Parker^{6} Tracy** (525.Lenora Jane^{5} Waybright, 155.Mary Elizabeth^{4}, 19.Jesse^{3}, 4.Rachel^{2} Arbogast, 1.John C.^{1}), b. Sep 28 1906 in West Virginia, d. Jan 2 1994 in Arbovale Cem., Arbovale, Pocahontas Co., WV.
Married Apr 23 1928, **Alma Vera Bly Moore**, b. May 6 1910.

***Children**:*

\+ 1954 i. Marian Ramona^{7} Tracy b. Aug 09 1928.
\+ 1955 ii. Helen Tracy.

1200. **Louise[6] Varner** (529.Estella[5] Calhoun, 155.Mary Elizabeth[4] Waybright, 19.Jesse[3], 4.Rachel[2] Arbogast, 1.John C.[1]), b. Nov 6 1934. S
he Married **William Sharpless.**

***Children*:**

1956 i. William Jr.[7] Sharpless.
1957 ii. Donnie Paul Sharpless.
1958 iii. Timothy John Sharpless.
1959 iv. Martha Louise Sharpless.

1201. **Retha Lucille[6] Varner** (529.Estella[5] Calhoun, 155.Mary Elizabeth[4] Waybright, 19.Jesse[3], 4.Rachel[2] Arbogast, 1.John C.[1]), b. Mar 20 1937. She
Married **F. R. Wright**.

***Children*:**

1960 i. Sherry[7] Wright.
1961 ii. Melinda Wright.
1962 iii. Randy Wright.

1222. **Mary[6] Waybright** (539.Thaddeus[5], 158.Mary Margaret[4], 21.Daniel[3], 4.Rachel[2] Arbogast, 1.John C.[1]), b. 1920. D/o Thaddeus and Alpha Hollie (Elza) Waybright. Mary is the same person as
Married Dec 3 1942, **Earl Frederick Kerr**, b. Sep 18 1918 in Randolph Co., WV (son of Orville Erry Kerr and Jessie Lucy Louk), d. Aug 6 1990.**Earl**: Ref: Randolph 1991: 33.

***Children*:**

\+ 1963 i. Margaret Ann[7] Kerr b. Jan 6 1949.

1228. **Darl Blaine[6] Waybright** (541.Oscar Blaine[5], 159.William Washington[4], 21.Daniel[3], 4.Rachel[2] Arbogast, 1.John C.[1]), b. Jun 16 1913 in Parsons, Tucker Co., WV, d. May 24 1999 in Logan General Hospital, Logan Co., WV, buried May 27 1999 in Highland Memorial Gardens Logan Co., WV. Darl was a retired miner from Island Creek Coal National mines with 35 years of service
Married Dec 17 1934 in Logan, Fayette Co., WV, **Mamie Tennessee Taylor**, b. Jun 5 1912 in Johnson City, Washington Co., TN, d. Mar 28 1998 in Logan General Hospital, Logan Co., WV, buried in Highland Memorial Gardens Logan Co., WV.

***Children*:**

1964 i. Edna Lois[7] Brewer b. Feb 1 1934 in Monaville Logan Co., WV, d. Apr 2 1988, buried in Highland Memorial Gardens Logan Co., WV.

1235. **Margie[6] Kisamore** (549.Perlie[5] Arbogast, 162.Cordelia[4] Waybright, 21.Daniel[3], 4.Rachel[2] Arbogast, 1.John C.[1]), b. Jul 27 1919 in Pendleton Co., WV, d. Mar 17 1990 in Tucker Co., WV. Married Jun 26 1938 in Tucker Co., WV, **George Clarence Gatto**, b. Jul 27 1917 in Henry, Grant Co., WV.

***Children*:**

\+ 1965 i. Kathryn Mae[7] Gatto b. Mar 16 1939.

1237. **Troy[6] Kisamore** (549.Perlie[5] Arbogast, 162.Cordelia[4] Waybright, 21.Daniel[3], 4.Rachel[2] Arbogast, 1.John C.[1]), b. in Tucker Co., WV.

(1) He Married **Lucille Taylor**.

***Children** by Lucille Taylor:*

1966 i. Troy Eugene[7] Kisamore b. Aug 03 1947.
1967 ii. Gary Williams Kisamore b. Nov 18 1948.
1968 iii. Gloria Dale Kisamore.

(2) He Married **Lorena (Unknown).**

***Children** by Lorena (Unknown):*

1969 iv. Troy Kisamore, Jr..

1238. **Glen[6] Kisamore** (549.Perlie[5] Arbogast, 162.Cordelia[4] Waybright, 21.Daniel[3], 4.Rachel[2] Arbogast, 1.John C.[1]), b. Oct 13 1927 in Barbour Co., WV.
Married Dec 24 1949 in Elkins, Randolph Co., WV, **Maria Bertha Kirkpatrick**, b. Jun 06 1929 in St. George, Washington Co., UT.

Children:

1970 i. Glen^{7} Kisamore, Jr. b. Feb 14 1952 in Baltimore, Baltimore Co., MD.
+ 1971 ii. Diana Marie Kisamore b. Aug 27 1954.

1240. **Guy^{6} Kisamore** (549.Perlie^{5} Arbogast, 162.Cordelia^{4} Waybright, 21.Daniel^{3}, 4.Rachel^{2} Arbogast, 1.John C.^{1}), b. Jan 18 1934 in Tucker Co., WV, d. Dec 24 1978 in Tucker Co., WV.
Married Apr 28 1953 in Oakland, Garrett Co., MD, **Mary Bell**, b. Dec 15 1934 in Tucker Co., WV.

Children:

+ 1972 i. Olive Pearl^{7} Kisamore b. Jul 26 1954.
1973 ii. Bernetti Ann Kisamore b. Oct 24 1955 in Tucker Co., WV, d. Oct 24 1955 in Tucker Co., WV.

1244. **Samuel Henry^{6} Arbogast** (550.Wilbur^{5}, 162.Cordelia^{4} Waybright, 21.Daniel^{3}, 4.Rachel^{2} Arbogast, 1.John C.^{1}), b. Jul 10 1928, d. Feb 13 1986 in Morgantown, Monongalia Co., WV.
Married Oct 15 1947, **Iva Marie Cree**, b. Jan 16 1931, d. Feb 13 1986 in Morgantown, Monongalia Co., WV, buried in Garards Fort, Greene Co., PA.

Children:

+ 1974 i. David Lee^{7} Arbogast b. Feb 14 1948.
1975 ii. Doyle Edward Arbogast b. 1950, d. May 16 1954.
1976 iii. Robert Allen Arbogast b. Jan 28 1951.
+ 1977 iv. Linda Arbogast b. Jul 06 1952.
+ 1978 v. Donald Arbogast b. May 05 1958.
1979 vi. Donna Darlene Arbogast b. Nov 1958, d. Nov 1958 in Garards Fort, Greene Co., PA.
+ 1980 vii. Connie Sue Arbogast b. Mar 16 1961.

1245. **Lovie May^{6} Arbogast** (550.Wilbur^{5}, 162.Cordelia^{4} Waybright, 21.Daniel^{3}, 4.Rachel^{2} Arbogast, 1.John C.^{1}), b. Aug 18 1929, d. Mar 10 1985 in Washington, PA, buried Garards Fort, Greene Co., PA.
Married Jul 31 1948, **Lloyd Francis Conrad**, b. Sep 1927. **Lloyd**: Son of Samuel and Martha Conrad.

Children:

+ 1981 i. Larry Francis^{7} Conrad b. May 13 1949.
+ 1982 ii. Randy Conrad b. Jul 25 1954.
+ 1983 iii. Patricia Ann Conrad b. Oct 31 1955.
+ 1984 iv. Debra Conrad b. Oct 08 1957.
+ 1985 v. Jerry Conrad b. Mar 08 1961.
1986 vi. Michael Conrad b. May 16 1962. He Married **Sue Davis**, b. Aug 08 1992.
1987 vii. Ricky Gene Conrad b. Nov 02 1971.

1246. **Wilbur Junior^{6} Arbogast** (550.Wilbur^{5}, 162.Cordelia^{4} Waybright, 21.Daniel^{3}, 4.Rachel^{2} Arbogast, 1.John C.^{1}), b. Jun 21 1932, d. May 19 1978 in Garards Fort, Greene Co., PA.
He Married **Mary Jane Fordyce**, b. Nov 25 1941.

Children:

1988 i. James Edward^{7} Arbogast b. Apr 16 1958.
+ 1989 ii. Roger Lee Arbogast b. Jan 04 1960.

1266. **Ellis Paul^{6} Waybright** (558.Burley McCoy^{5}, 164.John Edward^{4}, 21.Daniel^{3}, 4.Rachel^{2} Arbogast, 1.John C.^{1}), b. Mar 12 1941 in Elkins, Randolph Co., WV, d. Feb 22 1982.

Children:

1990 i. Anthony Burl^{7} Waybright.
1991 ii. Jeffrey Lynn Waybright b. Mar 23 1967, d. Mar 23 1967.
1992 iii. Ellis Paul Waybright b. Feb 5 1968, d. May 29 1995.

1280. **Bricel^{6} Waybright** (578.Bert^{5}, 167.Albert^{4}, 21.Daniel^{3}, 4.Rachel^{2} Arbogast, 1.John C.^{1}), b. Dec 13 1911 in Whitmer, Randolph Co., WV, d. Nov 12 1966 in Elkins, Randolph Co., WV.
He Married **Dollie Vorden Fansler**, b. 1916, d. 1971.

Children:

1993 i. Thomas L.^{7} Waybright d. 1991.
He Married **Marla (Unknown)**.
1994 ii. Bricel Roy Waybright.

1995 iii. Retha Waybright. (1) She Married **Neal Smith**. Neal: . (2) She Married **Roy Ware** (son of Jacob G. Ware and Sarah M Hamrick).
1996 iv. Richard L. Waybright b. Jun 6 1933, d. Aug 1987 in Dundalk Baltimore Co., MD.
1997 v. Billy Keith Waybright b. Jun 30 1935, d. Mar 1980.
1998 vi. Kenneth Gene Waybright b. Mar 4 1937 in Elkins, Randolph Co., WV, d. Oct 11 1993 in Las Vegas, Clark Co., NV.

1281. **Walter Lee[6] Blagg** (584.William Pearl[5] Waybright, 168.Andrew Jackson[4], 22.Nathan[3], 4.Rachel[2] Arbogast, 1.John C.[1]), b. Jun 5 1895 in Monterey, Highland Co., VA, d. Aug 28 1982 in Redondo Beach, Los Angeles Co., CA, buried in Pacific Crest Cem., Redondo Beach, Los Angele Co., CA.
Walter is a Uncle to Me Born Out Of wedlock
was a sewer inspector for the city of Redondo and County of Los Angeles
Married Dec 26 1914, **Emma Glander**.

Children:

1999 i. Thomas A.[7] Blagg b. Oct 20 1918, d. Oct 8 1944 in Belgium, buried in Henri Chapelle Cem., Belgium. Married in Austin, Williamson Co., TX, **Muriel Wiley**.

1282. **Merrill Frithoff[6] Waybright** (584.William Pearl[5], 168.Andrew Jackson[4], 22.Nathan[3], 4.Rachel[2] Arbogast, 1.John C.[1]), b. Jun 13 1902 in Monterey, Highland Co., VA, d. Jan 15 1980 in Redondo Beach, Los Angeles Co., CA, buried Jan 18 1980 in Pacific Crest Cem., Redondo Beach, Los Angele Co., CA.
Married May 9 1924 in Los Angeles, Los Angeles Co., CA, **Marjorie Catherine Hartman**, b. Sep 8 1905 in Salt Lake City, Salt Lake Co., UT, d. Jul 15 1981 in Redondo Beach, Los Angeles Co., CA, buried Jul 18 1981 in Pacific Crest Cem., Redondo Beach, Los Angele Co., CA.

Children:

2000 i. Everett Lee[7] Waybright b. Oct 6 1925 in Torrance, Los Angeles Co., CA.
Married 1950, **Marjorie Tufts**, b. Nov 1 1928.
\+ 2001 ii. Robert Merrill Waybright b. Jun 6 1927.
2002 iii. Kenneth Richard Waybright b. Oct 31 1928 in Redondo Beach, Los Angeles Co., CA.

1283. **Mabel Virginia[6] Waybright** (584.William Pearl[5], 168.Andrew Jackson[4], 22.Nathan[3], 4.Rachel[2] Arbogast, 1.John C.[1]), b. Sep 28 1904 in Monterey, Highland Co., VA, d. Sep 25 1993 in Whittier, Los Angeles Co., CA, buried Sep 30 1993 in Rose Hills Memorial Park, Whittier, Los Angeles County CA.
Married Mar 8 1923 in Redondo Beach, Los Angeles Co., CA, **Verle Ramon Marks**, b. Aug 9 1896 in Redfield, Bourbon Co., KA, d. Jul 27 1976 in Whittier, Los Angeles Co., CA, buried Jul 30 1976 in Rose Hills Memorial Park, Whittier, Los Angeles County CA.

Children:

2003 i. Betty Jo[7] Marks b. May 13 1924 in Redondo Beach, Los Angeles Co., CA. She Married **Wallace David**.
2004 ii. Viola Katherine Marks b. Aug 30 1925 in Redondo Beach, Los Angeles Co., CA. Married May 26 1944, Jack **Dayton Kramer**.
2005 iii. Mabel Verlene Marks b. Mar 26 1927 in Redondo Beach, Los Angeles Co., CA, d. Jul 17 1989 in Loma Linda, San Bernardino Co., CA. She Married **Harold Beecham**.
2006 iv. Clair Louise Marks b. Nov 17 1928 in La Puente, Los Angeles Co., CA. Married Jun 15 1946, **Robert William Stein**.

1285. **Thomas Mead[6] Waybright** (584.William Pearl[5], 168.Andrew Jackson[4], 22.Nathan[3], 4.Rachel[2] Arbogast, 1.John C.[1]), b. Mar 21 1909 in Monterey, Highland Co., VA, d. Feb 2 1979 in Torrance, Los Angeles Co., CA, buried in Pacific Crest Cem., Redondo Beach, Los Angele Co., CA.
(1) Married Jun 29 1937 in Redondo Beach, Los Angeles Co., CA, **Tressa Miriam Wenzel**, b. Mar 8 1919 in Hermosa Beach, Los Angeles Co., CA, d. Aug 15 1984 in Sparks Washoe Co., NV, buried Aug 20 1984 in Reno, Washoe Co., NV.

***Children** by Tressa Miriam Wenzel:*

2007 i. Clayton Mead[7] Waybright b. Feb 18 1938 in Torrance, Los Angeles Co., CA.
.(1) He Married **Justine La Verne Patten**. (2) He Married **Justine La Verne Patten**.
2008 ii. Diana Claudene Waybright b. Feb 21 1940. She Married **Ramon Benard Delack**. Ramon: .
.

(2) He Married **Florence Mildred Young**, b. Apr 10 1910 in Brooklyn, Kings Co., NY.

1306. **Ralph Scott[6] Simmons** (632.Fannie May[5] Hinkle, 189.Elbridge L.[4], 26.Martha Ann[3] Waybright, 4.Rachel[2] Arbogast, 1.John C.[1]) (See marriage to number 1144.)

1312. **Virgil^6 Rymer** (634.Clyde^5, 190.Susan^4 Hinkle, 26.Martha Ann^3 Waybright, 4.Rachel^2 Arbogast, 1.John C.^{1}), b. Nov 03 1908, d. Oct 18 1978.
Married Jun 04 1927, **Hazel Ferrebee**.

Children:

2009 i. Marie^7 Ferrebee.
2010 ii. Donna Ferrebee.
2011 iii. Debbie Ferrebee.

1317. **Cletis^6 Johnston** (636.Dolly^5 Mullenax, 191.Elizabeth C^4 Hinkle, 26.Martha Ann^3 Waybright, 4.Rachel^2 Arbogast, 1.John C.^{1}), b. Jul 31 1902, d. Nov 03 1993.
Married Oct 27 1938, **Ollie K. Warner**, b. Mar 1 1915.

Children:

\+ 2012 i. Mary Leta^7 Johnson.
\+ 2013 ii. Buford C Johnston.
2014 iii. Ann Lynn Johnston.

1319. **Jesse^6 Johnston** (636.Dolly^5 Mullenax, 191.Elizabeth C^4 Hinkle, 26.Martha Ann^3 Waybright, 4.Rachel^2 Arbogast, 1.John C.^{1}), b. Jul 2 1907, d. Dec 18 1971 in Bartow, Pocahontas Co., WV. He Married **Monna Raines**.

Children:

2015 i. Odell Raines^7 Johnston. He Married **Mildred Lambert**.

1321. **Georgia Ellen^6 Johnston** (636.Dolly^5 Mullenax, 191.Elizabeth C^4 Hinkle, 26.Martha Ann^3 Waybright, 4.Rachel^2 Arbogast, 1.John C.^{1}), b. Oct 01 1911, d. Mar 20 1975, buried in Pine Hill Cem., Brandywine, Pendleton Co., WV. She Married **Harry Srtife Eye**, b. 1909.

Children:

2016 i. Richard Hull^7 Eye b. Jul 09 1937, d. Jul 24 1968.
2017 ii. James Lee Eye b. Jan 30 1939.
2018 iii. Terry Sue Eye b. Sep 03 1943.

1327. **Verlie^6 Warner** (637.Lura^5 Mullenax, 191.Elizabeth C^4 Hinkle, 26.Martha Ann^3 Waybright, 4.Rachel^2 Arbogast, 1.John C.^{1}), b. Dec 27 1903, d. Nov 29 1969 in Circleville, Pendleton Co., WV, buried in Hunting Ground, Pendleton Co., (W)VA.
Married Apr-09-1928, **Ona Lucy Sponaugle**, b. Nov-21-1909 in Circleville Pendleton Co., WV (daughter of John Alonzo Sponaugle and Mary Dessie Vandevander), d. Dec-19-1992.
She Married Eldon J Wimer (son of Charles Amos Wimer and Zoe Etta Thompson).

Children:

\+ 2019 i. Mildred Mary^7 Warner b. Sep 1928.
2020 ii. Hilda Warner b. c 1931 in Cherry Grove, Pendleton Co., WV, d. Feb-26-1987 in Port St. Lucie, FL.
2021 iii. Geneva Warner.
2022 iv. Francis Warner.
2023 v. Jerrol Warner.
2024 vi. Jimmy Warner.
2025 vii. Johnnie Warner.
2026 viii. Caroline Ruth Warner.
2027 ix. Dennis Warner.
2028 x. Gail Warner.
2029 xi. Kermit Warner.

1329. **Betty^6 Warner** (637.Lura^5 Mullenax, 191.Elizabeth C^4 Hinkle, 26.Martha Ann^3 Waybright, 4.Rachel^2 Arbogast, 1.John C.^{1}), b. Jul 26 1913.
She Married **Conda Roy Sponaugle**, b. May-20-1912 in Circleville Pendleton Co., WV (son of John Alonzo Sponaugle and Mary Dessie Vandevander).

Children:

2030 i. Genevieve^7 Sponaugle.
2031 ii. Norms Jean Sponaugle. She Married **Kelley M. Mullenax**.
2032 iii. Billy Roy Sponaugle.
2033 iv. Brenda Sponaugle.

1330. **Judith⁶ Warner** (637.Lura⁵ Mullenax, 191.Elizabeth C⁴ Hinkle, 26.Martha Ann³ Waybright, 4.Rachel² Arbogast, 1.John C.¹), b. Dec 18 1915.
She Married **Brison Jay Sponaugle**, b. Apr 03 1911 in Hunting Ground, Pendleton Co., (W)VA (son of Gilbert Kenton Sponaugle and Annie Pressie Mallow), d. Jun 13 1992.

Children:

2034 i. M. Elaine⁷ Sponaugle. She Married **(unknown) Alt**.
2035 ii. Jenny K. Sponaugle. Married 0, **(unknown) Halterman.**
\+ 2036 iii. Harold Michael Sponaugle b. May-18-1936.

1332. **Brooks Burdette⁶ Mullenax** (638.Mcclelland⁵, 191.Elizabeth C⁴ Hinkle, 26.Martha Ann³ Waybright, 4.Rachel² Arbogast, 1.John C.¹), b. Apr 23 1918, d. Dec 15 1968 in Fayetteville, Cumberland Co., NC.
S/o McClelland and Anna B. (Calhoun) Mullenax; Brooks is same person as #22355 and is a descendant of both John (Volume I) and Mary (Volume III).
Married Jun 5 1944, **Nell Lorraine Beard**, b. Mar 19 1920 (daughter of Samuel Bryant Monroe Beard and Mary Inez Brown), d. Nov 15 2001 in Wake Medical Center, Raleigh Co., NC.

Children:

\+ 2037 i. Carolyn Jean⁷ Mullenax b. Nov 9 1952.

1333. **Harlan⁶ Mullenax** (639.Martha Ellen⁵, 191.Elizabeth C⁴ Hinkle, 26.Martha Ann³ Waybright, 4.Rachel² Arbogast, 1.John C.¹), b. May 11 1912. (
1) Married Dec 05 1934, **Ruby M. Johnson**. .

Children *by Ruby M. Johnson:*

2038 i. Doris Lee⁷ Mullenax b. Oct 06 1934.

(2) He Married **Ruth Bennett**

Children *by Ruth Bennett:*

\+ 2039 ii. David Lee Mullenax b. May 24 1949.

1334. **Halcie⁶ Mullenax** (639.Martha Ellen⁵, 191.Elizabeth C⁴ Hinkle, 26.Martha Ann³ Waybright, 4.Rachel² Arbogast, 1.John C.¹).
She Married **Virgil Vandevander** (son of Wayne Sylvester Vandevender and Lena Tingler).

Children:

2040 i. Wayne⁷ Vandevander.
2041 ii. Randall Vandevander.
2042 iii. Billy D. Vandevander.
2043 iv. Robert Vandevander.

1338. **Elmer P.⁶ Phares** (641.Cleat⁵, 192.Eliza Ann⁴ Hinkle, 26.Martha Ann³ Waybright, 4.Rachel² Arbogast, 1.John C.¹), b. 1908, d. Jan-02-1972.
He Married **Myrtle M Sponaugle**, b. Dec-13-1908 (daughter of Herman Henry Sponaugle and Etta Beulah Warner), d. Nov-27-1970 in Cherry Grove, Pendleton Co., WV.

Children:

\+ 2044 i. Richard Cleat⁷ Phares b. May-16-1928.
\+ 2045 ii. Ina Lee Phares b. Aug-07-1930.
\+ 2046 iii. James H. Phares b. Oct-19-1932.
\+ 2047 iv. Raymond Phares b. Sep-20-1934.
\+ 2048 v. Mary June Phares b. Dec-15-1936.
\+ 2049 vi. Dottie Lou Phares b. Aug-02-1944.

1348. **Ethel Mae⁶ Sponaugle** (653.Gilbert Kenton⁵, 199.Roseann⁴ Ketterman, 28.Alice³ Waybright, 5.Rebecca² Arbogast, 1.John C.¹) (See marriage to number 821.)

1350. **Brison Jay⁶ Sponaugle** (653.Gilbert Kenton⁵, 199.Roseann⁴ Ketterman, 28.Alice³ Waybright, 5.Rebecca² Arbogast, 1.John C.¹) (See marriage to number 1330.)

1354. **Herbert Charles⁶ Sponaugle** (656.William Letcher⁵, 199.Roseann⁴ Ketterman, 28.Alice³ Waybright, 5.Rebecca² Arbogast, 1.John C.¹), b. Sep 1 1913 in Pendleton Co., WV, d. Jun 24 1989 in Alliance, Stark Co., OH.

Married Mar 15 1944, **Sally Nola "Sallie" Sponaugle**, b. Jul 11 1910 in Cherry Grove, Pendleton Co., WV, d. Nov 12 2001 in Arbovale Cem., Arbovale, Pocahontas Co., WV.

Children:

2050 i. Jerlene Wilda[7] Sponaugle b. Sep 23 1935 in Pendleton Co., WV, d. Sep 16 1996. Married Mar 7 1953, **Solon Clarence Blosser** , Jr, b. Aug 18 1928.
\+ 2051 ii. Juanita Sponaugle b. Jun 12 1944.
\+ 2052 iii. Patrice Sponaugle.

1355. **Nola Lee[6] Sponaugle** (656.William Letcher[5], 199.Roseann[4] Ketterman, 28.Alice[3] Waybright, 5.Rebecca[2] Arbogast, 1.John C.[1]), b. Jan 21 1916 in Pendleton Co., WV, d. Mar 3 1973 in Rockingham Co., VA.
Married Oct 6 1935, **Marshall William Wimer**, b. Nov 26 1913, d. Nov 19 1985.

Children:

2053 i. James Sherwood[7] Wimer b. Aug 4 1954 in Weyers Cave, Augusta Co., VA, d. Mar 16 1965 in Harrisonburg, Rockingham Co., VA.

1360. **Roche Elijah[6] Sponaugle** (656.William Letcher[5], 199.Roseann[4] Ketterman, 28.Alice[3] Waybright, 5.Rebecca[2] Arbogast, 1.John C.[1]), b. Mar 1 1925 in Pendleton Co., WV, d. Dec 6 1968 in Baltimore, Baltimore Co., MD.
Married Apr 20 1947, **Harvey Jay Long**, b. Sep 20 1921 in West Virginia.

Children:

2054 i. Ronnie Jay[7] Long b. Dec 30 1946 in Petersburg, Grant Co., WV.

1362. **Rosie Zona[6] Sponaugle** (656.William Letcher[5], 199.Roseann[4] Ketterman, 28.Alice[3] Waybright, 5.Rebecca[2] Arbogast, 1.John C.[1]), b. Jul 20 1928 in Pendleton Co., WV.
Married Jan 17 1946, **Omar Wilson Sponaugle**, b. May 21 1921 in Pendleton Co., WV (son of Adam Harness Sponaugle and Levi Lillian Moyers).

Children:

2055 i. Terry Donthan[7] Sponaugle b. Nov 22 1954 in Pendleton Co., WV, d. Dec 12 1954 in Pendleton Co., WV.

1363. **Marvin Luther[6] Sponaugle** (657.Herman Henry[5], 199.Roseann[4] Ketterman, 28.Alice[3] Waybright, 5.Rebecca[2] Arbogast, 1.John C.[1]), b. Jun-08-1903, d. Oct-21-1990 in Franklin, Pendleton Co., WV. (1) He Married **Argyle Wimer**. .

***Children** by Argyle Wimer:*

\+ 2056 i. Loriraine L[7] Sponaugle b. Feb-03-1924.
\+ 2057 ii. Ruth Elaine Sponaugle b. May-05-1928.
\+ 2058 iii. Marvin Luther Sponaugle, Jr. b. May-05-1928.
2059 iv. Herbert W. Sponaugle b. Feb-26-1925, d. Apr-08-1925.
2060 v. Lucy Louise Sponaugle b. Jan-16-1932, d. Apr-08-1932.
\+ 2061 vi. Carroll Lee Sponaugle b. Mar-10-1933.
2062 vii. Betty Lou Sponaugle b. Jun-04-1934.
\+ 2063 viii. Loretta June Sponaugle b. Dec-27-1937.

(2) He Married **Wanda Grover**

1364. **Beulah[6] Sponaugle** (657.Herman Henry[5], 199.Roseann[4] Ketterman, 28.Alice[3] Waybright, 5.Rebecca[2] Arbogast, 1.John C.[1]), b. Jul-26-1901 in WV, d. 1998 in MD.
She Married **Jesse Forest Simmons**, b. 1898, d. 1977.

Children:

2064 i. Carl[7] Simmons.
2065 ii. Herman Simmons.
2066 iii. Hansel Simmons.

1365. **Raymond[6] Sponaugle** (657.Herman Henry[5], 199.Roseann[4] Ketterman, 28.Alice[3] Waybright, 5.Rebecca[2] Arbogast, 1.John C.[1]), b. Mar-09-1905 in Hunting Ground, Pendleton Co. WV, buried in Sponaugle Family Cem., Hunting Grounds Pendleton County WV, d. Dec-26-1981 in Cherry Grove, Pendleton Co., WV.
Married Sep-12-1925 in Pendleton Co., WV, **Pauline Warner**.

Children:

2067 i. Olin[7] Sponaugle.
2068 ii. Berlin Sponaugle.

2069 iii. Gaylon C Sponaugle.
2070 iv. Merle Sponaugle.

1366. **Alpha Cynyhia^{6} Sponaugle** (657.Herman Henry^{5}, 199.Roseann^{4} Ketterman, 28.Alice^{3} Waybright, 5.Rebecca^{2} Arbogast, 1.John C.^{1}), b. Dec-18-1907.
She Married **Curtis Bennett**, b. Oct-28-1902, d. Jun-30-1987.

Children:

2071 i. Raynond^{7} Bennett d. Mar-12-1925.
2072 ii. Hartsell Bennett d. Jul-22-1926.
2073 iii. Guy Bennett d. Jun-17-1940.
\+ 2074 iv. Delene Bennett.
2075 v. Paul Bennett.
2076 vi. Harlan Bennett.
\+ 2077 vii. Judy Bennett.

1367. **Myrtle M^{6} Sponaugle** (657.Herman Henry^{5}, 199.Roseann^{4} Ketterman, 28.Alice^{3} Waybright, 5.Rebecca^{2} Arbogast, 1.John C.^{1}) (See marriage to number 1338.)

1370. **Mary Kerlin^{6} Sponaugle** (657.Herman Henry^{5}, 199.Roseann^{4} Ketterman, 28.Alice^{3} Waybright, 5.Rebecca^{2} Arbogast, 1.John C.^{1}), b. Mar-07-1914, d. Jul-27-1971 in Davis Memorial Hospital, Elkins, Randolph Co., WV.
Married Mar-28-1932, **Ralph M. Landis**, b. May-17-1905, d. Dec-28-1975.

Children:

2078 i. Kitty^{7} Landis. She Married **Blain Simmons**.
2079 ii. Dottie Landis. She Married **Jery Propst**.
2080 iii. Charles H Landis.
2081 iv. Ralph M Landis, Jr..
2082 v. Olin R Landis.
2083 vi. John W Landis.
2084 vii. Robert J Landis.
2085 viii. Jimmy J Landis.
2086 ix. Larry Landis.

1371. **Levern^{6} Sponaugle** (657.Herman Henry^{5}, 199.Roseann^{4} Ketterman, 28.Alice^{3} Waybright, 5.Rebecca^{2} Arbogast, 1.John C.^{1}), b. Dec-16-1919.
She Married **H Stern Butcher**, b. Dec-12-1915.

Children:

2087 i. Hugh^{7} Butcher.
\+ 2088 ii. Sherry Butcher.
2089 iii. Douglas Butcher.

1372. **Roscoe^{6} Sponaugle** (657.Herman Henry^{5}, 199.Roseann^{4} Ketterman, 28.Alice^{3} Waybright, 5.Rebecca^{2} Arbogast, 1.John C.^{1}), b. May-10-1921. (1) He Married **Judith Bland**. .

***Children** by Judith Bland:*

\+ 2090 i. Sandra^{7} Sponaugle.

(2) He Married **Phyllis Fisher**

***Children** by Phyllis Fisher:*

\+ 2091 ii. Peggy Sue Sponaugle.

1376. **Ruth^{6} Sponaugle** (657.Herman Henry^{5}, 199.Roseann^{4} Ketterman, 28.Alice^{3} Waybright, 5.Rebecca^{2} Arbogast, 1.John C.^{1}), b. May-18-1918.
She Married **Theron A Harper**, b. Feb-14-1924, d. Mar-02-1964.

Children:

\+ 2092 i. Patsey Louisa^{7} Harper.
\+ 2093 ii. Dorothy Harper.
2094 iii. Elizabeth Ann Harper. Married Sep-03-1983, **Richard Allen Harper**.

1386. **Karl Janson^6 Arbaugh** (666.Louella^5 Pennington, 204.Ann Rebecca^4 Ketterman, 28.Alice^3 Waybright, 5.Rebecca^2 Arbogast, 1.John C.^{1}), b. Jul 06 1909 in Pendleton Co., WV, d. Mar 02 1985 in Alliance, Stark Co., OH.
Married Dec 31 1934, **Olive Madge Newcomb**, b. 1904, d. Oct. 1985.

Children:

2095 i. Karlin^7 Arbaugh.

1396. **Virginia C.^{6} Vest** (673.Molley^5 Strauder, 205.Susan P.^{4} Ketterman, 28.Alice^3 Waybright, 5.Rebecca^2 Arbogast, 1.John C.^{1}), b. 1910, d. 1993. She Married **Henry Bennett**.

Children:

\+ 2096 i. Henry E.^{7} Bennett b. Dec-17-1932.

1405. **Iona Patrica^6 Waybright** (678.Wilber Allen^5, 208.Churchill^4, 28.Alice^3, 5.Rebecca^2 Arbogast, 1.John C.^{1}), b. Apr 24 1894 in Job, Randolph Co., WV, d. Dec 08 1965 in Elkins, Randolph Co., WV.
She Married **Cecil Morgan Collins**, b. Aug 14 1896 in Boyer, Pocahontas Co., WV (son of Andrew Morgan Collins and Louella Maer Grogg), d. Apr 13 1952 in Hospital, Columbus, Franklin Co., OH, buried in Union Cem., Olentangy River, Columbus, Franklin Co., OH.

Children:

\+ 2097 i. Harold Cecil^7 Collins b. Aug 13 1916.
2098 ii. Wilma Dell Collins b. Jan 10 1918 in Sitlington Creek, Pocahontas Co., WV, d. Jul 14 1918 in Sitlington Creek, Pocahontas Co., WV.
\+ 2099 iii. Bernard Morris Collins b. Jan 30 1920.
2100 iv. Ruby Mae Collins b. Feb 10 1925 in Laurel Lick, Boyer, Pocahontas Co., WV, d. Sep 1925 in Laurel Lick, Boyer, Pocahontas Co., WV.

1407. **Ollie Katherine^6 Waybright** (680.Amby Stanton^5, 208.Churchill^4, 28.Alice^3, 5.Rebecca^2 Arbogast, 1.John C.^{1}), b. Sep 30 1903 in Winterburn Pocahontas Co., WV, d. Jan 2 1999 in Crystal Springs Nursing home Elkins Pendleton Co., WV, buried Jan 5 1999 in Arbovale Cem., Arbovale, Pocahontas Co., WV.
She Married **Carl Elza**, b. Apr 25 1902, d. Feb 1983.

Children:

2101 i. Clinton Charles^7 Elza b. Mar 28 1923.

1408. **Grace Elizabeth^6 Waybright** (680.Amby Stanton^5, 208.Churchill^4, 28.Alice^3, 5.Rebecca^2 Arbogast, 1.John C.^{1}), b. Jun 16 1905 in Pocahontas Co., WV, d. 1993.
(1) She Married **Charles Vandevander**. **George**: .

Children *by Charles Vandevander:*

2102 i. Dollie Irene^7 Vandevander b. Sep 30 1921.
2103 ii. Lottie Mae Vandevander b. Oct 24 1924, d. Jan 1 1970.
2104 iii. Vervie Vandevander b. Oct 26 1926.
2105 iv. Merle Vandevander b. Jul 19 1929.

. (2) She Married **George Starks**, b. Nov 5 1904, d. Dec 24 1980

1409. **Gertrude Lee^6 Waybright** (680.Amby Stanton^5, 208.Churchill^4, 28.Alice^3, 5.Rebecca^2 Arbogast, 1.John C.^{1}), b. Dec 2 1907 in Pocahontas Co., WV.
She Married **Sterling Bruce Gum**, b. Oct 18 1897 in Green Bank, Pocahontas Co., WV (son of William Crawford Gum and Rubina Ruth Sutton), d. May 13 1980 in Marlinton, Pocahontas Co., WV.

Children:

\+ 2106 i. Sterling Lee^7 Gum b. May 2 1925.

1410. **Rella K^6 Waybright** (680.Amby Stanton^5, 208.Churchill^4, 28.Alice^3, 5.Rebecca^2 Arbogast, 1.John C.^{1}), b. Sep 29 1908 in Pocahontas Co., WV, d. Jul 22 2001.
She Married **Henry Parker Arbogast**, b. May 1 1892 in Pocahontas Co., WV (son of Adam Crawford Arbogast and Rachel Nettie Galford), d. Sep 11 1979 in Pocahontas Co., WV, buried in Arbovale Cem., Arbovale, Pocahontas Co., WV. **Henry**: The line of Parker Henry from Tommie Arbogast Huggins and her copy of The Galford Ancestry, by Lloyd Pritt Galford, 1981, Gateway Press, Baltimore, MD; copy in file. For family with Rella Waybright see #15691.

Children:

\+ 2107 i. Rev. James Bert^7 Arbogast b. Aug 11 1927.

1412. **Edna Alice[6] Waybright** (680.Amby Stanton[5], 208.Churchill[4], 28.Alice[3], 5.Rebecca[2] Arbogast, 1.John C.[1]), b. Mar 27 1912 in Pocahontas Co., WV, d. May 28 1993.
She Married **Grant Vandevander**.

***Children*:**

2108 i. Helen Kathleen[7] Vandevander b. Jul 10 1928.
2109 ii. Eugene Charles Vandevander b. Feb 01 1930.
2110 iii. Grant Vandevander b. Jul 23 1934.
2111 iv. Francis Marie Vandevander b. Aug 28 1936.

1413. **Bertie Catherine[6] Warner** (682.Fransina Lee[5] Waybright, 208.Churchill[4], 28.Alice[3], 5.Rebecca[2] Arbogast, 1.John C.[1]), b. Jul 9 1903 in Churchville, Pendleton Co., WV, d. Feb 14 1937.
Married Oct 4 1923, **Fred Marshall Wimer**, b. Mar 1903, d. Nov 1961.

***Children*:**

2112 i. Dessie Ina[7] Wimer b. Mar-12-1922 in Hunting Ground, Pendleton Co. WV. She Married **Lynn Lambert**, b. May-28-1916 in Riverton, Pendleton, West Virginia (son of J. Elmer Lambert and Maggie Hedrick).
2113 ii. Floyd Herman Wimer b. Mar-24-1924, d. Dec-18-1975. He Married **Mary Ruth Armstrong**, b. Nov-22-1920 in Harmon, WV (daughter of Eli Armstrong and Kate Warner), d. Aug-31-1980 in Baltimore, Baltimore Co., MD.
2114 iii. Omer John Wimer b. Mar-14-1926 in Hunting Ground, Pendleton Co. WV. He Married **Viva Georgia Lambert**, b. Oct-25-1930 (daughter of Cam lambert and Tressie Bennett).
2115 iv. Homer Sylvarius Wimer b. Mar-14-1926 in Hunting Ground, Pendleton Co. WV, d. Jul-11-1986 in Baltimore, Baltimore Co., MD. He Married **Oddie Mclamb**, b. Apr-18-1916 in Columbia Co. SC (daughter of Cager McLamb and Hattie Watts).
2116 v. Berlie Brooks Wimer b. Feb-10-1928 in Hunting Ground, Pendleton Co. WV. He Married **Maxine Carrie Hartman**, b. Jul-24-1935 (daughter of Charles Okey Hartman and Pauline Elza Eye).
2117 vi. Eston Jennings Wimer b. Nov-03-1935 in Hunting Ground, Pendleton Co. WV. He Married **Lois Ann Holtz**, b. Jun-21-1937 in Minot, ND (daughter of Arthur Holtz and Mabel Forthun).
\+ 2118 vii. Bobby MCarthur Wimer b. May-10-1942.

1416. **Ollie Elizabeth[6] Mullenax** (686.Arbelia[5] Wimer, 212.Jeremiah Emanuel[4], 29.Sidney[3] Waybright, 5.Rebecca[2] Arbogast, 1.John C.[1]) (See marriage to number 1141.)

1421. **Nellie Susan[6] Mullenax** (686.Arbelia[5] Wimer, 212.Jeremiah Emanuel[4], 29.Sidney[3] Waybright, 5.Rebecca[2] Arbogast, 1.John C.[1]) (See marriage to number 1114.)

1448. **Noah Washington[6] Waybright** (728.Abel Washington[5], 224.George Washington[4], 32.Elijah[3], 5.Rebecca[2] Arbogast, 1.John C.[1]), b. May 12 1902 in Churchville, Pendleton Co., WV, d. Jul 16 1991.
Married Dec 24 1931, **Wilma Erma Bittinger**, b. Jun 21 1911 in Brookside, Preston Co., WV.

***Children*:**

2119 i. Janet W.[7] Waybright b. May 23 1939 in Brookside, Preston Co., WV, d. Jun 15 1997 in Ruby Memorial Hospital, Morgantown, Monongalia Co., WV, buried in Eglon, Preston Co., WV.

1449. **Josiah[6] Waybright** (728.Abel Washington[5], 224.George Washington[4], 32.Elijah[3], 5.Rebecca[2] Arbogast, 1.John C.[1]), b. Mar 6 1905 in Churchville, Pendleton Co., WV, d. Jul 31 1990 in Preston Co., WV, buried in Mount Israel Methodist Church Fellowsville, Preston Co., WV.
Married Dec 23 1930 in Oakland, Garrett Co., MD, **Mamie Hershman**, b. Apr 29 1912.

***Children*:**

2120 i. Jones Junior[7] Waybright b. Oct 2 1931 in Preston Co., WV, d. Aug 24 1932 in Preston Co., WV.
\+ 2121 ii. Richard Dean Waybright b. May 1 1938.

1450. **John[6] Waybright** (728.Abel Washington[5], 224.George Washington[4], 32.Elijah[3], 5.Rebecca[2] Arbogast, 1.John C.[1]), b. Jun 10 1907 in Churchville, Pendleton Co., WV, d. Oct 29 1972 in Churchville, Pendleton Co., WV, buried in Garden of Faith Cem., Baltimore, MD.
Married Mar 14 1928 in Oakland, Garrett Co., MD, **Lela Iva Jenetta Miller**, b. Dec 1 1910 in Breedlove, Preston Co., WV, d. Aug 10 1963, buried in Garden of Faith Cem., Baltimore, MD.

***Children*:**

2122 i. William Thomas[7] Waybright b. Nov 20 1928 in Pierce, Tucker Co., WV, d. Nov 20 1928 in Pierce, Tucker Co., WV, buried in Maple Springs Cem., Eglon, Preston Co., WV.

2123 ii. Washington Lee Waybright b. Nov 20 1928 in Pierce, Tucker Co., WV, d. Nov 20 1928 in Pierce, Tucker Co., WV, buried in Maple Springs Cem., Eglon, Preston Co., WV.

2124 iii. William Eugene Waybright b. Nov 1 1929 in Pierce, Tucker Co., WV. Married Feb 26 1950, **Eva Jullia Rohman**, b. Feb 13 1928.

1460. **Ethel Florence[6] Waybright** (730.Luther Lee[5], 224.George Washington[4], 32.Elijah[3], 5.Rebecca[2] Arbogast, 1.John C.[1]), b. Mar 12 1907 in Pendleton Co., WV, d. Sep 13 1993, buried in Mount Olive Cem., Lantz Ridge Road, Preston Co., WV.
Married 1925 in Preston Co., WV or Garrett County, MD, **Linsey Elliot Nice**, b. May 11 1905 in Rowlesburg, Preston Co., WV, d. Apr 2 1971, buried in Mount Olive Cem., Lantz Ridge Road, Preston Co., WV.

Children:

2125 i. Lawrence Hall[7] Nice b. Aug 20 1926, d. May 24 1985, buried in Mount Olive Cem., Lantz Ridge Road, Preston Co., WV.

1462. **Sadie Annie[6] Waybright** (730.Luther Lee[5], 224.George Washington[4], 32.Elijah[3], 5.Rebecca[2] Arbogast, 1.John C.[1]), b. Dec 11 1910 in Accident Cem., Preston Co., WV, d. Jul 17 1976 in York, Adams Co., PA.
Married 1927 in Oakland, Garrett Co., MD, **Arthur Blaine Smallwood**, b. Sep 4 1884 in Rowlesburg, Preston Co., WV, d. Jun 29 1956 in York, Adams Co., PA. **Arthur**: .

Children:

2126 i. Nellie[7] Smallwood b. Aug 31 1927 in Rowlesburg, Preston Co., WV, d. Aug 31 1927 in Rowlesburg, Preston Co., WV.

2127 ii. Robert Madison Smallwood b. Apr 15 1929 in Rowlesburg, Preston Co., WV, d. Apr 15 1929 in Rowlesburg, Preston Co., WV.

2128 iii. Pallie Susan Smallwood b. Apr 15 1929 in Rowlesburg, Preston Co., WV, d. Apr 15 1929 in Rowlesburg, Preston Co., WV.

2129 iv. Walter William Smallwood b. Nov 6 1943 in West Manchester, York Co., PA, d. Nov 7 1943 in West Manchester, York Co., PA.

1470. **George William[6] Waybright** (731.Hendricks Cleveland[5], 224.George Washington[4], 32.Elijah[3], 5.Rebecca[2] Arbogast, 1.John C.[1]), b. Apr 28 1919 in Pickins, Randolph Co., WV, d. Sep 11 1999 in Webster Memorial Hospital, Webster Springs, Webster Co., WV, buried in IMOF Cem., Pickens, Randolph Co., WV. He was a member of Webster Co. Republican Committee, the farm Bureau, VFW post 3738 American leg ion heavy equipment operator. a Navy veteran of ww2
(1) Married Jan 1 1939 in Webster Springs, Webster Co., WV, **Clara Rosa Lee Hicks**, b. Sep 12 1917 in Pickins, Randolph Co., WV, d. Aug 24 1975 in Morgantown, Monongalia Co., WV. **Clara**: .

Children *by Clara Rosa Lee Hicks:*

2130 i. Rose Marie[7] Waybright b. Aug 16 1944 in Elkins, Randolph Co., WV, d. Feb 13 1983.

(2) Married Dec 26 1977, **Wilma Gay Brady**, b. Jan 21 1928.

1476. **Leota M.[6] Warner** (732.Surrilda Florence[5] Waybright, 224.George Washington[4], 32.Elijah[3], 5.Rebecca[2] Arbogast, 1.John C.[1]), b. Feb 11 1912, d. Feb 21 1981. Married Jun 20 1938, **Woodford Arbaugh**, b. Jun 15 1917, d. Jun 4 1967.

Children:

2131 i. Ruth Arline[7] Sponaugle b. Aug 29 1931. Married in Cleveland, Cuyahoga Co., OH, **Vere Ray Arbogast**.

2132 ii. Larwence C Sponaugle b. Jun 04 1933. (1) He Married **Betty Thompson**. (2) He Married **Wilma Lambert**.

2133 iii. David A Arbaugh.

2134 iv. Gene W Arbaugh.

2135 v. Linda Arbaugh.

1478. **Peachie N.[6] Warner** (732.Surrilda Florence[5] Waybright, 224.George Washington[4], 32.Elijah[3], 5.Rebecca[2] Arbogast, 1.John C.[1]), b. Jun 29 1916 in West Virginia.
Married Oct 23 1937, **Owen C. Warner**.

Children:

\+ 2136 i. Jerri[7] Warner b. Mar-28-1959.

1493. **Eugene[6] Wimer** (747.Franklin Cameron[5], 227.Martha Ellen[4] Harold, 34.Catherine Elizabeth[3] Waybright, 5.Rebecca[2] Arbogast, 1.John C.[1]), b. Jan 24 1921 in Highland Co., VA, d. Feb 8 1995 in Alexandria, Fairfax Co., VA. He Married **Mary Madeline Waugh**, b. May 15 1915 in Marlinton, Pocahontas Co., WV (daughter of George Beverly Waugh and Mary Ellen Merritt), d. Feb 6 1990 in Alexandria, Fairfax Co., VA.

Children:

2137 i. Pamela Sue[7] Wimer b. Aug 8 1949.

1503. **Rizpah Florence[6] Waybright** (776.William Garrett[5], 241.Nicholas[4], 36.Miles[3], 5.Rebecca[2] Arbogast, 1.John C.[1]), b. Oct 4 1914 in Blue Grass Cem., Highland Co., VA, d. Feb 15 1990 in Woodstock Shenandoah Co., VA, buried Feb 18 1990 in Massanutten Cem., Woodstock Shenandoah Co., VA.

Children:

2138 i. Charles Newton[7] Boyden b. Aug 13 1933 in Highland Co., VA, d. Dec 26 1971 in Pulaski, Pulaski Co., VA., buried Dec 29 1971 in Lindale Mennonite Cem., Broadway, Highland Co., VA.

2139 ii. Linda Lou Boyden b. Jul 1 1946 in Woodstock Shenandoah Co., VA, d. Jul 28 1997 in Fairfax, Fairfax Co., VA, buried Jul 30 1997.

1504. **Alda Christine[6] Waybright** (776.William Garrett[5], 241.Nicholas[4], 36.Miles[3], 5.Rebecca[2] Arbogast, 1.John C.[1]), b. Sep 19 1917 in Blue Grass Cem., Highland Co., VA, d. Jan 12 1990 in Davis Memorial Hospital, Elkins, Randolph Co., WV, buried Jan 15 1990 in Mount State Memorial Gardens, Gilman, Randolph Co., WV.
Married Jun 13 1934, **Russell Valley Arbogast**, b. Jun 6 1914 in Cherry Grove, Pendleton Co., WV, d. Dec 2 1989 in Davis Memorial Hospital, Elkins, Randolph Co., WV, buried Dec 5 1989 in Mount State Memorial Gardens, Gilman, Randolph Co., WV.

Children:

2140 i. Delphia M[7] Arbogast b. May 12 1935.

\+ 2141 ii. Russell Valey Arbogast, Jr. b. Nov 11 1936.

2142 iii. Ray Garnett Arbogast b. Apr 18 1938 in Harman, Randolph Co., WV, d. May 20 1991 in Monongalia General Hospital, Morgantown, WV, buried May 23 1991 in Flanagan Cem., Dry Fork, Tucker Co., WV. Married Oct 06 1960 in Deep Creek, Garrett Co., MD, **Helen Pennington**.

1508. **Omar Wilson[6] Sponaugle** (788.Levi Lillian[5] Moyers, 242.Ann Elizabeth[4] Waybright, 36.Miles[3], 5.Rebecca[2] Arbogast, 1.John C.[1]) (See marriage to number 1362.)

1509. **George B.[6] Crew** (790.Saulsberry N[5] Chew, 257.Lucinda[4] Arbogast, 40.Lemuel[3], 6.Joseph E.[2], 1.John C.[1]), b. Aug 07 1904, d. Nov 26 1991.
He Married **Nellie Dessa Lambert**, b. Feb 19 1901 in Pendleton Co., WV, d. Mar 16 1990 in Harrisonburg, Rockingham Co., VA.

Children:

2143 i. Emma Mae[7] Chew.

1518. **Martin Boston[6] Bell** (792.Lettie Susan[5] Arbogast, 259.Martin Van Buren[4], 40.Lemuel[3], 6.Joseph E.[2], 1.John C.[1]), d. Sep 19 1983.
Married Aug 16 1937, **Nela Geneva Mallow**, b. Aug 15 1906.

Children:

\+ 2144 i. Joy Hallie[7] Bell b. Aug 16 1937.

1529. **Wineberg[6] Morral** (793.Mary Jane[5] Arbogast, 259.Martin Van Buren[4], 40.Lemuel[3], 6.Joseph E.[2], 1.John C.[1]), b. Apr 1895.
He Married **Delphia Helmick**, b. Mar 06 1894.

Children:

2145 i. Mabel M[7] Morral b. May 01 1915 in Jenningston, Tucker Co., WV, d. Dec 02 1993 in Onego, Pendleton Co., WV. She Married **Fred Hedrick**.

2146 ii. Effie Morral.

2147 iii. Ruby Morral.

2148 iv. Mary Morral.

2149 v. Ocie Morral.

2150 vi. Blake Morral.

2151 vii. Roy Morral b. Melvin.

2152 viii. Melvin Morral.

1532. **Arthur[6] Morral** (793.Mary Jane[5] Arbogast, 259.Martin Van Buren[4], 40.Lemuel[3], 6.Joseph E.[2], 1.John C.[1]), b. Jun 10 1902.
He Married **Dora Vance**, b. Apr 07 1905 in Pendleton Co., WV, d. Mar 20 1980.

Children:

2153 i. Bert^{7} Morral b. Dec 28 1923, d. Jul 15 1944.
Bert was killed in action WWII.
2154 ii. Gaythel Morral b. Jul 29 1925, d. 1959.
+ 2155 iii. Ernest Morral b. Feb 04 1927.
2156 iv. Ruth Morral b. Dec 29 1928, d. 1929.
2157 v. Rosalie Morral b. Aug 31 1930.
2158 vi. Richard Morral b. Nov 08 1933.
2159 vii. Troy Morral b. Aug 30 1935.
2160 viii. Hazel Morral b. Oct 29 1937.
2161 ix. Gerlean Morral b. Oct 12 1941.
2162 x. Tom Morral b. Dec 26 1943.
2163 xi. James Morral b. Dec 29 1945.
2164 xii. Juanita Morral b. Jun 19 1949.

1537. **Bertha Catherine^{6} Arbogast** (794.Robert Calvin^{5}, 259.Martin Van Buren^{4}, 40.Lemuel^{3}, 6.Joseph E.^{2}, 1.John C.^{1}), b. May 30 1903 in Pendleton Co., WV, d. Mar 07 1995 in Wintersville, Jefferson Co., OH.
She Married **Stephen C Warner**, b. Nov 14 1900 in Pendleton Co., WV, d. Feb 19 1983 in Steubenville, Jefferson Co., OH.: Son of Alvin Warner and Margaret Mauzy.

***Children**:*

2165 i. Dorothea^{7} Warner. She Married **Larwence Ford.**
2166 ii. Shirley Warner. She Married **John Ziklo**.
2167 iii. Leona Warner. She Married **Ronald Hodd**.
+ 2168 iv. Forrest Stephen Warner b. Mar 29 1925.
2169 v. Carol Warner. She Married **Larry Brigner.**
2170 vi. Boyd E Warner.
2171 vii. Lee O Warner.

1541. **Blanche Ann^{6} Arbogast** (794.Robert Calvin^{5}, 259.Martin Van Buren^{4}, 40.Lemuel^{3}, 6.Joseph E.^{2}, 1.John C.^{1}), b. Jan 31 1918.
She Married **Blake Vance**, b. Jul 07 1913, d. Feb 18 1994.

***Children**:*

2172 i. Bonnie Jean^{7} Vance b. Jul 24 1933. She Married **James Richard Miller**, b. Apr 15 1934.
2173 ii. Betty Jo Vance b. Nov 14 1935. She Married **Herman Elwood Kenney**, b. Mar 02 1928, d. Feb 15 1994 in Bridgewater, Rockingham Co., VA. Herman: Son of George H Kenney and Leona Guyer.
2174 iii. Boyd Jennings Vance b. Jun 22 1937, d. Jul 29 1937.
2175 iv. Ruby Gail Vance b. Aug 02 1939. She Married **Leon Shiffiett**.
2176 v. Nancy Mae Vance b. Dec 22 1942. She Married George Timothy Riffett, b. Jan 20 1938 in Briery Branch, Rockingham Co., VA.
2177 vi. Kenneth Dale Vance b. Dec 06 1945. He Married **Lana Faye Norman**, b. Jan 27 1949, d. Nov 21 1977 in Dayton, Rockingham Co., VA.

1544. **Allen^{6} Arbogast** (814.Samual^{5}, 267.Jacob A.^{4}, 40.Lemuel^{3}, 6.Joseph E.^{2}, 1.John C.^{1}), b. Mar 12 1927 in Randolph Co., WV, d. Jun 15 1991 in Randolph Co., WV.
He Married **Phyllis Rauseo**, b. in Boston, Suffolk Co., MA.

***Children**:*

+ 2178 i. Allen Gerald^{7} Arbogast b. Sep 28 1948.
2179 ii. James A. Arbogast b. Sep 10 1952.
2180 iii. Mark S Arbogast b. Nov 03 1962. Married Oct 09 1988, **Michelle Suzette Carter**.

1545. **Audrey Maxine^{6} Arbogast** (814.Samual^{5}, 267.Jacob A.^{4}, 40.Lemuel^{3}, 6.Joseph E.^{2}, 1.John C.^{1}), b. Apr 14 1928 in Randolph Co., WV.
(1) Married Aug 07 1946, **Houston M McCuley**, b. in West Virginia.

***Children** by Houston M McCuley:*

+ 2181 i. Sam Houston^{7} McCauley b. Jun 08 1947.

(2) She Married **Claude Wilcox**, d. Apr 04 1986 in Orwell, Ashtabula Co., OH.

***Children** by Claude Wilcox:*

+ 2182 ii. Robert Lee Wilcox b. Jun 03 1951.
+ 2183 iii. Dean Thea Wilcox b. Dec 05 1957.

1546. **Betty Jean**[6] **Arbogast** (814.Samual[5], 267.Jacob A.[4], 40.Lemuel[3], 6.Joseph E.[2], 1.John C.[1]), b. Aug 01 1929 in Randolph Co., WV.
She Married **Howard P Webley**, b. in Elkins, Randolph Co., WV.

Children:

+ 2184 i. Olive[7] Webley b. May 01 1949.
+ 2185 ii. Edgar H Webley b. Aug 24 1950.
+ 2186 iii. Audrey D Webley.
+ 2187 iv. James J Webley b. Mar 16 1955.

1547. **Jeff Jake**[6] **Arbogast** (814.Samual[5], 267.Jacob A.[4], 40.Lemuel[3], 6.Joseph E.[2], 1.John C.[1]), b. Oct 31 1930 in Randolph Co., WV. (
1) He Married **Wanda Collett**, b. in Elkins, Randolph Co., WV.

Children *by Wanda Collett:*

2188 i. Randy[7] Arbogast.

(2) He Married **Phyllis Hawley**, b. in Cabin Creek, Kanawha Co., WV.

Children *by Phyllis Hawley:*

+ 2189 ii. Mickey Arbogast.
2190 iii. Holly Arbogast.
+ 2191 iv. Dana Arbogast.

1551. **John Mutt**[6] **Arbogast** (814.Samual[5], 267.Jacob A.[4], 40.Lemuel[3], 6.Joseph E.[2], 1.John C.[1]), b. February 4, 1934, d. June 9, 1956.
He Married **Carolyn Jean Delauder**, b. May 22 1940 in Elkins, Randolph Co., WV.

Children:

+ 2192 i. Diana Lynn[7] Arbogast b. Aug 02 1957.
+ 2193 ii. Jonnie Sue Arbogast b. Sep 14 1958.
+ 2194 iii. Anita Kay Arbogast b. May 15 1961.
2195 iv. Michael Sam Arbogast b. Feb 19 1965.

1552. **Mary Bessie**[6] **Arbogast** (814.Samual[5], 267.Jacob A.[4], 40.Lemuel[3], 6.Joseph E.[2], 1.John C.[1]), b. Jan 25 1936 in Randolph Co., WV.
She Married **Howard B Luzander**, b. in Sutton, Braxton Co., WV.

Children:

2196 i. Howard B[7] Luzander, Jr. b. Aug 07 1957.
+ 2197 ii. Jeffery Allen Luzander b. Sep 03 1961.

1554. **Donald Lee**[6] **Arbogast** (814.Samual[5], 267.Jacob A.[4], 40.Lemuel[3], 6.Joseph E.[2], 1.John C.[1]), b. Jun 22 1937 in Randolph Co., WV.
He Married **Barbara Teter**, b. in Elkins, Randolph Co., WV.

Children:

+ 2198 i. Vickie Dawn[7] Arbogast.
+ 2199 ii. Cathy Sue Arbogast.
+ 2200 iii. Donald Lee Arbogast, Jr. b. Feb 11 1957.

1555. **Lois Ann**[6] **Arbogast** (814.Samual[5], 267.Jacob A.[4], 40.Lemuel[3], 6.Joseph E.[2], 1.John C.[1]), b. Jun 22 1937 in Randolph Co., WV.
Married 1957 in Ohio, **Woodrow Sarson Hoover**.

Children:

+ 2201 i. Deborah Ann[7] Gover b. Aug 18 1958.
+ 2202 ii. Andrea Lynn Hoover b. Nov 25 1959.

1585. **Monna**[6] **Bennett** (822.Ada M.[5] Arbogast, 270.Hannah Elizabeth[4], 42.Joseph Elili[3], 6.Joseph E.[2], 1.John C.[1]), b. Apr 14 1898, d. May 31 1987.
She Married **Arcellous Simmons**.

Children:

+ 2203 i. Nelva Marie[7] Simmons.
+ 2204 ii. Bessie May Simmons b. Nov 24 1937.

1586. **John B.[6] Bennett** (822.Ada M.[5] Arbogast, 270.Hannah Elizabeth[4], 42.Joseph Elili[3], 6.Joseph E.[2], 1.John C.[1]) (See marriage to number 1008.)

1587. **Kate Sadie[6] Bennett** (822.Ada M.[5] Arbogast, 270.Hannah Elizabeth[4], 42.Joseph Elili[3], 6.Joseph E.[2], 1.John C.[1]), b. 1905, d. 1945.
She Married **Robert Mick**, b. Apr 22 1902 in Pendleton Co., WV, d. Sep 27 1987 in Pendleton Co., WV.

Children:

2205 i. Donald Gerry[7] Mick b. Jun 2 1922 in Cherry Grove, Pendleton Co., WV, d. Mar 8 1958 in Cherry Grove, Pendleton Co., WV. He Married **Ruth Bennett**.
2206 ii. Virginia May Mick b. Aug 14 1924 in Cherry Grove, Pendleton Co., WV, d. Jul 28 2003 in Cherry Grove, Pendleton Co., WV.
2207 iii. Raymond Robert Mick b. Sep 25 1926 in Cherry Grove, Pendleton Co., WV, d. Mar 30 1987 in Harrisonburg, Rockingham Co., VA.

1588. **Ethel[6] Bennett** (822.Ada M.[5] Arbogast, 270.Hannah Elizabeth[4], 42.Joseph Elili[3], 6.Joseph E.[2], 1.John C.[1]), b. Jul 30 1910, d. Feb 24 1992 in Pendleton Co., WV.
Married May 1 1930, **Samuel Warner**, b. Jul 12 1909 in Preston Co., WV, d. Sep 7 1984 in Pendleton Co., WV.

Children:

2208 i. Willard[7] Warner.
2209 ii. Charles Warner.
2210 iii. Pauline Warner.
2211 iv. Joy Warner.
2212 v. Vallie Warner.
2213 vi. Wilma Warner.
2214 vii. Freddie Calvin Warner b. Jul 21 1930 in Cherry Grove, Pendleton Co., WV, d. 1983.
2215 viii. Rosco Gerald Warner b. Jul 21 1930 in Cherry Grove, Pendleton Co., WV, d. Nov 23 1986 in Elkins, Randolph Co., WV. Married Jan 3 1961, **Phyllis Schoonover**, d. c 1986.

1597. **Mary Dessie[6] Vandevander** (826.Wayne Sylvester[5] Vandevender, 273.Ruth Ellen[4] Arbogast, 42.Joseph Elili[3], 6.Joseph E.[2], 1.John C.[1]), d. Mar-05-1964, buried in Cedar Hill Cem., Pendleton Co., WV.
Married Feb 24 1905, **John Alonzo Sponaugle**, b. Feb 9 1884 in Randolph Co., WV (son of Adam Harness Sponaugle and Sarah Jane Nelson), d. Nov 26 1985, buried in Cedar Hill Cem., Pendleton Co., WV.

Children:

+ 2216 i. Christena Belle[7] Sponaugle b. Jun-08-1906.
2217 ii. Bead Alonzo Sponaugle b. Feb-10-1908 in Circleville Pendleton Co., WV. (1) Married Aug-12-1928, **Annie Pressie Mallow**, b. Nov-14-1986 in Circleville Pendleton Co., WV (daughter of Benjamin Franklin Mallow and Roxanna Nelson), buried in Sponaugle, Circleville, WV, d. Dec-27-1982 in Elkins, Randolph Co., WV. Annie: She had been Married twice. After her first husband, **Gilbert Sponaugle**, died in 1925, she Married **Bead Sponaugle**.
DEC 1982 in Randolph Co., WV Pendleton Times Obituary
. (2) He Married **Myrtle Warner Bennett**.
2218 iii. William Sponaugle b. Jan-10-1914.
+ 2219 iv. Nola M. Sponaugle b. Feb-21-1915.
+ 2220 v. Adam Harness Sponaugle b. Jul-01-1918.
+ 2221 vi. Paul R. Sponaugle b. Apr-15-1920.
+ 2222 vii. Isaac Jay Sponaugle b. Oct-08-1922.
+ 2223 viii. Vallie Verie Sponaugle b. Mar-10-1927.
+ 2224 ix. Anna Jo Sponaugle b. Oct-09-1928.
+ 2225 x. Mary Lou Sponaugle b. Jul-21-1933.
+ 2226 xi. Conda Roy Sponaugle b. May-20-1912.
+ 2227 xii. Ona Lucy Sponaugle b. Nov-21-1909.
+ 2228 xiii. Cranston John Sponaugle b. Dec-12-1924.

1602. **Virgil[6] Vandevander** (826.Wayne Sylvester[5] Vandevender, 273.Ruth Ellen[4] Arbogast, 42.Joseph Elili[3], 6.Joseph E.[2], 1.John C.[1]) (See marriage to number 1334.)

1610. **Irma Mae[6] Arbogast** (831.Truman[5], 274.Elijah J.[4], 42.Joseph Elili[3], 6.Joseph E.[2], 1.John C.[1]), b. Sep 27 1915 in Pendleton Co., WV, d. Apr 30 1995 in Bedford, Cuyahoga Co., OH.
(1) She Married **Warren S. Propst.** .

Children *by Warren S. Propst:*

2229 i. Eva Elizabeth[7] Propst b. Oct 11 1938 in Pendleton Co., WV, d. Apr 21 2003 in Harrisonburg, Rockingham Co., VA.

(2) She Married **Dolph Day**

1617. **Woodrow Richard[6] Johnson** (832.Bertie Kate[5] Arbogast, 274.Elijah J.[4], 42.Joseph Elili[3], 6.Joseph E.[2], 1.John C.[1]), b. Apr 2 1917 in Pendleton Co., WV, d. Jun 18 1997 in Tucker Co., WV.
Married Jan 8 1939 in Franklin, Pendleton Co., WV, **Mary Alice Hartman**, b. Jun 11 1914 in Pendleton Co., WV (daughter of Isaac Perry Hartman and Lucy Vandevander), d. Jan 8 1992 in Pendleton Co., WV.

Children:

2230 i. Bruce Boyd[7] Johnston b. Aug 16 1947 in Pendleton Co., WV, d. May 1 1963 in Pendleton Co., WV.

1623. **Nora Gustava[6] Calhoun** (839.William Cecil[5], 275.Hannah Catharine[4] Bennett, 43.Sidney Dean[3] Arbogast, 6.Joseph E.[2], 1.John C.[1]), b. Feb 28 1915.
Parents names from marriage record; d/o Cecil and Emma Susan (Graham) Calhoun.
Married May 11 1940 in Highland Co., VA, **Theodore Jennings Arbogast**, b. Feb 3 1912 in Pocahontas Co., WV (son of William Harrison Arbogast and Docie Belle Ervine), d. Mar 20 1983 in Randolph Co., WV, buried in Dunmore Cem., Dunmore, Pocahontas Co., WV. Birth and death dates from obituary.

Children:

\+ 2231 i. Beverly Ann[7] Arbogast b. Sep 24 1940.

1628. **Lula Pauline[6] Lough** (842.Nina Beth[5] Calhoun, 275.Hannah Catharine[4] Bennett, 43.Sidney Dean[3] Arbogast, 6.Joseph E.[2], 1.John C.[1]), b. 1902, d. 1969.
Married 1920, **Paul Alexander Riggleman**, b. Oct 3 1898, d. DEC 1975. **Paul**: Was employed as a carman for the B and O railroad.

Children:

2232 i. Hazel Pearl[7] Riggleman b. 1921. Married 1942, **Earl Edward Scheminant**, b. 1922. Earl: .
\+ 2233 ii. Helen Pauline Riggleman b. Feb 14 1923.
2234 iii. Mildred Ruth Riggleman b. 1924. Married 1948, **Albert G Parrott**, b. 1925..
2235 iv. William Paul Riggleman b. 1925. Married 1956, **Marie Bailey**, b. 1919.
2236 v. Robert Ray Riggleman b. 1929.

1647. **Oscar William[6] Kerr** (862.Orville Erry[5], 288.William Bailey[4], 51.Hannah V.[3] Arbogast, 7.Moses[2], 1.John C.[1]), b. Oct 10 1909 in Randolph Co., WV, d. Mar 14 1958.
Married 1934, **Golda Gaye Hannah**, b. Jul 17 1908 in Slatyfork, Pocahontas Co., WV (daughter of Samuel Hannah and Amanda Moore), d. Sep 29 2002 in Ashland, Boyd Co., KY. **Golda**: Ref: Pocahontas 1981: 310 D/o Samuel David and Amanda Margaret (Moore) Hannah.

Children:

2237 i. Robert David[7] Kerr b. 1948. He Married **Valerie Hilton**.

1648. **Eunice[6] Kerr** (862.Orville Erry[5], 288.William Bailey[4], 51.Hannah V.[3] Arbogast, 7.Moses[2], 1.John C.[1]), b. Jan 14 1912 in Randolph Co., WV, d. Jun 17 1989.
(1) She Married **S. Y. Sharp** (son of Luther Sharp and Laura Morgan).
(2) She Married **Harold David Gibson** (son of Forest Gibson and Allie Catherine Gibson).

Children *by Harold David Gibson:*

2238 i. Vicki[7] Gibson.
2239 ii. Pamela Gibson.

1651. **Earl Frederick[6] Kerr** (862.Orville Erry[5], 288.William Bailey[4], 51.Hannah V.[3] Arbogast, 7.Moses[2], 1.John C.[1]) (See marriage to number 1222.)

1654. **Betty Jane[6] Kerr** (862.Orville Erry[5], 288.William Bailey[4], 51.Hannah V.[3] Arbogast, 7.Moses[2], 1.John C.[1]), b. Jan 10 1925 in Bemis, Randolph County WV.
Source is family records of Betty Jane (Kerr) Lewis of Beverly, WV. See parents notes as descendants of Michael Arbogast' sons, George and John, as well as Adam.
Married Jun 1 1946 in Randolph Co., WV, **Charles Junior Lewis**, b. Nov 28 1923 in Beverly, Randolph Co., WV (son of George Lewis and Juanita Lewis). Source is family records of Betty Jane (Kerr) Lewis of Beverly, WV. S/o George Arnold and Juanita Esta Mae (Lewis) Lewis.

Children:

2240 i. Richard Lee[7] Lewis.
2241 ii. Carol Sue Lewis.
2242 iii. Charles Joe Lewis.
2243 iv. John Lynn Lewis.
2244 v. Terry Keith Lewis.
2245 vi. Tammy Joy Lewis.

1658. **Calvin William[6] Stalnaker** (873.Birdie Cleo[5] Channell, 326.Eva Jane[4] Arbogast, 60.Moses Wamsley[3], 7.Moses[2], 1.John C.[1]), b. Feb 20 1924, d. 1987.
Married in Unsure, **Eleanor Louise Currence**, b. Apr 13 1924.

Children:

2246 i. Bertie Pugh[7] Stalnaker b. Jun 23 1951.
2247 ii. William Calvin Stalnaker b. Dec 21 1956.
2248 iii. Louise Stalnaker.

1665. **Monnie Irene[6] Stout** (887.Oleva (Levy) Alice[5] Cawthon, 336.Mary Susan[4] Arbogast, 63.Adam Jr.[3], 8.Adam Sr.[2], 1.John C.[1]), b. Sep 26 1911 in Gilmer Co., WV, d. May 17 1995 in Gilmer Co., WV, buried in Union Turner Cem. Gilmer Co., WV.
Married Apr 17 1927 in Gilmer Co., WV, **John O. Furr**, b. Jul 22 1904 in Gilmer Co., WV. **John**: At the time this data was assembled this Family may have 4 living, unwed children (child), that are not included here.
.

Children:

2249 i. Michael Wayne[7] Furr b. Abt 1929 in Normantown, Gilmer Co., WV, d. Abt 1929 in Normantown, Gilmer Co., WV.

1677. **Ermal Lenore Cawthon[6] KUHL** (893.Lona Elizabeth[5] CAWTHON, 336.Mary Susan[4] Arbogast, 63.Adam Jr.[3], 8.Adam Sr.[2], 1.John C.[1]), b. Mar 10 1916 in Withers, Gilmer Co., WV.
Living in Barberton, OH.
Married Mar 31 1934 in Parkersburg, Wood Co., WV, **Arnett Blackburn Edwards**, b. Feb 16 1913 in Dulin, Wirt Co., WV, d. Apr 21 1981 in Akron, Summit Co., OH, buried in Greenlawn Cem. Akron, Summit Co., OH. **Arnett**: Cause of death, cancer and heart disease.

Children:

2250 i. Donzil Cleo[7] Edwards b. Apr 16 1937 in Parkersburg, Wood Co., WV, d. Aug 25 1993 in Barberton, Summit Co., OH, buried in Greenlawn Cem. Akron, Summit Co.,
Cause of death, cancer.

1678. **Edith Murl[6] Kuhl** (893.Lona Elizabeth[5] CAWTHON, 336.Mary Susan[4] Arbogast, 63.Adam Jr.[3], 8.Adam Sr.[2], 1.John C.[1]), b. 14 Oct. 1919 in Gilmer Co., WV, d. Oct 17 1995 in Parkersburg, Wood Co., WV, buried in Sunset Memory Gardens, Wood Co., WV. Was a victim of MS for years. Died after surgery for Cancer.
Married Sep 16 1939, **Victor Hamilton Rafferty**, b. Jun 30 1920 in Gilmer Co., WV.

Children:

2251 i. Shirley Ann[7] Rafferty b. 1940 in Parkersburg, Wood Co., WV, d. 1940 in Parkersburg, Wood Co., WV, buried in Union Turner Cem. Gilmer Co., WV.
2252 ii. James Victor Rafferty b. May 9 1943 in Parkersburg, Wood Co., WV, d. Oct 25 1997 in Tipp City, Miami Co., OH, buried in Maple Hill Cem., Tipp City, Miami County OH.
.

1681. **Winifred Elaine[6] Kuhl** (893.Lona Elizabeth[5] CAWTHON, 336.Mary Susan[4] Arbogast, 63.Adam Jr.[3], 8.Adam Sr.[2], 1.John C.[1]), b. Aug 20 1926 in Burnsville, Braxton Co., WV.
Lives in Vienna, WV.
(1) Married Dec 21 1970, **Edgar Ward Boston**, b. Aug 2 1923.
(2) Married Never Married, **Glenville Parsons**, b. Dec 3 1924.

(3) Married Abt 1945, **Vannie Eagle**, b. Abt 1926.

Children *by Vannie Eagle:*

2253 i. Gary Wayne[7] Eagle b. Oct 4 1947 in Wood Co., WV, d. Jul 15 1983 in Parkersburg, Wood Co., WV, buried in Evergreen South Cem., Wood Co., WV.

1697. **Russell G.[6] Colaw** (913.Glen Dyer[5], 355.Bertha Viola[4] Ketterman, 78.Nicholas Harper[3], 9.Mary Ann[2] Arbogast, 1.John C.[1]), b. Mar 28 1941, d. May 4 1984.

(1) He Married **Denny Holub**, b. in Wyoming. .

Children *by Denny Holub:*

2254 i. Glenn[7] Colaw.
Lived in Normal, IL

2255 ii. Gail Colaw b. in card.
Lives in Farmington, IL

2256 iii. Gary Colaw b. in Perkin, Tazewell Co., IL.

(2) Married in Bloomington, McLean Co., IL, **Dixie Harmon**

1701. **Leo Dwain[6] Ketterman** (920.Merle Nicholas[5], 356.Paul[4], 78.Nicholas Harper[3], 9.Mary Ann[2] Arbogast, 1.John C.[1]), b. Jan 17 1937.

He Married **Twila Johnsboen**, b. Dec 7 1939.

Children:

2257 i. Dan[7] Ketterman b. Nov 11 1957.

2258 ii. Greg Ketterman b. Mar 6 1959.

2259 iii. Michelle Ketterman b. Apr 13 1960. She Married **Ruban Lopez**, b. Dec 29 1958 in Los Angeles Co., CA.

1723. **Mabel[6] Shomo** (939.Margaret[5] Arbogast, 375.George McClelland[4], 84.George Washington[3], 10.John C.[2], 1.John C.[1]), b. Aug 06 1912 in Barbour Co., WV, d. May 17 1979 in Richland Co., SC.

She Married **Homor Corell Wagner**, b. May 10 1911 in Barbour Co., WV

Children:

2260 i. Margaret Ann[7] Wagner b. Sep 01 1934 in Barbour Co., WV, d. May 01 2000 in Camden, Kershaw Co., SC. She Married **Lloyd Nelson Woods**, b. Oct 05 1921 in Mill Creek, Randolph Co., WV.

Generation Seven

1740. **Shelby Ruth[7] Smith** (956.Wilbur Amos[6], 405.Minnie May[5] Arbogast, 98.Amos Cyrus[4], 12.George Washington[3], 3.Michael[2], 1.John C.[1]), b. Jun 17 1953.

Married Oct 01 1977, **George Stanley Hunt**.

Children:

2261 i. Gregory Allen[8] Hunt b. Jun 12 1978.

1745. **Kathy[7] Samples** (957.Wavie[6] Smith, 405.Minnie May[5] Arbogast, 98.Amos Cyrus[4], 12.George Washington[3], 3.Michael[2], 1.John C.[1]).

She Married **Ed Walker**.

Children:

2262 i. Matthew[8] Walker.

1748. **Michael Irving[7] Smith** (958.Oliver Irvin[6], 405.Minnie May[5] Arbogast, 98.Amos Cyrus[4], 12.George Washington[3], 3.Michael[2], 1.John C.[1]), b. May 13 1955.

(1) He Married **Juanita Harper**. .

Children *by Juanita Harper:*

2263 i. Michael Anthony[8] Smith.

(2) He Married **Carrie Leonard**

1750. **Edward Allen[7] Smith** (958.Oliver Irvin[6], 405.Minnie May[5] Arbogast, 98.Amos Cyrus[4], 12.George Washington[3], 3.Michael[2], 1.John C.[1]), b. Mar 07 1958.
He Married **Sandy Hanshaw**.

Children:

2264	i.	Edward Allen[8] Smith< Jr..
2265	ii.	James Jackson Smith.

1762. **Mary[7] Hughes** (963.Amos[6], 407.Mary[5] Arbogast, 98.Amos Cyrus[4], 12.George Washington[3], 3.Michael[2], 1.John C.[1]), b. Sep 02 1957.
She Married **Brad Madison**.

Children:

2266	i.	Melissa[8] Madison.

1778. **Phillip Brett[7] Eades** (980.Amos Cyrus[6], 409.Faye Elvira[5] Arbogast, 98.Amos Cyrus[4], 12.George Washington[3], 3.Michael[2], 1.John C.[1]), b. Feb 12 1952 in Ft. Polk, Beauregard Parish, LA.
Married May 02 1973, **Franlie Louise Pride**, b. Jan 08 1954.

Children:

+ 2267	i.	Krystal Karma[8] Eades b. Nov 30 1973.
2268	ii.	Phillip Brett Eades, Jr. b. Jan 24 1979 in Oak Ridge, Anderson Co., TN.

1780. **Kerrilou[7] Eades** (980.Amos Cyrus[6], 409.Faye Elvira[5] Arbogast, 98.Amos Cyrus[4], 12.George Washington[3], 3.Michael[2], 1.John C.[1]), b. Sep 27 1960 in Wilmington, Clinton Co., OH.
Married Feb 24 1988, **Charles Eric Harmon**, b. Dec 09 1958.

Children:

2269	i.	Laurel Lee[8] Harmon b. Apr 09 1988.
2270	ii.	Kira Rose Harmon b. Jun 16 1992.

1781. **Hertha Velma[7] Arbogast** (981.William Leanord[6], 409.Faye Elvira[5], 98.Amos Cyrus[4], 12.George Washington[3], 3.Michael[2], 1.John C.[1]), b. Feb 01 1952 in Bremerhaven, Germany.
Married Sep 05 1970 in Farmingdale, Monmouth Co., NJ, **Manuel Magouis**, b. Jan 28 1952 in Hackensack, Bergen Co., NJ.

Children:

2271	i.	Coressa[8] Magoulis b. Feb 12 1971.
2272	ii.	Jessica Magoulis b. Oct 10 1978.

1782. **Beverley[7] Arbogast** (981.William Leanord[6], 409.Faye Elvira[5], 98.Amos Cyrus[4], 12.George Washington[3], 3.Michael[2], 1.John C.[1]), b. Jan 12 1954.
She Married **Michael Holtz**, b. Aug 26 1951 in Salisbury, Wicomico Co., MD.

Children:

2273	i.	Danielle[8] Holtz b. Sep 13 1983.

1783. **Leonard Warren[7] Arbogast** (981.William Leanord[6], 409.Faye Elvira[5], 98.Amos Cyrus[4], 12.George Washington[3], 3.Michael[2], 1.John C.[1]), b. Nov 05 1957.
Married Jun 20 1986 in Jackson, Ocean Co., NJ, **Jackie Agens**, b. Dec 10 1962 in Trenton, Mercer Co., NJ.

Children:

2274	i.	William Leanorg[8] Arbogast b. Aug 22 1987.
2275	ii.	Cheryl Arbogast b. Aug 11 1990.

1786. **Paul Joseph[7] Neal** (982.Denver McDonald[6], 410.Jessie Sarah[5] Arbogast, 98.Amos Cyrus[4], 12.George Washington[3], 3.Michael[2], 1.John C.[1]), b. Feb 18 1954. Married May 31 1981 in Roanoke, Roanoke Co., VA, **Keran Woods**.

Children:

2276	i.	Danial Joseph[8] Neal b. Nov 08 1985.

1787. **Edna[7] Samples** (983.Violet Gustava[6] Neal, 410.Jessie Sarah[5] Arbogast, 98.Amos Cyrus[4], 12.George Washington[3], 3.Michael[2], 1.John C.[1]), b. Dec 19 1942 in Baltimore, Baltimore Co., MD. She Married **Don Jewell**, b. Jul 05 1939 in South Gate, Los Angeles Co., CA.

Children:

2277	i.	Robbie[8] Jewell b. Oct 08 1959 in Pomona, Los Angeles Co., CA.

+ 2278 ii. Todd Jewell b. Jan 09 1963.
+ 2279 iii. Jeff Jewell b. Mar 14 1965.
2280 iv. James Jewell b. Mar 18 1971.

1789. **Linda Fay[7] Samples** (983.Violet Gustava[6] Neal, 410.Jessie Sarah[5] Arbogast, 98.Amos Cyrus[4], 12.George Washington[3], 3.Michael[2], 1.John C.[1]), b. Sep 14 1947.
Married Jul 25 1967 in Seattle, King Co., WA, **Kenneth Solney**, b. Jul 25 1947 in Seattle, King Co., WA.

Children:

+ 2281 i. Kerry[8] Solney b. May 22 1965.
2282 ii. Kenny Solney b. Apr 23 1970 in Lakewood, Los Angeles Co., CA.
2283 iii. Jason Solney b. Nov 23 1973 in Lakewood, Los Angeles Co., CA.

1791. **Easter Susan[7] Samples** (983.Violet Gustava[6] Neal, 410.Jessie Sarah[5] Arbogast, 98.Amos Cyrus[4], 12.George Washington[3], 3.Michael[2], 1.John C.[1]), b. Apr 12 1954 in Dundon, Clay Co., WV. She Married **Author Gaytan**, b. Oct 15 1951 in Ventura, Ventura Co., CA.

Children:

2284 i. Jessica[8] Gaytan b. Jul 24 1972 in Artesia, Los Angeles Co., CA.

1792. **Kenneth Richard[7] Samples** (983.Violet Gustava[6] Neal, 410.Jessie Sarah[5] Arbogast, 98.Amos Cyrus[4], 12.George Washington[3], 3.Michael[2], 1.John C.[1]), b. Jun 03 1958 in Anaheim, Orange Co., CA.

Children:

2285 i. Sarah Grace[8] Samples b. Aug 24 1987 in Fullerton, Orange Co., CA.
2286 ii. Jacqueline Diana Samples b. Dec 09 1990 in Fullerton, Orange Co., CA.

1796. **Berry Andrew[7] Arbogast** (987.Oliver Wendell[6], 411.Joseph Monroe[5], 98.Amos Cyrus[4], 12.George Washington[3], 3.Michael[2], 1.John C.[1]), b. May 11 1957 in Charleston, Kanawha Co., WV. He Married **Patricia McCardie**.

Children:

2287 i. Lea[8] . Arbogast.
2288 ii. Cory Arbogast

1798. **Betsy Lynn[7] Samples** (988.Addie Ramona[6] Arbogast, 411.Joseph Monroe[5], 98.Amos Cyrus[4], 12.George Washington[3], 3.Michael[2], 1.John C.[1]), b. Feb 10 1953 in Charleston, Kanawha Co., WV. Married Oct 04 1972, **Newton Jack Stepgenson**, b. Jul 04 1949 in Spencer, Rhone Co., WV.

Children:

2289 i. Matthew Gordon[8] Stephenson b. Jan 09 1980 in Charleston, Kanawha Co., WV.

1801. **Carolyn Elizabeth[7] Adams** (989.Anna May[6] Arbogast, 411.Joseph Monroe[5], 98.Amos Cyrus[4], 12.George Washington[3], 3.Michael[2], 1.John C.[1]), b. May 11 1957 in Jersey City, Jersey City NJ. Married 1984, **G. Marty Price**.

Children:

2290 i. Robert Walter[8] Price b. Aug 17 1985 in Starkville, Oktibbeha Co., MS.
2291 ii. Allison Wendy Price b. Oct 14 1994 in Starkville, Oktibbeha Co., MS.

1802. **John Michael[7] Adams** (989.Anna May[6] Arbogast, 411.Joseph Monroe[5], 98.Amos Cyrus[4], 12.George Washington[3], 3.Michael[2], 1.John C.[1]), b. Jul 24 1958 in Jersey City, Jersey City NJ. He Married **Jenalee Elgin**, b. f.

Children:

2292 i. Michael Allen[8] Adams b. Sep 27 1983 in Alexandria Rapides Co., Louisiana.
2293 ii. Amy Christine Adams b. Aug 20 1986 in Shreveport, Caddo Co., LA.

1805. **Harold Lloyd[7] Meadows** (990.Joyce[6] Cantley, 412.Lucy Esta[5] Arbogast, 98.Amos Cyrus[4], 12.George Washington[3], 3.Michael[2], 1.John C.[1]), b. Oct 16 1946 in Charleston, Kanawha Co., WV. Married Nov 25 1971 in Odd, Raleigh Co., WV, **Judy Farley**, b. Dec 07 1949 in McDowell Co., WV.

Children:

+ 2294 i. Elizabeth Ann[8] Meadows b. Jun 20 1972.
2295 ii. Rebecca Jane Meadows b. Dec 02 1977 in Mullins, Wyoming Co., WV.

1806. **Jacquenlin[7] Cantley** (991.Jack[6], 412.Lucy Esta[5] Arbogast, 98.Amos Cyrus[4], 12.George Washington[3], 3.Michael[2], 1.John C.[1]), b. Dec 19 1947 in Beckley, Raleigh Co., WV.

(1) Married Jun 03 1971 in Las Vegas, Clark Co., NV, **Doris Harold Chester**, b. Jun 24 1932 in Wayland, Floyd Co., KY..

Children *by Doris Harold Chester:*

2296 i. Robert John^{8} Chester b. Sep 28 1968 in Los Angeles, Los Angeles Co., CA.

(2) She Married **James Clyde Acker**, b. Nov 17 1935 in Los Angeles, Los Angeles Co., CA

1807. **Clair^{7} Cantley** (991.Jack^{6}, 412.Lucy Esta^{5} Arbogast, 98.Amos Cyrus^{4}, 12.George Washington^{3}, 3.Michael^{2}, 1.John C.^{1}), b. Jun 30 1952.
Married Jul 07 1971 in Artesia, Los Angeles Co., CA, **Thomas G Howard**, b. Dec 06 1952 in Montebello, Los Angeles Co., CA.

Children*:*

2297 i. Brie Anne^{8} Howard b. Aug 23 1981 in Lakewood, Los Angeles Co., CA.
2298 ii. Shanna Lynne Howard b. Oct 31 1984 in Lakewood, Los Angeles Co., CA.
2299 iii. Thomas Lloyd Howard b. Jul 06 1986 in Lakewood, Los Angeles Co., CA.

1808. **Steven^{7} Cantley** (991.Jack^{6}, 412.Lucy Esta^{5} Arbogast, 98.Amos Cyrus^{4}, 12.George Washington^{3}, 3.Michael^{2}, 1.John C.^{1}), b. Dec 08 1953.
He Married **Maureen Levy**, b. Oct 03 1958 in Torrance, Los Angeles Co., CA.

Children*:*

2300 i. Sarah Marie^{8} Cantley b. Jul 27 1982 in Fullerton, Orange Co., CA.

1809. **Mary Esta^{7} Jones** (993.Naomi Rose^{6} Cantley, 412.Lucy Esta^{5} Arbogast, 98.Amos Cyrus^{4}, 12.George Washington^{3}, 3.Michael^{2}, 1.John C.^{1}), b. Aug 24 1952 in Crab Orchard, Raleigh Co., WV.
She Married **Paul Wayne Lilly**, b. Mar 10 1951 in Beckley, Raleigh Co., WV.

Children*:*

2301 i. Melissa Sue^{8} Lilly b. Feb 04 1977 in Beckley, Raleigh Co., WV.
2302 ii. Jennifer Michelle Lilly b. Feb 04 1977 in Beckley, Raleigh Co., WV.

1810. **Kathy Ann^{7} Jones** (993.Naomi Rose^{6} Cantley, 412.Lucy Esta^{5} Arbogast, 98.Amos Cyrus^{4}, 12.George Washington^{3}, 3.Michael^{2}, 1.John C.^{1}), b. Jul 07 1953 in Beckley, Raleigh Co., WV. Married Jul 15 1972 in Mabscott, Raleigh Co., WV, **Grant Carvil Petitt, Jr**, b. Jul 07 1952 in Mabscott, Raleigh Co., WV.

Children*:*

2303 i. Phillip Grant^{8} Petitt b. Dec 07 1973 in Beckley, Raleigh Co., WV.
2304 ii. Andrew Jason Petitt b. Oct 27 1977 in Beckley, Raleigh Co., WV.

1811. **John William^{7} Jones, Jr.** (993.Naomi Rose^{6} Cantley, 412.Lucy Esta^{5} Arbogast, 98.Amos Cyrus^{4}, 12.George Washington^{3}, 3.Michael^{2}, 1.John C.^{1}), b. Mar 23 1955 in Beckley, Raleigh Co., WV. Married Aug 15 1976 in Sabine, Wyoming Co., WV, **Norma Phillips**, b. Mar 02 1959.

Children*:*

2305 i. Kristine Leigh^{8} Jones b. Oct 27 1981 in Beckley, Raleigh Co., WV.

1812. **Lesa^{7} Calhoun** (994.Carolyn^{6} Cantley, 412.Lucy Esta^{5} Arbogast, 98.Amos Cyrus^{4}, 12.George Washington^{3}, 3.Michael^{2}, 1.John C.^{1}), b. Mar 08 1965 in College Park, Prince George's Co., MD. She Married **Samuel Peck**, b. Apr 14 1965 in Shady Springs, Raleigh Co., WV.

Children*:*

2306 i. Tiffany^{8} Peck b. Aug 20 1991 in Winston Salem, Forsyth Co., NC.

1815. **Denver Henry^{7} Judy** (996.Orpha Gladys^{6} Shreves, 421.Joanna^{5} Shreve, 102.Benjamin "Little Ben"^{4}, 13.Mary Magdalene.^{3} Arbogast, 3.Michael^{2}, 1.John C.^{1}), b. Aug 24 1924 in North Fork, Pendleton Co., VA.

Children*:*

2307 i. Roger Dale^{8} Judy b. Aug 3 1950 in Petersburg, Grant Co., WV, d. Aug 3 1950 in Petersburg, Grant Co., WV.

1825. **Madeline^{7} Woods** (1009.Mabel Perl^{6} Reedy, 450.Acinith Lieuticia^{5} Markle, 117.Sarah D.^{4} Arbogast, 15.Nichodemus^{3}, 3.Michael^{2}, 1.John C.^{1}), b. Aug 13 1923 in Bentree, Clay and Nicholas Counties, WV.
Married Jul 21 1945 in Huntington, Cabell Co., WV, **Robert James Sizemore**, b. Jun 18 1925 in Clay Co., WV (son of John Sizemore and Matilda Lockhart).

Children:

2308 i. Mary Catherine[8] Sizemore b. Apr 19 1946 in Morgantown, Monongalia Co., WV.
2309 ii. Robert Lee Sizemore b. Dec 21 1948 in Morgantown, Monongalia Co., WV.
2310 iii. Sara E. Sizemore b. May 26 1952 in Huntington, Cabell Co., WV.

1829. **Roger Lee[7] Wriston** (1017.Olive Doris[6] Reedy, 450.Acinith Lieuticia[5] Markle, 117.Sarah D.[4] Arbogast, 15.Nichodemus[3], 3.Michael[2], 1.John C.[1]), b. Feb 14 1949 in Montgomery, Fayette Co., WV.
Married Jun 12 1965, **Diana L Beverly**.

Children:

2311 i. Patricia Louise[8] Wriston b. Sep 18 1965 in Cleveland, Cuyahoga Co., OH. Married Jun 25 1988, Kevin Filko.
2312 ii. Roger Lee Wriston, Jr. b. Aug 19 1972 in Cleveland, Cuyahoga Co., OH.
2313 iii. Molly Lynae Wriston b. Aug 03 1975 in Cleveland, Cuyahoga Co., OH.

1836. **Carlton Watson[7] Stallworth** (1019.Alberta Maxine[6] Arbogast, 459.Albert Lee[5], 119.George Franklin[4], 15.Nichodemus[3], 3.Michael[2], 1.John C.[1]), b. Aug 30 1947.
He Married **Sarah June Ansley**, b. Oct 30 1947.

Children:

2314 i. Audrey Ansley[8] Stallworth b. Oct 23 1965.
\+ 2315 ii. Sloan Leigh Stallworth b. Oct 01 1966.
\+ 2316 iii. Selena Lane Stallworth b. Oct 01 1966.

1839. **Janet Gail[7] Perry** (1021.Lois Jean[6] Arbogast, 459.Albert Lee[5], 119.George Franklin[4], 15.Nichodemus[3], 3.Michael[2], 1.John C.[1]), b. Mar 11 1956 in Charleston, Kanawha Co., WV. Married Dec 06 1986 in Kanawha Co., WV, **Timothy Dale Sheldon**, b. Jul 15 1960 in Charleston, Kanawha Co., WV.

Children:

\+ 2317 i. Perry Kathryn[8] Sheldon b. Apr 26 1990.

1841. **Diana Sue[7] Arbogast** (1022.William Bert[6], 459.Albert Lee[5], 119.George Franklin[4], 15.Nichodemus[3], 3.Michael[2], 1.John C.[1]), b. Oct 19 1947 in Charleston, Kanawha Co., WV.
Married Aug 26 1965, **David McCormick**.

Children:

2318 i. Amy Elizabeth[8] McCormick b. Nov 10 1966 in Charleston, Kanawha Co., WV. Married Sep 12 1986 in Kanawha Co., WV, **Wayne Gibson**.
2319 ii. Sherry Diane McCormick b. Dec 01 1967 in Charleston, Kanawha Co., WV. Married Nov 28 1987 in Kanawha Co., WV, **Erie Hedrick.**
2320 iii. Heather Lee McCormick b. May 02 1975 in Kanawha Co., WV.

1845. **Patsy Jo[7] Hughes** (1025.Francis Vivian[6] Arbogast, 460.Joseph Martin[5], 119.George Franklin[4], 15.Nichodemus[3], 3.Michael[2], 1.John C.[1]), b. Feb 24 1939 in Chillicothe, Ross Co., OH.
(1) She Married **Richard Thomas Dallas**. .

***Children** by Richard Thomas Dallas:*

\+ 2321 i. Lachona Ann[8] Dallas b. Jun 17 1966.

2) She Married **Richard Pierce**

1846. **George[7] Hughes** (1025.Francis Vivian[6] Arbogast, 460.Joseph Martin[5], 119.George Franklin[4], 15.Nichodemus[3], 3.Michael[2], 1.John C.[1]), b. Feb 14 1941 in Chillicothe, Ross Co., OH.
He Married **Terry Lee Oldacre**.

Children:

2322 i. George[8] Hughes II b. Mar 14 1975 in Columbus, Franklin Co., OH.
2323 ii. Dirk Hughes b. Sep 27 1980 in Columbus, Franklin Co., OH.

1848. **Nancy[7] Martin** (1025.Francis Vivian[6] Arbogast, 460.Joseph Martin[5], 119.George Franklin[4], 15.Nichodemus[3], 3.Michael[2], 1.John C.[1]), b. About 1954.
(1) She Married **Donald Cain**. .

***Children** by Donald Cain:*

2324 i. Kevin[8] Cain b. About 1974 in Columbus, Franklin Co., OH.

(2) She Married **Kenneth Dible**

Children *by Kenneth Dible:*

2325 ii. Derek Dible b. About 1980 in Marion Co., OH.

1849. **William Levi[7] Collins** (1026.Masel[6] Arbogast, 460.Joseph Martin[5], 119.George Franklin[4], 15.Nichodemus[3], 3.Michael[2], 1.John C.[1]), b. Sep 05 1939.

Children:

+ 2326 i. William Levi[8] Collins, Jr. b. 1130 1964.
+ 2327 ii. Gina Collins b. Jan 06 1966.
2328 iii. Danial Collins b. Feb 13 1968.

1851. **Earl[7] Woodruff** (1028.Maggie Jo[6] Arbogast, 460.Joseph Martin[5], 119.George Franklin[4], 15.Nichodemus[3], 3.Michael[2], 1.John C.[1]), b. Oct 02 1942.
He Married **(unknown) Woodruff**.

Children:

2329 i. Elizabeth[8] Woodruff b. Jul 05 1962.
2330 ii. Richard Woodruff b. Apr 1963.
2331 iii. Joseph Woodruff b. Aug 18 1973.
2332 iv. Nicholas Woodruff b. Aug 02 1990.

1852. **Joyce[7] Woodruff** (1028.Maggie Jo[6] Arbogast, 460.Joseph Martin[5], 119.George Franklin[4], 15.Nichodemus[3], 3.Michael[2], 1.John C.[1]), b. Nov 08 1944.
She Married **(unknown) Freeman**.

Children:

2333 i. Thomas[8] Freeman b. Nov 08 1963.
2334 ii. Lisa Freeman.
2335 iii. Debra Freeman.

1854. **Tamara[7] Chrystal** (1029.Ethel Malinda[6] Arbogast, 460.Joseph Martin[5], 119.George Franklin[4], 15.Nichodemus[3], 3.Michael[2], 1.John C.[1]).
She Married **(unknown) Hackett**.

Children:

2336 i. Michael James[8] Hackett b. Jun 21 1990.

1856. **Mary Lou[7] Arbogast** (1030.Ralph Martin[6], 460.Joseph Martin[5], 119.George Franklin[4], 15.Nichodemus[3], 3.Michael[2], 1.John C.[1]).
She Married **(unknown) Sarka**.

Children:

2337 i. Mary Ann[8] Sarka b. Aug 17 1974.
2338 ii. Charlene Sarka b. Jan 07 1978.
2339 iii. Laura Sarka b. Nov 30 1981.

1857. **Donald Wesley[7] Collins, II** (1031.Clarissa Velma[6] Arbogast, 460.Joseph Martin[5], 119.George Franklin[4], 15.Nichodemus[3], 3.Michael[2], 1.John C.[1]), b. Jun 10 1947.
He Married **(unknown) Collins**.

Children:

2340 i. Donald Wesley[8] Collins, III b. Jun 15 1973.

1858. **Temara Jo[7] Collins** (1031.Clarissa Velma[6] Arbogast, 460.Joseph Martin[5], 119.George Franklin[4], 15.Nichodemus[3], 3.Michael[2], 1.John C.[1]), b. Apr 14 1958.
She Married **Foster Collins**.

Children:

2341 i. Samantha Ashley[8] Stulen b. Feb 27 1992.

1859. **George Lee[7] Arbogast** (1032.George Lee[6], 460.Joseph Martin[5], 119.George Franklin[4], 15.Nichodemus[3], 3.Michael[2], 1.John C.[1]), b. Aug 07 1960 in Columbus, Franklin Co., OH.

He Married **Vickie Louise Nash**, b. f08031962 in Muskingum Co., OH.

Children:

2342 i. Ashley Michellle[8] Arbogast b. Feb 13 1993 in Tampa, Pasco Co., FL.

1860. **Robert Larwence[7] Arbogast** (1032.George Lee[6], 460.Joseph Martin[5], 119.George Franklin[4], 15.Nichodemus[3], 3.Michael[2], 1.John C.[1]).
Married Apr 17 1981 in Dunedin, Pinellas Co., FL, **Jacqueline Ann Leavey**, b. Nov 22 1961.

Children:

2343 i. Robert Larwence[8] Arbogast, Jr. b. Jan 13 1981 in Clearwater, Pinellas Co., FL.
2344 ii. David Joseph Arbogast b. Apr 15 1983 in Dunedin, Pinellas Co., FL.
2345 iii. Angela Lynn Arbogast b. Jan 09 1990 in Dunedin, Pinellas Co., FL.

1861. **John Edward[7] Hart** (1034.Lucy Kathryn[6] Perkins, 462.Sarah Alice[5] Arbogast, 119.George Franklin[4], 15.Nichodemus[3], 3.Michael[2], 1.John C.[1]), b. Dec 03 1949 in Charleston, Kanawha Co., WV.
He Married **Delinda Jean Holley**, b. Mar 28 1946.

Children:

2346 i. Kathryn Jean[8] Hart b. Aug 23 1983 in Charleston, Kanawha Co., WV.

1862. **Teresa Yvonne[7] Hart** (1034.Lucy Kathryn[6] Perkins, 462.Sarah Alice[5] Arbogast, 119.George Franklin[4], 15.Nichodemus[3], 3.Michael[2], 1.John C.[1]), b. Mar 28 1955 in Charleston, Kanawha Co., WV.
She Married **Michale Freddie Spudlock**, b. Dec 23 1953.

Children:

2347 i. Rhyn Michael[8] Spudlock b. Nov 29 1983 in Huntington, Cabell Co., WV.
2348 ii. Weslie Tyler Spudlock b. Nov 30 1986 in Huntington, Cabell Co., WV.

1863. **Donald Wilson[7] Lanham** (1037.Louella Francis[6] Arbogast, 468.Fred Lee[5] Arbogast, 121.Thomas[4] Arbogast, 15.Nichodemus[3], 3.Michael[2], 1.John C.[1]), b. Aug 29 1934.
Married Nov 25 1959, **Mary C Hutton**, b. Oct 28 1939.

Children:

\+ 2349 i. Robert W[8] Lanham b. Dec 20 1967.

1864. **Bobby Lee[7] Casto** (1037.Louella Francis[6] Arbogast, 468.Fred Lee[5] Arbogast, 121.Thomas[4] Arbogast, 15.Nichodemus[3], 3.Michael[2], 1.John C.[1]), b. Jul 25 1947 in Dunbar, Kanawha Co., WV. Married Jul 15 1967, **Shirley Casto**, b. June 1947.

Children:

2350 i. Joseph A[8] Casto b. Jan 12 1969.
2351 ii. Bobbi Jo Casto b. Jan 20 1971.
2352 iii. Christopher Casto b. Sep 01 1981.

1865. **Olga[7] White** (1038.Florence Doris[6] Arbogast, 468.Fred Lee[5] Arbogast, 121.Thomas[4] Arbogast, 15.Nichodemus[3], 3.Michael[2], 1.John C.[1]), b. Oct 31 1936.
Married Mar 30 1954, **Rodney Lee Williams**, b. Jan 21 1934.

Children:

\+ 2353 i. Rodney Lee[8] Williams b. Oct 19 1954.
\+ 2354 ii. Roy Franklin Williams b. Jul 04 1957.
2355 iii. Stephen Williams b. Aug 10 1963. He Married Sherry (Unknown).

1866. **Sheree Joan[7] Arbogast** (1039.Samual Roy[6], 468.Fred Lee[5] Arbogast, 121.Thomas[4] Arbogast, 15.Nichodemus[3], 3.Michael[2], 1.John C.[1]), b. Jun 23 1954.
Married May 15 1976, **Joseph L Brosk**, b. Jan 22 1954.

Children:

2356 i. Joseph Leo[8] Brosk b. Jul 17 1980.
2357 ii. Emiley Louise Brosk b. Oct 03 1981.

1867. **Steven Samual[7] Arbogast** (1039.Samual Roy[6], 468.Fred Lee[5] Arbogast, 121.Thomas[4] Arbogast, 15.Nichodemus[3], 3.Michael[2], 1.John C.[1]), b. Oct 15 1958.
Married Dec 16 1977, **Marilyn Gail Cummings**, b. Jun 19 1958.

Children:

2358 i. Norissa Mae[8] Arbogast b. Feb 01 1979.
2359 ii. Jeremy Steven Arbogast b. Jun 18 1980.
2360 iii. Asa Arbogast b. Jun 24 1985.
2361 iv. Adam Arbogast b. Jun 24 1985.

1868. **Sheldon Douglas[7] Arbogast** (1039.Samual Roy[6], 468.Fred Lee[5] Arbogast, 121.Thomas[4] Arbogast, 15.Nichodemus[3], 3.Michael[2], 1.John C.[1]), b. Dec 02 1960.
Married Jun 30 1976, **Karen Sue (Unknown)**, b. Dec 05 1961.

Children:

2362 i. Dustin Sheldon[8] Arbogast b. Jul 09 1981.
2363 ii. Alex Andrew Arbogast b. Jul 29 1989.

1869. **Sheila Francis[7] Arbogast** (1039.Samual Roy[6], 468.Fred Lee[5] Arbogast, 121.Thomas[4] Arbogast, 15.Nichodemus[3], 3.Michael[2], 1.John C.[1]), b. Mar 12 1963.
Married May 22 1981, **Terry Harper**, b. Jul 11 1962.

Children:

2364 i. Samantha[8] Harper b. May -2 1983.
2365 ii. Ashley Marie Harper b. Mar 22 1985.
2366 iii. Terry Austin Harper b. Jun 15 1988.

1870. **Bradford Edward[7] Arbogast** (1040.Bernard Fredrick[6], 468.Fred Lee[5] Arbogast, 121.Thomas[4] Arbogast, 15.Nichodemus[3], 3.Michael[2], 1.John C.[1]), b. Jul 12 1944.
Married Feb 19 1971, **Dorothy Culbertson**, b. Oct 22 1952.

Children:

2367 i. Christopher[8] Arbogast b. Oct 29 1971.
2368 ii. Paul Arbogast b. Nov 19 1972.

1871. **Jack Ray[7] Arbogast** (1040.Bernard Fredrick[6], 468.Fred Lee[5] Arbogast, 121.Thomas[4] Arbogast, 15.Nichodemus[3], 3.Michael[2], 1.John C.[1]), b. Dec 04 1947.
Married Mar 28 1975, **Cynthia Wertz**, b. Feb 15 1954.

Children:

2369 i. Kelly Rea[8] Arbogast b. Nov 06 1979.
2370 ii. Kristen Arbogast b. Nov 17 1983.

1872. **Ronald Allen[7] Arbogast** (1040.Bernard Fredrick[6], 468.Fred Lee[5] Arbogast, 121.Thomas[4] Arbogast, 15.Nichodemus[3], 3.Michael[2], 1.John C.[1]), b. Sep 20 1950.
Married May 08 1974, **Linda Devine**, b. Mar 07 1950.

Children:

2371 i. Angela Mae[8] Arbogast b. Oct 14 1975.
2372 ii. Jerome Arbogast b. Nov 05 1977.

1878. **Theresa Lynn[7] Constantini** (1044.Ginger Lynn[6] Arbogast, 469.Robert L.[5], 121.Thomas[4], 15.Nichodemus[3], 3.Michael[2], 1.John C.[1]), b. Aug 22 1964.

Children:

2373 i. Joseph Christopher[8] Constantini b. May 11 1982.

1886. **Majorie[7] Keller** (1049.Roy Everett[6], 477.Harvey[5], 128.Emily Catharine[4] Arbogast, 16.Michael[3], 3.Michael[2], 1.John C.[1]).
She Married **Willard Palmer** (son of Arthur Palmer and Susan Hooper).

Children:

2374 i. Roy Edward[8] Palmer d. Jan 21 2004.
2375 ii. Jimmie Lee Palmer b. Oct 2 1940 in Waldo, Russell Co., KS, d. Oct 3 1979.

1892. **Mary Ollie[7] Thompson** (1094.Rhoda[6] Warner, 506.Ollie W.[5] Waybright, 151.James Bud[4], 19.Jesse[3], 4.Rachel[2] Arbogast, 1.John C.[1]).
Married Feb 14 1936, **Gilbert Fidler**.

Children:

2376 i. Delores Joan[8] Fidler b. 1936, d. 1963.

2377 ii. Marcella Fidler b. 1938.
2378 iii. Mary Elizabeth Fidler b. 1940.
2379 iv. Rhoda Karen Fidler b. 1943.

1893. **James Ralph^{7} Thompson** (1094.Rhoda^{6} Warner, 506.Ollie W.^{5} Waybright, 151.James Bud^{4}, 19.Jesse^{3}, 4.Rachel^{2} Arbogast, 1.John C.^{1}). Married Jun 16 1938, **Dolly Godwin**.

***Children**:*

2380 i. James E.^{8} Thompson.
2381 ii. Eloise Thompson.

1894. **Robert Isaac^{7} Thompson** (1094.Rhoda^{6} Warner, 506.Ollie W.^{5} Waybright, 151.James Bud^{4}, 19.Jesse^{3}, 4.Rachel^{2} Arbogast, 1.John C.^{1}).

(1) Married Aug 01 1948, **Lynne Craig**. .

***Children** by Lynne Craig:*

2382 i. Craig Allen^{8} Thompson.
2383 ii. Lyndean Thompson.

(2) Married Aug 23 1963, **Helen Crump**

1895. **Wilmer^{7} Thompson** (1094.Rhoda^{6} Warner, 506.Ollie W.^{5} Waybright, 151.James Bud^{4}, 19.Jesse^{3}, 4.Rachel^{2} Arbogast, 1.John C.^{1}).

Married Nov 24 1952, **Joann Smith**.

***Children**:*

2384 i. Steve^{8} Thompson.
2385 ii. Dorothy Thompson.

1896. **Leona Catherine^{7} Thompson** (1094.Rhoda^{6} Warner, 506.Ollie W.^{5} Waybright, 151.James Bud^{4}, 19.Jesse^{3}, 4.Rachel^{2} Arbogast, 1.John C.^{1}). (

1) She Married **Grayburn Cooper, Jr.**. .

***Children** by Grayburn Cooper, Jr.:*

2386 i. Melody^{8} Cooper.

(2) Married Nov 14 1959, **Forrest Hyre**

***Children** by Forrest Hyre:*

2387 ii. David Hyre.

1901. **Brooks^{7} Mullenax** (1105.James Edward^{6}, 507.Anna Elizabeth^{5} Waybright, 151.James Bud^{4}, 19.Jesse^{3}, 4.Rachel^{2} Arbogast, 1.John C.^{1}), b. Jul 17 1927.

He Married **Priscilla Lane Warner**, b. Apr-10-1934 (daughter of Charles Warner and Mary Ellen Wimer).

***Children**:*

\+ 2388 i. Shirley Ann^{8} Mullenax b. 1953.
2389 ii. Diana Fay Mullenax b. 1995.
2390 iii. Donald Brooks Mullenax b. 1960.
2391 iv. Rose Mary Mullenax b. 1964. She Married **Kevin Simmons** (son of Harlan Simmons and Kittie Warner).

1918. **Irene^{7} Nelson** (1109.Elva^{6} Mullenax, 507.Anna Elizabeth^{5} Waybright, 151.James Bud^{4}, 19.Jesse^{3}, 4.Rachel^{2} Arbogast, 1.John C.^{1}).

She Married **Leslie Varner**.

***Children**:*

\+ 2392 i. Debbie Jo^{8} Varner.

1934. **William Nevin^{7} Waybright** (1141.Kenny^{6}, 511.Jesse^{5}, 151.James Bud^{4}, 19.Jesse^{3}, 4.Rachel^{2} Arbogast, 1.John C.^{1}), b. Jan 25 1925 in Blue Grass Cem., Highland Co., VA, d. Oct 8 1997 in Arbovale Cem., Arbovale, Pocahontas Co., WV, buried Oct 11 1997 in Boyer, Pocahontas Co., WV.

He Married **Millie Ryder**.

***Children**:*

\+ 2393 i. William Nevin^{8} Waybright.
2394 ii. Timothy Scott Waybright b. Sep 5 1955 in Marlinton, Pocahontas Co., WV, d. Jun 10 1995.

2395 iii. (unknown) Waybright b. May 13 1961 in Marlinton, Pocahontas Co., WV, d. May 13 1961 in Marlinton, Pocahontas Co., WV.

1936. **George Samual[7] Waybright, Sr.** (1141.Kenny[6], 511.Jesse[5], 151.James Bud[4], 19.Jesse[3], 4.Rachel[2] Arbogast, 1.John C.[1]).
Married Feb 21 1954, **Anna B. Wilfong**, b. May 30 1936.

Children:

2396 i. Diana Kay[8] Waybright b. Jan 27 1955. She Married Gary Lane Cash Cash. Gary: .
\+ 2397 ii. George Samuel Waybright, Jr. b. Feb 3 1957.

1937. **Dollie Elizabeth[7] Waybright** (1141.Kenny[6], 511.Jesse[5], 151.James Bud[4], 19.Jesse[3], 4.Rachel[2] Arbogast, 1.John C.[1]).
Dau. of Kennie and Ollie Elizabeth (Mullenax) Waybright. For = Dollie at #22792 in line of John Arbogast, of Michael. Same = for her siblings and parents in line to Mary Arbogast.
Married Aug 19 1961, **William Dale Varner**, b. Oct 4 1941 (son of William Oaklyn Varner and Anna Mae Sayre).**William**: Same person as #24435 in Dollie's line to Mary Arbogast.

Children:

\+ 2398 i. Penelope Kaye[8] Varner b. May 26 1962.
2399 ii. Jenifer Lynn Varner b. May 16 1966.
From Wm. C. Varner.

1951. **Ralph David[7] Waybright** (1185.Delbert[6], 518.Clarence[5], 152.Alvah C.[4], 19.Jesse[3], 4.Rachel[2] Arbogast, 1.John C.[1]), b. Apr 19 1949 in Pocahontas Co., WV.
Married Aug 24 1970 in Bath Co., VA, **Marie Alice Bond**, b. Feb 05 1953 in Mineral Co., NV.

Children:

2400 i. Jeremiah David[8] Waybright b. Jan 20 1977 in Randolph Co., WV.
2401 ii. Andrew Zephaniah Waybright b. Mar 12 1990 in Randolph Co., WV.

1952. **Donna[7] Tracy** (1194.Leonard Lee[6], 525.Lenora Jane[5] Waybright, 155.Mary Elizabeth[4], 19.Jesse[3], 4.Rachel[2] Arbogast, 1.John C.[1]).
She Married **(unknown) Hawkins**.

Children:

2402 i. Elizabeth[8] Hawkins.
2403 ii. Thomas Hawkins.

1954. **Marian Ramona[7] Tracy** (1195.Glenn Parker[6], 525.Lenora Jane[5] Waybright, 155.Mary Elizabeth[4], 19.Jesse[3], 4.Rachel[2] Arbogast, 1.John C.[1]), b. Aug 09 1928.
She Married **Robert David Bittle**, b. Aug 19 1935.

Children:

\+ 2404 i. Ronert David[8] Brittle, II b. Oct 14 1953.
2405 ii. Mark Tracy Brittle b. Jun 08 1956. Married Aug 08 1990, Holly Anne Olden.
2406 iii. Lisa Anne Brittle b. Jul 31 1967.

1955. **Helen[7] Tracy** (1195.Glenn Parker[6], 525.Lenora Jane[5] Waybright, 155.Mary Elizabeth[4], 19.Jesse[3], 4.Rachel[2] Arbogast, 1.John C.[1]).
She Married **Gorege Loman**.

Children:

2407 i. Jina[8] Loman.
2408 ii. John Jones Loman.

1963. **Margaret Ann[7] Kerr** (1222.Mary[6] Waybright, 539.Thaddeus[5], 158.Mary Margaret[4], 21.Daniel[3], 4.Rachel[2] Arbogast, 1.John C.[1]), b. Jan 6 1949.
She
Married **Robert Nicholas Beckwith**, b. Dec 12 1945 in Morristown, Morris Co., NJ (son of Walton Beckwith and Olga Markom). **Robert**: Ref: Randolph 1991: 33; information from Robert S/o Walton and Olga (Markom) Beckwith.

Children:

2409 i. Beth Ann[8] Beckwith b. Oct 3 1969.
2410 ii. Tracy Lynn Beckwith b. Nov 23 1971.

1965. **Kathryn Mae[7] Gatto** (1235.Margie[6] Kisamore, 549.Perlie[5] Arbogast, 162.Cordelia[4] Waybright, 21.Daniel[3], 4.Rachel[2] Arbogast, 1.John C.[1]), b. Mar 16 1939 in Tucker Co., WV.
Married Feb 14 1959 in Washington, D.C., **Dwight Gorden Hoppes**.

Children:

2411 i. Dwayne Allen[8] Hoppes b. Aug 31 1960 in Wichita, Sedgwick Co., KS. Married Oct 25 1987, **Janet Shepler**.

1971. **Diana Marie[7] Kisamore** (1238.Glen[6], 549.Perlie[5] Arbogast, 162.Cordelia[4] Waybright, 21.Daniel[3], 4.Rachel[2] Arbogast, 1.John C.[1]), b. Aug 27 1954 in Baltimore, Baltimore Co., MD.
Married 1972, **David Personeus**.

Children:

2412 i. Mary Alicia[8] Personeus b. Sep 06 1972.
2413 ii. Melissa Personeus b. Jan 31 1981.

1972. **Olive Pearl[7] Kisamore** (1240.Guy[6], 549.Perlie[5] Arbogast, 162.Cordelia[4] Waybright, 21.Daniel[3], 4.Rachel[2] Arbogast, 1.John C.[1]), b. Jul 26 1954 in Tucker Co., WV.
Married in Baltimore, Baltimore Co., MD, **Henry Ross**.

Children:

2414 i. Henry[8] Ross, Jr. b. Mar 15 1973.
2415 ii. Selena Ross b. Jul 26 1975 in Baltimore, Baltimore Co., MD.
2416 iii. Christopher Guy Ross b. Dec 30 1977 in Baltimore, Baltimore Co., MD.

1974. **David Lee[7] Arbogast** (1244.Samual Henry[6], 550.Wilbur[5], 162.Cordelia[4] Waybright, 21.Daniel[3], 4.Rachel[2] Arbogast, 1.John C.[1]), b. Feb 14 1948 in Waynesburg, Greene Co., PA.
He Married **Linda Cummings**, b. Jul 11 1950.

Children:

\+ 2417 i. Quinten[8] Arbogast b. Aug 21 1970.
2418 ii. Duane Arbogast b. Jul 1973.

1977. **Linda[7] Arbogast** (1244.Samual Henry[6], 550.Wilbur[5], 162.Cordelia[4] Waybright, 21.Daniel[3], 4.Rachel[2] Arbogast, 1.John C.[1]), b. Jul 06 1952 in Waynesburg, Greene Co., PA. S
he Married **Donnie Ray Higgins**, b. Aug 08 1947.

Children:

2419 i. Brandy[8] Huggins b. Feb 14 1980.
2420 ii. Heather Higgins b. Dec 24 1982.
2421 iii. Samuel Raymond Higgins b. Feb 16 1990.

1978. **Donald[7] Arbogast** (1244.Samual Henry[6], 550.Wilbur[5], 162.Cordelia[4] Waybright, 21.Daniel[3], 4.Rachel[2] Arbogast, 1.John C.[1]), b. May 05 1958.
Married Apr 17 1982, **Kathy Dean**, b. Oct 18 1961.

Children:

2422 i. Nichol[8] Arbogast b. Sep 25 1982.
2423 ii. Travis Arbogast b. Jan 23 1984.

1980. **Connie Sue[7] Arbogast** (1244.Samual Henry[6], 550.Wilbur[5], 162.Cordelia[4] Waybright, 21.Daniel[3], 4.Rachel[2] Arbogast, 1.John C.[1]), b. Mar 16 1961 in Waynesburg, Greene Co., PA. She
Married **Kenneth Frost**, b. Apr 07 1952.

Children:

2424 i. Joshua[8] Frost b. Feb 27 1982.
2425 ii. Jeff Frost b. Apr 01 1983.
2426 iii. Jonathan Frost b. May 20 1986.

1981. **Larry Francis[7] Conrad** (1245.Lovie May[6] Arbogast, 550.Wilbur[5], 162.Cordelia[4] Waybright, 21.Daniel[3], 4.Rachel[2] Arbogast, 1.John C.[1]), b. May 13 1949 in Waynesburg, Greene Co., PA. Married Dec 30 1972, **Nadine Polize**.

Children:

2427 i. Nichole[8] Conrad b. 1972, d. Mar 11 1973.
2428 ii. Heidi Conrad b. Jun 02 1975 in Morgantown, Monongalia Co., WV.
2429 iii. Larry Francis Conrad b. Mar 03 1979 in Morgantown, Monongalia Co., WV.

1982. **Randy[7] Conrad** (1245.Lovie May[6] Arbogast, 550.Wilbur[5], 162.Cordelia[4] Waybright, 21.Daniel[3], 4.Rachel[2] Arbogast, 1.John C.[1]), b. Jul 25 1954. He
Married **Debra White**.

***Children**:*

2430 i. Darla Renna[8] Conrad b. Aug 18 1975 in Waynesburg, Greene Co., PA.
2431 ii. Christie Lynn Conrad b. Sep 20 1976 in Waynesburg, Greene Co., PA.
2432 iii. Robert Lee Conrad b. in Waynesburg, Greene Co., PA.

1983. **Patricia Ann[7] Conrad** (1245.Lovie May[6] Arbogast, 550.Wilbur[5], 162.Cordelia[4] Waybright, 21.Daniel[3], 4.Rachel[2] Arbogast, 1.John C.[1]), b. Oct 31 1955.
She Married **Gary Sappington**, b. Dec 31 1929 in Garards Fort, Greene Co., PA.

***Children**:*

2433 i. Angela Mae[8] Conrad b. Nov 03 1982 in Morgantown, Monongalia Co., WV.
2434 ii. Justin Lloyd Conrad b. Feb 18 1986 in Morgantown, Monongalia Co., WV.

1984. **Debra[7] Conrad** (1245.Lovie May[6] Arbogast, 550.Wilbur[5], 162.Cordelia[4] Waybright, 21.Daniel[3], 4.Rachel[2] Arbogast, 1.John C.[1]), b. Oct 08 1957.
Debra had two other children Glen E. Miller b 11-21-1978, at Uniontown, PA and Nichole Catherine Miller, b 1-11-1979 in Uniontown, PA. She also Married **Lane Harbarger**.
She Married **Billy King**, b. in Morgantown, Monongalia Co., WV.

***Children**:*

2435 i. William Authur[8] King b. Jan 03 1975 in Morgantown, Monongalia Co., WV.

1985. **Jerry[7] Conrad** (1245.Lovie May[6] Arbogast, 550.Wilbur[5], 162.Cordelia[4] Waybright, 21.Daniel[3], 4.Rachel[2] Arbogast, 1.John C.[1]), b. Mar 08 1961 in Waynesburg, Greene Co., PA.
He Married **Debbie Stewart**.

***Children**:*

2436 i. Jerry Lee[8] Conrad b. Dec 01 1982.
2437 ii. Jonathan Conrad b. Oct 08 1985.

1989. **Roger Lee[7] Arbogast** (1246.Wilbur Junior[6], 550.Wilbur[5], 162.Cordelia[4] Waybright, 21.Daniel[3], 4.Rachel[2] Arbogast, 1.John C.[1]), b. Jan 04 1960 in Waynesburg, Greene Co., PA.
(1) He Married **Lisa Murray**. .

***Children** by Lisa Murray:*

2438 i. Misty Lea[8] Arbogast b. Mar 10 1982.

(2) He Married **Sherry Murray**

***Children** by Sherry Murray:*

2439 ii. Narhon Scott Murray b. Jun 30 1988 in Morgantown, Monongalia Co., WV.

2001. **Robert Merrill[7] Waybright** (1282.Merrill Frithoff[6], 584.William Pearl[5], 168.Andrew Jackson[4], 22.Nathan[3], 4.Rachel[2] Arbogast, 1.John C.[1]), b. Jun 6 1927 in Redondo Beach, Los Angeles Co., CA.

***Children**:*

2440 i. Michele Eileen[8] Waybright b. Feb 4 1956 in Long Beach, Los Angeles Co., CA, d. Oct 16 1978 in Lake Havasu City, Mohave Co., AZ.

2012. **Mary Leta[7] Johnson** (1317.Cletis[6] Johnston, 636.Dolly[5] Mullenax, 191.Elizabeth C[4] Hinkle, 26.Martha Ann[3] Waybright, 4.Rachel[2] Arbogast, 1.John C.[1]).
She Married **James Morgan Rexrode** (son of Cecil Clark Rexrode and Jessie Wilfong).

***Children**:*

2441 i. Theresa Iola[8] Rexrode. She Married **Richard Creed**, b. Jun 19 1992 in Bozeman, Gallatin Co., MT.
2442 ii. Kim Rexrode.

2013. **Buford C[7] Johnston** (1317.Cletis[6], 636.Dolly[5] Mullenax, 191.Elizabeth C[4] Hinkle, 26.Martha Ann[3] Waybright, 4.Rachel[2] Arbogast, 1.John C.[1]).
He Married **Patrica Sponaugle** (daughter of Herbert Charles Sponaugle and Sally Nola "Sallie" Sponaugle).

***Children**:*

2443 i. Mary Ann[8] Johnston. She Married **William Vandevander**.
2444 ii. Janet L Johnston. She Married **Danny Vandevander**.
2445 iii. Ricky Johnston b. 1960.
2446 iv. Dotty Johnston b. 1964.

2019. **Mildred Mary[7] Warner** (1327.Verlie[6], 637.Lura[5] Mullenax, 191.Elizabeth C[4] Hinkle, 26.Martha Ann[3] Waybright, 4.Rachel[2] Arbogast, 1.John C.[1]), b. Sep 1928 in Hunting Ground, Pendleton Co., (W)VA.
She Married **Warden Guy Hartman**, b. Jan-11-1922 (son of Elemuel Ake Hartman and Mona Wimer), buried in Cedar Hill Cem., Pendleton Co., WV, d. Sep-30-1968.

Children:

2447 i. Dorothy Louise[8] Hartman. She Married Jimmy Stewart.
\+ 2448 ii. Steven Guy Hartman.

2036. **Harold Michael[7] Sponaugle** (1330.Judith[6] Warner, 637.Lura[5] Mullenax, 191.Elizabeth C[4] Hinkle, 26.Martha Ann[3] Waybright, 4.Rachel[2] Arbogast, 1.John C.[1]), b. May-18-1936.
(1) He Married **Peter Hebert**.
(2) Married Dec-31-1956 in Oakland, Garrett Co., MD, **Patricia Louvon Judy**, b. Apr-15-1937 in Smith Creek, Pendleton Co., WV (daughter of Early Thomas Judy and Monna Roxie Sponaugle).

***Children** by Patricia Louvon Judy:*

2449 i. Tamara Jo[8] Sponaugle b. Sep-11-1970 in Cleveland, Cuyahoga Co., OH.

2037. **Carolyn Jean[7] Mullenax** (1332.Brooks Burdette[6], 638.Mcclelland[5], 191.Elizabeth C[4] Hinkle, 26.Martha Ann[3] Waybright, 4.Rachel[2] Arbogast, 1.John C.[1]), b. Nov 9 1952 in Fuerth, Germany.
(1) She Married **Andrew Smith**.
(2) She Married **John Hair II**.

***Children** by John Hair II:*

2450 i. A. Forbes[8] Hair.

2039. **David Lee[7] Mullenax** (1333.Harlan[6], 639.Martha Ellen[5], 191.Elizabeth C[4] Hinkle, 26.Martha Ann[3] Waybright, 4.Rachel[2] Arbogast, 1.John C.[1]), b. May 24 1949.
He Married **Juanita Mallow**.

Children:

2451 i. Brenda Lyn[8] Mullenax.
2452 ii. Lonnie Lee Mullenax.

2044. **Richard Cleat[7] Phares** (1338.Elmer P.[6], 641.Cleat[5], 192.Eliza Ann[4] Hinkle, 26.Martha Ann[3] Waybright, 4.Rachel[2] Arbogast, 1.John C.[1]), b. May-16-1928.
He Married **Ruth M. Stites**, b. Oct-01-1933 (daughter of L.B. Sites and Gertrude Hoffman).

Children:

2453 i. Pamela Karla[8] Phares b. Jul-15-1932. She Married **Steven J. Kulback**, b. Jul-21-1953.
\+ 2454 ii. Richard Clete Phares, Jr. b. Dec-25-1953.
\+ 2455 iii. Kimberly Lynn Phares b. Dec-20-1957.
2456 iv. Sonnee Dee Phares b. Feb-14-1965. She Married **Kevin Barkley**, b. Dec-31-1958.

2045. **Ina Lee[7] Phares** (1338.Elmer P.[6], 641.Cleat[5], 192.Eliza Ann[4] Hinkle, 26.Martha Ann[3] Waybright, 4.Rachel[2] Arbogast, 1.John C.[1]), b. Aug-07-1930.
She Married **Blake R. Hedrick**, b. 102119255 (son of Glenn Hedrick and Myrtle Raines).

Children:

2457 i. Cathy Dianna[8] Hedrick b. Feb-04-1953. She Married **Harry McMorrow**, b. Jul-07-1951.
2458 ii. Patsy L. Hedrick b. Mar-16-1955. She Married **Douglas H. Wimer**.

2046. **James H.[7] Phares** (1338.Elmer P.[6], 641.Cleat[5], 192.Eliza Ann[4] Hinkle, 26.Martha Ann[3] Waybright, 4.Rachel[2] Arbogast, 1.John C.[1]), b. Oct-19-1932.
He Married **Beverly June Huffman**, b. Jun-12-1939 (daughter of Hensel Huffman and Wilma Raines).

Children:

2459 i. James Allen[8] Phares b. Oct-08-1956. He Married **Lenita Jill Calliton**.
2460 ii. Thomas Lee Phares b. May-29-1958. He Married **Cheryl Lynn Cooper**.

2461 iii. Benjamin Loren Phares b. Nov-23-1964.
2462 iv. Matthew H Phares b. Mar-11-1971.
2463 v. Marianne M. Phares b. Mar-11-1971.

2047. **Raymond[7] Phares** (1338.Elmer P.[6], 641.Cleat[5], 192.Eliza Ann[4] Hinkle, 26.Martha Ann[3] Waybright, 4.Rachel[2] Arbogast, 1.John C.[1]), b. Sep-20-1934.
He Married **Alta Rose Elkins**, b. May-07-1942 (daughter of Walter G Elkins and Ida Mae Miller).

***Children**:*

\+ 2464 i. Michael Elmer[8] Phares b. Dec-03-1963.
\+ 2465 ii. Raymond Edward Phares b. Aug-04-1965.
2466 iii. Georgia Lynn Phares b. Mar-17-1969.

2048. **Mary June[7] Phares** (1338.Elmer P.[6], 641.Cleat[5], 192.Eliza Ann[4] Hinkle, 26.Martha Ann[3] Waybright, 4.Rachel[2] Arbogast, 1.John C.[1]), b. Dec-15-1936.
Married Jan-10-1958, **Henry E. Bennett**, b. Dec-17-1932 (son of Henry Bennett and Virginia C. Vest).

***Children**:*

2467 i. Scott Allen[8] Bennett b. Jan-15-1971.

2049. **Dottie Lou[7] Phares** (1338.Elmer P.[6], 641.Cleat[5], 192.Eliza Ann[4] Hinkle, 26.Martha Ann[3] Waybright, 4.Rachel[2] Arbogast, 1.John C.[1]), b. Aug-02-1944.
She Married **Jerry M. Warner**.

***Children**:*

\+ 2468 i. Jeffery[8] Warner b. Jan-14-1966.
2469 ii. Melissa Daun Warner b. Jun-25-1965. She Married **Larry Allen Hoover**, b. Apr-01-1965 (son of Wilson Hoover and Betty Jean Warner).

2051. **Juanita[7] Sponaugle** (1354.Herbert Charles[6], 656.William Letcher[5], 199.Roseann[4] Ketterman, 28.Alice[3] Waybright, 5.Rebecca[2] Arbogast, 1.John C.[1]), b. Jun 12 1944.
Married Jul 22 1961, **Charles Albert Taylor**, b. Dec 9 1938 (son of Robert Daniel Taylor and Florence Henitz).

***Children**:*

\+ 2470 i. Joyce Juanita[8] Taylor b. Apr 16 1962.
\+ 2471 ii. Norma Jean Taylor b. Dec 23 1963.
\+ 2472 iii. Allen Ray Taylor b. Jun 21 1969.

2052. **Patrica[7] Sponaugle** (1354.Herbert Charles[6], 656.William Letcher[5], 199.Roseann[4] Ketterman, 28.Alice[3] Waybright, 5.Rebecca[2] Arbogast, 1.John C.[1]) (See marriage to number 2013.)

2056. **Loriraine L[7] Sponaugle** (1363.Marvin Luther[6], 657.Herman Henry[5], 199.Roseann[4] Ketterman, 28.Alice[3] Waybright, 5.Rebecca[2] Arbogast, 1.John C.[1]), b. Feb-03-1924.
She Married **Cranston Harper**.

***Children**:*

2473 i. Guy[8] Harper.
2474 ii. Gary Harper.

2057. **Ruth Elaine[7] Sponaugle** (1363.Marvin Luther[6], 657.Herman Henry[5], 199.Roseann[4] Ketterman, 28.Alice[3] Waybright, 5.Rebecca[2] Arbogast, 1.John C.[1]), b. May-05-1928.
She Married **William Harvey Bowers**.

***Children**:*

2475 i. William Harvy[8] Bowers, Jr..
\+ 2476 ii. Jeffery Stewart Bowers.

2058. **Marvin Luther[7] Sponaugle, Jr.** (1363.Marvin Luther[6], 657.Herman Henry[5], 199.Roseann[4] Ketterman, 28.Alice[3] Waybright, 5.Rebecca[2] Arbogast, 1.John C.[1]), b. May-05-1928.
(1) He Married **Martha Jean Bland**. .

***Children** by Martha Jean Bland:*

2477 i. Stephen Douglas[8] Sponaugle b. Jul-07-1954.
\+ 2478 ii. Martin Luther Sponaugle, III b. Apr-17-1956.

(2) He Married **Gayle Anderson**

2061. **Carroll Lee^{7} Sponaugle** (1363.Marvin Luther^{6}, 657.Herman Henry^{5}, 199.Roseann^{4} Ketterman, 28.Alice^{3} Waybright, 5.Rebecca^{2} Arbogast, 1.John C.^{1}), b. Mar-10-1933.
She Married **Phyllis Crigler**.

Children:

\+ 2479 i. Diane^{8} Sponaugle.

2063. **Loretta June^{7} Sponaugle** (1363.Marvin Luther^{6}, 657.Herman Henry^{5}, 199.Roseann^{4} Ketterman, 28.Alice^{3} Waybright, 5.Rebecca^{2} Arbogast, 1.John C.^{1}), b. Dec-27-1937.
She Married **John F Homan**.

Children:

2480 i. Sarah^{8} Homan.
2481 ii. Susan Homan.

2074. **Delene^{7} Bennett** (1366.Alpha Cynyhia^{6} Sponaugle, 657.Herman Henry^{5}, 199.Roseann^{4} Ketterman, 28.Alice^{3} Waybright, 5.Rebecca^{2} Arbogast, 1.John C.^{1}).
Married Dec-23-1946, **Albert Freeman Bland**, b. Dec-26-1923 (son of Donald Bland and Tina Huffman), d. Oct-30-1982.

Children:

2482 i. Peggy^{8} Bland b. Jun-22-1947. She Married **Robert Mills**.

2077. **Judy^{7} Bennett** (1366.Alpha Cynyhia^{6} Sponaugle, 657.Herman Henry^{5}, 199.Roseann^{4} Ketterman, 28.Alice^{3} Waybright, 5.Rebecca^{2} Arbogast, 1.John C.^{1}).
She Married **Arlie McQuain**.

Children:

2483 i. Chandra^{8} McQuain.

2088. **Sherry^{7} Butcher** (1371.Levern^{6} Sponaugle, 657.Herman Henry^{5}, 199.Roseann^{4} Ketterman, 28.Alice^{3} Waybright, 5.Rebecca^{2} Arbogast, 1.John C.^{1}).
She Married **Hank Murry**.

Children:

2484 i. Ashlet Rebecca^{8} Murry b. May-15-1978.
2485 ii. Meredith Butcher b. Oct-04-1981.

2090. **Sandra^{7} Sponaugle** (1372.Roscoe^{6} Sponaugle, 657.Herman Henry^{5}, 199.Roseann^{4} Ketterman, 28.Alice^{3} Waybright, 5.Rebecca^{2} Arbogast, 1.John C.^{1}).
She Married **Donald Boggs**.

Children:

2486 i. Rodney^{8} Boggs.
2487 ii. Derek Boggs.

2091. **Peggy Sue^{7} Sponaugle** (1372.Roscoe^{6}, 657.Herman Henry^{5}, 199.Roseann^{4} Ketterman, 28.Alice^{3} Waybright, 5.Rebecca^{2} Arbogast, 1.John C.^{1}).
She Married **Donald Waldron**.

Children:

2488 i. Tracey^{8} Waldron.
2489 ii. Crystal Waldron.

2092. **Patsey Louisa^{7} Harper** (1376.Ruth^{6} Sponaugle, 657.Herman Henry^{5}, 199.Roseann^{4} Ketterman, 28.Alice^{3} Waybright, 5.Rebecca^{2} Arbogast, 1.John C.^{1}). She Married **Jackie Dale Hinkle**.

Children:

\+ 2490 i. Angela Kay^{8} Hinkle.

2093. **Dorothy^{7} Harper** (1376.Ruth^{6} Sponaugle, 657.Herman Henry^{5}, 199.Roseann^{4} Ketterman, 28.Alice^{3} Waybright, 5.Rebecca^{2} Arbogast, 1.John C.^{1}).
She Married **Herbert Cooper**.

Children:

2491 i. Jaqueline[8] Cooper b. Oct-22-1965.
2492 ii. Michael Cooper b. Jan-07-1971.

2096. **Henry E.[7] Bennett** (1396.Virginia C.[6] Vest, 673.Molley[5] Strauder, 205.Susan P.[4] Ketterman, 28.Alice[3] Waybright, 5.Rebecca[2] Arbogast, 1.John C.[1]) (See marriage to number 2048.)

2097. **Harold Cecil[7] Collins** (1405.Iona Patrica[6] Waybright, 678.Wilber Allen[5], 208.Churchill[4], 28.Alice[3], 5.Rebecca[2] Arbogast, 1.John C.[1]), b. Aug 13 1916 in Columbus, Franklin Co., OH, d. Jul 8 1986 in Cleveland, Cuyahoga Co., OH.
He Married **Evelien S Hickman**, b. 1920 in Big Springs, Meigs Co., TN.

Children:

\+ 2493 i. Lowell Jene[8] Collins b. Aug 09 1939.
\+ 2494 ii. Atlos Martin Collins b. Oct 25 1942.

2099. **Bernard Morris[7] Collins** (1405.Iona Patrica[6] Waybright, 678.Wilber Allen[5], 208.Churchill[4], 28.Alice[3], 5.Rebecca[2] Arbogast, 1.John C.[1]), b. Jan 30 1920 in Bartow, Pocahontas Co., WV, d. Sep 28 2002 in Northfield, Franklin Co., MA.
He Married **Mildred Lee Varner**, b. 1924, d. Sep 28 1983 in Arbovale Cem., Arbovale, Pocahontas Co., WV.

Children:

\+ 2495 i. Carol Lee[8] Collins.
\+ 2496 ii. Rebecca Jeanne Collins.

2106. **Sterling Lee[7] Gum** (1409.Gertrude Lee[6] Waybright, 680.Amby Stanton[5], 208.Churchill[4], 28.Alice[3], 5.Rebecca[2] Arbogast, 1.John C.[1]), b. May 2 1925 in Bartow, Pocahontas Co., WV, d. Jul 27 1972 in Bartow, Pocahontas Co., WV.
He Married **Thelma Delores Slaven**, b. Nov 12 1930 in Pocahontas Co., WV (daughter of Dallas Slaven and Alice Seiler), d. Dec 25 2002 in Martinsburg, Berkeley Co., WV.

Children:

2497 i. Donna Lee[8] Gum b. Apr 10 1954 in Marlinton, Pocahontas Co., WV. She Married (unknown) Means.
2498 ii. Sandra Gum. She Married **(unknown) Mullin.**
2499 iii. Beverly Ann Gum b. o5241956 in Marlinton, Pocahontas Co., WV.
2500 iv. Pamela Marie Gum b. Mar 29 1957 in Bartow, Pocahontas Co., WV. She Married **(unknown) Butts.**
2501 v. David Sterling Gum b. Apr 15 1959 in Bartow, Pocahontas Co., WV.
2502 vi. Jacqueline Jean Gum b. Mar 8 1961 in Marlinton, Pocahontas Co., WV. She Married **(unknown) Cophenhaven**.
2503 vii. Patricia Jo Gum b. Dec 17 1965 in Marlinton, Pocahontas Co., WV. She Married **(unknown) Offutt**.
2504 viii. Tamara Gum.

2107. **Rev. James Bert[7] Arbogast** (1410.Rella K[6] Waybright, 680.Amby Stanton[5], 208.Churchill[4], 28.Alice[3], 5.Rebecca[2] Arbogast, 1.John C.[1]), b. Aug 11 1927.
Names of wife and children given by Jim and Rita Wooddell 1994
He Married **Rheba Hoffman**, b. Dec 11 1929 (daughter of Brown Hoffman and Mary Ann Stalnaker).**Rheba**: Ref: Stalnaker 259.

Children:

\+ 2505 i. Sue Ellen[8] Arbogast.
\+ 2506 ii. Sherry Lynnarbogast.

2118. **Bobby MCarthur[7] Wimer** (1413.Bertie Catherine[6] Warner, 682.Fransina Lee[5] Waybright, 208.Churchill[4], 28.Alice[3], 5.Rebecca[2] Arbogast, 1.John C.[1]), b. May-10-1942 in Hunting Ground, Pendleton Co. WV.
He Married **Patricia Vandevander** (daughter of Arlie Vandevander and Mary Harper).

Children:

2507 i. Timothy Allen[8] Wimer b. Feb-19-1967, d. Jul-22-1985 in auto accident, Circleville, WV.

2121. **Richard Dean[7] Waybright** (1449.Josiah[6], 728.Abel Washington[5], 224.George Washington[4], 32.Elijah[3], 5.Rebecca[2] Arbogast, 1.John C.[1]), b. May 1 1938 in Preston Co., WV, d. Nov 23 1981 in Shanks, Hampshire Co., WV, buried in Mount Zion Church Cem., Marques, Hampshire Co., WV. Married Jul 10 1968 in Romney, Hampshire Co., WV, **Mary Louise Reel**, b. Apr 17 1950 in Romney, Hampshire Co., WV, d. Nov 23 1981 in Shanks, Hampshire Co., WV, buried in Mount Zion Church Cem., Marques, Hampshire Co., WV.

Children:

2508 i. Richard Lee[8] Waybright b. Nov 7 1968 in Romney, Hampshire Co., WV, d. Nov 23 1981 in Shanks, Hampshire Co., WV, buried in Mount Zion Church Cem., Marques, Hampshire Co., WV.
2509 ii. Joseph Allen Waybright b. Jan 20 1970 in Morgantown, Monongalia Co., WV, d. Nov 23 1981 in Shanks, Hampshire Co., WV, buried in Mount Zion Church Cem., Marques, Hampshire Co., WV.
2510 iii. Katrina Marie Waybright b. Feb 2 1971 in Romney, Hampshire Co., WV, d. Nov 23 1981 in Shanks, Hampshire Co., WV, buried in Mount Zion Church Cem., Marques, Hampshire Co., WV.

2136. **Jerri[7] Warner** (1478.Peachie N.[6], 732.Surrilda Florence[5] Waybright, 224.George Washington[4], 32.Elijah[3], 5.Rebecca[2] Arbogast, 1.John C.[1]), b. Mar-28-1959.
She Married **Glenn Warner** (son of Dice G Warner and Annie Bennett).

***Children**:*

2511 i. Travis[8] Warner.
2512 ii. Steven Warner b. Dec 1983.

2141. **Russell Valey[7] Arbogast, Jr.** (1504.Alda Christine[6] Waybright, 776.William Garrett[5], 241.Nicholas[4], 36.Miles[3], 5.Rebecca[2] Arbogast, 1.John C.[1]), b. Nov 11 1936 in Harman, Randolph Co., WV.
(1) Married Jun 18 1979 in Oakland, Garrett Co., MD, **Vera (Wolford) Bennett**. (

2) Married Nov 10 1956 in Later Divorced, **Shelva J. Davis**.

***Children** by Shelva J. Davis:*

\+ 2513 i. Randall Lee[8] Arbogast b. Sep 07 1960.

2144. **Joy Hallie[7] Bell** (1518.Martin Boston[6], 792.Lettie Susan[5] Arbogast, 259.Martin Van Buren[4], 40.Lemuel[3], 6.Joseph E.[2], 1.John C.[1]), b. Aug 16 1937.
She Married **Gerald Wilson Day, Sr.**, b. Oct 28 1931.

***Children**:*

2514 i. Vera Dawn[8] Day b. Jan 11 1956.

2155. **Ernest[7] Morral** (1532.Arthur[6], 793.Mary Jane[5] Arbogast, 259.Martin Van Buren[4], 40.Lemuel[3], 6.Joseph E.[2], 1.John C.[1]), b. Feb 04 1927 in Elkins, Randolph Co., WV, d. Oct 24 1989.
Married Oct 24 1993 in Elkins, Randolph Co., WV, **Margaret V Kernes**, b. Oct 15 1922 in White Sulphur Springs, Greenbrier Co., WV.

***Children**:*

2515 i. Donald[8] Morral b. in Elkins, Randolph Co., WV.
2516 ii. Gary Morral b. in Elkins, Randolph Co., WV.
2517 iii. Virginia Morral b. in Elkins, Randolph Co., WV.
2518 iv. Sandra Morral b. in Elkins, Randolph Co., WV.
2519 v. Linda Morral b. in Elkins, Randolph Co., WV.
2520 vi. Margaret Morral b. in Elkins, Randolph Co., WV.
2521 vii. Joan Morral b. in Elkins, Randolph Co., WV.
2522 viii. Carolyn Morral b. in Elkins, Randolph Co., WV.

2168. **Forrest Stephen[7] Warner** (1537.Bertha Catherine[6] Arbogast, 794.Robert Calvin[5], 259.Martin Van Buren[4], 40.Lemuel[3], 6.Joseph E.[2], 1.John C.[1]), b. Mar 29 1925 in Pendleton Co., WV, d. May 06 1986 in Bergholz, Jefferson Co., OH.
He Married **Annabel Day**, d. 1986.

***Children**:*

2523 i. David[8] Warner.
2524 ii. Betty Jane Warner. She Married **Pete McMasters.**

2178. **Allen Gerald[7] Arbogast** (1544.Allen[6], 814.Samual[5], 267.Jacob A.[4], 40.Lemuel[3], 6.Joseph E.[2], 1.John C.[1]), b. Sep 28 1948 in Milford, Worcester Co., MA.
He Married **Lori Louise Marshall**.

***Children**:*

2525 i. Allen Jacob[8] Arbogast b. Feb 25 1979.
2526 ii. Corry Arbogast b. May 30 1985.
\+ 2527 iii. James A. Arbogast.

2181. **Sam Houston**^{7} **McCauley** (1545.Audrey Maxine^{6} Arbogast, 814.Samual^{5}, 267.Jacob A.^{4}, 40.Lemuel^{3}, 6.Joseph E.^{2}, 1.John C.^{1}), b. Jun 08 1947 in Randolph Co., WV.
He Married **Ruby M King**.

***Children**:*

+ 2528 i. Donna C^{8} McCauley.
2529 ii. Donald L McCauley.
2530 iii. Tracy L McCauley.

2182. **Robert Lee**^{7} **Wilcox** (1545.Audrey Maxine^{6} Arbogast, 814.Samual^{5}, 267.Jacob A.^{4}, 40.Lemuel^{3}, 6.Joseph E.^{2}, 1.John C.^{1}), b. Jun 03 1951.
(1) He Married **Debra F Johnson**, b. in Memphis, Shelby Co., TN .

***Children** by Debra F Johnson:*

2531 i. Sabrina Lee^{8} Wilcox..

(2) He Married **Sue Lee**

***Children** by Sue Lee:*

2532 ii. Jefferson A Wilcox.
2533 iii. Robert Lee Wilcox, Jr..
2534 iv. Adam M Wilcox.

2183. **Dean Thea**^{7} **Wilcox** (1545.Audrey Maxine^{6} Arbogast, 814.Samual^{5}, 267.Jacob A.^{4}, 40.Lemuel^{3}, 6.Joseph E.^{2}, 1.John C.^{1}), b. Dec 05 1957.
(1) He Married **Linda S Metz**

***Children** by Linda S Metz:*

2535 i. Dean Thea^{8} Wilcoz, Jr..
2536 ii. David Wilcox..

(2) He Married **Ronda S (Unknown)**.

***Children** by Ronda S (Unknown):*

2537 iii. Derek L Wilcox.

2184. **Olive**^{7} **Webley** (1546.Betty Jean^{6} Arbogast, 814.Samual^{5}, 267.Jacob A.^{4}, 40.Lemuel^{3}, 6.Joseph E.^{2}, 1.John C.^{1}), b. May 01 1949.
She Married **Dean Crow**.

***Children**:*

2538 i. Dean^{8} Crow, Jr..
2539 ii. Eric Von Crow.

2185. **Edgar H**^{7} **Webley** (1546.Betty Jean^{6} Arbogast, 814.Samual^{5}, 267.Jacob A.^{4}, 40.Lemuel^{3}, 6.Joseph E.^{2}, 1.John C.^{1}), b. Aug 24 1950.
He Married **Lis De Hart**.

***Children**:*

2540 i. Edgar H.^{8} Webley, Jr.. He Married **Kim Bennett**.

2186. **Audrey D**^{7} **Webley** (1546.Betty Jean^{6} Arbogast, 814.Samual^{5}, 267.Jacob A.^{4}, 40.Lemuel^{3}, 6.Joseph E.^{2}, 1.John C.^{1}).
She Married **Roger Paxton, II**.

***Children**:*

2541 i. Roger^{8} Paxton, III.
2542 ii. Angela K Paxton.

2187. **James J**^{7} **Webley** (1546.Betty Jean^{6} Arbogast, 814.Samual^{5}, 267.Jacob A.^{4}, 40.Lemuel^{3}, 6.Joseph E.^{2}, 1.John C.^{1}), b. Mar 16 1955.
He Married **Roxana Shifflet** .

***Children**:*

2543 i. Jared J^{8} Webley.
2544 ii. Tara L Webley.

2189. **Mickey**^{7} **Arbogast** (1547.Jeff Jake^{6}, 814.Samual^{5}, 267.Jacob A.^{4}, 40.Lemuel^{3}, 6.Joseph E.^{2}, 1.John C.^{1}).

She Married **Sam Elza**.

***Children**:*

2545 i. Casey J[8] Elza.
2546 ii. Tracy L Elza.

2191. **Dana[7] Arbogast** (1547.Jeff Jake[6], 814.Samual[5], 267.Jacob A.[4], 40.Lemuel[3], 6.Joseph E.[2], 1.John C.[1]).
She Married **Sandra Johnsom**.

***Children**:*

2547 i. Cody Jeff[8] Arbogast.

2192. **Diana Lynn[7] Arbogast** (1551.John Mutt[6], 814.Samual[5], 267.Jacob A.[4], 40.Lemuel[3], 6.Joseph E.[2], 1.John C.[1]), b. Aug 02 1957.
She Married **Claire E. Daft, Jr.**, b. in Beverly, Randolph Co., WV.

***Children**:*

2548 i. Heather Lunn[8] Daft b. Jul 03 1979 in Elkins, Randolph Co., WV.
2549 ii. Whitney Lynn Deft b. Jul 21 1987 in Beverly, Randolph Co., WV.

2193. **Jonnie Sue[7] Arbogast** (1551.John Mutt[6], 814.Samual[5], 267.Jacob A.[4], 40.Lemuel[3], 6.Joseph E.[2], 1.John C.[1]), b. Sep 14 1958.
She Married **Carl Edward Simmons**, b. in Beverly, Randolph Co., WV.

***Children**:*

2550 i. Dustin Carl[8] Simmons b. Apr 22 1983 in Elkins, Randolph Co., WV.

2194. **Anita Kay[7] Arbogast** (1551.John Mutt[6], 814.Samual[5], 267.Jacob A.[4], 40.Lemuel[3], 6.Joseph E.[2], 1.John C.[1]), b. May 15 1961.
She Married **Roger P. Brady**, b. in Memphis, Shelby Co., TN.

***Children**:*

2551 i. Jaran John[8] Brady b. Jul 08 1993 in Memphis, Shelby Co., TN.

2197. **Jeffery Allen[7] Luzander** (1552.Mary Bessie[6] Arbogast, 814.Samual[5], 267.Jacob A.[4], 40.Lemuel[3], 6.Joseph E.[2], 1.John C.[1]), b. Sep 03 1961.
He Married **Dorotha Kwiatkowski**, b. in Poland.

***Children**:*

2552 i. Phillip Leapole[8] Luzander b. Jun 10 1983.
2553 ii. Michael Allen Luzander b. Aug 13 1984.

2198. **Vickie Dawn[7] Arbogast** (1554.Donald Lee[6], 814.Samual[5], 267.Jacob A.[4], 40.Lemuel[3], 6.Joseph E.[2], 1.John C.[1]), b. in Elkins, Randolph Co., WV. She
Married **Dale Plum**.

***Children**:*

2554 i. Jessica D[8] Plum b. Feb 05 1887.

2199. **Cathy Sue[7] Arbogast** (1554.Donald Lee[6], 814.Samual[5], 267.Jacob A.[4], 40.Lemuel[3], 6.Joseph E.[2], 1.John C.[1]), b. in Elkins, Randolph Co., WV.
She Married **Allen R Langevin**.

***Children**:*

2555 i. Kyle R[8] Langevin b. Jan 14 1988 in Elkins, Randolph Co., WV.

2200. **Donald Lee[7] Arbogast, Jr.** (1554.Donald Lee[6], 814.Samual[5], 267.Jacob A.[4], 40.Lemuel[3], 6.Joseph E.[2], 1.John C.[1]), b. Feb 11 1957 in Elkins, Randolph Co., WV.
(1) He Married **Debarah Bailey** .

***Children** by Debarah Bailey:*

2556 i. Crystal N[8] Arbogast b. Sep 17 1979. .

(2) He Married **Inetta Kalar**

***Children** by Inetta Kalar:*

2557 ii. Ethan Q Arbogast b. Mar 21 1991.

2201. **Deborah Ann[7] Gover** (1555.Lois Ann[6] Arbogast, 814.Samual[5], 267.Jacob A.[4], 40.Lemuel[3], 6.Joseph E.[2], 1.John C.[1]), b. Aug 18 1958 in Ohio.
She Married **Steven P Amams**.

Children:

2558 i. David Scott[8] Adams.
2559 ii. Bo Lynn Adams b. Dec 09 1980.
2560 iii. Steven H Hoover b. Aug 16 1984.

2202. **Andrea Lynn[7] Hoover** (1555.Lois Ann[6] Arbogast, 814.Samual[5], 267.Jacob A.[4], 40.Lemuel[3], 6.Joseph E.[2], 1.John C.[1]), b. Nov 25 1959.
She Married **Gary W Light**.

Children:

2561 i. Gerrick Wayne[8] Light b. Apr 15 1980.
2562 ii. Brandon Alexander Light b. Aug 06 1981.

2203. **Nelva Marie[7] Simmons** (1585.Monna[6] Bennett, 822.Ada M.[5] Arbogast, 270.Hannah Elizabeth[4], 42.Joseph Elili[3], 6.Joseph E.[2], 1.John C.[1]).
From, William Nottingham, Jr. & Mary Arbogast of Pocahontas Co., = Descendants, by Mary Elizabeth (Nottingham) Skelton of Jamestown, =
She Married **Lester Amos Nottingham**, b. Jan 19 1921 in Pocahontas Co., WV (son of Austin Amos Nottingham and Alice Mary Stone), d. Jun 24 1993 in Morgantown, Monongalia Co., WV, buried in Nottingham Cem., Durbin, Pocahontas Co., WV.
Lester: From, William Nottingham, Jr. & Mary Arbogast of Pocahontas Co., = Descendants, by Mary Elizabeth (Nottingham) Skelton of Jamestown, = Durbin, WV.

Children:

\+ 2563 i. Judy Mae[8] Nottingham.
2564 ii. Harold Amos Nottingham b. Mar 11 1949. Married Jul 18 1970, **Beth Ann Leikala**.
2565 iii. Frances Marie Nottingham b. Mar 1 1953 in Elkins, Randolph Co., WV. Married Nov 18 1978 in Durbin, Pocahontas Co., WV, **Stephen Douglas Rider**.
\+ 2566 iv. Debra Jean Nottingham b. Jun 3 1963.
\+ 2567 v. Roberta Lynn Nottingham b. Sep 12 1964.

2204. **Bessie May[7] Simmons** (1585.Monna[6] Bennett, 822.Ada M.[5] Arbogast, 270.Hannah Elizabeth[4], 42.Joseph Elili[3], 6.Joseph E.[2], 1.John C.[1]), b. Nov 24 1937 in Durbin, Pocahontas Co., WV.
Married Jan 26 1958 in Baltimore, Baltimore Co., MD, **Ivan Clark Sutton**, b. Jun 5 1935 in Arbovale Cem., Arbovale, Pocahontas Co., WV (son of John Herbert Adam Sutton and Vada Lee Gum).

Children:

\+ 2568 i. Viviennne Rene[8] Sutton b. Mar 31 1960.
2569 ii. Susan Marie Sutton b. Aug 25 1961 in Sandy Springs, Montgomery Co., MD. Married Nov 1 1986, **Mickey Day**.

2216. **Christena Belle[7] Sponaugle** (1597.Mary Dessie[6] Vandevander, 826.Wayne Sylvester[5] Vandevender, 273.Ruth Ellen[4] Arbogast, 42.Joseph Elili[3], 6.Joseph E.[2], 1.John C.[1]), b. Jun-08-1906 in Circleville Pendleton Co., WV.
Married Aug-17-1929, **Jesse Howard Bennett**, b. Oct-15-1893 in Osceola Randolph Co., WV (son of Ruben D. Bennett and Emma vent), d. May-11-1963 in Martinsburg, Berkeley Co., WV.

Children:

\+ 2570 i. Hazel[8] Bennett.
\+ 2571 ii. Fred D. Bennett.
2572 iii. Fay Bennett. He Married **Dorothy Nelson**.

2219. **Nola M.[7] Sponaugle** (1597.Mary Dessie[6] Vandevander, 826.Wayne Sylvester[5] Vandevender, 273.Ruth Ellen[4] Arbogast, 42.Joseph Elili[3], 6.Joseph E.[2], 1.John C.[1]), b. Feb-21-1915.
She Married **Charles Miller**.

Children:

2573 i. Jackie[8] Miller.
2574 ii. Jerlean Miller.
2575 iii. Dickie Miller.
2576 iv. Gary Miller.

2220. **Adam Harness[7] Sponaugle** (1597.Mary Dessie[6] Vandevander, 826.Wayne Sylvester[5] Vandevender, 273.Ruth Ellen[4] Arbogast, 42.Joseph Elili[3], 6.Joseph E.[2], 1.John C.[1]), b. Jul-01-1918 in Circleville Pendleton Co., WV, buried in North Fork of South Branch, WV., d. May-11-1989 in Riverton, Pendleton Co., WV.
He Married **Mae Thompson**.

Children:

2577 i. Adam[8] Harness Sponaugle, Jr..

2221. **Paul R.[7] Sponaugle** (1597.Mary Dessie[6] Vandevander, 826.Wayne Sylvester[5] Vandevender, 273.Ruth Ellen[4] Arbogast, 42.Joseph Elili[3], 6.Joseph E.[2], 1.John C.[1]), b. Apr-15-1920.
He Married **Nellie Gum**.

Children:

2578 i. Larry[8] Sponaugle.
2579 ii. Ronald Sponaugle.
2580 iii. Sheila Sponaugle.

2222. **Isaic Jay[7] Sponaugle** (1597.Mary Dessie[6] Vandevander, 826.Wayne Sylvester[5] Vandevender, 273.Ruth Ellen[4] Arbogast, 42.Joseph Elili[3], 6.Joseph E.[2], 1.John C.[1]), b. Oct-08-1922.
He Married **Mary Elizabeth Frat**.

Children:

2581 i. Diane[8] Sponaugle.
2582 ii. Elizabeth Sponaugle.
2583 iii. Holly Sponaugle.

2223. **Vallie Verie[7] Sponaugle** (1597.Mary Dessie[6] Vandevander, 826.Wayne Sylvester[5] Vandevender, 273.Ruth Ellen[4] Arbogast, 42.Joseph Elili[3], 6.Joseph E.[2], 1.John C.[1]), b. Mar-10-1927 in Circleville Pendleton Co., WV.
She Married **Thomas Phalen**.

Children:

2584 i. Susan Lynn[8] Phalen.
2585 ii. Pamala Jane Phalen.
2586 iii. Regina Mary Phalen.
2587 iv. Timothy Edward Phalen.

2224. **Anna Jo[7] Sponaugle** (1597.Mary Dessie[6] Vandevander, 826.Wayne Sylvester[5] Vandevender, 273.Ruth Ellen[4] Arbogast, 42.Joseph Elili[3], 6.Joseph E.[2], 1.John C.[1]), b. Oct-09-1928 in Circleville Pendleton Co., WV.
(1) She Married **Raymond W. Hartman**. ((2) She Married **James Clyde Acker**, b. Nov 17 1935 in Los Angeles, Los Angeles Co., CA **Raymond Wade Hartman** (son of Elemuel Ake Hartman and Mona Wimer).

Children *by Raymond W. Hartman:*

2588 i. Joe[8] Hartman.
2589 ii. Jeannie Hartman.
2590 iii. Teddy Hartman.
2591 iv. Raymond Hartman, Jr..
2592 v. Luann Hartman.
2593 vi. Kim Hartman.

(2) She Married **James Clyde Acker**, b. Nov 17 1935 in Los Angeles, Los Angeles Co., CA

2225. **Mary Lou[7] Sponaugle** (1597.Mary Dessie[6] Vandevander, 826.Wayne Sylvester[5] Vandevender, 273.Ruth Ellen[4] Arbogast, 42.Joseph Elili[3], 6.Joseph E.[2], 1.John C.[1]), b. Jul-21-1933. She Married **David Lambert**.

Children:

2594 i. Janice[8] Lambert.
2595 ii. Lori Lambert.

2226. **Conda Roy[7] Sponaugle** (1597.Mary Dessie[6] Vandevander, 826.Wayne Sylvester[5] Vandevender, 273.Ruth Ellen[4] Arbogast, 42.Joseph Elili[3], 6.Joseph E.[2], 1.John C.[1]) (See marriage to number 1329.)

2227. **Ona Lucy[7] Sponaugle** (1597.Mary Dessie[6] Vandevander, 826.Wayne Sylvester[5] Vandevender, 273.Ruth Ellen[4] Arbogast, 42.Joseph Elili[3], 6.Joseph E.[2], 1.John C.[1]) (See marriage to number 1327.)

2228. **Cranston John^{7} Sponaugle** (1597.Mary Dessie^{6} Vandevander, 826.Wayne Sylvester^{5} Vandevender, 273.Ruth Ellen^{4} Arbogast, 42.Joseph Elili^{3}, 6.Joseph E.^{2}, 1.John C.^{1}), b. Dec-12-1924 in Circleville Pendleton Co., WV.
He Married **Jessie Warner**, b. Dec-02-1924.

Children:

2596 i. Danny^{8} Sponaugle.
2597 ii. Cranston Sponaugle.
2598 iii. Patricia Sponaugle.
2599 iv. Lonnie Sponaugle.

2231. **Beverly Ann^{7} Arbogast** (1623.Nora Gustava^{6} Calhoun, 839.William Cecil^{5}, 275.Hannah Catharine^{4} Bennett, 43.Sidney Dean^{3} Arbogast, 6.Joseph E.^{2}, 1.John C.^{1}), b. Sep 24 1940 in Pocahontas Co., WV.
Married Jul 14 1959 in Highland Co., VA, **Donald Raymond Nottingham**, b. Jul 20 1936 in Dunmore, Pocahontas Co., WV (son of Raymond Harvey Nottingham and Helen Grace Galford). **Donald**: S/o Raymond Harvey and Helen Grace (Galford) Nottingham.

Children:

+ 2600 i. Kimberly Susan^{8} Nottingham b. May 4 1960.
+ 2601 ii. Teresa Lynn Nottingham b. Jan 29 1962.
+ 2602 iii. John Leslie Nottingham b. Jan 23 1963.
+ 2603 iv. Randall Lee Nottingham b. Aug 3 1964.

2233. **Helen Pauline^{7} Riggleman** (1628.Lula Pauline^{6} Lough, 842.Nina Beth^{5} Calhoun, 275.Hannah Catharine^{4} Bennett, 43.Sidney Dean^{3} Arbogast, 6.Joseph E.^{2}, 1.John C.^{1}), b. Feb 14 1923.
Married OCT 1944, **Theodore Oberg**, b. Aug 25 1920.

Children:

2604 i. Karen Lois^{8} Oberg b. Oct 8 1948 in Baltimore, Baltimore Co., MD, d. Dec 5 1997 in Fairfax, Fairfax Co., VA.

Generation Eight

2267. **Krystal Karma^{8} Eades** (1778.Phillip Brett^{7}, 980.Amos Cyrus^{6}, 409.Faye Elvira^{5} Arbogast, 98.Amos Cyrus^{4}, 12.George Washington^{3}, 3.Michael^{2}, 1.John C.^{1}), b. Nov 30 1973 in Carson City, Ormsby Co., NV.
She Married **Alex Roger Cody**.

Children:

2605 i. Alex Roger Cody^{9} Eades b. Dec 13 1990 in Knoxville, Knox Co., TN.

2278. **Todd^{8} Jewell** (1787.Edna^{7} Samples, 983.Violet Gustava^{6} Neal, 410.Jessie Sarah^{5} Arbogast, 98.Amos Cyrus^{4}, 12.George Washington^{3}, 3.Michael^{2}, 1.John C.^{1}), b. Jan 09 1963 in Arcadia, Los Angeles Co., CA.
Married Mar 1985, **Sharon Lynn Hutton**, b. Jan 28 1967 in Pennsylvania.

Children:

2606 i. Karen^{9} Jewell b. Feb 15 1985 in Riverside, Riverside Co., CA.
2607 ii. Barron Jewell b. Dec 08 1989 in Fallbrook, San Diego Co., CA.

2279. **Jeff^{8} Jewell** (1787.Edna^{7} Samples, 983.Violet Gustava^{6} Neal, 410.Jessie Sarah^{5} Arbogast, 98.Amos Cyrus^{4}, 12.George Washington^{3}, 3.Michael^{2}, 1.John C.^{1}), b. Mar 14 1965.
He Married **Robin Rogers**, b. Sep 06 1965 in Torrance, Los Angeles Co., CA.

Children:

2608 i. Kalla^{9} Jewell b. Mar 16 1990.

2281. **Kerry^{8} Solney** (1789.Linda Fay^{7} Samples, 983.Violet Gustava^{6} Neal, 410.Jessie Sarah^{5} Arbogast, 98.Amos Cyrus^{4}, 12.George Washington^{3}, 3.Michael^{2}, 1.John C.^{1}), b. May 22 1965 in Long Beach, Los Angeles Co., CA. She Married **John Parr**, b. Jan 07 1963 in Norwalk, Los Angeles Co., CA.

Children:

2609 i. Melissa^{9} Parr b. Oct 07 1989 in Norwalk, Los Angeles Co., CA.

2294. **Elizabeth Ann[8] Meadows** (1805.Harold Lloyd[7], 990.Joyce[6] Cantley, 412.Lucy Esta[5] Arbogast, 98.Amos Cyrus[4], 12.George Washington[3], 3.Michael[2], 1.John C.[1]), b. Jun 20 1972 in Mullins, Wyoming Co., WV.
Married Jul 30 1990 in Beckley, Raleigh Co., WV, **Martin Sargent, Jr.**, b. Sep 30 1972 in Mullins, Wyoming Co., WV.

Children:

2610 i. Justin[9] Sargent b. Jun 03 1991 in Beckley, Raleigh Co., WV.

2315. **Sloan Leigh[8] Stallworth** (1836.Carlton Watson[7], 1019.Alberta Maxine[6] Arbogast, 459.Albert Lee[5], 119.George Franklin[4], 15.Nichodemus[3], 3.Michael[2], 1.John C.[1]), b. Oct 01 1966.
Married Aug 27 1987, **Daniel William Kelly**, b. Sep 06 1957 in Georgia.

Children:

2611 i. Shannon Ryan[9] Kelly b. Mar 22 1991.

2316. **Selena Lane[8] Stallworth** (1836.Carlton Watson[7], 1019.Alberta Maxine[6] Arbogast, 459.Albert Lee[5], 119.George Franklin[4], 15.Nichodemus[3], 3.Michael[2], 1.John C.[1]), b. Oct 01 1966.
She Married **Robert Coppert**.

Children:

2612 i. Sarah[9] Lane Coppert b. Dec 03 1984.
2613 ii. Carl Coppert b. May 23 1988 in Georgia.

2317. **Perry Kathryn[8] Sheldon** (1839.Janet Gail[7] Perry, 1021.Lois Jean[6] Arbogast, 459.Albert Lee[5], 119.George Franklin[4], 15.Nichodemus[3], 3.Michael[2], 1.John C.[1]), b. Apr 26 1990 in Charleston, Kanawha Co., WV.

Children:

2614 i. Kendall James[9] Perry.
2615 ii. Brenna Renee Perry.

2321. **Lachona Ann[8] Dallas** (1845.Patsy Jo[7] Hughes, 1025.Francis Vivian[6] Arbogast, 460.Joseph Martin[5], 119.George Franklin[4], 15.Nichodemus[3], 3.Michael[2], 1.John C.[1]), b. Jun 17 1966.
She Married **Jeffery B. Richter**, b. Aug 09 1963 in Chillicothe, Ross Co., OH.

Children:

2616 i. Sarah Ann[9] Richter b. Aug 18 1988 in Chillicothe, Ross Co., OH.
2617 ii. Jeffery Wayne Richter b. May 21 1992 in Chillicothe, Ross Co., OH.
2618 iii. Latherine Elizabeth Richter b. Sep 04 1993 in Chillicothe, Ross Co., OH.

2326. **William Levi[8] Collins, Jr.** (1849.William Levi[7], 1026.Masel[6] Arbogast, 460.Joseph Martin[5], 119.George Franklin[4], 15.Nichodemus[3], 3.Michael[2], 1.John C.[1]), b. 1130 1964. H
e Married **Dawn (Unknown)**.

Children:

2619 i. Megan[9] Collins b. Apr 05 1990.
2620 ii. Shelby Collins b. Oct 01 1992.

2327. **Gina[8] Collins** (1849.William Levi[7], 1026.Masel[6] Arbogast, 460.Joseph Martin[5], 119.George Franklin[4], 15.Nichodemus[3], 3.Michael[2], 1.John C.[1]), b. Jan 06 1966.
She Married **Danial O'Sullivan**.

Children:

2621 i. Shannon[9] O'Sullivan b. Mar 28 1988.
2622 ii. Maureen O'Sullivan b. Sep 18 1990.

2349. **Robert W[8] Lanham** (1863.Donald Wilson[7], 1037.Louella Francis[6] Arbogast, 468.Fred Lee[5] Arbogast, 121.Thomas[4] Arbogast, 15.Nichodemus[3], 3.Michael[2], 1.John C.[1]), b. Dec 20 1967. Married Jul 02 1991, **Lisa Jordan**, b. Jun 06 1969.

Children:

2623 i. Bobbi Jo[9] Lanham b. May 01 1992.

2353. **Rodney Lee[8] Williams** (1865.Olga[7] White, 1038.Florence Doris[6] Arbogast, 468.Fred Lee[5] Arbogast, 121.Thomas[4] Arbogast, 15.Nichodemus[3], 3.Michael[2], 1.John C.[1]), b. Oct 19 1954. Married May 25 1973, **Katherine Barnes**, b. Mar 13 1954.

Children:

2624 i. Rodney Lee[9] Williams, Jr. b. Nov 12 1974.
2625 ii. Alicia Lee Williams b. Nov 12 1974.

2354. **Roy Franklin[8] Williams** (1865.Olga[7] White, 1038.Florence Doris[6] Arbogast, 468.Fred Lee[5] Arbogast, 121.Thomas[4] Arbogast, 15.Nichodemus[3], 3.Michael[2], 1.John C.[1]), b. Jul 04 1957.
Married Oct 03 1975, **Beverly Arnett**, b. Mar 23 1956.

Children:

2626 i. Tiffany[9] Williams b. Sep 28 1978.
2627 ii. Tera Lynn Williams b. Aug 22 1988.

2388. **Shirley Ann[8] Mullenax** (1901.Brooks[7], 1105.James Edward[6], 507.Anna Elizabeth[5] Waybright, 151.James Bud[4], 19.Jesse[3], 4.Rachel[2] Arbogast, 1.John C.[1]), b. 1953.
Married 1972, **Michael C Bland**, b. 1954 (son of Byron Bland and Eula Vance).

Children:

2628 i. Rachel Denise[9] Bland.
2629 ii. Christopher Bland b. 1974.
2630 iii. Scott Allen Bland b. 1982.

2392. **Debbie Jo[8] Varner** (1918.Irene[7] Nelson, 1109.Elva[6] Mullenax, 507.Anna Elizabeth[5] Waybright, 151.James Bud[4], 19.Jesse[3], 4.Rachel[2] Arbogast, 1.John C.[1]).
Married Nov 20 1976 in Durbin, Pocahontas Co., WV, **Clarence Darrell Wright** (son of Boyd Wright and Daisy Rexrode).

Children:

2631 i. Darrell[9] Wright.
2632 ii. David Alan Wright b. Jan 23 1985.

2393. **William Nevin[8] Waybright** (1934.William Nevin[7], 1141.Kenny[6], 511.Jesse[5], 151.James Bud[4], 19.Jesse[3], 4.Rachel[2] Arbogast, 1.John C.[1]).
He Married **Regina Cassell**.

Children:

2633 i. Nevette Lagina[9] Waybright b. Jun 26 1972.
2634 ii. Javan Seth Waybright b. Jun 2 1977.

2397. **George Samuel[8] Waybright Jr.** (1936.George Samual[7], 1141.Kenny[6], 511.Jesse[5], 151.James Bud[4], 19.Jesse[3], 4.Rachel[2] Arbogast, 1.John C.[1]), b. Feb 3 1957 in Marlinton, Pocahontas Co., WV, d. Jan 1 1992.
He Married **Vickie Lynn McCarty**.

Children:

2635 i. Kagun Eugene[9] Waybright.

2398. **Penelope Kaye[8] Varner** (1937.Dollie Elizabeth[7] Waybright, 1141.Kenny[6], 511.Jesse[5], 151.James Bud[4], 19.Jesse[3], 4.Rachel[2] Arbogast, 1.John C.[1]), b. May 26 1962.
From Wm. C. Varner.

Children:

2636 i. Autumn Grace[9] Hunter b. Nov 14 1979, d. Dec 4 1991.

2404. **Ronert David[8] Brittle, II** (1954.Marian Ramona[7] Tracy, 1195.Glenn Parker[6], 525.Lenora Jane[5] Waybright, 155.Mary Elizabeth[4], 19.Jesse[3], 4.Rachel[2] Arbogast, 1.John C.[1]), b. Oct 14 1953. Married Mar 08 1985, **Dianne Whitlock Northern**.

Children:

2637 i. Travis Benjamin[9] Brittle b. Jan 08 1986.
2638 ii. Logan Bradford Brittle b. Oct 23 1988.
2639 iii. Tyler David Brittle b. Nov 06 1992.

2417. **Quinten[8] Arbogast** (1974.David Lee[7], 1244.Samual Henry[6], 550.Wilbur[5], 162.Cordelia[4] Waybright, 21.Daniel[3], 4.Rachel[2] Arbogast, 1.John C.[1]), b. Aug 21 1970.

Children:

2640 i. Ashley Marie[9] Arbogast b. Jan 21 1993.

2448. **Steven Guy[8] Hartman** (2019.Mildred Mary[7] Warner, 1327.Verlie[6], 637.Lura[5] Mullenax, 191.Elizabeth C[4] Hinkle, 26.Martha Ann[3] Waybright, 4.Rachel[2] Arbogast, 1.John C.[1]).

He Married **Robin Shull**.

Children:

2641 i. April[9] Hartman.
2642 ii. Adriana Hartman.

2454. **Richard Clete[8] Phares, Jr.** (2044.Richard Cleat[7], 1338.Elmer P.[6], 641.Cleat[5], 192.Eliza Ann[4] Hinkle, 26.Martha Ann[3] Waybright, 4.Rachel[2] Arbogast, 1.John C.[1]), b. Dec-25-1953.
He Married **Lisa Yvonne Launder**, b. May-01-1961 (daughter of Ruben Phares and Beverly Noel).

Children:

2643 i. Richard Clete[9] Phares, III b. Jun-08-1990.

2455. **Kimberly Lynn[8] Phares** (2044.Richard Cleat[7], 1338.Elmer P.[6], 641.Cleat[5], 192.Eliza Ann[4] Hinkle, 26.Martha Ann[3] Waybright, 4.Rachel[2] Arbogast, 1.John C.[1]), b. Dec-20-1957.
She Married **John Edsel Gowdin**, b. Jun 1953 (son of Charles Gowdin and Wilda Moore).

Children:

2644 i. John Richard[9] Gowdin b. Aug-29-1988.

2464. **Michael Elmer[8] Phares** (2047.Raymond[7], 1338.Elmer P.[6], 641.Cleat[5], 192.Eliza Ann[4] Hinkle, 26.Martha Ann[3] Waybright, 4.Rachel[2] Arbogast, 1.John C.[1]), b. Dec-03-1963.
He Married **Jill F. Phares**.

Children:

2645 i. Joshua Michael[9] Phares b. Nov-12-1990.

2465. **Raymond Edward[8] Phares** (2047.Raymond[7], 1338.Elmer P.[6], 641.Cleat[5], 192.Eliza Ann[4] Hinkle, 26.Martha Ann[3] Waybright, 4.Rachel[2] Arbogast, 1.John C.[1]), b. Aug-04-1965.
He Married **Susanna Thompson**.

Children:

2646 i. Stephen Edward[9] Phares b. Nov-25-1990.

2468. **Jeffery[8] Warner** (2049.Dottie Lou[7] Phares, 1338.Elmer P.[6], 641.Cleat[5], 192.Eliza Ann[4] Hinkle, 26.Martha Ann[3] Waybright, 4.Rachel[2] Arbogast, 1.John C.[1]), b. Jan-14-1966.
He Married **Pamala J. Craig**, b. Jun-18-1975.

Children:

2647 i. Clara Dawn[9] Craig b. Dec-01-1989.

2470. **Joyce Juanita[8] Taylor** (2051.Juanita[7] Sponaugle, 1354.Herbert Charles[6], 656.William Letcher[5], 199.Roseann[4] Ketterman, 28.Alice[3] Waybright, 5.Rebecca[2] Arbogast, 1.John C.[1]), b. Apr 16 1962 in Montgomery Co., MD.
(1) Married Jun 21 1980 in Green Bank, Pocahontas Co., WV, **James Franklin Tripplet** (son of G. F. Tripplet).
(2) Married Nov 9 1984, **Dempsey Michael Fox**.

***Children** by Dempsey Michael Fox:*

2648 i. Dustin Michael[9] Fox b. Sep 26 1986.

2471. **Norma Jean[8] Taylor** (2051.Juanita[7] Sponaugle, 1354.Herbert Charles[6], 656.William Letcher[5], 199.Roseann[4] Ketterman, 28.Alice[3] Waybright, 5.Rebecca[2] Arbogast, 1.John C.[1]), b. Dec 23 1963 in Virginia.
Married Nov 7 1987, **Joseph Michael Judy** (son of Joseph Judy).

Children:

2649 i. Brittany Nicole[9] Judy b. Feb 1 1990.

2472. **Allen Ray[8] Taylor** (2051.Juanita[7] Sponaugle, 1354.Herbert Charles[6], 656.William Letcher[5], 199.Roseann[4] Ketterman, 28.Alice[3] Waybright, 5.Rebecca[2] Arbogast, 1.John C.[1]), b. Jun 21 1969 in Elkins, Randolph Co., WV.
Married Jun 27 1998 in Arbovale Cem., Arbovale, Pocahontas Co., WV, **Holly Michele Gordon** (daughter of Ronald L. Gordon and Ramona Jane Carpenter).

Children:

2650 i. Jarred Allen[9] Taylor b. Feb 15 2000 in Davis Memorial Hospital, Elkins, Randolph Co., WV.
2651 ii. Alexa Raye Taylor b. Feb 17 2002 in Davis Memorial Hospital, Elkins, Randolph Co., WV.

2476. **Jeffery Stewart^8 Bowers** (2057.Ruth Elaine^7 Sponaugle, 1363.Marvin Luther^6, 657.Herman Henry^5, 199.Roseann^4 Ketterman, 28.Alice^3 Waybright, 5.Rebecca^2 Arbogast, 1.John C.^{1}). He Married **unknown Geary**.

Children:

2652 i. Jeffery^9 Stewart Bowers, Jr. b. Nov-08-1983.

2478. **Martin Luther^8 Sponaugle, III** (2058.Marvin Luther^7 Sponaugle, Jr., 1363.Marvin Luther^6, 657.Herman Henry^5, 199.Roseann^4 Ketterman, 28.Alice^3 Waybright, 5.Rebecca^2 Arbogast, 1.John C.^{1}), b. Apr-17-1956.
He Married **Dana Lynn Grant**.

Children:

2653 i. Ryan Christopher^9 Sponaugle b. Jan-28-1980.
2654 ii. Lindsay Noel Sponaugle b. May-11-1983.

2479. **Diane^8 Sponaugle** (2061.Carroll Lee^7, 1363.Marvin Luther^6, 657.Herman Henry^5, 199.Roseann^4 Ketterman, 28.Alice^3 Waybright, 5.Rebecca^2 Arbogast, 1.John C.^{1}).
She Married **Gary Paden**.

Children:

2655 i. Joshua Craig^9 Paden b. Jul-16-1982.
2656 ii. Michelle Paden b. Feb-02-1984.

2490. **Angela Kay^8 Hinkle** (2092.Patsey Louisa^7 Harper, 1376.Ruth^6 Sponaugle, 657.Herman Henry^5, 199.Roseann^4 Ketterman, 28.Alice^3 Waybright, 5.Rebecca^2 Arbogast, 1.John C.^{1}).
She Married **John W. Phares**.

Children:

2657 i. Nathaniel John^9 Phares b. May-17-1984.

2493. **Lowell Jene^8 Collins** (2097.Harold Cecil^7, 1405.Iona Patrica^6 Waybright, 678.Wilber Allen^5, 208.Churchill^4, 28.Alice^3, 5.Rebecca^2 Arbogast, 1.John C.^{1}), b. Aug 09 1939.
(1) He Married **Susan Alkire**. .

Children *by Susan Alkire:*

2658 i. Kelly Sue^9 Collins.

(2) He Married **Sharon Johnson**

Children *by Sharon Johnson:*

2659 ii. Christine Collins.
2660 iii. Andrew Jon Collins.

2494. **Atlos Martin^8 Collins** (2097.Harold Cecil^7, 1405.Iona Patrica^6 Waybright, 678.Wilber Allen^5, 208.Churchill^4, 28.Alice^3, 5.Rebecca^2 Arbogast, 1.John C.^{1}), b. Oct 25 1942 in Pocahontas Co., WV. (1) He Married **Judith Elaine Gill**.

Children *by Judith Elaine Gill:*

2661 i. Dawnne Renee^9 Collins b. Oct 01 1964.
2662 ii. Robin Leigh Collins b. Aug 01 1965. .
2663 iii. Virginia Lynn Collins b. Aug 19 1967.

(2) He Married **Tammy Jo Farnham**

Children *by Tammy Jo Farnham:*

2664 iv. Sonja Michelle Collins b. Feb 02 1979.

2495. **Carol Lee^8 Collins** (2099.Bernard Morris^7, 1405.Iona Patrica^6 Waybright, 678.Wilber Allen^5, 208.Churchill^4, 28.Alice^3, 5.Rebecca^2 Arbogast, 1.John C.^{1}).
She Married **Bill Waco Lambert**.

Children:

2665 i. Janie Marie^9 Lambert.
2666 ii. Billy W Lambert.
2667 iii. Jody Lynn Lambert.
2668 iv. Pamela Carol Lambert.
2669 v. Julie Ann Lambert.

2496. **Rebecca Jeanne^8 Collins** (2099.Bernard Morris^7, 1405.Iona Patrica^6 Waybright, 678.Wilber Allen^5, 208.Churchill^4, 28.Alice^3, 5.Rebecca^2 Arbogast, 1.John C.^{1}).

(1) She Married **Bob Shepherd**. .

***Children** by Bob Shepherd:*

2670 i. Kelly Ann[9] Shepherd.

2671 ii. Gred Rob Shepherd.

(2) She Married **Tom Nohe**

***Children** by Tom Nohe:*

2672 iii. Thomas Nohe.

2505. **Sue Ellen[8] Arbogast** (2107.Rev. James Bert[7], 1410.Rella K[6] Waybright, 680.Amby Stanton[5], 208.Churchill[4], 28.Alice[3], 5.Rebecca[2] Arbogast, 1.John C.[1]).
She Married **Lynn Doddrill**.

***Children**:*

2673 i. Matthew[9] Doddrill.

2506. **Sherry[8] Lynnarbogast** (2107.Rev. James Bert[7] Arbogast, 1410.Rella K[6] Waybright, 680.Amby Stanton[5], 208.Churchill[4], 28.Alice[3], 5.Rebecca[2] Arbogast, 1.John C.[1]).
Ref: Stalnaker 259
She Married **Dana Lemasters**.

***Children**:*

2674 i. Lisa Marie[9] Lemasters.

2513. **Randall Lee[8] Arbogast** (2141.Russell Valey[7], 1504.Alda Christine[6] Waybright, 776.William Garrett[5], 241.Nicholas[4], 36.Miles[3], 5.Rebecca[2] Arbogast, 1.John C.[1]), b. Sep 07 1960 in Elkins, Randolph Co., WV.
He Married **Sandra Miller**, b. Mar 12 1962 in Elkins, Randolph Co., WV.

***Children**:*

2675 i. Andrew J[9] Arbogast b. Sep 23 1989 in Elkins, Randolph Co., WV.

2676 ii. Rachel Lee Arbogast b. Mar 16 1994 in Elkins, Randolph Co., WV.

2527. **James A.[8] Arbogast** (2178.Allen Gerald[7], 1544.Allen[6], 814.Samual[5], 267.Jacob A.[4], 40.Lemuel[3], 6.Joseph E.[2], 1.John C.[1]).
Married Jul 20 1981, **Karen Ann Marshall**.

***Children**:*

2677 i. Jamie Janine[9] Arbogast b. Nov 22 1981.

2528. **Donna C[8] McCauley** (2181.Sam Houston[7], 1545.Audrey Maxine[6] Arbogast, 814.Samual[5], 267.Jacob A.[4], 40.Lemuel[3], 6.Joseph E.[2], 1.John C.[1]).
She Married **Thomas Houser**.

***Children**:*

2678 i. Melanie[9] Houser.

2679 ii. Thomas J Houser.

2563. **Judy Mae[8] Nottingham** (2203.Nelva Marie[7] Simmons, 1585.Monna[6] Bennett, 822.Ada M.[5] Arbogast, 270.Hannah Elizabeth[4], 42.Joseph Elili[3], 6.Joseph E.[2], 1.John C.[1]).
From, William Nottingham, Jr. & Mary Arbogast of Pocahontas Co., = Descendants, by Mary Elizabeth (Nottingham) Skelton of Jamestown, =
Married Jul 12 1972 in Durbin, Pocahontas Co., WV, **Jerry Allen Mathney** (son of Charles Matheny and Bonnie Hedrick).
From, William Nottingham, Jr. & Mary Arbogast of Pocahontas Co., = Descendants, by Mary Elizabeth (Nottingham) Skelton of Jamestown, =.

***Children**:*

2680 i. Christopher M.[9] Mathney.
From, William Nottingham, Jr. & Mary Arbogast of Pocahontas Co., = Descendants, by Mary Elizabeth (Nottingham) Skelton of Jamestown, =

2681 ii. Patrick Brian Mathney b. Jan 4 1976.
From, William Nottingham, Jr. & Mary Arbogast of Pocahontas Co., = Descendants, by Mary Elizabeth (Nottingham) Skelton of Jamestown, =

2566. **Debra Jean[8] Nottingham** (2203.Nelva Marie[7] Simmons, 1585.Monna[6] Bennett, 822.Ada M.[5] Arbogast, 270.Hannah Elizabeth[4], 42.Joseph Elili[3], 6.Joseph E.[2], 1.John C.[1]), b. Jun 3 1963.

(1) She Married **Wayne Thornton**.
(2) She Married **Glenn William Arbogast** (son of Green Arbogast and Dorothy Ryder).

***Children** by Glenn William Arbogast:*

2682 i. Andrew William^{9} Arbogast b. Dec 23 1982 in Davis Memorial Hospital, Elkins, Randolph Co., WV.
\+ 2683 ii. Stephanie Arbogast.

2567. **Roberta Lynn^{8} Nottingham** (2203.Nelva Marie^{7} Simmons, 1585.Monna^{6} Bennett, 822.Ada M.^{5} Arbogast, 270.Hannah Elizabeth^{4}, 42.Joseph Elili^{3}, 6.Joseph E.^{2}, 1.John C.^{1}), b. Sep 12 1964 in Marlinton, Pocahontas Co., WV.
She Married **Todd Jonah Shreve** (son of Frank Shreve and Madeline Sparks).

***Children**:*

2684 i. Eric Ryan^{9} Shreve b. May 20 1985 in Davis Memorial Hospital, Elkins, Randolph Co., WV. A stepchild

2568. **Viviennne Rene^{8} Sutton** (2204.Bessie May^{7} Simmons, 1585.Monna^{6} Bennett, 822.Ada M.^{5} Arbogast, 270.Hannah Elizabeth^{4}, 42.Joseph Elili^{3}, 6.Joseph E.^{2}, 1.John C.^{1}), b. Mar 31 1960 in Morgantown, Monongalia Co., WV.
Married Jun 19 1982, **William McGuinnis**.

***Children**:*

2685 i. Amber^{9} McGuinnis b. May 10 1988.
2686 ii. Bridgett McGuinnis b. Oct 6 1990.
2687 iii. Russell McGuinnis b. Sep 20 1993.

2570. **Hazel^{8} Bennett** (2216.Christena Belle^{7} Sponaugle, 1597.Mary Dessie^{6} Vandevander, 826.Wayne Sylvester^{5} Vandevender, 273.Ruth Ellen^{4} Arbogast, 42.Joseph Elili^{3}, 6.Joseph E.^{2}, 1.John C.^{1}).
She Married **Edgar Simmions**.

***Children**:*

2688 i. Douglas^{9} Simmions.
2689 ii. Mark Simmions.
2690 iii. Allan Simmions.

2571. **Fred D.^{8} Bennett** (2216.Christena Belle^{7} Sponaugle, 1597.Mary Dessie^{6} Vandevander, 826.Wayne Sylvester^{5} Vandevender, 273.Ruth Ellen^{4} Arbogast, 42.Joseph Elili^{3}, 6.Joseph E.^{2}, 1.John C.^{1}).
He Married **Joyce Mounts**.

***Children**:*

2691 i. Julie^{9} Bennett.
2692 ii. Fred D. Bennett, Jr,.
2693 iii. David W. Bennett.

2600. **Kimberly Susan^{8} Nottingham** (2231.Beverly Ann^{7} Arbogast, 1623.Nora Gustava^{6} Calhoun, 839.William Cecil^{5}, 275.Hannah Catharine^{4} Bennett, 43.Sidney Dean^{3} Arbogast, 6.Joseph E.^{2}, 1.John C.^{1}), b. May 4 1960 in Pocahontas Co., WV. (
1) She Married **Donald Frazee**. .

***Children** by Donald Frazee:*

2694 i. Spencer Pierce^{9} Nottingham b. Dec 14 1999 in Davis Memorial Hospital, Elkins, Randolph Co., WV.

(2) She Married **Frank Gardner**

***Children** by Frank Gardner:*

2695 ii. Frederica Suzanne Nottingham.

2601. **Teresa Lynn^{8} Nottingham** (2231.Beverly Ann^{7} Arbogast, 1623.Nora Gustava^{6} Calhoun, 839.William Cecil^{5}, 275.Hannah Catharine^{4} Bennett, 43.Sidney Dean^{3} Arbogast, 6.Joseph E.^{2}, 1.John C.^{1}), b. Jan 29 1962 in Pocahontas Co., WV.
(1) Married Apr 1 1980 in Bath Co., VA, **Winfred Rex Cassell**, b. Apr 26 1962 in Pocahontas Co., WV (son of John Cassell and Joan Brewster). **Winfred**: S/o John Berle and JoAnn Virginia (Brewster) Cassell.
(2) Married Apr 24 1999 in Pigeon Forge, Sevier Co., TN, **Trampas E. Hammons** (son of Harold Edward Hammons).

***Children** by Trampas E. Hammons:*

2696 i. Trevor Keegan Lee^{9} Hammons b. May 28 2000 in Ruby Memorial Hospital, Morgantown, Monongalia Co., WV.

2602. **John Leslie^{8} Nottingham** (2231.Beverly Ann^{7} Arbogast, 1623.Nora Gustava^{6} Calhoun, 839.William Cecil^{5}, 275.Hannah Catharine^{4} Bennett, 43.Sidney Dean^{3} Arbogast, 6.Joseph E.^{2}, 1.John C.^{1}), b. Jan 23 1963 in Pocahontas Co., WV.

He Married **Venchesia Angelo**, b. in Italy.

***Children**:*

2697 i. Vincent[9] Nottingham.

2698 ii. Angela Nottingham.

2603. **Randall Lee[8] Nottingham** (2231.Beverly Ann[7] Arbogast, 1623.Nora Gustava[6] Calhoun, 839.William Cecil[5], 275.Hannah Catharine[4] Bennett, 43.Sidney Dean[3] Arbogast, 6.Joseph E.[2], 1.John C.[1]), b. Aug 3 1964 in Pocahontas Co., WV.

(1) Married Mar 7 1993, **Tiana Rabel** (daughter of Daniel Rabel)

***Children** by Tiana Rabel:*

2699 i. Brandon Lee[9] Nottingham b. Aug 2 1993.

(2) He Married **Jacqueline Lynn Lambert**, b. Dec 4 1965 (daughter of Roy Lambert and Connie Cassell).

***Children** by Jacqueline Lynn Lambert:*

2700 ii. Amanda Lee Nottingham b. Jan 7 1992.

Generation Nine

2683. **Stephanie[9] Arbogast** (2566.Debra Jean[8] Nottingham, 2203.Nelva Marie[7] Simmons, 1585.Monna[6] Bennett, 822.Ada M.[5] Arbogast, 270.Hannah Elizabeth[4], 42.Joseph Elili[3], 6.Joseph E.[2], 1.John C.[1]). She Married **James Richard Cassell**, b. Aug 19 1967 (son of James Edward Cassell and Connie Jean Mullenax).

***Children**:*

2701 i. Madison Faith[10] Cassell b. Sep 8 2004 in Davis Memorial Hospital, Elkins, Randolph Co., WV.

Descendants of George Arbogast Ninth Child of Michael and Mary Elizabeth Samuels

Generation One

1. **George[1] Arbogast**, b. Jun 09 1772 in Crabbottom, Highland Co., VA (son of Michael Arbogast and Mary Elizabeth Samuels Amanapas), d. Mar 03 1844 in Crabbottom, Highland Co., VA.
All information from AAF. See Pendleton Co. deed from heirs of his brother, John. Married once, remained in the community where his father settled near the village of Crabbottom, Pendleton Co., VA/WV, now Blue Grass, Highland Co., VA. His place probably abutted the lands of his father and brother, Michael. It may be possible that he lived 2-3 miles from his fathers home, on Franks Run. His son, Daniel, lived at this location. Carl Arbogast, son of Abraham Arbogast lived there in 1971, per Amanda Forbes. Had 9 children. Deed of heirs filed in Pendleton Co., 1844 gives names of children. Died intestate. His dates are from a family bible in possession of Larry Roberts.
Bible was kept by Emanuel or some of his family who went to Illinois.
Married 1791 in Pendleton Co., WV, **Catherine Yeager**, b. Jun 17 1769 in Shenandoah Co., VA (daughter of Johann Andrew Yeager and Margaret Catherine Elizabeth Sommer), d. FEB 1848 in Crabbottom, Highland Co., VA. It is possible Catherine was born in Pennsylvania before her parents came to Shenandoah Co., VA. Birth and death dates are from family bible kept by her son, Emanuel, and now in possession of Larry Roberts. All research and records on this line from Amanda Crawford Arbogast Forbes.

Children:

+ 2 i. Hannah[2] Arbogast b. May 00 1790.
+ 3 ii. Daniel Arbogast b. About 1793.
+ 4 iii. Elizabeth L. Arbogast b. Aug 13 1797.
+ 5 iv. Catherine Arbogast b. About 1801.
+ 6 v. Emanuel Arbogast b. Mar 31 1803.
+ 7 vi. Leah Arbogast b. About 1806.
+ 8 vii. Mary "Polly" Arbogast b. About 1811.
9 viii. Adam Arbogast.
+ 10 ix. Henry W. Arbogast.

Generation Two

2. **Hannah[2] Arbogast** (1.George[1]), b. May 00 1790 in Crabbottom, Highland Co., VA, d. Jan 28 1856 in Crabbottom, Highland Co., VA.
Source of information is Amanda Arbogast Forbes research in file.. Children, George, John and Catharine from "Mullenax - Bales", by Katherine and Alvin Mullenax, April 1980, Manhattan, Kansas. Hannah's death reported by son, John, 65 years, 8 mos. from supplemental information by Helen J. Gasch research and family group record in file.
Married Jan 24 1814 in Pendleton Co., WV, **Jacob Mullenax**, b. About 1790 in Pendleton Co., WV (son of James Mullenax and Mary Elizabeth Arbogast), d. Aug 1846 in Highland Co., VA. Source is research and family records of Helen J. Gasch of Clarkston, WA. Veteran, War of 1812.

Children:

+ 11 i. John H.[3] Mullenax b. 1814.
+ 12 ii. George Mullenax b. About 1818.
+ 13 iii. Catharine Mullenax b. 1820.

3. **Daniel[2] Arbogast** (1.George[1]), b. About 1793 in Crabbottom, Highland Co., VA, d. Feb 13 1845 in Crabbottom, Highland Co., VA. The Crabbottom area of Pendleton Co., VA became part of Highland Co., VA when it was created in 1847. Daniel's exact birth date is unknown, estimated from census records. He served in war of 1812 as a private in Capt. Jesse Hinkle's Company of VA Militia, enlisting August, 1814 for six months at Norfolk, VA and discharged there on 6 Nov., 1914. Widow's application (Sarah Arbogast) for bounty land, Dec., 1850. Bounty Land File 51371 and file 189510. Date of

Daniel's death is from this application.
Pendleton Co. marriage records.
Highland Co., VA Circuit Court Case, drawer 21, packet 71, chancery suit, E.D. Clark, his wife and others v Daniel Arbogast heirs establishes children.
Marriages of children found in both Pendleton Co., WV and Highland Co., VA.
This family is well documented in "At the Sign of the Swan, Ancestry and Descendants of Hans Wendell Zwecker", by Amanda Crawford Arbogast Forbes.
Married Dec 02 1817 in Pendleton Co., WV, **Sarah Swecker**, b. Sep 16 1793 in Rockingham Co., VA, d. Jun 08 1858 in Crabbottom, Highland Co., VA. There are 2 spellings of her name. One Swacker and one Zwecker. Swacker is used here and shows 9 children, as does Zwecker. Details of both on children data varies. Included here is most detailed.

Children:

+ 14 i. William Samual[3] Arbogast b. Aug 13 1818.
+ 15 ii. Elizabeth Jane Arbogast b. 1820.
16 iii. George Arbogast b. 1822.
+ 17 iv. Leah Frances Arbogast b. 1824.
+ 18 v. Mary Arbogast b. Jan-10-1826.
+ 19 vi. Benjamin Franklin Arbogast b. 1829.
20 vii. Sarah A. Arbogast b. 1831 in Crabbottom, Highland Co., VA, d. Oct 11 1918 in Staunton, Augusta Co., VA.
+ 21 viii. John Wesley Arbogast b. Mar 16 1835.
+ 22 ix. Henry W. Arbogast b. 1837.

4. **Elizabeth L.[2] Arbogast** (1.George[1]), b. Aug 13 1797 in Crabbottom, Highland Co., VA, d. Dec 28 1875 in Pendleton Co., WV, buried in Sponaugle Family Cem., Hunting Grounds Pendleton County WV.
From research and family group record from Amanda Arbogast Forbes. Note from Glenn Huffman that Elizabeth's tombstone indicates birth as shown.
Married Feb 22 1821 in Pendleton Co., WV, **Jacob Phillip Sponaugle**, b. 1799 in Churchville, Pendleton Co., WV (son of Balsor Sponaugle and Sarah White), d. in Hunting Ground, Pendleton Co., (W)VA.

Children:

+ 23 i. William[3] Sponaugle b. Feb-14-1822.
+ 24 ii. George Washington Sponaugle b. Oct 16 1823.
+ 25 iii. Jesse Sponaugle b. ABT 1825.
+ 26 iv. Catherine Sponaugle b. Oct 1827.
+ 27 v. Lewis Martin Sponaugle b. AUG 1829.
+ 28 vi. Mary Elizabeth Sponaugle b. Feb8 1831.
+ 29 vii. Elizabeth Ann Sponaugle b. Jan 03 1833.
+ 30 viii. Leah Sponaugle b. Sep 17 1834.
+ 31 ix. Hannah Sponaugle b. Sep 30 1836.
+ 32 x. Sarah Sponaugle b. ABT 1839.
+ 33 xi. Jacob Sponaugle, Jr. b. 1841.

5. **Catherine[2] Arbogast** (1.George[1]), b. About 1801 in Crabbottom, Highland Co., VA, d. About 1852 in Monterey, Highland Co., VA.
Source is AAF Two additional children, Emanuel and Benjamin, died in infancy.
Married About 1825, **John A. Cook**, b. 1803 in Pendleton Co., WV (son of John Cook and Maey Ann Varner), d. Feb 28 1866 in Jacksonville, Lewis Co., WV.

Children:

+ 34 i. George[3] Cook b. Jan 02 1826.
+ 35 ii. Catherine Cook b. Jan 02 1826.
+ 36 iii. Elizabeth Cook b. 1828.
+ 37 iv. Emily Cook b. Jun 22 1830.
38 v. Mary Cook b. 1831 in Pendleton Co., WV.
She Married **Osborne Wade**, b. 1836, d. 1904.
+ 39 vi. Belinda Cook b. 1834.
+ 40 vii. John Wesley Cook b. 1836.
+ 41 viii. Christopher Columbus Cook b. 1845.

6. **Emanuel[2] Arbogast** (1.George[1]), b. Mar 31 1803 in Crabbottom, Highland Co., VA, d. Aug 13 1879 in Tazewell Co., IL.

347om Amanda Arbogast Forbes research, copy in file. Birth, marriages, children and death recorded in a family bible kept by Emanuel or his children now in possession of Larry Roberts at Hannibal, MO. Data confirmed by 1850 Highland Co., VA Census, by Matheny, pp. 58 and 59.; Marriages of Pendleton Co., VA 1788-1853, by Mary Harter, p. 2 and History of Highland Co., VA, by Morton. Emanuel also named in deed of heirs of George
Arbogast, his father, Pendleton Co., Deed Book 14, pp. 173 and 174, 1844. Other recorded events indicate Emanuel was one of the first justices of Highland Co. when it was formed in 1847. Appointed school commissioner in 1853. Appraised his brother, Daniel Arbogast's estate in 1845. He was influential in organizing the Methodist Church at Dry Run on land given earlier by the descendants of his grandfather, Michael. In 1847 Emanuel freed his slaves including Sam, who belonged to his father-in-law, Isaac Gum; see Deed Book1, p. 37, Highland Co., VA. Emanuel and Isabella deed land to trustees of M.E. Church, Deed Book 2, p. 104, 23 Jun 1853, Highland Co., VA. Emanuel and Isabella deed land to Ben Ami Hansel, 32ac, Deed Book 2, p. 388, 6 Aug 1855, Highland Co., VA. Emanuel, Isabella and some of his children went to Illinois
in late 1855 or 1856.

(1) Married Dec 26 1826 in Crabbottom, Highland Co., VA, **Jane Gum**, b. Jun 11 1805 in Crabbottom, Highland Co., VA, d. Mar 22 1837 in Crabbottom, Highland Co., VA.

Children:

- \+ 42 i. Jane Caroline[3] Arbogast b. Dec 13 1827.
- 43 ii. Margaret K. Arbogast b. About 1830 in Pendleton Co., WV.
  She Married **David Seiver**.
- 44 iii. Rachel Sidney Arbogast b. Oct 24 1831 in Pendleton Co., WV.
  She Married **James Bishop**.
- \+ 45 iv. Jeremiah Elderidge Arbogast b. Sep 14 1834.
- \+ 46 v. Norval Wilson Arbogast b. May 08 1837.

(2) Married Sep 19 1839 in Pendleton Co., WV, **Isabella Wimer**, b. Jun 26 1821 in Pendleton Co., WV, d. May 07 1886.

Children:

- 47 vi. Martha Elizabeth Arbogast b. Dec 15 1840 in Pendleton Co., WV.
- 48 vii. Andrew Clark Arbogast b. Feb 09 1842 in Pendleton Co., WV, d. Dec 01 1871 in Illinois.
  Married Jun-20-1866 in McLean Co., IL, **Eliza Jane Rexrode** (daughter of Solomon Arbogast).
- 49 viii. William Brison Arbogast b. Mar 03 1844 in Pendleton Co., WV, d. Feb 07 1925 in McLean Co., IL.
  Maybe died in IL.
- 50 ix. Frances Virginia Arbogast b. Jul 14 1846 in Pendleton Co., WV, d. in Illinois.
  She Married **Joseph P Janes**.
- \+ 51 x. James W. Arbogast b. About 1848.
- 52 xi. Eliza H. Arbogast b. Feb 1850 in Highland Co., VA.
- 53 xii. Lucy Arbogast b. About 1852 in Highland Co., VA.
- 54 xiii. Anna Arbogast b. Sep 06 1855 in Highland Co., VA.
- \+ 55 xiv. David Howard Arbogast b. Apr 01 1860.

7. **Leah[2] Arbogast** (1.George[1]), b. About 1806 in Crabbottom, Highland Co., VA, d. About 1885 in Waynesboro, Augusta Co., VA.
(1) Married Feb 01 1831 in Pendleton Co., WV, **William Chew**, b. 1803 in Pendleton Co., WV, d. 1847 in Pendleton Co., WV.

Children:

- 56 i. William[3] Chew b. July 1832 in Crabbottom, Highland Co., VA, d. 1918 in Waynesboro, Augusta Co., VA.

(2) Married Apr 30 1850 in Highland Co., VA, **Andrew Seybert**, b. 18094 in Pendleton Co., WV, d. Sep 04 1862 in Highland Co., VA.

8. **Mary "Polly"[2] Arbogast** (1.George[1]), b. About 1811 in Crabbottom, Highland Co., VA, d. About 1870 in Highland Co., VA.
Married Jan 11 1839 in Crabbottom, Highland Co., VA, **Joseph L. Chew**, b. About 1814 in Crabbottom, Highland Co., VA, d. 1860 in Crabbottom, Highland Co., VA.

Children:

- 57 i. John W.[3] Chew b. Mar 1840 in Crabbottom, Highland Co., VA, d. Nov 04 1861 in Crabbottom, Highland Co., VA.
- \+ 58 ii. George E. M. Chew b. About 1841.
- 59 iii. D. Stuart Chew b. May 07 1843 in Crabbottom, Highland Co., VA, d. Oct 06 1905 in Crabbottom, Highland Co., VA.
- 60 iv. Martha Catherine Chew b. About 1847 in Crabbottom, Highland Co., VA, d. Oct 09 1918 in Crabbottom, Highland Co., VA.

10. **Henry W.[2] Arbogast** (1.George[1]), d. 1928.
Known as squire Arbogast.
Married Jun 20 1867, **Susan Judy Arbogast**, b. Jul 6 1850, d. Jun 20 1937.

Children:

	61	i.	Florence (Dolly)[3] Arbogast b. 1874, d. 1967. She Married **Frank S. Ketterman**, d. 1950.
	62	ii.	George Arbogast.
	63	iii.	Lena Arbogast. She Married **Juss Lowther**.
	64	iv.	Sarah Arbogast. She Married **Jess H. Simmons.**
	65	v.	Bertha Arbogast d. 1965. She Married **George Arbogast**.
	66	vi.	Oddie Arbogast.
	67	vii.	Arthur Arbogast.
+	68	viii.	Orien Austin Arbogast b. Jul 16 1898.

Generation Three

11. **John H.[3] Mullenax** (2.Hannah[2] Arbogast, 1.George[1]), b. 1814 in Crabbottom, Highland Co., VA, d. Aug 19 1862 in Crabbottom, Highland Co., VA.
Married Mar 02 1837 in Crabbottom, Highland Co., VA, **Rachel Rexrode** (daughter of Christian Rexrode and Leah Seybert).

Children:

+	69	i.	Emily Jane[4] Mullenax.
	70	ii.	Ida Florence Mullenax.

12. **George[3] Mullenax** (2.Hannah[2] Arbogast, 1.George[1]), b. About 1818 in Crabbottom, Highland Co., VA, d. in Crabbottom, Highland Co., VA.
He Married **Elizabeth Lambert** (daughter of John Lambert and Nancy (Unknown)).

Children:

+	71	i.	Martha[4] Mullenax.

13. **Catharine[3] Mullenax** (2.Hannah[2] Arbogast, 1.George[1]), b. 1820 in Crabbottom, Highland Co., VA, d. in Highland Co., VA.
Married Mar 14 1840 in Pendleton Co., WV, **George Vandevender**, b. About 1818 in Pendleton Co., WV, d. 1895 in Highland Co., VA.

Children:

	72	i.	Almira J.[4] Mullenax.
	73	ii.	Jacob E. Mullenax.

14. **William Samual[3] Arbogast** (3.Daniel[2], 1.George[1]), b. Aug 13 1818 in Crabbottom, Highland Co., VA, d. Jan 30 1865 in Union Prison, Point Lookout, St. Mary's Co., MD.
Married 1843, **Catherine Eagle**.

Children:

+	74	i.	Samuel Benjamin[4] Arbogast b. 10 Dec 1844.
	75	ii.	Sarah T. Arbogast b. Aug 15 1850 in Highland Co., VA, d. Mar 03 1856 in Highland Co., VA.

15. **Elizabeth Jane[3] Arbogast** (3.Daniel[2], 1.George[1]), b. 1820 in Crabbottom, Highland Co., VA, d. Apr 28 1898 in Highland Co., VA, buried in Monterey Cem., Monterey, Highland Co., VA.
Married Feb-23-1857 in Pendleton Co., WV, **James Alfred Harding, MD**, b. 1813 (son of William Harting), buried in Monterey Cem., Monterey, Highland Co., VA, d. Feb-14-1877.

Children:

+	76	i.	Sallie Amanda[4] Harding b. May-28-1858.
	77	ii.	Lucy D Heading b. Dec-03-1860, d. Oct-28-1949. She Married **William M Arbogast.**

17. **Leah Frances[3] Arbogast** (3.Daniel[2], 1.George[1]), b. 1824 in Crabbottom, Highland Co., VA, d. Apr 05 1905 in Greenville, Augusta Co., VA.
He Married **Eramus D Claeke**, b. Dec-09-1924 in Crabbottom, Highland Co., VA, buried in Mt Cornford, Rockingham Co. VA, d. Feb-08-1902 in Greenville, Augusta Co., VA.

Children:

78 i. Sarah Gray[4] Clarke b. Mar-03-1853 in Highland Co., VA, d. Oct-26-1932 in Staunton, Augusta Co., VA.
79 ii. John Howard Clarke b. 1857, buried in Greenville, Augusta Co., VA, d. 1928.
He Married **Sue Minor**, b. 1868, d. 1957 in Augusta Stone church Cem., Augusta Co., VA.

18. **Mary[3] Arbogast** (3.Daniel[2], 1.George[1]), b. Jan-10-1826 in Crabbottom, Highland Co., VA, d. Apr 05 1905 in Franklin Co., WV.
She Married **John Anthony Marshall**, b. Oct-06-1828 in Fort Pleasany, VA (son of William Marshall and Matgilda Hoffman), d. 0311997 in Franklin, VA. Served with Stonewall Jackson during his Valley Camp again.

Children:

80 i. Sarah Alice[4] Marshal b. May-14-1852 in Franklin, Pendleton Co., WV, d. Sep-17-1917 in Charlottesville, VA.
81 ii. William Bernard Marshall b. Nov-28-1856 in Franklin, Pendleton Co., WV, d. Oct-17-1935 in Waskon, TX.
\+ 82 iii. Lelia Ada Marshall b. Oct-22-1860.
83 iv. Minor K. Marshall b. Mar-28-1866, d. Feb-14-1900.

19. **Benjamin Franklin[3] Arbogast** (3.Daniel[2], 1.George[1]), b. 1829 in Crabbottom, Highland Co., VA, d. Apr 09 1904 in Lexington, McLean Co., IL. Benjamin and Cynthia went to Illinois by wagon in 1856. He farmed for five years and then went into building and contracting successfully. According to Cynthia's obituary in the Lexington Unit Journal, she and Benjamin had 8 children, with four living in 1907. It is thought that some of the children died in infancy.
1880 Illinois census, Lexington Twp., McLean Co.; B. F. Arbogast age 51 born VA, wife Cynthia 46 born VA, son George B. 13 born IL and son Emmett B. 4 born IL. 1860 census, Lexington City and Township, McLean Co., IL, age 31 b. VA, wife Cynthia age 26 b. VA, and dau. Ella age 1 b. IL.
Married Sep-03-1855 in Highland Co., VA, **Cynthia A. Wilson**, b. May-02-1834 in Highland Co., VA, d. Dec-08-1907 in Levington, IL.

Children:

84 i. Ella Adelane[4] Arbogast b. Aug-06-1858, d. Jan-09-1929 in Lexington.KY.
She Married **Ezra Dawson**, b. May-25-1983 in McLean Co., IL.
85 ii. Virginia Lee Arbogast b. 1863, d. Mar-20-1950.
She Married **Frank Paul**, b. 1882.
86 iii. George "Bernie" Arbogast b. about 1867.
87 iv. David Arbogast b. about 1870.
\+ 88 v. Emmett Benjamin Arbogast b. May-28-1876.

21. **John Wesley[3] Arbogast** (3.Daniel[2], 1.George[1]), b. Mar 16 1835 in Highland Co., VA, d. Feb 10 1890 in Highland Co., VA.
Married Aug 04 1858 in Cumberland, Alleghany Co., MD, **Amanda Melvina Hansel**, b. May-01-1837 in Pendleton Co., VA (daughter of Ben Ami Hansel and Mary Wallace), d. Jun-21-1908 at Buena Vista, Rockbridge Co., VA.

Children:

\+ 89 i. Emery Matthew[4] Arbogast b. Jun-01-1862.
90 ii. Ella Texanna Arbogast b. Sep-13-1864 in Crabbottom, Highland Co., VA, d. Nov-08-1932 in Staunton, Augusta Co., VA, buried in Monterey Cem., Monterey, Highland Co., VA.
91 iii. Lula Kate Arbogast b. Jan-07-1867 at Crabbottom, Highland Co., VA, d. Jan-18-1940 in Hematite, Allegheny, VA.
\+ 92 iv. Arthur William Arbogast b. May-20-1869.
\+ 93 v. Charles Cameron Arbogast b. Sep-10-1871.
\+ 94 vi. John Edwin Arbogast b. Jan-16-1877.
95 vii. Sarah Belle Arbogast b. Aug-04-1861 to Monterey, Highland Co., VA, d. Jan-03-1961 in Univ of VA Hospital, Charlottesville, Charlottesville, VA, buried in Monterey Cem., Monterey, Highland Co., VA.
96 viii. Mary Elizabeth Arbogast b. Jun 01 1859 in Crabbottom, Highland Co., VA, d. Apr 09 1861 in Crabbottom, Highland Co., VA.
97 ix. Cora Addie Arbogast b. Jan 07 1861 in Crabbottom, Highland Co., VA, d. Aug 31 1861 in Crabbottom, Highland Co., VA.
98 x. Robert Wallace Arbogast b. Mar-03-1874 in Monterey, Highland Co., VA, buried in Monterey Cem., Monterey, Highland Co., VA, d. 25 Mar 1889 in Monterey, Highland Co., VA.
\+ 99 xi. Arthur William Arbogast b. May-29-1969.

22. **Henry W.[3] Arbogast** (3.Daniel[2], 1.George[1]), b. 1837 in Crabbottom, Highland Co., VA.
He was a school teacher and first Superintended of Schools in the county.
(1) Married Jun-20-1867 in Pendleton or Lewis Co., VA, **Susan Judy**, b. Jul-04-1950 in Pendleton Co., VA (daughter of Samuel Judy and Rebecca Carr).

Children:

100 i. Samuel Lawson[4] Arbogast b. Mar-11-1868 in Pendleton Co., VA, d. May-01-1889 in Pendleton Co., WV.
He Married **Erastus Carr**.
\+ 101 ii. Orien Austin Arbogast b. Feb-12-1870.
102 iii. Sarah Rebecca Arbogast b. Jun-14-1872, d. Jan-20-1943 in Florida City, FL.
She Married **J. H. Simmons**.
103 iv. William Arthur Arbogast b. Apr-04-1883, d. May-24-1906.
\+ 104 v. Ida Florence Arbogast b. Jun-09-1874.
\+ 105 vi. Lorena Elizabeth Arbogast b. Oct-11-1878.
106 vii. Bertha Fay Ellen Arbogast b. Feb-06-1887, d. Oct-08-1965 in Homestead, Miami-Dade Co., FL.
107 viii. Clarence Orten Arbogast b. Nov-30-1879, d. Jul-07-1976.
Married Jan-21-1926 in Petersburg, Grant Co., WV, **Myrtle Schaeffer**.

(2) He Married **Susan Judy**, b. Jul-04-1950 in Pendleton Co., VA (daughter of Samuel Judy and Rebecca Carr).

23. **William[3] Sponaugle** (4.Elizabeth L.[2] Arbogast, 1.George[1]), b. Feb-14-1822 in Hunting Ground, Pendleton Co., (W)VA, d. Jan 10 1892 in Doddridge Co., WV.
Note: From Pendleton County, Past & Present, pg. 215: William & wife Minerva had eleven children. They moved back and forth between Pendleton. 7 the "Sinks" in Randolph Co. before moving to Doddridge Co., WV where William died. Most of their children went to other counties except George m. Elizabeth Judy who lived on Smith Creek, and Adam m. Ann Ketterman, Sarah Nelson and Mary Kate m. Columbus Thompson, who lived near Circleville, WV.
Married Dec 5 1844 in Pendleton Co., WV, **Minerva (Teter) Fleisher**, b. Jan 10 1825 in Bland Hills, Pendleton Co., WV, d. May 2 1898 in Randolph Co., WV.

Children:

\+ 108 i. George Washington[4] Sponaugle b. Jan 25 1846.
\+ 109 ii. Mary Catherine Sponaugle b. Sep 15 1847.
\+ 110 iii. William Jackson Sponaugle b. Nov 08 1849.
\+ 111 iv. Elizabeth Jane Sponaugle b. Mar 10 1854.
\+ 112 v. Lucy A. Sponaugle b. 1856.
\+ 113 vi. Adam Harness Sponaugle b. Feb 4 1858.
\+ 114 vii. Eli Perry Sponaugle.
\+ 115 viii. John Wesley Sponaugle b. Mar 16 1860.
\+ 116 ix. Martha Sponaugle b. 1862.
\+ 117 x. Haymond Sponaugle b. Dec 25 1864.
\+ 118 xi. Levi Sponaugle b. Feb 28 1868.

24. **George Washington[3] Sponaugle** (4.Elizabeth L.[2] Arbogast, 1.George[1]), b. Oct 16 1823 in Straight Creek, Pendleton/Highland Co., VA, d. Nov 26 1881 in Pendleton Co., WV.
Married Oct 14 1865, **Ursula Thompson**, b. Nov 04 1839 in Riverton, Pendleton Co., WV, d. Apr 22 1916. daughter of Adam Harness BIBLE and Elizabeth THOMPSON.

Children:

119 i. Mary Elizabeth[4] Sponaugle b. Nov 27 1866 in Hunting Ground, Pendleton Co., (W)VA.
\+ 120 ii. Robert Boyd Sponaugle b. May 26 1868.
\+ 121 iii. Debby Jane Sponaugle b. Aug 01 1870.
122 iv. Ann Rebecca Sponaugle b. Oct 04 1872 in Hunting Ground, Pendleton Co., (W)VA, d. Jan 03 1960 in Hunting Ground, Pendleton Co., (W)VA.
\+ 123 v. Adam Harness Sponaugle b. Mar 12 1878.
124 vi. Sarah Levada Sponaugle b. Mar 04 1880 in Hunting Ground, Pendleton Co., (W)VA, d. Jan 03 1967 in Pendleton Co., WV.
She Married **George Andrew Bennett**, b. Aug-10-1872 in Pendleton Co., WV.

25. **Jesse[3] Sponaugle** (4.Elizabeth L.[2] Arbogast, 1.George[1]), b. ABT 1825 in Pendleton Co., WV, d. WFT Est 1878-1917.

Married May 6 1852 in Pendleton Co., WV, **Abigail Strawder**, b. ABT 1834, d. WFT Est 1879-1929.

Children:

125 i. Nathaniel Clarke[4] Sponaugle b. Apr 25 1855 in Pendleton Co., WV, d. WFT Est 1856-1945.
126 ii. Jacob Asbury Sponaugle b. 1858 in Pendleton Co., WV, d. WFT Est 1859-1948.
127 iii. Rebecca Alice Sponaugle b. 1860, d. WFT Est 1861-1954.
128 iv. William L. Jackson Sponaugle b. 1863, d. WFT Est 1864-1953.

129 v. Sarah E. Sponaugle b. 1865, d. WFT Est 1866-1959.
130 vi. Mary Ann Sponaugle b. 1868, d. WFT Est 1869-1962.
131 vii. Lucinda Sponaugle b. 1870, d. WFT Est 1871-1964.
132 viii. George W. Sponaugle b. 1873, d. WFT Est 1874-1963.
133 ix. Martha J. Sponaugle b. 1877, d. WFT Est 1878-1971.

26. **Catherine[3] Sponaugle** (4.Elizabeth L.[2] Arbogast, 1.George[1]), b. Oct 1827 in Straight Creek, Pendleton/Highland Co., VA. Married Aug 12 1848, **Joel Teter**, b. Aug 1829 (son of Solomon Teter and Mary Bland), d. Feb 05 1910.

Children:

134 i. Della[4] Teter.
She Married **Jonas E. Hodkin.**
135 ii. Margaret Teter.
136 iii. Martha Teter.
\+ 137 iv. Ruth Teter b. c182.
138 v. Savannah Teter.
She Married **Samuel Smith**.
\+ 139 vi. Mary Elizabeth Teter b. Jan 27 1853.
140 vii. Virginia C. (Jennie) Teter b. May 1860.
She Married **Isaac Teter**, b. Feb-17-1844 (son of Isaac Teter and Mahala Calhoun Teter), d. Jul-03-1928.

27. **Lewis Martin[3] Sponaugle** (4.Elizabeth L.[2] Arbogast, 1.George[1]), b. AUG 1829 in Pendleton Co., WV, d. 1907.

Married Nov 12 1856 in Pendleton Co., WV, **Mary Ann Teter**, b. 1836, d. AFT 1910.

Children:

141 i. Saulsberry[4] Sponaugle b. Aug 28 1857 in Hunting Ground, Pendleton Co., (W)VA, d.
He Married **Sarah Elza**.
\+ 142 ii. Cecelia (Celia) Sponaugle b. Aug 4 1859.
\+ 143 iii. Susan Sponaugle b. Feb 17 1861.
144 iv. Lewis C. Sponaugle b. Jan 4 1863 in Hunting Ground, Pendleton Co., (W)VA, d. BEF 1870.
\+ 145 v. Phoebe E. Sponaugle b. Apr 18 1864.
146 vi. Christena Sponaugle b. Apr 17 1866 in Hunting Ground, Pendleton Co., (W)VA, d. Nov 14 1877.
\+ 147 vii. Martha Alice Sponaugle b. May 30 1868.
148 viii. John Wilson Sponaugle b. Jan 28 1871 in Hunting Ground, Pendleton Co., (W)VA, d.
He Married **Lottie Raines**, b. about 1874.
\+ 149 ix. Norman Sponaugle b. May 2 1873.
150 x. Claddie C. Sponaugle b. FEB 1877 in Hunting Ground, Pendleton Co., (W)VA, d.
She Married **Jacob Pirkey**.

28. **Mary Elizabeth[3] Sponaugle** (4.Elizabeth L.[2] Arbogast, 1.George[1]), b. Feb 8 1831 in Hunting Ground, Pendleton Co., (W)VA, d. May 21 1903 in Homeplace, Hunting Ground.
(1) Married Nov 17 1853 in Pendleton Co., WV, **William Strawder**, b. ABT 1832, d. BEF 1860.

Children:

151 i. Jacob McKendry[4] Strawder b. Mar 25 1854 in Hunting Ground, Pendleton Co., (W)VA, d. 1930 in Randolph Co., WV.
Married Mar-17-1858, Susan P. Ketterman, b. Mar 17 1858 in Pendleton Co., WV (daughter of Esau Lacey Ketterman and Alice Waybright), d. in Glady, WV.

(2) Married Jun 17 1860 in Pendleton Co., WV, **Jacob Wimer**, b. Oct 11 1832 in Hunting Ground, Pendleton Co., (W)VA, d. Aug 20 1907 in Tiberius Wimer, Home, Hunting Ground.

Children:

\+ 152 ii. James Patrick Wimer b. Feb 7 1861.
153 iii. Ashbee L. Wimer b. Feb 17 1863 in Hunting Ground, Pendleton Co., (W)VA, d. Jan 3 1865.

+ 154 iv. Silverbush Wimer b. Sep 23 1865.

155 v. Debby Wimer b. Nov 21 1867 in Hunting Ground, Pendleton Co., (W)VA, d. Nov 24 1868.

156 vi. Edgar J. Wimer b. Jan 3 1870 in Hunting Ground, Pendleton Co., (W)VA, d. Mar 14 1936 in Hunting Ground, Pendleton Co., (W)VA.

157 vii. Leander (Lee) Wimer b. Feb 24 1872 in Hunting Ground, Pendleton Co., (W)VA, d. Nov 12 1904 in Hunting Ground, Pendleton Co., (W)VA.

+ 158 viii. Albert Wimer b. Apr 22 1877.

+ 159 ix. Tiberius Wimer b. May-19-1973.

29. **Elizabeth Ann[3] Sponaugle** (4.Elizabeth L.[2] Arbogast, 1.George[1]), b. Jan 03 1833 in Pendleton Co., WV, d. Jul 15 1881 in County Farm, Upper Tract, Pendleton Co., WV.

<u>Married</u> Jun 23 1857 in Pendleton Co., WV, **Henry Teter**, b. About 1827, d. Mar 06 1868.

Children:

160 i. Susan[4] Teter b. About 1856.

161 ii. Mary Elizabeth Teter b. About 1857.
She <u>Married</u> **Jasper Lauck** .

162 iii. Joel Teter b. 1860.

163 iv. Noah W. Warner b. 1868.

30. **Leah[3] Sponaugle** (4.Elizabeth L.[2] Arbogast, 1.George[1]), b. Sep 17 1834 in Pendleton Co., WV, d. Sep 17 1897 in Tucker Co., WV.

<u>Married</u> May 22 1855 in Pendleton Co., WV, **John Jackson Teter**, b. ABT 1833, d. AFT 1880.

Children:

+ 164 i. Louis Clark[4] Teter b. 1856.

+ 165 ii. Virginia Catherine (Jennie) Teter b. Apr 16 1859.

+ 166 iii. Andrew Teter b. Abt 1863.

+ 167 iv. William Patterson Teter b. ABT 1865.

+ 168 v. John Jackson Teter, Jr. b. 1869.

169 vi. Cora Teter b. 1871, d. WFT Est 1872-1965.
She <u>Married</u> **Enoch Carr**, b. 1858.

+ 170 vii. Elizabeth Mary Teter b. 1873.

+ 171 viii. Alice Grace Teter b. c 1875.

172 ix. Boena Teter b. 1879, d. WFT Est 1880-1973.

31. **Hannah[3] Sponaugle** (4.Elizabeth L.[2] Arbogast, 1.George[1]), b. Sep 30 1836 in Pendleton Co., WV, d. Feb 07 1893 in Pendleton Co., WV.

<u>Married</u> Jun 02 1858 in Pendleton Co., WV, **Hezekiah Tingler**, b. About 1835, d. Mar 04 1867.

Children:

173 i. (infant)[4] Tingler d. Feb 25 1859.

174 ii. Mary Tingler b. Mar 23 1860.

175 iii. Martha E. Tingler b. Feb 06 1863, d. 1865.

176 iv. Anna C. Tingler b. Oct 16 1865.
She <u>Married</u> **Mclennan Judy**.

177 v. Ada Tingler b. May 1870.

32. **Sarah[3] Sponaugle** (4.Elizabeth L.[2] Arbogast, 1.George[1]), b. ABT 1839 in Pendleton Co., WV, d. WFT Est 1885-1934.

<u>Married</u> Oct 6 1858 in Pendleton Co., WV, **Zebulon Tingler**, b. ABT 1835, d. WFT Est 1885-1927.

Children:

178 i. Miles[4] Tingler b. 1860,

179 ii. Jacob Tingler b. 1862, ..
He <u>Married</u> **Florence Thompson**.

180 iii. Elizabeth Jane Tingler .
She <u>Married</u> **William P Warner**.

181 iv. Della Tingler b. 1867,
(1) She <u>Married</u> **Isaac Turner**.
(2) She <u>Married</u> **Paul Bland.**

182 v. Kenny Tingler b. 1869,.

Married Mar-14-1900 in Pendleton Co., WV, **Cloe Warner**.

183 vi. Mary Tingler· b. 1872·
(1) She Married **Isaac Harper**.
(2) She Married **Blanche Teter.**

184 vii. Charles Tingler· b. 1875,·

185 viii. Cora Tingler· b. 1878,·
(1) She Married **Noah W. Warner**.
(2) She Married **Wilson Sponaugle**.

\+ 186 ix. Lena Tingler b. Aug 26 1883.

33. **Jacob[3] Sponaugle, Jr.**· (4.Elizabeth L.[2] Arbogast, 1.George[1]), b. 1841 in Pendleton Co., WV,· d. Sep 13 1880 in Pendleton Co., WV.·
He Married **Roseann Ketterman**, b. 1848 in Pendleton Co., WV (daughter of Esau Lacey Ketterman and Alice Waybright), buried in Sponaugle Family Cem., Hunting Grounds Pendleton County WV.

Children:

\+ 187 i. Ashby[4] Sponaugle b. 1868.

\+ 188 ii. Gilbert Kenton Sponaugle b. Jan 2 1870.

189 iii Eli Perry Sponaugle· b. Jan 28 1871 in Hunting Ground, Pendleton Co., (W)VA,· d. Jan 15 1893.·

190 iv. Flora Anna Sponaugle· b. JUN 1874 in Hunting Ground, Pendleton Co., (W)VA,· d. Dec 26 1947,· buried in Sponaugle Family Cem., Hunting Grounds Pendleton County WV.

\+ 191 v. William Letcher Sponaugle b. Sep 16 1875.

\+ 192 vi. Herman Henry Sponaugle b. Jan 13 1877.

34. **George[3] Cook** (5.Catherine[2] Arbogast, 1.George[1]), b. Jan 02 1826 in Pendleton Co., WV, d. Aug 23 1900.
Married Sep-20-1947 in Pendleton Co., VA, **Eliza Bird**, b. 1830, d. 1803.

Children:

193 i. Elizabeth Jane[4] Cook b. Jul-18-1850 in Highland Co., VA, d. Feb-17-1878 in Weston, WV.

194 ii. Cora Alice Cook b. Nov-20-1851 in Highland Co., VA, d. Apr-17-1898 in Sand Fork, VA.
She Married **Albert Hammer**.

\+ 195 iii. John Alstoyshus Cook b. Jan-16-1853.

196 iv. Margaret Catherine Cook b. Feb-26-1855 in Highland Co., VA.
lived in Omaha, NB school teacher.

\+ 197 v. Mary Virginia Cook b. Jun-01-1856.

198 vi. Ann Eliza Cook b. Jul-04-1858 in Highland Co., VA, d. May-30-1894.

\+ 199 vii. Emma Estella Cook b. Mar-02-1860.

200 viii. Lucy Ellen Cook b. Dec-13-1861 in Highland Co., VA, d. Nov 1909.
She Married **J.P. Jackson**. Family moved to Omaha, NB.

201 ix. George Jackson Cook b. Sep-25-1864 in Highland Co., VA, d. Aug-04-1911 in Weston, Wood County OH.

\+ 202 x. William Franklin Cook b. Jul-03-1867.

\+ 203 xi. Gertrude Victoria Cook b. Sep-16-1870.

\+ 204 xii. Harry Bland Cook b. Oct-02-1872.

35. **Catherine[3] Cook** (5.Catherine[2] Arbogast, 1.George[1]), b. Jan 02 1826 in Pendleton Co., WV.
John was sheriff of Highland co., VA.
Married Mar-24-1847, **John Rexrode**, b. 1820, d. 1890.

Children:

205 i. George Kenna[4] Rexrode.

206 ii. Lillie Belle Rexrode.

207 iii. William Tell Rexrode.

36. **Elizabeth[3] Cook** (5.Catherine[2] Arbogast, 1.George[1]), b. 1828 in Pendleton Co., WV.
Married in Died as an infant, **Valentine Bird**.

Children:

208 i. Columbus T[4] Bird b. Jan-17-1853, d. 1918.

209 ii. Jane Bird.
She Married Dr., **Samuel Bond**.

210 iii. Clara Bird b. May-01-1855, d. c 1926.
She Married **Benjamin Matthew**.

211 iv. Mary Bird.
She Married **unknown Ellis**, b. in Glenville, Gilmer Co., WV.
212 v. Ida Florence Bird b. Sep-22-1958.
She Married **unknown Schieffer**.
. 213 vi. Anna Bird b. Feb-02-1861.
She Married **Mansfield Hevener**.
214 vii. Will Bird d. c1926.
215 viii. Charles Bird d. c 1923.
216 ix. John Lee Bird b. Jan-25-1865.
217 x. Eliza Bird d. in as an infant.

37. **Emily[3] Cook** (5.Catherine[2] Arbogast, 1.George[1]), b. Jun 22 1830, d. Sep 29 1894.
Married Nov 27 1850, **Andrew Jackson Bird**, b. Oct 07 1826 in Pendleton Co., WV, d. Jul 18 1858. son of John BIRD and Margaret Rebecca DAHMER.

Children:

218 i. George Johnson[4] Bird b. Nov-27-1851, d. Dec-30-1913.
Married Oct-31-1876, **Laura Alice Crouch**.
219 ii. Edwin Calvin Bird b. Oct 07 1857, d. Mar 17 1925.
Married Sep 06 1883, **Ella Ann Harrison**.
220 iii. Margaret Catherine Bird b. Apr-15-1855, d. Dec-15-1929.
\+ 221 iv. Mary Elizabeth Bird b. Sep-10-1953.
\+ 222 v. Ollie Mae Bird.

39. **Belinda[3] Cook** (5.Catherine[2] Arbogast, 1.George[1]), b. 1834 in Pendleton Co., WV.
She Married **Elmer Rohrbough**.

Children:

223 i. Ida Florence[4] Rohrbough b. Feb-05-1856, d. Oct-12-1933.
Married 1876, **S. K, Spalding**.

40. **John Wesley[3] Cook** (5.Catherine[2] Arbogast, 1.George[1]), b. 1836 in Pendleton Co., WV, d. Nov 05 1908 in Kuttawa, Lyon Co., KY.
He Married **Mary C. Rolston**, b. Aug-15-1841 (daughter of Samuel Rolston and Eliza Rolston), buried in Monterey Cem., Monterey, Highland Co., VA, d. Oct-08-1901.

Children:

\+ 224 i. Frank H.[4] Cook b. May-07-1858.
225 ii. Elizabeth Cook b. 1862, d. Jun-25-1927.
Married 1899, **Charles J. Shumate**, b. 1854, d. 1930.

41. **Christopher Columbus[3] Cook** (5.Catherine[2] Arbogast, 1.George[1]), b. 1845 in Pendleton Co., WV.
He Married **Jurusha Dmron**.

Children:

226 i. Carrie[4] Cook.
She Married **unknown Caldwell**.
227 ii. Ida Cook.
She Married **Jack Welsh**.
228 iii. Jennie Cook.
She Married **Harry Krebs**.
229 iv. Ora Cook.
She Married **Guy Dann**.
230 v. Ethel Cook.
She Married **unknown Miller.**
231 vi. Carl Cook.

42. **Jane Caroline[3] Arbogast** (6.Emanuel[2], 1.George[1]), b. Dec 13 1827 in Pendleton Co., WV, d. Feb 28 1868 in Lexington, McLean Co., IL.
Married Mar-21-1849 in Alleghany Co., MD, **Dr. Charles T. Gray**.

Children:

232 i. Sarah Jane[4] Gray b. 1850, d. 1879.

She Married **Wesley Goddard**.
233 ii. Lucy C Gray b. 1851, d. 1979.
She Married **Shelby Bull.**
234 iii. Amelia C. Gray b. Sep 1583.
She Married **Arthur Scroggin**.
235 iv. Mary V. Gray.
236 v. Walter Gray.

45. **Jeremiah Elderidge[3] Arbogast** (6.Emanuel[2], 1.George[1]), b. Sep 14 1834 in Pendleton Co., WV, d. Oct 02 1895 in Crabbottom, Highland Co., VA, buried in Crabbottom, Highland Co., VA.
He Married **Mary J. Hidy**, b. May-01-1836 in Crabbottom, Highland Co., VA (daughter of John . Hidy and Matilda Penninger), d. Dec-09-1906 in Wimer Family Cem., Pendleton Co., WV.

Children:

\+ 237 i. Carrie E.[4] Arbogast b. Apr-10-1858.
\+ 238 ii. William Gum Arbogast b. Jul-05-1861.
239 iii. John L. Arbogast b. Jul-05-1861 in Highland Co., VA, d. 121281888.

46. **Norval Wilson[3] Arbogast** (6.Emanuel[2], 1.George[1]), b. May 08 1837 in Pendleton Co., WV, d. c 1880 in McLean Co., IL.
Married 1924, **Luvy C, Bishop**, b. 1845 in IL, buried in Kampf Mem. Cem., Wt. Hope, McLean Co., IL.

Children:

240 i. John[4] Arbogast b. c 1871.
241 ii. Elizabeth Arbogast b. c 1873.
242 iii. Fannie Arbogast b. c1874.
243 iv. Eva Arbogast b. c 1875.
244 v. Arabella Arbogast b. c 1877.
245 vi. Grace Arbogast b. c 1877, d. 1938.

51. **James W.[3] Arbogast** (6.Emanuel[2], 1.George[1]), b. About 1848 in Pendleton Co., WV, d. Jun 06 1882 in Tazewell Co., IL.
He Married **Lucy Ann (unknown)**, b. c 1852 in MO.

Children:

246 i. Roberta[4] Arbogast b. Dec-21-1871, d. May-05-1937.
247 ii. Luetta Arbogast b. Jun-15-1873, d. Apr-23-1943.
248 iii. Alice Arbogast b. c1875, d. c 1947.
She Married **John Bishop**.
249 iv. James Arbogast b. c 1876, d. c1945.
250 v. Mary Arbogast b. c1877, d. c1947.
251 vi. Effie Arbogast b. c 1879, d. c 1943.
252 vii. Daisy Arbogast b. Aug-16-1881 in Warrenburg, MO, buried in Pleasant Hill Cem., Lexington, IL, d. Mar-30-1947 in Chicago, Cook Co., IL.
Married Jul-27-1909, **unknown Bishop**.

55. **David Howard[3] Arbogast** (6.Emanuel[2], 1.George[1]), b. Apr 01 1860 in Lexington, McLean Co., IL, d. Sep 11 1948 in Foster, Bates Co., MO.
Married Feb-29-1880 in Lexington, McLean Co., IL, **Rozetta Melvina Rowland**, b. Jun-08-1858 in Macon City, Macon Co., MO (daughter of James M Rowland and Icefine C. Barnet), d. Dec-05-1927 in Foster, Bates Co., MO.

Children:

253 i. Fred D[4] Arbogast b. Jan-03-1881 in MO.
254 ii. Fresalia May Arbogast b. Oct-31-1982 in MO.
255 iii. Dee Lee Arbogast b. Dec-02-1886 in MO.
256 iv. Howard Emanuel Arbogast b. Feb-18-1890 in MO.
257 v. James Rowland Arbogast b. Dec-29-1892.
\+ 258 vi. Ada Neil Arbogast b. Jun-02-1894.
259 vii. Norvall Wilson Arbogast b. Jun-01-1896, d. Oct-23-1951.
260 viii. Grover Cleveland Arbogast b. Nov-04-1884 in MO.
261 ix. Joseph Arbogast b. May-07-1900, d. Feb-14-1955.
262 x. Daisy Arbogast b. Aug-16-1881 in Warrenburg, MO, buried in Pleasant Hill Cem., Lexington, IL, d. Mar-30-1947 in Chicago, Cook Co., IL.
Married Jul-27-1909, **unknown Bishop**.

58. **George E. M.[3] Chew** (8.Mary "Polly"[2] Arbogast, 1.George[1]), b. About 1841 in Crabbottom, Highland Co., VA, d. in Crabbottom, Highland Co., VA.
He Married **Lucinda Arbogast**, b. May 1 1840 in Churchville, Pendleton Co., WV (daughter of Lemuel Arbogast and Susan Bennett), d. Mar 31 1913 in Blue Grass, Highland Co., WV.

Children:

+ 263 i. Saulsberry N[4] Chew b. Dec 1879.
+ 264 ii. Lillie May Chew b. Nov 09 1882.

68. **Orien Austin[3] Arbogast** (10.Henry W.[2], 1.George[1]), b. Jul 16 1898 in Davis, Tucker Co., WV, d. Mar 28 1969 in Homestead, Miami-Dade Co., FL, buried in Parsons, Tucker Co., WV.
He Married **Edith Shrader**.

Children:

265 i. Ernst Arthur[4] Arbogast b. Jul 4 1922 in Thornwood, Pocahontas Co., WV, d. May 4 1975.
Married Jan 26 1945 in Parsons, Tucker Co., WV, Josie Kinsey, b. Apr 18 1918 in Simpson, Taylor Co., WV.
+ 266 ii. Margaret Jean Arbogast b. Apr 13 1924.
+ 267 iii. Kathryn Eloise Arbogast b. Dec 1 1927.
268 iv. Kenneth Alan Arbogast b. Sep 13 1931.

Generation Four

69. **Emily Jane[4] Mullenax** (11.John H.[3], 2.Hannah[2] Arbogast, 1.George[1]).
She Married **James J. Grogg**.

Children:

+ 269 i. Louella Maer[5] Grogg b. Apr 17 1874.

71. **Martha[4] Mullenax** (12.George[3], 2.Hannah[2] Arbogast, 1.George[1]).
Married Nov 24 1842, **Daniel Waybright, Jr.**, b. 1823 in Pendleton Co., WV (son of Daniel Waybright and Rachel Arbogast), d. 1879 in Pendleton Co., WV.

Children:

+ 270 i. Columbus P.[5] Waybright b. Jul 1845.
+ 271 ii. Mary Jane Waybright b. 1847.
+ 272 iii. Albert Waybright b. May 1848.

74. **Samuel Benjamin[4] Arbogast** (14.William Samual[3], 3.Daniel[2], 1.George[1]), b. 10 Dec 1844 in Pendleton Co., VA, d. 8 Jul 1915 in Albemarle Co., VA.
Enlisted in. Enlisted in Company F, Virginia 25th Infantry Regiment on 11 Jun 1861.Mustered out on 01 Apr 1862.
.(1) Married Jan 19 1864, **Margaret Hinkle Teter**, b. Mar 23 1844 in Circleville Pendleton Co., WV, d. Aug 31 1872 in Pendleton Co., WV.

Children:

273 i. Della[5] Arbogast b. 1867 in Pendleton Co., VA, d. Apr-01-1868 in Pendleton Co., VA.
+ 274 ii. Lulu Arbogast b. Mar-19-1869.

(2) Married Dec-27-1874 in Pendleton Co., WV, **Barbara Ellen Harper,**, b. Sep-27-1836 in Pendleton Co., VA (daughter of Jacob Harper and Catherine McClure), d. Sep-27-1936 in Albemarle Co., VA.

Children:

275 iii. Katherine (Kate) Arbogast b. Nov-06-1975 in Circleville Pendleton Co., WV, d. Jul-23-1967 in Charlottesville, Albemarle Co., VA.
276 iv. Richard A. Arbogast b. Aug-10-1877 in Circleville Pendleton Co., WV, d. Apr-13-1954.
277 v. Sarah T. Arbogast b. 1878 in Circleville Pendleton Co., WV, d. 1954 in Earlysville, Va.
Married 1902, **James M. Wood**, b. 1898 in Circleville Pendleton Co., WV, d. 1954 in Earlysville, Va.
278 vi. Mayme L. Arbogast b. Jan-17-1880 in Circleville Pendleton Co., WV, d. after 1974.
279 vii. Frank M. Arbogast, b. 1881 in Circleville Pendleton Co., WV, d. 1942 in Charlottesville, Albemarle Co., VA.
Married 1927, **May Biley**.
280 viii. Jay Arbogast b. 1983 in Locust Dale, VA, d. 1893 in Union Mills, Va.

281 ix. John Paul Arbogast b. Nov-20-1984 in Union Mills, VA, d. Sep 1973 in Alexandria, Va.
Married 1910**, Essie Bruffey**.
282 x. Maggie Belle Arbogast b. 1886 in Union Mills, VA, d. after 1973.
283 xi. Riegart Hamilton Arbogast b. Jul-22-1887 in Union Mills, VA, d. Aug-16-1965 in Lindsay, VA.
Married 1925, **Blanche Bickers**.
284 xii. Marjorie Arbogast b. 1888 in Union Mills, VA, d. after 1865 in prob. Earlysville, Va.
Married 1920, **Henry C. Garrison**.
285 xiii. Ella Arbogast b. 1890 in Union Mills, VA, d. after 1965 in Winter Park, Fl.
Married 1931, **Leo V. Renfro**, b. 1890, d. after1965.

286 xiv. William Harper Arbogast b. Aug-09-1891 in Union Mills, VA, d. Aug-16-1947 in Alexandria, Va.
287 xv. Samuel Benjamin Jr. Arbogast b. 1892, d. 1968 in Charlottesville, Va.
Married 1923, **Carrie Dean**, d. Mar-23-1968.
288 xvi. Barbara Ellen Arbogast b. 1894, d. 1965 to Winter Park, Fl.
Married 1923, **V. R. Lindsay.**
289 xvii. Juanita Maude Arbogast b. 1896, d. 1965 in Prb. Redding, Ca.
Married 1920, **Frank Weast**.

76. **Sallie Amanda[4] Harding** (15.Elizabeth Jane[3] Arbogast, 3.Daniel[2], 1.George[1]), b. May-28-1858, d. 1921 in Staunton, Augusta Co., VA.
She Married **Silis Westly Crummett** (son of Henry Washington Crummett and Amanda Jan Dove), d. Feb 1914 in Staunton, Augusta Co., VA.

Children:

290 i. Silis Berlin[5] Crummett b. May-28-1958, d. 1965.
Married 1915, **Helen Ivy**.
291 ii. Elizabeth Marie Crummett b. 1893, d. 1912.
292 iii. Richard Harting Crummett b. 1897, d. 1967.
Married 1913, **Mary Lou Heavner.**

82. **Lelia Ada[4] Marshall** (18.Mary[3] Arbogast, 3.Daniel[2], 1.George[1]), b. Oct-22-1860 in Buckhannon, Upshur Co., WV, d. Apr-24-1914 in Charlottesville, Albemarle Co., VA.
She Married **William Edwin Wilson**, b. May-15-1854 in Franklin, Pendleton Co., WV (son of John Edwin Wilson and Mary Jane Hille), d. Mar-18-1933 in Charlottesville, Va.

Children:

293 i. Mary Marshall[5] Wilson b. Mar-22-1884 in Franklin, Pendleton Co., WV, d. Jul-18-1957 in Charlottesville, Albemarle Co., VA.
294 ii. Fred Hille Wilson b. Dec-22-1886 in Monterey, Highland Co., VA, d. Oct-16-1960.
He Married **Lola Minton.**
295 iii. William Ronald Wilson b. Mar-13-1888 in Monterey, Highland Co., VA, d. Oct-15-1960.
He Married **Anna Thomas Noakes**.
296 iv. Harry Minor Wilson b. Mar-08-1883 in Monterey, Highland Co., VA, d. 1881.
(1) He Married **Catherine Elizabeth Vasseur**.
(2) He Married **Myrtle Watts Haggerty**.
297 v. Lelia Alice Wilson b. Apr-13-1885 in Monterey, Highland Co., VA, d. Apr-01-1960 in Charlottesville, Albemarle Co., VA.
298 vi. Lois Wilson b. May-23-1881 in Charlottesville, Albemarle Co., VA, d. 1984,.

88. **Emmett Benjamin[4] Arbogast** (19.Benjamin Franklin[3], 3.Daniel[2], 1.George[1]), b. May-28-1876 in Lexington, McLean Co., IL, d. May-02-1950 in Cleveland, MS.
Married Nov-24-1897, **Mildred E. Baird**.

Children:

299 i. Mildred[5] Arbogast b. May-29-1900, d. Oct-15-1919 in Lexington, McLean Co., IL.
300 ii. Theodore Emmett Arbogast, b. Dec-27-1901 in Lexington, McLean Co., IL, d. Oct-03-1972 in Cleveland, MS.
301 iii. Franklin Martin Arbogast b. 1907, d. 1967 in Memphis, TN.
302 iv. Duane Jennings Arbogast, b. Sep-24-1914, d. Feb-08-1975 in Memphis, TN.

89. **Emery Matthew[4] Arbogast** (21.John Wesley[3], 3.Daniel[2], 1.George[1]), b. Jun-01-1862 in Crabbottom, Highland Co., VA, d. Dec-28-1929 in Los Angeles Co., CA.

Information on this family from, At The Sign Of The Swan, Ancestry and Descendants of Hans Wendell Swecker, by Amanda Arbogast Forbes, Gateway Press, Baltimore, MD, 1987, copy in file. "Through investments in timber land and real estate, Emory became a wealthy man. He was sheriff of Highland County, VA, following his father, from 1889 to 1899 but moved to Marlinton, WV about 1900. He later moved to Winchester, KY and about 1924, moved to Los Angeles, CA. He returned frequently to visit in Highland County and Marlinton".
Married 2231881 in Highland Co., VA, **Annie Laurie Mc Nulty**, b. Jun-07-1868 in Highland Co., VA, d. Feb-18-1952 in Albuquerque, Bernalillo Co., NM.

Children:

\+ 303 i. Elmo Mead^{5} Arbogast b. Jun-26-1883.
304 ii. John Robert Arbogast b. Jul-04-1897 in Monterey, Highland Co., VA, d. 1987 in New Cumberland, Hancock Co., WV.
Married Jun-06-1925, **Grace Helen Dare**, b. Jun-10-1903, d. Oct 1974.
\+ 305 iii. Virginia Arbogast.

92. **Arthur William^{4} Arbogast** (21.John Wesley^{3}, 3.Daniel^{2}, 1.George^{1}), b. May-20-1869 in Crabbottom, Highland Co., VA, d. Jun-12-1934 in Hematite, Allegheny, Virginia, buried in Monterey Cem., Monterey, Highland Co., VA.
Married Dec-31-1912 in Alderson, WV, **Teresa "Tessie" Dougher**, b. Aug-02-1885 in Tuscarora, Pa, d. Jul-09-1872 in White Sulphur Springs, Greenbrier Co., VA.

Children:

\+ 306 i. John Arthur^{5} Arbogast b. May-29-1869.
\+ 307 ii. Charles Edward Arbogast b. Mar-05-1915.
\+ 308 iii. Robert William Arbogast b. Jun-11-1916.
309 iv. James Alexander Arbogast b. Nov 10 in Ronceverte, Greenbrier Co., WV, d. Mar-15-1986 in Fairlea, Greenbrier Co., WV.
310 v. Ralph Thomas Arbogast, b. Aug-13-1926 in White Sulphur Springs, Greenbrier Co., WV.
311 vi. John Scott Arbogast b. Nov-24-1988 in Roanoke, Roanoke Co., VA.

93. **Charles Cameron^{4} Arbogast** (21.John Wesley^{3}, 3.Daniel^{2}, 1.George^{1}), b. Sep-10-1871 in Monterey, Highland Co., VA, d. Apr-04-1940 in Monterey, Highland Co., VA, buried in Monterey Cem., Monterey, Highland Co., VA.
Married Apr 1913 in Grant Co. WV, **Katherine Viola Naedle**, b. Nov-27-1887 in Petersburg Area, VA, d. Feb-02-1942 in Marysville, WV. Widow of Williams Naedle

Children:

\+ 312 i. Russell Cameron^{5} Arbogast b. Apr-14-1914.
\+ 313 ii. Paul Gae Arbogast b. Feb-02-1916.

94. **John Edwin^{4} Arbogast** (21.John Wesley^{3}, 3.Daniel^{2}, 1.George^{1}), b. Jan-16-1877 in Monterey, Highland Co., VA, d. May-06-1954 in Monterey, Highland Co., VA, buried in Monterey Cem., Monterey, Highland Co., VA.
Married Jul-25-1912 in Parnassus, Augusta Co., VA, **Margaret Crawford Gilkeson**, b. Oct-03-1885 in Parnassus, Augusta Co., VA (daughter of Aurelius Rodney Gilkerson and Mary Elizabeth Hiner), d. Jun-07-1967 in Charlottesville, Albemarle Co., VA.

Children:

\+ 314 i. Amanda Crawford^{5} Arbogast b. Aug-16-1920.

99. **Arthur William^{4} Arbogast** (21.John Wesley^{3}, 3.Daniel^{2}, 1.George^{1}), b. May-29-1969 in Crabbottom, Highland Co., VA, d. Jun-12-1934 in Hematite, Allegheny, Virginia.
Married Dec-31-1912 in Alderson Cem., Greenbrier Co., WV, **Teresa Dougher**.

Children:

\+ 315 i. Robert William^{5} Arbogast b. Jun 11 1916.
\+ 316 ii. James Alexander Arbogast b. Nov-02-1918.
\+ 317 iii. Ralph Thomas Arbogast b. Aug-13-1926.

101. **Orien Austin^{4} Arbogast** (22.Henry W.^{3}, 3.Daniel^{2}, 1.George^{1}), b. Feb-12-1870, d. Sep-30-1929.
Married May-28-1897, **Ida Huffman**, b. Nov 18 1872, d. Sep 25 1950.

Children:

318 i. Roscoe^{5} Arbogast.
He Married **Edith Shrader**.
319 ii. Frank Arbogast b. Jul 7 1912, d. 1979.
320 iii. Leo Arbogast b. May-16-1900 in Davis, Tucker Co., WV, d. Dec 1980 in Florida.
\+ 321 iv. Delbert E. Arbogast, b. Dec-02-1902.

104. **Ida Florence⁴ Arbogast** (22.Henry W.³, 3.Daniel², 1.George¹), b. Jun-09-1874, d. Sep-02-1967 in Morgantown, Monongalia Co., WV.
Married Jul-04-1873 in Cumberland, Alleghany Co., MD, **B. Franklin H. Ketterman**, b. Apr-28-1867.

Children:

322 i. Glenn Whitter[5] Ketterman b. Jan-26-1893 in Davis, Tucker Co., WV.
323 ii. Randall Ketterman b. Apr-28-1867 in Harmon, WV, d. 1914.
324 iii. Otto Ketterman b. Feb-09-1897 in Riverton, Pendleton Co., WV, d. 1902.
325 iv. Okareda Ketterman, b. Aug-15-1899 in Davis, Tucker Co., WV, d. 1944.
326 v. Nell Ketterman b. Feb-14-1901 in Davis, Tucker Co., WV, d. After 1975.
327 vi. Jody Ketterman, b. Jul-03-1903 in Coalton, WV.

105. **Lorena Elizabeth[4] Arbogast** (22.Henry W.[3], 3.Daniel[2], 1.George[1]), b. Oct-11-1878, d. Oct-31-1958 in Clarksburg, Harrison Co., VA.
She Married **A. J. Lowthers**.

Children:

328 i. Jewell Wilmington[5] Lowthers b. Oct-11-1876 in Davis, Tucker Co., WV.
329 ii. Pearl Williams Lowthers b. Dec-06-1888.

108. **George Washington[4] Sponaugle** (23.William[3], 4.Elizabeth L.[2] Arbogast, 1.George[1]), b. Jan 25 1846 in Hunting Ground, Pendleton Co., (W)VA, d. Jan 15 1928 in Zigler, Smith Creek, Pendleton Co., WV, buried UNKNOWN in Sponaugle Cem., Smith Creek, Pendleton Co., WV.

NOTE from Pendleton City, Past and Present, page 216 - George Washington Sponaugle was 15 years old when he volunteered for service in the Confederate Army of the Civil War, at Hightown, Virginia. The year was1861. He was in Company "E" of the 25th Virginia Regiment. During the winter of 1861-62, George was at West View, several miles west of Staunton, Virginia. He fought in several battles under Stonewall Jackson and also fought in the battle of Gettysburg. George is buried in Sponaugle Cemetery, Smith Creek, Pendleton City, WV.

George was born Jan 25, 1846 on Hunting Ground and was the son of William and Minerva (Teter) Sponaugle. He was the oldest of 11 children, all large and strong. William provided for his family by hunting the game that was plentiful on Hunting Ground. George was a great hunter using muzzle-loading rifle,

After the war, on December 25, 1867, George Married Elizabeth Susan Judy. She was the daughter of John and Mary Lambert Judy. They made their home on Smith Creek, at the lower end of John Judy's land. They raised 9 children, all of them being of large stature. George provided
or his family by farming and hunting.

Elizabeth died of breast cancer on March 28, 1907. George died of stomach cancer on Jan. 15, 1928, just 10 days from his 82nd birthday. They are buried in the Sponaugle family cemetery on Smith Creek.

Notes: 25th VA Infantry & 9th Battalion VA Infantry by Richard L Armstrong Sponaugle, George W - Private. 2nd Company E. (b - Smith Creek,1844, age 16, laborer, Franklin, Pendleton Co, VA/WV, 1860 census. Enlisted Camp Shenandoah April 5, 1862, age 16 (?), Absent 4/30/1862 to2/28/1863, deserted. Served in 2nd Co. C, 62nd VA Mtd. Infantry. Postwar resident of Zigler and Franklin, WV. Age 35, carpenter, Circleville District, Pendleton Co, WV, 1880 census.

Married Dec 25 1867 in Pendleton Co., WV, **Elizabeth Susan Judy**, b. in Smith Creek, Pendleton Co., WV, d. Mar 28 1907 in Smith Creek, Pendleton Co., WV.

Children:

\+ 330 i. Serilda C[5] Sponaugle b. Nov 01 1868.
\+ 331 ii. Carrie E Sponaugle b. May 12 1870.
\+ 332 iii. Minerva Sponaugle b. Jan 20 1873.
\+ 333 iv. William Okay Sponaugle b. Aug 25 1875.
\+ 334 v. Green Judy Sponaugle b. Oct 19 1877.
\+ 335 vi. Mary Perlie Sponaugle b. Apr 23 1880.
\+ 336 vii. Martha Lucretia Sponaugle b. Apr 29 1882.
337 viii. Savannah E Sponaugle b. Jul 04 1885 in Pendleton Co., WV, d. Feb 26 1962.
She Married **Whitney D Simmons**,
\+ 338 ix. George Arthur Sponaugle b. Jul 18 1887.

109. **Mary Catherine[4] Sponaugle** (23.William[3], 4.Elizabeth L.[2] Arbogast, 1.George[1]), b. Sep 15 1847 in Hunting Ground, Pendleton Co., (W)VA, d. Jun 17 1922 in Middle Timber Ridge, Pendleton Co., WV.
Married Apr 12 1870 in Pendleton Co., WV, **Christopher Columbus Thompson**, b. MAR 1844 in Riverton, Pendleton Co., WV, d. 1921 in Middle Timber Ridge, Pendleton Co., WV.

Children:

339 i. William Lee[5] Wimer b. MAR 1866, d. WFT Est 1907-1957.
(1) Married May 20 1887, **Salome Cooper**, b. APR 1863, d. ABT 1900.
(2) Married Mar 10 1902, **Mary B. Harman**, b. ABT 1875, d. ABT 1922 in Columbus, Franklin Co., OH.
\+ 340 ii. Mary Ida Teter b. 1869.
\+ 341 iii. Jenettie Catherine Thompson b. Jan 10 1871.
\+ 342 iv. Melissa A. Thompson b. ABT 1873.
\+ 343 v. Jacob Kenny Thompson b. Mar 15 1874.
\+ 344 vi. Sylvanus Harper Thompson b. Dec 15 1875.
\+ 345 vii. James C. Thompson b. ABT 1878.
346 viii. Arthur Columbus Thompson b. Jul 2 1880, d. Nov 25 1963.
Married, **Alice B. Simmons**, .
\+ 347 ix. Opie Enders Thompson b. JAN 1882.
348 x. Virginia Alfa Thompson b. Dec 22 1883 in Pendleton Co., WV, d. Mar 31 1972.
Married, **Isaac J. Arbaugh**, b. Apr 26 1878 in Churchville, Pendleton Co., WV, d. Jul 15 1964 in Newark, Licking Co., OH.
349 xi. Emory G. Thompson b. Nov 22 1889 in Pendleton Co., WV, d. Aug 14 1966 in Cass, Pocahontas Co., WV.
Married Dec 13 1914 in Churchville, Pendleton Co., WV, **Mary J. Mallow**, b. FEB 1896, d. ABT 1982.

110. **William Jackson[4] Sponaugle** (23.William[3], 4.Elizabeth L.[2] Arbogast, 1.George[1]), b. Nov 08 1849 in Highland Co., VA, d. Dec 26 1883 in Doddridge Co., WV.
(1) Married Feb 17 1867, **Lucinda Lamb**,
(2) Married c1872, **Sarah C.E. Dinkle**, d. 1942, buried in Clover Hill, Rockingham Co., VA.

Children:

\+ 350 i. Arthur Dinkle[5] Sponaugle b. Jan 14 1874.
351 ii. Martin Luther Sponaugle b. About 1875.
Maybe born in Lewis County, WV.
352 iii. Florence Sponaugle b. Abt 1878 in Churchville, Pendleton Co., WV.
353 iv. Charles H. Sponaugle b. July 1880 in Pendleton Co., WV.
Married Jan-28-1903 in Rockingham Co., VA, **Savilla F.Kible,** b. Dec 1977.
354 v. Ollie B. Sponaugle b. July 1880.
Married Dec-29-1898 in Rockingham Co., VA, **John L. Thacker**.
355 vi. Willie Elizabeth Sponaugle b. Mar 15 1884 in Doddridge Co., WV, d. May 23 1972 in Harrisonburg, Rockingham Co., VA, buried in Clover Hill, Rockingham Co., VA.
Married Mar 15 1905 in Rockbridge Co., VA, **Jon Solomon Garber**.

111. **Elizabeth Jane[4] Sponaugle** (23.William[3], 4.Elizabeth L.[2] Arbogast, 1.George[1]), b. Mar 10 1854, d. Apr 29 1919.
Married Sep 20 1874 in Randolph Co., WV, **John Francis Louk**, b. 1850, d. Jan 10 1893.

Children:

\+ 356 i. Flora Anna[5] Louk b. Jun 12 1876.
357 ii. Webster Beef Louk b. Nov 03 1877, d. Jan-10-1993.
Did not marry.
358 iii. Martha Jane Louk b. Feb 20 1879, d. 1930.
She Married **Clinton F. Taylor**, b. 1873, d. 1960 in Randolph County, WV.
\+ 359 iv. Ora Idella Louk b. Apr-10-1882.
\+ 360 v. Ida Louella Louk b. Apr 10 1882.
361 vi. William Fred Louk b. Aug 01 1888, d. 1919.
Buried in Military Cemetery in France from WW I. From Elkins, WV.
Married **Viola Smith** 15 Sep 1914.
\+ 362 vii. Jessie Lucy Louk b. Jan 17 1892.

112. **Lucy A.[4] Sponaugle** (23.William[3], 4.Elizabeth L.[2] Arbogast, 1.George[1]), b. 1856.
(1) She Married **James C Teeter**, d. UNKNOWN.
(2) She Married **Louis Clark Teter**, b. 1856, (son of John Jackson Teter and Leah Sponaugle), d. WFT Est 1884-1947.

Children:

363 i. Alfred[5] Teter b. 1878 in Tucker Co., WV.
364 ii. Martha Teter b. 1880.

113. **Adam Harness^4 Sponaugle** (23.William^3, 4.Elizabeth L.^{2} Arbogast, 1.George^1), b. Feb 4 1858 in Pendleton Co., WV, d. Sep 6 1945 in Randolph Co., WV.
(1) Married Dec 20 1876 in Pendleton Co., WV, **Ann (Rebecca) Ketterman**, b. About 1855 in Pendleton Co., WV, d. UNKNOWN.

Children:

- 365 i. Verlie Berlie^5 Sponaugle d. UNKNOWN.
- 366 ii. Ostella Sponaugle d. UNKNOWN.
- \+ 367 iii. James Dyer Sponaugle b. Mar 23 1878.

(2) Married Jun 22 1881 in Pendleton Co., WV, **Sarah Jane Nelson**, d. Apr 26 1944 in Churchville, Pendleton Co., WV, b. May 24 1856 in Pendleton Co., WV. Daughter of Isaac J. NELSON and Susan PORTER.

Children:

- 368 iv. Annabelle Sponaugle b. Mar 12 1880 in Randolph Co., WV, b. Mar 12 1880 in Osceola Randolph Co., WV, d. Jun 8 1894 in Randolph Co., WV, buried in Nelson Fam. Cem., Timber Ridge, WV.
- \+ 369 v. Lee Paris Sponaugle b. Mar 17 1882.
- \+ 370 vi. John Alonzo Sponaugle b. Feb 9 1884.
- 371 vii. William Cleveland Sponaugle b. Mar 8 1886 in Randolph Co., WV, d. Jun 8 1968.
  (1) Married May 30 1908 in Pendleton Co., WV, **Lillie M Vandevander** (daughter of Joe Irvin Vandevander and Mahala Caton), d. Jun-20-1892, d. Oct-20-1934.
  (2) He Married **Dorothy Lee Howell**, .
- 372 viii. Louvary Sponaugle b. Jul 7 1888 in Job, Randolph Co., WV, d. Feb 16 1902 in Timber Ridge, Hampshire Co., WV, buried in Nelson Fam. Cem., Timber Ridge, WV.
- \+ 373 ix. Zola Adam Sponaugle b. Jul 7 1890.
- \+ 374 x. Fannie Minerva Sponaugle b. Aug 25 1892.
- \+ 375 xi. Martha Hester Sponaugle b. Jan 25 1894.
- \+ 376 xii. Monna Roxie Sponaugle b. Jun 3 1896.

114. **Eli Perry^4 Sponaugle** (23.William^3, 4.Elizabeth L.^{2} Arbogast, 1.George^1), d. Oct 27 1923.
Married Oct 23 1873, **Anna Rebecca Kile**, d. Jul 03 1920, b. Oct 23 1855.

Children:

- 377 i. Eli^5 Sponaugle.
- 378 ii. Carrie Ellen Sponaugle b. Jun 26 1874, d. Oct 11 1944.
- \+ 379 iii. Charles Walter Sponaugle b. Mar 04 1876.
- 380 iv. Albert Sponaugle b. Sep 11 1877, d. Jul 03 1928.
  He Married unknown Shreves.
- 381 v. William C. Sponaugle b. Mar 12 1879, d. Feb 28 1956.
  He Married Myrtle O'Hara, d. Dec-14-1936.
- 382 vi. Emery Sponaugle b. Jan 10 1881, d. July 1962.
- 383 vii. Lillian Sponaugle b. Mar 05 1884.
- 384 viii. C. H. Sponaugle b. Jul 08 1889.
- 385 ix. Florence Sponaugle b. Aug 19 1897.

115. **John Wesley^4 Sponaugle** (23.William^3, 4.Elizabeth L.^{2} Arbogast, 1.George^1), b. Mar 16 1860, d. WFT Est 1909-1952.
Married Jan 13 1887 in Randolph Co., WV, **Isabelle Cunningham**, b. Nov 27 1865, d. 1942.

Children:

- 386 i. Alpha^5 Sponaugle b. Dec 14 1887, d. Feb 16 1960.
  Married Jul-07-1908, **Melvin E. Hickman.**
- 387 ii. Renaz Sponaugle b. Sep 11 1889, d. WFT Est 1890-1983.
- 388 iii. Alvin Sponaugle b. Nov 3 1891, d. WFT Est 1892-1981.
- 389 iv. Minerva Malenna Sponaugle b. Feb 16 1894, d. WFT Est 1895-1988.
- \+ 390 v. Tiny Sponaugle b. Jul 23 1896.
- 391 vi. Brian Sponaugle b. Aug 19 1900, d. WFT Est 1901-1990.
- 392 vii. Bricie Sponaugle b. Aug 19 1900, d. 1989 in Bartow, Polk Co., FL.
- 393 viii. Jessie Sponaugle b. Feb 7 1903, d. 1989 in Parsons, Tucker Co., WV.
- 394 ix. Bodkin Sponaugle b. WFT Est 1882-1908, d. WFT Est 1888-1988.
- 395 x. Bessie Sponaugle .
- 396 xi. William Clarence Sponaugle .
- 397 xii. Lennie Sponaugle .
- 398 xiii. Lorenza Sponaugle .

116. **Martha[4] Sponaugle** (23.William[3], 4.Elizabeth L.[2] Arbogast, 1.George[1]), b. 1862.
Married Nov 23 1882, **Frederick Bodie**, d. in Doddridge Co., WV, b. 1855 in Doddridge Co., WV. Son of William BODIE and Margaret M. BODIE.

Children:

399 i. Willie[5] Bodie b. About 1882.

117. **Haymond[4] Sponaugle** (23.William[3], 4.Elizabeth L.[2] Arbogast, 1.George[1]), b. Dec 25 1864, d. Dec 15 1952.
(1) Married May 11 1887 in Randolph Co., WV, **Charlotte White**, b. DEC 1868, d. WFT Est 1899-1962.

Children:

400 i. William B.[5] Sponaugle b. 1887, d. WFT Est 1888-1977.

401 ii. Brooks Sponaugle b. JAN 1889, d. WFT Est 1890-1979.
402 iii. Pearl Sponaugle b. 1891, d.
She Married **unknown Schwartz**.
403 iv. Woodford Sponaugle b. 1893,
404 v. Harry W. Sponaugle b. 1896,
405 vi. Grover Sponaugle .
406 vii. Thelma Sponaugle .
(2) Married Sep 4 1911 in Randolph Co., WV, **Anna White**, b. WFT Est 1861-1894, d. WFT Est 1916-1981.

Children:

407 viii. Frank Sponaugle
408 ix. Edith Sponaugle
409 x. Muriel Sponaugle .
410 xi. Georgia Sponaugle .
411 xii. John W. Sponaugle .

118. **Levi[4] Sponaugle** (23.William[3], 4.Elizabeth L.[2] Arbogast, 1.George[1]), b. Feb 28 1868 in Randolph Co., WV, d. Mar 1 1949 in Canada.
Married Jun 30 1892 in Randolph Co., WV, **Lucy Birdella Pennington**, b. Feb 04 1872 in Randolph Co., WV, d. 1955.

Children:

412 i. William Cody[5] Sponaugle b. Mar 28 1893 in Pendleton Co., WV, d. SEP 1969 in Kamloops, Brit. Columbia, Canada.
Married Jun 23 1917 in Alberta, Canada, Zilla McGhee, d. UNKNOWN.
\+ 413 ii. Delbert Sponaugle b. Apr 08 1900.

120. **Robert Boyd[4] Sponaugle** (24.George Washington[3], 4.Elizabeth L.[2] Arbogast, 1.George[1]), b. May 26 1868 in Hunting Ground, Pendleton Co., (W)VA, d. Jan 19 1942.
She Married **Louisa Vent**.

Children:

414 i. George C.[5] Sponaugle.
He Married **Mable Warner**, b. Aug-13-1910 in Hunting Ground, Pendleton Co., (W)VA (daughter of Charles Warner and Mary Ellen Wimer).

121. **Debby Jane[4] Sponaugle** (24.George Washington[3], 4.Elizabeth L.[2] Arbogast, 1.George[1]), b. Aug 01 1870 in Hunting Ground, Pendleton Co., (W)VA, d. Jan 26 1960, buried in Cedar Hill Cem., Pendleton Co., WV.
(1) She Married **Amby H. Warner**, b. Jun 20 1868 in Hunting Ground, Pendleton Co., (W)VA, d. Jun 19 1955, buried in Warner Cem., Hunting Ground, Pendleton Co., VA/WV.

Children:

415 i. Okey[5] Oscar Warner.
416 ii. Curtis R. Warner b. Jun 16 1904, d. Jul 9 1980.
He Married **Bessie R Warner**, b. Dec 2 1924 in West Virginia (daughter of Amby H. Warner and Surrilda Florence Waybright).

(2) She Married **John W. Warner**, b. May 15 1874 in Pendleton Co., WV, d. Sep 5 1960, buried in Warner Cem., Hunting Ground, Pendleton Co., VA/WV.

Children:

417 iii. William J. Warner b. Aug 1894 in Churchville, Pendleton Co., WV, d. Nov 1969.

(1) He Married **Martha Clayton**.
(2) He Married **Lou Warner Hedrick.**

418 iv. Alice Etta Warner b. Aug 12 1898 in Churchville, Pendleton Co., WV, d. Nov 1 1970.
She Married **Charles Zickefoose**, b. Aug 1893, d. Feb 1968.

419 v. Adam Harness Warner b. Jun 30 1902 in Churchville, Pendleton Co., WV, d. Nov 1987 in Harrisonburg, Rockingham Co., VA.
He Married **Jessie Elza** (daughter of James Elza and Zella Swagger).

123. **Adam Harness[4] Sponaugle** (24.George Washington[3], 4.Elizabeth L.[2] Arbogast, 1.George[1]), b. Mar 12 1878 in Hunting Ground, Pendleton Co., (W)VA, d. Oct 27 1968 in Cherry Grove, Pendleton Co., WV.
He Married **Levi Lillian Moyers** (daughter of Henry Markwood Moyers and Ann Elizabeth Waybright).

Children:

\+ 420 i. Omar Wilson[5] Sponaugle b. May 21 1921.

137. **Ruth[4] Teter** (26.Catherine[3] Sponaugle, 4.Elizabeth L.[2] Arbogast, 1.George[1]), b. c182.
Married Jun-23-1881, **James Patrick Wymer**, b. Feb 7 1861 in Hunting Ground, Pendleton Co., (W)VA, (son of Jacob Wimer and Mary Elizabeth Sponaugle), d. Oct 22 1926 in Evenwood, Randolph Co., WV.

Children:

421 i. Ory Ester[5] Wymer b. 1882.
422 ii. Artie Wymer b. 1886.
423 iii. Belvie Wymer b. 1890.
He Married **Riley Hedrick**.
\+ 424 iv. Mary Elizabeth Wymer b. 1895.
425 v. Dillon Wymer b. 1892.
He Married **Zona Tingler.**
426 vi. I.H. Wymer b. Oct-05-1900, d. Mar-01-1901.
427 vii. Ora Ester Wymer b. 1882.
He Married **Anna R. Killingsworth**.

139. **Mary Elizabeth[4] Teter** (26.Catherine[3] Sponaugle, 4.Elizabeth L.[2] Arbogast, 1.George[1]), b. Jan 27 1853, d. Apr 19 1886.

She Married **John A. Warner**, b. Aug-13-1848.

Children:

428 i. Okey[5] Warner.
He Married **Ann Turner**.
\+ 429 ii. Walter Warner b. May-18-1874.
430 iii. Alvah Warner.
431 iv. Blanche Warner.
432 v. Flick Warner.
433 vi. Glenn Warner.
434 vii. Chloe Warner.

142. **Cecelia (Celia)[4] Sponaugle** (27.Lewis Martin[3], 4.Elizabeth L.[2] Arbogast, 1.George[1]), b. Aug 4 1859 in Hunting Ground, Pendleton Co., (W)VA, d. May 27 1914.
(1) Married Jan-31-1885, **Ashby Warner**, b. Jan 1862.

Children:

435 i. Lurie M.[5] Warner b. Dec 1895.
She Married **Alonzo Clarence Arbaugh**, b. Nov 1883. Information from, Teter Descendants of Hans Jorg and Maria Dieter, by Eva A. (Teter) Winfield of Ridgeley, WV, 1992.
436 ii. Thurman Warner b. Nov 1888, d. Dec-01-1888.
437 iii. J. Lloyd Warner b. Jun 1887.
438 iv. Laura Alice Warner b. Oct 1889, d. 1920.
She Married **Albert Solon Nelson**, b. Jul 1882, buried in Teter Gap, Circleville, Pendleton Co., WV, d. 1958.
\+ 439 v. Tina Warner b. Sep-12-1892.
\+ 440 vi. Zola Denver Warner b. Jul 1893.
441 vii. Roy Warner b. Jun 1885, d. 1918.
442 viii. Jesse Warner b. Oct 1897.
He Married **Mary Warner**.

+ 443 ix. Grace Warner b. Jul 1899.
444 x. Zoa Warner.
445 xi. Steelman Warner b. Oct 1902, d. Oct 1902.
446 xii. infant Warner b. 1903, d. 1903.

(2) She Married **Pearlie Thompson**.

143. **Susan⁴ Sponaugle** (27.Lewis Martin³, 4.Elizabeth L.² Arbogast, 1.George¹), b. Feb 17 1861 in Hunting Ground, Pendleton Co., (W)VA, d. Aug-14-1910.
Married 1892 in Hunting Ground, Pendleton Co. WV, **Martin John Raines**, b. Aug-26-1848 in Pendleton Co., VA, d. Dec-12-1896 in Pendleton Co., WV.

Children:

447 i. Sylvester⁵ Raines b. 1857.
+ 448 ii. Mary Alice Raines b. Sep-18-1892.
449 iii. George W Raines.
450 iv. Phoebe Ellen Raines.
451 v. Virginia Raines.

145. **Phoebe E.⁴ Sponaugle** (27.Lewis Martin³, 4.Elizabeth L.² Arbogast, 1.George¹), b. Apr 18 1864 in Hunting Ground, Pendleton Co., (W)VA, d. Feb 6 1938, buried in Jacob Sponaugle Cem., Pendleton Co. WV.
She Married **John Wesley Warner**, b. 1849, d. 1929.

Children:

452 i. Bertha A.⁵ Sponaugle b. Sep 1885.
Bertha was the daughter of Wm. L. Jackson Sponaugle, son of Jesse.
453 ii. Verdie N. Warner b. May 1888.
454 iii. Don W. Warner b. Apr-18-1890, d. Apr-06-1973.
455 iv. Ellis C, Warner b. Aug 1893.
456 v. Ezra Thurman Warner b. May-13-1894, d. Nov-20-1968.
He Married **Vergie Vandevander**, b. May-12-1906 in Cherry Grove, Pendleton Co., WV (daughter of Henry Vandevander and Alice Howdtshell), d. Jun-21-1980.
457 vi. Lester Warner b. May-1898.
458 vii. Darrie E. Warner b. Mar-20-1900, d. Oct-04-1982.
Married Jul-02-1924, **Michael Smith**, b. Oct-29-1898 in Riverton, Pendleton Co., WV, d. Jul-15-1998 in Davis Memorial Hospital, Elkins, Randolph Co., WV.
459 viii. Delmar R. Warner b. 1903, d. Sep 1981.
He Married **Kte Bennett**, b. 1929.
460 ix. Zona Warner b. 1906.
461 x. Richard Warner b. 1911, d. Mar-9-1964.
462 xi. Stanley Warner b. 1912, d. Feb-01-1938.

147. **Martha Alice⁴ Sponaugle** (27.Lewis Martin³, 4.Elizabeth L.² Arbogast, 1.George¹), b. May 30 1868 in Hunting Ground, Pendleton Co., (W)VA, d.
(1) She Married **Paschal Warner**.

Children:

+ 463 i. Mary Clara⁵ Warner b. Oct-27-1890.
464 ii. Eva L. Sponaugle b. Dec 1899.
465 iii. Infant Warner.
(
2) She Married **Joel Teter**.

149. **Norman⁴ Sponaugle** (27.Lewis Martin³, 4.Elizabeth L.² Arbogast, 1.George¹), b. May 2 1873 in Hunting Ground, Pendleton Co., (W)VA, d. Jan 11 1939.
(1) He Married **Lottie Raines**, b. about 1874.

Children:

466 i. Lester⁵ Sponaugle b. Apr-22-1896, d. 1900.
467 ii. Kennie Sponaugle b. Dec-31-1905 in Hunting Ground, Pendleton Co., (W)VA, d. Feb-09-1992 in Franklin, Pendleton Co., WV.

(1) He Married **Ella Vandevander**, b. Mar-23-1903 (daughter of Jacob Lee Vandevander and Mahala Caton), d. 1931.
(2) He Married **Lizetta Hedrick**, b. 1910 (daughter of Leonard Hedrick and Betty Puffenburger).

468 iii. Coy Sponaugle b. 1908.
He Married **Eva Vent** (daughter of Isaac Vent and Esta Maude Nelson).

469 iv. Gracie Hicle Sponaugle b. Mar-23-1910 in Hunting Ground, Pendleton Co., (W)VA, d. May-24-1978.
Married Oct-16-1929, **Henry Edward Hartman**, b. Apr-17-1891, d. Nov-12-1959 in Harrisonburg, Rockingham Co., VA.

470 v. Georgie E. Sponaugle b. 1912 in Hunting Ground, Pendleton Co., (W)VA.
Married Oct-23-1930, **Robert French Raines**, b. Mar-12-1905 in Riverton, Pendleton Co., WV (son of Watson Raines and Della Bland), d. Oct-03-1972.

471 vi. Comie Sponaugle.

472 vii. Theodore Sponaugle b. May-11-1915 in Hunting Ground, Pendleton Co., (W)VA, d. Jul-12-1990 in Hunting Ground, Pendleton Co., (W)VA.
He Married **Edith Thompson**.

473 viii. John Opie Sponaugle.
He Married **Dora Lou Bennett**, b. in Hunting Ground, Pendleton Co., (W)VA.

474 ix. Mazie Belle Sponaugle b. Feb-22-1927 in Hunting Ground, Pendleton Co., (W)VA, buried in Oak Lawn Gardens Staunton Augusta Co., VA, d. 1964 in Staunton, Augusta Co., VA.
Married Oct-12-1947, **Elmer L. Nicely**.

(2) Married May-21-1960, **Ardena Bennett**, b. May-06-1885.

152. **James Patrick[4] Wymer** (28.Mary Elizabeth[3] Sponaugle, 4.Elizabeth L.[2] Arbogast, 1.George[1]) (See marriage to number 137.)

154. **Sylverius[4] Wimer** (28.Mary Elizabeth[3] Sponaugle, 4.Elizabeth L.[2] Arbogast, 1.George[1]), b. Sep 23 1865 in Hunting Ground, Pendleton Co., (W)VA, d. Sep 28 1943 in Hunting Ground, Pendleton Co., (W)VA.
At the time of his death Sylvester was living with Maggie Arbogast Bennett back of Spruce Knob Lake. (Huffman research).
Married Dec-05-1890, **Martha Susan Thompson**, b. Aug-20-1866 in Timberridge, Pendleton Co., WV (daughter of Amos Thompson and Mary Hedrick), buried in Wilmer Cem, Hunting Ground, Pendleton Co., (W)VA, d. Mar-13-1955 in Hunting Ground, Pendleton Co., (W)VA.

Children:

\+ 475 i. Albert Harness[5] Wimer b. Apr-27-1891.
\+ 476 ii. Mary Ellen Wimer b. Oct-07-1892.
\+ 477 iii. Hassie Blanche Wimer b. Sep-20-1994.
\+ 478 iv. Lou Catherine Wimer b. Apr-08-1896.
\+ 479 v. Charles Amos Wimer b. Mar-20-1898.
480 vi. George Wimer b. May-21-1901 in Hunting Ground, Pendleton Co. WV, buried in Hunting Ground, Pendleton Co. WV, d. Jul-28-1906.

158. **Albert[4] Wimer** (28.Mary Elizabeth[3] Sponaugle, 4.Elizabeth L.[2] Arbogast, 1.George[1]), b. Apr 22 1877 in Hunting Ground, Pendleton Co., (W)VA, d. Sep 24 1946 in Harrisonburg, Rockingham Co., VA, buried in Sponaugle Family Cem., Hunting Grounds Pendleton County WV.
Married Jul-22-1901, **Rachel Milvinie Thompson**, b. Aug-05-1883 in Timber Ridge, Pendleton Co.,, WV (daughter of Amos Thompson and Mary Hedrick), buried in Thompson Cem. Timber ridge, Pendleton Co., WV, d. Mar-02-1978 in Colonial Beach, Westmoreland Co., VA.

Children:

\+ 481 i. Carson Elmer[5] Wymer b. Apr-03-1902.
\+ 482 ii. Maycel Wimer b. Aug-09-1911.
\+ 483 iii. Treve Mary Wimer b. Jul-18-1914.
484 iv. Freda Wimer b. Jul-18-1914, buried in Wimer Cem, Hunting Ground, Pendleton Co., WV, d. Jul-18-1914.

159. **Tiberius[4] Wimer** (28.Mary Elizabeth[3] Sponaugle, 4.Elizabeth L.[2] Arbogast, 1.George[1]), b. May-19-1973 in Hunting Ground, Pendleton Co. WV, buried in Wimer Cem, Hunting Ground, Pendleton Co., WV, d. Dec-28-1952 in Harrisonburg, Rockingham Co., VA.
Married Apr-24-1895 in Timber Ridge, Pendleton Co.,, WV, **Cora Ellen Thompson**, b. Oct-14-1873 in Timber Ridge, Pendleton Co.,, WV (daughter of Amos Thompson and Mary Hedrick), d. Dec-28-1952 in Elkins, Randolph Co., WV.

Children:

+ 485 i. Lillie Mae[5] Wimer b. Jun-24-1895.
+ 486 ii. Leanna Wimer b. Apr-19-1897.
+ 487 iii. Mona Wimer b. Dec-12-1900.
+ 488 iv. Amos Wimer b. 1902.
+ 489 v. Grace Elizabeth Wimer b. 1905.
+ 490 vi. Russell Jennings Wimer b. 1907.
+ 491 vii. Iva Phillis Wimer b. 1909.
+ 492 viii. Willie Clinton Wimer b. 1911.

164. **Louis Clark[4] Teter** (30.Leah[3] Sponaugle, 4.Elizabeth L.[2] Arbogast, 1.George[1]) (See marriage to number 112.)

165. **Virginia Catherine (Jennie)[4] Teter** (30.Leah[3] Sponaugle, 4.Elizabeth L.[2] Arbogast, 1.George[1]), b. Apr 16 1859 in Hunting Ground, Pendleton Co., (W)VA, d. Dec 10 1936 in Weippe, Clearwater Co., ID.
Married Sep-30-1980 in Hendricks, Tucker Co., WV, **Charles Edward Long**, b. Feb-06-1862 in Randolph Co., WV, d. Oct-11-1940 in Weippe, Clearwater Co., ID.

Children:

+ 493 i. Rosetta[5] Long b. Dec-28-1881.
+ 494 ii. Elmina Long b. Apr-26-1884.
+ 495 iii. John William Long b. Feb-11-1887.
+ 496 iv. Arta Long b. Jul-11-1889.
+ 497 v. Florence Long b. Feb-01-1891.
+ 498 vi. Ada Long b. Oct-23-1894.
499 vii. Della Grace Long b. May-05-1898, d. Feb-06-1985.
She Married **Roy Erb**, b. May-10-1895.

166. **Andrew[4] Teter** (30.Leah[3] Sponaugle, 4.Elizabeth L.[2] Arbogast, 1.George[1]), b. Abt 1863, d. May 28 1934, buried in Teter Cem, Gladwin, WV.
He Married **Rachel Ann Tusing** (daughter of Chris Tusing and Margaret Canfield).

Children:

+ 500 i. Edward[5] Teter.
+ 501 ii. Clifton Andrew Teter b. Mar-05-0893.
+ 502 iii. Delpha Teter b. Dec-15-1894.
503 iv. John Teter.
He Married **Susie Sunnerfield.**
504 v. Zerne Teter.
She Married **Olan Harper**.
505 vi. Ina Teter.
She Married **Laurence Allen.**
+ 506 vii. Howard Teter.
507 viii. Blain Teter.
He Married **Opal Mallow**.
508 ix. Viola Teter.
Died at age two, house fire.
509 x. Cael Teter d. 1945Killed in WWII.
He Married **Oda Ketterman**.
510 xi. Burly Teter d. Jul-13-1944.
Burley died from drowning.
He Married **Mabel Roy**.
+ 511 xii. Izabelle Teter b. Jun 18 1891.

167. **William Patterson[4] Teter** (30.Leah[3] Sponaugle, 4.Elizabeth L.[2] Arbogast, 1.George[1]), b. ABT 1865, d. Mar 12 1926, buried in Parson City Cem., WV.
Married 1887, **Samantha Jane Summerfield**, b. Jan-30-1865 (daughter of Geo. Wash. Summerfield), d. Jul-08-1956.

Children:

+ 512 i. Selena[5] Teter b. Apr-08-1889.
513 ii. Blanche Teter b. Apr-12-1894.
(1) She Married **unknown Stahl.**
(2) She Married **George Michales.**

514 iii. Charles Teter b. Oct-28-1896.
\+ 515 iv. Virginia Teter b. Sep-26-1897.
\+ 516 v. George Wesley Grimm b. Oct-13-1899.
517 vi. Bessie Mae Teter b. Apr-08-1902, d. 1937.
518 vii. Lawrence Victor Teter b. Jun-21-1906, d. Jul-11-1958.
519 viii. Lylayh Ann Teter b. Jul-09-1913.

168. **John Jackson[4] Teter, Jr.** (30.Leah[3] Sponaugle, 4.Elizabeth L.[2] Arbogast, 1.George[1]), b. 1869, d. Jan 12 1947.
Married Apr-05-1896, **Amanda Bell Long**, b. 1016878, d. Oct-08-1962.

Children:

\+ 520 i. Mary Ann[5] Teter b. Jan-05-1897.

170. **Elizabeth Mary[4] Teter** (30.Leah[3] Sponaugle, 4.Elizabeth L.[2] Arbogast, 1.George[1]), b. 1873, d. 1917.
Married 1937, **Sylvanus James Bright**, b. 1867 (son of George Washington Bright and Phebe White).

Children:

521 i. Luther[5] Bright b. 1890, d. 1969.
He Married **Clara Bell Carr**, b. 1895, d. 1983.
522 ii. Harry Edward Bright b. 1893, d. 1973.
Married 1921, **Clara Bell Carr**, b. 1895, d. 1983.
\+ 523 iii. Rosa Bell Bright b. 1897.
524 iv. Garber Lee Bright b. 1904.
Married 1923, **Evelyn Ruth Jackson**, b. 1905.
525 v. Gladys Lulu Bright b. 1905.
Married 1921, **George Phillips,** b. 1900.
526 vi. Hilda Bright b. 1907.
She Married **Loy Lough**, b. in Pine Bluff, WY.
527 vii. Minnie Bright.
She Married **Cyrus Phillips.**
528 viii. Clesta Bright b. 1915.
She Married **Dale Luther Carr**.

171. **Alice Grace[4] Teter** (30.Leah[3] Sponaugle, 4.Elizabeth L.[2] Arbogast, 1.George[1]), b. c 1875, d. Nov 5 1958, buried in Smith Cem., Tyler Co., WV.
She Married **Solomon Smith**.

Children:

\+ 529 i. Orpha[5] Smith b. 1905.
\+ 530 ii. Oakey Smith b. 1894.
531 iii. Garber Smith b. 1896, buried in near Hines, WV, d. Apr-25-1975.
He Married **Mollie Samples**.
\+ 532 iv. Gilbert P. Smith b. Apr-12-1899.
533 v. Morren Smith b. 1901, buried in Smith Cem., Tyler Co., WV, d. May-14-1967.
He Married **Delphia Pennington**.
534 vi. Don Smith b. 1903, d. May-25-1973.
He Married **Alta Bonner.**
535 vii. Joel Smith b. 1907, buried in Smith Cem., Tyler Co., WV.
\+ 536 viii. Rosa Alice Smith b. c 1910.
\+ 537 ix. Omer Smith b. Feb-17-1912.
\+ 538 x. Sylvia Smith b. May-24-1914.
539 xi. Straudie Virginia Smith b. 1916.
540 xii. Billie Smith d. in died at 10 mos.
541 xiii. Jackeline Smith.
She Married **unknown Cooper.**
542 xiv. Geraldine Smith.
543 xv. Boyd Smith.
He Married **Susanna Thompson**.
544 xvi. Lewis Smith.
He Married **Anne Lee Breckridge**.
545 xvii. Virginia Smith.

546 xviii. Dorothy Smith.
She Married **Frank Ramsey**.
547 xix. Mary Alice Smith.
She Married **Delbert Pitzenberger.**

186. **Lena[4] Tingler** (32.Sarah[3] Sponaugle, 4.Elizabeth L.[2] Arbogast, 1.George[1]), b. Aug 26 1883, d. May 5 1962.
(1) She Married **Wayne Sylvester Vandevender**, b. About 1885 (son of Adam H. Vandevender and Ruth Ellen Arbogast).

Children:

548 i. Adam[5] Vandevander.
549 ii. Joseph Vandevander.
\+ 550 iii. Mary Dessie Vandevander.
551 iv. Sylvia Mae Vandevander b. Oct 12 1910 in Pendleton Co., WV, d. Jun 16 2003 in Pendleton Co., WV.
She Married **Mason Thompson**, b. 1906, d. Apr 29 1968 in Pendleton Co., WV.
552 v. Willie Vandevander b. Apr 6 1914 in Pendleton Co., WV, d. May 21 1999 in Pendleton Co., WV.
He Married **Grethal Lee Lambert**, b. Oct 30 1913 in Cherry Grove, Pendleton Co., WV, d. Mar 6 2005 in Elkins, Randolph Co., WV.
553 vi. Betty Vandevander b. About 1918.
554 vii. Belva Vandevander b. About 1921.
\+ 555 viii. Virgil Vandevander.

(2) She Married **Sylvester Vandevander**.
(3) She Married **Branson Shears**.

187. **Ashby[4] Sponaugle** (33.Jacob[3], 4.Elizabeth L.[2] Arbogast, 1.George[1]), b. 1868 in Hunting Ground, Pendleton Co., (W)VA, d. Feb 24 1945.
Married Feb-12-1889 in Randolph County, WV, **Mary Catherine Mullenax**.

Children:

556 i. Glenn[5] Sponaugle.

188. **Gilbert Kenton[4] Sponaugle** (33.Jacob[3], 4.Elizabeth L.[2] Arbogast, 1.George[1]), b. Jan 2 1870 in Hunting Ground, Pendleton Co., (W)VA, d. Dec 30 1924, buried in Sponaugle Family Cem., Hunting Grounds Pendleton County WV.
He Married **Annie Pressie Mallow**, b. Nov-14-1986 in Circleville Pendleton Co., WV (daughter of Benjamin Franklin Mallow and Roxanna Nelson), buried in Sponaugle, Circleville, WV, d. Dec-27-1982 in Elkins, Randolph Co., WV. She had been Married twice. After her first husband, Gilbert Sponaugle, died in 1925, she Married Bead Sponaugle.
DEC 1982 in Randolph Co., WV Pendleton Times Obituary

Children:

557 i. Shirley Arlene[5] Sponaugle b. Jan 13 1914 in Pendleton Co., WV, d. Apr 19 1974 in Springville, Utah Co., UT.
(1) Married Sep 9 1933 in Pendleton Co., WV, **William Guy Johnston,** b. Mar 17 1913 in Pendleton Co., WV (son of Robert Boyd Johnston and Bertie Kate Arbogast), d. Jul 13 2003 in Provo, Utah Co., UT.
(2) She Married **Thomas Lynn Johnston**, b. Dec 18 1954 in Randolph Co., WV, d. Oct 8 1980 in Boise, Ada Co., ID.
\+ 558 ii. Ethel Mae Sponaugle b. Aug-06-1906.
559 iii. Zallie Sponaugle b. 1908, d. 1910.
\+ 560 iv. Brison Jay Sponaugle b. Apr 03 1911.
561 v. Benjamin Franklin Sponaugle b. Jun-06-1916 in Pendleton Co., WV, d. Sep-28-1999.
He Married **Ruthene Marie Vanaman Blankenship**, b. Jul-23-1927 (daughter of Charles Isaac Vanaman and Minnie Belle Bishop), buried in Arlington, Arlington VA, d. Feb-13-1974.
562 vi. John Eber Sponaugle b. Jun-07-1918 in Hunting Ground, Pendleton Co. WV, buried in Sponaugle Cem., Smith Creek, Pendleton Co., WV, d. Sep-21-1940 in Hunting Ground, Pendleton Co. WV.
informant, Isaac Mallow - cause of death, Suicide (gun shot in right side of head - place of death, School Ground
563 vii. Mary Wilda Sponaugle b. Jun-14-1922 in Hunting Ground, Pendleton Co. WV, d. Dec-16-2012 in Cuyahoga Co., OH.
She Married **Lloyd E Bennett**, b. Jan-18-1925, buried in Sponaugle Family Cem., Hunting Grounds Pendleton County WV, d. May-28-1901.

191. **William Letcher[4] Sponaugle** (33.Jacob[3], 4.Elizabeth L.[2] Arbogast, 1.George[1]), b. Sep 16 1875 in Hunting Ground, Pendleton Co., (W)VA, d. May 21 1960.

He Married **Leona Arbogast**, b. Aug 18 1899 in Pendleton Co., WV (daughter of Elijah J. Arbogast and Roberta Prudence Arbaugh), d. Aug 27 1992 in Harrisburg, Raleigh Co., VA.

Children:

+ 564 i. Herbert Charles[5] Sponaugle b. Sep 1 1913.
+ 565 ii. Nola Lee Sponaugle b. Jan 21 1916.
566 iii. Olin Raymond Sponaugle b. Jan 15 1918 in Cherry Grove, Pendleton Co., WV, d. May 10 1992 in Hunting Ground, Pendleton Co., (W)VA.
567 iv. Sudie Sponaugle b. Nov 29 1919 in Cherry Grove, Pendleton Co., WV, d. Aug 16 1932.
568 v. Thelma Sponaugle b. Sep 4 1921 in Cherry Grove, Pendleton Co., WV.
She Married **James William Sponaugle**, b. May 17 1914 in Pendleton Co., WV, d. Nov 30 1996 in Raleigh Co., NC.
569 vi. Jacob Cenior Sponaugle b. Apr 20 1923 in Pendleton Co., WV.
Married Jul 8 1949, **Emma Lee Wilson**, b. Feb 14 1928.
+ 570 vii. Roche Elijah Sponaugle b. Mar 1 1925.
571 viii. Merlie Sponaugle b. Dec 14 1926 in Pendleton Co., WV.
+ 572 ix. Rosie Zona Sponaugle b. Jul 20 1928.

192. **Herman Henry[4] Sponaugle** (33.Jacob[3], 4.Elizabeth L.[2] Arbogast, 1.George[1]), b. Jan 13 1877 in Hunting Ground, Pendleton Co. WV, d. Sep 25 1953 in Pendleton Co., WV.
Married Jun-08-1902, **Etta Beulah Warner**.

Children:

+ 573 i. Marvin Luther[5] Sponaugle b. Jun-08-1903.
+ 574 ii. Beulah Sponaugle b. Jul-26-1901.
+ 575 iii. Raymond Sponaugle b. Mar-09-1905.
+ 576 iv. Alpha Cynyhia Sponaugle b. Dec-18-1907.
+ 577 v. Myrtle M Sponaugle b. Dec-13-1908.
578 vi. Elsie Mildred Sponaugle b. Apr-17-1919.
She Married **Stanley White.**
579 vii. Kitty Belle Sponaugle b. Apr 24 1912 in Churchville, Pendleton Co., WV.
Married in Franklin Co., WV, **Morris Waybright**, b. Sep 30 1905 in Rich Mountain, Pendleton Co., WV (son of Wilber Allen Waybright and Sena White).
+ 580 viii. Mary Kerlin Sponaugle b. Mar-07-1914.
+ 581 ix. Levern Sponaugle b. Dec-16-1919.
+ 582 x. Roscoe Sponaugle b. May-10-1921.
583 xi. Idelta Rebecca Sponaugle b. Nov-01-1925.
584 xii. Jacob Sponaugle.
585 xiii. Clifford Sponaugle.
+ 586 xiv. Ruth Sponaugle b. May-18-1918.

195. **John Alstoyshus[4] Cook** (34.George[3], 5.Catherine[2] Arbogast, 1.George[1]), b. Jan-16-1853 in Highland Co., VA, d. Oct-04-1914. He Married **Ella Weatherwax**.

Children:

587 i. Thomas[5] Cook.
588 ii. George Cook.
589 iii. Lynn Cook.
590 iv. Mora Cook.

197. **Mary Virginia[4] Cook** (34.George[3], 5.Catherine[2] Arbogast, 1.George[1]), b. Jun-01-1856 in Highland Co., VA, d. Dec-07-1990. She Married **Adam Simmons**.

Children:

591 i. Edith[5] Simmons.
592 ii. William Simmons.
593 iii. Glen Simmons.
594 iv. Mabel Simmons.

199. **Emma Estella[4] Cook** (34.George[3], 5.Catherine[2] Arbogast, 1.George[1]), b. Mar-02-1860 in Highland Co., VA, d. Dec-09-1833. She Married **Charles Smith**. Family moved to CO.

Children:

595 i. Eva^{5} Smith.
596 ii. Bertha Smith.
597 iii. Olive Smith.

202. **William Franklin^{4} Cook** (34.George^{3}, 5.Catherine^{2} Arbogast, 1.George^{1}), b. Jul-03-1867 in Highland Co., VA.
Moved to David City, NB.
Married 1891, **Margaret Stacy Spataz**.

Children:

598 i. Hazel^{5} Cook.
599 ii. Blanche Cook.

She Married **Charles Schwexer**.
600 iii. Helen Cook.
601 iv. Louis Cook.
Was a WW i Aviation flyer.

203. **Gertrude Victoria^{4} Cook** (34.George^{3}, 5.Catherine^{2} Arbogast, 1.George^{1}), b. Sep-16-1870 in Highland Co., VA.
Married 1884, **Charles Rhodes**. Moved to N. Yakima, WA.

Children:

602 i. Lynn^{5} Rhodes.
603 ii. Archie Rhodes.
604 iii. Stanley Rhodes.
605 iv. Gertrude Rhodes.

204. **Harry Bland^{4} Cook** (34.George^{3}, 5.Catherine^{2} Arbogast, 1.George^{1}), b. Oct-02-1872.
Married 1905 in Kiption, Lorraine o., OH, **Alice Marie Branchland**.

Children:

606 i. Robert Jackson^{5} Cook.
607 ii. Margaret Alice Cook.

221. **Mary Elizabeth^{4} Bird** (37.Emily^{3} Cook, 5.Catherine^{2} Arbogast, 1.George^{1}), b. Sep-10-1953, d. Jul-11-1935.
(1) She Married **Washington Enlow**.

Children:

608 i. Bessie L^{5} Enlow b. Jul-23-1980.
She Married Dr. **Hoye John Arbogast**.

(2) She Married **C.P. French**.

222. **Ollie Mae^{4} Bird** (37.Emily^{3} Cook, 5.Catherine^{2} Arbogast, 1.George^{1}).
She Married **unknown Rice**.

Children:

\+ 609 i. OllieMae^{5} Rice.

224. **Frank H.^{4} Cook** (40.John Wesley^{3}, 5.Catherine^{2} Arbogast, 1.George^{1}), b. May-07-1858.
He Married **Margaret Jones**.

Children:

610 i. Harry D.^{5} Cook.
He Married **Elizabeth Baldwin**.
611 ii. Gertie Cook.
She Married **William Gray**.

237. **Carrie E.^{4} Arbogast** (45.Jeremiah Elderidge^{3}, 6.Emanuel^{2}, 1.George^{1}), b. Apr-10-1858 in New Hampden, Highland Co., VA, d. Sep-27-1933 in Hightown, Highland Co., VA.
Married Nov-06-1876, **Charles H. Slaven**, b. 1848.

Children:

\+ 612 i. Caddie^{5} Slaven b. Jun-15-1895.

238. **William Gum[4] Arbogast** (45.Jeremiah Elderidge[3], 6.Emanuel[2], 1.George[1]), b. Jul-05-1861 in Highland Co., VA, d. Dec-28-1888, buried in Wimer Family Cem., Highland Co, VA.
Married 1881 in Harpers Ferry, Jefferson Co., VA, **Mary Kinked** (daughter of William P. kinked and Grace Mauzy).

Children:

+ 613 i. Howard K.[5] Arbogast b. Dec-02-1882.
+ 614 ii. William G. Arbogast b. Jul-03-1887.

258. **Ada Neil[4] Arbogast** (55.David Howard[3], 6.Emanuel[2], 1.George[1]), b. Jun-02-1894, d. Jun-20-1869.
She Married **Charles Lee Roberts**, b. Oct-15-1893 in Mulberry, MO (son of Samuel Roberts and Angelina Hobs), d. Aug-23-1976 in Fort Collins, CO.

Children:

+ 615 i. Charles Howard[5] Roberts b. Apr-30-1918.

263. **Saulsberry N[4] Chew** (58.George E. M.[3], 8.Mary "Polly"[2] Arbogast, 1.George[1]), b. Dec 1879.
He Married **Edith Catherine Lambert**, b. Apr 06 1881, d. Aug 17 1965.

Children:

+ 616 i. George B.[5] Crew b. Aug 07 1904.

264. **Lillie May[4] Chew** (58.George E. M.[3], 8.Mary "Polly"[2] Arbogast, 1.George[1]), b. Nov 09 1882, d. Sep 06 1936.
Married Dec 21 1902 in Highland Co., VA, **George Washington Wimer**, b. Dec 03 1874, d. Nov 30 1950.

Children:

617 i. Alvenza Morgan[5] Wimer b. 1904.
618 ii. Louisanna Wimer b. 1906.
619 iii. Lora Wimer b. 1908.
620 iv. Claricy Wimer b. 1910.
621 v. Lona Wimer b. 1914.
622 vi. Vernon Wimer b. 1917.
623 vii. Luther Harold Wimer b. 1920.

266. **Margaret Jean[4] Arbogast** (68.Orien Austin[3], 10.Henry W.[2], 1.George[1]), b. Apr 13 1924 in Parsons, Tucker Co., WV, d. Sep 17 1988 in St. Petersburg, Pinellas Co., FL, buried Sep 20 1988 in St Petersburg, Pinellas Co., FL.
Married Jan 20 1945 in Elkins, Randolph Co., WV, **Stanley J. Flanagan**, b. Jun 13 1920 in Davis, Tucker Co., WV (son of Sol Flanagan and Bertha Harper), d. May 16 1983 in St. Petersburg, Pinellas Co., FL, buried May 19 1983 in St. Petersburg, Pinellas Co., FL.

Children:

+ 624 i. Dennis Keith[5] Flanagan b. Dec 20 1946.
625 ii. Barbara Jean Flanagan b. Oct 18 1956 in Charleston, Kanawha Co., WV.
Barbara was previously Married to John William Ferrari, and divorced in 1987.
Married Mar 27 1987 in St. Petersburg, Pinellas Co., FL, **Clayton S. Campbell,** b. Nov 29 1947 in Atlanta, Fulton Co., GA (son of George Bennett Campbell and Corinne Huguley). Clayton was previously Married to Ronda Noname and to Sharon Noname. Clayton's parents were George Bennett Campbell and Corinne Huguley.

267. **Kathryn Eloise[4] Arbogast** (68.Orien Austin[3], 10.Henry W.[2], 1.George[1]), b. Dec 1 1927, d. Dec 12 1980.
Kathryn was
Married to two other men. Her first husband was **Tom Powell**, her second was **Bryce Winnowson**, who had two children to a previous marriage (Leon and Richard), and her third husband was Hubert Freeman, also previously Married with three children to an earlier wife (Mark, Steven, and Pamela).
She Married **Tom Powell**.

Children:

626 i. Patrica[5] Powell.
627 ii. Kathi Powell.

Generation Five

269. **Louella Maer[5] Grogg** (69.Emily Jane[4] Mullenax, 11.John H.[3], 2.Hannah[2] Arbogast, 1.George[1]), b. Apr 17 1874 in Crabbottom, Highland Co., VA, d. Apr 12 1949 in Boyer, Pocahontas Co., WV.
Married Aug 19 1890 in Pocahontas Co., WV, **Andrew Morgan Collins**, b. in Pocahontas Co., WV, d. Nov 28 1942 in Boyer, Pocahontas Co., WV.

Children:

+ 628 i. Floyd William[6] Collins b. Nov 25 1893.
+ 629 ii. Cecil Morgan Collins b. Aug 14 1896.

270. **Columbus P.[5] Waybright** (71.Martha[4] Mullenax, 12.George[3], 2.Hannah[2] Arbogast, 1.George[1]), b. Jul 1845 in Pendleton Co., WV, d. in Huntington, Cabell Co., WV.
Married Dec 7 1865, **Phoebe Jane Huffman**, b. 1848 in Pendleton Co., WV.

Children:

630 i. Mona[6] Waybright.
631 ii. (infant) Waybright b. Jul 27 1860 in Pendleton Co., WV.
632 iii. Mary Bella Waybright b. 1867 in Pendleton Co., WV.
633 iv. Martha J. Waybright b. Aug 1870 in Pendleton Co., WV.

271. **Mary Jane[5] Waybright** (71.Martha[4] Mullenax, 12.George[3], 2.Hannah[2] Arbogast, 1.George[1]), b. 1847.
She Married **Perry Vance**, b. 1843.

Children:

634 i. Phoebe C.[6] Vance b. About 1866.
635 ii. Martha E Vance b. About 1868.
636 iii. Sarah Vance b. About 1869.
637 iv. Mary J Vance b. About 1869.

272. **Albert[5] Waybright** (71.Martha[4] Mullenax, 12.George[3], 2.Hannah[2] Arbogast, 1.George[1]), b. May 1848 in Whitmer, Randolph Co., WV, d. Feb 27 1909, buried in Seneca Creek, Pendleton Co., VA/WV.
Married Oct 20 1876 in Pendleton Co., WV, **Dorothy Dolly**, b. Apr 16 1858 in Pendleton Co., WV, d. Oct 29 1904, buried in Waybright Cem., Pendleton Co., WV.

Children:

638 i. Lloyd[6] Waybright b. Jan 1878 in Pendleton Co., WV.
639 ii. Rosie Waybright b. May 1882 in Pendleton Co., WV.
640 iii. Jasper Waybright b. Oct 3 1884 in Pendleton Co., WV, d. Feb 18 1904 in Onego, Pendleton Co., WV, buried in Seneca Creek, Pendleton Co., VA/WV.
He Married **Rachel Turner**.
641 iv. Henry V. Waybright b. Sep 1887 in Pendleton Co., WV.
+ 642 v. Bert Waybright b. Oct 1890.
643 vi. Myrtle Waybright b. Aug 1893.
644 vii. Martha Jane Waybright b. Aug 1895 in Pendleton Co., WV.
She Married **Frank Huffman**.
645 viii. Arthur Waybright b. Apr 1897 in Pendleton Co., WV.

274. **Lulu[5] Arbogast** (74.Samuel Benjamin[4], 14.William Samual[3], 3.Daniel[2], 1.George[1]), b. Mar-19-1869 in Pendleton Co., VA, d. Jan-26-1906 in Circleville Pendleton Co., WV.
She Married **McCollett Lambert**, b. Jun 1871 (son of William Taylor Lambert and Eubice Teer).

Children:

646 i. (infant)[6] Lambert b. Jan-05-1895, d. Jan-06-1895.
+ 647 ii. Marie Lambert b. May-23-1896.
648 iii. Conway C Lambert b. Oct 1898.

303. **Elmo Mead[5] Arbogast** (89.Emery Matthew[4], 21.John Wesley[3], 3.Daniel[2], 1.George[1]), b. Jun-26-1883 in Monterey, Highland Co., VA, d. Jan-03-1972 in Albuquerque, Bernalillo Co., NM.
Married Feb-23-1920, **Priscilla Sloan**, b. Oct-31-1886 in Marlinton, Pocahontas Co., WV, d. Jul-22-1922 in Albuquerque, Bernalillo Co., NM.

Children:

649 i. Meade Sloan[6] Arbogast b. May-20-1922 in Marlinton, Pocahontas Co., WV, d. about 1970 in Albuquerque, Bernalillo Co., NM.

Married Jan 1944, **Mary Perth Nelson**. Adopted son, Halsey, and adopted daughter, Mary Marcia.
\+ 650 ii. Frances Ann Arbogast, b. Dec-03-1925.

305. **Virginia[5] Arbogast** (89.Emery Matthew[4] Arbogast, 21.John Wesley[3], 3.Daniel[2], 1.George[1]).
Married 1924, **Roy Quackenbush**, b. in Portland, Multnomah Co., OR.

Children:

651 i. Robert[6] Quackenbush.
Married **Marjorie ________**, a son, Piet. Robert is a commercial artist and noted author of children's books. NYC, NY.
\+ 652 ii. Anna Laurie Quackenbush.
653 iii. Roy Emery Quackenbush b. Jun-30-1930 in Phoenix, Maricopa Co., AZ, d. Oct 1991 in Phoenix, Maricopa Co., AZ.
Married **Doris Poenkoe**, has two sons.

306. **John Arthur[5] Arbogast** (92.Authur William[4], 21.John Wesley[3], 3.Daniel[2], 1.George[1]), b. May-29-1869 in Lewisburg, Greenbrier Co., WV, d. Jun-12-1934 in Hematite, Allegheny, Virginia.
Living children
Owned and managed Rainbow Lumber Company Inc. in White Sulphur Springs, WV for 38 years, sold business and retired about 1985. Letter in file from John dated 17 Oct. 1992. Information on his spouse, their marriage, children, his and his spouse parents and his siblings from a most interesting writing of 28 pages from John Arthur Arbogast written in 1990 from John Arthur Arbogast. The writing is entertaining as well as informative.
He Married **Dorothy Louise Villa** (daughter of Lewis Joseph Villa and Julia Martha Reggetts).

Children:

654 i. Daniel Joseph[6] Arbogast b. Jun-18-1950 in Covington, Allegheny Co., VA.
\+ 655 ii. John Kent Arbogast b. Nov-18-1951.

307. **Charles Edward[5] Arbogast** (92.Authur William[4], 21.John Wesley[3], 3.Daniel[2], 1.George[1]), b. Mar-05-1915 in Ronceverte, Greenbrier Co., WV, d. Dec-07-1993 in White Sulphur Springs, Greenbrier Co., WV.
Living children.
He Married **Nora Hefner**, b. Feb-06-1930 in Lewisburg, Greenbrier Co., VA (daughter of Virgil Hefner and Eva Wiley), d. Dec-07-1993 in White Sulphur Springs, Greenbrier Co., VA.

Children:

656 i. Kim[6] Renee Arbogast, Ph.D. b. Jun-27-1956 in Covington, Allegheny Co., VA.
Kim and Steven hold degrees from Mich State Univ.
She Married Steven McBride. Ph.D..
657 ii. Shane Ervine Arbogast b. Oct-12-1962 in Covington, Allegheny Co., VA.

308. **Robert William[5] Arbogast** (92.Authur William[4] Arbogast, 21.John Wesley[3], 3.Daniel[2], 1.George[1]), b. Jun-11-1916 in Lewisburg, Greenbrier Co., WV, d. Mar-09-1984 in Roanoke, Roanoke Co., VA.
Married Nov-22-1942 in Victorville, Ca, **Elizabeth Whiting**, b. Nov-14-1915 in Keyford, WV, d. Sep-19-1990 in Roanoke, Roanoke Co., VA.

Children:

658 i. Vincent Patrick[6] Arbogast b. Aug 1950, buried in Homestead Hotel, Hot Springs, VA, d. Aug 1950 in Huntington, Cabell Co., WV.
Killed in auto accident.

312. **Russell Cameron[5] Arbogast** (93.Charles Cameron[4], 21.John Wesley[3], 3.Daniel[2], 1.George[1]), b. Apr-14-1914 in Keyser, Mineral Co., WV, d. July 1984 in Petersburg, Grant Co., WV.
(1) He Married **Lillian Martin**, b. 1914, d. 1978.

Children:

659 i. Lawrence Cameron[6] Arbogast.
660 ii. Lames Martin Arbogast b. 1946.
661 iii. Greggory Gae Arbogast b. 1948.
662 iv. Pamela Lou Arbogast b. 1952.
She Married **Phillip Williams**.

(2) Married 1980, **Ruth Thorne**.

313. **Paul Gae[5] Arbogast** (93.Charles Cameron[4], 21.John Wesley[3], 3.Daniel[2], 1.George[1]), b. Feb-02-1916 in Keyser, Mineral Co., WV, d. May-22-1953 in Memphis, Shelby Co., TN.
He Married **Tresa Marie Cappadona**, b. Jun-09-1951.

Children:

663 i. Charles Cameron[6] Arbogast b. Mar-23-1952, d. in Memphis, Shelby Co., TN.

314. **Amanda Crawford[5] Arbogast** (94.John Edwin[4], 21.John Wesley[3], 3.Daniel[2], 1.George[1]), b. Aug-16-1920 in Monterey, Highland Co., VA, d. Oct-28-1896 in Johns Hopkins, Hosp., Baltimore, Md.
She Married **John Alexander Forbes, Jr.**, b. Aug-18-1915 in Clayton , Johnson county, NC.

Children:

\+ 664 i. Patricia Crawford[6] Forbes b. Jan-29-1945.
665 ii. John Alexander Forbes MIII b. May-15-1947 in Staunton, Augusta Co., VA.
\+ 666 iii. James Edwin Forbes b. Feb-10-1975.

315. **Robert William[5] Arbogast** (99.Arthur William[4], 21.John Wesley[3], 3.Daniel[2], 1.George[1]), b. Jun 11 1916 in Ronceverte, Greenbrier Co., WV, d. Mar 09 1984 in Green Bank, Pocahontas Co., WV.
He Married **Gertrude Elizabeth Whiting**, b. Nov 14 1915 in Kayford, Kanawha Co., WV (daughter of Harry Ebenezer Whiting and Mayme Settle), d. Sep 19 1990 in Roanoke, Roanoke Co., VA.

Children:

\+ 667 i. Theresa[6] Arbogast b. Sep 03 1943.
\+ 668 ii. Diane Patricia Arbogast b. Nov 29 1946.
\+ 669 iii. Robert Michael Arbogast b. Nov 22 1947.
670 iv. Vincent P. Arbogast b. Aug 30 1950 in Green Bank, Pocahontas Co., WV, d. Aug 30 1950 in Green Bank, Pocahontas Co., WV, buried in White Sulphur Springs, Greenbrier Co., WV.

316. **James Alexander[5] Arbogast** (99.Arthur William[4], 21.John Wesley[3], 3.Daniel[2], 1.George[1]), b. Nov-02-1918 in Ronceverte, Greenbrier Co., WV, buried in White Sulphur Springs, Greenbrier Co., VA, d. Mar-09-1984 in Fairlea, Greenbrier Co., WV.
He Married **Veronica Jastremski**, b. Feb-03-1920 in Plains, PA (daughter of Adam Jastremski and Catherine Inglot).

Children:

671 i. Janes Andrew[6] Arbogast b. Jan-23-1948 in Aberdeen, Harford Co., MD.
He Married **Karen Tilley**.
672 ii. Barbara Marie Arbogast b. Dec-08-1949 in Ronceverte, Greenbrier Co., WV.
Married Apr-22-1972 in White Sulphur Springs, Greenbrier Co., VA, **Edward Smallwood**.
673 iii. Kathryn Theresa Arbogast b. Nov-24-1951 in Covington, Allegheny Co., VA.
Married Jun-07-1980 in Burke, VA, **Michael Schoelles**.
674 iv. Mary Veronica Arbogast b. Sep-09-1955 in White Sulphur Springs, Greenbrier Co., WV.
Married Aug-06-1977 in White Sulphur Springs, Greenbrier Co., WV, **John Michael Kessler**.

317. **Ralph Thomas[5] Arbogast** (99.Arthur William[4], 21.John Wesley[3], 3.Daniel[2], 1.George[1]), b. Aug-13-1926 in White Sulphur Springs, Greenbrier Co., WV.
He Married **Patricia J. Peterson**, b. Nov-07-1931 in Chicago, Cook Co., IL (daughter of Myron J. Peterson and Cleo Fatetta Swanson).

Children:

\+ 675 i. Maureen[6] Arbogast b. Apr-10-1956.
\+ 676 ii. Thomas Arbogast b. Jun-16-1958.
677 iii. William Joseph Arbogast b. Sep-20-1963 in Waukegan, Il.

321. **Delbert E.[5] Arbogast** (101.Orien Austin[4], 22.Henry W.[3], 3.Daniel[2], 1.George[1]), b. Dec-02-1902 in Davis, Tucker Co., WV, d. about 1980.
Married May-29-1929 in Homestead, Miami-Dade Co., FL, **Opal Grace Mahle**, b. May-08-1907 in Davis, Tucker Co., WV.

Children:

678 i. Carol[6] Arbogast.
679 ii. Doris Arbogast.
680 iii. Betty Sue Arbogast.

330. **Serilda C[5] Sponaugle** (108.George Washington[4], 23.William[3], 4.Elizabeth L.[2] Arbogast, 1.George[1]), b. Nov 01 1868 in Pendleton Co., WV, d. Jan 16 1962.

Married Aug-23-1891 in Pendleton Co., WV, **Robert Edward C** (son of Samuel Mullenax and Sarah S. Zickafoose), d. Oct-14-1945 in Cedar Hill Cem., Pendleton Co., WV, b. Jun-11-1868.

Children:

681 i. Etta Carrie[6] Mullenax b. 1892, d. 1994.
682 ii. Edward Jacob Mullenax b. 1892, d. 1918.
683 iii. Mary Ellen Mullenax b. 1894.
+ 684 iv. Luther Lee Mullenax b. Sep-19-1896.
685 v. Carrie Susan Mullenax.
Married **Mr. Propst**.
+ 686 vi. Myrtle Annie Mullenax b. Dec-16-1905.
687 vii. Fannie Macel Mullenax b. 1905.
688 viii. Mattie Lucille Mullenax b. Jan-05-1915, d. Nov-28-1973.
Married Jun-25-1933, **John E. Nelson**.

331. **Carrie E[5] Sponaugle** (108.George Washington[4], 23.William[3], 4.Elizabeth L.[2] Arbogast, 1.George[1]), b. May 12 1870 in Pendleton Co., WV, d. Dec 2 1937 in Smith Creek, Pendleton Co., WV, buried in Perry Hartman Cem., Pendleton Co., WV. Died in Son Melvin Earls Home.
Married Dec 18 1885 in Pendleton Co., WV, **James W Hartman**, b. Nov 24 1860 in Pendleton Co., WV, d. Jan 28 1938 in Hawes Hills Pendleton Co., WV.

Children:

689 i. William H[6] Hartman b. Jan 3 1888 in Pendleton Co., WV, d. Mar 21 1903 in Pendleton Co., WV. Killed by falling tree.
690 ii. John T Hartman b. Mar 20 1890 in Pendleton Co., WV, d. Jul 6 1914 in Pendleton Co., WV.
691 iii. Henry Edward Hartman b. Apr 17 1891 in Pendleton Co., WV, d. Nov 12 1959 in Pendleton Co., WV.
He Married Grace **Hicle Sponaugle**, d. UNKNOWN.
+ 692 iv. George Edgar Hartman b. Mar 27 1894.
+ 693 v. Alpha Susan Hartman b. Dec 22 1897.
+ 694 vi. James Arthur Hartman b. Jun 1 1899.
+ 695 vii. Denny Herman Hartman b. Jun 2 1902.
+ 696 viii. Melvin Earl Hartman b. Sep 3 1904.
+ 697 ix. Charles Okey Hartman b. Jan 22 1907.
698 x. Lizzy C. Hartman b. Oct 18 1913 in Pendleton Co., WV, d. Jun 1 1914 in Pendleton Co., WV.
699 xi. Viola Hartman b. May 18 1913 in Pendleton Co., WV, d. Jun 4 1914 in Pendleton Co., WV.
+ 700 xii. Robert Paul Hartman b. Feb 24 1914.
701 xiii. Henry Arthur Hartman b. Oct-24-1953.
Married Oct-26-1971, **Carolyn June Pritt.**

332. **Minerva[5] Sponaugle** (108.George Washington[4], 23.William[3], 4.Elizabeth L.[2] Arbogast, 1.George[1]), b. Jan 20 1873 in Pendleton Co., WV, d. Feb 18 1956 in Pendleton Co., WV.
Married Sep 30 1894 in Pendleton Co., WV, **John Clark Hartman**, b. Aug 29 1865 in Pendleton Co., WV, d. Feb 26 1927 in Pendleton Co., WV.

Children:

+ 702 i. John Esby[6] Hartman.
703 ii. Sidney Glenn Flemming Hartman d. Aug-21-1934, b. Aug-04-1903.

333. **William Okay[5] Sponaugle** (108.George Washington[4], 23.William[3], 4.Elizabeth L.[2] Arbogast, 1.George[1]), b. Aug 25 1875, d. Jun 16 1965.
He Married **Emma Warner**, d. UNKNOWN.

Children:

704 i. Joseph Arvel[6] Sponaugle.
705 ii. Ralph Sponaugle.
706 iii. Richard Sponaugle.
707 iv. Steryl Sponaugle.

334. **Green Judy[5] Sponaugle** (108.George Washington[4], 23.William[3], 4.Elizabeth L.[2] Arbogast, 1.George[1]), b. Oct 19 1877 in Pendleton Co., WV, d. Mar 16 1966 in Harrisonburg Hospital, VA.
Married Nov-06-1901 in Pendleton Co., WV, **Frances Etna Bland** (daughter of Isaac J. Bland and Susan Hedrick), d. Nov-23-1923, d. Mar-16-1966 in Harrisonburg Hospital, VA, buried in Sponaugle Cem., Smith Creek, Pendleton Co., WV.

Children:

+ 708 i. Russell McClure[6] Sponaugle b. Dec-23-1903.
709 ii. Alta Sponaugle b. Apr-06-1902, d. Apr-06-1902.
+ 710 iii. Elizabeth Susan Sponaugle b. Feb-12-1906.
711 iv. Leslie Gree Sponaugle b. Sep-14-1908, d. Feb-24-1909.
+ 712 v. Rhea Mae Sponaugle b. Feb-26-1910.
+ 713 vi. Walter Glenn Sponaugle b. Aug-03-1912.
+ 714 vii. Mary Ruth Sponaugle b. Feb-03-1915.
+ 715 viii. George Isaac Sponaugle b. Jun-09-1917.
+ 716 ix. Joie Catherine Sponaugle b. Aug-08-1919.
+ 717 x. William Joseph Sponaugle b. Apr-12-1922.

335. **Mary Perlie[5] Sponaugle** (108.George Washington[4], 23.William[3], 4.Elizabeth L.[2] Arbogast, 1.George[1]), b. Apr 23 1880, d. Jul 28 1960 in Cedar Hill Cem., Pendleton Co., WV.
She Married **Herman Evick**, d. UNKNOWN.

Children:

+ 718 i. Cletus[6] Evick b. Jan-31-1903.
719 ii. Olie Evick.
720 iii. James W. Evick.
721 iv. Emory Evick.
722 v. Glenna Evick.

336. **Martha Lucretia[5] Sponaugle** (108.George Washington[4], 23.William[3], 4.Elizabeth L.[2] Arbogast, 1.George[1]), b. Apr 29 1882 in Pendleton Co., WV, d. Jan 19 1976 in Lebanon, Lebanon Co., PA.
She Married **Solomon Warner**, b. Jul-1966.

Children:

+ 723 i. Emily[6] Warner.
724 ii. Joie Warner b. c 1902.
She Married **Harry Winters**.
725 iii. George R Warner b. c1902.
726 iv. Roscoe S. Warner b. 1908.

338. **George Arthur[5] Sponaugle** (108.George Washington[4], 23.William[3], 4.Elizabeth L.[2] Arbogast, 1.George[1]), b. Jul 18 1887, d. Jul 1 1954.
He Married **Meredith Gladys Hartman**, b. Sep 22 1895, (daughter of Job Hartman and Mary Alice Kline), d. Dec 6 1956.

Children:

+ 727 i. Eva Pearl[6] Sponaugle .
728 ii. Jessie Ray Sponaugle b. Oct-02-1916.
729 iii. Ervin Arthur Sponaugle b. Apr-04-1923, d. Aug-11-1992 in Harrisonburg Hospital, VA.
He Married **Wynona Evick**.

340. **Mary Ida[5] Teter** (109.Mary Catherine[4] Sponaugle, 23.William[3], 4.Elizabeth L.[2] Arbogast, 1.George[1]), b. 1869, d.
Married 1899, **William J.K. Adams**, b. ABT 1868,.

Children:

730 i. Sadie A.[6] Teter b. 1892, d.
+ 731 ii. Kate L. Cook b. 1895.
+ 732 iii. Kennie Andress Adams b. 1902.
+ 733 iv. Erma V. Adams.

341. **Jenettie Catherine[5] Thompson** (109.Mary Catherine[4] Sponaugle, 23.William[3], 4.Elizabeth L.[2] Arbogast, 1.George[1]), b. Jan 10 1871 in Pendleton Co., WV, d. Mar 2 1952 in Falls, Grant Co., WV.
Married Jul 21 1887 in Churchville, Pendleton Co., WV, **Jacob Lee Nelson**, b. May 31 1867 in Churchville, Pendleton Co., WV, d. Jul 3 1953 in Falls, Grant Co., WV.

Children:

734 i. Effie Lee[6] Nelson b. Jan 14 1887, d. Nov 2 1949.
Married, **(unknown) Casteel,**
735 ii. Anna Lena Nelson b. Jul 8 1889, d. Sep 2 1971.

Married, **Asa Joseph Weimer**,

736 iii. Sarah Catherine Nelson b. Jan 14 1891 in Pendleton Co., WV, d. Jan 14 1891 in Pendleton Co., WV.
\+ 737 iv. Clarice May Nelson b. Jun 15 1892.
738 v. John Clement Enders Nelson b. Apr 17 1894, d. Apr 22 1965 in Cumberland, Alleghany Co., MD.
739 vi. Goldie Marie Nelson b. Aug 28 1899, d. Aug 30 1900 in Pendleton Co., WV.

\+ 740 vii. Lacie Madonna Nelson b. Feb 18 1901.

342. **Melissa A.[5] Thompson** (109.Mary Catherine[4] Sponaugle, 23.William[3], 4.Elizabeth L.[2] Arbogast, 1.George[1]), b. ABT 1873 in Pendleton Co., WV, d. WFT Est 1918-1968.
Married **William D. Nelson**, b. 1869 in Pendleton Co., WV, d. WFT Est 1918-1961.

Children:

741 i. William C.[6] Nelson b. d.
742 ii. Zula B. Nelson .
743 iii. Tressie P. Nelson .
744 iv. Codia C. Nelson .
745 v. William H. Nelson .

343. **Jacob Kenny[5] Thompson** (109.Mary Catherine[4] Sponaugle, 23.William[3], 4.Elizabeth L.[2] Arbogast, 1.George[1]), b. Mar 15 1874, d. 1948.
Married 1904, **Lula Fay Caton/ Bland**, b. 1876, d. 1964.

Children:

\+ 746 i. Orie D.[6] Thompson b. Mar 16 1892.
747 ii. Eva L. Caton/ Thompson b. 1895, d. 1984.
Married 1965, **Clarence Rhaerd Cooper**, b. 1889.
\+ 748 iii. Leslie E. Thompson b. 1906.
749 iv. John Riley Thompson b. 1907, d. 1971.
(1) He Married **Mattie M. Nelson**, b. 1911, d. 1986.
(2) He Married **Bernice Wymer Batsdorff.**

344. **Sylvanus Harper[5] Thompson** (109.Mary Catherine[4] Sponaugle, 23.William[3], 4.Elizabeth L.[2] Arbogast, 1.George[1]), b. Dec 15 1875, d. 1966.
Married 1897, **Jennie L. Cunningham**, b. 1878, d. 1959.

Children:

750 i. Emmett Cassiday[6] Thompson b. MAR 1897, d. 1967.
Married 1974, **Efffie Lambert,** b. 1897.

345. **James C.[5] Thompson** (109.Mary Catherine[4] Sponaugle, 23.William[3], 4.Elizabeth L.[2] Arbogast, 1.George[1]), b. ABT 1878, d. 1959.
Married **Jennie Cunningham**, b. 1882, d. 1977.

Children:

751 i. Charlie[6] Thompson b. 1897, d. 1969.
Married, **Katie (Lamb) Raines**, b. 1905, d. 1972.

347. **Opie Enders[5] Thompson** (109.Mary Catherine[4] Sponaugle, 23.William[3], 4.Elizabeth L.[2] Arbogast, 1.George[1]), b. JAN 1882, d. OCT 1953.
Married 1903, **Rosa Pearl Vandevander**, b. Apr 4 1886, d. 1963.

Children:

752 i. William[6] Thompson b. 1907, d. 1944.

350. **Arthur Dinkle[5] Sponaugle** (110.William Jackson[4], 23.William[3], 4.Elizabeth L.[2] Arbogast, 1.George[1]), b. Jan 14 1874 in Churchville, Pendleton Co., WV, d. Aug 06 1942 in Rich Hill, Bates Co., MO, buried in Green Lawn Cem., Rich Hill, MO.
Married Mar-18-1903 in Clover Hill, Rockingham Co., VA, **Mollie Gertrude Funk**, b. 1883 in Circleville, Pickaway Co., OH.

Children:

753 i. Marion Clark[6] Sponaugle.

754 ii. Francis Alberta Sponaugle.
755 iii. Arthur Newton Sponaugle.
756 iv. Myrtie Virginia Sponaugle b. Feb-07-1910.
757 v. Minnie Irene Sponaugle b. Mar-08-1911, d. Jan 1972.
758 vi. Porter Wilson Sponaugle.
759 vii. Charles Luther Sponaugle.
760 viii. Elmer Elmo Sponaugle.
761 ix. Ralph Frederick Sponaugle.
762 x. August William Sponaugle.
763 xi. Louise Dinkle Sponaugle.

356. **Flora Anna[5] Louk** (111.Elizabeth Jane[4] Sponaugle, 23.William[3], 4.Elizabeth L.[2] Arbogast, 1.George[1]), b. Jun 12 1876, d. Nov 29 1909.
She Married **Eliot Daniels**, b. 1895.

Children:

764 i. Ethel Mae[6] Daniels.
765 ii. Guy Wesley Daniels.
766 iii. Clifford Daniels.
767 iv. Nellie Daniels.

359. **Ora Idella[5] Louk** (111.Elizabeth Jane[4] Sponaugle, 23.William[3], 4.Elizabeth L.[2] Arbogast, 1.George[1]), b. Apr-10-1882, d. Jan 28 1952.
Married Sep-15-1960, **Herman S. Rhodes,**, b. Oct-04-1877.

Children:

768 i. Jessie J.[6] Rhodes b. Oct-15-1903, d. Dec-24-1989.
Married Apr-07-1938 in Randolph Co., WV, **Patty S. Weese**.
769 ii. Orville E. Rhodes, b. Feb-09-1905, d. Jul-17-1969.
770 iii. Gladys B. Rhodes b. Jan-03-1907, d. Dec-12-1981.
771 iv. Hester H. Rhodes b. Apr-11-1908, d. Dec 1973.
772 v. Artie E. Rhodes b. Feb-20-1911, d. Nov-03-1979.
773 vi. Grant L. Rhodes b. Oct-16-1912, d. Jan-14-1992.
He Married **Virginia Rexrode**..
774 vii. Ila L. Rhodes, b. Feb-12-1919, d. Oct-15-1988.
She Married **Willard Gee**..
775 viii. Frank W. Rhodes b. Dec-05-1920, d. May-18-1931.
776 ix. Robert Randolph Rhodes b. Feb-22-1923, d. Nov-16-1973.
777 x. Clarence Stanley Rhodes, b. Oct 1926, d. Jan-19-41990.
He Married **Irene Simmons**..
778 xi. Ida V. Rhodes b. Feb-14-1916.
She Married **James Varner**.

360. **Ida Louella[5] Louk** (111.Elizabeth Jane[4] Sponaugle, 23.William[3], 4.Elizabeth L.[2] Arbogast, 1.George[1]), b. Apr 10 1882.
She Married **Harvey Rhodes**.

Children:

779 i. Icie[6] Rhodes.
780 ii. Cluster (Custer) Rhodes.
781 iii. Russell Rhodes.
782 iv. Bonnie Rhodes.

362. **Jessie Lucy[5] Louk** (111.Elizabeth Jane[4] Sponaugle, 23.William[3], 4.Elizabeth L.[2] Arbogast, 1.George[1]), b. Jan 17 1892 in Glady, Randolph Co., WV, d. Apr 06 1962 in Weston, Lewis Co., WV.B Kerr and Mary Elizabeth Burner), d. Nov 26 1956 in Spencer, Rhone Co., WV. Source is family records of Betty Jane (Kerr) Lewis of Beverly, WV. Same person as #7736 in line of Michael Arbogast's son, George.

Children:

783 i. Martha Elizabeth[6] Kerr b. Dec 21 1907 in Randolph Co., WV, d. Apr 25 1989.
Married Nov 15 1926 in Randolph Co., WV, **Gordon Atkins Ricketts**.
\+ 784 ii. Oscar William Kerr b. Oct 10 1909.
\+ 785 iii. Eunice Kerr b. Jan 14 1912.

786 iv. Rita Irene Kerr b. 1914 in Randolph Co., WV.
She Married **Edward I. Roberts**.

787 v. Dorothy Bernice Kerr b. Dec 14 1916 in Randolph Co., WV, d. Sep 10 1981.
She Married **Bruce Haden White**.

\+ 788 vi. Earl Frederick Kerr b. Sep 18 1918.

789 vii. Alfred Lee Kerr b. Sep 18 1920 in Randolph Co., WV, d. Sep 23 1987.
He Married **Freda Bennett**.

790 viii. Hilda Helen Kerr b. Mar 7 1923 in Randolph Co., WV, d. Jun 9 1979.
She Married **Creed Runner**.

\+ 791 ix. Betty Jane Kerr b. Jan 10 1925.

792 x. Kenneth Kermit Kerr b. Sep 13 1926 in Randolph Co., WV, d. Sep 2 1962.
Married Patricia Johnson, 2nd Carolyn Sutton.
(1) He Married **Patricia Johnson**.
(2) He Married **Carolyn Sutton**.

793 xi. Raymond Harold Kerr b. Aug 7 1928 in Randolph Co., WV, d. May 31 1977.
(1) He Married **Dawn Sherman**.
(2) He Married **Alma Everson**.

794 xii. Mary Lourean Kerr b. Dec 31 1930 in Randolph Co., WV, d. Nov 12 1991.
(1) She Married **Elza Lambert**, b. Apr 16 1923.
(2) She Married **John Elza**.

367. **James Dyer[5] Sponaugle** (113.Adam Harness[4], 23.William[3], 4.Elizabeth L.[2] Arbogast, 1.George[1]), b. Mar 23 1878.
(1) Married Sep-21-1906 in Randolph Co., WV, **Erma H. Poling**, b. A 1890.
(2) Married Aug-06-1899 in Randolph Co., WV, **Bettie Lantz Bennett**, b. Sep 1870 in Pendleton Co., WV (daughter of Abraham Lantz and Martha Harold).

Children:

795 i. Verlie Berlie[6] Sponaugle d. UNKNOWN.

369. **Lee Paris[5] Sponaugle** (113.Adam Harness[4], 23.William[3], 4.Elizabeth L.[2] Arbogast, 1.George[1]), b. Mar 17 1882 in Timber Ridge, Hampshire Co., WV, d. May 6 1982 in Hopemont, Terra Alta, Garrett Co., WV, buried in Maple Springs Cem., Eglon, Preston Co., WV.
(1) Married Mar 27 1901 in Pendleton Co., WV, **Mary Selma Grady**, d. UNKNOWN.

Children:

796 i. Okey D.[6] Sponaugle b. Nov-29-1902 in Horton, Randolph Co., WV, buried in Maple Springs Cem., Eglon, Preston Co., WV, d. Jan-20-1918.

797 ii. Ethel F. Sponaugle b. Mar-06-1905 in Horton, Randolph Co., WV, buried in Timber Ridge, Franklin Co., WV, d. Feb-21-1909.

798 iii. Vergie Sponaugle b. Dec-15-1907 in Horton, Randolph Co., WV, d. Dec-15-1907.

\+ 799 iv. Willis Raymond Sponaugle b. Apr-10-1909.

\+ 800 v. Milford Jay Sponaugle b. Sep-18-1913.

(2) Married 1960, **Freda L. Munson**, b. Sep-09-1892, d. 1964.

370. **John Alonzo[5] Sponaugle** (113.Adam Harness[4], 23.William[3], 4.Elizabeth L.[2] Arbogast, 1.George[1]), b. Feb 9 1884 in Randolph Co., WV, d. Nov 26 1985, buried in Cedar Hill Cem., Pendleton Co., WV.
Married Feb 24 1905, **Mary Dessie Vandevander** (daughter of Wayne Sylvester Vandevender and Lena Tingler), d. Mar-05-1964, buried in Cedar Hill Cem., Pendleton Co., WV.

Children:

\+ 801 i. Christena Belle[6] Sponaugle b. Jun-08-1906.

802 ii. Bead Alonzo Sponaugle b. Feb-10-1908 in Circleville Pendleton Co., WV.
(1) Married Aug-12-1928, Annie Pressie Mallow, b. Nov-14-1986 in Circleville Pendleton Co., WV (daughter of Benjamin Franklin Mallow and Roxanna Nelson), buried in Sponaugle, Circleville, WV, d. Dec-27-1982 in Elkins, Randolph Co., WV. She had been Married twice. After her first husband, Gilbert Sponaugle, died in 1925, she Married Bead Sponaugle.
DEC 1982 in Randolph Co., WV Pendleton Times Obituary

(2) He Married Myrtle Warner Bennett.

803 iii. William Sponaugle b. Jan-10-1914.

+ 804 iv. Nola M. Sponaugle b. Feb-21-1915.
+ 805 v. Adam Harness Sponaugle b. Jul-01-1918.
+ 806 vi. Paul R. Sponaugle b. Apr-15-1920.
+ 807 vii. Isaic Jay Sponaugle b. Oct-08-1922.
+ 808 viii. Vallie Verie Sponaugle b. Mar-10-1927.
+ 809 ix. Anna Jo Sponaugle b. Oct-09-1928.
+ 810 x. Mary Lou Sponaugle b. Jul-21-1933.
+ 811 xi. Conda Roy Sponaugle b. May-20-1912.
+ 812 xii. Ona Lucy Sponaugle b. Nov-21-1909.
+ 813 xiii. Cranston John Sponaugle b. Dec-12-1924.

373. **Zola Adam[5] Sponaugle** (113.Adam Harness[4], 23.William[3], 4.Elizabeth L.[2] Arbogast, 1.George[1]), b. Jul 7 1890 in Randolph Co., WV, d. Aug 7 1970 in Buckhannon, Upshur Co., WV.
Married Oct 5 1912 in Buckhannon, Upshur Co., WV, **Cora Balyard**, d. UNKNOWN.

Children:

814 i. Rosalee[6] Sponaugle.
She Married **Raymond Lockwood**.
815 ii. Lela Sponaugle.

374. **Fannie Minerva[5] Sponaugle** (113.Adam Harness[4], 23.William[3], 4.Elizabeth L.[2] Arbogast, 1.George[1]), b. Aug 25 1892 in Randolph Co., WV, d. Sep 20 1985 in Elkins, Randolph Co., WV, buried in Lambert Cem. Wymer, WV.
Married Oct 20 1912 in Oakland, Garrett Co., MD, **George Washington Lambert**, d. Jan-07-1958.

Children:

816 i. Lindsay[6] Lambert b. Oct-14-1913, d. 1940.
817 ii. Brycie Lambert b. Apr-01-1916, d. Jan-25-1979.
818 iii. Vernard H. Lambert b. Jan-23-1918.
He Married **Marie Waldren.**
819 iv. Louvary Jane Lambert b. May-26-1920, buried in Elkins, Randolph Co., WV.
She Married **Virgil Ray**.
820 v. Lynettas Lambert b. Oct-06-1922, d. in Elkins, Randolph Co., WV.
She Married **Steve E. Knutti.**
821 vi. Curley Lambert.
Died young.
822 vii. George Charles Lambert.
Died Young.
823 viii. Katherine Lambert.
She Married **Hoy Waldren**.
824 ix. Edith Jean Lambert b. Jun-08-1932.
(1) She Married **Charles Mullenax**.
(2) She Married **Don Ryan**.
825 x. Hershel C. Lambert b. Jul-10-1937.

375. **Martha Hester[5] Sponaugle** (113.Adam Harness[4], 23.William[3], 4.Elizabeth L.[2] Arbogast, 1.George[1]), b. Jan 25 1894 in Randolph Co., WV, d. Aug 17 1979 in Elkins, Randolph Co., WV.
Married Oct 27 1912 in Pendleton Co., WV, **Okey Oscar Warner**, d. Sep-06-1970, b. Oct-18-1892 in Grant Mem. Hosp., Petersburg, WV, buried in Cedar Hill Cem., Pendleton Co., WV.

Children:

826 i. Vergie B.[6] Warner b. Aug-06-1913.
827 ii. Lacie J. Warner b. Mar-03-1916, d. Oct-04-1916, buried in Nelson Fam. Cem., Timber Ridge, WV.
+ 828 iii. Louvary Warner b. Dec-10-1917.
+ 829 iv. Otis Joy Warner b. Jul-18-1920.
+ 830 v. Thelma Jean Warner b. Sep-09-1922.
+ 831 vi. Mary Bernice Warner.
+ 832 vii. Alice Lucy Warner.
+ 833 viii. Izetta Jewel Warner b. Mar-21-1390.
+ 834 ix. William Guy Warner b. Aug-19-1937.
+ 835 x. Hilbert Oneal Warner b. Nov-10-1935.
836 xi. Herman Isaac Warner b. Jul-21-1939.

He Married **Christina Ann Barnasky**, b. Mar-13-1943 in Frank, Pocahontas Co., WV (daughter of Steve Barnasky and Blanch Moates), d. May-23-1981 in Charlottesville, Albemarle Co., VA.

376. **Monna Roxie[5] Sponaugle** (113.Adam Harness[4], 23.William[3], 4.Elizabeth L.[2] Arbogast, 1.George[1]), b. Jun 3 1896 in Randolph Co., WV, d. Sep 6 1990 in Smith Creek, Pendleton Co., WV.
Married Jul-04-1915 in Timber Ridge, Franklin Co., WV, **Early Thomas Judy**, b. d.

Children:

+ 837 i. Guy William[6] Judy b. Apr-09-1916.
+ 838 ii. Kermit Adam Judy b. Mar-03-1918.
+ 839 iii. Ethel Susan Judy b. Jan-09-1921.
+ 840 iv. Bernice Evangeline Judy b. Apr-04-1924.
+ 841 v. Richard Thomas Judy b. Jul-24-1926.
+ 842 vi. Ina Judy b. May-17-1928.
+ 843 vii. Gayle Edward Judy b. Jan-08-1932.
+ 844 viii. Early Thomas Judy, Jr. b. Dec-02-1934.
+ 845 ix. Patricia Louvon Judy b. Apr-15-1937.
+ 846 x. Gary Nelson Judy b. Oct-16-1940.

379. **Charles Walter[5] Sponaugle** (114.Eli Perry[4], 23.William[3], 4.Elizabeth L.[2] Arbogast, 1.George[1]), b. Mar 04 1876, d. Nov 28 1949.
(1) He Married **Laurie Cunningham**, b. 1876/77.

Children:

847 i. Catl Walter[6] Sponaugle b. Apr-17-1910.

(2) He Married **Bess Ann Arbogast** (daughter of Martin Van Buren Arbogast and Martha Ellen Helmick).

Children:

848 ii. Helen Sponaugle.

390. **Tiny[5] Sponaugle** (115.John Wesley[4], 23.William[3], 4.Elizabeth L.[2] Arbogast, 1.George[1]), b. Jul 23 1896, d. Jan-27-1995 in Elkins, Randolph Co., WV, buried in Dade Me. Park, Cem., Dade Co., FL.
(1) Married 1943, **Pete Nucilli**, d. 1975.
(2) Married 1916, **Osbern Bodkin**.

Children:

849 i. Woodrow[6] Bodkin.
850 ii. Leo Bodkin.
851 iii. Delmar Bodkin.
852 iv. James Bodkin.
853 v. Virginia Bodkin.
Married 1995 in Rawlings, MD, **unknown Lawrence**.
854 vi. Freda Bodkin.
Married 1995 in Hephzibah, GA, **Unknown Smith.**
855 vii. Eva Bodkin.

413. **Delbert[5] Sponaugle** (118.Levi[4], 23.William[3], 4.Elizabeth L.[2] Arbogast, 1.George[1]), b. Apr 08 1900.
He Married **Ruth Channell**.

Children:

856 i. Dale[6] Sponaugle.
857 ii. Paul Sponaugle.

420. **Omar Wilson[5] Sponaugle** (123.Adam Harness[4], 24.George Washington[3], 4.Elizabeth L.[2] Arbogast, 1.George[1]), b. May 21 1921 in Pendleton Co., WV.
Married Jan 17 1946, **Rosie Zona Sponaugle**, b. Jul 20 1928 in Pendleton Co., WV (daughter of William Letcher Sponaugle and Leona Arbogast).

Children:

858 i. Terry Donthan[6] Sponaugle b. Nov 22 1954 in Pendleton Co., WV, d. Dec 12 1954 in Pendleton Co., WV.

65424. **Mary Elizabeth[5] Wymer** (137.Ruth[4] Teter, 26.Catherine[3] Sponaugle, 4.Elizabeth L.[2] Arbogast, 1.George[1]), b. 1895.
She Married **Jesse Thurman Louk**.

Children:

859 i. Emery Gerald[6] Louk.

860 ii. Grover Louk.

861 iii. Claude Louk.

862 iv. Lucille Louk.
She Married **unknown Harper**.

863 v. Belvie Louk.
She Married **unknown Lewhead**.

429. **Walter[5] Warner** (139.Mary Elizabeth[4] Teter, 26.Catherine[3] Sponaugle, 4.Elizabeth L.[2] Arbogast, 1.George[1]), b. May-18-1874, d. Jan-18-1937.
He Married **Virginia Mauzy**, b. 1876, d. May-06-1922.

Children:

864 i. Clifton[6] Warner b. Jan-09-1898, d. Jun-18-1982.

\+ 865 ii. Dice G Warner b. Apr-01-1902.

\+ 866 iii. Beulah Warner.

867 iv. Sally Warner.
She Married **Jesse Tiangler,** b. in Elkins, Randolph Co., WV.

868 v. Lee O. Warner.

\+ 869 vi. Verlin Warner.

439. **Tina[5] Warner** (142.Cecelia (Celia)[4] Sponaugle, 27.Lewis Martin[3], 4.Elizabeth L.[2] Arbogast, 1.George[1]), b. Sep-12-1892, d. Dec-31-1965.
She Married **Olie Judy**, b. Feb-28-1887, d. Jun-29-1964.

Children:

\+ 870 i. Ona Austie[6] Judy.

871 ii. Tina Judy.
She Married **Emory J. Warner**, b. Jan 9 1913 in Churchville, Pendleton Co., WV (son of John W. Warner and Fransina Lee Waybright), d. Apr 19 1994.

\+ 872 iii. Nellie Judy.

873 iv. Richard Judy b. Jun-06-1921 in Riverton, Pendleton, West Virginia, d. Sep-24-1987 in Baltimore, Baltimore City, MD.
He Married **Martha Ann Wimer**, b. Jan-08-1924 (daughter of Charles Amos Wimer and Zoe Etta Thompson).

22 874 v. Virgie Judy.
He Married **Rev Harding Nelson**.

875 vi. Roy T Judy b. Oct 1919 in Riverton, Pendleton Co., WV, d. Jun-11-1985 in Harrisonburg, Rockingham Co., VA.
Married Mar-23-1940, **Mary Eloise Arbogast**, d. in Riverton, Pendleton Co., WV.

\+ 876 vii. Nellie Mae Judy b. Aug-13-1914.

440. **Zola Denver[5] Warner** (142.Cecelia (Celia)[4] Sponaugle, 27.Lewis Martin[3], 4.Elizabeth L.[2] Arbogast, 1.George[1]), b. Jul 1893 in Circleville Pendleton Co., WV, buried in Ashby Warner Cem. Teter Gap, WV, d. Aug-21-1976.
He Married **Lillie Mae Wimer**, b. Jun-24-1895 (daughter of Tiberius Wimer and Cora Ellen Thompson), buried in Maple Hill Cem. Petersburg, Grant Co., WV, d. Aug-21-1976 in Denmar, Pocahontas Co., WV.

Children:

877 i. Gae Nell[6] Warner b. Jun-13-1917.
She Married **Jami Smith**, b. Jul-22-1917 in Riverton, Pendleton Co., WV, buried in North Fork, Mem. Cem. Pendleton Co., VA, d. May-09-1982 in Germany Valley, Pendleton, West Virginia,.

878 ii. Ralph Hansel Warner b. Jul-05-1921 in Hunting Ground, Pendleton Co. WV, d. Jun-06-1944 in Normandy, France.
Ralph died on D-day 1944 on Normandy Beach.

443. **Grace[5] Warner** (142.Cecelia (Celia)[4] Sponaugle, 27.Lewis Martin[3], 4.Elizabeth L.[2] Arbogast, 1.George[1]), b. Jul 1899, d. May-24-1983.
She Married **Curtis Patrick Bland**, b. Jan-23-1889, d. Oct-23-1961.

Children:

\+ 879 i. Roy Dewey[6] Bland.

880 ii. Mildred Wilma Bland.
She Married **Herbert Glenn Nelson**.

+ 881 iii. Eva Lee Bland.
882 iv. Rebecca Grace Bland.
She Married **unknown Hartman**.
883 v. Katherine Bland.
She Married **Elmer Sponaugle, Jr.**.
884 vi. Shirley Bland.
885 vii. Celia Bland b. Sep-05-1919, d. 1920.
886 viii. Hartsel Bland.
+ 887 ix. Marshall Bland b. Dec-17-1916.

448. **Mary Alice[5] Raines** (143.Susan[4] Sponaugle, 27.Lewis Martin[3], 4.Elizabeth L.[2] Arbogast, 1.George[1]), b. Sep-18-1892 in Circleville Pendleton Co., WV, d. Jun-10-1879 in Jacksonville, Duval Co., FL.
She Married **Summers D. Webster**.

Children:

888 i. Freda V.[6] Webster.
889 ii. Maxine Webster.
890 iii. Kisamore Webster.

463. **Mary Clara[5] Warner** (147.Martha Alice[4] Sponaugle, 27.Lewis Martin[3], 4.Elizabeth L.[2] Arbogast, 1.George[1]), b. Oct-27-1890 in London, Gallia Co., OH, d. Dec-04-1970 in Elkins, Randolph Co., WV.
She Married **Charles Hedrick**, b. Jul-01-1890 in Hightown, Highland Co., VA, buried in Whitmer, Randolph Co., WV, d. Oct-12-1950 in Durbin, Pocahontas Co., WV.

Children:

891 i. Pauline[6] Hedrick b. Jun-17-1911 in Whitmer, Randolph Co., WV, d. in as an infant.
892 ii. Paul Hedrick b. Aug-01-1912 in Whitmer, Randolph Co., WV, d. in as an infant.
893 iii. Edgar Hedrick b. Aug-17-1913 in Whitmer, Randolph Co., WV, d. in as an infant.
894 iv. Jesse Brooks Hedrick b. Nov-15-1914 in Whitmer, Randolph Co., WV.
He Married Helen East.
+ 895 v. Richard Pascal Hedrick b. Jul-14-1916.
896 vi. Catherine Virginia Hedrick b. Mar-01-1918 in Whitmer, Randolph Co., WV.
(1) She Married **Mack Herdrick**.
(2) She Married **Dick Simmons**.
897 vii. Mack Hedrick b. Jan-31-1922.
898 viii. Thelma Jane Hedrick b. Mar-01-1923 in Whitmer, Randolph Co., WV.
She Married **Charles Renz**.
899 ix. Bonnie Viva Hedrick b. Feb-13-1928 in Whitmer, Randolph Co., WV, d. Feb-26-1982.
She Married **Denver Davis**.

475. **Albert Harness[5] Wimer** (154.Sylverius[4], 28.Mary Elizabeth[3] Sponaugle, 4.Elizabeth L.[2] Arbogast, 1.George[1]), b. Apr-27-1891 in Simoda, Pendleton Co. WV, buried in North Fork, Mem. Cem. Pendleton Co., VA, d. Apr-04-1966 in Franklin, Pendleton Co., WV.
He Married **Kittie Dyer Warner**, b. Jul-31-1889 in Hunting Ground, Pendleton Co., (W)VA (daughter of Noah Warber and Rebecca Tetar), buried in North Fork, Mem. Cem. Pendleton Co., VA, d. Jul-21-1973 in Roots Run, Pendleton Co., WV.

Children:

+ 900 i. William Harness[6] Wimer b. Sep-06-1914.
+ 901 ii. Harlan Warner Wimer . Feb-16-1920.

476. **MaryEllen[5] Wimer** (154.Sylverius[4], 28.Mary Elizabeth[3] Sponaugle, 4.Elizabeth L.[2] Arbogast, 1.George[1]), b. Oct-07-1892 in Hunting Ground, Pendleton Co., (W)VA, buried in North Fork, Mem. Cem. Pendleton Co., VA, d. Jul-06-1977.
She Married **Charles Warner**, b. Feb-23-1886 in Hunting Ground, Pendleton Co., (W)VA (son of Noah Tetar and Rebecca Warner), buried in North Fork, Mem. Cem. Pendleton Co., VA, d. May-19-1955.

Children:

+ 902 i. Mable[6] Warner b. Aug-13-1910.
+ 903 ii. Arlie Warner b. Nov-20-1912.
904 iii. Ollice C Warner b. Mar-01-1915.
He Married **CLETUS Johnston** (daughter of Solomon Harvey Johnston and Dolly Mullenax).
+ 905 iv. Roy Warner b. Jan-17-1917.
+ 906 v. Ray Warner b. Mar-03-1919.

+ 907 vi. Dewitt Warner b. May-24-1921.
+ 908 vii. Charles Warner, Jr. b. Jul-29-1928.
+ 909 viii. Merl Noah Warner b. Mar-05-1930.
+ 910 ix. Priscilla Lane Warner b. Apr-10-1934.
+ 911 x. Paul Warner b. Oct-10-1935.

477. **Hassie Blanche[5] Wimer** (154.Sylverius[4], 28.Mary Elizabeth[3] Sponaugle, 4.Elizabeth L.[2] Arbogast, 1.George[1]), b. Sep-20-1994, d. Jun-10-1989.
She Married **Willie Nathen Gatewood** (son of Dewitt Clinton Gatewood and Minnie Nelson).

Children:

912 i. Virginia Russie[6] Gatewood b. Jun-13-1920.
She Married **Edwin Duncan Dilworth**.
913 ii. Dewitt Clinton Gatewood b. Mar-02-1922, d. Apr-15-1981.
He Married **Dorothy Adams.**
914 iii. Wilma Gatewood b. 1926.
Married Dec 19 1944, **Robert Lewis Waybright**, b. Aug 22 1924 in Montrose, Randolph Co., WV (son of Guy Daniel Waybright and Toy Helen Bennett).
915 iv. Martha Mae Gatewood b. Mar-07-1924.
She Married **Arthur E Pascoe.**
916 v. Bonnie Lou Gatewood b. Jan-17-1928.
She Married **Scott Standord Hockenberry** (son of Charles Scott Hockenberry and Cora Wimer).
917 vi. Emily Elizabeth Gatewood b. 1931, d. c 1935.
918 vii. Mary Lee Gatewood b. Jul-30-1935.
She Married **Robert Earl Lambert**.

478. **Lou Catherine[5] Wimer** (154.Sylverius[4], 28.Mary Elizabeth[3] Sponaugle, 4.Elizabeth L.[2] Arbogast, 1.George[1]), b. Apr-08-1896, d. Jan-14-1978.
She Married **Lafayette Hedrick**, b. Mar-19-1982 in Highland Co., VA (son of Jonas Hedrick and Mary Susan Wimer), buried in Sinks, Randolph co. WV, d. Oct-14-1941 in Hunting Ground, Pendleton Co., (W)VA.

Children:

+ 919 i. Reva Kerlin[6] Hinkle b. Jan-02-1915.

479. **Charles Amos[5] Wimer** (154.Sylverius[4], 28.Mary Elizabeth[3] Sponaugle, 4.Elizabeth L.[2] Arbogast, 1.George[1]), b. Mar-20-1898, d. Aug-25-1975.
He Married **Zoe Etta Thompson**, b. Feb 1905 in Hunting Ground, Pendleton Co., (W)VA.

Children:

920 i. Edna[6] Wimer.
She Married **Garnet (Buck) Fallon**..
921 ii. Martha Ann Wimer b. Jan-08-1924.
She Married **Richard Judy**, b. Jun-06-1921 in Riverton, Pendleton, West Virginia (son of Olie Judy and Tina Warner), d. Sep-24-1987 in Baltimore, Baltimore City, MD.
922 iii. Charles Mack Wimer b. in Hunting Ground, Pendleton Co. WV.
He Married **Violet Sponaugle** (daughter of Virgil Sponaugle).
923 iv. Leona Jea Wimer b. Sep-08-1928.
She Married **Paul Nicholas**, b. September 27, 1925 (son of Charles Edward Nicholas and Argie Arbogast), d. August 18, 1995.
924 v. Eldon J Wimer.
He Married **Hilda Warner**, b. c 1931 in Cherry Grove, Pendleton Co., WV (daughter of Verlie Warner and Ona Lucy Sponaugle), d. Feb-26-1987 in Port St. Lucie, FL.

481. **Carson Elmer[5] Wymer** (158.Albert[4] Wimer, 28.Mary Elizabeth[3] Sponaugle, 4.Elizabeth L.[2] Arbogast, 1.George[1]), b. Apr-03-1902, buried in Burns Cem., Riverton. WV, d. Apr-13-1974 in Rockingham Memorial Hospital, Harrisonburg Rockingham Co., VA.
Married May-25-1919, **Mucie Kay Burns**, b. Feb-03-1898 in Riverton, Pendleton Co., WV (daughter of Henry Burns and Sarah Bland), d. Dec-29-1978 in Elkins, Randolph Co., WV.

Children:

+ 925 i. Richard Harold[6] Wymer b. Apr-28-1920.
+ 926 ii. Aleta Macie Wymer b. May-26-1926.

+ 927 iii. Bernice Kay Wymer.
+ 928 iv. Vivian Wymer b. Jul-06-1934.
929 v. Berlin Wymer d. in at birth.
930 vi. Granville Wymer.

482. **Maycel^5 Wimer** (158.Albert^4, 28.Mary Elizabeth^3 Sponaugle, 4.Elizabeth L.^{2} Arbogast, 1.George^1), b. Aug-09-1911, d. Feb-09-1961.
She Married **William Stancil.**

Children:

931 i. Fred^6 Stancil.
932 ii. Treva Stancil.
She Married **George Devers**.

483. **Treve Mary^5 Wimer** (158.Albert^4, 28.Mary Elizabeth^3 Sponaugle, 4.Elizabeth L.^{2} Arbogast, 1.George^1), b. Jul-18-1914, d. Sep-22-1965.
(1) She Married **Bealie Smith**.

Children:

933 i. Bealie^6 P. Smith.
She Married **Joanna Wood**.

(2) She Married Brownie Collins.

Children:

934 ii. Linda Collins.

485. **Lillie Mae^5 Wimer** (159.Tiberius^4, 28.Mary Elizabeth^3 Sponaugle, 4.Elizabeth L.^{2} Arbogast, 1.George^1), b. Jun-24-1895, buried in Maple Hill Cem. Petersburg, Grant Co., WV, d. Aug-21-1976 in Denmar, Pocahontas Co., WV.
(1) She **Married Zola Denver Warner** (See marriage to number 440).

Children:

(See marriage to number 440)

(2) Married Dec-27-1920 in Cherry Grove, Pendleton Co., WV, **Pickney Bradey Wimer** (son of Samuel Wimer and Nancy Buzzard), d. Jan-07-1963 in VA hospital., Martinsburg WV.

Children:

+ 935 iii. Mildred Marie Wimer b. Jan-20-1923.
+ 936 iv. Wilda Mae Wilmer b. Nov-07-1926.

486. **Leanna^5 Wimer** (159.Tiberius^4, 28.Mary Elizabeth^3 Sponaugle, 4.Elizabeth L.^{2} Arbogast, 1.George^1), b. Apr-19-1897.
She Married Ora Horbart Kissmore, b. Oct-28-1897 in Lower Timber Ridge Pendleton Co. WV, buried in Wimer Cem, Hunting Ground, Pendleton Co., WV, d. Nov-03-1964 in Harrisonburg, Rockingham Co., VA.

Children:

937 i. Donald Ray^6 Kissmore b. Jun-08-1918 in Hunting Ground, Pendleton Co. WV, d. Aug-05-1920 in Back Ridge, Hunting Ground, Pendleton Co. WV.
+ 938 ii. Roy Richard Kissmore b. May-02-1921.
939 iii. Evaline Peggy Kissmore b. Apr-20-1926, d. Dec-28-1975.
940 iv. Mary Ellen Kissmore b. Dec-10-1928 in Back Ridge, Hunting Ground, Pendleton Co. WV, d. Jun-19-1931 in Back Ridge, Hunting Ground, Pendleton Co. WV.

487. **Mona^5 Wimer** (159.Tiberius^4, 28.Mary Elizabeth^3 Sponaugle, 4.Elizabeth L.^{2} Arbogast, 1.George^1), b. Dec-12-1900 in Hunting Ground, Pendleton Co., (W)VA, buried in Cedar Hill Cem., Pendleton Co., WV, d. Oct-14-1981 in Rockingham Memorial Hospital, Harrisonburg Rockingham Co., VA.
Married Sep-25-1921 in West Dry Run, Pendleton Co. WV, **Elemuel Ake Hartman**, b. Nov-15-1997 to West Dry Run, Pendleton Co,, WV (son of James Hartman and Josephine Lambert), buried in Cedar Hill Cem., Pendleton Co., WV, d. Jun-16-1972 in Rockingham Memorial Hospital, Harrisonburg Rockingham Co., VA.

Children:

+ 941 i. Warden Guy^6 Hartman b. Jan-11-1922.
942 ii. Raymond Wade Hartman.

Married Oct-31-1947 in Circleville Pendleton Co., WV, **Anna Jo Sponaugle**, b. Oct-09-1928 in Circleville Pendleton Co., WV (daughter of John Alonzo Sponaugle and Mary Dessie Vandevander).

943 iii. Irean Cory Hartman b. 1925.
She Married **Edward Hahn**.

944 iv. Betty Jo Hartman b. 1926.
She Married **Leo Christopher Connolly**, b. 1929.

945 v. Mary Virginia Hartman b. 1928.
(1) She Married **Clarence Northcraft**.
(2) She Married **Grover Hollomon**.
(3) She Married **Donald k. Elyard, b. 1928.**

946 vi. Junior Ake Hartman **b. 1931.**
(1) He Married **Mary Bodkin**.
(2) He Married **Joann Colaw**, b. 1938.

947 vii. Jerry Robert Hartman b. 1934.
He Married **Ellen Paugh.**

948 viii. Joan Hartman b. 1936.
She Married **Richard M. Lambert**, b. 1935.

949 ix. Jimmie Glenn Hartman b. 1936.
He Married **Gloria May**.

488. **Amos[5] Wimer** (159.Tiberius[4], 28.Mary Elizabeth[3] Sponaugle, 4.Elizabeth L.[2] Arbogast, 1.George[1]), b. 1902, d. 1969.
He Married **Edith Fannie Humphreys**, b. 2106, d. 1984.

Children:

950 i. Ruth Maxine[6] Wimer b. 1924.
She Married **Donald L. Slayton**, b. 1924.

951 ii. Richard McRaynolds Wimer b. 1925.

952 iii. William Lewis Wimer b. 1926.
(1) He Married **Carolyn Triplett.**
(2) He Married **Nelma Carter**, b. 1931.

953 iv. James Edward Wimer b. 1929, d. 1929.

954 v. Earl Eugene Wimer b. 1932.
He Married **Neva Lea Keterman,** b. 1928.

955 vi. Amos Wimer, Jr. b. 1933.
He Married **Florence Joan Beal.**

956 vii. Deloris Lean Wimer b. 1934.
She Married **Derrell Lee Cooper**, b. 1935.

957 viii. Robert Dale b. 1939, d. 1946.

489. **Grace Elizabeth[5] Wimer** (159.Tiberius[4], 28.Mary Elizabeth[3] Sponaugle, 4.Elizabeth L.[2] Arbogast, 1.George[1]), b. 1905, d. 1985.
(1) She Married **Jessie Wimer**, b. 1901, d. 1985.

Children:

958 i. Maxine[6] Tingler b. 1925.
She Married **Brice Edward Weese**, b. 1921.

959 ii. Jesse Tingler, Jr. b. 1929, d. 1965 in 1965.

(2) She Married **Denver Nelson**, b. 1909, d. 1984.

Children:

960 iii. Ella Sue Nelson b. 1941.
She Married **Choice Kelley Clark**, b. 1937.

961 iv. Clinton Caleb Nelson b. 1944.
He Married **Joyce Crawfod Kruger.**

490. **Russell Jennings[5] Wimer** (159.Tiberius[4], 28.Mary Elizabeth[3] Sponaugle, 4.Elizabeth L.[2] Arbogast, 1.George[1]), b. 1907, d. 1985.
(1) He Married **Bertha Lane Hedrick**, b. 1898, d. 1969.
(2) He Married **Thelma Lee Thompson Elmore**, b. 1911.
(3) He Married **Mona Arveta Hinkle**, b. 1912.

Children:

962 i. Ralph Jennings^6 Hinkle b. 1943.
He Married **Mary Rose Gordon**.

491. **Iva Phillis^5 Wimer** (159.Tiberius^4, 28.Mary Elizabeth^3 Sponaugle, 4.Elizabeth L.^{2} Arbogast, 1.George^1), b. 1909.
She Married **Rudolph Bernard Huffman**, b. 16906, d. 1991.

Children:

963 i. Glenn^6 Huffman b. 1953.

492. **Willie Clinton^5 Wimer** (159.Tiberius^4, 28.Mary Elizabeth^3 Sponaugle, 4.Elizabeth L.^{2} Arbogast, 1.George^1), b. 1911.
He Married **Eltha Jane Vandevander**, b. 1918.

Children:

964 i. Curtis Glenn^6 Wimer b. 1946.
He Married **Sharon Lee Smallwood,** b. 1947.

493. **Rosetta^5 Long** (165.Virginia Catherine (Jennie)^4 Teter, 30.Leah^3 Sponaugle, 4.Elizabeth L.^{2} Arbogast, 1.George^1), b. Dec-28-1881, d. 1966.
Married Jun-06-1901 in ID, **Edgar Crosby**, b. Dec-28-1881 in WV.

Children:

\+ 965 i. Orpha^6 Crosby.

494. **Elmina^5 Long** (165.Virginia Catherine (Jennie)^4 Teter, 30.Leah^3 Sponaugle, 4.Elizabeth L.^{2} Arbogast, 1.George^1), b. Apr-26-1884 in WV, d. Apr-21-1945.
Married Jan-27-1904, **Burton Mosley**.

Children:

\+ 966 i. George Otis^6 Mosley b. Jan-20-1905.
\+ 967 ii. Grace Levin Mosley b. Mar-29-1908.
\+ 968 iii. Johnny Mosley b. Sep-26-1910.
\+ 969 iv. Opel Irene Mosley b. May-22-1913.

495. **John William^5 Long** (165.Virginia Catherine (Jennie)^4 Teter, 30.Leah^3 Sponaugle, 4.Elizabeth L.^{2} Arbogast, 1.George^1), b. Feb-11-1887 in WV, d. Mar-06-1953 in Idaho.
He Married **Hazel Gilmore.**

Children:

\+ 970 i. Dorothy Leone^6 Long b. Nov-23-1914.
971 ii. John Emery Long b. Feb-04-1918, d. Jul-05-1920.
\+ 972 iii. Lorna Doone Long b. Jul-26-1919.
973 iv. Forrest Long b. May-06-1923.
Forrest Married **four times**, and had children with three of them.
He Married **Edith Stanfield**.
\+ 974 v. Mary Virginia Long b. Jun-17-1929.

496. **Arta^5 Long** (165.Virginia Catherine (Jennie)^4 Teter, 30.Leah^3 Sponaugle, 4.Elizabeth L.^{2} Arbogast, 1.George^1), b. Jul-11-1889.
He Married **Charles Wesley O'Bryan**, b. Nov-25-1889, d. May-03-1963.

Children:

\+ 975 i. Gordon Charles^6 O'Bryan b. Oct-12-1912.

497. Florence^5 Long (165.Virginia Catherine (Jennie)^4 Teter, 30.Leah^3 Sponaugle, 4.Elizabeth L.^{2} Arbogast, 1.George^1), b. Feb-01-1891, d. Dec-10-1968.
Married Oct-15-1910, **Hugh Douglas Dillon**, b. Dec 1884, d. Dec-28-1954.

Children:

976 i. Elmer^6 Dillon b. Sep-08-1911, d. Dec-21-1937.
\+ 977 ii. Zona Dillon b. Feb-02-1914.

498. **Ada^5 Long** (165.Virginia Catherine (Jennie)^4 Teter, 30.Leah^3 Sponaugle, 4.Elizabeth L.^{2} Arbogast, 1.George^1), b. Oct-23-1894 in WV, d. Jun-06-1921.
Married Jun-30-1914, **Leopold Summers**, b. Jul-01-1889.

Children:

\+ 978 i. Robert Harold[6] Summers b. Sep-19-1915.
\+ 979 ii. Juanita Rilla Summers b. Jan-23-1917.

500. **Edward[5] Teter** (166.Andrew[4], 30.Leah[3] Sponaugle, 4.Elizabeth L.[2] Arbogast, 1.George[1]).
He Married **Flossie Wolford**.

Children:

980 i. Nora[6] Teter.
981 ii. Nina Teter.
982 iii. Marvin Teter.
He Married **Nellie Davis**.
983 iv. Dorothy Teter.
984 v. Olyn Teter.
He Married **Helen Ranck.**
985 vi. Holley Teter.
986 vii. Raymond Teter.

501. **Clifton Andrew[5] Teter** (166.Andrew[4], 30.Leah[3] Sponaugle, 4.Elizabeth L.[2] Arbogast, 1.George[1]), b. Mar-05-0893.
(1) Married 1917, **Etta bell Roy**, d. 1966.

Children:

\+ 987 i. Roy Clifton[6] Teter b. Aug-11-1918.

(2) He Married Ethel J Johnson, b. 1886 in Macedonia, Morgan Co., IL, d. Sep 9 1956.

502. **Delpha[5] Teter** (166.Andrew[4], 30.Leah[3] Sponaugle, 4.Elizabeth L.[2] Arbogast, 1.George[1]), b. Dec-15-1894.
She Married **Henry Lawrence Nester**, b. Mar-03-1892. Hans Jorg and Maria Dieter : born in Germany and emigrated to America in 1727. [Eva A Teter Winfield]

. *Children:*

988 i. Gerald[6] Nester.
He Married **Irene Kissmore**.
989 ii. Sandy Nester.

506. **Howard[5] Teter** (166.Andrew[4], 30.Leah[3] Sponaugle, 4.Elizabeth L.[2] Arbogast, 1.George[1]).
He Married **Orpha Smith**, b. 1905 (daughter of Solomon Smith and Alice Grace Teter).

Children:

990 i. Savannah[6] Teter.
(1) She Married **Harvey White**.
(2) She Married **Charles Rhodes**.
991 ii. Lucille Teter.
She Married **unknown Fortney**.
992 iii. Marie Teter.
She Married **Wayne Schoolover**.
993 iv. Gerald Teter.
He Married **Jean Moore**.
994 v. Ruth Teter.
She Married **G L Harman**.

511. **Irabelle[5] Teter** (166.Andrew[4], 30.Leah[3] Sponaugle, 4.Elizabeth L.[2] Arbogast, 1.George[1]), b. Jun 18 1891 in Tucker Co., WV, d. 1958 in Tucker Co., WV, buried in Red Creek, Tucker Co., WV.
Married Dec 10 1909 in Garrett Co., MD, **Don Waybright**, b. Oct 2 1888 in Tucker Co., WV (son of Isaac P Waybright and Sidney Ellen Arbogast), d. Apr 1963 in Elkins, Randolph Co., WV, buried in Red Creek, Tucker Co., WV.

Children:

995 i. Eva Pearl[6] Waybright b. Sep 9 1911 in Osceola Randolph Co., WV.
She Married **Ivan Eye.**
996 ii. Carl Waybright b. 1915 in Osceola Randolph Co., WV.
997 iii. Jesse Willard Waybright b. Mar 26 1917 in Osceola Randolph Co., WV, d. Oct 1975, buried in Flanagan Hill Cem., Tucker Co., WV.

He Married **Savannah White**.

998 iv. Cornelia Ruth Waybright b. Jan 9 1919 in Osceola Randolph Co., WV, d. 1971.

999 v. Alma Helen Waybright b. Jun 1919 in Osceola Randolph Co., WV.

1000 vi. Sturl Robert Waybright b. Feb 9 1921 in Osceola Randolph Co., WV.
(2) He Married **Ruth Thomson**.

1001 vii. Freddie Rachel Waybright b. Jan 6 1923 in Osceola Randolph Co., WV.
Married Dec 10 1945, **Thomas Lindsy Bonner**.

1002 viii. Earl Donald Waybright b. Oct 20 1925 in Tucker Co., WV, d. 1951.

1003 ix. Erma Gertrude Waybright b. Aug 6 1927 in Tucker Co., WV.
She Married **Blair Gordon**.

1004 x. Andrew Jerald Waybright b. Jun 19 1929 in Shavers Mountain, Tucker Co., WV.

512. **Selena[5] Teter** (167.William Patterson[4], 30.Leah[3] Sponaugle, 4.Elizabeth L.[2] Arbogast, 1.George[1]), b. Apr-08-1889.
She Married **Chester Foy**.

Children:

1005 i. Warren[6] Foy.

1006 ii. John Foy.

+ 1007 iii. Virginia Foy.

515. **Vigrinia[5] Teter** (167.William Patterson[4], 30.Leah[3] Sponaugle, 4.Elizabeth L.[2] Arbogast, 1.George[1]), b. Sep-26-1897.
She Married **Lee Gillespie**.

Children:

1008 i. Orin[6] Gillespie.
Lost at sea during WWII.

1009 ii. Bruce Gillespie d. 1975.

+ 1010 iii. Patti Lynn Gillespie.

516. **George Wesley[5] Grimm** (167.William Patterson[4] Teter, 30.Leah[3] Sponaugle, 4.Elizabeth L.[2] Arbogast, 1.George[1]), b. Oct-13-1899, buried in Parson City Cem., WV, d. Aug-16-1976.
Married May-20-1975, **Ada May Kearns**, b. Mar-17-1903.

Children:

+ 1011 i. Darrell[6] Teter b. Feb-24-1920.

1012 ii. Leonard Orville Teter b. Sep-14-1921, buried in Kerns Cem., Middle Mountain, Sully, WV, d. Jun-01-1923.

1013 iii. Paul William Teter b. Sep-19-1923, buried in Kerns Cem., Middle Mountain, Sully, WV, d. Aug-22-1925.

520. **Mary Ann[5] Teter** (168.John Jackson[4], 30.Leah[3] Sponaugle, 4.Elizabeth L.[2] Arbogast, 1.George[1]), b. Jan-05-1897, buried in Bright Chapel Cem., Dry Fork, WV.
Married Apr-13-1913, **John Add Bright**, b. Apr-27-1888 (son of Thomas Wesley Bright and Martha Alice Cooper). source: Ancestory.com Liptrap family.

Children:

1014 i. Dessie Gladys[6] Bright b. Oct-09-1914 in Mountain State Memorial Gardens Elkins Randolph Co., WV.
She Married **Perry Hall Phillips**, b. May-11-1907, d. Feb-07-1979.

1015 ii. Ethel Hazel Bright b. Oct-27-1916.
(1) She Married **Ralph Burns**.
(2) She Married **Kensel E. Stephens**, b. Sep-24-1920.

1016 iii. Eva Mae Bright b. Dec-26-1918, buried in East Oak Grove Cem., Morgantown, WV.
(1) She Married **Clarence William Fister**.
(2) Married Oct-02-1972, **Kenneth Paul Breakiron**, b. Aug-23-1906.

+ 1017 iv. Flossie Mabel Bright b. Aug-17-1920.

1018 v. Fanny Ruth Bright b. Sep-10-1922.

1019 vi. Burley Lee Bright b. Nov-27-1924, d. Nov-03-1971.

1020 vii. Texie Marie Bright b. Jan-02-1928.

1021 viii. Robert Earl Bright b. Jan-16-1931.
Married Jun-04-1958, **Jacquie Sue Thornhill**, b. Mar-28-1939.

1022 ix. Nellie Blanche Bright b. Aug-13-1933.
She Married **Junior Cordell Shreve**, b. Jul-08-1939.

1023 x. Alice Belle Bright b. Apr-19-1936.
She Married **Henry Cecil Tharp**, b. Aug-22-1922.

1024 xi. Daniel Perry Bright b. Aug-15-1940, buried in Maplewood Cem., Elkins, Randolph Co., WV, d. Jun-05-1981. Married Aug-16-1965, **Joyce Lynn Bland**, b. Sep-06-1947.

523. **Rosa Bell[5] Bright** (170.Elizabeth Mary[4] Teter, 30.Leah[3] Sponaugle, 4.Elizabeth L.[2] Arbogast, 1.George[1]), b. 1897, d. 1980.
(1) She Married **Robert Mace Davis**, b. 1892.

Children:

+ 1025 i. Genevieve Marie[6] Davis b. 1914.
+ 1026 ii. Herbert William Davis b. 1919.
+ 1027 iii. Londa Ruby Davis b. 1923.
+ 1028 iv. Howard Ernest Davis b. 1926.
+ 1029 v. Hallena Bell Davis b. 1928.
+ 1030 vi. Martin VanBuren Davis b. 1929.

(2) Married 1955, **Martin VanBuren Bonner**, b. 1865.

Children:

+ 1031 vii. Calvin Collage Bright b. 1932.
1032 viii. Nathan Hale Bright b. 1933.
1033 ix. Eva Hasta Bright b. 1935.
She Married **James Moore, Jr..**
1034 x. Benjamin Cleon Bright b. 1938.
He Married **Shirley Rosenburg.**
1035 xi. Ellen Mae Bright b. 1941.
(1) She Married **James Young**.
(2) She Married **Robert Zekus**.

529. **Orpha[5] Smith** (171.Alice Grace[4] Teter, 30.Leah[3] Sponaugle, 4.Elizabeth L.[2] Arbogast, 1.George[1]) (See marriage to number 506.)

530. Oakey[5] Smith (171.Alice Grace[4] Teter, 30.Leah[3] Sponaugle, 4.Elizabeth L.[2] Arbogast, 1.George[1]), b. 1894, buried in Rich Mountain, Pendleton Co., WV, d. Nov-05-1958.
He Married **Gertie Allen**.

Children:

1036 i. Magdaline[6] Smith.
She Married **unknown Spencer**.
1037 ii. Nettie Smith.
She Married **unknown Cassidy.**
1038 iii. Oakey Smith, Jr..
1039 iv. Myrtle Smith.
She Married **unknown Bailey**.
1040 v. Dale Smith.
He Married **Betty Summerfield.**
1041 vi. Lavene Smith.
She Married **unknown Burns.**
1042 vii. Nannie Smith.
She Married **unknown Miller**.

532. **Gilbert P.[5] Smith** (171.Alice Grace[4] Teter, 30.Leah[3] Sponaugle, 4.Elizabeth L.[2] Arbogast, 1.George[1]), b. Apr-12-1899, buried in Davis, Tucker Co., WV, d. May-11-1971.
He Married **Bessie Susan Blizzard**.

Children:

1043 i. Alice Jan[6] Smith b. 1942, d. in Stillborn.
1044 ii. Gilbert P. Smith, Jr. b. 1943, d. in Stillborn.

536. **Rosa Alice[5] Smith** (171.Alice Grace[4] Teter, 30.Leah[3] Sponaugle, 4.Elizabeth L.[2] Arbogast, 1.George[1]), b. c 1910, buried in Fort Ashby Cem. WV, d. Oct-01-1985.
She Married **Norman Daniel White**.

Children:

1045 i. Donald[6] Smith.

+ 1046 ii. Andrew White.

537. **Omer[5] Smith** (171.Alice Grace[4] Teter, 30.Leah[3] Sponaugle, 4.Elizabeth L.[2] Arbogast, 1.George[1]), b. Feb-17-1912.
He Married **Nina Blizzard**.

Children:

+ 1047 i. Sarah Louise[6] Smith.
1048 ii. Kaye P Smith.
She Married **Wilma Foltz.**

538. **Sylvia[5] Smith** (171.Alice Grace[4] Teter, 30.Leah[3] Sponaugle, 4.Elizabeth L.[2] Arbogast, 1.George[1]), b. May-24-1914.
She Married **Don Burgess**.

Children:

1049 i. Richard[6] Burgess b. 1938, d. 1938 in at birth.
+ 1050 ii. David Burgess.
+ 1051 iii. Kenneth Burgess.
+ 1052 iv. Nancy Burgess.
1053 v. Sharon Burgess.
She Married **Roger Mullenax**.
+ 1054 vi. Betty Burgess.

550. **Mary Dessie[5] Vandevander** (186.Lena[4] Tingler, 32.Sarah[3] Sponaugle, 4.Elizabeth L.[2] Arbogast, 1.George[1]) (See marriage to number 370.)

555. Virgil[5] Vandevander (186.Lena[4] Tingler, 32.Sarah[3] Sponaugle, 4.Elizabeth L.[2] Arbogast, 1.George[1]).
He Married **Halcie Mullenax** (daughter of Otha Lambert and Martha Ellen Mullenax).

Children:

1055 i. Wayne[6] Vandevander.
1056 ii. Randall Vandevander.
1057 iii. Billy D. Vandevander.
1058 iv. Robert Vandevander.

558. **Ethel Mae[5] Sponaugle** (188.Gilbert Kenton[4], 33.Jacob[3], 4.Elizabeth L.[2] Arbogast, 1.George[1]), b. Aug-06-1906, d. Oct-29-1992.
Married Mar-11-1992, **Marlin Arbogast**, b. Oct-06-1904 (son of Alfred T. Arbogast and Sarah E. Wyant Arbogast), buried in Rest Haven Mem Gar, Harrisonburg VA.

Children:

1059 i. Mike[6] Arbogast b. Mar-11-1926 in Glady, Randolph Co., WV, d. Jan-05-1998 in Harrisonburg, Rockingham Co., VA.
He Married **Charlotte Swecker**, d. Aug-02-1987 in Harrisonburg, Rockingham Co., VA.
1060 ii. Merl Arbogast b. Nov-18-1929, d. Dec-06-2014 in Flagler County, FL.
He Married **Carmela Ida Arbogast**, b. Mar-27-1926, d. Aug-15-1999.
1061 iii. Cam Arbogast b. Sep-28-1927 in Circleville Pendleton Co., WV, d. May-01-2014 in Harrisonburg, Rockingham Co., VA.

560. **Brison Jay[5] Sponaugle** (188.Gilbert Kenton[4], 33.Jacob[3], 4.Elizabeth L.[2] Arbogast, 1.George[1]), b. Apr 03 1911 in Hunting Ground, Pendleton Co., (W)VA, d. Jun 13 1992.
He Married **Judith Warner,** b. Dec 18 1915 (daughter of Pet Warner and Lura Mullenax).

Children:

1062 i. M. Elaine[6] Sponaugle.
She Married **(unknown) Alt.**
1063 ii. Jenny K. Sponaugle.
Married **(unknown) Halterman**.
+ 1064 iii. Harold Michael Sponaugle b. May-18-1936.

564. **Herbert Charles[5] Sponaugle** (191.William Letcher[4], 33.Jacob[3], 4.Elizabeth L.[2] Arbogast, 1.George[1]), b. Sep 1 1913 in Pendleton Co., WV, d. Jun 24 1989 in Alliance, Stark Co., OH.
Married Mar 15 1944**, Sally Nola "Sallie" Sponaugle**, b. Jul 11 1910 in Cherry Grove, Pendleton Co., WV, d. Nov 12 2001 in Arbovale Cem., Arbovale, Pocahontas Co., WV.

Children:

1065 i. Jerlene Wilda[6] Sponaugle b. Sep 23 1935 in Pendleton Co., WV, d. Sep 16 1996.
Married Mar 7 1953, Solon Clarence Blosser , Jr, b. Aug 18 1928.

+ 1066 ii. Juanita Sponaugle b. Jun 12 1944.

+ 1067 iii. Patrica Sponaugle.

565. **Nola Lee[5] Sponaugle** (191.William Letcher[4], 33.Jacob[3], 4.Elizabeth L.[2] Arbogast, 1.George[1]), b. Jan 21 1916 in Pendleton Co., WV, d. Mar 3 1973 in Rockingham Co., VA.

Married Oct 6 1935, **Marshall William Wimer**, b. Nov 26 1913, d. Nov 19 1985.

Children:

1068 i. James Sherwood[6] Wimer b. Aug 4 1954 in Weyers Cave, Augusta Co., VA, d. Mar 16 1965 in Harrisonburg, Rockingham Co., VA.

570. **Roche Elijah[5] Sponaugle** (191.William Letcher[4], 33.Jacob[3], 4.Elizabeth L.[2] Arbogast, 1.George[1]), b. Mar 1 1925 in Pendleton Co., WV, d. Dec 6 1968 in Baltimore, Baltimore Co., MD.
Married Apr 20 1947, **Harvey Jay Long**, b. Sep 20 1921 in West Virginia.

Children:

1069 i. Ronnie Jay[6] Long b. Dec 30 1946 in Petersburg, Grant Co., WV.

572. **Rosie Zona[5] Sponaugle** (191.William Letcher[4], 33.Jacob[3], 4.Elizabeth L.[2] Arbogast, 1.George[1]) (See marriage to number 420.)

573. **Marvin Luther[5] Sponaugle** (192.Herman Henry[4], 33.Jacob[3], 4.Elizabeth L.[2] Arbogast, 1.George[1]), b. Jun-08-1903, d. Oct-21-1990 in Franklin, Pendleton Co., WV.
(1) He Married **Argyle Wimer.**

Children:

+ 1070 i. Loriraine L[6] Sponaugle b. Feb-03-1924.

+ 1071 ii. Ruth Elaine Sponaugle b. May-05-1928.

+ 1072 iii. Marvin Luther Sponaugle, Jr. b. May-05-1928.

1073 iv. Herbert W. Sponaugle b. Feb-26-1925, d. Apr-08-1925.

1074 v. Lucy Louise Sponaugle b. Jan-16-1932, d. Apr-08-1932.

+ 1075 vi. Carroll Lee Sponaugle b. Mar-10-1933.

1076 vii. Betty Lou Sponaugle b. Jun-04-1934.

+ 1077 viii. Loretta June Sponaugle b. Dec-27-1937.

(2) He Married Wanda Grover.

574. **Beulah[5] Sponaugle** (192.Herman Henry[4], 33.Jacob[3], 4.Elizabeth L.[2] Arbogast, 1.George[1]), b. Jul-26-1901 in WV, d. 1998 in MD.
She Married **Jesse Forest Simmons**, b. 1898, d. 1977.

Children:

1078 i. Carl[6] Simmons.

1079 ii. Herman Simmons.

1080 iii. Hansel Simmons.

575. **Raymond[5] Sponaugle** (192.Herman Henry[4], 33.Jacob[3], 4.Elizabeth L.[2] Arbogast, 1.George[1]), b. Mar-09-1905 in Hunting Ground, Pendleton Co. WV, buried in Sponaugle Family Cem., Hunting Grounds Pendleton County WV, d. Dec-26-1981 in Cherry Grove, Pendleton Co., WV.
Married Sep-12-1925 in Pendleton Co., WV, **Pauline Warner**.

Children:

1081 i. Olin[6] Sponaugle.

1082 ii. Berlin Sponaugle.

1083 iii. Gaylon C Sponaugle.

1084 iv. Merle Sponaugle.

576. **Alpha Cynyhia[5] Sponaugle** (192.Herman Henry[4], 33.Jacob[3], 4.Elizabeth L.[2] Arbogast, 1.George[1]), b. Dec-18-1907.
She Married **Curtis Bennett**, b. Oct-28-1902, d. Jun-30-1987.

Children:

1085 i. Raynond^{6} Bennett d. Mar-12-1925.
1086 ii. Hartsell Bennett d. Jul-22-1926.
1087 iii. Guy Bennett d. Jun-17-1940.
\+ 1088 iv. Delene Bennett.
1089 v. Paul Bennett.
1090 vi. Harlan Bennett.
\+ 1091 vii. Judy Bennett.

577. **Myrtle M^{5} Sponaugle** (192.Herman Henry^{4}, 33.Jacob^{3}, 4.Elizabeth L.^{2} Arbogast, 1.George^{1}), b. Dec-13-1908, d. Nov-27-1970 in Cherry Grove, Pendleton Co., WV.
She Married **Elmer P. Phares**, b. 1908 (son of Cleat Phares and Edith C Hammer), d. Jan-02-1972.

Children:

\+ 1092 i. Richard Cleat^{6} Phares b. May-16-1928.
\+ 1093 ii. Ina Lee Phares b. Aug-07-1930.
\+ 1094 iii. James H. Phares b. Oct-19-1932.
\+ 1095 iv. Raymond Phares b. Sep-20-1934.
\+ 1096 v. Mary June Phares b. Dec-15-1936.
\+ 1097 vi. Dottie Lou Phares b. Aug-02-1944.

580. **Mary Kerlin^{5} Sponaugle** (192.Herman Henry^{4}, 33.Jacob^{3}, 4.Elizabeth L.^{2} Arbogast, 1.George^{1}), b. Mar-07-1914, d. Jul-27-1971 in Davis Memorial Hospital, Elkins, Randolph Co., WV.
Married Mar-28-1932, **Ralph M. Landis**, b. May-17-1905, d. Dec-28-1975.

Children:

1098 i. Kitty^{6} Landis.
She Married **Blain Simmons**.
1099 ii. Dottie Landis.
She Married **Jery Propst**.
1100 iii. Charles H Landis.
1101 iv. Ralph M Landis, Jr..
1102 v. Olin R Landis.
1103 vi. John W Landis.
1104 vii. Robert J Landis.
1105 viii. Jimmy J Landis.
1106 ix. Larry Landis.

581. **Levern^{5} Sponaugle** (192.Herman Henry^{4}, 33.Jacob^{3}, 4.Elizabeth L.^{2} Arbogast, 1.George^{1}), b. Dec-16-1919.
She Married **H Stern Butcher**, b. Dec-12-1915.

Children:

1107 i. Hugh^{6} Butcher.
\+ 1108 ii. Sherry Butcher.
1109 iii. Douglas Butcher.

582. **Roscoe^{5} Sponaugle** (192.Herman Henry^{4}, 33.Jacob^{3}, 4.Elizabeth L.^{2} Arbogast, 1.George^{1}), b. May-10-1921.
(1) He Married **Judith Bland.**

Children:

\+ 1110 i. Sandra^{6} Sponaugle.

(2) He Married **Phyllis Fisher**.

Children:

\+ 1111 ii. Peggy Sue Sponaugle.

586. **Ruth^{5} Sponaugle** (192.Herman Henry^{4}, 33.Jacob^{3}, 4.Elizabeth L.^{2} Arbogast, 1.George^{1}), b. May-18-1918.
She Married Theron A Harper, b. Feb-14-1924, d. Mar-02-1964.

Children:

\+ 1112 i. Patsey Louisa^{6} Harper.
\+ 1113 ii. Dorothy Harper.

1114 iii. Elizabeth Ann Harper.
Married Sep-03-1983, **Richard Allen Harper**.

609. **OllieMae[5] Rice** (222.Ollie Mae[4] Bird, 37.Emily[3] Cook, 5.Catherine[2] Arbogast, 1.George[1]).
She Married **unknown Murphy**.

Children:

1115 i. Martha[6] Murphy.

612. **Caddie[5] Slaven** (237.Carrie E.[4] Arbogast, 45.Jeremiah Elderidge[3], 6.Emanuel[2], 1.George[1]), b. Jun-15-1895 in New Hampton, VA, buried in Blue Grass Cem., Highland Co., VA, d. Aug-12-1990 in Harrisonburg, Rockingham Co., VA.
She Married **A. Frank McNulty**, d. 1965.

Children:

1116 i. Nancy[6] McNulty.
1117 ii. Mary McNulty.
1118 iii. James F. McNulty.

613. **Howard K.[5] Arbogast** (238.William Gum[4], 45.Jeremiah Elderidge[3], 6.Emanuel[2], 1.George[1]), b. Dec-02-1882 in Hightown, Highland Co., VA, d. Aug-29-1956 in Swoope, Augusta Co., VA, buried in McKinley, VA.
Married Dec-24-1903 in Blue Grass Cem., Highland Co., VA, **Lucy D. Fox**, b. Feb-02-1878 in Blue Grass, Highland Co., VA (daughter of Charpes H. Fox and Louvina Hinkle), d. Jun-18-1939, buried in Wimer Family Cem., Highland Co, VA.

Children:

\+ 1119 i. Argyle Grace[6] Arbogast b. Sep-09-1905.

614. **William G.[5] Arbogast** (238.William Gum[4], 45.Jeremiah Elderidge[3], 6.Emanuel[2], 1.George[1]), b. Jul-03-1887 in Highland Co., VA.
Married 1911, **May J. Wallace**, b. 1889.

Children:

1120 i. Thelma[6] Arbogast b. 1916 in Rainier, Columbia Co., OR, d. 1961.
Married 1935 in Rainelle, Greenbrier Co. WV, **Homer L. Gibbs**.
\+ 1121 ii. William G. Arbogast, Jr. b. 1919.

615. **Charles Howard[5] Roberts** (258.Ada Neil[4] Arbogast, 55.David Howard[3], 6.Emanuel[2], 1.George[1]), b. Apr-30-1918, d. Feb-01-1983.
He Married **Deloris Lien**, b. Mar-12-1925 in Blooming Prairie, MN .

Children:

\+ 1122 i. Larry Howard[6] Roberts b. Jun-06-1946.

616. **George B.[5] Crew** (263.Saulsberry N[4] Chew, 58.George E. M.[3], 8.Mary "Polly"[2] Arbogast, 1.George[1]), b. Aug 07 1904, d. Nov 26 1991.
He Married **Nellie Dessa Lambert,** b. Feb 19 1901 in Pendleton Co., WV, d. Mar 16 1990 in Harrisonburg, Rockingham Co., VA.

Children:

1123 i. Emma Mae[6] Chew.

624. **Dennis Keith[5] Flanagan** (266.Margaret Jean[4] Arbogast, 68.Orien Austin[3], 10.Henry W.[2], 1.George[1]), b. Dec 20 1946 in Elkins, Randolph Co., WV.
Married Dec 17 1971, **Carolyn Breese.**

Children:

1124 i. Jason Jay[6] Flanagan b. Dec 19 1974.
1125 ii. James Ryan Flanagan b. May 29 1980.

Generation Six

628. **Floyd William[6] Collins** (269.Louella Maer[5] Grogg, 69.Emily Jane[4] Mullenax, 11.John H.[3], 2.Hannah[2] Arbogast, 1.George[1]), b. Nov 25 1893, d. May 20 1968 in Frank, Pocahontas Co., WV.

Ref: Pocahontas 1981: 257 S/o Andrew Morgan and Louella Mae (Grogg) Collins. Louella is the same person as #7634, a descendant of George; see Volume III for her lineage.
Married Nov 26 1914 in Pocahontas Co., WV, **Bertie Ruth Ervine**, b. Jul 18 1894 (daughter of Edward Newton Ervine and Phoebe Rebecca Bright), d. May 20 196

Children:

+ 1126 i. Paul Hunter[7] Collins b. Dec 9 1915.
1127 ii. Donald Eugene Collins b. 1917, d. 1936 in Circleville, Pendleton Co., WV.
Died in accident.

629. **Cecil Morgan[6] Collins** (269.Louella Maer[5] Grogg, 69.Emily Jane[4] Mullenax, 11.John H.[3], 2.Hannah[2] Arbogast, 1.George[1]), b. Aug 14 1896 in Boyer, Pocahontas Co., WV, d. Apr 13 1952 in Hospital, Columbus, Franklin Co., OH, buried in Union Cem., Olentangy River, Columbus, Franklin Co., OH.
He Married **Iona Patrica Waybright**, b. Apr 24 1894 in Job, Randolph Co., WV (daughter of Wilber Allen Waybright and Sena White), d. Dec 08 1965 in Elkins, Randolph Co., WV.

Children:

+ 1128 i. Harold Cecil[7] Collins b. Aug 13 1916.
1129 ii. Wilma Dell Collins b. Jan 10 1918 in Sitlington Creek, Pocahontas Co., WV, d. Jul 14 1918 in Sitlington Creek, Pocahontas Co., WV.
+ 1130 iii. Bernard Morris Collins b. Jan 30 1920.
1131 iv. Ruby Mae Collins b. Feb 10 1925 in Laurel Lick, Boyer, Pocahontas Co., WV, d. Sep 1925 in Laurel Lick, Boyer, Pocahontas Co., WV.

642. **Bert[6] Waybright** (272.Albert[5], 71.Martha[4] Mullenax, 12.George[3], 2.Hannah[2] Arbogast, 1.George[1]), b. Oct 1890 in Pendleton Co., WV.
(1) He Married **Minnie V. (Unknown),** b. Oct 3 1891, d. Jan 1981 in Alleghany Co., MD.

Children:

1132 i. Ruth V.[7] Waybright.
1133 ii. (unknown) Waybright.
1134 iii. (unknown) Waybright.
1135 iv. Edsel Waybright b. Jul 24 1919.
1136 v. Gerald Waybright b. Jul 10 1922.

(2) He Married **Artie Dolly Hedrick**, b. May 10 1894, d. Jan 15 1968 in Elkins, Randolph Co., WV.

Children:

+ 1137 vi. Bricel Waybright b. Dec 13 1911.

647. **Marie[6] Lambert** (274.Lulu[5] Arbogast, 74.Samuel Benjamin[4], 14.William Samual[3], 3.Daniel[2], 1.George[1]), b. May-23-1896, d. Mar-03-1987 in Berkeley Springs, WV.
She Married **Charles Allen Kline**, d. 1934.

Children:

1138 i. Betty Lou[7] Kline.
She Married **Unknown Harminson**.

650. **Frances Ann[6] Arbogast** (303.Elmo Mead[5], 89.Emery Matthew[4], 21.John Wesley[3], 3.Daniel[2], 1.George[1]), b. Dec-03-1925 in Hollywood, CA, d. Dec-27-1991 in Albuquerque, Bernalillo Co., NM.
living family.
She Married **John William Hardwick**, D.D.S., b. Mar-14-1924 in Camden, NJ.

Children:

+ 1139 i. John William[7] Hardwick b. Jun-08-1947.
+ 1140 ii. Maetha Ann Hardwick.

652. **Anna Laurie[6] Quackenbush** (305.Virginia[5] Arbogast, 89.Emery Matthew[4] Arbogast, 21.John Wesley[3], 3.Daniel[2], 1.George[1]).
Married Bruce **Marvin Marvin Haston** in 1956. Children are Laura and Roger.

Children:

1141 i. Laura[7] Haston.
1142 ii. Roger Haston.

655. **John Kent^6 Arbogast** (306.John Arthur^5, 92.Authur William^4, 21.John Wesley^3, 3.Daniel^2, 1.George^1), b. Nov-18-1951 in Covington, Allegheny Co., VA.
He <u>Married</u> **Marilyn Schmidt**, b. Aug-09-1954 (daughter of Harold Schmidt and Mary Dehart).

Children:

1143 i. Brian^7 Arbogast b. Mar-20-1983 in Roanoke, Roanoke Co., VA.

664. **Patricia Crawford^6 Forbes** (314.Amanda Crawford^5 Arbogast, 94.John Edwin^4, 21.John Wesley^3, 3.Daniel^2, 1.George^1), b. Jan-29-1945 to Chattanooga, Hamilton Co., TN.
She <u>Married</u> William Harper Girvin, b. Dec-07-1944 in Bethesda, Montgomery Co., MD.

Children:

1144 i. Abigail Crawgord^7 Girvin b. Dec-31-1970 in Lansing, MI.

666. **James Edwin^6 Forbes** (314.Amanda Crawford^5 Arbogast, 94.John Edwin^4, 21.John Wesley^3, 3.Daniel^2, 1.George^1), b. Feb-10-1975 in Bethesda, Montgomery Co., MD, buried in Monterey Cem., Monterey, Highland Co., VA, d. May-06-1954 in Charlottesville, Albemarle Co., VA.
He <u>Married</u> **Kathleen Annete Bililes**, b. 1957 in Bethesda, Montgomery Co., MD.

Children:

1145 i. Kyle Alexabder^7 Forbes b. Mar-19-1994.

667. **Theresa^6 Arbogast** (315.Robert William^5, 99.Arthur William^4, 21.John Wesley^3, 3.Daniel^2, 1.George^1), b. Sep 03 1943 in Green Bank, Pocahontas Co., WV.
(1) <u>Married</u> 0941965 in Morgantown, Monongalia Co., WV, **Robert Stephen Kun**, b. Apr-04-1945.

<u>Children:</u>

\+ 1146 i. Katrena Maxhelle^7 Kun b. May-28-1965.
1147 ii. Thomas Brandan Kun b. Sep-22-1977.

(2) <u>Married</u> Jul-19-1992 in Osceola, MO, **James Leroy Estes**, b. May-18-1935.

668. **Diane Patricia^6 Arbogast** (315.Robert William^5, 99.Arthur William^4, 21.John Wesley^3, 3.Daniel^2, 1.George^1), b. Nov 29 1946 in Greensboro, Guilford Co., NC.
She <u>Married</u> **Melvin Roy Buzzard**, b. Apr 30 1945 (son of Arnold Dean Buzzard and Lillie Lee Ryder).

Children:

1148 i. Diane Patricia^7 Buzzard b. Apr 3 1969.
1149 ii. Stephanie Christine Buzzard b. Feb 10 1974.

669. **Robert Michael^6 Arbogast** (315.Robert William^5, 99.Arthur William^4, 21.John Wesley^3, 3.Daniel^2, 1.George^1), b. Nov 22 1947 in Greensboro, Guilford Co., NC.
He <u>Married</u> **Clara Lou Widley**, b. Apr-25-1949.

Children:

1150 i. Michele Denise^7 Arbogast b. May-26-1970, d. Jun-06-1992.
She <u>Married</u> **Timothy Haden Elmore**.
1151 ii. Michael Christopher Arbogast b. Sep-03-1976.
1152 iii. Holly Elizabeth Arbogast b. Jan-02-1980.

675. **Maureen^6 Arbogast** (317.Ralph Thomas^5, 99.Arthur William^4, 21.John Wesley^3, 3.Daniel^2, 1.George^1), b. Apr-10-1956 in Stevens Point, WI.
<u>Married</u> Sep-13-1975 in Durwood's Glen, Baraboo, WI, **Chuck Rehberg.**

Children:

1153 i. Danielle^7 Rehberg b. Apr-28-1979.
1154 ii. Monica Rehberg b. Aug-01-1981.
1155 iii. Maek Rexburg b. Jul-18-1986.
1156 iv. Jaclyn Rehberg b. Sep-24-1988.

676. **Thomas^6 Arbogast** (317.Ralph Thomas^5, 99.Arthur William^4, 21.John Wesley^3, 3.Daniel^2, 1.George^1), b. Jun-16-1958 in Cleveland, Cuyahoga Co., OH.
<u>Married</u> Feb-26-1983 in East Lansing, Ingham Co., MI, **Carolyn Snyder**, b. Jul-25-1957 in Kitchener, Ontario, CA (daughter of Harvey Snyder and Dorothy Brubacher).

Children:

1157 i. Michael[7] Arbogast b. Mar-13-1986.
1158 ii. Laura Arbogast b. Mar-03-1988.
1159 iii. Sarah Arbogast b. Mar-21-1991.

684. **Luther Lee[6] Mullenax** (330.Serilda C[5] Sponaugle, 108.George Washington[4], 23.William[3], 4.Elizabeth L.[2] Arbogast, 1.George[1]), b. Sep-19-1896, d. Dec-20-1974.
He Married **Viola Jane Bible**, d. 1948.

Children:

1160 i. Leo[7] Mullenax.
Leo Married and had at least one child Viola Jean. She Married **Genn Riggleman** and **William Mullenax**.
1161 ii. George Mullenax.
Spouse unknown. Had two children Ann and Dorothy.

686. **Myrtle Annie[6] Mullenax** (330.Serilda C[5] Sponaugle, 108.George Washington[4], 23.William[3], 4.Elizabeth L.[2] Arbogast, 1.George[1]), b. Dec-16-1905, buried in Cedar Hill Cem., Pendleton Co., WV, d. Nov-28-1975 in Alliance, Stark Co., OH.
She Married **John Amos Judy**, b. Jul-16-1893 (son of George Judy and Cynthia Cook), buried in Cedar Hill Cem., Pendleton Co., WV, d. Jan-16-1967.

Children:

1162 i. Alma Catherine[7] Hartman b. ___-29-1923.
Daughter of Myrtle and Okey Hartman.
She Married **Robert Eye.**
1163 ii. Roy Edward Hartman b. May-20-1926.
Daughter of Myrtle and Dennis Hartman.. Cherry, Grove.
1164 iii. Maxine R. Judy.
1165 iv. Glenna Marie Judy b. Aug-28-1930, d. Apr-10-1982.
1166 v. Yvonne Judy.
She Married **Kenneth Shriver**.
1167 vi. Carrie L. Judy b. Mar-21-1934, d. Aug-05-1951.
\+ 1168 vii. John Delano Judy b. Nov-18-1937.
1169 viii. Martin Dale Judy.
He Married **Anita Pearl Wimer**, b. Sep-21-1939 (daughter of Arnold Eldora Wimer and Eva Pearl Sponaugle).

692. **George Edgar[6] Hartman** (331.Carrie E[5] Sponaugle, 108.George Washington[4], 23.William[3], 4.Elizabeth L.[2] Arbogast, 1.George[1]), b. Mar 27 1894 in Pendleton Co., WV, d. Feb 24 1961 in Pendleton Co., WV.
(1) Married Sep 5 1914, **Margie Belle Warner**, d. Dec1938, b. in Riverton, Pendleton Co., WV, buried in Teter Gap, Circleville, Pendleton Co., WV.

Children:

1170 i. Nola Lee[7] Hartman b. Apr-14-1921 in Franklin, Pendleton Co., WV, d. in Brandywine, Pendleton Co., VA.
(1) She Married **Charles Raymond Simmons**.
(2) She Married **Loreb Bryant**.
(3) Married in Franklin, Pendleton Co., WV, **Luther Tison Nesselrodt**.
1171 ii. Etta May Hartman b. Sep-04-1918 in Franklin, Pendleton Co., WV.
1172 iii. Linnie Ann Hartman b. Jun-04-1916 in Franklin, Pendleton Co., WV.

(2) He Married **Jean Lillian Hurlet,** .

693. **Alpha Susan[6] Hartman** (331.Carrie E[5] Sponaugle, 108.George Washington[4], 23.William[3], 4.Elizabeth L.[2] Arbogast, 1.George[1]), b. Dec 22 1897 in Pendleton Co., WV, d. Oct 11 1960.
Married Jul 31 1914, **Clyde William Johnson** (son of Samson Johnson and Ellen Thompson), d. 1971, b. Aug-13-1883 in Riverton, Pendleton Co., WV, buried in Cedar Hill Cem., Pendleton Co., WV.

. ***Children:***

1173 i. Roy Glen[7] Johnson b. Apr-08-1915, d. May-10-1974 in Staunton, Augusta Co., VA, buried in Oak Lawn Gardens Staunton Augusta Co., VA.
He Married **Bertha Simmons**.
1174 ii. Maurice Johnson b. Feb-15-1917, d. Sep-29-1976.
1175 iii. Robert Johnson b. 1921, d. Mar-18-1949.
1176 iv. Margie Etta Johnson b. Sep-23-1923.

She Married **William Blair Clower.**

1177 v. Arvel Johnson b. Sep-23-1923 in Macksville, d. May-11-1977 in Harrisonburg, Rockingham Co., VA, buried in Co., WV.
Married Jan-23-1950**, Rose Lee Colaw.**

1178 vi. Roscoe Johnson b. Apr-03-1926
He Married **Rettie Hedrick**.

1179 vii. Brozie Johnson b. Jun-16-1932, d. 1976 in Harrisonburg, Rockingham Co., VA.
He Married **Martha Wimer**.

1180 viii. Myrtle Pauline Johnson .

1181 ix. Leo Johnson b. Jun 1934.
She Married **Pollyanna Dahmer**.

694. **James Arthur[6] Hartman** (331.Carrie E[5] Sponaugle, 108.George Washington[4], 23.William[3], 4.Elizabeth L.[2] Arbogast, 1.George[1]), b. Jun 1 1899 in Pendleton Co., WV, d. Feb 7 1966.
He Married **Laura Ellen Harper**, .

Children:

1182 i. Geneva Laura[7] Hartman .
Married Oct-06-1945 in Moorefield, Grant County, WV, **Arlie Edwin Thomson**.

1183 ii. Juanita Hartman .

695. **Denny Herman[6] Hartman** (331.Carrie E[5] Sponaugle, 108.George Washington[4], 23.William[3], 4.Elizabeth L.[2] Arbogast, 1.George[1]), b. Jun 2 1902 in Pendleton Co., WV, d. May 12 1968 in Pendleton Co., WV, buried UNKNOWN in Cedar Hill Cem., Pendleton Co., WV.
Denny and Virgie resided in various places - Hidden Valley on Smith Creek, the North Fork area and then back to Goshen on Smith Creek.
He Married **Annie Myrtle Mullenax**, .

Children:

1184 i. Dorothy Helen[7] Hartman .

696. **Melvin Earl[6] Hartman** (331.Carrie E[5] Sponaugle, 108.George Washington[4], 23.William[3], 4.Elizabeth L.[2] Arbogast, 1.George[1]), b. Sep 3 1904 in Pendleton Co., WV, d. Apr 3 1976 in Pendleton Co., WV.
Married Jul-25-1926 in Cave, Pendleton Co., WV, **Mary Ellen Lambert**, b. Aug-24-1907 in Zigler, Smith Creek, Pendleton Co., WV, buried in Cedar Hill Cem., Pendleton Co., WV.

Children:

1185 i. Melvin John[7] Hartman b. Mar-24-1926.
Married May-10-1947, **Charlotte Louise Eye**. Retired Teacher, forest ranger.

1186 ii. Leslie Weldon Hartman b. Sep-11-1928.
Married Apr-08-1950 in Franklin, Pendleton Co., WV, **Marthenna Cornelia Simmons**.

1187 iii. Lucy Jean Hartman b. Nov-15-1930.
Married Mar-05-1947 in Smith Creek, Pendleton Co., WV, **Samuel Bowers Propst**.

1188 iv. Mary Kathleen Hartman b. May-27-1933.
Married Aug-13-1950, **Roy Abrem Mitchell**.

1189 v. James Otis Hartman b. Sep-05-1935.
Married in Monterey, Highland Co., VA, **Shirley Arlene Rexroad**.

\+ 1190 vi. Cornelia Etta Hartman b. Jan-30-1937.

1191 vii. Loy Allen Hartman b. Aug-10-1939.
Married Mar-31-1957, **Joy E. Vandevander**.

1192 viii. Nancy Mae Hartman b. Dec-19-1941.
(1) She Married **Harry Barnett**, b. Jan-05-1961 in Cumberland, KY.
(2) Married Mar-15-1958 in Laurel, MD, **John Herbert Kipp**.

697. **Charles Okey[6] Hartman** (331.Carrie E[5] Sponaugle, 108.George Washington[4], 23.William[3], 4.Elizabeth L.[2] Arbogast, 1.George[1]), b. Jan 22 1907 in Smith Creek, Pendleton Co., WV, d. Oct 17 1981 in Pendleton Co., WV, buried in Hartman Cem., Arbovale, Pocahontas Co., WV.
Married Jul-17-1926 in Moyers, Pendleton Co., WV, **Ottie Jane Eye**, b. Jul-25-1910 (daughter of William Henry Eye and Ida Jane Simmons), d. Jan-18-1989 in Brandywine, Pendleton Co., VA, buried in Pine Hill Cem., Brandywine, Pendleton Co., WV.

Children:

1193 i. Alma Catherine[7] Hartman b. Oct-29-1923.

Alma Catherine Hartman and her brother Care the biological children of Charles Okey Hartman and Ottie jane Eye, but are also listed with John Amos Judy and Robert Eye who apparently raised them. Thus these two people are duplicated with two families.

1194 ii. William Irvin Hartman b. Jan-15-1927 in Brandywine, Pendleton Co., WV, d. in Dayton, Montgomery Co., OH.

1195 iii. Kenneth Leon Hartman b. Mar-16-1930 in Brandywine, Pendleton Co., VA.

1196 iv. Colleen Hartman b. Jul-26-1933.
She Married a **Mr. Shipley**, Sparta, WI.

1197 v. Carrie Maxine Hartman b. Jul-24-1935.
Married Jan-06-1953, **Berlie Brooks Wimer**.

700. **Robert Paul⁶ Hartman** (331.Carrie E⁵ Sponaugle, 108.George Washington⁴, 23.William³, 4.Elizabeth L.² Arbogast, 1.George¹), b. Feb 24 1914 in Pendleton Co., WV, d. Jul 27 1982 in Pendleton Co., WV.
Married Sep-06-1934, Ella Charlotte Lambert, b. Sep-04-1918 (daughter of Robert Harvey Lambert and Janet Leona Hartman), d. in Franklin, Pendleton Co., WV.

Children:

1198 i. Bobby Lee⁷ Hartman b. Jan-23-1935, d. in Franklin, Pendleton Co., WV.
Married May-27-1953, **Mabel Marie Beach**.

1199 ii. Paul Hartman b. Apr-08-1937, d. Apr-08-1937.

1200 iii. Theodore Lambert Hartman b. 040701938.
Married Aug-17-1963, **Anna Elizabeth Eye**, b. Apr-07-1938, d. in Smith Creek, Pendleton Co., WV.

1201 iv. William Harvey Hartman b. Apr-30-1940.
Married Aug-03-1959, **Retha Lee Joyce**.

1202 v. Paula Diana Hartman b. Jun-18-1950.
Married Apr-05-1969, **James Michael Waybright**.

1203 vi. Leona Charlotte Hartman b. Apr-30-1940.
Married Apr-16-1951, **Berlie May Botkin**.

1204 vii. Danny Edward Hartman b. Dec-10-1944.
Married Sep-17-1968, **Ruby Mae Mitchell**.

1205 viii. Luther Patrick Hartman b. Sep-26-1946.
He Married **Mary Jane Cervinski**, b. Jul-01-1666.

1206 ix. David Marcell Hartman b. Nov-22-1948.
Married Jun-29-1973 in Martinsburg, Berkeley Co., WV, **Debra Kay Wimer**.

1207 x. Robert Paul Hartman b. 0231951, buried in Smith Creek, Pendleton Co., WV, d. Sep-10-1952.

1208 xi. Henry Arthur Hartman b. Oct-24-1953.
Married Oct-26-1971, **Carolyn June Pritt**.

1209 xii. Christena Elizabeth Hartman b. Mar-08-1955.
Married Jul-03-1971, **Ronald Wayne Bawers.**

702. **John Esby⁶ Hartman** (332.Minerva⁵ Sponaugle, 108.George Washington⁴, 23.William³, 4.Elizabeth L.² Arbogast, 1.George¹), d. UNKNOWN, d. Dec-01-1968 in Smith Creek, Pendleton Co., WV.
Married Mar-15-1912 in Pendleton Co., WV, **Mary Lena Simmons**, b. Mar-11-1893 in Franklin, Pendleton Co., WV (daughter of James Zebulon Simmons and Lara Nancy Hartman), buried in Smith Creek, Pendleton Co., WV, d. May-16-1978 in Harrisonburg Hospital, VA.

Children:

1210 i. Geneva Ruth⁷ Hartman b. Jan-22-1913 in Zigler, Smith Creek, Pendleton Co., WV, buried in Hartman Cem. Franklin, Pendleton Co., WV, d. Jul-06-1914 in Zigler, Smith Creek, Pendleton Co., WV.
Married Apr-27-1946 in Harrisonburg, Rockingham Co., VA, **Ira Ray Riddle**.

1211 ii. John Layman Hartman b. Jun-22-1914, buried in Smith Creek, Pendleton Co., WV, d. Jul-06-1914.

1212 iii. Ruby Gail Hartman b. Jun-14-1915 in Zigler, Smith Creek, Pendleton Co., WV, buried in Hartman Cem. Franklin, Pendleton Co., WV, d. Jun-14-1945 in Zigler, Smith Creek, Pendleton Co., WV.

1213 iv. Mable Marie Hartman b. Aug-18-1916 in Zigler, Smith Creek, Pendleton Co., WV.
She Married **Gail Campbell.**

1214 v. Ortha Glenn Hartman b. Feb-20-1918 in Pendleton Co., WV, buried in Hartman Cem. Franklin, Pendleton Co., WV, d. Oct-22-1922 in Zigler, Smith Creek, Pendleton Co., WV.

1215 vi. Lester Harold Hartman b. Apr-12-1919 in Zigler, Smith Creek, Pendleton Co., WV, buried in Hartman Cem. Franklin, Pendleton Co., WV, d. Jun-23-1968 in Franklin, Pendleton Co., WV.

1216 vii. Charles Reese Hartman b. Nov-16-1924, d. Dec-22-1915.

1217 viii. Jesse Wayne Hartman b. Jul-18-1926 in Zigler, Smith Creek, Pendleton Co., WV, d. Aug-11-1982 in Franklin, Pendleton Co., WV.

1218 ix. Richard Esby Hartman b. Aug-27-1927 in Franklin, Pendleton Co., WV, d. Jun-10-1928 in Franklin, Pendleton Co., WV.

1219 x. Dorothy Lucille Hartman b. 121419+28 in Franklin, Pendleton Co., WV, d. Apr-23-1927 in Franklin, Pendleton Co., WV.

1220 xi. Ivan Leroy Hartman b. Sep-12-1930 in Franklin, Pendleton Co., WV, d. Apr-06-1915 in Franklin, Pendleton Co., WV.

1221 xii. Martha Geniel Hartman b. Jul-11-1933 in Franklin, Pendleton Co., WV, d. Nov-30-2004 in New Market, Shenandoah County, VA.
She Married **Brian Hartman**.

1222 xiii. Weldon Harold Hartman b. Nov-06-1923 in Zigler, Smith Creek, Pendleton Co., WV, d. Nov- 6-1923 in Smith Creek, Pendleton Co., WV.

1223 xiv. Juanita May Hartman.
Married Jan-19-1934, **Harold Edward Self.**

708. **Russell McClure[6] Sponaugle** (334.Green Judy[5], 108.George Washington[4], 23.William[3], 4.Elizabeth L.[2] Arbogast, 1.George[1]), b. Dec-23-1903 in Zigler, Smith Creek, Pendleton Co., WV, d. Dec-14-1985.
Married Dec-24-1926, Iva Jane Lambert, b. Dec-23-1903 (daughter of Charles Lambert and Cora Maud Eye), buried in Cedar Hill Cem., Pendleton Co., WV, d. Dec-14-1985 in Franklin, Pendleton Co., WV.

Children:

\+ 1224 i. Harlan Dale[7] Sponaugle, M.D. b. Feb-13-1926.

710. **Elizabeth Susan[6] Sponaugle** (334.Green Judy[5], 108.George Washington[4], 23.William[3], 4.Elizabeth L.[2] Arbogast, 1.George[1]), b. Feb-12-1906.
Married 0830124 in Pendleton Co., WV, **Joseph Walter Judy**, b. Oct-15-1898 in Zigler, Smith Creek, Pendleton Co., WV (son of William Harvey Judy and Susan C. Hartman), d. Jul-15-1949 in Dayton, Rockingham Co., VA.

Children:

1225 i. Madeline Susan[7] Judy b. Dec-16-1924.
(1) Married Feb 1956, **John Welby Spencer**.
(2) She Married **Edward Freeman**, d. Dec 1960.

1226 ii. Joseph Wreford Judy b. Nov-07-1926.
Married Sep-20-1958, **Leona Mad Keller**.

1227 iii. Fannie Ramona Judy b. Jun-06-1926.
Married Sep-10-1955, **Ralph Warren Crowe**.

1228 iv. Raeburn Ingles Judy b. Apr-05-1932.
Married Sep 1959, **Carol Watkins**.

712. **Rhea Mae[6] Sponaugle** (334.Green Judy[5], 108.George Washington[4], 23.William[3], 4.Elizabeth L.[2] Arbogast, 1.George[1]), b. Feb-26-1910 in Zigler, Smith Creek, Pendleton Co., WV.
Married Dec-24-1934 in Smith Creek, Pendleton Co., WV, **Earlie Lee Simmons**, b. Sep-01-1909 in Franklin, Pendleton Co., WV (son of Sebaldis Simmons and Della Zenna Lambert), buried in Cedar Hill Cem., Pendleton Co., WV, d. Nov-14-1978 in Harrisonburg Hospital, VA.

Children:

\+ 1229 i. Naomi[7] Simmons b. Dec-11-1937.

713. **Walter Glenn[6] Sponaugle** (334.Green Judy[5], 108.George Washington[4], 23.William[3], 4.Elizabeth L.[2] Arbogast, 1.George[1]), b. Aug-03-1912 in Zigler, Smith Creek, Pendleton Co., WV, d. Dec-12-1987.
(1) Married Sep-14-1936 in Franklin, Pendleton Co., WV, **Maycel Gladys Warner,** b. Jul-12-1915 in Franklin, Pendleton Co., WV (daughter of Flick Warner and Ursula Mauzy), buried in Sponaugle Cem., Smith Creek, Pendleton Co., WV, d. Jun-09-1973 in Harrisonburg Hospital, VA.

Children:

\+ 1230 i. Debera Jane[7] Sponaugle b. Jun-20-1952.

\+ 1231 ii. Brenda Sue Sponaugle b. Jul-07-1956.

(2) Married Apr-23-1983, **Mary Ellen Lambert**.

714. **Mary Ruth^{6} Sponaugle** (334.Green Judy^{5}, 108.George Washington^{4}, 23.William^{3}, 4.Elizabeth L.^{2} Arbogast, 1.George^{1}), b. Feb-03-1915, d. Dec-10-1984.
Married Apr-09-1938 in Christiansburg, VA, **Hurl Wilber Lambert**, b. Jun-19-1911 in Smith Creek, Pendleton Co., WV (son of William Edward Lambert and Sarah Margret Lambert), d. Dec-02-1980 in Harrisonburg, Rockingham Co., VA.

Children:

1232 i. Dennis Hurl^{7} Lambert b. Dec-31-1939 in Franklin, Pendleton Co., WV.
(1) He Married **Helen Francis Goldstein**.
(2) Married Dec-09-1972, **Chrustine Anita Vier.**
1233 ii. Margaret Louise Lambert b. Sep-01-1941 in Franklin, Pendleton Co., WV.
She Married **Nelson Eugene Huffman**, b. Oct-15-1961 in Dayton, Rockingham Co., VA.
1234 iii. William Judy Lambert b. Nov-04-1944 in Smith Creek, Pendleton Co., WV.
1235 iv. Larry Wade Lambert b. May-20-1947 in Dayton, Rockingham Co., VA.
Married Oct-16-1971 in Bridgewater, Rockingham Co., VA, **Phyllis Kay Liskey**.
1236 v. Joseph Wayne Lambert b. Aug-17-1951 in Dayton, Rockingham Co., VA.
(1) Married Apr-06-1968 in Dayton, Rockingham Co., VA, **Wanda Kay Smith**.
(2) Married Jun-21-1980 in Fluvanna County, VA, **Kathleen Paula Beahnke**.
1237 vi. Herl Wilber Lambert, Jr. b. Feb-09-1956 in Harrisonburg, Rockingham Co., VA.
Married May-07-1963 in Fairfax, Fairfax Co., VA, **Sherry Lee Salovitz**.

715. **George Isaac^{6} Sponaugle** (334.Green Judy^{5}, 108.George Washington^{4}, 23.William^{3}, 4.Elizabeth L.^{2} Arbogast, 1.George^{1}), b. Jun-09-1917.
Married Dec-31-1937, **Ronna Harper**, b. Nov-09-1916 (daughter of Mauzy Harper and Bessie Harper).

Children:

\+ 1238 i. George Isaac^{7} Sponaugle II b. Jun-09-1917.
\+ 1239 ii. James Harper Sponaugle.

716. **Joie Catherine^{6} Sponaugle** (334.Green Judy^{5}, 108.George Washington^{4}, 23.William^{3}, 4.Elizabeth L.^{2} Arbogast, 1.George^{1}), b. Aug-08-1919.
Married Jun 1939s, **Olin Brownie Simmons**, b. Dec-06-1914 in Zigler, Smith Creek, Pendleton Co., WV (son of Sebaldis Simmons and Della Zenna Lambert), d. Oct-29-1966.

Children:

1240 i. Hestor Della^{7} Simmons b. Nov-21-1929 in Franklin, Pendleton Co., WV.
Married Jun-15-1957 in Smith Creek, Pendleton Co., WV, **Gayle Edwards Judy**.
1241 ii. Janet Sue Simmons b. Aug-22-1941 in Franklin, Pendleton Co., WV.
Married Nov-01-1958 in Oak Park, MD, **Charles Jerry Lambert**.
1242 iii. Joie Etnona Simmons b. Jan-09-1945.
She Married **Phillip N. Nelson**.
1243 iv. Betty Simmons b. Nov-17-1949.
She Married **Rexford R. Leonard**.
1244 v. Jeffery Olin Simmons b. Jul-27-1960.
\+ 1245 vi. Heata Della Simmons b. Nov-21-1939.

717. **William Joseph^{6} Sponaugle** (334.Green Judy^{5}, 108.George Washington^{4}, 23.William^{3}, 4.Elizabeth L.^{2} Arbogast, 1.George^{1}), b. Apr-12-1922 in Zigler, Smith Creek, Pendleton Co., WV.
(1) Married Jun-01-1946, **Ellen Elizabeth Campbell**.

Children:

1246 i. William Joseph^{7} Sponaugle, Jr..
\+ 1247 ii. Ruth Ann Sponaugle.
1248 iii. Linda Lou Sponaugle b. Jul-07-1956.
1249 iv. Timothy Craig Sponaugle.
Married Sep-15-1984, **Cleda Ann Toatello**.
1250 v. Christopher James Sponaugle.
1251 vi. Danial Lee Sponaugle.

(2) He **Married Joyce Young**.

718. **Cletus^{6} Evick** (335.Mary Perlie^{5} Sponaugle, 108.George Washington^{4}, 23.William^{3}, 4.Elizabeth L.^{2} Arbogast, 1.George^{1}), b. Jan-31-1903, d. Feb-22-1984.

Married Dec-05-1928, **Florence Hoover**.

Children:

1252 i. J.Reid[7] Hoover.
1253 ii. Carey Hoover.

723. **Emily[6] Warner** (336.Martha Lucretia[5] Sponaugle, 108.George Washington[4], 23.William[3], 4.Elizabeth L.[2] Arbogast, 1.George[1]). She Married **Louis Curry**.

Children:

1254 i. Ardith[7] Curry.
1255 ii. Rebecca Curry.

727. **Eva Pearl[6] Sponaugle** (338.George Arthur[5], 108.George Washington[4], 23.William[3], 4.Elizabeth L.[2] Arbogast, 1.George[1]), . Married Jan-28-1929 in Franklin, Pendleton Co., WV, **Arnold Eldora Wimer**, b. Apr-26-1911 in Salt Lake City, Salt Lake Co., UT (son of Edgar Wimer and Pearl May Boyce), d. Apr-10-1984 in Harrisonburg Hospital, VA.

Children:

1256 i. Betty Lou[7] Wimer b. Sep-28-1933.
Married Apr-16-1949 in Franklin, Pendleton Co., WV, **Glenn Carlson Vandevander**.
1257 ii. Anita Pearl Wimer b. Sep-21-1939.
(1) She Married **Stanley Mitchell**.
(2) She Married **Martin Dale Judy** (son of John Amos Judy and Myrtle Annie Mullenax).

1258 iii. **William Arthur Wilmer** b. Dec-05-1941.
Married Mar-17-1961 in Franklin, Pendleton Co., WV, **Barbara May**.

1259 iv. Edward Arnold Wimer b. Feb-05-1946.
(1) He Married **Getta Jean Lambert**.
(2) He Married **Jamie Lynn Mohler**.

731. Kate L.[6] Cook (340.Mary Ida[5] Teter, 109.Mary Catherine[4] Sponaugle, 23.William[3], 4.Elizabeth L.[2] Arbogast, 1.George[1]), b. 1895, d. 1966.
Married, William Jennings Bryan Vandevander, b. 1894, d. 1982.

Children:

1260 i. Nola[7] Vandevander b. 1917, d. 1991.
She Married **Stanley R. Phares**.
1261 ii. Christopher Gerald Vandevander b. 1919, d. 1985.
He Married **Gertrude Nelson**.
1262 iii. Harper Keith Vandevander .
He Married **Edith Kisamore**.

732. **Kennie Andress[6] Adams** (340.Mary Ida[5] Teter, 109.Mary Catherine[4] Sponaugle, 23.William[3], 4.Elizabeth L.[2] Arbogast, 1.George[1]), b. 1902, d. 1985.
(1) Married, Peachie Mae White, b. 1899, d. 1990.

Children:

1263 i. Mary C.[7] Adams.
She Married **William M. Vandevander**.

(2) Married Private, Eva Lena Smith, .

Children:

1264 ii. Jack Adams.

733. **Erma V.[6] Adams** (340.Mary Ida[5] Teter, 109.Mary Catherine[4] Sponaugle, 23.William[3], 4.Elizabeth L.[2] Arbogast, 1.George[1]). She Married **Charles Judy**,.

Children:

1265 i. Nellie[7] Judy.
1266 ii. Chester Judy.
1267 iii. Lester Judy.

737. Clarice May[6] Nelson (341.Jenettie Catherine[5] Thompson, 109.Mary Catherine[4] Sponaugle, 23.William[3], 4.Elizabeth L.[2] Arbogast, 1.George[1]), b. Jun 15 1892 in Pendleton Co., WV, d. Mar 2 1986 in Morgantown, Monongalia Co., WV.
Married Mar 26 1912 in Cumberland, Alleghany Co., MD, **Anthony Joseph Degler**, b. Nov 6 1883 in Scottsdale, Fayette Co., PA, d. Jan 17 1945 in Morgantown, Monongalia Co., WV.

Children:

1268 i. Crist Anthony Warren[7] Degler b. Aug 23 1914 in Cumberland, Alleghany Co., MD, d. Oct 24 1971 in Oxnard, Ventura Co., CA.
Married, **Pearl Bright Lieberger**, , d. Feb 3 1971 in Oxnard, Ventura Co., CA.

1269 ii. Alexander Joseph Degler b. Jul 1 1917 in Westernport, Washington Co., MD, d. Mar 11 1991 in Morgantown, Monongalia Co., WV.
Married, **Geneva Gould**, in Morgantown, Monongalia Co., WV.

1270 iii. Joseph Junior Degler b. Jul 26 1919 in Westernport, Washington Co., MD, d. Jul 13 1990 in Texas.
Married **Erma Lynda Scaparro**, .

1271 iv. Paul Nelson Degler b. Jun 8 1922 in Westernport, Washington Co., MD, d. Dec 30 1984 in Pittsburgh, Allegheny Co., PA.
Married Private, **Wanda Frome**, .

1272 v. Leslie Allen Degler .

1273 vi. Marie Virginia Degler .
Married, **Wilfred L. Clulo**, in Morgantown, Monongalia Co., WV.

\+ 1274 vii. Clair Fern Anne Degler .

740. Lacie Madonna[6] Nelson (341.Jenettie Catherine[5] Thompson, 109.Mary Catherine[4] Sponaugle, 23.William[3], 4.Elizabeth L.[2] Arbogast, 1.George[1]), b. Feb 18 1901 in Beverly, Randolph Co., WV, d. Mar 3 1974 in Richmond, Henrico Co., VA.

(1) Married Jan 12 1917 in LA Vale, Allegany Co., MD, **Thomas Albert Clarke, Jr.**, b. ABT 1897, d. WFT Est 1923-1988.

Children:

1275 i. Keith Allen[7] Clarke b. Nov 19 1917 in Cumberland, Alleghany Co., MD, d. Feb 3 1976 in St. Petersburg, Pinellas Co., FL.
(1) Married Private, **Lillian Minday**, .
(2) Married Private, **Anna Fedick Lewicki**, .

(2) Married Jul 26 1932 in Washington, PA, Arnold Wesley Ozment, b. Aug 4 1911 in Greensboro, Guilford Co., NC, d. Dec 12 1975 in Richmond, Henrico Co., VA.

Children:

\+ 1276 ii. Dwight Wesley Ozment b. Sep-23-1933.

746. Orie D.[6] Thompson (343.Jacob Kenny[5], 109.Mary Catherine[4] Sponaugle, 23.William[3], 4.Elizabeth L.[2] Arbogast, 1.George[1]), b. Mar 16 1892, d. May 29 1970.
Married 1915, **Julia May Teter**, b. Mar 28 1894, d. Sep 24 1972.

Children:

1277 i. Worth[7] Thompson b. 1920, d. 1925.

1278 ii. Glenn Thompson b. WFT Est 1912-1939, d. WFT Est 1918-1996 in Teterton, Pendleton Co., WV.

1279 iii. Guy A. Thompson b. 1918.
He Married **Audrey Taken**.

1280 iv. Joseph H. Thompson b. Feb-09-1922.

1281 v. Kenneth R. Thompson b. Jun-25-1925.
Married 1948, **Clare Lee Miller**.

\+ 1282 vi. Naomi K. Thompson b. Jun-11-1929.

748. Leslie E.[6] Thompson (343.Jacob Kenny[5], 109.Mary Catherine[4] Sponaugle, 23.William[3], 4.Elizabeth L.[2] Arbogast, 1.George[1]), b. 1906, d. 1948.
He Married **Bessie Vandevander**.

Children:

1283 i. Leslie[7] Thompson b. 1929, d. 1971.

1284 ii. John Wayne Thompson.

784. Oscar William[6] Kerr (362.Jessie Lucy[5] Louk, 111.Elizabeth Jane[4] Sponaugle, 23.William[3], 4.Elizabeth L.[2] Arbogast, 1.George[1]), b. Oct 10 1909 in Randolph Co., WV, d. Mar 14 1958.

Married 1934, **Golda Gaye Hannah**, b. Jul 17 1908 in Slatyfork, Pocahontas Co., WV (daughter of Samuel Hannah and Amanda Moore), d. Sep 29 2002 in Ashland, Boyd Co., KY. Ref: Pocahontas 1981: 310 D/o Samuel David and Amanda Margaret (Moore) Hannah.

Children:

1285 i. Robert David^{7} Kerr b. 1948.
He Married **Valerie Hilton**.

785. Eunice^{6} Kerr (362.Jessie Lucy^{5} Louk, 111.Elizabeth Jane^{4} Sponaugle, 23.William^{3}, 4.Elizabeth L.^{2} Arbogast, 1.George^{1}), b. Jan 14 1912 in Randolph Co., WV, d. Jun 17 1989.
(1) She Married **S. Y. Sharp** (son of Luther Sharp and Laura Morgan).
(2) She Married Harold David Gibson (son of Forest Gibson and Allie Catherine Gibson).

Children:

1286 i. Vicki^{7} Gibson.
1287 ii. Pamela Gibson.

788. Earl Frederick^{6} Kerr (362.Jessie Lucy^{5} Louk, 111.Elizabeth Jane^{4} Sponaugle, 23.William^{3}, 4.Elizabeth L.^{2} Arbogast, 1.George^{1}), b. Sep 18 1918 in Randolph Co., WV, d. Aug 6 1990.
Ref: Randolph 1991: 33.
Married Dec 3 1942, **Mary Waybright**, b. 1920 (daughter of Thaddeus Waybright and Alpha Hollie Elza). D/o Thaddeus and Alpha Hollie (Elza) Waybright. Mary is the same person as.

Children:

\+ 1288 i. Margaret Ann^{7} Kerr b. Jan 6 1949.

791. Betty Jane^{6} Kerr (362.Jessie Lucy^{5} Louk, 111.Elizabeth Jane^{4} Sponaugle, 23.William^{3}, 4.Elizabeth L.^{2} Arbogast, 1.George^{1}), b. Jan 10 1925 in Bemis, Randolph County WV.
Source is family records of Betty Jane (Kerr) Lewis of Beverly, WV. See parents notes as descendants of Michael Arbogast' sons, George and John, as well as Adam.
Married Jun 1 1946 in Randolph Co., WV, **Charles Junior Lewis**, b. Nov 28 1923 in Beverly, Randolph Co., WV (son of George Lewis and Juanita Lewis). Source is family records of Betty Jane (Kerr) Lewis of Beverly, WV. S/o George Arnold and Juanita Esta Mae (Lewis) Lewis.

Children:

1289 i. Richard Lee^{7} Lewis.
1290 ii. Carol Sue Lewis.
1291 iii. Charles Joe Lewis.
1292 iv. John Lynn Lewis.
1293 v. Terry Keith Lewis.
1294 vi. Tammy Joy Lewis.

799. Willis Raymond^{6} Sponaugle (369.Lee Paris^{5}, 113.Adam Harness^{4}, 23.William^{3}, 4.Elizabeth L.^{2} Arbogast, 1.George^{1}), b. Apr-10-1909 in Horton, Randolph Co., WV, buried in Cannan Valley, WV, d. Mar-13-1904 in Monterville, Randolph Co., WV.
Was killed in coal mine.
He Married **Margery Opel Allman**, b. Apr-21-1903 in Cannan Valley, WV.

Children:

\+ 1295 i. Norma Lee^{7} Sponaugle b. Apr-14-1928.
\+ 1296 ii. Norman Willis Sponaugle b. May-02-1931.

800. Milford Jay^{6} Sponaugle (369.Lee Paris^{5}, 113.Adam Harness^{4}, 23.William^{3}, 4.Elizabeth L.^{2} Arbogast, 1.George^{1}), b. Sep-18-1913 in Stemple Ridge, WV, d. Sep-13-1984.
Married Sep-18-1933 in Davis, Tucker Co., WV, **Anna Virginia Winters**, b. Feb-26-1915 in Frostburg, Allegany Co., MD (daughter of Lloyd F. Winters and Margar Leah Lewis), buried in Davis, Tucker Co., WV, d. Sep-13-1984 in Thomas, Tucker Co., WV.

Children:

\+ 1297 i. Shirley Ann^{7} Sponaugle b. Sep-18-1937.
\+ 1298 ii. Aaron Charles Sponaugle b. May-08-1938.
\+ 1299 iii. Gloria Carrol Sponaugle b. Oct-16-1941.
1300 iv. Frederick Lee Sponaugle b. Feb-07-1946.

He Married **Hellen Kathleen Vandevender**.
+ 1301 v. Tena Ann Myers b. May-13-1964.

801. Christena Belle^{6} Sponaugle (370.John Alonzo^{5}, 113.Adam Harness^{4}, 23.William^{3}, 4.Elizabeth L.^{2} Arbogast, 1.George^{1}), b. Jun-08-1906 in Circleville Pendleton Co., WV.
Married Aug-17-1929, **Jesse Howard Bennett**, b. Oct-15-1893 in Osceola Randolph Co., WV (son of Ruben D. Bennett and Emma Vint), d. May-11-1963 in Martinsburg, Berkeley Co., WV.

Children:

+ 1302 i. Hazel^{7} Bennett.
+ 1303 ii. Fred D. Bennett.
1304 iii. Fay Bennett.
He Married **Dorothy Nelson**.

804. Nola M.^{6} Sponaugle (370.John Alonzo^{5}, 113.Adam Harness^{4}, 23.William^{3}, 4.Elizabeth L.^{2} Arbogast, 1.George^{1}), b. Feb-21-1915.
She Married **Charles Miller**.

Children:

1305 i. Jackie^{7} Miller.
1306 ii. Jerlean Miller.
1307 iii. Dickie Miller.
1308 iv. Gary Miller.

805. Adam Harness^{6} Sponaugle (370.John Alonzo^{5}, 113.Adam Harness^{4}, 23.William^{3}, 4.Elizabeth L.^{2} Arbogast, 1.George^{1}), b. Jul-01-1918 in Circleville Pendleton Co., WV, buried in North Fork of South Branch, WV., d. May-11-1989 in Riverton, Pendleton Co., WV.
He Married **Mae Thompson**.

Children:

1309 i. Adam^{7} Harness Sponaugle, Jr..

806. Paul R.^{6} Sponaugle (370.John Alonzo^{5}, 113.Adam Harness^{4}, 23.William^{3}, 4.Elizabeth L.^{2} Arbogast, 1.George^{1}), b. Apr-15-1920.
He Married **Nellie Gum**.

Children:

1310 i. Larry^{7} Sponaugle.
1311 ii. Ronald Sponaugle.
1312 iii. Sheila Sponaugle.

807. Isaic Jay^{6} Sponaugle (370.John Alonzo^{5}, 113.Adam Harness^{4}, 23.William^{3}, 4.Elizabeth L.^{2} Arbogast, 1.George^{1}), b. Oct-08-1922.
He Married **Mary Elizabeth Frat**.

Children:

1313 i. Diane^{7} Sponaugle.
1314 ii. Elizabeth Sponaugle.
1315 iii. Holly Sponaugle.

808. Vallie Verie^{6} Sponaugle (370.John Alonzo^{5}, 113.Adam Harness^{4}, 23.William^{3}, 4.Elizabeth L.^{2} Arbogast, 1.George^{1}), b. Mar-10-1927 in Circleville Pendleton Co., WV.
She Married **Thomas Phalen**.

Children:

1316 i. Susan Lynn^{7} Phalen.
1317 ii. Pamala Jane Phalen.
1318 iii. Regina Mary Phalen.
1319 iv. Timothy Edward Phalen.

809. Anna Jo^{6} Sponaugle (370.John Alonzo^{5}, 113.Adam Harness^{4}, 23.William^{3}, 4.Elizabeth L.^{2} Arbogast, 1.George^{1}), b. Oct-09-1928 in Circleville Pendleton Co., WV.
(1) She Married **Raymond W. Hartman**.

Children:

1320 i. Joe[7] Hartman.
1321 ii. Jeannie Hartman.
1322 iii. Teddy Hartman.
1323 iv. Raymond Hartman, Jr..
1324 v. Luann Hartman.
1325 vi. Kim Hartman.

(2) Married Oct-31-1947 in Circleville Pendleton Co., WV, **Raymond Wade Hartman** (son of Elemuel Ake Hartman and Mona Wimer).

810. Mary Lou[6] Sponaugle (370.John Alonzo[5], 113.Adam Harness[4], 23.William[3], 4.Elizabeth L.[2] Arbogast, 1.George[1]), b. Jul-21-1933.
She Married **David Lambert**.

Children:

1326 i. Janice[7] Lambert.
1327 ii. Lori Lambert.

811. Conda Roy[6] Sponaugle (370.John Alonzo[5], 113.Adam Harness[4], 23.William[3], 4.Elizabeth L.[2] Arbogast, 1.George[1]), b. May-20-1912 in Circleville Pendleton Co., WV.
He Married **Betty Warner**, b. Jul 26 1913 (daughter of Pet Warner and Lura Mullenax).

Children:

1328 i. Genevieve[7] Sponaugle.
1329 ii. Norms Jean Sponaugle.
She Married **Kelley M. Mullenax.**
1330 iii. Billy Roy Sponaugle.
1331 iv. Brenda Sponaugle.

812. Ona Lucy[6] Sponaugle (370.John Alonzo[5] Sponaugle, 113.Adam Harness[4], 23.William[3], 4.Elizabeth L.[2] Arbogast, 1.George[1]), b. Nov-21-1909 in Circleville Pendleton Co., WV, d. Dec-19-1992.
Married Apr-09-1928, **Verlie Warner**, b. Dec 27 1903 (son of Pet Warner and Lura Mullenax), d. Nov 29 1969 in Circleville, Pendleton Co., WV, buried in Hunting Ground, Pendleton Co., (W)VA.

Children:

\+ 1332 i. Mildred Mary[7] Warner b. Sep 1928.
1333 ii. Hilda Warner b. c 1931 in Cherry Grove, Pendleton Co., WV, d. Feb-26-1987 in Port St. Lucie, FL.
She Married **Eldon J Wimer** (son of Charles Amos Wimer and Zoe Etta Thompson).
1334 iii. Geneva Warner.
1335 iv. Francis Warner.
1336 v. Jerrol Warner.
1337 vi. Jimmy Warner.
1338 vii. Johnnie Warner.
1339 viii. Caroline Ruth Warner.
1340 ix. Dennis Warner.
1341 x. Gail Warner.
1342 xi. Kermit Warner.

813. Cranston John[6] Sponaugle (370.John Alonzo[5], 113.Adam Harness[4], 23.William[3], 4.Elizabeth L.[2] Arbogast, 1.George[1]), b. Dec-12-1924 in Circleville Pendleton Co., WV.
He Married **Jessie Warner**, b. Dec-02-1924.

Children:

1343 i. Danny[7] Sponaugle.
1344 ii. Cranston Sponaugle.
1345 iii. Patricia Sponaugle.
1346 iv. Lonnie Sponaugle.

828. Louvary[6] Warner (375.Martha Hester[5] Sponaugle, 113.Adam Harness[4], 23.William[3], 4.Elizabeth L.[2] Arbogast, 1.George[1]), b. Dec-10-1917.
She Married **Chuck Vanicek**.

Children:

1347 i. Betty Jo^{7} Vanicek.
1348 ii. Charles Vanicek.
1349 iii. Wayne Vanicek.

829. Otis Joy^{6} Warner (375.Martha Hester^{5} Sponaugle, 113.Adam Harness^{4}, 23.William^{3}, 4.Elizabeth L.^{2} Arbogast, 1.George^{1}), b. Jul-18-1920.
He <u>Married</u> **Mary McClure.**

Children:

1350 i. Roy^{7} Warner.
1351 ii. Ricky Warner.
1352 iii. Randy Warner.
1353 iv. Robert Warner.

830. Thelma Jean^{6} Warner (375.Martha Hester^{5} Sponaugle, 113.Adam Harness^{4}, 23.William^{3}, 4.Elizabeth L.^{2} Arbogast, 1.George^{1}), b. Sep-09-1922.
She <u>Married</u> **unknown Carr.**

Children:

1354 i. Billy^{7} Carr.
1355 ii. Sharon Carr.
She <u>Married</u> **George Phares**

.

831. Mary Bernice^{6} Warner (375.Martha Hester^{5} Sponaugle, 113.Adam Harness^{4}, 23.William^{3}, 4.Elizabeth L.^{2} Arbogast, 1.George^{1}).
She <u>Married</u> **Mearl Scott**.

Children:

1356 i. Richard^{7} Scott.
1357 ii. Bridgett Scott.

832. Alice Lucy^{6} Warner (375.Martha Hester^{5} Sponaugle, 113.Adam Harness^{4}, 23.William^{3}, 4.Elizabeth L.^{2} Arbogast, 1.George^{1}).
She <u>Married</u> **Robert Longonette**.

Children:

1358 i. Donna^{7} Longonette.
1359 ii. Barbara Longonette.

833. Izetta Jewel^{6} Warner (375.Martha Hester^{5} Sponaugle, 113.Adam Harness^{4}, 23.William^{3}, 4.Elizabeth L.^{2} Arbogast, 1.George^{1}), b. Mar-21-1390.
She <u>Married</u> **Joseph Stealoski**.

Children:

1360 i. Mary Jo^{7} Stealoski.
1361 ii. Debra Stealoski.
1362 iii. Joey Stealoski.

834. William Guy^{6} Warner (375.Martha Hester^{5} Sponaugle, 113.Adam Harness^{4}, 23.William^{3}, 4.Elizabeth L.^{2} Arbogast, 1.George^{1}), b. Aug-19-1937.
He <u>Married</u> **Marble Thompson.**

<u>Children:</u>

1363 i. Gloria^{7} Warner.
1364 ii. Kay Warner.
1365 iii. Ella Warner.
1366 iv. Sarah Warner.
1367 v. David Warner.

835. Hilbert Oneal^{6} Warner (375.Martha Hester^{5} Sponaugle, 113.Adam Harness^{4}, 23.William^{3}, 4.Elizabeth L.^{2} Arbogast, 1.George^{1}), b. Nov-10-1935 in Hunting Ground, Pendleton Co., (W)VA.
He <u>Married</u> **Dorothy Elaine Lambert**.

Children:

1368 i. Roger Oneal^{7} Warner b. May-12-1966 in Cleveland, Cuyahoga Co., OH.

He Married **Bonnie Jean Pardee**.
1369 ii. Judirg Ann Warner b. May-12-1966 in Cleveland, Cuyahoga Co., OH.

837. Guy William[6] Judy (376.Monna Roxie[5] Sponaugle, 113.Adam Harness[4], 23.William[3], 4.Elizabeth L.[2] Arbogast, 1.George[1]), b. Apr-09-1916 in Timberridge, Pendleton Co., WV, d. Jan-30-1989 in Kennewick, Benton Co., WA, buried in Sunset Mem. Gard. Richmond, WA.
(1) Married Sep 1934, **Ada Rose Cox**, b. in Fairmont, Marion Co., WV (daughter of Ben Cox).

Children:

+ 1370 i. James Arthur[7] Judy b. Dec-01-1939.
+ 1371 ii. John Ben Judy b. Jun-07-1941.

(2) He Married Elaine Hartman.

Children:

+ 1372 iii. Susan Ann Marie Judy b. Oct-17-1955.

(3) He Married **Thelma Pearl Lemley**, b. Mar-24-1918 in Mt. Morris, PA.

Children:

+ 1373 iv. Linda Gaye Judy b. Dec-09-1952.
+ 1374 v. Teresa Lynn Judy b. May-10-1953.
1375 vi. William Keith Judy b. Jun-11-1955 in Kennewick, Benton Co., WA.
+ 1376 vii. Jacklyn Joyce Judy b. Oct-08-1956.
1377 viii. Loren Earl Judy b. Jul-15-1960 in Kennewick, Benton Co., WA.
Married Nov-16-1991, **Diane Marie Moore** (daughter of Don Moore and Belauh Moore).

838. Kermit Adam[6] Judy (376.Monna Roxie[5] Sponaugle, 113.Adam Harness[4], 23.William[3], 4.Elizabeth L.[2] Arbogast, 1.George[1]), b. Mar-03-1918 in Zigler, Smith Creek, Pendleton Co., WV.
He Married **Buanna Cornelia Hartman**, b. Apr-11-1921 in Timberridge, Pendleton Co., WV (daughter of Isaac Perry Hartman and Lucy Vandevander).

Children:

+ 1378 i. Bambara Joan[7] Judy b. Jul-08-1939.
+ 1379 ii. Harriet Levon Judy b. Oct-01-1941.
+ 1380 iii. Jennie Lou Judy b. May-01-1950.

839. Ethel Susan[6] Judy (376.Monna Roxie[5] Sponaugle, 113.Adam Harness[4], 23.William[3], 4.Elizabeth L.[2] Arbogast, 1.George[1]), b. Jan-09-1921 in Cherry Grove, Pendleton Co., WV.
Married Jun-21-1940 in Franklin, Pendleton Co., WV, **Robert Oliver Hall**, b. Jan-31-1918 (son of Hatvey Hall and Hazel Davis).

Children:

+ 1381 i. Linda Jean[7] Hall b. Jun-14-1941.
+ 1382 ii. Mary Susan Hall b. May-03-1945.

840. Bernice Evangeline[6] Judy (376.Monna Roxie[5] Sponaugle, 113.Adam Harness[4], 23.William[3], 4.Elizabeth L.[2] Arbogast, 1.George[1]), b. Apr-04-1924 in Circleville Pendleton Co., WV.
She Married **Howard Campbell Fortner, Jr**., b. Jun-13-1914 in Monograph, WV (son of Howard Campbell Fortner and Winfred Grace Flemming).

Children:

+ 1383 i. Howard Campbell[7] Fortner III b. Jun-03-1949.

841. Richard Thomas[6] Judy (376.Monna Roxie[5] Sponaugle, 113.Adam Harness[4], 23.William[3], 4.Elizabeth L.[2] Arbogast, 1.George[1]), b. Jul-24-1926 in Beverly, Randolph Co., WV.
He Married **Evelyn Mae Sites**, b. Aug-05-1932 in Franklin, Pendleton Co., WV (daughter of Perry Lester Sites and Laura Jane Propst).

Children:

1384 i. Jerry Lee[7] Judy b. Feb-17-1952 in Fairmont, Marion Co., WV.
+ 1385 ii. Katherine Ann Judy b. Oct-22-1958.

842. Ina^{6} Judy (376.Monna Roxie^{5} Sponaugle, 113.Adam Harness^{4}, 23.William^{3}, 4.Elizabeth L.^{2} Arbogast, 1.George^{1}), b. May-17-1928 in Elkins, Randolph Co., WV.
She Married **Richard Jones**, b. Jul-10-1930 in Chicago, Cook Co., IL (son of John Christian Frederick Kuehl and Josephine Louise Schmidt).

Children:

\+ 1386 i. Diane Louise^{7} Kuehl b. Aug-20-1953.

843. Gayle Edward^{6} Judy (376.Monna Roxie^{5} Sponaugle, 113.Adam Harness^{4}, 23.William^{3}, 4.Elizabeth L.^{2} Arbogast, 1.George^{1}), b. Jan-08-1932 in Princeton, Mercer Co., WV.

Married Jun-15-1957 in Smith Creek, Pendleton Co., WV, **Heata Della Simmons**, b. Nov-21-1939 in Franklin, Pendleton Co., WV (daughter of Olin Brownie Simmons and Joie Catherine Sponaugle).

Children:

\+ 1387 i. Edward^{7} Judy b. Jul-28-1960.

844. Early Thomas^{6} Judy, Jr. (376.Monna Roxie^{5} Sponaugle, 113.Adam Harness^{4}, 23.William^{3}, 4.Elizabeth L.^{2} Arbogast, 1.George^{1}), b. Dec-02-1934 in Smith Creek, Pendleton Co., WV.
He Married **Betty Lou Sponaugle**, b. Jan-19-1939 in Franklin, Pendleton Co., WV (daughter of Percy Carl Sponaugle and Arle Evelyn Dahmer).

Children:

1388 i. Carla Lynn-Nichoe^{7} Judy b. Dec-04-1960 in Washington, D.C.
Married Sep-10-1988 in Warrenton Fauquier Co., VA, **Thomas Vernon Martin, Jr.**.
1389 ii. Pamala Denise Judy b. Apr-11-1966 in Bethesda , MD.
Married Aug-12-1989 in Bethesda, Montgomery Co., MD, **David Charles Nilsen**.

845. Patricia Louvon^{6} Judy (376.Monna Roxie^{5} Sponaugle, 113.Adam Harness^{4}, 23.William^{3}, 4.Elizabeth L.^{2} Arbogast, 1.George^{1}), b. Apr-15-1937 in Smith Creek, Pendleton Co., WV.
Married Dec-31-1956 in Oakland, Garrett Co., MD, **Harold Michael Sponaugle**, b. May-18-1936 (son of Brison Jay Sponaugle and Judith Warner).

Children:

1390 i. Tamara Jo^{7} Sponaugle b. Sep-11-1970 in Cleveland, Cuyahoga Co., OH.

846. Gary Nelson^{6} Judy (376.Monna Roxie^{5} Sponaugle, 113.Adam Harness^{4}, 23.William^{3}, 4.Elizabeth L.^{2} Arbogast, 1.George^{1}), b. Oct-16-1940 in Smith Creek, Pendleton Co., WV.
Married Jun-16-1962 in Riverdale, MD, **Carole Faye Harper**, b. Aug-31-1942 (daughter of Leon Harper and Mary Jean Mowery).

Children:

1391 i. Janice Lynn^{7} Judy b. Dec-27-1966 in Lexington, Rockbridge Co., VA.
Married Jun-09-1990 in Lexington, Rockbridge Co., VA, **Gregory Dale Buckner**.

865. Dice G^{6} Warner (429.Walter^{5}, 139.Mary Elizabeth^{4} Teter, 26.Catherine^{3} Sponaugle, 4.Elizabeth L.^{2} Arbogast, 1.George^{1}), b. Apr-01-1902.
Married 1925, Annie Bennett.

Children:

\+ 1392 i. Nola Eda^{7} Warner b. Jul-27-1927.
\+ 1393 ii. Roy B. Warner.
1394 iii. Ralph Warner.
1395 iv. William Warner.
\+ 1396 v. unknown Warner.
\+ 1397 vi. Glenn Warner.
1398 vii. Ted Warner.
1399 viii. Olin Warner.
1400 ix. Florence Warner.

866. Beulah^{6} Warner (429.Walter^{5}, 139.Mary Elizabeth^{4} Teter, 26.Catherine^{3} Sponaugle, 4.Elizabeth L.^{2} Arbogast, 1.George^{1}).
(1) She Married **Austin Judy**.

Children:

\+ 1401 i. Hansel[7] Judy b. Jul-02-1922.
1402 ii. Dessie Judy b. Jul-27-1924.
She Married **Charles Brendle**.
1403 iii. Martha Judy b. Feb-13-1926.
\+ 1404 iv. Henry Edsel Judy b. Mar-11-1928.
\+ 1405 v. Norma Judy b. Apr-11-1929.

(2) She Married **Hansel Nelson**.

869. Verlin[6] Warner (429.Walter[5], 139.Mary Elizabeth[4] Teter, 26.Catherine[3] Sponaugle, 4.Elizabeth L.[2] Arbogast, 1.George[1]).
Married May-20-1940, **Lona Mae Simmons**, d. Dec-07-1977.

Children:

1406 i. Rose Darlene[7] Warner.
1407 ii. Verlin D. Warner.

870. Ona Austie[6] Judy (439.Tina[5] Warner, 142.Cecelia (Celia)[4] Sponaugle, 27.Lewis Martin[3], 4.Elizabeth L.[2] Arbogast, 1.George[1]).
He Married **Russell Lee Bland**.

Children:

\+ 1408 i. Herman[7] Bland b. Nov-24-1932.
\+ 1409 ii. Bryan Bland.
\+ 1410 iii. Dale Worth Bland b. Feb-08-1937.

872. Nellie[6] Judy (439.Tina[5] Warner, 142.Cecelia (Celia)[4] Sponaugle, 27.Lewis Martin[3], 4.Elizabeth L.[2] Arbogast, 1.George[1]).
She Married **William Wimer**.

Children:

1411 i. John William[7] Wimer.

876. Nellie Mae[6] Judy (439.Tina[5] Warner, 142.Cecelia (Celia)[4] Sponaugle, 27.Lewis Martin[3], 4.Elizabeth L.[2] Arbogast, 1.George[1]), b. Aug-13-1914 in Riverton, Pendleton Co., WV, d. Jul-23-1986 in Harrisonburg, Rockingham Co., VA.
Married Sep-30-1933 in Pendleton Co., WV, **William Harness Wimer**, b. Sep-06-1914 in Hunting Ground, Pendleton Co., (W)VA (son of Albert Harness Wimer and Kittie Dyer Warner).

Children:

1412 i. Mary Ellen[7] Wimer b. Mar-01-1935, d. Mar-01-1935.
\+ 1413 ii. John William Wimer b. Feb-16-1937.

879. Roy Dewey[6] Bland (443.Grace[5] Warner, 142.Cecelia (Celia)[4] Sponaugle, 27.Lewis Martin[3], 4.Elizabeth L.[2] Arbogast, 1.George[1]).
He Married **Betty Jo Perry**.

Children:

\+ 1414 i. Roy Dewey[7] Bland, Jr..
\+ 1415 ii. Betty Darlene Bland.
1416 iii. Curtis Corbett Bland b. Aug-17-1952.
(1) He Married **Ann Kimmons**.
(2) He Married **Kathy Holt**.
1417 iv. Donald Wayne Bland b. Jul-18-1956.
He Married **Jeanette Henry**.

881. Eva Lee[6] Bland (443.Grace[5] Warner, 142.Cecelia (Celia)[4] Sponaugle, 27.Lewis Martin[3], 4.Elizabeth L.[2] Arbogast, 1.George[1]).
She Married **Sherman Thompson**.

Children:

1418 i. Larry Sherman[7] Thompson.
\+ 1419 ii. Terry Allen Thompson.

887. Marshall[6] Bland (443.Grace[5] Warner, 142.Cecelia (Celia)[4] Sponaugle, 27.Lewis Martin[3], 4.Elizabeth L.[2] Arbogast, 1.George[1]), b. Dec-17-1916.
He Married **Hope Chatterbuck**.

Children:

+ 1420 i. Charles Wesley^7 Bland.
+ 1421 ii. Janis Sue Bland.

895. Richard Pascal^6 Hedrick (463.Mary Clara^5 Warner, 147.Martha Alice^4 Sponaugle, 27.Lewis Martin^3, 4.Elizabeth L.^{2} Arbogast, 1.George^1), b. Jul-14-1916 in Whitmer, Randolph Co., WV.
Married Jul-15-1940 in Monterey, Highland Co., VA, **Kathryn Gail Mullenax**, b. Jun-06-1919 in Whitmer, Randolph Co., WV (daughter of Kennie Oscar Mullenax and Rebecca Cunningham).

Children:

1422 i. Judith Gail^7 Hedrick b. Dec-10-1940 in Elkins, Randolph Co., WV.
(1) She Married **Donovan Elmo Shrader, Jr.**.
(2) Married May-16-1961 in Temple, Bell Co., TX, Vernon Ray Martin.
1423 ii. Richard Junior Hedrick b. Nov-17-1942 in Cheat Bridge, WV.
Married Jul-30-1966, **Erma Lucille Collins**.
1424 iii. Randall Wayne Hedrick b. Apr-10-1946 in Durbin, Pocahontas Co., WV.
Married Jul-30-1971, **Catherine Mendiola**.
1425 iv. Keren Sue Hedrick b. Aug-28-1953 in Marlinton, Pocahontas Co., WV.
Married Jun-20-1973, **Larry Orland Conley**.
1426 v. Kathy Kaye Hedrick b. Oct-04-1960 in Marlinton, Pocahontas Co., WV.
1427 vi. Delores Faye Hedrick b. Oct-04-1960 in Marlinton, Pocahontas Co., WV, d. Oct-05-1960.

900. William Harness^6 Wimer (475.Albert Harness^5, 154.Sylverius^4, 28.Mary Elizabeth^3 Sponaugle, 4.Elizabeth L.^{2} Arbogast, 1.George^1), b. Sep-06-1914 in Hunting Ground, Pendleton Co., (W)VA.
(1) Married Sep-30-1933 in Pendleton Co., WV, **Nellie Mae Judy** (See marriage to number 876).

Children:

(See marriage to number 876)

(2) He Married **Violet Genevieve Martin**.

Children:

1428 iii. Mary Ann Wimer b. Jul-21-1961.
She Married **Harold Martin**.
1429 iv. Kitty Dyer Wimer b. Jul-21-1961.

901. Harlan^6 Warner (475.Albert Harness^5 Wimer, 154.Sylverius^4, 28.Mary Elizabeth^3 Sponaugle, 4.Elizabeth L.^{2} Arbogast, 1.George^1), b. Feb-16-1920 in Hunting Ground, Pendleton Co., (W)VA, d. Apr-11-1967 in Brandywine, Pendleton Co., WV.
He Married **Texie Leah Bland**, b. Dec-22-1921 in Hunting Ground, Pendleton Co., (W)VA (daughter of Charles Bland and Virginia Warner).

Children:

+ 1430 i. Larry Harlan^7 Wimer b. Aug-23-1940.
1431 ii. Nathan Wimer b. Apr-17-1942, d. Apr-17-1942.
1432 iii. Carolyn June Wimer.
+ 1433 iv. Christopher Lee Wimer b. 1950.
1434 v. Rebecca Ellen Wimer.

902. Mable^6 Warner (476.MaryEllen^5 Wimer, 154.Sylverius^4, 28.Mary Elizabeth^3 Sponaugle, 4.Elizabeth L.^{2} Arbogast, 1.George^1), b. Aug-13-1910 in Hunting Ground, Pendleton Co., (W)VA.
(1) Married Jun-29-1929 in Flintstone, Allegheny Co., MD, **Jimmie Jay Bennett**, b. Jul-01-1912 in Circleville Pendleton Co., WV (son of Adam Jay Bennett and Edie Murphy), d. Nov-02-1969 in Rockingham Co., VA.

Children:

+ 1435 i. Glenn Richard^7 Bennett b. 1930.
1436 ii. Merl Edwin Bennett b. 1932.
1437 iii. Mable Ruth Bennett b. 1934.
She Married **Vernon Clay Simmons**.

(2) She Married **George C. Sponaugle** (son of Louisa Vent and Robert Boyd Sponaugle).

903. Arlie^6 Warner (476.MaryEllen^5 Wimer, 154.Sylverius^4, 28.Mary Elizabeth^3 Sponaugle, 4.Elizabeth L.^{2} Arbogast, 1.George^1), b. Nov-20-1912.
He Married **Vera White**.

Children:

+ 1438 i. Ronald Lee[7] Warner.
+ 1439 ii. Sandra Warner.

905. Roy[6] Warner (476.MaryEllen[5] Wimer, 154.Sylverius[4], 28.Mary Elizabeth[3] Sponaugle, 4.Elizabeth L.[2] Arbogast, 1.George[1]), b. Jan-17-1917.
He Married Sadie Kathryn Bennett (daughter of Adam Jay Bennett and Edie Murphy).

Children:

+ 1440 i. Thomas Gartrh[7] Warner b. 1939.
1441 ii. Jerry William Warner b. 1942.
He Married **Evelyn Richards**.
1442 iii. Wanda Joy Warner b. 1948.

906. Ray[6] Warner (476.MaryEllen[5] Wimer, 154.Sylverius[4], 28.Mary Elizabeth[3] Sponaugle, 4.Elizabeth L.[2] Arbogast, 1.George[1]), b. Mar-03-1919.
He Married **Nola Eda Warner**, b. Jul-27-1927 (daughter of Dice G Warner and Annie Bennett).

Children:

+ 1443 i. Olin Ray[7] Warner b. Dec-19-1944.
+ 1444 ii. Nancy Lee Warner b. 1947.
1445 iii. Doris Ann Warner b. Oct-21-1952.
She Married **Dennis Michael Koch**.

907. Dewitt[6] Warner (476.MaryEllen[5] Wimer, 154.Sylverius[4], 28.Mary Elizabeth[3] Sponaugle, 4.Elizabeth L.[2] Arbogast, 1.George[1]), b. May-24-1921.
He Married **Millie J Marsh**.

Children:

1446 i. Terry[7] Warner.

908. Charles[6] Warner, Jr. (476.MaryEllen[5] Wimer, 154.Sylverius[4], 28.Mary Elizabeth[3] Sponaugle, 4.Elizabeth L.[2] Arbogast, 1.George[1]), b. Jul-29-1928.
He Married **Betty Lea Cornell**, b. Aug-27-1931 in Orange Co., VA (daughter of James Lee Cornell and Alva Mills).

Children:

+ 1447 i. Roy Lee[7] Warner.
1448 ii. Linda Sue Warner b. 1950.

909. Merl Noah[6] Warner (476.MaryEllen[5] Wimer, 154.Sylverius[4], 28.Mary Elizabeth[3] Sponaugle, 4.Elizabeth L.[2] Arbogast, 1.George[1]), b. Mar-05-1930.
He Married **Margaret Jean Mullenax**.

Children:

1449 i. Randy[7] Bennett.
1450 ii. Jimmie Bennett.

910. Priscilla Lane[6] Warner (476.MaryEllen[5] Wimer, 154.Sylverius[4], 28.Mary Elizabeth[3] Sponaugle, 4.Elizabeth L.[2] Arbogast, 1.George[1]), b. Apr-10-1934.
She Married **Brooks Mullenax**, b. Jul 17 1927 (son of James Edward Mullenax and Gertrude Lee Waybright).

Children:

+ 1451 i. Shirley Ann[7] Mullenax b. 1953.
1452 ii. Diana Fay Mullenax b. 1995.
1453 iii. Donald Brooks Mullenax b. 1960.
1454 iv. Rose Mary Mullenax b. 1964.
She Married **Kevin Simmons** (son of Harlan Simmons and Kittie Warner).

911. Paul[6] Warner (476.MaryEllen[5] Wimer, 154.Sylverius[4], 28.Mary Elizabeth[3] Sponaugle, 4.Elizabeth L.[2] Arbogast, 1.George[1]), b. Oct-10-1935.
He Married **Pauline Arbogast**.

Children:

1455 i. Paul[7] Warner, Jr..

1456 ii. Paula Jean Warner.

919. Reva Kerlin^6 Hinkle (478.Lou Catherine^5 Wimer, 154.Sylverius^4, 28.Mary Elizabeth^3 Sponaugle, 4.Elizabeth L.^{2} Arbogast, 1.George^1), b. Jan-02-1915 in Hunting Ground, Pendleton Co., (W)VA, buried in Cemetery, Elkton, MD and all individuals with events at this location, d. Apr-24-1987 in Union Hosp., Elkton, Md.
Daughter of Jasper Hinkle. Lived at Cecil Co., MD. Kept her mother's name. This comment copied. There is confusion on the part of recorder about who parents are of Reva. Limited information does no add u.
She Married **John William Johnston**, b. May-31-1909 (son of William Wallace Johnston and Solinda Bennett), d. Oct-16-1972.

Children:

1457 i. Arnold Lee^7 Johnston b. Dec-22-1931, d. Aug 1945.
\+ 1458 ii. John William Johnston, Jr. b. Jul-30-1934.
\+ 1459 iii. Emma Lou Johnston b. Jul-21-1937.
\+ 1460 iv. Sue Johnston b. Nov-05-1939.
\+ 1461 v. Marian Johnston b. Feb-08-1942.
\+ 1462 vi. Eveline Kay Johnston.
\+ 1463 vii. Bruce Dallas Johnston.

925. Richard Harold^6 Wymer (481.Carson Elmer^5, 158.Albert^4 Wimer, 28.Mary Elizabeth^3 Sponaugle, 4.Elizabeth L.^{2} Arbogast, 1.George^1), b. Apr-28-1920 in Cherry Grove, Pendleton Co., WV, d. Sep-14-1981 in Riverton, Pendleton Co., WV.
He Married **Bonnie Blanche Murphy**, b. Oct-22-1916 (daughter of Isaac Murphy and Lena Lambert).

Children:

\+ 1464 i. Elaine^7 Wymer.

926. Aleta Macie^6 Wymer (481.Carson Elmer^5, 158.Albert^4 Wimer, 28.Mary Elizabeth^3 Sponaugle, 4.Elizabeth L.^{2} Arbogast, 1.George^1), b. May-26-1926.
Married Feb-17-1945, Leo Stelman Pennington, b. Jun-21-1924 (son of Ora Pennington and Erva Simmons).

Children:

1465 i. Leon Carlson^7 Pennington b. Jun-23-1946, d. Mar-28-1967 in Vandenberg AFB,,CA.
\+ 1466 ii. Rita Lynn Pennington b. Nov-14-1949.

927. Bernice Kay^6 Wymer (481.Carson Elmer^5, 158.Albert^4 Wimer, 28.Mary Elizabeth^3 Sponaugle, 4.Elizabeth L.^{2} Arbogast, 1.George^1).
(1) She Married **Richard Barzdorff**.

Children:

\+ 1467 i. Angeletta^7 Wymer.
\+ 1468 ii. Robrietta Barzdorff.

(2) She Married **Glen H. DePue**, b. Apr-02-1914 in Creston, Wirt Co., WV (son of John A. DePue and Lula M. Douglass), d. May-25-1993 in Franklin, Pendleton Co., WV.

928. Vivian^6 Wymer (481.Carson Elmer^5, 158.Albert^4 Wimer, 28.Mary Elizabeth^3 Sponaugle, 4.Elizabeth L.^{2} Arbogast, 1.George^1), b. Jul-06-1934.
She Married **Richard LaValley**.

Children:

1469 i. Kevin James^7 LaValley b. May-17-1965 in Washington, D.C., buried in Waldorf, Charles Co., MD, d. May-06-1987 in Prince George Co., MD.

He Married S. **Renee Murphy**.

1470 ii. Craig L LaValley.
1471 iii. Keith E. LaValley.

935. Mildred Marie^6 Wimer (485.Lillie Mae^5, 159.Tiberius^4, 28.Mary Elizabeth^3 Sponaugle, 4.Elizabeth L.^{2} Arbogast, 1.George^1), b. Jan-20-1923.
She Married **James Luther Vance**, b. Dec-18-1920 in Petersburg, Grant Co., WV, buried in Cedar Hill Cem., Grant Co., WV, d. Mar-16-1968 in Morgantown, Monongalia Co., WV.

Children:

+ 1472 i. Virgil Lee[7] Wimer b. Dec-10-1942.
+ 1473 ii. Linda Kay Vance b. Jan-08-1947.

936. Wilda Mae[6] Wilmer (485.Lillie Mae[5] Wimer, 159.Tiberius[4], 28.Mary Elizabeth[3] Sponaugle, 4.Elizabeth L.[2] Arbogast, 1.George[1]), b. Nov-07-1926 in Circleville Pendleton Co., WV.
She Married **Ralph Roscoe Hartman**, b. May-07-1927 in Petersburg, Grant Co., WV, d. Oct-16-1953 in Parkersburg, Wood Co., WV.

Children:

+ 1474 i. Stoney Roscoe[7] Hartman b. Nov-24-1952.

938. Roy Richard[6] Kissmore (486.Leanna[5] Wimer, 159.Tiberius[4], 28.Mary Elizabeth[3] Sponaugle, 4.Elizabeth L.[2] Arbogast, 1.George[1]), b. May-02-1921 in Back Ridge, Hunting Ground, WV.
He Married **Christena Lou Lambert**, b. Aug-01-1928 in Dry Run, Pendleton Co., WV (daughter of Troy Leslie lambert and Elsie Bird).

Children:

+ 1475 i. Mary Ann[7] Kissamore b. Dec-27-1945.
+ 1476 ii. Dorothy Mae Kissamore b. Aug-14-1947.
+ 1477 iii. Donald Marion Lilly.

1478 iv. Joseph Ray Kissamore b. Feb-12-1950 to Fort Run, Hardy Co., WV.
(1) Married Sep-19-1971 in Rockingham Co., VA, **Shirley Temple**, b. Aug-19-1943 (daughter of Henry McAvoy and Leta Simmons).
(2) He Married **Sharon Jean Vandevander**, b. May-08-1946 in WV.

1479 v. Allan Dale Kissmore b. Feb-15-1948 in Petersburg, Grant Co., WV.
He Married **Debbie Lynn Ellis**, b. Aug-27-1962 in Hampton, VA (daughter of Fay Ellis and Carylon Hopkins).

+ 1480 vi. Evaline Peggy Kissamore` b. Apr-20-1926.

941. Warden Guy[6] Hartman (487.Mona[5] Wimer, 159.Tiberius[4], 28.Mary Elizabeth[3] Sponaugle, 4.Elizabeth L.[2] Arbogast, 1.George[1]), b. Jan-11-1922, buried in Cedar Hill Cem., Pendleton Co., WV, d. Sep-30-1968.
(1) Married Jun-24-1942 in Pendleton Co., WV, **Alma Corinne Calhoun**, b. 1923 in Pendleton Co., WV (daughter of Russell Calhoun and Nola Judy), d. Jan-24-1987 in Baltimore Co., MD.
(2) He Married **Mildred Mary Warner**, b. Sep 1928 in Hunting Ground, Pendleton Co., (W)VA (daughter of Verlie Warner and Ona Lucy Sponaugle).

Children:

1481 i. Dorothy Louise[7] Hartman.
She Married Jimmy Stewart.

+ 1482 ii. Steven Guy Hartman.

965. Orpha[6] Crosby (493.Rosetta[5] Long, 165.Virginia Catherine (Jennie)[4] Teter, 30.Leah[3] Sponaugle, 4.Elizabeth L.[2] Arbogast, 1.George[1]), d. Jun-07-1970.
She Married **Kennie Simmons**, d. Mar-06-1970.

Children:

+ 1483 i. Artis E[7] Simmons b. Jun-21-1921.

1484 ii. Dale Simmons.
He Married **Dorthea O'Dell**.

1485 iii. Phillip Simmons.

966. George Otis[6] Mosley (494.Elmina[5] Long, 165.Virginia Catherine (Jennie)[4] Teter, 30.Leah[3] Sponaugle, 4.Elizabeth L.[2] Arbogast, 1.George[1]), b. Jan-20-1905, d. Feb-17-1942.
He Married **Mildred unknown**.

Children:

+ 1486 i. Charles Roy[7] Mosley b. Oct-08-1935.
+ 1487 ii. Burton Taylor Mosley b. Nov-30-1937.
+ 1488 iii. Donald Clyde Mosley b. Apr-11-1939.
+ 1489 iv. Ruby Pauline Mosley b. Jul-01-1940.

+ 1490 v. Betty Darleen b. Nov-08-1941.

967. Grace Levin[6] Mosley (494.Elmina[5] Long, 165.Virginia Catherine (Jennie)[4] Teter, 30.Leah[3] Sponaugle, 4.Elizabeth L.[2] Arbogast, 1.George[1]), b. Mar-29-1908.
She Married **Larry Aukamp**, b. Dec-28-1897.

Children:

1491 i. James[7] Aukamp b. Jan-30-1924.
+ 1492 ii. Harry Glenn Aukamp b. Nov-26-1927.
+ 1493 iii. Shirley Aukamp b. Apr-25-1936.

968. Johnny[6] Mosley (494.Elmina[5] Long, 165.Virginia Catherine (Jennie)[4] Teter, 30.Leah[3] Sponaugle, 4.Elizabeth L.[2] Arbogast, 1.George[1]), b. Sep-26-1910, d. Jun-29-1968.
(1) He Married **Katherine Unknown**.

Children:

+ 1494 i. Barkley Allen[7] Mosley b. Sep-07-1937.
1495 ii. Michal Deering Mosley b. Mar-06-1944.
He Married **Judy Freze** (daughter of Lee Freze and Lee Ann Mosley).
1496 iii. Robert Pruitt Mosley.

(2) He Married **Darlean Dakota**.

969. Opel Irene[6] Mosley (494.Elmina[5] Long, 165.Virginia Catherine (Jennie)[4] Teter, 30.Leah[3] Sponaugle, 4.Elizabeth L.[2] Arbogast, 1.George[1]), b. May-22-1913.

She Married **Bart Gayman**, b. May-08-1910.

Children:

+ 1497 i. Rodney[7] Gayman b. Mar-21-1931.
+ 1498 ii. Irean Gayman b. Dec-20-1933.
1499 iii. Sharon Gayman d. 1992.

970. Dorothy Leone[6] Long (495.John William[5], 165.Virginia Catherine (Jennie)[4] Teter, 30.Leah[3] Sponaugle, 4.Elizabeth L.[2] Arbogast, 1.George[1]), b. Nov-23-1914.
(1) She Married **Mike Gynkiss**.

Children:

1500 i. Sondra[7] Gynkiss b. Jul-01-1937.

(2) She Married **Leonard Erickson**.

Children:

+ 1501 ii. Ronald Lee Erickson b. Apr-07-1940.

972. Lorna Doone[6] Long (495.John William[5], 165.Virginia Catherine (Jennie)[4] Teter, 30.Leah[3] Sponaugle, 4.Elizabeth L.[2] Arbogast, 1.George[1]), b. Jul-26-1919.
Married Nov-01-1937, **Edward Long**, b. Jan-20-1906, d. Jul 1963.

Children:

+ 1502 i. Joyce[7] Long b. Nov-14-1941.
+ 1503 ii. Michael John Long b. Jan-27-1947.

974. Mary Virginia[6] Long (495.John William[5], 165.Virginia Catherine (Jennie)[4] Teter, 30.Leah[3] Sponaugle, 4.Elizabeth L.[2] Arbogast, 1.George[1]), b. Jun-17-1929.
She Married **Daniel Hoyrup**, b. Oct-16-1924.

Children:

1504 i. John Lewis[7] Hoyrup b. May-03-1955.
1505 ii. Diann Lee Hoyrup b. Dec-17-1960.
1506 iii. Catherine Elizabeth Hoyrup b. Feb-19-1965.

975. Gordon Charles[6] O'Bryan (496.Arta[5] Long, 165.Virginia Catherine (Jennie)[4] Teter, 30.Leah[3] Sponaugle, 4.Elizabeth L.[2] Arbogast, 1.George[1]), b. Oct-12-1912.

He Married **Dorothy Dingler**, b. Jul-02-1909.

Children:

+ 1507 i. Ann Elizabeth[7] O'Bryan b. May-09-1941.
+ 1508 ii. Arta Jean O'Bryan b. Mar-17-1945.
+ 1509 iii. Charles Francis O'Bryan b. Feb-07-1946.

977. Zona[6] Dillon (497.Florence[5] Long, 165.Virginia Catherine (Jennie)[4] Teter, 30.Leah[3] Sponaugle, 4.Elizabeth L.[2] Arbogast, 1.George[1]), b. Feb-02-1914.
(1) Married Jun-28-1937, **James Galbreath**, b. Nov-28-1901.

Children:

+ 1510 i. Howard[7] Galbreath b. Sep-13-1948.

(2) Married May-13-1953, Carl G. Speck, b. Jun-16-1905.

978. Robert Harold[6] Summers (498.Ada[5] Long, 165.Virginia Catherine (Jennie)[4] Teter, 30.Leah[3] Sponaugle, 4.Elizabeth L.[2] Arbogast, 1.George[1]), b. Sep-19-1915.
He Married **Maxine Pearsall**, b. Mar-08-1920.

Children:

+ 1511 i. Jack Harold[7] Summers b. Jun-31-1939.

979. Juanita Rilla[6] Summers (498.Ada[5] Long, 165.Virginia Catherine (Jennie)[4] Teter, 30.Leah[3] Sponaugle, 4.Elizabeth L.[2] Arbogast, 1.George[1]), b. Jan-23-1917.
She Married **Harry Munds**, b. Apr-20-1907.

Children:

+ 1512 i. Juanita Mae[7] Munds b. Mar-18-1935.
+ 1513 ii. James Robert Munds b. Sep-26-1936.
1514 iii. Barbara Lee Munds b. Mar-08-1939.
+ 1515 iv. Glenn Munds b. Sep-02-1944.

987. Roy Clifton[6] Teter (501.Clifton Andrew[5], 166.Andrew[4], 30.Leah[3] Sponaugle, 4.Elizabeth L.[2] Arbogast, 1.George[1]), b. Aug-11-1918.
He Married **Delphia Workman**.

Children:

1516 i. Roy Clifton[7] Teter Jr..
1517 ii. Paul Teter b. Aug-12-1920.

1007. Virginia[6] Foy (512.Selena[5] Teter, 167.William Patterson[4], 30.Leah[3] Sponaugle, 4.Elizabeth L.[2] Arbogast, 1.George[1]).
She Married **Woodrow Wilson**.

Children:

1518 i. Susan[7] Wilson.
1519 ii. Donald Wilson.
1520 iii. James Wilson.
1521 iv. Barbara Wilson.

1010. Patti Lynn[6] Gillespie (515.Vigrinia[5] Teter, 167.William Patterson[4], 30.Leah[3] Sponaugle, 4.Elizabeth L.[2] Arbogast, 1.George[1]).
She Married **Allen Grimm**.

Children:

1522 i. Aaron[7] Grimm.
1523 ii. Jacob Grimm.

1011. Darrell[6] Teter (516.George Wesley[5] Grimm, 167.William Patterson[4] Teter, 30.Leah[3] Sponaugle, 4.Elizabeth L.[2] Arbogast, 1.George[1]), b. Feb-24-1920, buried in Kerns Cem., Middle Mountain, Sully, WV, d. Jul-12-1984.
He Married **Marie B. Nield**, b. Jan-16-1934.

Children:

1524 i. Mary Jane[7] Teter b. Apr-01-1957, d. Apr-01-1957.
1525 ii. Vickie Lynn Teter b. Dec-14-1964.

Married May-10-1985, **Christopher A, Keister**, b. Nov-03-1960.

1017. Flossie Mabel[6] Bright (520.Mary Ann[5] Teter, 168.John Jackson[4], 30.Leah[3] Sponaugle, 4.Elizabeth L.[2] Arbogast, 1.George[1]), b. Aug-17-1920.
Married Mar-02-1940, Daniel Hardy, b. Mar-27-1913, d. Mar-08-1986.

Children:

+ 1526 i. Shirley Grace[7] Hardy b. 1941.
+ 1527 ii. Thomas Daniel Hardy b. 1943.
+ 1528 iii. Linda Lou Hardy b. 1945.
1529 iv. Jerry Lee Hardy b. 1948.
1530 v. Harry Webster Hardy b. 1950.

1025. Genevieve Marie[6] Davis (523.Rosa Bell[5] Bright, 170.Elizabeth Mary[4] Teter, 30.Leah[3] Sponaugle, 4.Elizabeth L.[2] Arbogast, 1.George[1]), b. 1914.
1) She Married **Clyde Barkley**, b. 1914, d. 1983.

Children:

1531 i. Harold Kingston[7] Barkley b. 1933.
1532 ii. Sharett Juanita Barkley b. 1935.
1533 iii. Clara Rosie Barkley.
1534 iv. Robert Lee Barkley b. 1937.
1535 v. Virginia Evelyn Barkley.

(2) She Married **John Penscoski**.

1026. Herbert William[6] Davis (523.Rosa Bell[5] Bright, 170.Elizabeth Mary[4] Teter, 30.Leah[3] Sponaugle, 4.Elizabeth L.[2] Arbogast, 1.George[1]), b. 1919.
He Married **Violet Virginia Shrout**.

Children:

1536 i. Jerry Leon[7] Davis b. 1944.
1537 ii. Coby Grant Davis b. 1949.

1027. Londa Ruby[6] Davis (523.Rosa Bell[5] Bright, 170.Elizabeth Mary[4] Teter, 30.Leah[3] Sponaugle, 4.Elizabeth L.[2] Arbogast, 1.George[1]), b. 1923.
She Married **Michael Bowman**.

Children:

1538 i. Linda Rae[7] Bowman.
1539 ii. Michael Gordon Bowman.

1028. Howard Ernest[6] Davis (523.Rosa Bell[5] Bright, 170.Elizabeth Mary[4] Teter, 30.Leah[3] Sponaugle, 4.Elizabeth L.[2] Arbogast, 1.George[1]), b. 1926.
He Married **June Teter**, b. 1932 in Parsons, Tucker Co., WV.

Children:

1540 i. Victoria[7] Davis.
1541 ii. Betty Jean Davis.

1029. Hallena Bell[6] Davis (523.Rosa Bell[5] Bright, 170.Elizabeth Mary[4] Teter, 30.Leah[3] Sponaugle, 4.Elizabeth L.[2] Arbogast, 1.George[1]), b. 1928.
She Married **George Deitz**, b. in Meadow Bridge, Fayette Co., WV.

Children:

+ 1542 i. Sandra Kay[7] Deitz b. 1952.

1030. Martin VanBuren[6] Davis (523.Rosa Bell[5] Bright, 170.Elizabeth Mary[4] Teter, 30.Leah[3] Sponaugle, 4.Elizabeth L.[2] Arbogast, 1.George[1]), b. 1929.
He Married **Phyllis Jean Hardy**, b. in Hendricks, Tucker Co., WV.

Children:

1543 i. Cathy Lucille[7] Hardy b. 1955.
1544 ii. Robert John Davis b. 1958.

1031. Calvin Coolage[6] Bright (523.Rosa Bell[5], 170.Elizabeth Mary[4] Teter, 30.Leah[3] Sponaugle, 4.Elizabeth L.[2] Arbogast, 1.George[1]), b. 1932.
Married 1964, **Leona Clifton**, b. 1936 in Upshur Co., WV.

Children:

1545 i. Rose Marie[7] Bright b. 1958.
1546 ii. Patrick Lesley Bright b. 1960.

1046. Andrew[6] White (536.Rosa Alice[5] Smith, 171.Alice Grace[4] Teter, 30.Leah[3] Sponaugle, 4.Elizabeth L.[2] Arbogast, 1.George[1]).
He Married **Roberta Deloris Burkhart**.

Children:

1547 i. Mark[7] Burkhart.
1548 ii. Robert Glenn Smith.
1549 iii. Russell E. Smith.
1550 iv. Harry D Smith.
\+ 1551 v. Norman D Smith.
1552 vi. Coley Smith.
Killed in Viet Nam.
1553 vii. Easter M Smith.
She Married **unknown Rinker**.
1554 viii. Ursula A Smith.
She Married **unknown McDonald**.

1047. Sarah Louise[6] Smith (537.Omer[5], 171.Alice Grace[4] Teter, 30.Leah[3] Sponaugle, 4.Elizabeth L.[2] Arbogast, 1.George[1]).

She Married **Clifford Danials**.

Children:

1555 i. Melissa Dawn[7] Danials.

1050. David[6] Burgess (538.Sylvia[5] Smith, 171.Alice Grace[4] Teter, 30.Leah[3] Sponaugle, 4.Elizabeth L.[2] Arbogast, 1.George[1]).
He Married **Tylyn Huffman**.

Children:

1556 i. Teresa[7] Burgess.
1557 ii. Dwight Burgess.
1558 iii. Rebecca Burgess.
1559 iv. Darrell Burgess.

1051. Kenneth[6] Burgess (538.Sylvia[5] Smith, 171.Alice Grace[4] Teter, 30.Leah[3] Sponaugle, 4.Elizabeth L.[2] Arbogast, 1.George[1]).
He Married S**haron Tingler**.

Children:

1560 i. Jodi Shupp[7] Burgess.
1561 ii. Michelle Burgess.
1562 iii. Shelby Burgess.

1052. Nancy[6] Burgess (538.Sylvia[5] Smith, 171.Alice Grace[4] Teter, 30.Leah[3] Sponaugle, 4.Elizabeth L.[2] Arbogast, 1.George[1]).
She Married **John Mann**.

Children:

1563 i. John Wesley[7] Mann.

1054. Betty[6] Burgess (538.Sylvia[5] Smith, 171.Alice Grace[4] Teter, 30.Leah[3] Sponaugle, 4.Elizabeth L.[2] Arbogast, 1.George[1]).
She Married **Mike Betler**

Children:

1564 i. Raymond[7] Butler.

1064. Harold Michael^6 Sponaugle (560.Brison Jay^5, 188.Gilbert Kenton^4, 33.Jacob^3, 4.Elizabeth L.^{2} Arbogast, 1.George^1), b. May-18-1936.
(1) He Married **Peter Hebert.**
(2) Married Dec-31-1956 in Oakland, Garrett Co., MD, **Patricia Louvon Judy** (See marriage to number 845).

Children:
(See marriage to number 845)

1066. Juanita^6 Sponaugle (564.Herbert Charles^5, 191.William Letcher^4, 33.Jacob^3, 4.Elizabeth L.^{2} Arbogast, 1.George^1), b. Jun 12 1944.
Married Jul 22 1961, **Charles Albert Taylor**, b. Dec 9 1938 (son of Robert Daniel Taylor and Florence Henitz).

Children:
+ 1565 i. Joyce Juanita^7 Taylor b. Apr 16 1962.
+ 1566 ii. Norma Jean Taylor b. Dec 23 1963.
+ 1567 iii. Allen Ray Taylor b. Jun 21 1969.

1067. Patrica^6 Sponaugle (564.Herbert Charles^5, 191.William Letcher^4, 33.Jacob^3, 4.Elizabeth L.^{2} Arbogast, 1.George^1).
She Married **Buford C Johnston** (son of Cletis Johnston and Ollie K. Warner).

Children:
1568 i. Mary Ann^7 Johnston.
She Married **William Vandevander**.
1569 ii. Janet L Johnston.
She Married **Danny Vandevander**.
1570 iii. Ricky Johnston b. 1960.
1571 iv. Dotty Johnston b. 1964.

1070. Loriraine L^6 Sponaugle (573.Marvin Luther^5, 192.Herman Henry^4, 33.Jacob^3, 4.Elizabeth L.^{2} Arbogast, 1.George^1), b. Feb-03-1924.
She Married Cranston Harper.

Children:
1572 i. Guy^7 Harper.
1573 ii. Gary Harper.

1071. Ruth Elaine^6 Sponaugle (573.Marvin Luther^5, 192.Herman Henry^4, 33.Jacob^3, 4.Elizabeth L.^{2} Arbogast, 1.George^1), b. May-05-1928.
She Married **William Harvey Bowers**.

Children:
1574 i. William Harvy^7 Bowers, Jr..
+ 1575 ii. Jeffery Stewart Bowers.

1072. Marvin Luther^6 Sponaugle, Jr. (573.Marvin Luther^5, 192.Herman Henry^4, 33.Jacob^3, 4.Elizabeth L.^{2} Arbogast, 1.George^1), b. May-05-1928.
(1) He Married **Martha Jean Bland**.

Children:
1576 i. Stephen Douglas^7 Sponaugle b. Jul-07-1954.
+ 1577 ii. Martin Luther Sponaugle, III b. Apr-17-1956.

(2) He Married Gayle Anderson.

1075. Carroll Lee^6 Sponaugle (573.Marvin Luther^5, 192.Herman Henry^4, 33.Jacob^3, 4.Elizabeth L.^{2} Arbogast, 1.George^1), b. Mar-10-1933.
She Married **Phyllis Crigler**.

Children:
+ 1578 i. Diane^7 Sponaugle.

1077. Loretta June^6 Sponaugle (573.Marvin Luther^5, 192.Herman Henry^4, 33.Jacob^3, 4.Elizabeth L.^{2} Arbogast, 1.George^1), b. Dec-27-1937.
She Married **John F Homan**.

Children:

1579 i. Sarah^7 Homan.
1580 ii. Susan Homan.

1088. Delene^6 Bennett (576.Alpha Cynyhia^5 Sponaugle, 192.Herman Henry^4, 33.Jacob^3, 4.Elizabeth L.^{2} Arbogast, 1.George^1).
Married Dec-23-1946, **Albert Freeman Bland**, b. Dec-26-1923 (son of Donald Bland and Tina Huffman), d. Oct-30-1982.

Children:

1581 i. Peggy^7 Bland b. Jun-22-1947.
She Married Robert Mills.

1091. Judy^6 Bennett (576.Alpha Cynyhia^5 Sponaugle, 192.Herman Henry^4, 33.Jacob^3, 4.Elizabeth L.^{2} Arbogast, 1.George^1).
She Married **Arlie McQuain**

Children:

1582 i. Chandra^7 McQuain.

1092. Richard Cleat^6 Phares (577.Myrtle M^5 Sponaugle, 192.Herman Henry^4, 33.Jacob^3, 4.Elizabeth L.^{2} Arbogast, 1.George^1), b. May-16-1928.
He Married **Ruth M. Stites**, b. Oct-01-1933 (daughter of L.B. Sites and Gertrude Hoffman).

Children:

1583 i. Pamala Karla^7 Phares b. Jul-15-1932.
She Married **Steven J. Kulback**, b. Jul-21-1953.
\+ 1584 ii. Richard Clete Phares, Jr. b. Dec-25-1953.
\+ 1585 iii. Kimberly Lynn Phares b. Dec-20-1957.
1586 iv. Sonnee Dee Phares b. Feb-14-1965.
She Married **Kevin Barkley**, b. Dec-31-1958.

1093. Ina Lee^6 Phares (577.Myrtle M^5 Sponaugle, 192.Herman Henry^4, 33.Jacob^3, 4.Elizabeth L.^{2} Arbogast, 1.George^1), b. Aug-07-1930.
She Married **Blake R. Hedrick**, b. 102119255 (son of Glenn Hedrick and Myrtle Raines).

Children:

1587 i. Cathy Dianna^7 Hedrick b. Feb-04-1953.
She Married Harry **McMorrow**, b. Jul-07-1951.
1588 ii. Patsy L. Hedrick b. Mar-16-1955.
She Married **Douglas H. Wimer**.

1094. James H.^{6} Phares (577.Myrtle M^5 Sponaugle, 192.Herman Henry^4, 33.Jacob^3, 4.Elizabeth L.^{2} Arbogast, 1.George^1), b. Oct-19-1932.
He Married **Beverly June Huffman**, b. Jun-12-1939 (daughter of Hensel Huffman and Wilma Raines).

Children:

1589 i. James Allen^7 Phares b. Oct-08-1956.
He Married **Lenita Jill Calliton**.
1590 ii. Thomas Lee Phares b. May-29-1958.
He Married **Cheryl Lynn Cooper**.
1591 iii. Benjamin Loren Phares b. Nov-23-1964.
1592 iv. Matthew H Phares b. Mar-11-1971.
1593 v. Marianne M. Phares b. Mar-11-1971.

1095. Raymond^6 Phares (577.Myrtle M^5 Sponaugle, 192.Herman Henry^4, 33.Jacob^3, 4.Elizabeth L.^{2} Arbogast, 1.George^1), b. Sep-20-1934.
He Married **Alta Rose Elkins**, b. May-07-1942 (daughter of Walter G Elkins and Ida Mae Miller).

Children:

\+ 1594 i. Michael Elmer^7 Phares b. Dec-03-1963.
\+ 1595 ii. Raymond Edward Phares b. Aug-04-1965.
1596 iii. Georgia Lynn Phares b. Mar-17-1969.

1096. Mary June^6 Phares (577.Myrtle M^5 Sponaugle, 192.Herman Henry^4, 33.Jacob^3, 4.Elizabeth L.^{2} Arbogast, 1.George^1), b. Dec-15-1936.
Married Jan-10-1958, **Henry E. Bennett**, b. Dec-17-1932 (son of Henry Bennett and Virginia C. Vest).

Children:

1597 i. Scott Allen[7] Bennett b. Jan-15-1971.

1097. Dottie Lou[6] Phares (577.Myrtle M[5] Sponaugle, 192.Herman Henry[4], 33.Jacob[3], 4.Elizabeth L.[2] Arbogast, 1.George[1]), b. Aug-02-1944.
She Married **Jerry M. Warner**.

Children:

\+ 1598 i. Jeffery[7] Warner b. Jan-14-1966.
1599 ii. Melissa Daun Warner b. Jun-25-1965.
She Married Larry Allen Hoover, b. Apr-01-1965 (son of Wilson Hoover and Betty Jean Warner).

1108. Sherry[6] Butcher (581.Levern[5] Sponaugle, 192.Herman Henry[4], 33.Jacob[3], 4.Elizabeth L.[2] Arbogast, 1.George[1]).
She Married **Hank Murry**.

Children:

1600 i. Ashlet Rebecca[7] Murry b. May-15-1978.
1601 ii. Meredith Butcher b. Oct-04-1981.

1110. Sandra[6] Sponaugle (582.Roscoe[5] Sponaugle, 192.Herman Henry[4], 33.Jacob[3], 4.Elizabeth L.[2] Arbogast, 1.George[1]).
She Married **Donald Boggs**.

Children:

1602 i. Rodney[7] Boggs.
1603 ii. Derek Boggs.

1111. Peggy Sue[6] Sponaugle (582.Roscoe[5], 192.Herman Henry[4], 33.Jacob[3], 4.Elizabeth L.[2] Arbogast, 1.George[1]).
She Married **Donald Waldron**.

Children:

1604 i. Tracey[7] Waldron.
1605 ii. Crystal Waldron.

1112. Patsey Louisa[6] Harper (586.Ruth[5] Sponaugle, 192.Herman Henry[4], 33.Jacob[3], 4.Elizabeth L.[2] Arbogast, 1.George[1]).
She Married **Jackie Dale Hinkle**.

Children:

\+ 1606 i. Angela Kay[7] Hinkle.

1113. Dorothy[6] Harper (586.Ruth[5] Sponaugle, 192.Herman Henry[4], 33.Jacob[3], 4.Elizabeth L.[2] Arbogast, 1.George[1]).
She Married **Herbert Cooper**.

Children:

1607 i. Jaqueline[7] Cooper b. Oct-22-1965.
1608 ii. Michael Cooper b. Jan-07-1971.

1119. Argyle Grace[6] Arbogast (613.Howard K.[5], 238.William Gum[4], 45.Jeremiah Elderidge[3], 6.Emanuel[2], 1.George[1]), b. Sep-09-1905 in Hightown, Highland Co., VA, buried in Blue Grass Cem., Highland Co., VA, d. Jul-03-1985 in Harrisonburg, Rockingham Co., VA.
Married Oct-12-1921 in Highland Co., VA, **Elmer Harry Nicholas**, b. Aug-06-1902 in Pendleton Co., (son of John A Nicholas and Louise Rachel Arbogast), d. Aug-03-1966 in Hightown, Highland Co., VA.

Children:

1609 i. Lucy lorraine[7] Nicholas b. Feb-26-1923.
1610 ii. Maxine Nicholas.

1121. William G.[6] Arbogast, Jr. (614.William G.[5], 238.William Gum[4], 45.Jeremiah Elderidge[3], 6.Emanuel[2], 1.George[1]), b. 1919 in Rainelle, Greenbrier Co. WV, d. 1961.
Married 1938, **Thelma Jo Orms**r.

Children:

1611 i. William David[7] Arbogast b. 1939, d. 1961.
He Married **Karen Walker.**

1122. Larry Howard[6] Roberts (615.Charles Howard[5], 258.Ada Neil[4] Arbogast, 55.David Howard[3], 6.Emanuel[2], 1.George[1]), b. Jun-06-1946.
He Married **Nancy Ellen Dale**, b. Sep-28-1947 in El Dorado Springs, MO.

Children:

1612 i. Aaron Howard[7] Roberts b. Oct-26-1972 in Springfield, Greene Co., MO.
1613 ii. Justin Dale Roberts b. Nov-29-1972 in Springfield, Greene Co., MO.

Generation Seven

1126. Paul Hunter[7] Collins (628.Floyd William[6], 269.Louella Maer[5] Grogg, 69.Emily Jane[4] Mullenax, 11.John H.[3], 2.Hannah[2] Arbogast, 1.George[1]), b. Dec 9 1915.
He Married **Georgia Goodsell Frazier**.

Children:

1614 i. Karyl Lynn[8] Collins.
1615 ii. Kaye Adair Collins.

1128. Harold Cecil[7] Collins (629.Cecil Morgan[6], 269.Louella Maer[5] Grogg, 69.Emily Jane[4] Mullenax, 11.John H.[3], 2.Hannah[2] Arbogast, 1.George[1]), b. Aug 13 1916 in Columbus, Franklin Co., OH, d. Jul 8 1986 in Cleveland, Cuyahoga Co., OH.
He Married **Evalene S Hickman**, b. 1920 in Big Springs, Meigs Co., TN.

Children:

\+ 1616 i. Lowell Jene[8] Collins b. Aug 09 1939.
\+ 1617 ii. Atlos Martin Collins b. Oct 25 1942.

1130. Bernard Morris[7] Collins (629.Cecil Morgan[6], 269.Louella Maer[5] Grogg, 69.Emily Jane[4] Mullenax, 11.John H.[3], 2.Hannah[2] Arbogast, 1.George[1]), b. Jan 30 1920 in Bartow, Pocahontas Co., WV, d. Sep 28 2002 in Northfield, Franklin Co., MA.
He Married **Mildred Lee Varner**, b. 1924, d. Sep 28 1983 in Arbovale Cem., Arbovale, Pocahontas Co., WV.

Children:

\+ 1618 i. Carol Lee[8] Collins.
\+ 1619 ii. Rebecca Jeanne Collins.

1137. Bricel[7] Waybright (642.Bert[6], 272.Albert[5], 71.Martha[4] Mullenax, 12.George[3], 2.Hannah[2] Arbogast, 1.George[1]), b. Dec 13 1911 in Whitmer, Randolph Co., WV, d. Nov 12 1966 in Elkins, Randolph Co., WV.
He Married **Dollie Vorden Fansler,** b. 1916, d. 1971.

Children:

1620 i. Thomas L.[8] Waybright d. 1991.
He Married **Marla (Unknown)**.
1621 ii. Bricel Roy Waybright.
1622 iii. Retha Waybright.
(1) She Married **Neal Smith.**
(2) She Married **Roy Ware** (son of Jacob G. Ware and Sarah M Hamrick).
1623 iv. Richard L. Waybright b. Jun 6 1933, d. Aug 1987 in Dundalk Baltimore Co., MD.
1624 v. Billy Keith Waybright b. Jun 30 1935, d. Mar 1980.
1625 vi. Kenneth Gene Waybright b. Mar 4 1937 in Elkins, Randolph Co., WV, d. Oct 11 1993 in Las Vegas, Clark Co., NV.

1139. John William[7] Hardwick (650.Frances Ann[6] Arbogast, 303.Elmo Mead[5], 89.Emery Matthew[4], 21.John Wesley[3], 3.Daniel[2], 1.George[1]), b. Jun-08-1947 in Omaha, Douglas Co., NE.
He Married **Mary Amanda Trimble**.

Children:

1626 i. Meaum[8] Hardwick.
1627 ii. Marshall Hardwick.

1140. Maetha Ann[7] Hardwick (650.Frances Ann[6] Arbogast, 303.Elmo Mead[5], 89.Emery Matthew[4], 21.John Wesley[3], 3.Daniel[2], 1.George[1]).
(1) She Married **James Alarid**.

Children:

1628 i. Rachel[8] Alarid.
1629 ii. Renee Alarid.

(2) She Married **Bruce Bertin.**

1146. Katrena Maxhelle[7] Kun (667.Theresa[6] Arbogast, 315.Robert William[5], 99.Arthur William[4], 21.John Wesley[3], 3.Daniel[2], 1.George[1]), b. May-28-1965.
Married Aug 1984, Timothy Scott Taylor, b. Sep 1958.

Children:

1630 i. Tiffany Nicole[8] Taylor b. Aug-01-1959.

1168. John Delano[7] Judy (686.Myrtle Annie[6] Mullenax, 330.Serilda C[5] Sponaugle, 108.George Washington[4], 23.William[3], 4.Elizabeth L.[2] Arbogast, 1.George[1]), b. Nov-18-1937, d. May-26-1967 in Snowy Mountain, WV.
He Married Ruth Allene Hartman, b. Mar-05-1940 in Goshen, Smith Creek, WV, d. May-26-1967.

Children:

1631 i. Anthony Roy[8] Judy b. 1957.
He Married **Kathy Hudson.**
1632 ii. Winona Ruth Judy b. 1958.
She Married **Bradley Hott.**
1633 iii. Rita Juawan Judy b. 1959.
She Married **Jon L. Todd.**
1634 iv. Jonny Mark Judy b. 1963.
He Married **Pamala White.**

1190. Cornelia Etta[7] Hartman (696.Melvin Earl[6] Hartman, 331.Carrie E[5] Sponaugle, 108.George Washington[4], 23.William[3], 4.Elizabeth L.[2] Arbogast, 1.George[1]), b. Jan-30-1937.
Married Dec-13-1958 in Petersburg, Grant Co., WV, **John Mitchell Teter**.

Children:

1635 i. Judy Looraine[8] Teter b. Mar-06-1962.
She Married **Oliver Cromwell Mowery III**.
1636 ii. Jackie Lynn Teter b. Jul-06-1963.

She Married **William Henry Sisson**.
1637 iii. Sandra Teter.
1638 iv. William Teter b. Sep-18-1959 in Harrisonburg, Rockingham Co., VA, buried in Cedar Hill Cem., Pendleton Co., WV, d. Aug-08-1998.

1224. Harlan Dale[7] Sponaugle, M.D. (708.Russell McClure[6], 334.Green Judy[5], 108.George Washington[4], 23.William[3], 4.Elizabeth L.[2] Arbogast, 1.George[1]), b. Feb-13-1926 in Franklin, Pendleton Co., WV.
Optomologist.
Married Aug-24-1957**, Orva Uvon Hammer**, b. Aug-18-1937.

Children:

1639 i. Susan Hammer[8] Sponaugle b. Mar-05-1962 in Philadelphia, PA .
Married Jul-18-1987 in Portsmouth, VA, **Roger Winfield Newsom**, b. Mar-14-1964.
1640 ii. Patrick McClure Sponaugle b. Jul-14-1964 in Guantanamo, Cuba.

1229. Naomi[7] Simmons (712.Rhea Mae[6] Sponaugle, 334.Green Judy[5], 108.George Washington[4], 23.William[3], 4.Elizabeth L.[2] Arbogast, 1.George[1]), b. Dec-11-1937.
(1) Married Sep 1961, **David Allen Dyer**.

Children:

1641 i. Jody Allison[8] Dyer b. May-04-1964.
1642 ii. Gregory Alled Dyer b. Jan-21-1967.
1643 iii. Lee Grail Simmons b. Sep-06-1939.
He Married **Patricia Ann Shaw**.
\+ 1644 iv. Jerry Price Simmons b. Apr-18-1941.

(2) She Married B

1230. Debera Jane^{7} Sponaugle (713.Walter Glenn^{6} Sponaugle, 334.Green Judy^{5}, 108.George Washington^{4}, 23.William^{3}, 4.Elizabeth L.^{2} Arbogast, 1.George^{1}), b. Jun-20-1952.
(1) Married Aug-29-1970, **Gary Alston Thompson.**

Children:

1645 i. Jeremt^{8} Thompson b. Dec-29-1971.
1646 ii. Anthony Thompson b. 1976.

1231. Brenda Sue^{7} Sponaugle (713.Walter Glenn^{6}, 334.Green Judy^{5}, 108.George Washington^{4}, 23.William^{3}, 4.Elizabeth L.^{2} Arbogast, 1.George^{1}), b. Jul-07-1956.
Married Apr-29-1972, **David Simmons.**

Children:

1647 i. Tonya^{8} Simmons b. Nov-13-1972.
1648 ii. Trisha LeAnn Simmons b. Nov-29-1979.

1238. George Isaac^{7} Sponaugle II (715.George Isaac^{6}, 334.Green Judy^{5}, 108.George Washington^{4}, 23.William^{3}, 4.Elizabeth L.^{2} Arbogast, 1.George^{1}), b. Jun-09-1917.
Married Dec-31-1937, **Kathy Moyers.**

Children:

1649 i. George Isaac^{8} Sponaugle III.
1650 ii. Erin Brooks Sponaugle .

1239. James Harper^{7} Sponaugle (715.George Isaac^{6}, 334.Green Judy^{5}, 108.George Washington^{4}, 23.William^{3}, 4.Elizabeth L.^{2} Arbogast, 1.George^{1}).
Married May-10-1980, **Debra Lynn Jackson**.

Children:

1651 i. Ashley E^{8} Sponaugle.
1652 ii. Sarah Michelle Sponaugle.
1653 iii. Alexander David Sponaugle.

1245. Heata Della^{7} Simmons (716.Joie Catherine^{6} Sponaugle, 334.Green Judy^{5}, 108.George Washington^{4}, 23.William^{3}, 4.Elizabeth L.^{2} Arbogast, 1.George^{1}) (See marriage to number 843.)

1247. Ruth Ann^{7} Sponaugle (717.William Joseph^{6}, 334.Green Judy^{5}, 108.George Washington^{4}, 23.William^{3}, 4.Elizabeth L.^{2} Arbogast, 1.George^{1}).
She Married **Gregory Skoglund.**

Children:

1654 i. John David^{8} Skoglund.

1274. Clair Fern Anne^{7} Degler (737.Clarice May^{6} Nelson, 341.Jenettie Catherine^{5} Thompson, 109.Mary Catherine^{4} Sponaugle, 23.William^{3}, 4.Elizabeth L.^{2} Arbogast, 1.George^{1}), .
Married P, **Jacob Edward Hare**, b. May 31 1917 in Morgantown, Monongalia Co., WV, d. Jun 20 1992 in Morgantown, Monongalia Co., WV.

Children:

1655 i. Janice Mae^{8} Hare b. Mar 21 1942 in Morgantown, Monongalia Co., WV, d. Feb 13 1943 in Morgantown, Monongalia Co., WV.

1276. Dwight Wesley^{7} Ozment (740.Lacie Madonna^{6} Nelson, 341.Jenettie Catherine^{5} Thompson, 109.Mary Catherine^{4} Sponaugle, 23.William^{3}, 4.Elizabeth L.^{2} Arbogast, 1.George^{1}), b. Sep-23-1933.
(1) Married Jun-27-1974 in St. Petersburg, FL, **Zelma Mae Pelton**, b. Dec-01-1936 in Tyler, Smith Co., TX.

Children:

\+ 1656 i. Sylvia Lynn^{8} Ozment b. Apr-21-1955.

(2) Married Sep-06-1975 in Petersburg, PVA, **Mary Jo Tudor**, b. May-31-1943 in Richmond, Chesterfield Co., VA.

Children:

1657 ii. Daniel Wesley Ozment b. Apr-12-1978.

1658 iii. Michael Tudor Ozment b. Apr-20-1982.

1282. Naomi K.[7] Thompson (746.Orie D.[6], 343.Jacob Kenny[5], 109.Mary Catherine[4] Sponaugle, 23.William[3], 4.Elizabeth L.[2] Arbogast, 1.George[1]), b. Jun-11-1929.
She Married David Johnson.

Children:

1659 i. Janet[8] Johnson.
1660 ii. James David Johnson.
1661 iii. Judith Caroline Johnson.

1288. Margaret Ann[7] Kerr (788.Earl Frederick[6], 362.Jessie Lucy[5] Louk, 111.Elizabeth Jane[4] Sponaugle, 23.William[3], 4.Elizabeth L.[2] Arbogast, 1.George[1]), b. Jan 6 1949.
She Married **Robert Nicholas Beckwith**, b. Dec 12 1945 in Morristown, Morris Co., NJ (son of Walton Beckwith and Olga Markom). Ref: Randolph 1991: 33; information from Robert S/o Walton and Olga (Markom) Beckwith.

Children:

1662 i. Beth Ann[8] Beckwith b. Oct 3 1969.
1663 ii. Tracy Lynn Beckwith b. Nov 23 1971.

1295. Norma Lee[7] Sponaugle (799.Willis Raymond[6], 369.Lee Paris[5], 113.Adam Harness[4], 23.William[3], 4.Elizabeth L.[2] Arbogast, 1.George[1]), b. Apr-14-1928.
(1) She Married **unknown Cannon**.

Children:

1664 i. Theresa May[8] Cannon.
1665 ii. Willis Kay Cannon.

(2) She Married **unknown Waggner**.

Children:

1666 iii. Debbie Waggner.
Adopter.

1296. Norman Willis[7] Sponaugle (799.Willis Raymond[6], 369.Lee Paris[5], 113.Adam Harness[4], 23.William[3], 4.Elizabeth L.[2] Arbogast, 1.George[1]), b. May-02-1931.
He Married **Betty Carr**.

Children:

1667 i. Donald Lee[8] Sponaugle.
1668 ii. Cariellie Sponaugle.
1669 iii. Margaret Angle Sponaugle.
1670 iv. Michelle Sponaugle.
1671 v. Raymond Willis Sponaugle.

1297. Shirley Ann[7] Sponaugle (800.Milford Jay[6], 369.Lee Paris[5], 113.Adam Harness[4], 23.William[3], 4.Elizabeth L.[2] Arbogast, 1.George[1]), b. Sep-18-1937.
She Married **Glenneth Edward Lester**, b. Dec-04-1937 in Longer, WV.

Children:

1672 i. Tommy Lynn[8] Lester b. Oct-05-1957 in Cleveland, Cuyahoga Co., OH.
She Married **Alan Junkie**.
\+ 1673 ii. Glenneth Edward Lester, Jr. b. Feb-27-1950.
1674 iii. Thurman Jay Lester b. Oct-23-1961.
He Married **Terry Workman**.
1675 iv. Eric Joseph Lester b. Jun 1965 in Cleveland, Cuyahoga Co., OH.

1298. Aaron Charles[7] Sponaugle (800.Milford Jay[6], 369.Lee Paris[5], 113.Adam Harness[4], 23.William[3], 4.Elizabeth L.[2] Arbogast, 1.George[1]), b. May-08-1938 in Davis, Tucker Co., WV, d. Dec-26-1985.
(1) He Married Clota Gibson.

Children:

\+ 1676 i. Lloyd Aaron[8] Sponaugle b. Feb-28-1958.
1677 ii. Milford Ryhan Sponaugle b. Sep-11-1950 in Youngstown, Mahoning Co., OH.

(2) He Married Mary Smith.

1299. Gloria Carrol^{7} Sponaugle (800.Milford Jay^{6}, 369.Lee Paris^{5}, 113.Adam Harness^{4}, 23.William^{3}, 4.Elizabeth L.^{2} Arbogast, 1.George^{1}), b. Oct-16-1941 in Davis, Tucker Co., WV.
She Married Fred Alan Myers, b. Jul-06-1938 in Ben Bush, WV.

Children:

- 1678 i. Fred^{8} Alan Myers, Jr. b. Jun-09-1962 in Newfoundland, Canada.
  He Married **Sylvia Marie Clark**.
- 1679 ii. Robert Lee Myers b. Jun-15-1963 in Parsons, Tucker Co., WV.
  He Married **Rose Marie Brotosky**.

1301. Tena Ann^{7} Myers (800.Milford Jay^{6} Sponaugle, 369.Lee Paris^{5}, 113.Adam Harness^{4}, 23.William^{3}, 4.Elizabeth L.^{2} Arbogast, 1.George^{1}), b. May-13-1964 in Elkins, Randolph Co., WV.
She Married **Eddie Lee Canfield**, b. Nov-08-1965 in Parsons, Tucker Co., WV.

Children:

- 1680 i. Julieann Michelle^{8} Canfield b. May-13-1984 in Elkins, Randolph Co., WV.
- 1681 ii. Randal Lee Canfield b. Mar 1987.

1302. Hazel^{7} Bennett (801.Christena Belle^{6} Sponaugle, 370.John Alonzo^{5}, 113.Adam Harness^{4}, 23.William^{3}, 4.Elizabeth L.^{2} Arbogast, 1.George^{1}).
She Married **Edgar Simmions**.

Children:

- 1682 i. Douglas^{8} Simmions.
- 1683 ii. Mark Simmions.
- 1684 iii. Allan Simmions.

1303. Fred D.^{7} Bennett (801.Christena Belle^{6} Sponaugle, 370.John Alonzo^{5}, 113.Adam Harness^{4}, 23.William^{3}, 4.Elizabeth L.^{2} Arbogast, 1.George^{1}).
He Married **Joyce Mounts**.

Children:

- 1685 i. Julie^{8} Bennett.
- 1686 ii. Fred D. Bennett, Jr,.
- 1687 iii. David W. Bennett.

1332. Mildred Mary^{7} Warner (812.Ona Lucy^{6} Sponaugle, 370.John Alonzo^{5} Sponaugle, 113.Adam Harness^{4}, 23.William^{3}, 4.Elizabeth L.^{2} Arbogast, 1.George^{1}) (See marriage to number 941.)

1370. James Arthur^{7} Judy (837.Guy William^{6}, 376.Monna Roxie^{5} Sponaugle, 113.Adam Harness^{4}, 23.William^{3}, 4.Elizabeth L.^{2} Arbogast, 1.George^{1}), b. Dec-01-1939 in Monongahela, Marion Co., WV.
Married Jan-08-1962 in Coeur D Alene, Kootenai Co., ID, **Bonnie Clary**, b. Apr-02-1943 in Columbia, SC (daughter of LeRoy Buryle Clary and Helen Mae Clarey).

Children:

- \+ 1688 i. Jill Lynn^{8} Judy b. Sep-28-1962.
- 1689 ii. Jana Lee Judy b. Nov-13-1967 in Pasco, WA.

1371. John Ben^{7} Judy (837.Guy William^{6}, 376.Monna Roxie^{5} Sponaugle, 113.Adam Harness^{4}, 23.William^{3}, 4.Elizabeth L.^{2} Arbogast, 1.George^{1}), b. Jun-07-1941 in Fairmont, Marion Co., WV.
(1) He Married **Mary Esther Gressel**, b. May-14-1941 in Logan, Cashe Co., UT (daughter of Homer John Gesselm and Elen Ackley).

Children:

- 1690 i. Keri Ellen^{8} Judy b. Jan-12-1965.
  Married Jul-22-1989 in Richmond, King Co., WA, Kevin Lee Neswick.
- 1691 ii. Jay Ben Judy b. Mar-06-1966 in Kennewick, Benton Co., WA.
- 1692 iii. Darin Wayne Judy b. Aug-20-1968 in Kennewick, Benton Co., WA.

(2) He Married **Suzanne Dorothy Pleasic** (daughter of Ambrose Arthur Pleasic and Anna Mae Potts).

Children:

1693 iv. Corrin Ann Judy b. Aug-09-1982 in Richland, Benton Co. WA.
1694 v. Derek Scott Judy b. Mar-20-1984 in Richland, Benton Co. WA.

1372. Susan Ann Marie[7] Judy (837.Guy William[6], 376.Monna Roxie[5] Sponaugle, 113.Adam Harness[4], 23.William[3], 4.Elizabeth L.[2] Arbogast, 1.George[1]), b. Oct-17-1955.
She Married **William Lamb.**

Children:

1695 i. Electra Lael[8] Lamb b. Jul-12-1986 in Houston, TX.
1696 ii. Theron Lamb b. May-08-1989.

1373. Linda Gaye[7] Judy (837.Guy William[6], 376.Monna Roxie[5] Sponaugle, 113.Adam Harness[4], 23.William[3], 4.Elizabeth L.[2] Arbogast, 1.George[1]), b. Dec-09-1952.
Married Nov-10-1973 in Kennewick, Benton Co., WA, **Michael Roy Saling,** b. May-10-1951 in Pasco, WV (son of Clifford Scott Saling and Violet Marie Bozarth).

Children:

1697 i. Tyler Russell[8] Saling b. Jul-30-1979 in Portland, Multnomah Co., OR.
1698 ii. Mollie Marie Saling b. Jun-24-1981 in Portland, Multnomah Co., OR.

1374. Teresa Lynn[7] Judy (837.Guy William[6], 376.Monna Roxie[5] Sponaugle, 113.Adam Harness[4], 23.William[3], 4.Elizabeth L.[2] Arbogast, 1.George[1]), b. May-10-1953 in Kennewick, Benton Co., WA.
Married Nov 1981 in Reno, Washoe Co., NV, **David Vandatti.**

Children:

1699 i. Vincent Michael[8] Vandatti b. Jul-12-1982 in Richland, Benton Co. WA.

1376. Jacklyn Joyce[7] Judy (837.Guy William[6], 376.Monna Roxie[5] Sponaugle, 113.Adam Harness[4], 23.William[3], 4.Elizabeth L.[2] Arbogast, 1.George[1]), b. Oct-08-1956 in Kennewick, Benton Co., WA.
She Married **unknown Goin.**

Children:

1700 i. Chanel Pearl[8] Goin.
1701 ii. Sterling Goin b. Oct-18-1986 in Kennewick, Benton Co., WA.

1378. Barbara Joan[7] Judy (838.Kermit Adam[6], 376.Monna Roxie[5] Sponaugle, 113.Adam Harness[4], 23.William[3], 4.Elizabeth L.[2] Arbogast, 1.George[1]), b. Jul-08-1939 in Smith Creek, Pendleton Co., WV.
She Married Kelly **William Harman**, b. Jul-16-1939 (son of John William Harman and Freda Armentrout).

Children:

\+ 1702 i. Gregory Alan[8] Harman b. Mar-12-1962.
\+ 1703 ii. Tracy Michele Harman b. Nov-12-1964.

1379. Harriet Levon[7] Judy (838.Kermit Adam[6], 376.Monna Roxie[5] Sponaugle, 113.Adam Harness[4], 23.William[3], 4.Elizabeth L.[2] Arbogast, 1.George[1]), b. Oct-01-1941 in Franklin, Pendleton Co., WV.
She Married **George Osborne Wilson**. Jr., b. Jul-28-1940 (son of George Osborne and Bonnie Gum).

Children:

1704 i. Matthew Lynn[8] Wilson b. Apr-11-1970 in Harrisonburg, Rockingham Co., VA.
Married Aug-01-1992 in Kensington, Montgomery Co., MD, **Victoria Lynn Crow**.
1705 ii. Lori Levon Wilson b. Nov-07-1971 in Harrisonburg, Rockingham Co., VA.

1380. Jennie Lou[7] Judy (838.Kermit Adam[6], 376.Monna Roxie[5] Sponaugle, 113.Adam Harness[4], 23.William[3], 4.Elizabeth L.[2] Arbogast, 1.George[1]), b. May-01-1950 in Franklin, Pendleton Co., WV.
She Married **Jeffrey Eldon Hott**, b. Jan-24-1951 in Petersburg, Grant Co., WV (son of Eldon Elwood Hott and Ruth Sreinee).

Children:

1706 i. Abbie Loranne[8] Hott b. Jan-12-1974.
1707 ii. Allie Rebecca Hott b. Jan-19-1976.
1708 iii. Emilie Will Hott b. Sep-06-1979.
1709 iv. Adam Jeffery Hott b. Jun-03-1985.

1381. Linda Jean[7] Hall (839.Ethel Susan[6] Judy, 376.Monna Roxie[5] Sponaugle, 113.Adam Harness[4], 23.William[3], 4.Elizabeth L.[2] Arbogast, 1.George[1]), b. Jun-14-1941 in Fairmont, Marion Co., WV.

Married Aug 1966, **George Lewis Yergy II**, b. Feb-27-1936.

Children:

1710 i. George Lewis^{8} Yergy III b. Aug-12-1968.
1711 ii. Robert Allen Yergy b. Feb-05-1971.
1712 iii. Michael Thomas Yergy b. May-02-1972.

1382. Mary Susan^{7} Hall (839.Ethel Susan^{6} Judy, 376.Monna Roxie^{5} Sponaugle, 113.Adam Harness^{4}, 23.William^{3}, 4.Elizabeth L.^{2} Arbogast, 1.George^{1}), b. May-03-1945 in Fairmont, Marion Co., WV.
She Married **David Howard Jones**, b. Jun-07-1943.

Children:

1713 i. Jamison Hall^{8} Jones b. Jun-03-1974 in Winchester, Frederick Co., VA.
1714 ii. Stephanie Susan Jones b. Dec-02-1975 in Hagerstown, Washington Co., MD.

1383. Howard Campbell^{7} Fortner III (840.Bernice Evangeline^{6} Judy, 376.Monna Roxie^{5} Sponaugle, 113.Adam Harness^{4}, 23.William^{3}, 4.Elizabeth L.^{2} Arbogast, 1.George^{1}), b. Jun-03-1949 in Fairmont, Marion Co., WV.
Married Mar-21-1981 in Monterey, Highland Co., VA, **Velda Elizabeth Knapp**, b. Mar-01-1957 in Harrisonburg, Rockingham Co., VA (daughter of Ralph Norman Knapp and Etta Marie Heverner).

Children:

1715 i. Sarah Elizabeth^{8} Fortner b. Oct-16-1981 in Fairmont, Marion Co., WV.
1716 ii. Christopher Shawn Fortner b. Dec-28-1983 in Fairmont, Marion Co., WV.

1385. Katherine Ann^{7} Judy (841.Richard Thomas^{6}, 376.Monna Roxie^{5} Sponaugle, 113.Adam Harness^{4}, 23.William^{3}, 4.Elizabeth L.^{2} Arbogast, 1.George^{1}), b. Oct-22-1958 in Fairmont, Marion Co., WV.
She Married **Christopher Robin Hardy**, b. Aug-30-1956 in Washington, D.C. (son of Edwyn Worrell Hardy and Ruth Bertha Annings).

Children:

1717 i. Tristan Thomas^{8} Hardy b. Apr-30-1984.
1718 ii. Btittanie Anning Hardy b. Jun-13-1987 in Falls Church, Fairfax Co., VA.

1386. Diane Louise^{7} Kuehl (842.Ina^{6} Judy, 376.Monna Roxie^{5} Sponaugle, 113.Adam Harness^{4}, 23.William^{3}, 4.Elizabeth L.^{2} Arbogast, 1.George^{1}), b. Aug-20-1953 in Great Lakes Navel Base, IL.
Married Nov-07-1981 in Midland, MI, Nicholas Roque De Peter, Jr., b. Dec-23-1945 in Chicago, Cook Co., IL (son of Nicholas Roque De Peter and Ruth Mae Kostner).

Children:

1719 i. Mathew Nicholas^{8} **DE Peder** b. Jan-09-1989 in Atlanta, Fulton Co., GA.
1720 ii. Dale Richard Kuehl b. Aug-09-1959 in St. Louise, MO.
1721 iii. Kathryn Lee Kuehl b. Aug-07-1964 in East Baton Rouge Parish, LA.
Married Oct-07-1989 in Midland Co., MI, **David Hugh Cramer**, b. Sep-30-1963 (son of Donald Harmon Cramer and Eileen Carol Yeager).

1387. Edward^{7} Judy (843.Gayle Edward^{6}, 376.Monna Roxie^{5} Sponaugle, 113.Adam Harness^{4}, 23.William^{3}, 4.Elizabeth L.^{2} Arbogast, 1.George^{1}), b. Jul-28-1960 in Harrisonburg, Rockingham Co., VA.
He Married **Jean Elaine Vaughn**, b. Oct-05-1962 in Luray, Page Co., VA.

Children:

\+ 1722 i. Luke Thomas^{8} Judy b. Mar-13-1981.
1723 ii. Rodney Shannon Judy b. Apr-14-1962 in Harrisonburg, Rockingham Co., VA.
Married Aug-02-1985 in Luray, Page Co., VA, **Deloris Ann Leake** (daughter of Jerry Olin Leake and Deloris Gray).
1724 iii. Kimberly Jill Judy b. Sep-16-1963 in Harrisonburg, Rockingham Co., VA.

1392. Nola Eda^{7} Warner (865.Dice G^{6}, 429.Walter^{5}, 139.Mary Elizabeth^{4} Teter, 26.Catherine^{3} Sponaugle, 4.Elizabeth L.^{2} Arbogast, 1.George^{1}) (See marriage to number 906.)
1393. Roy B.^{7} Warner (865.Dice G^{6}, 429.Walter^{5}, 139.Mary Elizabeth^{4} Teter, 26.Catherine^{3} Sponaugle, 4.Elizabeth L.^{2} Arbogast, 1.George^{1}).
He Married **unknown Warner**.

Children:

\+ 1725 i. Roy B^{8} Warner, Jr..

1396. unknown^{7} Warner (865.Dice G^{6}, 429.Walter^{5}, 139.Mary Elizabeth^{4} Teter, 26.Catherine^{3} Sponaugle, 4.Elizabeth L.^{2} Arbogast, 1.George^{1}).
He Married **Mike Lambourne**.

Children:

1726 i. Kathy^{8} Lambourne.

1397. Glenn^{7} Warner (865.Dice G^{6}, 429.Walter^{5}, 139.Mary Elizabeth^{4} Teter, 26.Catherine^{3} Sponaugle, 4.Elizabeth L.^{2} Arbogast, 1.George^{1}).
He Married **Jerri Warner**, b. Mar-28-1959 (daughter of Owen C. Warner and Peachie N. Warner).

Children:

1727 i. Travis^{8} Warner.
1728 ii. Steven Warner b. Dec 1983.

1401. Hansel^{7} Judy (866.Beulah^{6} Warner, 429.Walter^{5}, 139.Mary Elizabeth^{4} Teter, 26.Catherine^{3} Sponaugle, 4.Elizabeth L.^{2} Arbogast, 1.George^{1}), b. Jul-02-1922.
He Married **Donna Hedrick**.

Children:

1729 i. Steve^{8} Judy.
1730 ii. Barbara Judy.

1404. Henry Edsel^{7} Judy (866.Beulah^{6} Warner, 429.Walter^{5}, 139.Mary Elizabeth^{4} Teter, 26.Catherine^{3} Sponaugle, 4.Elizabeth L.^{2} Arbogast, 1.George^{1}), b. Mar-11-1928.
He Married **unknown Rose**.

Children:

1731 i. Anthony^{8} Judy b. 1961, d. 1977.
1732 ii. Roxanne Judy.

1405. Norma^{7} Judy (866.Beulah^{6} Warner, 429.Walter^{5}, 139.Mary Elizabeth^{4} Teter, 26.Catherine^{3} Sponaugle, 4.Elizabeth L.^{2} Arbogast, 1.George^{1}), b. Apr-11-1929.
She Married **George Smith**.

Children:

\+ 1733 i. Jerry^{8} Smith.
\+ 1734 ii. George Smith, Jr..
\+ 1735 iii. Mary Francis Smith.
1736 iv. Susan Smith.
She Married **Jerry Burns**.
1737 v. Vickie Smith.

1408. Herman^{7} Bland (870.Ona Austie^{6} Judy, 439.Tina^{5} Warner, 142.Cecelia (Celia)^{4} Sponaugle, 27.Lewis Martin^{3}, 4.Elizabeth L.^{2} Arbogast, 1.George^{1}), b. Nov-24-1932.
Wife and mother not identified.

Children:

1738 i. Debra Joyce^{8} Bland b. Nov-28-1935.
1739 ii. Larry Michael Bland b. Oct-24-1956.
1740 iii. Thomas Ray Bland b. May-11-1961.
1741 iv. Anita Bland.

1409. Bryan^{7} Bland (870.Ona Austie^{6} Judy, 439.Tina^{5} Warner, 142.Cecelia (Celia)^{4} Sponaugle, 27.Lewis Martin^{3}, 4.Elizabeth L.^{2} Arbogast, 1.George^{1}).
He Married **Jane Propst**.

Children:

1742 i. Gary^{8} Bland.
1743 ii. Karen Bland.

1410. Dale Worth^{7} Bland (870.Ona Austie^{6} Judy, 439.Tina^{5} Warner, 142.Cecelia (Celia)^{4} Sponaugle, 27.Lewis Martin^{3}, 4.Elizabeth L.^{2} Arbogast, 1.George^{1}), b. Feb-08-1937.

Wife & mother not identified.
He Married **Nile Jane Propst** (daughter of Grant Propst and Edna J. Harper).

Children:

1744 i. Tammy Jane[8] Bland.
1745 ii. Andy Bland.

1413. John William[7] Wimer (876.Nellie Mae[6] Judy, 439.Tina[5] Warner, 142.Cecelia (Celia)[4] Sponaugle, 27.Lewis Martin[3], 4.Elizabeth L.[2] Arbogast, 1.George[1]), b. Feb-16-1937.
He Married **Marian Shockly**.

Children:

1746 i. Darryl Jay[8] Wimer b. Jun-23-1960.
1747 ii. Kim Sue Wimer b. Jan-01-1966.
She Married **Troy Croson.**
1748 iii. Ty Wimer b. Dec-09-1967.
1749 iv. Gy Wimer b. Dec-09-1967.
He Married **Tabirha Bennett**.

1414. Roy Dewey[7] Bland, Jr. (879.Roy Dewey[6], 443.Grace[5] Warner, 142.Cecelia (Celia)[4] Sponaugle, 27.Lewis Martin[3], 4.Elizabeth L.[2] Arbogast, 1.George[1]).
(1) He Married **Sherry Dale Hutchins.**

Children:

1750 i. Robin[8] Bland b. Oct-07-1966.
1751 ii. Robin Bland b. Oct-07-1966.

(2) He Married **Dianore George**.

Children:

1752 iii. Tammy Bland b. Jan 1964.
1753 iv. Tommy Bland b. Jun-11-1969.

1415. Betty Darlene[7] Bland (879.Roy Dewey[6], 443.Grace[5] Warner, 142.Cecelia (Celia)[4] Sponaugle, 27.Lewis Martin[3], 4.Elizabeth L.[2] Arbogast, 1.George[1]).
(1) She Married **Raymond Wilkenson**.

Children:

1754 i. Timothy Raynond[8] Wilkenson b. Feb-10-1966.

(2) She Married **John Goin.**

(3) She Married **Pete Nixon**.

1419. Terry[7] Allen Thompson (881.Eva Lee[6] Bland, 443.Grace[5] Warner, 142.Cecelia (Celia)[4] Sponaugle, 27.Lewis Martin[3], 4.Elizabeth L.[2] Arbogast, 1.George[1]).
He Married Mary **Jane Riggleman**.

Children:

1755 i. Terry[8] Allen Thompson, Jr..
1756 ii. Andrew Scott Thompson.

1420. Charles Wesley[7] Bland (887.Marshall[6], 443.Grace[5] Warner, 142.Cecelia (Celia)[4] Sponaugle, 27.Lewis Martin[3], 4.Elizabeth L.[2] Arbogast, 1.George[1]).
He Married **Norma Diana Nelson**.

Children:

1757 i. Tammy Lyn[8] Bland.
1758 ii. Tracy Dawn Bland.

1421. Janis Sue[7] Bland (887.Marshall[6], 443.Grace[5] Warner, 142.Cecelia (Celia)[4] Sponaugle, 27.Lewis Martin[3], 4.Elizabeth L.[2] Arbogast, 1.George[1]).
She Married **Orville Harper, Jr.**.

Children:

1759 i. William[8] Harper.
1760 ii. Marshall Harper.
1761 iii. Glyn Harper.
1762 iv. Sabrina Harper.
1763 v. Heather Harper.

1430. Larry Harlan[7] Wimer (901.Harlan[6] Warner Wimer, 475.Albert Harness[5] Wimer, 154.Sylverius[4], 28.Mary Elizabeth[3] Sponaugle, 4.Elizabeth L.[2] Arbogast, 1.George[1]), b. Aug-23-1940.
He Married **Jean Armentrout**.

Children:

1764 i. Blenda[8] Wimer.
1765 ii. Jan Wimer.
1766 iii. Karen Wimer.

1433. Christopher Lee[7] Wimer (901.Harlan[6] Warner Wimer, 475.Albert Harness[5] Wimer, 154.Sylverius[4], 28.Mary Elizabeth[3] Sponaugle, 4.Elizabeth L.[2] Arbogast, 1.George[1]), b. 1950.
(1) He Married **Norme Gee Dice**, b. c 1954 (daughter of Melvin Dice and Lonnie Thompson).

Children:

1767 i. Christopher[8] Wimer b. c 1976.
1768 ii. Jennifer Dawn Wimer b. Dec-17-1979.

(2) He Married Lucy Miller.

Children:

1769 iii. Crista Lee Wimer b. 1982.

1435. Glenn Richard[7] Bennett (902.Mable[6] Warner, 476.MaryEllen[5] Wimer, 154.Sylverius[4], 28.Mary Elizabeth[3] Sponaugle, 4.Elizabeth L.[2] Arbogast, 1.George[1]), b. 1930.
He Married **Barbara Lou Sutton**.

Children:

1770 i. Billie[8] Bennett.
1771 ii. Richard Bennett.
He Married **Wendy Hoffman**.
1772 iii. Leah Bennett.
1773 iv. David Lee Bennett b. Oct-21-1964, d. Jul-19-1980.
1774 v. Lori Bennett.

1438. Ronald Lee[7] Warner (903.Arlie[6], 476.MaryEllen[5] Wimer, 154.Sylverius[4], 28.Mary Elizabeth[3] Sponaugle, 4.Elizabeth L.[2] Arbogast, 1.George[1]).
He Married **Linda Williams**.

Children:

1775 i. Kevin[8] Warner.
1776 ii. Rex Werner.

1439. Sandra[7] Warner (903.Arlie[6], 476.MaryEllen[5] Wimer, 154.Sylverius[4], 28.Mary Elizabeth[3] Sponaugle, 4.Elizabeth L.[2] Arbogast, 1.George[1]).
She Married **Wilmouth Cooper**.

Children:

1777 i. Harrison[8] Cooper b. 1979.

1440. Thomas Gartrh[7] Warner (905.Roy[6], 476.MaryEllen[5] Wimer, 154.Sylverius[4], 28.Mary Elizabeth[3] Sponaugle, 4.Elizabeth L.[2] Arbogast, 1.George[1]), b. 1939.
He Married **Gloria Arbogast**.

Children:

1778 i. Debbie[8] Warner.
1779 ii. Kathy Warner.
1780 iii. Danny Warner.

1443. Olin Ray[7] Warner (906.Ray[6], 476.MaryEllen[5] Wimer, 154.Sylverius[4], 28.Mary Elizabeth[3] Sponaugle, 4.Elizabeth L.[2] Arbogast, 1.George[1]), b. Dec-19-1944.
He Married **Janet Sue Cox**.

Children:

1781 i. David Michael[8] Warner.
1782 ii. Jodi Michelle Warner b. Jul-09-1970.

1444. Nancy Lee[7] Warner (906.Ray[6], 476.MaryEllen[5] Wimer, 154.Sylverius[4], 28.Mary Elizabeth[3] Sponaugle, 4.Elizabeth L.[2] Arbogast, 1.George[1]), b. 1947.
She Married **Ralph Shaffer Swain**.

Children:

1783 i. Mark Ralph[8] Swain b. 1966.
1784 ii. Glenn Ray Swain b. Sep-15-1968.

1447. Roy Lee[7] Warner (908.Charles[6], 476.MaryEllen[5] Wimer, 154.Sylverius[4], 28.Mary Elizabeth[3] Sponaugle, 4.Elizabeth L.[2] Arbogast, 1.George[1]).
He Married **Evangeline Scordos**, b. 1957 in Washington, D.C.

Children:

1785 i. Michal Kosta[8] Warner b. 1974.
1786 ii. Roy Lee Warner, Jr. b. 1975.

1451. Shirley Ann[7] Mullenax (910.Priscillia Lane[6] Warner, 476.MaryEllen[5] Wimer, 154.Sylverius[4], 28.Mary Elizabeth[3] Sponaugle, 4.Elizabeth L.[2] Arbogast, 1.George[1]), b. 1953.
Married 1972, **Michael C Bland**, b. 1954 (son of Byron Bland and Eula Vance).

Children:

1787 i. Rachel Denise[8] Bland.
1788 ii. Christopher Bland b. 1974.
1789 iii. Scott Allen B. Land b. 1982.

1458. John William[7] Johnston, Jr. (919.Reva Kerlin[6] Hinkle, 478.Lou Catherine[5] Wimer, 154.Sylverius[4], 28.Mary Elizabeth[3] Sponaugle, 4.Elizabeth L.[2] Arbogast, 1.George[1]), b. Jul-30-1934.
He Married **Mabel Leone Reynolds.**

Children:

1790 i. John William[8] Johnston, III.
1791 ii. Thomas Eugene Johnston.
1792 iii. Karen Ann Johnston.
1793 iv. Charles Mark Johnston.

1459. Emma Lou[7] Johnston (919.Reva Kerlin[6] Hinkle, 478.Lou Catherine[5] Wimer, 154.Sylverius[4], 28.Mary Elizabeth[3] Sponaugle, 4.Elizabeth L.[2] Arbogast, 1.George[1]), b. Jul-21-1937.
She Married **Larry Rhodes Kline**.

Children:

1794 i. Brenda Sue[8] Kline.
1795 ii. Larry Preston Kline.
1796 iii. Julia Yvonne Kline.

1460. Sue[7] Johnston (919.Reva Kerlin[6] Hinkle, 478.Lou Catherine[5] Wimer, 154.Sylverius[4], 28.Mary Elizabeth[3] Sponaugle, 4.Elizabeth L.[2] Arbogast, 1.George[1]), b. Nov-05-1939.
She Married **Townsend Harvey Johnson**.

Children:

1797 i. Christi Lynn[8] Johnson.
1798 ii. Teresa Ann Johnson.

1461. Marian[7] Johnston (919.Reva Kerlin[6] Hinkle, 478.Lou Catherine[5] Wimer, 154.Sylverius[4], 28.Mary Elizabeth[3] Sponaugle, 4.Elizabeth L.[2] Arbogast, 1.George[1]), b. Feb-08-1942.
She Married **Ralph Hazel Jr. Eveland**.

Children:

1799 i. Jamie Todd.[8] Eveland b. 1961.
1800 ii. Ralph Hazel Eveland, III b. 1967.
1801 iii. Jodie Lee Eveland b. 1968.

1462. Eveline Kay[7] Johnston (919.Reva Kerlin[6] Hinkle, 478.Lou Catherine[5] Wimer, 154.Sylverius[4], 28.Mary Elizabeth[3] Sponaugle, 4.Elizabeth L.[2] Arbogast, 1.George[1]).
She Married **Herman Raymond Aaronson**.

Children:

1802 i. Lisa Kay[8] Aaronson.
1803 ii. Herman Raymond Aaronson, III.

1463. Bruce Dallas[7] Johnston (919.Reva Kerlin[6] Hinkle, 478.Lou Catherine[5] Wimer, 154.Sylverius[4], 28.Mary Elizabeth[3] Sponaugle, 4.Elizabeth L.[2] Arbogast, 1.George[1]).
He Married **Kathy Joyce Slingbaum**.

Children:

1804 i. Bruce Dallas[8] Johnston, Jr..
1805 ii. Gregory Jeffrey Johnston.

1464. Elaine[7] Wymer (925.Richard Harold[6], 481.Carson Elmer[5], 158.Albert[4] Wimer, 28.Mary Elizabeth[3] Sponaugle, 4.Elizabeth L.[2] Arbogast, 1.George[1]).
She Married **Phillip D. Flemion**.

Children:

\+ 1806 i. Bonnie[8] Flemion.
1807 ii. Brian Richard Flemion b. Donald P. Flemion.
Married Mar-13-1991, Rebecca Lynn Crafton.
1808 iii. Donald P Flemion.

1466. Rita Lynn[7] Pennington (926.Aleta Macie[6] Wymer, 481.Carson Elmer[5], 158.Albert[4] Wimer, 28.Mary Elizabeth[3] Sponaugle, 4.Elizabeth L.[2] Arbogast, 1.George[1]), b. Nov-14-1949.
She Married **Edward McInturff**.

Children:

1809 i. Melissa[8] McInturff b. May-21-1979.

1467. Angeletta[7] Wymer (927.Bernice Kay[6], 481.Carson Elmer[5], 158.Albert[4] Wimer, 28.Mary Elizabeth[3] Sponaugle, 4.Elizabeth L.[2] Arbogast, 1.George[1]).
She Married **Sheldon Ruddle**.

Children:

1810 i. Roy Lee[8] Ruddle.

1468. Robrietta[7] Barzdoff (927.Bernice Kay[6] Wymer, 481.Carson Elmer[5], 158.Albert[4] Wimer, 28.Mary Elizabeth[3] Sponaugle, 4.Elizabeth L.[2] Arbogast, 1.George[1]).
She Married **Jack Paul Lambert (son** of Oscar Lambert and Ethel Moyers).

Children:

1811 i. Derek Riley[8] Lambert b. Dec-12-1983.
1812 ii. Keeley Marie Lambert b. Apr-26-1988.

1472. Virgil Lee[7] Wimer (935.Mildred Marie[6], 485.Lillie Mae[5], 159.Tiberius[4], 28.Mary Elizabeth[3] Sponaugle, 4.Elizabeth L.[2] Arbogast, 1.George[1]), b. Dec-10-1942.
He Married **Alice Lee Reggleman**, b. Nov-23-1944 in Moorefield, Hardy County, WV (daughter of Brook Riggleman and Evelyn Newhous2).

Children:

1813 i. Michael Ralph[8] Wimer b. Jan-13-1970 in Alexandria, Fairfax Co., VA.

1473. Linda Kay[7] Vance (935.Mildred Marie[6] Wimer, 485.Lillie Mae[5], 159.Tiberius[4], 28.Mary Elizabeth[3] Sponaugle, 4.Elizabeth L.[2] Arbogast, 1.George[1]), b. Jan-08-1947.
Married Jun-17-1967, **Willian Wilson Kile** (son of Harlan Kile and Pauline Lambert).

Children:

1814 i. Cassandra Ann[8] Kile b. Jun-30-1972 in Harrisonburg, Rockingham Co., VA.

1474. Stoney Roscoe[7] Hartman (936.Wilda Mae[6] Wilmer, 485.Lillie Mae[5] Wimer, 159.Tiberius[4], 28.Mary Elizabeth[3] Sponaugle, 4.Elizabeth L.[2] Arbogast, 1.George[1]), b. Nov-24-1952 in Columbus, Franklin Co., OH.

He Married **Sherry Melisa Redmond**, b. May-15-1952.

Children:

1815 i. Tarina Yvette[8] Hartman b. Jul-16-1971.
1816 ii. Jeremy Ralph Hartman b. Sep-29-1977.

1475. Mary Ann[7] Kissamore (938.Roy Richard[6] Kissmore, 486.Leanna[5] Wimer, 159.Tiberius[4], 28.Mary Elizabeth[3] Sponaugle, 4.Elizabeth L.[2] Arbogast, 1.George[1]), b. Dec-27-1945 in Franklin, Pendleton Co., WV.

She Married Franklin Herbert Cline, b. Jan-18-1940 in Burketown, Augusta, Co., VA (son of Orvin Kline and Esther Garber).

Children:

1817 i. Troy Edward[8] Cline b. May-02-1969 in Harrisonburg, Rockingham Co., VA.
\+ 1818 ii. Cathy Anna Cline b. Apr-28-1971.

1476. Dorothy Mae[7] Kissamore (938.Roy Richard[6] Kissmore, 486.Leanna[5] Wimer, 159.Tiberius[4], 28.Mary Elizabeth[3] Sponaugle, 4.Elizabeth L.[2] Arbogast, 1.George[1]), b. Aug-14-1947 in Fort Run, hearty Co., WV.
She Married **Donald Marion Lilly** (son of Roy Richard Kissmore and Christena Lou Lambert).

Children:

1819 i. Donna Marie[8] Lilly b. Jun-17-1974 in Harrisonburg, Rockingham Co., VA.
1820 ii. Douglas Lester Lilly b. Feb-06-1976 in Harrisonburg, Rockingham Co., VA.

1477. Donald Marion[7] Lilly (938.Roy Richard[6] Kissmore, 486.Leanna[5] Wimer, 159.Tiberius[4], 28.Mary Elizabeth[3] Sponaugle, 4.Elizabeth L.[2] Arbogast, 1.George[1]) (See marriage to number 1476.)

1480. Evaline **Peggy[7] Kissamore**` (938.Roy Richard[6] Kissmore, 486.Leanna[5] Wimer, 159.Tiberius[4], 28.Mary Elizabeth[3] Sponaugle, 4.Elizabeth L.[2] Arbogast, 1.George[1]), b. Apr-20-1926 in Back Ridge, Hunting Ground, Pendleton Co. WV, buried in South Branch Mem Gardens, Petersburg WV, d. Dec-28-1975 in Petersburg, Grant Co., WV.
Married Jan-14-1948 in Westernport, Washington Co., MD, Burl Randolph Barb, b. Jun-02-1923 in Moorefield, Hardy County, WV (son of Ashley Barb and Cora Ratcliffe).

Children:

\+ 1821 i. Betty Ellen[8] Barb b. Jan-16-1949.
\+ 1822 ii. Norman Randolph Barb b. Jun-25-1951.
\+ 1823 iii. Wanda Mae Barb b. Sep-22-1952.

1482. Steven Guy[7] Hartman (941.Warden Guy[6], 487.Mona[5] Wimer, 159.Tiberius[4], 28.Mary Elizabeth[3] Sponaugle, 4.Elizabeth L.[2] Arbogast, 1.George[1]).
He Married **Robin Shull**.

Children:

1824 i. April[8] Hartman.
1825 ii. Adriana Hartman.

1483. Artis E[7] Simmons (965.Orpha[6] Crosby, 493.Rosetta[5] Long, 165.Virginia Catherine (Jennie)[4] Teter, 30.Leah[3] Sponaugle, 4.Elizabeth L.[2] Arbogast, 1.George[1]), b. Jun-21-1921.
She Married **Oscar P Lewis**.

Children:

\+ 1826 i. John Warren[8] Lewis b. Feb-01-1950.
1827 ii. Michael Edwin Lewis b. Jun 25.
1828 iii. Oscar Lewis, Jr. b. Feb-25-1954.
Married Aug-26-1976, **Katherine Redden**.

1486. Charles Roy[7] Mosley (966.George Otis[6], 494.Elmina[5] Long, 165.Virginia Catherine (Jennie)[4] Teter, 30.Leah[3] Sponaugle, 4.Elizabeth L.[2] Arbogast, 1.George[1]), b. Oct-08-1935.

Married Sep-04-1957, Loveta Gardner.

Children:

1829 i. Kenneth Eugene[8] Mosley b. Dec-31-1958.
1830 ii. Marvin Lee Mosley b. Apr-11-1960.
1831 iii. Debra Sue Mosley b. May-10-1953.

1487. Burton Taylor[7] Mosley (966.George Otis[6], 494.Elmina[5] Long, 165.Virginia Catherine (Jennie)[4] Teter, 30.Leah[3] Sponaugle, 4.Elizabeth L.[2] Arbogast, 1.George[1]), b. Nov-30-1937.
Married May-29-1955, **Betty Anderson**.

Children:

1832 i. Terrie[8] Mosley b. Mar-12-1956.

1488. Donald Clyde[7] Mosley (966.George Otis[6], 494.Elmina[5] Long, 165.Virginia Catherine (Jennie)[4] Teter, 30.Leah[3] Sponaugle, 4.Elizabeth L.[2] Arbogast, 1.George[1]), b. Apr-11-1939.
He Married Carol Hagan, b. Mar 1966.

Children:

1833 i. Tammy[8] Mosley b. Sep-06-1967.
1834 ii. Darey Mosley b. Jul-16-1970.

1489. Ruby Pauline[7] Mosley (966.George Otis[6], 494.Elmina[5] Long, 165.Virginia Catherine (Jennie)[4] Teter, 30.Leah[3] Sponaugle, 4.Elizabeth L.[2] Arbogast, 1.George[1]), b. Jul-01-1940.
Married Mar-29-1964, Larry Hutton.

Children:

1835 i. Pauline[8] Hutton.
1836 ii. Billy Hutton b. Aug-24-1967.
1837 iii. Carlo Hutton b. Oct-30-1970.

1490. Betty[7] Darleen (966.George Otis[6] Mosley, 494.Elmina[5] Long, 165.Virginia Catherine (Jennie)[4] Teter, 30.Leah[3] Sponaugle, 4.Elizabeth L.[2] Arbogast, 1.George[1]), b. Nov-08-1941.
Married Mar-28-1964, Bob Wheeler.

Children:

1838 i.
Judy[8] Wheeler b. Sep-07-1964.
1839 ii. Lynn B> Wheeler b. Oct-01-1966.

1492. Harry Glenn[7] Aukamp (967.Grace Levin[6] Mosley, 494.Elmina[5] Long, 165.Virginia Catherine (Jennie)[4] Teter, 30.Leah[3] Sponaugle, 4.Elizabeth L.[2] Arbogast, 1.George[1]), b. Nov-26-1927.
He Married **Edith Smith**.

Children:

1840 i. Michael Glenn[8] Aukamp b. Sep-01-1954.

1493. Shirley[7] Aukamp (967.Grace Levin[6] Mosley, 494.Elmina[5] Long, 165.Virginia Catherine (Jennie)[4] Teter, 30.Leah[3] Sponaugle, 4.Elizabeth L.[2] Arbogast, 1.George[1]), b. Apr-25-1936.
She Married **Ray Martin**, b. Shirleen Martin.

Children:

1841 i. Shirleen[8] Martin b. May-18-1955, d. Jul-28-1966.
1842 ii. Cary Martin b. Dec-04-1959.
Married May-14-1977, **Teresa Marne Whitaker**.
1843 iii. Jim Martin b. May-22-1963.

1494. Barkley Allen[7] Mosley (968.Johnny[6], 494.Elmina[5] Long, 165.Virginia Catherine (Jennie)[4] Teter, 30.Leah[3] Sponaugle, 4.Elizabeth L.[2] Arbogast, 1.George[1]), b. Sep-07-1937.

He Married **Kay Nixon**.

Children:

1844 i. Wesley^8 Mosley.
1845 ii. Johnny Mosley.
1846 iii. Denise Mosley.

1497. Rodney^7 Gayman (969.Opel Irene^6 Mosley, 494.Elmina^5 Long, 165.Virginia Catherine (Jennie)^4 Teter, 30.Leah^3 Sponaugle, 4.Elizabeth L.^{2} Arbogast, 1.George^1), b. Mar-21-1931.
He Married **Jeanette Pratt,** b. Jul-28-1931.

Children:

1847 i. Vickie Jean^8 Gayman b. May-01-1955.

1498. Irean^7 Gayman (969.Opel Irene^6 Mosley, 494.Elmina^5 Long, 165.Virginia Catherine (Jennie)^4 Teter, 30.Leah^3 Sponaugle, 4.Elizabeth L.^{2} Arbogast, 1.George^1), b. Dec-20-1933.
She Married George Corliss, b. Jun-13-1927.

Children:

\+ 1848 i. Carolyn^8 Corliss b. Jan-02-1952.
1849 ii. Jacqueline Corliss b. Dec-15-1953.
1850 iii. Marylyn Corliss b. Dec-15-1953.
1851 iv. Joseph Corliss b. Jun-05-1965.

1501. Ronald Lee^7 Erickson (970.Dorothy Leone^6 Long, 495.John William^5, 165.Virginia Catherine (Jennie)^4 Teter, 30.Leah^3 Sponaugle, 4.Elizabeth L.^{2} Arbogast, 1.George^1), b. Apr-07-1940 in Oregon City, OR.
(1) Married Aug-05-1962, **Linda Ann Giogri**.

Children:

1852 i. Karl Leonard^8 Erickson b. May-04-1963.
1853 ii. Mark Joseph Erickson b. Nov-06-1967.

(2) Married Oct-11-1969, **Charlotte Taylor.**

1502. Joyce^7 Long (972.Lorna Doone^6, 495.John William^5, 165.Virginia Catherine (Jennie)^4 Teter, 30.Leah^3 Sponaugle, 4.Elizabeth L.^{2} Arbogast, 1.George^1), b. Nov-14-1941.
Married Jun-19-1965, **Joseph Pavlinac.**

Children:

1854 i. Joey^8 Pavlinac b. May-05-1966.
1855 ii. Jamie Pavlinac b. Jul-25-1971.

1503. Michael John^7 Long (972.Lorna Doone^6, 495.John William^5, 165.Virginia Catherine (Jennie)^4 Teter, 30.Leah^3 Sponaugle, 4.Elizabeth L.^{2} Arbogast, 1.George^1), b. Jan-27-1947.
Married Sep-15-1973, **Suzanne Neer**.

Children:

1856 i. Jennifer Marie^8 Long b. Jan-23-1974.

1507. Ann Elizabeth^7 O'Bryan (975.Gordon Charles^6, 496.Arta^5 Long, 165.Virginia Catherine (Jennie)^4 Teter, 30.Leah^3 Sponaugle, 4.Elizabeth L.^{2} Arbogast, 1.George^1), b. May-09-1941.
Married , **Phillip Kane.**

Children:

1857 i. Susan Elizabeth^8 Kane b. Nov-28-1964.
1858 ii. Steven Christian Kane b. May 21.
1859 iii. Debra Ann Kane b. Jul-02-1970.

1508. Arta Jean^7 O'Bryan (975.Gordon Charles^6, 496.Arta^5 Long, 165.Virginia Catherine (Jennie)^4 Teter, 30.Leah^3 Sponaugle, 4.Elizabeth L.^{2} Arbogast, 1.George^1), b. Mar-17-1945.
Married Dec 1970, **Robert Ross**.

Children:

1860 i. Gordon Robert^8 Ross b. Aug-03-0971.

1509. Charles Francis[7] O'Bryan (975.Gordon Charles[6], 496.Arta[5] Long, 165.Virginia Catherine (Jennie)[4] Teter, 30.Leah[3] Sponaugle, 4.Elizabeth L.[2] Arbogast, 1.George[1]), b. Feb-07-1946.
He Married **Martha Wright**.

Children:

1861 i. Jeff Charles[8] O'Bryan b. Oct-01-1970.

1510. Howard[7] Galbreath (977.Zona[6] Dillon, 497.Florence[5] Long, 165.Virginia Catherine (Jennie)[4] Teter, 30.Leah[3] Sponaugle, 4.Elizabeth L.[2] Arbogast, 1.George[1]), b. Sep-13-1948.
Married May-12-1961, **Judy Grasser,** b. May-24-1942.

Children:

1862 i. Scott David[8] Galbreath b. Oct-20-1970.

1511. Jack Harold[7] Summers (978.Robert Harold[6], 498.Ada[5] Long, 165.Virginia Catherine (Jennie)[4] Teter, 30.Leah[3] Sponaugle, 4.Elizabeth L.[2] Arbogast, 1.George[1]), b. Jun-31-1939.
Married Jul-01-1961, **Sharron Dale**.

Children:

1863 i. Teresa Lynn[8] Summers b. Jan-15-1962.
1864 ii. Jull Denice Summers b. Dec-31-1953.
1865 iii. Stacey Lee Summers b. Nov-23-1965.
1866 iv. Greg Robert Summers b. Jun-09-1967.

1512. Juanita Mae[7] Munds (979.Juanita Rilla[6] Summers, 498.Ada[5] Long, 165.Virginia Catherine (Jennie)[4] Teter, 30.Leah[3] Sponaugle, 4.Elizabeth L.[2] Arbogast, 1.George[1]), b. Mar-18-1935.
She Married **Frank Agost**, b. Mar-22-1929.

Children:

1867 i. Dale[8] Agost b. Dec-03-1952, d. Jul-31-1972.
\+ 1868 ii. Debbie Louise Agost b. Feb-12-1953.

1513. James Robert[7] Munds (979.Juanita Rilla[6] Summers, 498.Ada[5] Long, 165.Virginia Catherine (Jennie)[4] Teter, 30.Leah[3] Sponaugle, 4.Elizabeth L.[2] Arbogast, 1.George[1]), b. Sep-26-1936.
He Married **Lois Dickerson,** b. Jun-06-1938.

Children:

1869 i. Cheryl Elaine[8] Munds b. May-07-1960.
1870 ii. Karen Lynn Munds b. Jul-19-1961.
1871 iii. Christine Munds b. Mar-12-1964.

1515. Glenn[7] Munds (979.Juanita Rilla[6] Summers, 498.Ada[5] Long, 165.Virginia Catherine (Jennie)[4] Teter, 30.Leah[3] Sponaugle, 4.Elizabeth L.[2] Arbogast, 1.George[1]), b. Sep-02-1944.
He Married **Claudia Ladd**, b. Sep-12-1945.

Children:

1872 i. Tareena Louis[8] Munds b. Jun-28-1963.
1873 ii. Stephanie Renee Munds b. Apr-21-1966.

1526. Shirley Grace[7] Hardy (1017.Flossie Mabel[6] Bright, 520.Mary Ann[5] Teter, 168.John Jackson[4], 30.Leah[3] Sponaugle, 4.Elizabeth L.[2] Arbogast, 1.George[1]), b. 1941.
She Married **Kenneth Lacy Moody**, b. 1939.

Children:

\+ 1874 i. Kenneth Lacy[8] Moody, Jr. b. 1960.
\+ 1875 ii. Jeffery Clay Moody b. 1961.

1527. Thomas Daniel[7] Hardy (1017.Flossie Mabel[6] Bright, 520.Mary Ann[5] Teter, 168.John Jackson[4], 30.Leah[3] Sponaugle, 4.Elizabeth L.[2] Arbogast, 1.George[1]), b. 1943.
He Married **Sandy Kisamore**, b. 1948.

Children:

1876 i. Tammy Lee[8] Hardy b. 1965.
1877 ii. Brenda Kay Hardy b. 1977.

1528. Linda Lou^{7} Hardy (1017.Flossie Mabel^{6} Bright, 520.Mary Ann^{5} Teter, 168.John Jackson^{4}, 30.Leah^{3} Sponaugle, 4.Elizabeth L.^{2} Arbogast, 1.George^{1}), b. 1945.
She Married **Charles Daniel Vest**, b. 1943 in Newport News, Newport News Co., VA.

Children:

1878 i. Elizabeth Diane^{8} Vest b. 1967.
1879 ii. James Allen Vest b. 1971.
1880 iii. Rebecca Lynn Vest b. 1979.

1542. Sandra Kay^{7} Deitz (1029.Hallena Bell^{6} Davis, 523.Rosa Bell^{5} Bright, 170.Elizabeth Mary^{4} Teter, 30.Leah^{3} Sponaugle, 4.Elizabeth L.^{2} Arbogast, 1.George^{1}), b. 1952.
Married 1980, **Ronald Cook**.

Children:

1881 i. Keith Bradley^{8} Cook b. 1982.

1551. Norman D^{7} Smith (1046.Andrew^{6} White, 536.Rosa Alice^{5} Smith, 171.Alice Grace^{4} Teter, 30.Leah^{3} Sponaugle, 4.Elizabeth L.^{2} Arbogast, 1.George^{1}).
He Married **Vickie Pryor**.

Children:

1882 i. Danielle Nicole^{8} White.

1565. Joyce Juanita^{7} Taylor (1066.Juanita^{6} Sponaugle, 564.Herbert Charles^{5}, 191.William Letcher^{4}, 33.Jacob^{3}, 4.Elizabeth L.^{2} Arbogast, 1.George^{1}), b. Apr 16 1962 in Montgomery Co., MD.
(1) Married Jun 21 1980 in Green Bank, Pocahontas Co., WV, **James Franklin Tripplet** (son of G. F. Tripplet).
(2) Married Nov 9 1984, **Dempsey Michael Fox**.

Children:

1883 i. Dustin Michael^{8} Fox b. Sep 26 1986.

1566. Norma Jean^{7} Taylor (1066.Juanita^{6} Sponaugle, 564.Herbert Charles^{5}, 191.William Letcher^{4}, 33.Jacob^{3}, 4.Elizabeth L.^{2} Arbogast, 1.George^{1}), b. Dec 23 1963 in Virginia.
Married Nov 7 1987, **Joseph Michael Judy** (son of Joseph Judy).

Children:

1884 i. Brittany Nicole^{8} Judy b. Feb 1 1990.

1567. Allen Ray^{7} Taylor (1066.Juanita^{6} Sponaugle, 564.Herbert Charles^{5}, 191.William Letcher^{4}, 33.Jacob^{3}, 4.Elizabeth L.^{2} Arbogast, 1.George^{1}), b. Jun 21 1969 in Elkins, Randolph Co., WV.
Married Jun 27 1998 in Arbovale Cem., Arbovale, Pocahontas Co., WV, **Holly Michele Gordon** (daughter of Ronald L. Gordon and Ramona Jane Carpenter).

Children:

1885 i. Jarred Allen^{8} Taylor b. Feb 15 2000 in Davis Memorial Hospital, Elkins, Randolph Co., WV.
1886 ii. Alexa Raye Taylor b. Feb 17 2002 in Davis Memorial Hospital, Elkins, Randolph Co., WV.

1575. Jeffery Stewart^{7} Bowers (1071.Ruth Elaine^{6} Sponaugle, 573.Marvin Luther^{5}, 192.Herman Henry^{4}, 33.Jacob^{3}, 4.Elizabeth L.^{2} Arbogast, 1.George^{1}).
He Married **unknown Geary.**

Children:

1887 i. Jeffery^{8} Stewart Bowers, Jr. b. Nov-08-1983.

1577. Martin Luther^{7} Sponaugle, III (1072.Marvin Luther^{6} Sponaugle, Jr., 573.Marvin Luther^{5}, 192.Herman Henry^{4}, 33.Jacob^{3}, 4.Elizabeth L.^{2} Arbogast, 1.George^{1}), b. Apr-17-1956.
He Married **Dana Lynn Grant**.

Children:

1888 i. Ryan Christopher^{8} Sponaugle b. Jan-28-1980.
1889 ii. Lindsay Noel Sponaugle b. May-11-1983.

1578. Diane^{7} Sponaugle (1075.Carroll Lee^{6}, 573.Marvin Luther^{5}, 192.Herman Henry^{4}, 33.Jacob^{3}, 4.Elizabeth L.^{2} Arbogast, 1.George^{1}).
She Married **Gary Paden**.

Children:

1890 i. Joshua Craig[8] Paden b. Jul-16-1982.
1891 ii. Michelle Paden b. Feb-02-1984.

1584. Richard Clete[7] Phares, Jr. (1092.Richard Cleat[6], 577.Myrtle M[5] Sponaugle, 192.Herman Henry[4], 33.Jacob[3], 4.Elizabeth L.[2] Arbogast, 1.George[1]), b. Dec-25-1953.
He Married **Lisa Yvonne Launder**, b. May-01-1961 (daughter of Ruben Phares and Beverly Noel).

Children:

1892 i. Richard Clete[8] Phares, III b. Jun-08-1990.

1585. Kimberly Lynn[7] Phares (1092.Richard Cleat[6], 577.Myrtle M[5] Sponaugle, 192.Herman Henry[4], 33.Jacob[3], 4.Elizabeth L.[2] Arbogast, 1.George[1]), b. Dec-20-1957.
She Married **John Edsel Gowdin**, b. Jun 1953 (son of Charles Gowdin and Wilda Moore).

Children:

1893 i. John Richard[8] Gowdin b. Aug-29-1988.

1594. Michael Elmer[7] Phares (1095.Raymond[6], 577.Myrtle M[5] Sponaugle, 192.Herman Henry[4], 33.Jacob[3], 4.Elizabeth L.[2] Arbogast, 1.George[1]), b. Dec-03-1963.
He Married **Jill F. Phares**.

Children:

1894 i. Joshua Michael[8] Phares b. Nov-12-1990.

1595. Raymond Edward[7] Phares (1095.Raymond[6], 577.Myrtle M[5] Sponaugle, 192.Herman Henry[4], 33.Jacob[3], 4.Elizabeth L.[2] Arbogast, 1.George[1]), b. Aug-04-1965.
He Married **Susanna Thompson.**

Children:

1895 i. Stephen Edward[8] Phares b. Nov-25-1990.

1598. Jeffery[7] Warner (1097.Dottie Lou[6] Phares, 577.Myrtle M[5] Sponaugle, 192.Herman Henry[4], 33.Jacob[3], 4.Elizabeth L.[2] Arbogast, 1.George[1]), b. Jan-14-1966.
He Married **Pamala J. Craig**, b. Jun-18-1975.

Children:

1896 i. Clara Dawn[8] Craig b. Dec-01-1989.

1606. Angela Kay[7] Hinkle (1112.Patsey Louisa[6] Harper, 586.Ruth[5] Sponaugle, 192.Herman Henry[4], 33.Jacob[3], 4.Elizabeth L.[2] Arbogast, 1.George[1]).
She Married **John W. Phares**.

Children:

1897 i. Nathaniel John[8] Phares b. May-17-1984.

Generation Eight

1616. Lowell Jene[8] Collins (1128.Harold Cecil[7], 629.Cecil Morgan[6], 269.Louella Maer[5] Grogg, 69.Emily Jane[4] Mullenax, 11.John H.[3], 2.Hannah[2] Arbogast, 1.George[1]), b. Aug 09 1939.
(1) He Married **Susan Alkire.**

Children:

1898 i. Kelly Sue[9] Collins.

(2) He Married Sharon Johnson.

Children:

1899 ii. Christine Collins.
1900 iii. Andrew Jon Collins.

1617. Atlos Martin^{8} Collins (1128.Harold Cecil^{7}, 629.Cecil Morgan^{6}, 269.Louella Maer^{5} Grogg, 69.Emily Jane^{4} Mullenax, 11.John H.^{3}, 2.Hannah^{2} Arbogast, 1.George^{1}), b. Oct 25 1942 in Pocahontas Co., WV.

(1) He Married Judith Elaine Gill.

Children:

1901 i. Dawnne Renee^{9} Collins b. Oct 01 1964.
1902 ii. Ribin Leigh Collins b. Aug 01 1965.
1903 iii. Virginia Lynn Collins b. Aug 19 1967.

(2) He Married **Tammy Jo Farnham**.

Children:

1904 iv. Sonja Michelle Collins b. Feb 02 1979.

1618. Carol Lee^{8} Collins (1130.Bernard Morris^{7}, 629.Cecil Morgan^{6}, 269.Louella Maer^{5} Grogg, 69.Emily Jane^{4} Mullenax, 11.John H.^{3}, 2.Hannah^{2} Arbogast, 1.George^{1}).

She Married **Bill Waco Lambert**.

Children:

1905 i. Janie Marie^{9} Lambert.
1906 ii. Billy W Lambert.
1907 iii. Jody Lynn Lambert.
1908 iv. Pamela Carol Lambert.
1909 v. Julie Ann Lambert.

1619. Rebecca Jeanne^{8} Collins (1130.Bernard Morris^{7}, 629.Cecil Morgan^{6}, 269.Louella Maer^{5} Grogg, 69.Emily Jane^{4} Mullenax, 11.John H.^{3}, 2.Hannah^{2} Arbogast, 1.George^{1}).

(1) She Married **Bob Shepherd.**

Children:

1910 i. Kelly Ann^{9} Shepherd.
1911 ii. Gred Rob Shepherd.

(2) She Married **Tom Nohe.**

Children:

1912 iii. Thomas Nohe.

1644. Jerry Price^{8} Simmons (1229.Naomi^{7}, 712.Rhea Mae^{6} Sponaugle, 334.Green Judy^{5}, 108.George Washington^{4}, 23.William^{3}, 4.Elizabeth L.^{2} Arbogast, 1.George^{1}), b. Apr-18-1941.

He Married **Evelyn Katgaleen Rumer.**

Children:

1913 i. Steven^{9} Simmons.
1914 ii. Teresa Ann Simmons.

1656. Sylvia Lynn^{8} Ozment (1276.Dwight Wesley^{7}, 740.Lacie Madonna^{6} Nelson, 341.Jenettie Catherine^{5} Thompson, 109.Mary Catherine^{4} Sponaugle, 23.William^{3}, 4.Elizabeth L.^{2} Arbogast, 1.George^{1}), b. Apr-21-1955.

(1) Married Mar 1972 in Chesterfield Co., VA, **Robert Charles Boyd.**

Children:

1915 i. Robert Charles^{9} Boyd b. Mar-26-1974 in Richmond, Chesterfield Co., VA.
1916 ii. Matthew Bradley Boyd b. Apr-11-1976 in Richmond, Chesterfield Co., VA.

(2) Married Apr-21-1991 in Wilmington, NC, Franklin Dyson.

1673. Glenneth Edward^{8} Lester, Jr. (1297.Shirley Ann^{7} Sponaugle, 800.Milford Jay^{6}, 369.Lee Paris^{5}, 113.Adam Harness^{4}, 23.William^{3}, 4.Elizabeth L.^{2} Arbogast, 1.George^{1}), b. Feb-27-1950 in Cleveland, Cuyahoga Co., OH.

He Married **Cindy Christie**.

Children:

1917 i. Natsaha Marie^{9} Lester b. Dec-07-1984 in Cleveland, Cuyahoga Co., OH.
1918 ii. Elizabeth Ann Lester b. Aug-12-1985 in Thruman, SC.

1676. Lloyd Aaron^{8} Sponaugle (1298.Aaron Charles^{7}, 800.Milford Jay^{6}, 369.Lee Paris^{5}, 113.Adam Harness^{4}, 23.William^{3}, 4.Elizabeth L.^{2} Arbogast, 1.George^{1}), b. Feb-28-1958 in Youngstown, OH.
He Married **Lorena Patos**.

Children:

1919 i. Aaron Michael^{9} Sponaugle b. Apr-10-1879 in Youngstown, Mahoning Co., OH.
1920 ii. Rebecca Ann Sponaugle b. Apr-19-1985 in Youngstown, Mahoning Co., OH.
1921 iii. Eric Lee Sponaugle b. Dec-29-1985 in Youngstown, Mahoning Co., OH.

1688. Jill Lynn^{8} Judy (1370.James Arthur^{7}, 837.Guy William^{6}, 376.Monna Roxie^{5} Sponaugle, 113.Adam Harness^{4}, 23.William^{3}, 4.Elizabeth L.^{2} Arbogast, 1.George^{1}), b. Sep-28-1962 in Kennewick, Benton Co., WA.
She Married **Thomas Michael Thoelke**, b. Sep-05-1953.

Children:

1922 i. Heather Linn^{9} Thoelke b. Mar-13-1982 in Kennewick, Benton Co., WA.
1923 ii. Haley Renee Thoelke b. Jan-14-1985 in Kennewick, Benton Co., WA.
1924 iii. Ross Michael Thoelke b. Sep-12-1988 in Kennewick, Benton Co., WA.

1702. Gregory Alan^{8} Harman (1378.Babbara Joan^{7} Judy, 838.Kermit Adam^{6}, 376.Monna Roxie^{5} Sponaugle, 113.Adam Harness^{4}, 23.William^{3}, 4.Elizabeth L.^{2} Arbogast, 1.George^{1}), b. Mar-12-1962 in Washington, D.C.
He Married **Cathy Ann Brewer**, b. Feb 1964 (daughter of Jack Harman and Ann Russell).

Children:

1925 i. Michael alan^{9} Harman b. Mar-18-1989 in Charlotte, Mecklenburg Co., NC.
1926 ii. Christopher John Harman b. May-11-1991 in Charlotte, Mecklenburg Co., NC.

1703. Tracy Michele^{8} Harman (1378.Babbara Joan^{7} Judy, 838.Kermit Adam^{6}, 376.Monna Roxie^{5} Sponaugle, 113.Adam Harness^{4}, 23.William^{3}, 4.Elizabeth L.^{2} Arbogast, 1.George^{1}), b. Nov-12-1964 in Harrisonburg, Rockingham Co., VA.
She Married **John Russell Brewer**, b. Jun-08-1962 in Texas (son of Jack Russell and Ann Brewer).

Children:

1927 i. Steven John^{9} Russell b. Apr-12-1988 in Provo, Utah Co., UT.
1928 ii. Jason Danial Brewer b. Jun-04-1990 in Atlanta, Fulton Co., GA.

1722. Luke Thomas^{8} Judy (1387.Edward^{7}, 843.Gayle Edward^{6}, 376.Monna Roxie^{5} Sponaugle, 113.Adam Harness^{4}, 23.William^{3}, 4.Elizabeth L.^{2} Arbogast, 1.George^{1}), b. Mar-13-1981 in Harrisonburg, Rockingham Co., VA.
He Married **Cara Jo Sottosanti**.

Children:

1929 i. Orlin Kaleb^{9} Judy b. Jul-04-1990 in Harrisonburg, Rockingham Co., VA.

1725. Roy B^{8} Warner, Jr. (1393.Roy B.^{7}, 865.Dice G^{6}, 429.Walter^{5}, 139.Mary Elizabeth^{4} Teter, 26.Catherine^{3} Sponaugle, 4.Elizabeth L.^{2} Arbogast, 1.George^{1}).
He Married **unknown Patterson.**

Children:

1930 i. Kimberly Diane^{9} Warner b. Jan-17-1983.

1733. Jerry^{8} Smith (1405.Norma^{7} Judy, 866.Beulah^{6} Warner, 429.Walter^{5}, 139.Mary Elizabeth^{4} Teter, 26.Catherine^{3} Sponaugle, 4.Elizabeth L.^{2} Arbogast, 1.George^{1}).
He Married **Debbie Warner.**

Children:

1931 i. Candace^{9} Smith.
1932 ii. Charity Smith.

1734. George^{8} Smith, Jr. (1405.Norma^{7} Judy, 866.Beulah^{6} Warner, 429.Walter^{5}, 139.Mary Elizabeth^{4} Teter, 26.Catherine^{3} Sponaugle, 4.Elizabeth L.^{2} Arbogast, 1.George^{1}).
He Married **Diane Warner.**

Children:

1933 i. Tracy^{9} Smith.

1735. Mary Francis^{8} Smith (1405.Norma^{7} Judy, 866.Beulah^{6} Warner, 429.Walter^{5}, 139.Mary Elizabeth^{4} Teter, 26.Catherine^{3} Sponaugle, 4.Elizabeth L.^{2} Arbogast, 1.George^{1}).
She Married Ralph Gerald Hise II, b. Oct 1 1946 (son of Clarence Wimer Hise and Lena Virginia Halterman).

Children:

1934 i. Laure^{9} Hise.
1935 ii. Luke Hise.
1936 iii. Lee Hise.
1937 iv. Benjamin Jeremiah Hise.

1806. Bonnie^{8} Flemion (1464.Elaine^{7} Wymer, 925.Richard Harold^{6}, 481.Carson Elmer^{5}, 158.Albert^{4} Wimer, 28.Mary Elizabeth^{3} Sponaugle, 4.Elizabeth L.^{2} Arbogast, 1.George^{1}).
Married 1985, **William A. Mitchell**.

Children:

1938 i. Dane^{9} Mitchell.

1818. Cathy Anna^{8} Cline (1475.Mary Ann^{7} Kissamore, 938.Roy Richard^{6} Kissmore, 486.Leanna^{5} Wimer, 159.Tiberius^{4}, 28.Mary Elizabeth^{3} Sponaugle, 4.Elizabeth L.^{2} Arbogast, 1.George^{1}), b. Apr-28-1971 in Henry Co., VA.
Married Apr-25-1992 in Harrisonburg, Rockingham Co., VA, **Curtis Darnell Skates**, b. Feb-03-1971 in Washington, D.C. (son of Victor Sanders Skates and Roxie Virginia Skates).

Children:

1939 i. Eric Trent^{9} Skates b. Mar-21-1989 in Harrisonburg, Rockingham Co., VA.
1940 ii. Curtis Darnell Skates b. Aug-19-1921 in Harrisonburg, Rockingham Co., VA.
1941 iii. Corey Douglas Skates b. Aug-16-1992 in Harrisonburg, Rockingham Co., VA.

1821. Betty Ellen^{8} Barb (1480.Evaline Peggy^{7} Kissamore`, 938.Roy Richard^{6} Kissmore, 486.Leanna^{5} Wimer, 159.Tiberius^{4}, 28.Mary Elizabeth^{3} Sponaugle, 4.Elizabeth L.^{2} Arbogast, 1.George^{1}), b. Jan-16-1949 in Petersburg, Grant Co., WV.
Married Apr-19-1969 in Moorefield, Hardy County, WV, **Roger Ervin Ours**, b. Apr-02-1946 in Grant County, WV (son of Ervin Ours and Lena Mongold).

Children:

+ 1942 i. Tina Marie^{9} Ours b. May-14-1971.
1943 ii. Amy Elizabeth Ours b. Nov-23-1977 in Petersburg, Grant Co., WV.

1822. Norman Randolph^{8} Barb (1480.Evaline Peggy^{7} Kissamore`, 938.Roy Richard^{6} Kissmore, 486.Leanna^{5} Wimer, 159.Tiberius^{4}, 28.Mary Elizabeth^{3} Sponaugle, 4.Elizabeth L.^{2} Arbogast, 1.George^{1}), b. Jun-25-1951 in Petersburg, Grant Co., WV.
Married Jun-02-1976 in Moorefield, Hardy County, WV, **Mary Alice Ours** (daughter of Ervin Ours and Lena Mongold).

Children:

1944 i. Tyler Randolph^{9} Barb b. Apr 1989.

1823. Wanda Mae^{8} Barb (1480.Evaline Peggy^{7} Kissamore`, 938.Roy Richard^{6} Kissmore, 486.Leanna^{5} Wimer, 159.Tiberius^{4}, 28.Mary Elizabeth^{3} Sponaugle, 4.Elizabeth L.^{2} Arbogast, 1.George^{1}), b. Sep-22-1952.
Married Apr-24-1976 in Moorefield, Hardy County, WV, **Steven Lee Watchford** (son of Carl Watchford and Mary Jo Southerly).

Children:

1945 i. Steven Lee^{9} Watchford b. Feb-04-1978 in Petersburg, Grant Co., WV.
1946 ii. Burl Randolph Watchford b. May-30-1979 in Petersburg, Grant Co., WV.
1947 iii. Briab Keith Watchford b. Mar-09-1982 in Winchester, Frederick Co., VA.

1826. John Warren^{8} Lewis (1483.Artis E^{7} Simmons, 965.Orpha^{6} Crosby, 493.Rosetta^{5} Long, 165.Virginia Catherine (Jennie)^{4} Teter, 30.Leah^{3} Sponaugle, 4.Elizabeth L.^{2} Arbogast, 1.George^{1}), b. Feb-01-1950.
He Married Pamela Billings.

Children:

1948 i. John^{9} Warren Lewis, Jr..

1848. Carolyn^{8} Corliss (1498.Irean^{7} Gayman, 969.Opel Irene^{6} Mosley, 494.Elmina^{5} Long, 165.Virginia Catherine (Jennie)^{4} Teter, 30.Leah^{3} Sponaugle, 4.Elizabeth L.^{2} Arbogast, 1.George^{1}), b. Jan-02-1952.
Married Sep-18-1970, **David Stiefel**.

Children:

1949 i. Trista Irene[9] Stiefel b. Jan-30-1976.

1868. Debbie Louise[8] Agost (1512.Juanita Mae[7] Munds, 979.Juanita Rilla[6] Summers, 498.Ada[5] Long, 165.Virginia Catherine (Jennie)[4] Teter, 30.Leah[3] Sponaugle, 4.Elizabeth L.[2] Arbogast, 1.George[1]), b. Feb-12-1953.
<u>Married</u> Aug-28-1970, **Kimberly Hanson**.

Children:

1950 i. Jona Daniella[9] Agost b. May-28-1973.
1951 ii. Jason Agost.

1874. Kenneth Lacy[8] Moody, Jr. (1526.Shirley Grace[7] Hardy, 1017.Flossie Mabel[6] Bright, 520.Mary Ann[5] Teter, 168.John Jackson[4], 30.Leah[3] Sponaugle, 4.Elizabeth L.[2] Arbogast, 1.George[1]), b. 1960.
He <u>Married</u> **Jennifer McClung**, b. 1965.

Children:

1952 i. Heather Lee[9] McClung b. 1982.

1875. Jeffery Clay[8] Moody (1526.Shirley Grace[7] Hardy, 1017.Flossie Mabel[6] Bright, 520.Mary Ann[5] Teter, 168.John Jackson[4], 30.Leah[3] Sponaugle, 4.Elizabeth L.[2] Arbogast, 1.George[1]), b. 1961.
He <u>Married</u> **Lucille Evens**, b. 1961.

Children:

1953 i. Eric Scott[9] Moody b. 1980.

Generation Nine

1942. Tina Marie[9] Ours (1821.Betty Ellen[8] Barb, 1480.Evaline Peggy[7] Kissamore`, 938.Roy Richard[6] Kissmore, 486.Leanna[5] Wimer, 159.Tiberius[4], 28.Mary Elizabeth[3] Sponaugle, 4.Elizabeth L.[2] Arbogast, 1.George[1]), b. May-14-1971 in Petersburg, Grant Co., WV.
She <u>Married</u> **Charlie Raybolds**.

Children:

1954 i. Tiffany Dinise[10] Reynolds b. Jun-16-1990 in Petersburg, Grant Co., WV.

About The Author

Nancy Elizabeth Arbogast, a fourth generation off spring rom German born Michael Arbogast ,produced a sixth generation male child who gave a dam about his relatives . This chap is the product of four pioneering families who settled in the heart of the Alleghany Mountains, and with the help of other pioneers turned the wilderness into a most hospitable place to live.

Edyth Laura Morrison had gone to Pocahontas County in 1916 to teach school in Frost. On September 3, 1923 she and Mitchell Sharp were married. Curtis was their third child, born October 31 1929 in his parent's home on Knapps Creek, two days after the October 29, 1929 bank crash. The land on which the house stood was a part of the holdings acquired by pioneer John Sharp (born c1757). It had passed from Pioneer John through multiple Sharp generations to Mitchell. Two years later Mitchell and Edyth lost the land and house for debts owed to a brother, cousin, neighbor and sister-in-law. The goodness and greatness of the Morrison family burst forward, and Mitchell, Edyth and the three boys had a place to land.

From 1931 through his retirement in 1994, Curtis rarely returned to Pocahontas County. After retirement, he began accumulating genealogical data and history on the ancestors of his four grandparents. *John Sharp and Margaret Blain Sharp Family History* was published in 2014., and *A Morrison Family, History and Descendants of Nathaniel Morrison* in 2016. This volume is a third result of that 20 plus year effort.

Curtis has been married to Peggy Bell Sharp for 60 years, has 4 children, 11 grandchildren and one great grandchild. This, a three volume effort, will be his sixth book since retirement. The first, *Blessings and Burdens, Growing up Poor and Rich,* is about his parent's upbringing, their downfall and recovery, and his early life. Being born poor and being the child of Mitchell and Edyth are among his greatest blessings.

His 40-year professional career with the U. S. Department of Agriculture focused on using vegetation for solving soil and water conservation problems. His forth post retirement book, *Conservation Plants, A USDA Success Story*, discussed the people and products resulting from the first 75 years history of this Program.

Index

---

[i] Price

Made in the USA
Coppell, TX
08 July 2023